PRESERVING THE
WORLD'S GREAT CITIES

PRESERVING THE WORLD'S GREAT CITIES

THE DESTRUCTION AND RENEWAL OF THE HISTORIC METROPOLIS

ANTHONY M. TUNG

THREE RIVERS PRESS
NEW YORK

Front cover painting (detail) by Canaletto, courtesy of Staatliche Museen Zu Berlin, Preussischer Kulturbesitz Gemäldegalerie; spine photograph of Xizhimen Gate (Beijing) by Donald Mennie, 1920

Published by Three Rivers Press, New York, New York.
Member of the Crown Publishing Group, a division of Random House, Inc.
www.randomhouse.com

THREE RIVERS PRESS and the Tugboat design are registered trademarks of Random House, Inc.

Originally published in hardcover by Clarkson Potter/Publishers in 2001.

Printed in the United States of America

Design by Caitlin Daniels Israel

Library of Congress Cataloging-in-Publication Data
Tung, Anthony M.
        Preserving the world's great cities: the destruction and renewal of the historic metropolis/
Anthony M. Tung.
        Includes bibliographical references and index.
        1. Architecture—conservation and restoration.   2. Historic districts—conservation and
restoration. 3. City planning. I. Title.
    NA9053.C6 T86 2001
    711'.4—dc21   2001021276

ISBN 0-609-80815-X

10   9   8   7   6   5   4   3

First Paperback Edition

To Jan

CONTENTS

THE WIDENING ETHIC OF PRESERVATION

The city, however, does not tell its past, but contains it like the lines of a hand.

—ITALO CALVINO, *Invisible Cities*

INTRODUCTION

*I*n March 1995 I embarked on a journey to twenty-two of the world's great cities to study how architectural preservation worked and failed in some of the most artistically and historically significant places around the globe. I set out to learn how different people in different places conserved their urban heritage, but I discovered instead a tragedy of history: I learned that during the twentieth century not only has modern civilization destroyed much of the architectural fabric inherited from previous generations, creating a widening chasm between us and our past, but, worse, on every continent we have adopted a culture of destruction that presages further loss.

This negative history and these destructive policies raise fundamental questions about how we design cities and what we understand the purpose of urban areas to be, for today and for tomorrow. Why is it crucial that we save the architectural accomplishments of previous generations as part of the vital substance of urban life? If the historic cores of major cities are vigorously protected and their architectural forms are fixed in time, as if they were living museums, can such metropolises prosper in the unforgiving world of global economic competition? Have we arrived at a moment when urban architectural conservation assumes an unprecedented urgency because of the historically unparalleled power of modern humans to alter whole cityscapes overnight?

My concerns when I embarked on this journey were practical. For many years I had been a member of the New York City Landmarks Preservation Commission and I knew from experience that the most useful information for informing the civic debate on architectural conservation was derived from lessons learned in other places. Too often we were reinventing the wheel, when other cities had already come to grips with the same problems. It was time to gather in one place, in one language, a body of very basic information about urban culture and to look at the practice of urban preservation across the world as a single related phenomenon.

Actually visiting these cities was the only way to evaluate the success of conservation efforts in different urban areas. Today virtually all major countries and great metropolises have conservation laws; and, in most places, planning for preservation is an important part of charting the future of urban areas. But what is the reality of conservation practice in the world's great cities, where power, poverty, politics, money, corruption, and the drive for economic growth often distort law, order, and rationality? If we look beyond the self-serving official rhetoric of governments and scrutinize the actual physical results of preservation efforts in various cities, are we truly conserving our historic architectural patrimony? Are we saving the evidence of our history?

The first thing I learned in my effort to answer such questions was that every city had to be studied differently. For instance, although the content and structure of preservation law was important to understand in each place, it was only part of the story, for in cities like Cairo, Rome, Moscow, Mexico City, Athens, and Jerusalem, the law was often not obeyed. In Beijing, the realities of preservation were determined less by law and more by the changeable policies of an omnipotent Communist Party.

A wide expanse of urban history needed to be scanned. Although the science and law of preservation is a relatively modern discipline, significant historical events affecting the conservation of cities have occurred at various times, in various places, and the lessons of preservation reach back to the early history of human settlement. One of the first documented preservation statutes was issued in imperial Rome 1,500 years ago, in the waning days of the empire, when Emperor Majorian forbade by edict the burning of the marble blocks of monuments to make lime. A singular feature of contemporary preservation in Amsterdam is its large number of proactive conservation societies which, together, have saved many hundreds of historic buildings in the old city's core. Why are Amsterdammers more aggressively involved in conserving their city than citizens in other places? Part of the answer can be traced back to the practices of medieval communal water boards, which preserved the dikes that protected the Netherlands from flooding by the sea. In Venice, where the preservation of the historic cityscape is inextricably tied to conserving the ecological balance of its surrounding lagoon, a sophisticated program of measured environmental interventions was developed during the Renaissance at the University in Padua. Failure to continue this program during most of the twentieth century is one of the reasons that Venice has begun to sink in the modern era. In Warsaw, in the 1940s, a Nazi plan to destroy the city's landmarks was implemented by German demolition squads. As the buildings were being dynamited, a group of Polish architecture professors— in direct violation of German occupation orders—surreptitiously removed to safety years of careful documentation of urban historic structures, risking death to save the evidence of their patrimony so it could be rebuilt in the future.

In the writing of this book the meaning of the words "preservation" and "conservation" had to be considered with care. In the United States, we use the term "preservation" in our legal language when referring to architectural and historical matters that Europeans and the rest of the world often mean when they say "conservation." In Italy a further distinction is made: there "preservation" connotes a reactive policy, such as waiting for new development to threaten an old building before designating it a landmark—a last-minute intervention that frequently angers the owners of private properties. Italians specifically use the term "conservation" to describe proactive thinking, which anticipates problems before they occur. An example of a proactive Italian conservation measure would be the creation of a program of government grants for the maintenance of listed properties, which attracts owners of historic buildings to request designation in order to receive financial support. In this way the government becomes a much-desired partner in the effort to remodel historic structures rather than an antagonist to be suffered or avoided.

In Western civilization to "preserve" a historic structure has most often meant to retain as much as possible of the original fabric, or material, of old buildings. In Europe and the United States, we go to great lengths to keep the actual brick, stone, glass, and wood of which our landmarks were made, because the processes by which these materials were manufactured are no longer practiced or because their sources in the natural world are exhausted. We want old things to look old, and we value the distortions and patina of age as part of the truth of an object. On the Acropolis, for example, the Parthenon does not look at all like the multicolored original, yet we revere its fragmented ruins bleached white by the sun.

In Asia, where verisimilitude is important, to "preserve" often means to retain the original aesthetic of a great building. Many monuments in Japan and China are periodically dismantled, and aged and misshapen parts are replaced, so that buildings continue to look the way they did when first constructed. This tradition has maintained historic construction arts; and when disaster strikes, these cultures can more easily reconstruct or duplicate centuries-old artifacts. But the visitor to a temple or palace site that has been reassembled many times never knows to what degree the artifact is an accurate door to the past.

In the interests of consistency, however, I have used the terms "preservation" and "conservation" interchangeably throughout the text when I refer to the effort to save original historic fabric. More exact distinctions are made in the course of specific explanations, as in the Traditional Building Preservation Districts in contemporary Kyoto, where the street elevations of buildings must comply with standard designs that scholars have judged to be consistent with historic norms. Here the terms "conservation," "preservation," and "restoration" do not accurately characterize either the result or the intent, which I have described as an effort to reestablish the culture of historic wooden architectural construction in the city.

In every city, I found that an understanding of local politics was critical, because politics often accounts for the failure of law to be applied logically, in appropriate measure, in all the instances where it is merited by the facts. The most extreme case that I encountered of the politicization of conservation was in Jerusalem. Here, Jewish municipal authorities have had great difficulty extending conservation initiatives to neighborhoods of old buildings where Palestinian Muslims live. Many Muslims fear that construction activity by the Israeli government might be a disguise for territorial expropriation—resulting in the destruction of their homes rather than in their rehabilitation—thereby requiring Muslims to relocate outside historic Jerusalem and reducing their representation among the city's populace. In actuality, one of the first acts of the Israeli government when it gained control of the city in 1967, after the destruction of the historic Jewish quarter of the city by the retreating Jordanian Muslims, was to demolish a historic neighborhood of Palestinian Muslim houses in order to create a plaza in front of the Wailing Wall. This of course exacerbated political tensions and undermined the credibility of conservation authorities. It is not uncommon in Jerusalem today to see historic structures of the same significance and age restored on one side of a street and continuing to decay on the other side, which invariably is the Muslim side.

Economics is inextricably tied to these matters. Many of the cities of our emerging modern urban civilization suffer from problems of economic marginalization similar to those in Cairo where massive population growth, extensive poverty, widespread infant mortality, and an endemic culture of illegal settlement cause numerous inhabitants to perceive the allocation of resources for architectural conservation as a lesser priority. Meanwhile a magnificent medieval Muslim cityscape is being lost to decades of deferred maintenance and a devastating attack from environmental pollution. In this context, the general economic problems of Cairo, and of Egypt as a whole, are a crucial element in the preservation story, and the pioneering work of Peruvian economist Hernando de Soto offers hope in alleviating tragic and overwhelming urban dilemmas. De Soto's proposal that black market holdings be converted into legalized assets for capital investment would empower marginalized Cairenes and give them a more palpable stake in their city's future. Otherwise, we must ask: Can any metropolis be well governed when large numbers of its residents do not fully share the benefits of citizenship?

Virtually every historic metropolis endures the loss of architectural character due to unrestrained speculative real estate development. In Singapore, the
rush toward achieving economic prosperity needlessly consumed much of the
city's remarkable colonial heritage. This erasure of exotic cross-cultural Asian
and European tropical architectural form is now bemoaned by many of the
city's inhabitants, and an aggressive conservation program has been mounted
by the government, since a lack of historical assets detracts from the modern
city's ability to draw tourists, who in the jet age are a major source of revenue
for all historic cities.

An enigma becomes apparent. In cities on all continents, the new developments that herald economic well-being frequently result in a threat to the continuation of landmarks and historic neighborhoods. Yet it was just such
prosperity that gave rise to the buildings that are the great landmarks of today.
Moreover, without economic success, we are unable to afford to maintain our
architectural patrimony. And without such financial achievement tomorrow,
architects, contractors, developers, institutions, and governments will be
unable to create the landmarks of our future. The pursuit of money creates the
resources to make landmarks, and to save landmarks, but it is also the justification for destroying them.

Though the cities I went to differed in many respects, I applied one constant measure to them all: I judged what I saw with my own eyes. This was the
central idea of the project—to write a book about the preservation of some of
the most important large cities across the world, to account for the differences
between one place and another, and to measure the final physical results in
urban and architectural form against a single standard. In other words,
regardless of mitigating social, political, economic, and cultural circumstances, how do the material results of preservation efforts in each place compare with the results of such efforts in other places? The book is an attempt to
compress time and distance and to compare cities with one another as if they
were immediate neighbors and could be seen simultaneously.

My judgments are, inevitably, informed by my experience. As a young man
I studied architecture at the Cooper Union in New York and was exposed to the
thinking of such influential avant-garde architects as John Hejduk, Richard
Meier, Charles Gwathmey, Ricardo Scofidio, and Peter Eisenman. I learned to
respect the achievement of excellence in architecture. Eight years later I was
appointed a landmarks commissioner for the city of New York and served for
three terms—that is, nine years—from 1979 until 1988. I was one of eleven
members empowered by law to make all decisions in regard to architectural
conservation in the city. The New York City Landmarks Preservation Commission designates landmarks and historic districts; once properties are listed,

their owners are required to have official approval before making any changes to their buildings or grounds. In open public hearings, the commission regulates such varied applications as the replacement of a window in the front elevation of a brownstone in Greenwich Village, the design of a shop front in a former factory building in SoHo, the proposal for an addition to the Whitney Museum in the Upper East Side Historic District, and the plans for a sixty-story office building on Fifth Avenue, in midtown Manhattan.

In my final year on the commission in the midst of a real estate boom, I was involved in the regulation of about three-quarters of a billion dollars of new construction (about 3.7 billion French francs, 6 billion Chinese yuan, or 4 trillion Russian rubles). Although the position was unpaid, I was dedicated to it and spent almost twenty hours a week on commission business. I visited most of the sites that we regulated and virtually all the buildings that we considered for designation. In all, across the nine years, this amounted to about 2,600 proposals for new construction at historic sites and approximately 4,000 properties designated as individual landmarks or as buildings in historic districts. Since the practice of preservation in New York generally meets the highest international standards of professionalism, I came to understand the application of these principles in the field. My architectural preservationist's eye was trained.

Further, as the years went by and I gradually acquired some influence, I learned to stick by my judgments under various forms of duress. During my tenure, I was offered bribes, I received anonymous threatening phone calls, and I was coerced by the Mob. In later years I was frequently cautioned to be more flexible when evaluating those construction projects politically blessed by City Hall. Since I did not comply with these suggestions, the mayor's office announced that I was to be removed from office. This caused most of the more than sixty citizen preservation groups in New York to rise in defense of the political independence of the commission. I served my last fourteen months as a commissioner in the eye of this public storm.

In short, I became familiar with some of the temptations and dilemmas of wielding power; I learned not to be surprised by the smell of impropriety or malfeasance; and I was introduced to the realities of land-use regulation in a major metropolis where people came to amass great wealth in real estate.

Perhaps the most important lesson I learned came several years after I left the commission, when I systematically conducted a review of buildings constructed in controversial preservation cases. These were all matters in which the commission had weighed imperfect solutions to complex problems. In many of these instances, I had concurred with the majority opinion and had voted to approve projects that were the result of concession and expediency. To this day I can remember my troubled feelings as I voted to approve those designs. Years later, standing in the shadow of these compromised second-class buildings, I saw that I had been complicit in wounding the cityscape, for in New York, to accept the architectural status quo often means to accept the crass and mundane products of a mercantile culture. Disheartened, I realized that most of these mistakes would outlive me. The echo of the words spoken in behalf of expediency had long ago faded; what remained was a permanently injured city. This was the lesson: that the final arbiter in all preservation issues should be the quality of the physical results themselves, which would affect the city for decades and sometimes centuries. I learned not to let the better judgment of my well-trained eye be fooled by the illusions of the temporal human comedy.

Most of these compromised approvals involved the sanctioning of modern high-rises next to low-scale historic monuments. During my travels, in lectures I would give abroad, foreign audiences were often stunned or driven to laughter when seeing what the commission in New York had sanctioned. When I tried to convey the logic behind our thinking, the bewilderment of my listeners only increased. I began to realize that these particular cases were interesting as expressions of a peculiar New York aesthetic blind spot. To a resident of Manhattan, where extraordinary and abrupt leaps of scale are common and where four-story buildings can abut sixty-story towers, a disparity of only a dozen stories between neighboring structures can seem only moderately egregious, whereas to a Venetian, whose native city is constituted entirely of buildings comprising two to six stories, a building of twelve stories is monstrous. What in one place may be an improvement, in another is an absurdity.

I soon found that peculiar aesthetic predispositions often existed in the cultures of the cities I traveled to. These differences were significant, and in order to recognize them, it became very important for me to maintain critical objectivity. Many attempts to preserve our urban architectural heritage are obvious failures when seen by an outsider, although within a society, the reasons for such cultural myopia may be contradictory and complex.

In the years that followed my departure from the Landmarks Commission, I became a citizen advocate for landmarks preservation, served on the transition team for a new mayoral administration, wrote opinion pieces on conservation matters for a local newspaper, and taught courses on the preservation of New York's architectural heritage. These experiences in politics and public life seemed invaluable when, six years later, I set out to learn about the realities of preservation in other large cities of the world.

Before I set foot on foreign soil, I was faced with a dilemma. From my years in government, I knew that subversion of the lawful preservation process was part of the politics of preservation in New York. Still, such misbehavior was seldom written about and difficult to prove on the basis of verifiable evidence. (The people who commit such improprieties often go to great lengths to camouflage their activities.) Nonetheless, not to speak about such occurrences would distort the facts for those not familiar with the city. In my own town, my experience and years of combing the press for news items on these subjects substantiated the phenomenon. In my travels, would it be possible to establish such behavior (as it affected the conservation of historic buildings), when and if it presented itself? This question was soon answered, once I was abroad.

In Cairo, I learned that foreign conservation missions to Egypt either con-tracted for the construction of their own projects themselves or, if working through the Egyptian government, wrote off as much as 50 percent of the budget to various illicit payoffs. Here there were published university studies of such bureaucratic misconduct, while the preservation of the city's landmarks suffered from a widespread lack of funds. In Rome about once every ten years, the government institutes a period of *condo* (amnesty), when the violators of municipal codes can declare their illegal acts and pay a fine as reparation. The lines during a period of *condo* are reported to be quite long, and this is but one aspect of a widely documented culture of illegality affecting innumerable his-toric buildings in Rome. Similar problems besiege Athens and several other cities I have profiled. The larger dilemma is fundamental: architectural con-servation requires continuity of practice and therefore a continuity of law. Landmarks can be preserved assiduously for many decades or centuries, but one momentary lapse in safeguarding them can result in irrevocable loss. Meanwhile, in economically marginalized megacities, governments have abdi-cated their responsibility to provide municipal services for millions of illegal settlers. As in Cairo, how can these inhabitants be asked to honor the social contract, when their families are excluded from its protections and benefits?

A final technical problem that I should speak about is the question of lan-guage. Although much has been written about conservation in various places, only some of this material has been translated into English, or any other single language, and few of these materials are available in libraries outside the coun-try in which the documents originated. Even such obviously desirable tools as translations of preservation statutes are surprisingly difficult to find; they must be constantly updated and require that the translator be expert in the termi-nology of conservation law in two cultures. Few such works exist even in the libraries of a multilingual organization such as UNESCO, and preservation-ists are often poorly informed about conservation efforts in other places. As a result, in order to gather a view of international urban conservation I had to go out into the world and collect it.

Before describing the organization of this text I must acknowledge an important historical element: intellectual honor—the honor of a great artist and architect of the Italian Renaissance who challenged a pope in regard to practices that resulted in destruction of the ancient monuments of Rome; the honor of a respected Roman academic who refused to sanction the ruinous urban renewal policies of a Fascist dictator; and the honor of Russian city planners who registered their dissent in opposition to Communist plans to modernize Moscow by cutting roads unnecessarily through the heart of the historic cityscape. Posterity is indebted to these people and others like them who, at critical historic junctures, recorded for following generations that there were options to the common wisdom of the time: that alternatives to self-inflicted destruction were available, explicated, but not embraced. It is through such dissent that we can trace the evolution of an ethic of urban architectural conservation.

Here is a map of this book. The first section, "The Awakening of a Conservation Ethic," describes how the practices of warfare and the modernization of the metropolis in the twentieth century resulted in unprecedented destruction of historic urban environments and, in answer to these policies, how modern conservation statutes were created spontaneously in almost every major historic city of the world. Next comes the story of Rome. In its 2,000-year history, during which an extraordinary urban legacy was slowly deconstructed, we see an urban populace gradually acquire out of dispute an understanding of the importance of architectural preservation to their cultural identity.

The middle section, "The Culture of Conservation in Cities," is composed of a series of urban conservation profiles that trace the evolving preservation ethic of various cities across their cultural history. (In all, I have described in varying detail eighteen of the cities I visited, although my studies of all twenty-two have informed the book throughout.) Here the central issues of architectural conservation are revealed in the actions of people embroiled in the realities of urban adaptation.

The painstaking and heroic reconstruction of Warsaw after World War II is a testament to the enduring meaning of culture for the human spirit. Moscow and Beijing exemplify the destruction of heritage for ideological reasons. Amsterdam and Vienna are models for the construction of beautiful socially subsidized housing, but in Vienna acts of social conscience led to policies that reduced its legendary beauty, whereas in Amsterdam, a remarkable solution was formulated to the combined problems of social housing, urban redevelopment, and historic conservation. In Athens, can the Acropolis survive the pollution and mismanagement of the modern city? And will we ever see the artistry of the Parthenon reassembled in all its glory? After World War II, erosion of the beautiful skylines of London and Paris raised questions about the dearness of each city's historic visage to its residents and nation. Different approaches evolved in each place in reconciling modernization and historic conservation—with two quite different results. Supreme legacies are imperiled in Cairo: the Pyramids are endangered by the gross exploitation of tourism, and the medieval Muslim settlement is threatened by the desperate problems of the impoverished megacity. In Singapore, where a noteworthy economic equity was achieved for a destitute populace, is the city's newfound commitment to preserving the material evidence of its unique multiethnic culture too late to matter? And across the world, are we exchanging urban cultural diversity for a homogenous urban monoculture? The singular cityscape of Venice is threatened by highly complex problems. Can modern Venice maintain an ecological balance with its surrounding natural environment? And will it continue to be a living city that sustains the lives and culture of Venetians, or will it become an exclusive theme park for tourists from other countries? In New York, based on my experiences as a landmarks commissioner in the city, I discuss in detail the participatory political process through which the soaring contemporary metropolis weighs the meaning of its architectural culture. Will the beautiful city of skyscrapers be consumed for private profit? And in Kyoto, might the destruction of its singular medieval heritage be reversed? Shall its traditional wooden building culture be reestablished within the chaotic modern Japanese cityscape? Can the currents of history and time itself be inverted?

In the final section of the book, "The Widening Ethic of Preservation," in the first of two chapters, "The City Redeemed," in Berlin, Moscow, New York, and Mexico City historic crimes against humanity have been physically memorialized and modern preservation has assumed a moral aspect involving the admission of wrongdoing and the desire of urban societies to make amends among their populations and the nations of the world. Does the city have a collective continuing soul? The last chapter, "The City As a Living Museum," is composed of a summary of the persisting destructive practices of contemporary urbanization, and an account of two important conservation initiatives I found with the potential to offset such self-negating tendencies. In Charleston a modest housing program of traditional vernacular structures is a blend of sound urban design, historic preservation, and social justice in the largest point of entry in the United States for Africans kidnapped into slavery. In Jerusalem a new modern housing project whose forms evoke the ambience of the recently dynamited historic Jewish Quarter of the Old City is both a place to live and a place to learn. Here the metropolis becomes a living museum. In places like these, and many others, where acts of human invention opened new doors to the future, I found the city triumphant.

On March 6, 1995, I boarded a flight for Athens—the first of a number of such trips. Upon arriving I planned to go to the legendary architectural heart of each city: the Acropolis, Saint Peter's Square, the Forbidden City, the Ringstrasse, Red Square, the Imperial Palace, the Piazza San Marco, the Place de la Concorde, the Brandenburg Gate, the Temple Mount. Here were places of potent magic, beyond the measure of conventional thinking, unique unto themselves, radiating important ideas out into the world beyond.

In the following days, I would explore the back alleys, looking for vestiges of the texture of the historic city, largely composed of modest vernacular structures, sometimes abandoned, decayed, forgotten. These were the neighborhoods of the history of everyday life, testifying to our capacity to endow the built environment with grace and meaning. Sometimes such places were woven together organically in marvelous symphonies of urban form. But were they being saved?

For some time we have lived in danger of the irreversible destruction of the gardens of nature as our civilization rushes forward, wrecking vast tracts of wilderness without fully comprehending the consequences. Now, across the world another question is being asked: How well have we tended the fruitful gardens of our creation—the gardens that are our cities?

As the plane to Athens left the tarmac, I anticipated the many wondrous places I would see. For years I had studied the architecture of civilization from afar; now I would experience it. Photography tends to isolate our monuments from their surroundings. Soon I would behold the great landmarks in context—amid their cityscapes and historic urban cultures. I felt the globe spread out before me. Yet when the plane touched down in some places, I was too late. The beauty I had longed to know had already been eradicated. For in many of the great cities of the world the wealth of cultural diversity and architectural expression that still existed at the beginning of the twentieth century had in the intervening hundred years been purposely, thoughtlessly, and sometimes with malice, removed from the earth forever.

THE AWAKENING OF A
CONSERVATION ETHIC

The Masai when they moved from their old country, north of the railway line, to the present reserve, took with them the names of their hills, plains, and rivers, and gave them to the hills, plains, and rivers in the new country. It is a bewildering thing to the traveler. The Masai were carrying their cut roots with them as a medicine.

—ISAK DINESEN, *Out of Africa*

As the Masai were the land and the land was the Masai, embodying their myths and symbols, so do urban societies living in the human-made agglomeration have a mutual relationship with their surroundings. The physical forms of Paris, for example, are a product of the social culture of its inhabitants, just as the evolving social culture of the Parisians grows out of the built construction in which they live.

Although the Masai were able in their minds to move the hills, plains, and rivers of their history, in the modern city a different physical reality determines the continuity of culture. Human-made environments gain value from being immovable, as succeeding generations erect beautiful buildings in the same place over centuries. Additions to the cityscape often require the removal of other structures. As a result, since the first construction of dense urban settlements in the distant past, the adaptation of historic cities to social, economic, political, and technological changes has always involved the basic question of whether or not to preserve old buildings as part of the city of the future. Over the millennia, this seemingly elementary question has become a complex metaphysical one. Like the Masai, if we remove the physical manifestations of our cultural identity, to what extent do we change who we are as a people?

The rise of an urban conservation ethic occurs in two distinct stages. In the history of Rome we see the incremental evolution of an awareness among a city's inhabitants of the cultural ties that bind them to their past. And in the unparalleled massive destruction of historic cities after the Industrial Revolution, we see the spontaneous creation of urban conservation statutes in response to a sudden, pervasive, and continuing threat. Whereas the Masai moved the landmarks of the earth with their imaginations, in the twentieth century civilization gained the power to refashion the settings of life in as brief a moment as it took to drop atomic bombs on the cities of Hiroshima and Nagasaki.

CHAPTER ONE
THE CENTURY OF DESTRUCTION

Whoever studies the behavior of human beings cannot escape the conclusion that we must reckon with an enemy within the lines. It becomes increasingly evident that some of the destruction that curses the earth is self-destruction; that the extraordinary propensity of the human being to join hands with external forces in an attack upon his own existence is one of the most remarkable of biological phenomena.

—KARL A. MENNINGER, *Man Against Himself,* 1938

The twentieth century was the century of destruction. This is the first and foremost fact concerning the preservation of historic cities around the world. It was a century of dramatic urban expansion, improvement, and redefinition, but it was also a century when urban architectural culture was destroyed at a rate unmatched in human history.

In two world wars and numerous regional conflicts, millions of tons of explosives have been detonated in ancient urban centers. In metropolitan areas across the globe, huge tracts of historic architecture, which might have been rehabilitated, were leveled instead, in waves of so-called urban renewal that frequently did not renew centuries-old handcrafted buildings so much as replace them with highways clogged with cars and with mass-produced anonymous structures of concrete, glass, and steel. By the end of the century, in underdeveloped nations, numerous old urban centers were surrounded by vast impoverished megacities where a culture of illegality—affecting virtually all aspects of urban management—subjected surviving historic structures to continuous hostile environmental siege. Meanwhile, across the century and around the clock, a progressively incalculable amount of human, industrial, and vehicular waste was spewed into our urban areas. In numerous places, this continuous flow of pollutants has caused the once-sustaining waters of life to become so acid—and so corrosive—that they melt the very stone of the architectural masterworks of history.

Between the years 1900 and 2000, nearly one-quarter of the landmarks of Amsterdam were leveled by Amsterdammers. More than half of the indexed buildings of Islamic Cairo—one of the few intact medieval Muslim cities out of several that had existed at the beginning of the century—were destroyed by Cairenes. Singapore razed the exotic colonial emporium that once attracted ships from across the world. Turks allowed the preponderance of the wooden buildings of Ottoman Istanbul to become so deteriorated that they barely continue to stand. Thousands of New York's beautiful old buildings were demolished by New Yorkers. In Athens all but a minute fraction of a lovely but quickly passing nineteenth-century achievement in city design was wrecked by Athenians. Communist rulers decimated the picturesque skyline of onion domes and gilded bell towers of czarist Moscow. Hardly a building in Venice was not eroded by decay due to heightened modern pollution caused by Venetians. Radical post–World War II modernization by Japan erased most of the refined wooden architectural cityscape of imperial Kyoto. Romans demolished a third of Rome's historic structures. The Viennese stripped of their beauty large parts of elegant fin de siècle Vienna. And after six hundred years the towering and fabled walls of ancient Beijing were dismantled by the Chinese, who then bulldozed block upon block of their city's traditional courtyard houses.

As damaging as these practices have been, in many places they continue. Meanwhile, in an attempt to stop the wreckage, an imaginative new urban planning practice has arisen in historic cities across the world, the effort of modern societies to conserve the architectural culture of the civilizations of the past. Yet even as the new urban conservation ethic emerged, the process of destruction has continued, and saving the culture of cities has become a race against time and self-negating human impulses.

The Third Reich demolished the landmarks of Warsaw as a punitive action against the Poles. The Allies firebombed Dresden as a punitive action against the Germans. The historic cores of Hamburg and Coventry were both despoiled. The preponderance of Japan's wooden cityscapes were incinerated. Vast armadas of planes pulverized Weimar Berlin. The venerated Jewish Quarter of Old Jerusalem was laid waste. Only yesterday, so was Sarajevo, and in the jungles of Cambodia the Khmer Rouge looted the temples of their ancestors to buy weapons with which to kill their neighbors.

The ruin resulting from warfare in our era continues an age-old pattern— Alexander burned Persepolis, Caesar set aflame the library at Alexandria, the

Mongols put the torch to Baghdad—and in the twentieth century, as modern arsenals have been unleashed upon historic cities, unprecedented desolation has ensued. Our ability to be barbaric has increased by a quantum leap.

And yet, by comparison, the vast and rapid devastation resulting from urban renewal and city building has been even more extensive. Half a century after the Second World War numerous planners throughout Europe, including Germany, have concluded that far more architectural history was destroyed in the urban redevelopment that followed the fighting than by the tens of millions of bombs themselves. Moreover, in many cities it has come to be perceived that much of the loss incurred in the rush to remodel the metropolis was avoidable, unnecessary, largely irreversible, and therefore tragic.

In the twentieth century, after thousands of years of city building, the shape and character of the historic metropolis was fundamentally changed. During an unprecedented period of metropolitan growth, the historic parts of many older cities came to be surrounded by dense urban and suburban rings whose aesthetic and environmental qualities clashed with the character of the traditional cityscape. Frequently, the original historic city became alienated within a larger conurbation. Numerous old places of urban settlement became fractured in scale, form, and spirit—with disrelated zones of modern and historic buildings set in disquieting juxtaposition.

For thousands of years prior to this transformation, even the largest cities of the world could be perceived in their totality from a high point near or in the city. The naked eye could encompass the expanse of the city and the beginning of the countryside beyond. Today, with few exceptions, we can discern the extent of the human-made environment only when looking down from an airplane. The modern metropolis became too large to be comprehended from any viewpoint on the earth.

The fantastic growth of our cities has been the consequence of a staggering worldwide increase in urban populations. In 1900, about 220 million people, or about 13.6 percent of the world's population, lived in urban areas; the largest city by far was London, with 6.5 million inhabitants, and only eight cities exceeded or even verged upon a million. By the year 2000, however, 323 cities had a million residents apiece. It is estimated that forty will soon house 15 million people each, and several will surpass 20 million. Early in the twenty-first century, for the first time in history, more people will live inside cities than outside them. The United Nations predicts that by 2025 about 61 percent of the population of the world, or 5.2 billion people, will reside in urban areas. In a hundred years, global urban population has increased more than tenfold, and it is still growing.

This eruption in population has fueled several massive building explosions. Myriad historic conurbations that had evolved over many hundreds of years soared to two, three, four, five—as much as ten times their size within a century, a half-century, a quarter-century.

The first stages of this rapid urban transformation began in the latter half of the 1800s in the United States and Europe as a result of the Industrial Revolution. As this development continued and spread into the twentieth century, new technologies irrevocably altered city life and city form.

THE MODERNIZATION OF CITIES

The change was both quantitative and qualitative. The modernization of the metropolis required its expansion as well as an effort to raise the standard of living for all the city's inhabitants. At the beginning of the Industrial Revolution, as people were driven off farms and into cities, life in metropolitan areas was bitter and unhealthy for large segments of an impoverished population. Many sections of older cities lacked sewage removal and sanitary water. A statistical survey of London in 1887 estimated that over 35 percent of its population—about one million people—were living in poverty in slums (that survey was taken before London subsumed several neighboring towns and further leaped in size). Inhabitants were crowded together at intolerable densities. Toilet facilities were inadequate or nonexistent, as were the accommodations for bathing, washing clothes, and cleaning. Several buildings often shared a single drinking-water tap. Crime, unemployment, hunger, disease, social unrest, hopelessness, and child mortality were prevalent. In Paris, it was judged that about 330,000 people were living in conditions worse than those in London. And in the eleventh ward in New York, more than 700 people were packed into each acre of tenements. Here the congestion was greater than in any other slum on the planet. The initial urbanization caused by the first machine age had engendered cities of despair.

But although industrialization was a root of the problem, it also offered a potential solution. The new machinery and mass production of the industrialized world not only mechanized agriculture but also created new products, new industries, and new jobs, and made possible the radical re-formation of the metropolis in virtually all of its aspects. During the nineteenth and twentieth centuries, as the populations of cities multiplied, the metropolis was simultaneously expanded and transformed in several dimensions. Cities became so big, so complex, and so multifaceted that human intellectual capacity was stretched to its limit to comprehend, control, and plan urban areas.

While cities at various levels of economic development on various continents would undergo such transfigurations to various degrees and at various times, the overall pattern of change in developed nations, and the desired result in all nations, would be similar in many ways.

- Dams and aqueducts were built and vast infrastructures were put in place to pump freshwater in and wastewater out of the city, ameliorating sanitary conditions.
- Gaslights made the metropolis safer at night, and cities like Paris became celebrated for their nocturnal beauty.
- Railroad tracks pierced the urban fabric as nations were united by rapid transport systems, and major cities became hubs for the movement of people, materials, and products.
- Monumental railway terminals, public parks, public schools, universities, hospitals, courts, museums, zoos, and opera houses were built. Department stores and apartment buildings proliferated. Countless government offices for the extensive bureaucracies of modern society inundated the cityscape.
- Avenues, boulevards, and streets were broadened to facilitate heightened vehicular traffic flow. Suspension bridges and tunnels spanned wide waterways and linked landmasses.
- Warehouses, factories, and rail yards occupied extended industrial zones.
- Mass transit systems were established above and below ground and horse-drawn trolleys were followed by electric trams and subways.
- Electric lighting replaced gas.
- Middle-class families moved to garden suburbs along commuter rail lines.
- The automobile proliferated, and cities were retrofitted to serve the needs of cars, trucks, and buses.
- The elevator and the skyscraper further increased the density of the metropolis.
- Immense networks of telephone lines were installed.
- Air conditioned high-rise central business districts rose up out of the city's mass.
- An extensive system of highways crisscrossed nations and encircled and cut through the metropolis.
- The suburbs expanded beyond all expectations; endless numbers of commuters clogged freeways.
- Industry moved out of the city's center.
- The wide suburban rings around cities were dotted with industrial and corporate parks, shopping malls, and asphalt parking lots.
- Airports were constructed on the urban periphery, and the great metropolis was joined to a global network of cities.

The extensive remodeling of the metropolis constituted nothing less than a physical and spiritual metamorphosis. Among a greatly expanded middle class in cities of the first wave of industrialized nations, greater health, happiness, and freedom from abject poverty were, to some degree, the end products of the physical alterations. And in every city, the most significant constructions, in terms of both their physical and their social implications, were the massive amounts of housing needed: more and more people were accommodated, with an increasing measure of better-quality living space for each person.

Housing the population of the growing metropolis was often a task of heroic proportions, mobilizing whole societies across decades. In the Communist capitals of Moscow and Beijing, the many clusters and rows of new residential blocks represented a major step forward, as vast populations of for-mer serfs and farmers were provided with greatly improved living conditions. In Amsterdam, Paris, New York, Vienna, Kyoto, Singapore, Berlin, London, and most other cities of the first and following waves of industrialization, numerous older inhabitants can still recall the days when several families were packed into one room, unwashed and with meager options for betterment. When first constructed, the armada of upgraded residential facilities seemed to be palpable evidence of an evolving social and economic equity. But in many of these places, for many people, as the gloss of newness wore thin, so did the promise of improvement.

While many aspects of the modernization of the city were profoundly posi-tive, as Karl A. Menninger has observed, there was "an enemy within the lines." A lurking human propensity for self-destruction caused this transfor-mation to have several negative by-products: the physical and social fracturing of the city, extensive urban poverty and illegal settlement in underdeveloped nations, urban environmental pollution of an unprecedented magnitude, and widespread radical depletion of urban architectural culture. In this regard, a fundamental change during the twentieth century in the way buildings were conceived and fabricated would eventually pose a complex and far-reaching environmental dilemma.

THE MODERN ARCHITECTURAL PARADOX

As the wholesale reconfiguration of the metropolis occurred, the economics, philosophy, aesthetics, and technology of architecture were undergoing an equally radical transformation. Until the twentieth century, throughout the world the thinking that gave form to buildings and cities had evolved slowly, with each new stage referring substantially to some earlier architectural style or construction technology. In Western culture, a direct aesthetic line connected the architecture of classical Greece, imperial Rome, the Romanesque period, the Renaissance, the Baroque, the Rococo, and all the forms of classical revival that followed. Even such divergent local traditional styles as French Gothic,

English Tudor, the architecture of the Greek Orthodox church, and the Islamic architecture of Andalusian Spain utilized many common architectonic elements such as columns, capitals, pediments, and cornices. Openings for windows and doorways were punched into bearing walls and supported by lintels, sills, and masonry archways. In important larger buildings interior spaces were spanned by vaults, pendentives, and domes. These architectural effects were the basic phrases of a time-honored and familiar sculptural language. (Similar deeply rooted architectonic traditions would evolve in Eastern culture as well.) In cityscapes composed of such structures, each generation of stylistic change became part of a larger visual dialogue that engaged the buildings of preceding eras. In many places, across the centuries, an extensive urban architectural harmony was achieved. The legendary cities of beauty—Paris, Kyoto, Vienna, Cairo, Amsterdam, Mexico City, Venice, Beijing, Prague—became great symphonies of thousands of interrelated buildings, composed of myriad interrelated building elements, made of common materials drawn from the surrounding natural environment, constructed by workers with skills evolved over centuries, and woven together by generations of inhabitants into unified visual themes, small and greater urban crescendos, and one or a few or many preeminent architectural high notes.

Early in the twentieth century, however, many of these age-old aesthetic compositions were abruptly interrupted by the jarring tone of a new architecture, built at an alien scale, of different materials, by new methods, and according to a philosophy of design that consciously sought a *lack* of relationship with the long continuum of preceding form. In the headlong and often idealistic rush to build a better metropolis, the patrimony of many old cities would be set into harsh juxtaposition with new buildings whose underlying cultural intent was to *not* relate to their older neighbors.

The modern architecture that emerged out of the Industrial Revolution would constitute a sweeping change in the aesthetics of building. It was a moment in history that illuminated great talent. Particularly through the groundbreaking designs of such master architects as Frank Lloyd Wright (1869–1959), Walter Gropius (1883–1969), Ludwig Mies van der Rohe (1886–1969), Le Corbusier (1887–1969), and Louis Kahn (1902–1974), the brave new world of mass production, interglobal travel, and instantaneous long-distance communication was given an elegant new architectural language.

As the Industrial Revolution progressed, its many inventions suggested that innumerable aspects of modern living would be radically different from the features of preindustrial society. A world of form began to evolve in which the new products based on new technologies gradually took on a modern, streamlined aesthetic. Typewriters, telephones, electric lamps, adding machines, refrigerators, vacuum cleaners, washing machines, dryers, sewing machines, fans, air conditioners, radios, record players, tape recorders, steamships, automobiles, motorcycles, and airplanes had few direct precedents in shape or function. Soon architects, industrial designers, engineers, interior decorators, graphic designers, and furniture makers began to conceive of an aesthetic philosophy by which every object in the modern world would be configured. Mass production of these products, at lower cost per item, promised to elevate the quality of life of whole societies.

Modernists believed that superficial decoration should be eliminated from the design of objects, that new products should look like the result of machine-age manufacturing rather than adopting the old aesthetics of handcraftsmanship, that new design should promote a common nationless culture, and that form should follow function.

It was a true international movement. In Holland, *De Stijl* magazine, whose express object was "to contribute to the development of a new consciousness of beauty," advanced a universal style based on primary colors and simple rectilinear compositions, as reflected in the abstract paintings of Piet Mondrian and the architecture and furniture of Gerrit Rietveld. In Moscow, the Russian Constructivists proposed an idealized modernism of angular geometric shapes for the classless society of the Communist revolution. In Vienna, architect Adolf Loos declared that "ornament is crime." In the American Midwest, architect Louis Sullivan advocated stripped-down, Chicago School skyscrapers, and Frank Lloyd Wright prophesied: "The old structural forms, which up to the present time have been called architecture, are decayed." In France, Le Corbusier proposed a "Dom-Ino" house, which was "a machine for living." In Germany, in 1919, a school was established with the express purpose of creating a new design process for all the material objects of life. This was, of course, the Bauhaus, and its teachers, students, and philosophy altered in innumerable ways the visual character of our world. "The Bauhaus believes the machine to be our modern medium of design and seeks to come to terms with it."

This aesthetic revolution did not occur overnight. For almost one hundred years, from the mid-nineteenth to the mid-twentieth century, designers of every kind were engaged in a war of ideas, pitting traditionalists against modernists. Although this ideological struggle caused many designers to approach their work with the zeal of revolutionaries, in architecture, the ultimate success of the modernists was inevitable.

As the twentieth century proceeded the wider social-welfare obligations of nations throughout the industrialized world altered the economics of building. The cost of labor, materials, and transport spiraled. Taxes, insurance, and professional fees rose. A larger part of every building's budget came to be expended on its interior environmental technology—its heating, air conditioning, plumbing, electricity, artificial lighting, and its connection to an electronic world of global communication. Factory production of prefabricated building parts offered savings, which decreased the cost of construction. Giant mobile machines such as cranes, concrete mixers, and bulldozers increased the pace of fabrication. Many old construction skills, performed on-site and handed down across the centuries, dwindled and began to disappear. And an ever smaller proportion of a building's total construction budget was devoted to the quality, detail, and articulation of its external skin, further reducing traditional hand-fashioned exterior details.

The development of manufactured high-strength steel made large buildings easier to erect and, with the invention of the elevator, structures like the Flatiron Building, the Woolworth Building, and the Empire State Building in New York raced upward. In just fifty years, office buildings soared from 400 feet to 800 feet to 1,200 feet. Eventually, apartment buildings, hotels, and government buildings also sped skyward, and urban settlement around the world assumed a new scale.

Moreover, industrialization caused fundamental changes in the way buildings were conceived in the mind of the architect. The wider anatomic possibilities of modern materials and advances in structural engineering opened new realms of aesthetic possibility. Many contemporary buildings became minimal and streamlined.

Steel-frame building technology allowed tall, open structures, and the age-old convention—of puncturing the thick external masonry bearing-walls of buildings to let in light through windows—was widely superseded. The availability of industrial-quality, mass-produced glass and metal panels permitted the surface skin of whole structures to become transparent, thin, flat planes. This curtain-wall construction technology, when combined with the new environmental advance of air conditioning, made possible giant hermetically sealed prisms. In the Lever House (Gordon Bunshaft) and the Seagram Building (Mies van der Rohe), the mass of the structure is suspended above the ground plane by columns. One enters such buildings by walking beneath their volume and being carried upward by elevator. Steel-reinforced concrete offered a new language of complex curvilinear shapes and extreme cantilevers. Airline terminals, museums, auditoriums, concert halls, theaters, and religious structures often became giant free-form sculptural masses. Buildings like the Guggenheim Museum (Frank Lloyd Wright), the TWA Terminal in New York (Eero Saarinen) and the Church of Notre-Dame-du-Haut in Ronchamp, France (Le Corbusier), introduced startling combinations of volume and interior space never before seen at such size. And the new materials, when harnessed by sophisticated structural engineering, made it possible to span great distances and enclose mammoth areas for public assembly with light space frames, thin concrete shells, and high-flying tensile structures, as in the

Olympic arenas and stadiums of Pier Luigi Nervi in Rome, of Kenzo Tange in Tokyo, and of Frei Otto in Munich.

Increasingly, these large minimal forms of different materiality and aesthetic aura appeared jarring when juxtaposed with traditional buildings. The shift to modernism seemed to call for a reconsideration of the design of every object in the human-made world, and many architects extended the underlying aesthetic principles that shaped their buildings to the objects within and around them. Walter Gropius produced a series of designs for automobiles. Mies van der Rohe, Le Corbusier, Frank Lloyd Wright, Alvar Aalto, and Marcel Breuer created classics of contemporary furniture. At Cranbrook Academy in the United States, Eliel Saarinen, with the aid of his wife and his son, the architect Eero Saarinen, laid out the master plan of the whole institution and designed all its buildings, walkways, gardens, fountains, furniture, lamps, tapestries, wrought-iron gateways, fences, flower planters, rugs, leaded-glass windows, and silverware—right down to his own tea and coffee services.

How, then, to reconcile modern architecture with the centuries-old built heritage of cities, when the prime generator of the movement was a rejection of the past? In the heat of forging a revolution, the question of how to make the new buildings meld with the forms that had been abandoned was rarely asked, and rarely answered. In the profusion of architectural drawings created during this period, hardly ever were new buildings depicted in a historical context. Modern structures were shown sitting apart, in combination with other modern buildings, or in visionary drawings of a world constituted entirely of objects of modern design, but never next to the historic monument or old vernacular building that would be its real-life neighbor.

For those swept away with revolutionary fervor, the natural consequence of the wholesale reconception of architecture seemed to be the complete remaking of the built environment. From the very beginnings of the movement, modernists had explored this possibility. Their drawings—often impractical in regard to the complex realities of the living city—were nonetheless a search for the shape of the new utopia. Thus, in Italy in 1914, Antonio Sant' Elia envisioned a metropolis of fantastic industrial skyscrapers and multilevel circulation in *La Città Nuova.* "I conclude in disfavor of preservation, reconstruction, reproduction of ancient monuments," he declared. In France in 1918, Tony Garnier drew in great picturesque detail *La Cité Industrielle,* a complete regional industrial village. In America in 1934, Frank Lloyd Wright constructed a vast miniature model of his imaginary modern town called Broadacre City. But it was the great Swiss-born Parisian architect Le Corbusier who, more than any of the other modern masters, devoted his energies to envisioning the consequences of modern architectural form upon the shape of the contemporary metropolis. His drawings were beautiful, abstract, and widely influential. In 1921–1922 he unveiled his design for a giant urban settlement, *"Une ville contemporaine pour 3 millions d'habitants,"* and by 1933 he had further developed his thinking in *La Ville Radieuse,* the Radiant City. Throughout his career Le Corbusier would offer numerous idealized poetic sketches as solutions to the complicated problems of real urban places such as the South American cities of Rio de Janeiro, São Paulo, Montevideo, Buenos Aires, and Bogotá; the African city of Algiers; and the French provincial cities of La Rochelle and Saint-Dié. One of his large urban conceptions—a design for the governmental center of Chandigarh, India—was constructed posthumously. It is one of the great tours de force of sculptural composition in the history of architecture, but it was soon surrounded by extended slums and illegal settlements of squatters' huts.

In 1925, in his Voisin Plan, Le Corbusier confronted the dilemma of the intersection of modernism with the history of civilization. It was a warning siren that largely went unheeded. He proposed a vast reconstruction of the center of historic Paris. The images were elegant. Mammoth structures, ten times taller and several hundred times larger than the typical buildings of the historic capital, would stand isolated in green superblocks. Slums would be eradicated, parklands increased, vast amounts of new housing erected, and a network of wide highways built to speed battalions of cars to the center of the city. Yet also inherent to his plan was the demolition of whole neighborhoods of historic buildings, the alienating juxtaposition of gigantic modern architecture with existing low-scale urban fabric, and the rupture of neighborhoods by the automobile.

Perhaps most damaging to the historic city was his proposal that modern structures should break with the sculptural system by which individual buildings in European cities became part of a larger urban whole. It was a drastic concept. Since the Renaissance, European cities had been configured by integrating individual buildings into the larger sculptural mass of the block and allotting the negative space between blocks of buildings to serve as the circulation network of the metropolis. In this system, the front face of each building lines up with its neighbors to form a continuous street wall, and the open space between the street walls is devoted to sidewalks and roadways. Thus each building, no matter how idiosyncratic, is still part of a larger urban design. In the Voisin Plan, Le Corbusier suggested that the whole idea of the historic city block as a unifying sculptural mass should be abandoned—that modern buildings should not adhere to this age-old architectural social contract but should stand in open spaces, disconnected from their historic neighbors. As a result, not only would the design of his buildings be radically different and their size enormous, but the centuries-old dialogue of buildings, wherein each structure's design entered the communal urban architectural conversation, would be ended. The modern buildings of the Voisin Plan would deliberately dissociate themselves from the architectural symphony of the historic city. In hindsight, it was a prescription for a choked and schizophrenic environment and a formula for cultural negation, which—in numerous cities across the world, to varying degrees—would often be implemented.

A seductive but paradoxical conception had gestated. The masters of modern architecture would construct a dazzling array of beautiful buildings to serve the different functions of modern life and modern society. One could imagine the glories of whole environments constituted of such structures. But in fact, only the most infinitesimal percentage of the vast armada of buildings that would alter the cityscapes of the world would be designed by the master architects or constructed to the standards of their masterpieces.

The early modern archetypes purported to be demonstrations of the new machine-age architecture by which the lot of all humankind would be advanced. In reality, although they often utilized factory-produced parts, these buildings were one-of-a-kind demonstrations whose construction required meticulous hand assembly, and thus were expensive to build. The finely articulated use of materials in the curtain-wall elements of the Seagram Building would evoke in bronze and glass the subtlety of detail of traditional Japanese wood construction. But across the world, speculative development would reduce the hundreds of thousands of new curtain-wall office structures that inundated cities to cheap, poorly constructed parodies of the beautiful paradigms by Mies. Similarly, the rich sculptural massing of such concrete apartment blocks as the Unité d'Habitation of Le Corbusier—using carefully modulated proportional systems from the Renaissance—were only in the least superficial way related to the thousands of proportionless, massive, low-cost, prefabricated government housing blocks that would be built in cities on every continent. But while the beautiful building forms of the modern master architects would rarely be achieved, the alienating urban design principles upon which modernism was founded would be reflected in the preponderance of new construction, throughout the world, for decades.

By the end of World War II, a new and giant wave of metropolitan expansion and modernization had begun; an unrivaled magnitude of urban material change. Having started in the United States prior to the war, then spread to the industrialized nations of Europe, this change continued across the globe as various societies endeavored to achieve developmental and economic parity. By now, decades of diminished maintenance due to worldwide economic depression and the destruction and shortages of two world wars had reduced to a distressing condition large areas of older cities in Europe, Asia, Africa, the Middle East, and the Americas. Whole historic areas and whole historic cityscapes were long overdue for conversion to reasonable densities of habitation, proper sanitation, new uses, and modern environmental technologies. Yet beneath the outward layer of decay, many of these sectors held buildings of remarkable historic and aesthetic value from the earliest periods of urban growth. Here, in fact, was the global cultural portfolio of myriad landmarks and interwoven ensembles of historic buildings built across hundreds and thousands of years and embodying the development of distinct urban cultures and the singular high achievements of civilizations.

THE INVENTION OF MODERN URBAN PRESERVATION

At every stage in the industrialization, expansion, and modernization of the historic city, old urban fabric was destroyed. This was, of course, to some degree simply a part of the process of urban evolution. Yet the decisive break of modern architecture from the long historic continuum of traditional building culture fundamentally altered the developmental equation. Old cities of hand-crafted buildings, largely made of natural materials from the immediate geographic location of cities, and reflecting the distinct physical characteristics and values of unique urban cultures, now constituted a finite resource from a closed period of human cultural evolution.

From the middle of the nineteenth century forward, as the changes in cities escalated in speed and breadth, as more and more historic urban fabric was lost, and as modern architecture became increasingly universal as a cultural expression and further departed from traditional building aesthetics, inhabitants in many of the most beautiful historic cities of the world became alarmed. Particularly in Europe and America, where the effects of industrialization were felt first, a belief began to emerge that old buildings and old urban fabric were a precious resource that ought to be conserved.

At the heart of the matter lay a mystery. As Amsterdammers watched old Amsterdam be lessened, as Parisians saw the beauty of historic Paris being reduced, the fear that emerged was not just that beloved old buildings might be destroyed. Something of far more profound value was embodied in the collective historic cityscape. For if human beings and human society have a propensity for self-destruction, the beauty of historic cities is evidence of a positive creative potential. Moreover, the different environmental aesthetic milieus in collective historic Prague, collective historic Kyoto, collective historic Cairo, and in old Vienna, Istanbul, Beijing, New York, and Jerusalem exemplify the diverse possibilities of life-affirming social invention.

Yet what makes each of these special places singular? Why is the beauty of historic Amsterdam so completely different from the comparable beauty of historic Venice? We know that the story of each city is unique in many ways. But it is more than that. The angle of the sun is different as it passes across each cityscape during the course of the year. The quality of light in the particular climatic conditions of each city is different. The colors of the surrounding earth, the sounds of the indigenous language, the sounds of indigenous music, and the sounds of each city itself are different. Across their histories, the collective social achievements of Amsterdam and Venice are different. The foods of these cities, their social norms, their religious practices, their customs of government, differ. And all these things, and innumerable other factors together form the mystery of the florescence of cities. And it was the loss of this ultimately unquantifiable social chemistry that people feared, the loss of the spirit of the city made palpable in the beautiful interwoven forms of the historic cityscape.

Thus even as the metropolis was transformed and modernized, human creativity in many of the great and beautiful cities of the world was directed toward finding social mechanisms by which that greatness and beauty might be saved. Some places mobilized successfully to save their historic architectural patrimony; some places failed. The story of how this sensibility grew to become a general urban planning practice, and established in law, would vary from city to city, nation to nation, culture to culture. A different balance of life-affirming and self-negating impulses would have to be realized via the imperfect political processes through which urban societies build consensus.

Until recently our cities have held the achievements and lessons of our past. Now in many places we verge on breaking that historic continuum irrevocably. While the motivations for the eradication of culture may differ from one place to another, the devastation of cities has usually been a result of human volition. Neither God nor nature has made the metropolis. Human settlement is a product of the human mind. And the destruction or conservation of the mysterious architectural beauty of our urban areas is in the final analysis a matter of choice, a reflection of our propensity to destroy and our propensity to create.

In seeking the great cities of the world, in the first glimpse of the metropolis through the window of a train or airplane, the modern traveler must wonder: To what degree has this special place—its architectural culture, its urban beauty, its high material accomplishments, its civic dignity, and the spirit of this metropolis itself—survived our century of self-inflicted destruction?

CHAPTER TWO
THE CITY THAT DEVOURED ITS GLORY

IMPERIAL AND RENAISSANCE ROME

We, the rulers of the state, with a view to restoring the beauty of our venerable city, desire to put an end to the abuses which have already long excited our indignation. It is well known that in several instances public buildings have been destroyed with the criminal permission of the authorities, on the pretext that the materials were necessary for public works. Splendid ancient buildings have been overthrown, and the great has been everywhere destroyed in order to erect the little. . . . We accordingly command, by universal law, that all buildings which were of old erected for the public use or ornament, be they temples or other monuments, shall henceforth be neither destroyed nor touched by anyone whomsoever.

—EMPEROR MAJORIAN OF ROME, EDICT OF A.D. 458

It is the mother of all cities and has twice been the center of the universe. Its shifts of time and character are many and dislocating. Within its ancient walls, from across more than two thousand years, in a single compacted gathering are the towering fragments of a great yet brutal civilization, the intact sublime perfection of the Pantheon, a twisting medieval maze, the dramatic straight vistas cut through the cityscape by the popes (which have influenced the building of all cities ever since), the flawless Tempietto of Bramante, the artful logic of Michelangelo on the Campidoglio, Saint Peter's, the brilliant fountains of Bernini, a colossal lumbering monument to the founding of the Italian nation-state known as the Monumento a Vittorio

Emanuele II, the zones of archaeology uncovered by Mussolini, and the highway he built on top of the forums of the Caesars—all amid the current chaos, pollution, and noise of crowded streets lined with elegant modern shops. In this one place, both the magnitude of historic architectural greatness, and the magnitude of historic architectural destruction are awesome. How was it that the same metropolis created, saved, and eradicated so much beauty? In comprehending the history of the preservation of architecture in cities, first there is Rome.

That the architecture of the past should be saved as part of the city of the future is both a very recent and a very old idea. While the widespread enactment of preservation statutes in cities around the world is primarily a phenomenon of the twentieth century, the development of cities has always required periodic consideration of how much of the old metropolis to preserve as part of the new conurbation. Two objects cannot occupy the same space at the same time. When a city continues in the same location, questions of preservation are bound to arise.

In Mesopotamia, in the seventh century B.C., anyone who ruined the appearance of the Royal Road of Nineveh was hanged from the roof of his own house. This was a clear, if somewhat zealous, policy in favor of urban architectural conservation. It may be said that the Royal Road of Nineveh is the earliest known protected historic district.

With the passage of time, in those locations where human settlement has flourished and survived the vicissitudes of famine, war, fire, and flood, an accrual of historical, architectural, and environmental value often occurs. More and more parts of the city acquire layers of significant meaning. Correspondingly, this makes more complex the question of how much of the old city to retain.

Rome is where architectural preservation first became a function of deliberate urban planning, because it is a nexus of rare historic events. It is one of the few cases in which the capital of one empire was built on top of the capital of another. It is a place where architectural value grew enormously and later was put into contention with a new urge to build. Only two other cities are comparable: Ottoman Istanbul, constructed within the remains of Byzantine Constantinople; and Mexico City, the home of one of the three viceroys of colonial Spain, built amid the ruins of Aztec Tenochtitlán. In these cities a great architectural patrimony was endangered by the emergence of a new and powerful civilization.

In Mexico City, the heritage of the Aztecs was purposely obliterated as part of a plan to subjugate a conquered people. In Istanbul, the new Muslim civilization reorganized the urban structure of an earlier and alien culture. Generally, in both of these places, the past was considered expendable because in the minds of the new rulers, the emerging city would have undisputed primacy over the historic one. In Rome, a somewhat different attitude evolved: the new culture would consciously take part of its identity from the older culture. The architectural aesthetics of the Italian Renaissance were predicated on a reinterpretation of the glories of Roman antiquity. As a result, the new Renaissance city and the old imperial city were both revered, and the intellectual powers of society were mobilized to resolve the intense spatial conflict between them. Rome, in the era of Raphael and Michelangelo, became the boiling pot from which the concepts of urban conservation would be distilled.

The story of how architectural preservation evolved in Rome has many abrupt starts, stops, and turns, as would the evolution of modern conservation practice in the twentieth century. This reflects the character of large cities, where conflicting interests, vision, common sense, and folly all coexist. Yet in Rome the contradictions somehow seem greater than in other places. Perhaps this is because to speak of imperial Rome as if it were like any other place is to distort its true dimensions. The size, intricacy, problems, and advances of the ancient city make it a place out of time, with few historical precedents or peers, and unsurpassed in some respects until the twentieth century.

IMPERIAL ROME

As the center of a great empire, Imperial Rome was the largest and most magnificent of the ancient cities. Many historians estimate that sometime in the second century it became the first place of urban habitation to reach a population of one million people. No other city in Europe would attain this size until London did so in the 1820s during the Industrial Revolution.

The first Rome—ancient Rome—was one of humankind's early experiments in managing a giant urban populace. The city was a step forward in human thinking, a glorious architectural conglomeration, a vast slum, and a place of unfathomable cruelty. These clashing characteristics are fundamental to understanding the ancient metropolis.

The immensity of ancient Rome was due to the fact that Roman military omnipotence directed the wealth of a vast empire to the building of a splendid capital. It was also due to the advances made by Roman civilization in support of dense urban settlement. During an extended period of Roman political hegemony, Roman law and administration facilitated the management of ever larger urban areas. Roman architects and engineers invented an array of buildings and infrastructures to serve the needs of an increasingly greater number of urban inhabitants. This particular assemblage of constructions would make the metropolis quite unlike any other city, before or since.

One of the principal Roman inventions that elevated the quality of life in cities was the segregation of water supply from human waste removal. Aqueducts, cisterns, reservoirs, and public fountains brought in clean water, while sewers were constructed to carry away filth. Fountains and taps were designed to continuously run and overflow so that a perpetual stream of water washed the city's filth into its sewers. These improvements in urban sanitation curbed the spread of infectious diseases and thus allowed large numbers of people to live together in one location. Today we regard this concept as a major contribution of Roman civilization to the science of city building. Yet although this technology was applied to Rome in the form of the Cloaca Maxima—the world's oldest sewer still in service after more than 2,500 years—it did not benefit all of the city or all of its populace. The private houses of the privileged had water closets, fountains, and bathrooms. The inhabitants of the city's poorest multistory tenements—the *insulae,* which housed about two hundred people apiece at the height of the city's density—had to lug water up to their living quarters from neighborhood fountains or from a common building tap. They would later deposit their sewage in cisterns at the bottom of stairwells, turning public hallways into communal septic tanks. (Better-quality *insulae* also accommodated the middle class and sometimes the wealthy.)

Other advances in urbanism were likewise haphazardly applied. Many Roman cities, particularly colonial cities, were laid out in rational grids with paved roads that made dense conglomerations more comprehensible, and movement within them easier. But in the capital—although several long vistas were created down major avenues—the street pattern grew largely without plan or regulation. Frequently the streets became so narrow that wheeled vehicles could barely pass. This danger to the lives and limbs of pedestrians compelled Julius Caesar to restrict delivery vehicles to the nighttime hours only. Fires caused by jamming buildings close together resulted in the poorer areas of the city being razed and rebuilt several times over. Thus while the colonial cities of the empire were models for Western town planning long into the future, the people of Rome itself did not benefit from this advance in the organization of the urban environment.

As we picture ancient Rome in our mind's eye, a simple distinction emerges. At its ceremonial center, monumental buildings were arranged in dramatic spatial relationships to create long vistas and imposing architectural effects. In its extensive residential quarters, thousands of multistory tenements, built via speculative development, were crammed together in arbitrary disorder. In areas of wealth and public spectacle, all the technology of Roman city building was applied and an elevated quality of urban life was achieved that would not be replicated for more than a thousand years. In the areas of common habitation, where the mass of the population lived, sanitation and amenity diminished, and the city became a slum.

In order to build these many different and extensive structures, the Romans perfected the use of concrete and masonry. Roman engineering and construction techniques raised the building of urban infrastructure to a high art. Not only were such edifices as the aqueducts made to last—and indeed they have endured across the millennia—but they were frequently conceived with beautiful proportions and with a refined sensitivity to detail and the expression of materials. The failure to apply this technical skill in the building of the *insulae*—which from time to time collapsed and buried their inhabitants—is a tale much repeated across history, a story of avarice, exploitation, and uncontrolled real estate development.

Although, in the earlier period of the republic many structures in the Roman city were utilitarian volumes of brick and aggregate concrete, eventually Roman buildings were adorned by stonework—often of marble or travertine, a form of local limestone—and inspired by the aesthetics of classical Greek architecture. In this regard, the boast of the first emperor, Augustus (63 B.C. to A.D. 14), is often cited: he inherited a city made of brick and left a city made of marble. Indeed, from the era of Augustus forward, the public areas of Rome gradually became an unrestrained exhibit of the architectural achievements of each new imperial administration; an impressive environment of elaborately carved and molded stone. Thus Roman architecture integrated sophisticated engineering with aesthetic refinement to produce huge, highly articulated marble-clad buildings for public assembly. In the center of the city, these gleaming white structures rose to unprecedented heights of Roman Baroque opulence.

At the city's core a vast public area was constructed over several centuries. These were the great forums, linked together to make an extended zone of the most important buildings of Roman government. High, proud basilicas held the courts of law, imposing curias housed the legislatures, ornate arches illuminated Rome's triumphs, and numerous temples in many architectural configurations paid homage to the gods of the city. There was a public-records office, or *tabularium,* as well as a prison, a mint, offices for the central bureaucracy, and a variety of market buildings—all beautifully constructed and classically proportioned. To this day, the majestic forum of Rome, existing for the most part only in our imaginations—with its rows of tall, fluted columns, its ornate capitals, its sweeping cornices, its vast coffered arches, vaults, and domes, and its floors of fine mosaics or of elaborate colored-marble geometric patterns—has been a model for the design of civic centers in almost every major city and town throughout the Americas, Europe, and wherever the European powers colonized.

Yet, as impressive as the buildings of the forum were, there were still greater structures that towered above them. In imperial Rome, the largest and most dominant buildings were neither governmental nor religious but were devoted to the collective pursuits of all the citizens of the metropolis. There were the great public baths, arenas, and amphitheaters. Here was a phenomenon never previously achieved and perhaps never after equaled (except in fin de siècle Vienna)—a giant city whose facilities for public gathering could hold more than half of the city's population at one time.

Here also was Rome's enlightenment and great shame. Of its wisdom, one might say that the public baths—immense constructions arguably as large and luxurious as any other public edifices built in human history—were the ultimate achievement of Roman city building. These magnificent structures, whose spans marked a pinnacle of engineering science, were a physical manifestation of a progression of values: buildings devoted to the health and social intercourse of Roman society were given symbolic primacy over all other buildings in the capital. It has been estimated that at the height of Rome's glory, over 60,000 citizens could bathe at one time. In the baths, Romans cleansed, gathered, enjoyed themselves, and read, for libraries were often a part of the vast complexes. Never before had the world seen such an idea: structures with huge interior spaces dedicated to the civic discourse and social interaction of broad segments of a city's population as a facet of daily life.

How do we reconcile or even begin to comprehend that for hundreds of years this same society habitually encouraged the death and mutilation of human beings as a popular form of public entertainment? It is a chilling question. In Rome, over a period of several hundred years and eventually on half the days of each year, spectacles of human suffering were witnessed by large segments of the populace. The 45,000 places in the Colosseum and the seating capacity of the many other arenas of the city testify to the popular demand to view violent death. The number of killings over this span of time is unknown, but some sources indicate it may have been close to a million.

This, then, is the city of Rome—brutal yet enlightened, ugly yet beautiful, a horror not to be repeated or forgotten, a new forward step for civilization. Many of its urban ills continue to plague the cities of today. Several of its accomplishments have yet to be matched. Across the surrounding countryside, its eleven long aqueducts point to Rome's towers and walls. On the outside edges of the metropolis, threatening the public health, lay open pits (*puticuli*), into which were piled the bodies of dead slaves, criminals, gladiators, and animals as well as general refuse. Inside Rome's arched triumphal gateways, an inventory of its structures—from a municipal survey of A.D. 312–315, cited and expanded by Lewis Mumford in *The City in History,* included the following:

- the curia of the senate
- the palaces of the emperor
- the administrative buildings of the state
- the public market buildings
- 10 basilicas
- 423 temples
- 28 libraries
- 11 great public baths
- 36 marble arches
- 37 ceremonial gateways
- 926 private bathhouses
- 3 public theaters
- 2 public amphitheaters
- 2 circuses, or stadiums
- 4 gladiatorial schools
- 290 storehouses and warehouses
- 5 water theaters for nautical spectacles
- 254 public bake houses
- 1,790 private palaces
- 46,602 *insulae,* or multistory tenements
- 18 public squares
- 8 public recreational fields
- 30 public parks and gardens
- 700 public pools and basins
- 1,212 fountains supplied by 247 reservoirs
- 8 bridges
- 6 obelisks
- 22 great sculptured horses
- 10,000 public statues

Never again would such a vast artistic and architectural legacy be purposely demolished by a city's own inhabitants. Neither the damage done by the vandalism of its conquerors, nor the disintegration caused by time and the elements can compare to the relentless attack—over a thousand years—of the changing populace of the city. What is left to us today is but a minuscule part of what once existed, and but a small fraction of what might have been saved.

THE FALL OF IMPERIAL ROME

The destruction of the city is merely part of the larger story of the decline and fall of the empire. Many historians cite several reasons for this degeneration: the erosion of the Roman civic spirit, the despotic rule of the emperors, the rise of Christianity, and the moral corruption of a society supported by slavery, living on the public dole, and entertained by spectacles of human slaughter. But the most widely cited harbinger of the waning of Rome is the loss of its status as the administrative center of the empire and, in A.D. 330, the establishment of Constantinople by Constantine as the capital of what would eventually be called the Byzantine Empire. No longer would the treasure of the world flow into Rome's coffers.

Also in the fourth century, the closing of the state marble-quarry administration, the *statio marmorum,* heralds the decline of the physical fabric of the city. From this moment forward, for a millennium, no building would be constructed in Rome of newly quarried stone. A culture of architectural cannibalism would evolve. Although the city would gradually diminish in population by roughly 99 percent, from one million in the fourth century to 10,000 people in the fourteenth, the damage to the heritage of the city would be extensive. Like a cancer slowly working its way across the centuries, the people of Rome would dismantle stone by stone their city's architectural glory in order to reuse the raw materials.

In A.D. 380, Christianity became the official religion of the Roman Empire, and by 385 the temples of the pagan gods of Rome were closed, their privileges and revenues abolished. In 402 the garbage pit surrounding the city's fortifications was covered with dirt and leveled. In 404 Honorius banned gladiatorial contests for the 250,000 people who remained. In 408 the Visigoths plundered the city, and in 455 the Vandals arrived.

In 458 Emperor Majorian decreed that magistrates who gave permission for imperial monuments to be stripped of their stone should be fined 25 kilograms of gold, and that the workmen who carried out such work should be scourged and have their hands cut off. This is one of the earliest recorded preservation statutes in history, and certainly one of the most severe, yet it failed to stop the destruction.

In the year 500, Theodoric the Great, from his capital in Ravenna, reestablished the ancient Roman office of *curator statuarum* to protect the statues of Rome from further dismemberment, and instructed the architects of the state to restore the damaged imperial city: "These excellent buildings are my delight, the image of the empire's power and witnesses of its grandeur and glory. It is my wish that you preserve in its original splendor all that is ancient and that whatever you may add will conform to it in style. . . . To leave to future generations, to humanity, monuments that will fill them with admiration is a service full of honor and worthy of every man's strongest desire." Fourteen hundred years later, modern archaeologists would rarely uncover an ancient building or site in Rome without discovering bricks from Theodoric's reign—evidence of the many repairs of his architects.

Yet the decline proceeded. In 536 the Goths sacked the city and by 537 water no longer flowed to the Baths of Caracalla. In the seventh century, the Pantheon became a church for Christian worship, thus protecting its magnificent interior from cannibalization. By 750, visitors to the vastly diminished city still spoke of seeing statues by Phidias, the master sculptor of the Parthenon, though the gold had long ago been stripped from the baths and palaces. In the sacking and fire of 1082, the obelisks were toppled, the last private houses and *insulae* were destroyed, and the vestigial markings of the street pattern of the residential parts of the old metropolis were obliterated. As the centuries passed, uncleared debris and garbage caused the ground level to rise 10 to 20 feet throughout the city, and the deserted monuments of the empire, jutting up from the weed-covered soil, partly buried and foreshortened, stood silent and covered with moss.

Medieval Rome was a small town of 30,000 people living along a bend in the Tiber. Surrounding them were swamplands infested with malaria now that they were no longer drained by the Cloaca Maxima, which was hidden in the depths below, unbroken but lost to memory. The technology that had raised the mammoth vaults and domes of the city's ruins had passed from human knowledge. Perhaps thousands of ancient sculptures lay buried beneath the ground. Aqueducts, reservoirs, and fountains had dried up. The decaying walls of ancient fortifications stretched for 12 miles across an empty countryside, pockmarked by eerie giant ruins and intermittent agricultural plots. The *marmorarii*, the marble cutters, slowly dismembered the remnants, and beautiful handcrafted marbles were crushed to fill rubble walls, recarved into fresh blocks, or shipped across Europe to decorate the monuments of the new religion: the cathedral of Aix-la-Chapelle in Aachen (built in 796–804), the cathedral in Pisa (1063–1118), the cathedral in Lucca (1064–1070), the cathedral in Monte Cassino (1066), the cathedral of San Mateo in Salerno (1084), the cathedral of San Andrea in Amalfi (eleventh century), the baptistery of San Giovanni in Florence (1100), the monastery of Nostra Signoria in Sardinia (1321–1360), and Westminster Abbey in London.

Calcararii, or lime makers, raised kilns within various ruins in which thousand-year old marble blocks were burned to make lime for concrete and whitewash. The supply of material must have seemed endless. Thousands of cartloads of finely carved marble could be removed from a monument such as the Circus Maximus and make only a minor dent in the vast white skin of the structure.

By the time of the Renaissance, the lime makers had discovered that the finest whitewash for painting came from the burning of these ancient statues, particularly the earliest marbles from classical Greece. The marble cutters found that breaking classical sculptures down into chips and grinding them into powder produced a plaster of the ultimate luminosity.

In the nineteenth century, archaeologists would unearth rubble foundation walls containing the shattered remains of whole artworks. This evidence confirms that many statues had been intact—perhaps for as long as 1,500 years—before they were purposely broken to make shards. We do not know what happened to the works of Phidias, one of the great artistic genuises of Western civilization.

In 1420, Pope Martin V returned the papacy to Rome—now a squalid, dangerous, and disease-ridden city. A recent outbreak of the Black Death had reduced the population to about 10,000. The streets were strewn with garbage and filth, and bands of outlaws terrorized its neighborhoods from their dens in such labyrinthine ruins as the Colosseum. Sometime in that same century, it is believed that a Florentine goldsmith named Filippo Brunelleschi wandered the strange landscape of the half-buried city, studying the immense vaulted and domed structures. He was searching for the secret of their construction.

To the north, in Florence, a massive cathedral stood unfinished. The Florentines had been working on this building for over a hundred years, with no realistic idea of how to complete it. An octagonal drum 149 feet wide, perched on a roof 180 feet high, lay open to the sky, waiting for an unbuttressed dome to be constructed across the opening. None of the structural methods of the Middle Ages could accomplish such a feat, for they all relied on wooden trusses to support the construction as it proceeded. The span and weight of this dome were beyond the strength of wood, as used by the technology of the time. The answer to the problem lay in Rome, amid the bracken and vines. Here was actual proof that such an engineering feat could be accomplished; by extrapolation, Brunelleschi was able to envision a structure that supported itself independently as it grew upward and inward. The heritage of the past had shown him that something beyond his immediate reach was nonetheless possible.

RENAISSANCE ROME

Brunelleschi's completion of the Duomo in Florence, using principles derived from the Pantheon and the roofs of the imperial baths, signaled the beginning of the architectural aspect of the Italian Renaissance. Soon monies from the powerful city-states of northern Italy—Florence, Venice, Pisa, Genoa, Bologna—would enable the popes to build a capital city for Christianity amid the mysterious landscape enclosed by the age-old Roman walls. The form of the dome of the Duomo would be refined in miniature by Bramante in his Tempietto, then brought to consummation by Michelangelo in the dome of Saint Peter's. And all of these would be reflected in many of the most symbolically important buildings of the next five centuries. The artists of the Italian Renaissance would come to Rome at the service of the popes and create an unparalleled aesthetic legacy. The architects of the Renaissance, inspired by the age-old ruins, would give birth to an architecture that adapted the classical style to the new values of a changing society, and this process of reinterpreting classical form would continue in the Mannerist and Baroque styles that followed and in numerous succeeding periods of classical revival for hundreds of years thereafter. With these new forms, Renaissance architects would erect such a vast collection of beautiful structures in Christian Rome that only one other city up to that point in the development of Western civilization could rival it: ancient Rome itself.

No one knows exactly how many of the great public buildings of classical Rome remained by the beginning of the Renaissance. Several medieval itineraries for pilgrims and partial records from the period show that major parts of the old metropolis were still intact. (The itineraries are a very interesting source. Different religious institutions throughout Europe had in their possession detailed descriptions of the sacred sites and significant landmarks of Rome. Specific walking tours through the city were prescribed. Hundreds of years later, these itemized traveler's guides, located in libraries across the continent, when translated and cross-referenced, constituted a record of the changing face of the city—of the demise of principal imperial sights.) We do know that a substantial architectural heritage, albeit much reduced, still existed at the time Martin V brought the papacy back to the city. Over the next two hundred years it became common practice before building any new structure to first identify the precise ruins to be cannibalized for their materials. Gaining possession of an ancient building to be used as a quarry was called securing a *petraria,* and abundant documentation exists of the granting of such warrants. Moreover, it was rare that any major ruin did not also have a permanent kiln located within its remains to reduce its substance to powder, and many of these permissions are also recorded. For example, during the fifteenth century, it is established that the loggia of the old Cathedral of Saint Peter would incorporate marble from these sites:

- The Colosseum
- The Temple of Jupiter Capitolinus
- The Forum Julium

- The Senate House
- The bridge of Nero
- The Temple of Dea Dia
- The portico of Octavia
- The Templum Sacrae Urbis
- The ruins at Ostia
- The Milvian Bridge
- The tombs of Via Flaminia
- The Baths of Caracalla

Subsequently, when this structure was destroyed to make way for the new Saint Peter's of Bramante, Michelangelo, Maderna, and Bernini, further cannibalization of stone would occur from imperial monuments not yet fully stripped or leveled.

The first phase of the destruction of the great monuments of imperial Rome, which lasted eleven centuries, had been gradual and involved several different agents: nature, man, and the tide of events. In the second phase, a mammoth amount of destruction would be accomplished in a far shorter period of time—about two hundred years. Only one major building, the Pantheon, would survive with its interior intact, and only one major structure, the Colosseum, would be left with any significant part of its exterior marble skin remaining. The perfect condition of the Pantheon, and the fact that the immense vaulted spans of the great baths of the city had stood the test of several earthquakes, testifies to the superb construction quality of Roman buildings.

Today, on any spring, summer, or fall morning, while queuing up outside the ruins of the Forum, amid an international gathering of people, one inevitably wonders how even more extraordinary Rome might be if just a half-dozen major structures had been left undiminished. The fact that a significant part of the imperial legacy of Rome was not passed down to us is largely a matter of choice—primarily the choice of the popes, who not only used the ruins as a source of cheap materials but sometimes directly sold and profited from the granting of demolition rights. Two things were thus accomplished simultaneously: the buildings of the Catholic city were far more opulent and greater in number than they would otherwise have been, and the buildings of the pagan empire no longer competed with them in size and magnificence. The general mass of Saint Peter's (dome aside) is equivalent to the mass of the Baths of Diocletian, or Caracalla. In other words, only the great Cathedral of Saint Peter—its dome rising above all other structures in the Christian cityscape—equaled or exceeded the size of the larger pagan monuments.

Once the pope was reinstalled in the city, the transformation of Rome was radical and rapid. The medieval settlement had occupied an area approximately one-thirtieth of the size of the imperial city, as indicated by the old ring of fortifications. Now the metropolis reversed the process of growth, and by the end of the seventeenth century the popes had half-filled the area once occupied by the imperial capital.

The economic and political strength brought to the papacy by the commercial success of the northern Italian cities allowed the popes to see Rome in an entirely new way. They had the means to reshape the city. At first they set out to make a dangerous and unruly place civilized, clean, and orderly. Eventually it was possible to conceive of building a metropolis whose grandeur would compete with that of the ancient empire. In the process, a transformation occurred in the way Westerners thought about the design of cities.

Working in collaboration with one of the greatest collections of artists and architects ever gathered in one place, the popes of the Renaissance built a metropolis in which the elements of the cityscape were consciously interrelated to yield artistic effects. Though the ancient Romans had arranged the buildings of the Forum in dramatic juxtaposition with one another, they had at the same time allowed the immense neighborhoods of tenements to become a discordant tangle. By comparison, the designers of Renaissance Rome saw that it was possible to make all the elements of the cityscape part of a larger artistic and rational whole. They recognized the city, intellectually, as an object that could be designed.

As a consequence, several fundamental changes in the conception of urban architecture occurred. They are so integral to the way we build cities today, and so elemental and important, that it is hard to imagine what architecture had been like before. For Western culture, however, Rome during the Renaissance was the most important laboratory for these experiments in city making. A second great patrimony came into being in the same geographic location as the first one.

The most basic conceptual change was the realization that the structures of the city had two concurrent functions. The mass of each building provided interior spaces for various private human needs, while the outer walls framed the public circulation channels of the city. In this way, the negative spaces of the townscape—the voids left between the solid masses of the buildings—became organized into a plan, a rational network of circulatory and public spaces. Now the total design of the metropolis could be expressed in an accurate drawing that was neither symbolic nor metaphorical but a map of the city's physical reality: the plan of its streets, the plan of its voids. In this form, the configuration of the cityscape could be discussed and thought about in precise terms. The metropolis as a large yet integrated complex could be pictured in the imagination.

In order to make the network of streets more usable and to allow access for emergency assistance, delivery vehicles, and garbage removal, the popes widened the circulation system to accommodate carriages, of which there were 883 in Rome by 1594. This established a common minimum width for streets, and gradually, over several hundred years, the buildings of Rome were made to conform to this standard. One of the earliest streets that was cut through the existing fabric of the medieval settlement was the Via Giulia, which the popes made straight to ensure the safety of pilgrims as they traveled through what had been a dangerous maze of alleys.

Another very elemental concept with important aesthetic implications then emerged: the idea that when buildings were aligned along the street they became a unified sculptural wall—a street wall. The visual potency of this simple idea is easy to underestimate. We can see its most positive effects in the parts of Western cities built in the seventeenth, eighteenth, and nineteenth centuries. Here, in places like the Baroque city plan of Paris or the grid of New York, the observance of street walls allows the technical needs of the city's vehicular and pedestrian circulation systems to relate harmoniously to the sculptural massing of the metropolis. Street walls help individual buildings to take their proper place in the larger urban composition, yet still express a particular architectural personality. As we look down the street, each building aligns itself with its neighbor to create a unified blockfront, which, in turn, lines up with other blockfronts to create an avenue, like the Via del Corso, Park Avenue, or the Champs-Élysées. Thus, no matter how eclectic the design of a building might be, by being aligned with the street wall it is subsumed into the larger sculptural order of the city; it becomes a part of a visually organized whole. One of the earliest deliberate attempts to create an avenue with street walls in Rome was the 1562 plan for the Via Pia by Michelangelo for Pius IV.

The concept of the street wall reconciles the aesthetic relationship between public and private needs. During the Renaissance, as this new awareness emerged, the architects of Rome came to understand that when they designed the outer surfaces of buildings they were fulfilling simultaneously both an obligation to their client and an obligation to the cityscape. Architectural facades were both the sculptural skin of a building's interior functions and an artistic enrichment of the public zones of the city.

Soon it became clear that buildings arranged in a street wall could delineate more than just the parallel edges of an avenue; they could also enclose geometrically configured public piazzas. One of the earliest and most remarkable of these in Rome is the Piazza Navona, whose elongated form echoes the shape of the ruined Roman circus that lies beneath its surface, thereby expressing an imperial Roman mass as a void in the Renaissance cityscape. The role of the piazza as an urban room was quite different from the voids that made up the network of streets. The space of the piazza provided for public gatherings, communal ceremonies, marketplaces, and psychological relief from the oppressive density of closely massed buildings. Piazzas allowed air and sunlight to burst into the city. Moreover, spaces like the Piazza Navona, which was adorned with fountains and sculptures by Bernini, were also places for the public display of fine art.

Before long, the popes rediscovered a dramatic spatial effect that the ancient Romans had sometimes utilized—the long axial vista. Two basic elements are required to produce this result: a straight clear line of sight and a visual element at the end that attracts the eye. Renaissance city builders discovered a way to enhance the experience. When they built two street walls along the parallel sides of an axial view, the pedestrian's sense of the depth of the perspective was greatly heightened, as the facade of each building in the street wall was foreshortened, in sequence, off into the distance. When people looked down such streets, the diminution of the street wall gave them an idea of just how far away the culmination of the panorama was. In dense urban fabric, the long axial street wall introduced the drama of distance and gave a feeling for the immensity of the city.

Finally, the development of perspective drawing had an indirect and very positive effect on the conception of the city. As Renaissance artists explored the use of perspective in imaginary architectural environments such as stage sets and paintings like Raphael's *School of Athens,* they discovered that the use of architectural symmetry in axial views created dramatic and harmonious compositions. They learned that the purposeful arrangement of building elements—for example, the horizontal alignment of cornices or the creation of identical facades on either side of a long vista—produced a cityscape whose interrelated architectural masses heightened the effect of urban perspectives. Gradually, this understanding resulted in unified architectural conceptions: the twin churches by Rinaldi on the Piazza del Popolo that frame the long perspective view down the Via del Corso, the symmetrical colonnade by Bernini that forms the elliptical shape of the Piazza San Pietro, the dramatic entrance up the grand steps to the Basilica of Saint Peter.

This palette of visual urban effects was used by the popes to create a new kind of city. The street pattern of Rome was delineated by long, straight vistas crisscrossing the metropolis and making clear pathways of circulation. At the end of these powerful lines, the dense urban fabric opened up into squares and piazzas framed by the walls of buildings. Tall Egyptian obelisks brought to Rome in the era of the caesars—later toppled but now re-erected—and extraordinary sculptures and fountains by Italian artists were located at the nexus points in the piazzas, where the axial lines crossed. These markers could be seen from great distances, orienting people and drawing them to the sculptural and architectural events of the piazzas. Using the drawn plan of the city's street

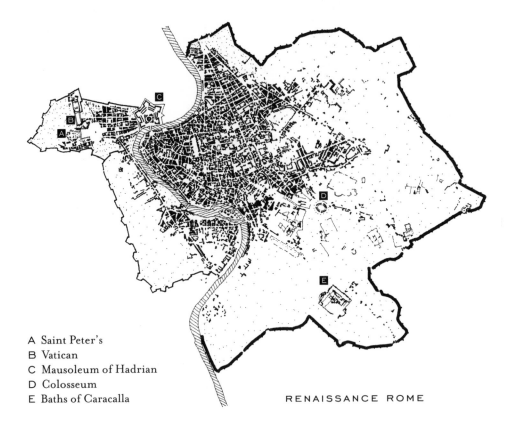

A Saint Peter's
B Vatican
C Mausoleum of Hadrian
D Colosseum
E Baths of Caracalla

RENAISSANCE ROME

pattern as a way to visualize the larger urban composition, the popes deliberately built a city that was a work of art, a stage set for urban living. Within this construct, the architects of the Renaissance created a collection of singular architectural masterpieces; Rome's churches held many of the great paintings of Western civilization; Michelangelo, Bernini, and others adorned the city with sculpture; and even the more prosaic buildings of the city were of a style, massing, and configuration that related harmoniously to the larger whole. The new Rome gave birth to the idea that the metropolis, in all its parts, could become a unified composition of form and a product of the rational mind.

Meanwhile, as the concepts that shaped the new Rome emerged and then were refined and realized, a simultaneous and convoluted dance occurred. The ancient city was revered. It was further destroyed. The greater splendor of the new city was celebrated. The destruction was condemned but then begun anew. And Renaissance Rome was further glorified as another ancient monument disappeared. For the inhabitants, such incongruities were visible on a daily basis, as stone by stone the still vast remains of the once-even-vaster imperial city continued to be erased. Out of this conflict, in many winding steps, even-

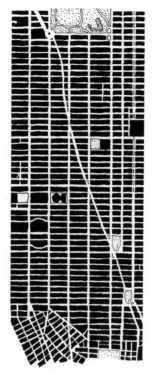

A contrast in urban structure: The street pattern of Renaissance Rome (from a 1748 drawing by Giovan Battista Nolli) compared to a fragment of the street pattern of contemporary Midtown Manhattan.

• In Rome, medieval urban organization has been followed by Baroque urban design, and straight avenues have been introduced to an organic pattern of buildings, blocks, and streets. The city has almost half-filled the area enclosed by its ancient Roman walls. West of the Tiber, and around St. Peter's, the Vatican, and the Mausoleum of Hadrian, the popes have added new lines of fortifications.

• In Manhattan, a modern grid plan presents a different size and method of urban organization. Blocks are bigger, streets are wider, buildings taller, and population density has increased dramatically. (*Both drawings at the same scale.*)

MODERN MIDTOWN MANHATTAN

tually was born a commitment by Roman society to preserve its architectural patrimony.

Throughout this process, the architects of the Renaissance, both in Rome and from elsewhere, studiously measured and examined the ancient buildings, often decrying their destruction. Influential architectural treatises of the time disseminated understanding of the complex aesthetic rules of classical building across Europe, and the author of one of these, Leon Battista Alberti, would also state: "If any Roman ruins exist upon the site, they ought to be preserved." But Alberti spoke from Florence, a commercial city with ample resources to quarry new stone for its buildings. In Rome, the extensive enhancement envisioned by the popes was unaffordable at the price of newly quarried and transported stone. Thus while each new beautiful architectural creation to some degree furthered the loss of another ancient monument, even if their designers condemned such destruction, how could they not answer the call to embellish the capital city of their religion? Is it not the vocation of architects to build?

Similar intellectual paradoxes befell the popes. Across several centuries, in between periods of destruction, one pope after another issued edicts against the decimation of the classical patrimony. Some of these popes were corrupt, their practices eventually inciting the Reformation. Some were sincere in lamenting the evisceration of their culture. Others continued the devastation, and some of these were sincere as well, destroying the old but raising new edifices that glorified their god, their religion, and the city that symbolized the triumph of their faith. Eugenius IV (1431–1447) appointed a *magistri aedificiorum* to protect the ancient monuments and halted the destruction of the Colosseum. Nicholas V (1447–1455) demolished the arches of Valentinian, Gratian, Theodosius, Arcadius, and Honorius. Pius II (1458–1464) imposed severe fines on those who destroyed ancient remains and personally inspected the age-old monuments. Alexander VI (1492–1503) reaped one-third of the profits from the marble quarries he allowed to function among the ruins.

All the while, admiration of Roman antiquities spread. In time, private individuals and the popes themselves collected the classical sculptures discovered by excavators. The city was a mine of buried treasure, and during the Renaissance the recovery and sale of Greek and Roman artworks became a trans-European business. In 1506, the *Laocoön*—a legendary Greek statue known to have been brought to imperial Rome—was unearthed, reassembled, and made part of the great art collection of the Vatican. The concept of publicly accessible art collections was born, and in 1645 one of the world's first museums was opened on the Capitoline Hill. Yet in other corners of the city, similar sculptures continued to be burned for lime or pounded into rubble or plaster dust.

Since the popes were the principal patrons of art and architecture, it was unwise for artists to criticize them. To do so was to jeopardize their careers. Yet to remain silent in regard to the destruction was a rational and spiritual contradiction. Significantly, documents of the period suggest that the painter and architect Raphael was associated with a letter sent to Pope Leo X (1513–1522) that criticized the papacy for "more willful destruction than the Goths and Vandals themselves." Raphael's connection to the letter must have been known, since in 1515, Leo X responded by making the artist commissioner of the city's antiquities with a mandate to inventory the remains.

Not many years later, Paul III (1534–1549) declared ruefully, "Not without deep sorrow are we aware that our greed and cunning have torn down, destroyed, and squandered the venerable adornments of the city." It was then decreed by papal edict that the penalty for destroying ancient works of art and architecture would be death. Yet in 1540, Paul III gave papal license to cannibalize ruins in order to acquire stone for the construction of Saint Peter's.

By the mid-sixteenth century, as the city grew westward across the Tiber, absorbing the rural landscape and the ruins that stood in its way, Christian Rome extended to the Capitoline Hill. Just east of the hill lay the site of the old

Roman Forum. For centuries it had been a dumping ground; now remnants of the center of the ancient empire, partially excavated, rose up out of the ground in a strange panorama. Here the popes stopped and deflected the growth of the city. Had they not done so, one of the most important archaeological sites in the Western world would have been buried beneath the living metropolis. Atop the Capitoline a complex of buildings was constructed around the Piazza del Campidoglio to house the municipal government of the contemporary city. The architect was Michelangelo Buonarroti and he would introduce an alternative approach to the intellectual contradictions that besieged the city.

Michelangelo's planning and architectural work in Rome was highly sensitive to the surrounding historical context. At the Porta Pia he erected a distinctive gateway in the Mannerist style and sited it to face inward to the new city, while leaving intact the existing ancient Roman gateway, which faced out to the surrounding countryside. At the Baths of Diocletian he erected a church inside the tepidarium of the baths, making modest changes to the original Roman architecture. Both of these projects might be described as instances of adaptive reuse. Rather than destroying the landmarks and beginning over again, Michelangelo updated the old structures for current and continuing functions. In neither case was the architect wary of the comparison of old to new. In regard to the Porta Pia, he set the two gateways apart, letting each entrance have its own separate integrity. In the church, where the great baths towered high above, he called for a minimalist treatment, leaving the original engineering stark and undecorated, a celebration of the accomplishment of his Roman forebears. (Later generations, however, would apply a thick layer of ornament to the interior.)

On the Capitoline, Michelangelo created one of the most revered designs in Western architectural history. Three historic structures already existed on the top of the hill surrounding an arbitrarily configured and ungainly public space of strange divergent angles. To the north of the piazza was the thirteenth-century church of Santa Maria in Aracoeli, whose long, steep stairway climbed down the western side of the hill toward the growing city. To the south of the piazza was a medieval guild hall of vernacular design set at an awkward angle to the church. On the eastern side of the hilltop was the Senators' Palace, an irregularly massed urban medieval fortress that utilized as its foundation the ruins of the ancient Roman *tabularium* (records office), which was built into the side of the Capitoline facing out to the Roman Forum. From these disparate elements, Michelangelo had been asked to fashion a new and noble urban complex.

The medieval guild hall was recloaked in a handsomely proportioned classical stone facade. On the opposite side of the piazza, the architect constructed a duplicate of the guild hall's front elevation in a narrow building that screened the view of the side of the church. These twin Renaissance structures formed a trapezoidal public space in alignment with the center of the Senators' Palace, which was reshaped as a symmetrical and balanced architectural mass crowned by a tall campanile and with a pair of monumental staircases leading to an ornate central entrance door.

Into the pavement pattern of the Piazza del Campidoglio, an intricate geometric design was woven in a great ellipse. All the elements of the piazza were now stylistically and aesthetically of one artistic piece. Michelangelo then created a long steep stairway from the plaza down the hillside; that intersected at the base of the hill with the long, steep stairway from Santa Maria in Aracoeli. The whole Campidoglio complex was adorned with large sculptures from antiquity; at the head of the stairway were giant Roman marbles of Castor and Pollux; in the center of the piazza stood an equestrian statue of Marcus Aurelius; at the base of the Senators' Palace were ancient figures of the river gods.

With deference to the existing structures on the Capitoline Hill, Michelangelo had redirected the arbitrary geometries of history to form a subtle and beautiful design. Elements of ancient, medieval, and Renaissance Rome were knit together and reconnected to the cityscape. The juxtaposition of the two stairways—marching up the Capitoline at different angles and pitches, each to its own architectural culmination—formed a memorable urban intersection, a moment of high architectural tension. His use of the accidental angle of the guild hall to form a trapezoid framed by matching facades of repetitive bays and columns resulted in vistas of heightened perspective power. His placement of impressive Roman statues at architecturally dramatic points gave these symbols of antiquity a position of primacy in the composition and linked the new Capitoline to its neighboring imperial heritage in the Forum. And since all the spatial relationships of the Piazza del Campidoglio were generated in response to the position of the *tabularium,* by implication the ancient Roman monument (though set in the hillside out of sight) was honored as the most significant element in the architectural hierarchy; it was literally and philosophically the foundation. In the Piazza del Campidoglio (completed posthumously) Michelangelo had given Rome a vision of an alternative cityscape in which a continuity of culture was achieved through accommodating new and old urban fabric within a single design of uncompromised brilliance.

Yet even Michelangelo was not disassociated from the process of raising great new works of architecture with material taken from the old, and his term as the chief architect of Saint Peter's and the designer of its great dome inevitably contributed to the destruction of other monuments of antiquity. After Michelangelo's death, Sixtus V (1585–1590) perhaps did more than any other pope to fully realize a great Renaissance city of straight avenues with long vistas and powerful culmination points set in open piazzas. His master plan was an exciting vision of a metropolis tied together by axial roads with Egyptian obelisks moved to critical focal points such as the piazza in front of Saint Peter's, and at the axial juncture in the center of the Piazza del Popolo. In addition, Sixtus V was the first pope to restore an ancient Roman aqueduct and through such efforts Catholic Rome eventually had the most abundant water supply of any city in Europe. Once again the metropolis became a city of fountains. Inevitably, this dramatic reorganization of the cityscape required the elimination of many medieval and ancient Roman structures that stood in the pathway of straight avenues or cluttered the new expanded plazas.

Thus, the term of Sixtus V was also a significant moment in the birth of an urban conservation awareness in Rome. Public opposition to the eradication of ancient architecture and artworks had for some time been slowly mounting. Gradually, the legislative body of the city's municipal government, its city council, had pitted itself against the popes in an effort to stop the destruction. In 1540 the council had condemned an edict by Paul III to quarry stone from the Forum and the Via Sacra. Soon afterward, the municipal senate issued a decree that no standing monuments under its protection were to be endangered by the papal search for stone. In 1580 a delegation from the city asked the pope to halt the desecration of ancient ruins, but to little avail. In reaction to the extensive program of public works by Sixtus V, the municipal authorities frequently intervened on behalf of endangered landmarks. Several ancient buildings, including the tomb of Cecilia Metella, were thereby preserved. In 1590, upon the death of Sixtus V, a municipal document read: "Today our most Holy Lord has departed this life, amid the rejoicing and mutual congratulations of all classes of citizens."

An important metamorphosis had occurred. Public opposition to the continued eradication of Rome's imperial heritage became part of the political culture of the city. The artists and intellects of the Renaissance had established a link between the culture of antiquity and the culture of the present—a continuity in the process of civilization. The beautiful new city that Christian Romans now inhabited reflected in its most glorious aspects and symbolically important buildings the aesthetic sensibilities of their ancestors. Deeper understanding of the past had led to a growth of knowledge, by which the great Renaissance domes were achieved and the flow of water through ancient aqueducts was restored. The expertise of imperial Romans was no longer perceived as arcane or of an alien people, but rather looked upon with pride as the mastery of the city's forbears. The works of Michelangelo had shown that the beautification of the new city could be accomplished in sympathetic relationship with the remains of the old one. Now, by popular mandate, the people of Rome were asserting that the new metropolis accommodate the ancient city rather than destroy it. For a new civilization, architectural preservation of an old civilization had become an important goal in the planning of the city. Out of ferment, and perhaps with greater intensity and at an earlier date than in any other place, Rome had awakened to the ethic of conservation.

Although the destructive policies of the Vatican would continue, it would be in a climate of increasing criticism. Paul V (1605–1621) leveled the Baths of Constantine and the temple of Minerva. Urban VIII (1623–1644) formed a commission to safeguard Roman monuments while he simultaneously benefited from the sale of stones from imperial landmarks and allowed marble to be stripped from the Colosseum to build his family palace, the Palazzo Barberini. Upon his passing, a pamphlet of the day declared: "What the barbarians did not do, the Barberinis did."

By the end of the seventeenth century, the hub of European commerce had shifted from the Italian city-states to the cities on the Atlantic coast. The once important connection to Asia via the silk road through Constantinople, and then by sea to Europe, was bypassed by the transoceanic fleets of the Dutch, Spanish, Portuguese, and English. The flow of wealth from northern Italy had lessened substantially and would further decline. The popes had taxed the papal states into destitution. The bribery and corruption of the papacy had diminished the influence of Rome throughout the Christian world, and precipitated the Reformation and Counter-Reformation. The reduced papacy could no longer afford to build on such a grandiose scale.

An eminent capital for Christianity had already been built. As the new city emerged, it attracted visitors—princes, architects, artists, and intellects—from all over Europe. For the second time in its history, the aesthetic accomplishments of Rome would set a standard against which all other cities were measured. As the volume of construction declined, the practices of destruction slowed. Something on the order of 90 to 95 percent of the ancient Roman heritage had been obliterated. War, pillage, and fire had leveled the residential half of the city, its neighborhoods of insulae and mansions. Cannibalization of stone and art had almost erased the public half of the city, its great monumental center of beautifully carved stone. Yet astoundingly, a large part of this mammoth assemblage is still in the same geographical place. The triumph we today celebrate as Renaissance-Baroque Rome was accomplished by reconstituting the substance of imperial Rome. The city had devoured its glory.

CHAPTER THREE
THE CITY THAT REWROTE ITS PAST

FASCIST AND MODERN ROME

I should like to divide the problems of Rome, the Rome of this twentieth century, into two categories: the problems of necessity and the problems of grandeur. One cannot confront the latter unless the first has been solved. The problems of necessity rise from the growth of Rome and are encompassed in this binomial: housing and communications. The problems of grandeur are of another kind: we must liberate all of ancient Rome from the mediocre construction that disfigures it, but side by side with the Rome of antiquity and Christianity we must also create the monumental Rome of the twentieth century. Rome cannot, must not, be solely a modern city, in the by now banal sense of that word; it must be a city worthy of its glory, and that glory must be revivified tirelessly to pass it on as the legacy of the Fascist era to generations to come!

— BENITO MUSSOLINI, APRIL 21, 1924

*I*n 1870, papal rule of the city came to an end. The taking of Rome completed the unification of Italy, and the Italian general Giuseppe Garibaldi had created a new nation-state, a parliamentary monarchy, with the ancient metropolis as its capital. The pope withdrew into what would become the independent city-state of the Vatican under the Lateran Treaty of 1929.

Since the Reformation and Counter-Reformation, the stream of funds from the papal states had drastically lessened. As this happened, the city was compelled to rely increasingly on its own resources. It had never been, nor

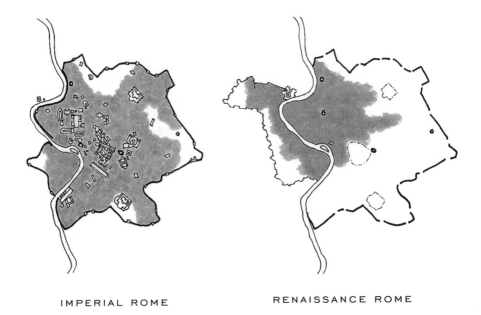

IMPERIAL ROME   RENAISSANCE ROME

The growth of the Rome conurbation across two millennia · In Imperial Rome, the city's built-up area (dark gray tone), including its great civic monuments, fills the area encircled by its fortifications. (By the end of the Renaissance, a new built-up area serving a much smaller number of inhabitants has been created. All that remains of the imperial capital are its outlying walls (broken black line), a handful of stripped monuments, and zones of fragmented ruins (demarked in thin dotted lines). · In the extended modern conurbation, the Renaissance cityscape and the remnants of the Imperial city have become a precious legacy within the expanded built-up area (pale gray tone) of the contemporary capital of the modern nation-state. (*All drawings at the same scale.*)

would it ever be, a major center of manufacturing, although since the Middle Ages it had gradually become a city that produced luxury goods and, in particular, copies and restorations of fine art. By 1790 the Vatican, as the center of the Christian world, would employ as much as a quarter of the city's workforce in the papal bureaucracy. Yet this percentage declined in proportion to Rome's population with every passing decade. Nonetheless, Rome possessed another significant commodity that would contribute to its continued viability as an important city long into the future: the interest its many faces of beauty held for the peoples of Western civilization.

For more than a thousand years, tourists had been coming to Rome. During the days of the empire, they had come to see the greatest city of the ancient world. Since the emergence of the Christian Roman Empire and throughout the Middle Ages, they had been coming to worship at the sacred sites of Christian history. During the Renaissance, they had come to study the

MODERN ROME

remnants of classical culture; and by the end of this period, they had come
to study the marvels of the new Catholic capital. By 1600 Rome's resident
population had risen to 100,000. In that same year it attracted five times
as many travelers and pilgrims. In 1644, visitors to Saint Peter's could make
use of established confessional seats in Hebrew, Greek, Latin, Spanish, Italian,
French, English, Irish, Welsh, Dutch, and several Slavic languages.

At the end of the sixteenth century, the French essayist Montaigne had
described the city as "the only town which is universal and common to everyone." In the seventeenth century, Louis XIV would establish an Académie de
France in Rome, to enable French artists, historians, and intellects to study the
art and artifacts of the city in its ancient and modern incarnations. Eventually
several other nations would create similar institutions. The culture of Rome
had come to be perceived as belonging to the universal story of all humankind.

Yet by the year 1700, visitors described Rome as lacking in the amenities
common to the other major cities of the day. It had limited sanitation facilities, inadequately paved roads, and no street signs or lighting. The glorious
cityscape that had reached its culmination in the work of Sixtus IV, while a

revelatory accomplishment in artistic urban form and architecture, had not continued to develop in its infrastructure and management. Moreover, the metropolis that had so recently established the standard for Western urbanism could no longer afford to remain in the forefront of city building. To varying degrees, Rome's financial woes would continue into the middle of the twentieth century. Increasingly, Italy would fall behind the rest of Europe economically and developmentally. As a result, tourism grew in its importance to the economy of Rome, and architectural preservation acquired a new significance. Under these conditions, loss of historical monuments would threaten the city's ability to attract visitors. In the most fundamental way, conservation had become tied to the long-term well-being of the metropolis.

Throughout this period—as Rome became frayed at the edges from lack of maintenance, as it lagged behind advances pioneered by such economically vibrant places as Paris and London—new structures continued to be built. Although the diminished economic power of the papacy and of Roman aristocrats, who were bound to an agricultural economy, were insufficient to modernize the city as a whole, the artistic vision of the Renaissance cityscape would be further refined in such unique landmarks as the Spanish Steps (1726), a marvelous sculptural cascade of intertwining stone stairways, and the Trevi Fountain (1762)—a vast Baroque sculpture of water spouts, gamboling horses, and ancient oceanic gods and goddesses celebrating the sweet water of the city's fountains. During a period of relative decline, Rome became an even more extensive harmonious assemblage as it slowly continued the long process of refilling the container of the ancient metropolis.

In this climate, another remarkable reversal began. Major fragments of the imperial past were rediscovered and painstakingly brought back to life in the cityscape. Existing ancient monuments were carefully repaired and maintained. An entirely new vision of the metropolis had emerged in which heroic efforts would be made to save, rehabilitate, and understand the historic legacy.

The new excavations in archaeological zones were no longer random treasure hunts but scientifically disciplined examinations of the past. Careful documentation of each site provided important data about the life and culture of the imperial city. One of the first scientific excavations of the Forum Romanum occurred in 1788 under the auspices of the Swedish ambassador, beginning a process of methodical reconstruction of this important site that continues to this day. Around 1800, a number of analyses were undertaken by Italian scholars to determine the original appearance of Trajan's Column, the Arch of Titus, and the Colosseum.

One of the basic questions in the art of architectural conservation concerns the target date of restoration: To what point in its history should an ancient structure be restored? Many imperial landmarks had been reused and adapted several times in their thousand-year lifetimes. For instance, across 1500 years the Theater of Marcellus, constructed by Augustus, became a medieval housing complex, a market for the city's butchers, and during the Renaissance, a palace for Italian nobility. Should such adaptations be preserved, or should historic monuments be returned to their original condition as when first constructed? In the nineteenth century, as the city began an effort to reconstitute its lost and deteriorated landmarks, the new discipline of archaeology would establish objective measures to determine how buildings had been altered over time and by whom.

In 1803 Pope Pius VII (1800–1823) had the ancient Roman paving around the Arch of Constantine uncovered and restored (1805–1807), so that the monument could be viewed in its original context. And on the basis of new scientific information, he began a thoughtful restoration of the Colosseum. For hundreds of years it had been mined for marble blocks and lime, and most of its stone features were long gone, particularly its interior stadium seating. Several later popes would continue to rehabilitate the remains of this long-abused monument. The carefully proportioned exterior marble skin of the arena had played a significant role in inspiring the architectural aesthetics of the Renaissance. Thus, in reconstituting and stabilizing the wounded structure, Pope Leo XII (in 1823–1829) differentiated new construction from historic construction by the use of contrasting materials (in 1825–1826), and made a clear record for posterity of what was genuine in the Colosseum and what was not. Similarly, the 1821 restoration of the Arch of Titus carefully distinguished newer material from the original by the use of subtly contrasting stone.

Pope after pope joined in the effort to reclaim fragments of the lost heritage that many of their predecessors had once sold for profit. As the science of restoration advanced, each step of reclamation became slower, costlier, and more painstaking. The fragments of ancient buildings constituted a puzzle of immense complexity. Years of scholarly expertise were expended to identify small segments. Much destruction had been wreaked in the seconds it took to swing a sledgehammer or lever a crowbar, and the resulting artifacts had often been sold for pennies. In the fullest sense, it was impossible to undo such damage. A structure refabricated in the 1800s is not the same as a structure made by the hands of ancient Romans and colored by more than a thousand years of wear. What was lost was lost forever and could be only partly redeemed. The greater significance of the application of archaeological science in Rome was the transformation of values that it signaled. Curatorial disciplines were being developed to secure the longevity of ancient remains. And because it was understood that the physical character of objects could convey meaning, speaking to us about the past, the popes and their archaeologists tried to ensure that reconstituted ancient structures spoke truthfully. Parts of the living city were now being handled as carefully as priceless objects in a museum.

Rome became one of the most important places in the world for the development of archaeology. It was an international gathering place for scholars and a site of ongoing excavation. In time, the evolution of the science led to more exacting methods of preserving all historic structures, and the analytic tools that explained the riddles of ancient Rome were used to gain a more accurate understanding of the construction of buildings from subsequent eras. Gradually, the theory, technical disciplines, and practice of architectural conservation became a specialized study, with Rome as its center. The intellectual conflicts of the Renaissance had given birth to a new urban consciousness in which architectural preservation was regarded as a principal determinant of the city's welfare.

In 1850 Pius IX (1846–1878) created the first supervisory body (*sovrintendenza*) responsible for the protection of all cultural properties in the Vatican State, which at that time still included the entire city of Rome. This was the administrative precursor of a branch of the city's modern conservation bureaucracy, eventually known as the Sovrintendenza delle Belle Arti and responsible for all municipally owned properties of cultural value. Thereafter, in acts consistent with a history fraught with contradiction, and after establishing a policy to save the landmarks of Rome, Pius IX also became the last pope to destroy an imperial monument: he eradicated the remains of a Roman bath and dismantled one of the better-conserved Roman gates. And then, removed from his city-wide authority in 1870, the pope withdrew into the Vatican.

CAPITAL OF THE CONSTITUTIONAL MONARCHY OF ITALY

After 450 years, since the reestablishment of the papacy in Rome in 1420, the fate of the city was returned to the hands of its inhabitants, and their first concern was to attain those municipal improvements that were being achieved in other great capitals. The subsequent modernization of Rome was accomplished in a discontinuous sequence by various national governments, as Italy evolved from a constitutional monarchy with Victor Emmanuel II as king, to a fascist dictatorship under Benito Mussolini, to a representative democracy by the end of World War II. Each of these administrations would strive to convert the country from an agricultural to an industrial economy. This common goal was motivated by the fact that at the beginning of the twentieth century the standard of life in Italy was far behind that of the leading modern nations. Some 75 percent of Italy's population consisted of illiterate peasants living in impoverished rural areas. Only 10 percent of Italian households had a bath or shower, and only 30 percent had a flushing toilet. These conditions were not fully alle-viated until after the Second World War, when the country completed an economic miracle, the cities of northern Italy were industrialized, and the urbanized citizens of the postindustrial nation came to enjoy the fifth-highest standard of living in the world.

Meanwhile, from the moment Rome was established as the capital of the nation-state, it began to acquire an enormous governmental bureaucracy, which—along with tourism, banking, and services—was the basis of its modern economy. Consequently, its population increased dramatically, from about 226,000 in 1870 to 500,000 by World War I and to a million by 1930.

Since the industrialization of Italy occurred primarily in the north, the modernization of historic Rome largely involved protecting it from seasonal flooding by the Tiber, making the city accessible to contemporary forms of transportation, and converting the principal city of the papal state into the capital city of a modern nation. These narrow causes had wide effects. In the process of accomplishing these goals, a major portion of the city's historic buildings were destroyed and the character of the cityscape altered dramati-cally.

Almost everything about this season of destruction was different from the devastation that had come before. To begin with, this damage was planned. One of the first actions of the government of the nation of Italy was to pass a law, on November 17, 1870 (Bill no. 2359), empowering the city of Rome to prepare a master plan, a *piano regolatore,* for the city's physical development. Thereafter, at different multiyear intervals, one plan or another would be in official effect. Although many of the ideas set forth in these plans were never realized, and a few ideas not set forth in the plans *were* realized, henceforth the design of the city involved a process of public decision-making.

Over the course of several decades and several master plans, consensus built in regard to a number of attributes fundamental to the character of Rome. It was generally recognized that the frame for the historic city would be the encircling Aurelian Walls of the empire. The major monuments of the Christian Renaissance-Baroque metropolis and the remains of the capital of imperial Rome would be treated as inviolate. Within the walls, the newer buildings of modern Rome would not be preeminent, and zoning limitations for the height of contemporary structures would keep them in appropriate scale with the historic cityscape. Also, new development inside the walls would be built at a moderate density, less than that which currently existed. Future growth would take place in an extended conurbation outside the line of old fortifications.

The effect of these basic decisions was profound. While the footprint of Christian Rome occupied a single and generally continuous area, the remnants of imperial Rome involved a number of disconnected sites. The new buildings of the expanding metropolis would now be wedged into leftover locations between important historic areas. Many of these contemporary incursions, designed in the neoclassical style, were the large office buildings of Italy's extensive bureaucracies. As a result, modern Rome became a city of haunting ruins (the imperial city) and glorious decay (the Renaissance city), juxtaposed with the scattered buildings of the contemporary city. These shifts of time and history were interspersed throughout the metropolis, becoming a fundamental part of its character.

Although a general commitment had been made to conserve the city, and various bureaucracies safeguarded its individual landmarks and archaeological sites, the modernization of Rome suffered from a liability shared with other European cities of this period. There was no commitment in law to protect historic areas as interconnected environments. Thus the texture and milieu of older parts of the city, whose thousands of modest historic buildings embodied much of the particular story of the evolution of Rome, were not protected by statute—and therefore not assured of consideration—as major urban changes were executed.

Modernization began with two significant urban surgeries. Under Pius IX, in the waning days of the papal state, Rome was linked to the transcontinental railway network by a line that ran around the southern segment of the imperial wall, penetrating the city near the Porta San Lorenzo and ending in a modern terminal near the ruins of the Baths of Diocletian. The creation of this rail line caused little destruction of historic assets, but it began covering land that still held uncharted archaeological material. Following this, in the early years of the nation-state, the shores of the Tiber as it meandered through the western end of the city were stabilized by flood walls, destroying a picturesque medieval-Renaissance aspect of the city while protecting remaining historic buildings from the damage due to periodic flooding. Thus started the process of selective urban demolition.

Next, one of the major dilemmas of historic cities was confronted. How could Rome be made accessible to contemporary forms of surface transportation—the trolley, the bus, the truck, and the car? The solution to this problem had extensive repercussions. The difficulty was that the significant historic core of Rome was too big, while its streets were too narrow.

Throughout Europe, the constricted and angular circulation pattern of medieval centers made simultaneous navigation by autos and pedestrians forbidding. The older the city, the more perplexing was the problem. In most of these places, there was little room for sidewalks, and cars would typically jump the curbs in search of space to park. This would force pedestrians to walk out in the roadways. For visitors from modern cities, a first trip to Europe can be unnerving. Why are these cities so dangerous? The answer, of course, is that such historic places were built long before the invention of the internal-combustion engine, and the discord between vehicular traffic and pedestrians is the product of a larger compromise. Historic urban settlement that could not be made to accommodate the automobile would not be torn down. Inefficiency in the living city was accepted as the price for retaining the assemblage of ancient buildings.

Still, some degree of penetration by modern vehicles was neccessary if the historic city was to serve modern life, for as the population of cities expanded as a result of industrialization, the volume of people and goods that needed to be transported within cities expanded as well. With more people in the core area, movement became increasingly difficult and the centers of large cities became clogged. In several historic cities, the configuration of the metropolis lent itself more readily to modern conveyances. The broad avenues of Haussmann's Paris, once sidewalks were narrowed and rows of trees eliminated, and the wide thoroughfares of medieval Beijing, once the historic pailou, or commemorative arches, were removed, could accommodate multiple lanes of automobiles. And the canals of Venice allowed vaporetti. But infiltrating Rome with modern transit was more problematic. There were several possible solutions, and obstacles to all of them.

First, there was the choice between moving people by mass transit or by individually owned vehicles. One of the simpler ways to avoid the navigational difficulties of the labyrinth of older street patterns is to tunnel lines for subways below the city. But Rome does not lend itself readily to this solution. Much of the hilly area circumscribed by the ancient walls has archaeological value. Tunnels and stations for subway lines would need to be deep under the ground to avoid compromising important archaeological material. Finally, when tunneling beneath standing historic structures, excavators must take great care to avoid doing damage to their foundations.

Eventually Rome did build a subway line, but it was a costly and slow endeavor with unsatisfactory results. A large area of winding streets and archaeological ruins—about 2,500 meters, or 1.5 miles, wide in all directions—was not serviced by the subway: north from the Piazza del Popolo, south to the Circus Maximus, east from the Baths of Diocletian, and west to Vatican City on the west side of the Tiber. Traversing this angular maze via surface transport took considerable time and effort. Although the city of the popes had been designed with long axial lines for carriages, these were not wide enough for a multi-lane flow of modern vehicles, nor did the avenues of the popes extend all the way across the much larger modern metropolis that had sprung up. By 1930 there were 30,000 motor vehicles in the city, with many more on the way. Thus for reasons of general practicality and public safety (to allow access to fire engines, police cars, and ambulances), it was decided to adapt the historic city center of Rome to automobiles and trolley and bus lines.

In a few instances this could be achieved by tunneling short distances under the hills of Rome. But for the most part, making the city accessible to cars required widening a select number of streets and cross-arteries and chopping off minor bits and pieces of numerous buildings along the way. It is easy to draw such pencil lines across the plan of the city, but performing this surgery in reality required substantial effort. The facades of many buildings had to be torn down and rebuilt several meters away. In total, to make a little more room at innumerable junctures was a task of mammoth proportions extending over about half a century. A set of seemingly modest adjustments required thousands of small and difficult cuts in the living tissue of the city.

Nor were all the losses aboveground. As the first stages of the modernization of Rome unfolded—as new roads were cut, ministry buildings constructed, and housing developed on open land—the city lacked a sufficiently large and properly staffed government archaeology program. Thus, few archaeological records were created for lands that, once built upon, were henceforth permanently hidden from examination. A golden opportunity to shed more light on Rome's history was lost.

These operations were further complicated by another consideration: somewhere within the city's urban fabric its function as the capital of the new nation-state needed to be expressed symbolically. This was an unusually difficult problem in Rome. Unlike Moscow, where the historic administrative center of the city—the Kremlin—could be appropriated by the newly empowered Communist government, Vatican City remained under the rule of the popes. Moreover, parts of the municipal government were already housed in Michelangelo's elegant complex on the Capitoline Hill, while the ruins of the proud imperial forums haunted the center of the city. In Rome, creating a noteworthy monumental presence required building something big—such as an ostentatious giant white marble wedding cake like the Monumento a Vittorio Emanuele II, or the Vittoriano.

This monument to the first king of Italy, Victor Emmanuel II, rose at a crucial nexus on the north side of the Capitoline, next to the Campidoglio, adjacent to the Forum of Caesar and in front of the Piazza Venezia. Here a number of important cross-arteries were obstructed by the dense historic growth of the city. Much of the area was a closely packed slum known as the Jewish Ghetto. A district slated for improvement, it was similar to decayed historic neighborhoods in many other cities of the world, where poor living conditions and social inequities tempted municipal governments to solve such problems by making them disappear via slum clearance. Yet this environment, which at first glance seemed chaotic and discordant, told an important story about the metropolis. Woven together organically were old Roman ruins, medieval accretions, and Renaissance additions. Here all the chapters of the first two thousand years of Rome's history were intertwined, revealing a medieval consciousness and order that contrasted with later conceptions of the city. Soon this milieu was to be purged.

This was a critical point in the urban history of Rome. In order to make the monument to Victor Emmanuel a dominant presence in the cityscape, the lines of sight needed to be cleared. Since important avenues of circulation converged and met in the forecourt at the base of the monument, expanding these lanes for traffic and axial views would result in the destruction of an enormous amount of the surrounding urban fabric. A scrupulously thoughtful process was called for—at the precise moment Benito Mussolini came to power.

FASCIST ROME

The leader of the Fascist state can fairly be credited with both the revitalization and the diminishment of Rome's historical assets. The government that had preceded Mussolini, guiding Italy in the first fifty years of its nationhood, had already opened up many roadways in the historic capital and had almost completed the Vittoriano when Mussolini ended parliamentary rule in 1928 and assumed dictatorial authority. Just as he made the trains of Italy more efficient, Mussolini made the street widenings wider and the straightenings straighter. Such urban operations thus became far more destructive. Further, since Mussolini wished to symbolically identify the Fascist state with the imperial city of Roman history, he began a program to reestablish the primacy of ruins in the cityscape, and escalated the devastation of medieval areas.

Up to this point, the modernization of Rome had caused substantial but carefully limited damage. One of the reasons for such moderation was the persistent advocacy of one of the Italy's leading conservationists—the architect, planner, engineer, and historian Gustavo Giovannoni. As director of the school of architecture in Rome from 1927 to 1935 and as a teacher of historic conservation from 1935 until his death in 1947, Giovannoni perceived the built fabric of the city as an interrelated whole. Ahead of his time, he understood the significance of saving the minor architecture of the city—the non-monuments that he described as constituting the "architectural prose" of everyday life. As a member of various commissions, as a consultant, and as a critic, Giovannoni suggested that the modernization be achieved by a thoughtful thinning-out of buildings (*diradamento edilizio*). The opening of the Corso Vittorio Emanuele is an excellent example of this approach. The gently winding course of the widened street was far more efficient than the narrow angular path that had preceded it, and planners minimized the amount of damage to significant urban tissue by not trying to make a perfectly straight thoroughfare. Giovannoni's *diradamento edilizio* led to a useful compromise between expediency and common sense. It was a way of modernizing Rome while preserving it. Giovannoni, who prized much of the historic fabric that surrounded the Vittoriano, suggested a restrained clearing that would leave intact the accretions of history. Mussolini advocated a more brutal surgical clearance (*sventramento*), or disemboweling. Few conservationists were likely to object; only Giovannoni, like Raphael, raised a critical voice while others remained silent. This did not stop the Fascists, but it stamped the integrity of Giovannoni's thinking into the memory of the city.

Il Duce wanted clear lines of sight to the Vittoriano, so as to heighten its aura of majesty. He considered straight, wide avenues an expression of Fascist efficiency and directed that the monuments of the Roman Empire were to stand unfettered in the cityscape. Hordes of workers armed with picks and shovels began clearing away the accrued historic urban fabric near the Capitoline. (Mussolini preferred manual labor, since it employed greater numbers of people.) A straight gash was cut from the Vittoriano to the Colosseum, destroying 5,500 habitable housing units and numerous historic structures. As a result of this clearance, 80,000 square meters of the Roman Forum were revealed and a careful archaeological study was undertaken. Afterward, 67,000 square meters of the site were reburied by the new roadway, which cut diagonally across the Forum and divided it in two. One era of history had been destroyed in the process of uncovering another, which was then once more hidden by a broad band of asphalt.

To the south of the Vittoriano lay the Campidoglio, the Jewish Ghetto, and the Teatro di Marcello. For hundreds of years, Michelangelo's capital and the ancient theater been casually interwoven with the gritty texture of everyday life. In the new Rome, infringing structures were leveled and imperial monuments set in open parklands. A wide avenue was opened southward around the hill and down to the Tiber. Also freed of the accretions of history, surrounded by greenery, and reestablished at their historic grade levels were the Arch of Janus, the Temple of Vesta, and the Temple of Fortuna Virilis.

The Mausoleum of Augustus—which had been a tomb, a fort, a pleasure garden, a bullfighting ring, a sculptor's studio, and a concert hall—was disconnected from the growth of the city, converted to a historical ruin, and set within a park, which in turn was set within a traffic circle. One hundred twenty multistory tenements were demolished in the process.

As each of these locations was opened, hundreds of dispossessed families were moved out of the city to hastily constructed public housing projects called *borgate,* or "scraps of the city,"as they came to be commonly known. In isolated areas, rows of single-family dwellings shared communal toilets and water taps.

Such communities had none of the amenities of a new town; there was barely a park, hospital, community center, cinema, school, or library. The disenfranchised poor were thus displaced to a no-man's-land from which they had to commute into the capital to work. (Actually, this was to some degree an improvement over the pre-Fascist policy for slum clearance, which had made virtually no allowance for those evicted, so that by 1920 there were over 50,000 baraccanti, or illegal shacks, in the countryside outside the city's walls.) Crooked streets had been straightened, imperial grandeur had been reestablished, and slums had been eradicated, but the city was now surrounded by several physically and economically impoverished zones.

The final piece of urban surgery to clear the historic city for traffic and majestic axial views was begun by the fascists and completed after World War II. This was the construction of the Via della Conciliazione, which opened Saint Peter's and its piazza to an axial view from the Tiber. The idea of creating a formal axis for Saint Peter's had first been proposed by Bernini. Many different groups supported this enhancement of the city, which required the destruction of the existing historic townscape along the line of sight. And it was done.

Thus was achieved the modernization of Rome. One-third of the historic buildings within Rome's imperial walls were demolished. Several hundred acres of archaeological value were covered over. Much of the story of the organic evolution of the form of the historic metropolis, particularly its medieval aspect, was erased through the destruction. The architectural story of Rome, as it was embodied in the cityscape, had been rewritten. Yet the ancient walls were saved, and the architectural unity of the extensive Renaissance core was maintained. Substantial plots of open land (about one-eighth of the area of the historic city) were set aside in perpetuity as archaeological parks for the ruins of the imperial past and the explorations of scholars. The largest of these areas was a central zone of the city extending from the Roman Forum through the Palatine Hill, the Colosseum, the Circus Maximus, and the Baths of Caracalla, to the Appian Way. Tall, oversize modern buildings, which violated many other cities generally did not cast shadows over the historic center, but a sizable ring of highways, middle-class suburbs, dilapidated public housing, shoddy contemporary construction, and numerous illegal settlements grew up around it. In the course of the twentieth century, the city's population multiplied tenfold, reaching 2.7 million inhabitants. The area within the ancient walled city eventually represented but 4 percent of the modern municipality.

The historic city was opened to traffic, which promptly clogged the new and wider streets. Automotive exhaust pollution contributed to the high acidic content of Roman rain, which in turn caused advanced deterioration of marble and travertine throughout the urban area. Since the clearing of Rome for traffic was integrated with the program to uncover more of the city's ancient ruins, much of this pollution was generated in the immediate proximity of the newly revealed monuments. The combination of the two programs has thus brought to light numerous precious historical assets while simultaneously producing an environmental condition that is destroying the stones of which these historic buildings are made. While modernization of the city was necessary, one cannot help but wonder if Rome would have been better served had the vision of Giovannoni prevailed over that of the Fascist dictator.

CONTEMPORARY ROME

By 1962 the master plan for the city called for safeguarding all historic structures within the ancient Roman walls. Rome had finally established protections for the whole historic cityscape.

From the reign of the emperors through the rule of the popes, Rome had known no shortage of preservation edicts, proclamations, and statutes. Some of these called for death, dismemberment, and scourging as penalties for the destruction of historic assets. Yet the effect of these controls throughout the history of the city had been minimal because each new ruler was free to follow or reject the practices of his predecessors. Many newly won advances in preservation policy had been short-lived. One of the prinicipal improvements of the nation-state was to create continuity in law. Although each new administration might differ in the degree of its commitment to conservation, the controls provided by statutes would continue to be in effect from one form of government to another. This allowed the body of law that governed society to be adjusted and refined over the decades.

Today the bureaucratic apparatus by which the historic city is administered is labyrinthine, vast, and inefficient. A complex overlay of different legislative strictures and uncoordinated agencies makes it almost impossible for many property owners and institutions to know with certainty their exact rights and responsibilities. As a result, Rome is simultaneously one of the most overprotected historic urban environments in the world as it is seen by the public, but it is extraordinarily prone to unregulated violations of its law in all those places that the public cannot see.

Five basic legal instruments guard the character of the historic cityscape: two national conservation statutes; a municipal preservation agency; a municipal building and zoning code; and a national planning law that is implemented by the Commune di Roma.

In the long story of Roman preservation law, dating back almost 1,500 years to the decrees of Emperor Majorian, two nationwide laws enacted in 1939 establish much of the basis for the regulation of historic properties today. Article 1089 of the 1939 statute establishes the power of the state to list privately owned buildings as landmarks; many important structures within the city are thus protected by being designated as *vincola*—"restricted," or "restrained." Article 1497 establishes automatic protection for every significant historical and architectural feature of every property owned by a public institution. It is a blanket designation. Thus a public institution must assume liability for the elements of its property, both aboveground and below. In effect the government is saying that if you are a public institution, every feature of your property that we might deem valuable is protected. The institution must figure out which features these are, and apply for permission before changing them, or it will be held liable retroactively.

Each of these statutes is enforced by the national Ministry for Cultural Properties, the Ministero per i Beni Culturali e Ambientali, which is divided into three superintending offices (*sovrintendente*). The Archaeological Sovrintendente is responsible for all antiquities predating A.D. 476. The Architectural and Environmental Sovrintendente is responsible for all landmarked buildings constructed after A.D. 476 (they must be at least fifty years old before they can be designated). The Artistic and Historical Sovrintendente is responsible for the protection of all movable objects such as frescoes, paintings, mosaics, and architectural sculpture. This is a common feature in modern European conservation statutes, and one notes that frescoes and mosaics are movable only if they are first detached from the structure into which they have been incorporated, a practice not uncommon in the past in order to facilitate the sale of such artifacts to museums and private collectors.

Reponsibility for municipally owned properties of cultural value, including all city monuments, walls, gateways, gardens, villas, and fountains, is administered by the municipal Sovrintendenza delle Belle Arti of the Comune di Roma. Between the municipal and the national *sovrintendente*, the most outstanding principal features of historic Rome are protected. Further, the general zoning and building code provisions of the city ensure that the height, color, and materials of all new buildings within the Aurelian walls must be compatible with the general historical character of the area.

Yet all these protections together would still leave unprotected numerous structures which, although not singular works of architecture, nonetheless contribute to the general historic ambience. These are restricted under the city's current *piano regulatore*, drawn up in 1989, which declares that the area within the Aurelian and Vatican walls must meet Italy's master planning standards for a Zone A—a central historic preservation zone. All changes to properties within this area must be regulated or reviewed by the national authorities.

The Romans, like the citizens of many other cities in Europe, finally protected the whole urban ensemble not by extending existing preservation laws but by using city-planning decrees. A balance of benefits and obligations was then created for the owners of historic properties. Every building listed as historic is free of property and inheritance taxes, and the state may reimburse owners for as much as 40 percent of the cost of preserving such properties. But in return, owners must make some provision for public access in order to receive reimbursement for the cost of maintenance. In addition, the state can require owners to perform mandatory maintenance; and if an owner wishes to sell a property, the state may purchase it at a legitimately established market value.

In total, these regulations make it extremely difficult for anyone to tear down a major or minor structure of the historic city, much less to erect an unsightly building in its place. At the same time, the numerous uncoordinated overlays of conservation regulations require citizens to undertake arduous and time-consuming expeditions through the Italian bureaucracy in order to make the slightest change to their properties.

The byzantine complexity of conservation laws is exacerbated by the widespread laxity of service on the part of public bureaucracies. As part of the process of modernizing Italy and providing employment for a displaced agrarian society, a giant administrative machine was created, which has become an obstacle to the functioning of daily life. The complexity of this machine makes it easy to hide all sorts of illegal and quasi-illegal infractions. (In the 1990s, experts estimated that Italian politicians and government officials stole or received kickbacks *(tangenti)* totaling $6 billion to $12 billion a year.) A culture of illegality is bred by the overcomplication of government rules, which serve as an obstacle to accountability.

Although many social commentators on contemporary Italy have described this phenomenon, the most telling proof of its persistence is an unusual practice of Roman law: the declaration of a period of *condo* every ten years or so. At this time, all violators of state and municipal codes are given the opportunity to undo their hidden infractions by declaring their illegal acts to the authorities and paying a fine as restitution. The lines at governmental offices during a *condo* are often exceedingly long. This practice gives credence to statements by Roman conservationists who claim that extended illegal modernization of the city is occurring behind its historic facades. Other places in the world have decided to allow such transformations to historic buildings, but in Rome much of this transformation goes unregulated. This vast gentrification and upgrading has driven the working classes from the historic center, and with them the neighborhood services of community life. As a result, an exclusive modern city is being built within the shell of the Renaissance-Baroque city.

This phenomenon has one other idiosyncratic cultural dimension. Over the long historic course of dealing with questions of preservation, a highly sophisticated tradition of conservation theory and practice has evolved in Italy. At its most refined levels, Italian conservationists have integrated the problems of preservation with the problems of housing and the maintenance of the social mix of the urban environment. In order to make it possible for poorer populations to stay in the center of historic cities, and to prevent working-class families, artists, and the elderly from being pushed out of their neighborhoods by gentrification, several municipal governments have begun reclaiming historic buildings for use as government-sponsored housing. Such restorations are carefully analyzed, and a proper mix between the new interior uses and the architectural character of the historic shell is maintained. In Rome, for instance, the guardrooms in the Aurelian walls now house studios for Roman artists, and a medieval monastery with many small rooms was recently converted into a college dormitory. Here, preservation has been blended with social equity, common sense, and farsighted urbanism. Sadly, just as imperial Rome's enlightened and technical sophistication benefited only part of the city, recent advances in Italian conservation are undermined by an intractable bureaucratic complexity.

LESSONS VIA ROME

Preservation evolves out of conflict. It is a choice between urban change by destruction of the past and urban change by integration with the past. The story of Rome is the most important early story in the evolution of urban conservation, because the destruction of a legacy of seminal importance to the development of Western civilization ignited an intellectual and political debate within Roman society from which evolved the principles and values of urban conservation.

Across the historic evolution of the city we witness the emergence of a number of very fundamental ideas about the preservation of cities. In the era of Majorian, as the empire began its decline, we see the realization that parts of the architectural heritage are irreplaceable, that a pinnacle of artistic building achieved by an earlier generation may be beyond our ability to duplicate. During the age of Byzantium, in the beneficent works of Theodoric the Great, we see the advent of the idea that saving the fabric of our architectural heritage requires our intervention through purposeful acts of conservation. The city is built by human volition, destroyed by human volition, conserved by human volition. The designs of Michelangelo at the Porta Pia, at the Baths of Diocletian, and at the Campidoglio demonstrate a sensitive approach to the architectural problems of adapting old structures to new uses and of deriving new designs from historic urban relationships. Michelangelo reminds us of the power of human creativity—that with each imaginative act, it is within our capacity to bring into existence works that extend the grace of the human-made universe.

The idea that tourism could be a major consideration in the commercial life of the city gradually emerged in Rome after the Reformation and Counter-Reformation. The city had always attracted a stream of visitors, but with the decline of the financial strength of the popes, tourism and conservation slowly became linked as intertwined pieces of the city's economy. The development of the science and art of archaeology, and the reclamation of imperial ruins in the nineteenth and twentieth centuries, gave birth to the idea that one of the functions of the city is to be a living museum of the architecture of the past—that the physical body of the metropolis has an educational purpose: to teach us about who we once were and who we might become.

Raphael and Giovannoni are linked across four hundred years by their integrity. One confronted a Fascist dictatorship; the other confronted an all-powerful papacy. The story of Giovannoni embodies the universal condition of the preservationist, who in thwarting the destructive tendencies of politically, economically, and socially powerful forces is armed only with knowledge, common sense, and a commitment to the public welfare. Today, few cities can successfully manage their built heritage without the help of citizen preservationists acting as sentinels. In the modern era, the degree to which the ethics of urban conservation have prevailed often is testimony to the perseverance of civic-minded individuals.

The lingering contradictions of the modern conservation effort in Rome reflect the complexity of governing large cities, where competing interests often cause urban policies to be compromised in illogical but politically expedient ways. Thus, rational interests are often not served in a rational manner. Hence the *condo*, for the violators of a punitive preservation code that breeds illegality by its unreasonable complexity.

In the end, there is a price for such folly, because in preservation one principle is absolute: we cannot replace the past once we have destroyed it. We may build facsimiles; but having forfeited the original, we have no way to judge how exact our copies are or what subtle but telling characteristic of human evolution has been erased.

A walk through this city of complex parts yields many thought-provoking contrasts of past and present. Rome's outlying walls are historic resources unique in the world. Originally more than 12 miles long, their ramparts and towers have been punctured, cropped, and gored in every imaginable way to make holes for trolleys, buses, cars, and pedestrians. Today, after 1,700 years, the ancient brick structure of the fortifications is simultaneously a treasured object of museological value and a casual part of daily life. Here, the city of the past is reconciled with subsequent generations. One walks toward the Porta

Pia, past blinking modern traffic lights, through the once forbidding fortified barrier—now rendered impotent by a hole cut by a Fascist traffic engineer—to discover a lofty white marble archway designed by Michelangelo and standing amid a painted macadam roadbed.

Wandering Rome's antiquated byways, navigating narrow sidewalks with fashionably dressed modern Italians, one is inevitably drawn to the Pantheon. The stripped-down masonry structure of simple eternal geometries is awkwardly embraced on three sides by the constricted Renaissance cityscape. A jumbled mix of bright-yellow Roman taxis, umbrella-covered café tables, and modern street furniture is part of the ambience of the small piazza that faces this sublime moment in the history of architecture.

Inside, a beam of light shines down through the circular hole in the peak of the dome. Fragments of clouds slide across the shutter-like opening. The richly detailed classical Roman interior is a breathtaking 1,500-year step back into history. How has this ethereal building survived in such a perfect state? How has this perilous feat of engineering, the graceful inverted shell of the great coffered dome, come down through the ages intact, while the rest of the ancient city is a patchwork of fragments? The answer is sadly obvious. The excellent condition of the Pantheon is a reminder that large parts of the legacy of ancient Rome could very well have been bequeathed to us. In the sun-drenched piazzas of the enlightened Renaissance city, a haunting admission echoes: "This mammoth deed of cultural and historical negation was committed by us, the inhabitants of the city. We desecrated our past in order to achieve this new glory. For centuries on end, we fractured the beautiful monuments and, piece by piece, dismembered the achievements of our ancestors." In all, it took nearly a thousand years to efface this singular manifestation of human accomplishment. The by-product of this vast and disputed act of destruction—the lesson for subsequent generations—was the emergence of the idea that it should have been tempered by reason and by consideration for the future of humankind.

THE CULTURE OF
CONSERVATION IN CITIES

Cities, like dreams, are made of desires and fears, even if the
thread of their discourse is secret, their rules are absurd, their
perspectives deceitful, and everything conceals something else.
—ITALO CALVINO, *Invisible Cities*

The culture of cities has always been as complex, contradictory,
cruel, and wondrous as the general blend of darkness and light
manifested by our species as a whole. As the metropolis has
grown to a hundred thousand, a million, twenty million inhabitants—with just
as many "dreams made of desires and fears"—the culture of cities has, to different degrees, offset this chaotic diversity and binds together the inhabitants of
urban places in life-affirming common purpose.

In this book I ask why some cities preserve their heritage better or more
readily than others. My years of investigation have shown that the most truth-
ful, all-encompassing, and succinct answer to this question is that a sensitivity
to conservation has evolved in their culture. There are of course specific legal,
economic, historical, social, political, and physical circumstances involved in
this question, but their complex interrelationship can only be described as
cultural. Preservation is different in different places because the culture of
every great city is unique. And in our age of globalization and creeping homogeneity, it is exactly this uniqueness that is in need of saving.

The culture of cities is both visible and invisible, palpable and elusive. On
the one hand, we know the culture of urban environments from the experience
of being in them. Paris feels like Paris and noplace else, just as the smells,
sounds, sights, aura, and rhythms of life in Beijing, Amsterdam, Kyoto,
Venice, Jerusalem, and Mexico City become singularly etched in our memories
after just one visit. Yet while we may recognize the cultures of different places,
we cannot quantify any particular culture in exact terms, in part because a city's
culture is always evolving—growing out of the past and changing at the moment
we attempt to define it.

In response to this dilemma, my work on this book became, in part, a search for the genesis of the conservation impulse, for moments when the significance of saving urban culture was crystallized. Nonetheless, I was somewhat shocked when I found that just such a decisive confirmation of the tangible significance of historic buildings was activated by none other than Adolf Hitler during World War II, when in order to subdue the Poles he ordered the destruction of the monuments of Warsaw. In seeking to destroy his enemies' courage, Hitler identified a primal source of their strength.

Three decades later, in *Invisible Cities,* Italo Calvino showed the meaning of the culture of cities to an equally decisive degree, by writing about imaginary urban places in poetic prose and capturing the essence of urban identity through metaphors. In order to solve the similar problem of making comprehensible the contradictions of cities, where often "the thread of their discourse is secret, their rules are absurd, their perspectives deceitful, and everything conceals something else," I have chosen to write about the drama of urban conservation by identifying important moments in history when human events culminated in a clear clash of values—when common sense, logic, law, and sometimes even the principles of physics were defied. And because the corporeal material of the metropolis is one of the elements that tie a city's people by invisible threads to the past, I have endeavored to set such moments in the context of each city's history, in urban profiles, so that tensions among cultural values can be seen in terms of cultural evolution. The preservation of great cities is ultimately the story of how different urban societies created environments of extraordinary meaning, were affected by their cityscapes through centuries of habitation, and came to realize that the loss of old buildings involved much more than just the visible destruction of ancient bricks and stones.

CHAPTER FOUR

THE HERITAGE OF WAR

WARSAW

Warsaw has to be pacified, that is, razed to the ground.

—ADOLF HITLER, 1944

Things have different costs in different places. In the ancient heart of Warsaw ice cream is inexpensive and on Sunday afternoons the lines in front of popular vendors are long and noisy, as grandparents, children, fathers, mothers, aunts, uncles, and friends debate what flavors to sample. A few of these people are foreign visitors, but most of them are Poles. They purchase their ice cream on cones and stroll through the historic medieval city, which has been meticulously re-created down to the finest detail after its destruction in World War II. Surrounded by the facsimile of their lost birthright, there is a palpable feeling of pride in the air. It is one of the most wonderful urban celebrations to be found anywhere in the world.

How important is our architectural heritage? What limits will we place on the city's future in order to preserve our cultural identity? What price are we willing to pay to conserve a record of our history? Few places have given as clear an answer to these questions as Warsaw. Here people established the value of their monuments by what they were willing to sacrifice. In Warsaw, a city's inhabitants endangered their lives to save their past.

❀

In Warsaw they fought. That is the first and most important fact.

The Poles fought the Germans again and again and again, refusing to be subdued. They died by the hundreds of thousands in battles, concentration camps, and ad hoc daily executions. And it was here, in the Warsaw Ghetto, that members of the Jewish resistance—realizing the ultimate futility of their desperate struggle and equipped with but a few stolen guns, bricks, and homemade bombs—pitted themselves against storm troopers wielding the most modern of military hardware.

Citizens in Warsaw resisted the Third Reich, and by their dissent and death they put a price on their metropolis. They established the price they would not pay to keep it whole. They would not sell the soul of their city in order to save its body. They would not refrain from resistance in order to spare their metropolis from becoming a battleground. And once it was evident that the cost of their defiance would be the destruction of the city, Varsovian architects, planners, and teachers, in a perilous act of disobedience, documented their architectural past so it could be rebuilt sometime in an unknown but better future.

In Warsaw they fought, and as a result the city and its people were almost totally eradicated, and not just by the missiles, bombs, and bullets of combat. In Warsaw the Nazis devised a systematic program of cultural annihilation.

German architects carefully identified the historic monuments of the city: the most beautifully proportioned buildings, the buildings designed by distinguished architects, the buildings where famous Varsovians had lived, the places where important historic events had taken place, the buildings with gracious sculptural decoration, the buildings of symbolic importance, the best examples of different architectural styles, the most meaningful buildings of various periods, the proudest churches, the richest palaces, the most beautiful homes, and the neighborhoods where the architecture of Warsaw was knit into an artistic whole—the panoply of Warsaw's pride, built across seven hundred years of history. Then, having ascertained the patrimony of the metropolis, the German occupational forces sent out squads to rob these places, to strip them of their art and artifacts and, afterward, to dynamite the architectural accomplishments of Polish culture. The structural integrity of buildings was analyzed. Explosives were set and detonated from a safe distance. In World War II, it became German national policy that the culture of Warsaw be erased as a way to quash the spirit of resistance among the Polish people.

OLD WARSAW

"She defies the storm!" That was the motto of the city long before the Germans attacked. Across hundreds of years of history, Warsaw and the rest of Poland had endured defeat, annihilation, betrayal, and subjugation by the Tartars, Teutonic knights, Swedes, Hungarians, Transylvanians, Russians, French,

Austrians, and Germans. In European history, Poland was a country not allowed to become a nation.

Caught by geography and fate between some of the major competing continental powers, Poland was established as an autonomous kingdom in 1526, but by 1655 it had already lost its independence to the Swedes. The country was erased from the map of Europe by Russia, Prussia, and Austria in three consecutive partitions in 1722, 1793, and 1795. It was taken by the French in 1806, ruled by Russia under the Congress of Vienna, subjugated once more after the Russo-Polish War, and occupied by the Germans in World War I. Finally, in 1918, the country was given back its independence, and thereafter, until the German invasion in World War II, it experienced a brief and tantalizing era of freedom.

As in other European countries, whose continuity of preservation law is anchored in the first national statute promulgated after the emergence of the nation-state, Poland began the effort to identify and conserve its heritage immediately following its independence in 1918. A Ministry of Culture and Arts responsible for the conservation of historic monuments was established, and ten years later, in 1928, a remarkably comprehensive statute was adopted by the Polish national legislature. The new law protected landmarks, their surroundings, parks, gardens, monuments of nature, and historic districts in urban areas. This is the earliest modern preservation statute to recognize the significance of protecting entire historic neighborhoods. It predates the special zoning statutes of both Charleston (1931) and New Orleans (1932) in the United States, as well as those in Paris, London, Amsterdam, Rome, and Vienna, which had formulated national preservation laws long before Poland but had not empowered conservation authorities to restrict the development of whole urban areas.

Having been denied a national identity for centuries, the Polish people had a strong desire to protect those manifestations of culture that were unique to them. Even before Polish independence, several architects and historians had attempted to identify a national architectural style and to inventory the country's singular historic buildings. One of the most important architectural clusters lay in the heart of the capital city. The environment that had evolved here embodied the historic building traditions of the nation more thoroughly than any other place in Poland.

The Old Town of Warsaw was first built up around a market square as a modest fortified trading settlement and regional administrative center sometime in the 1300s. By the fifteenth century it had become a ducal seat. In 1447 it expanded to include a New Town just to the north. As Poland took its place as the breadbasket of Europe, the burghers of Warsaw grew prosperous and transformed their wooden houses into handsome masonry structures. In 1611, during the reign of Sigismund Augustus III, the royal court was established in the city. An elegant castle was erected, based on the designs of architects imported from Italy. Numerous other noblemen's mansions soon embellished the growing capital town and its suburbs. Within a few years, there were over one hundred such elaborate residences and four grand palaces. Most of these were in the Baroque style, and before long the burghers' houses were undergoing similar stylistic transformations. The settlement's medieval defensive walls were periodically expanded. Numerous beautiful churches were built, both within and outside the Old Town walls. Across hundreds of years of building, the city had become a cherished architectural ensemble.

There was a Great Fire in 1607. In 1620, Warsaw was struck by plague. In 1660, it was laid waste by the Swedes, Hungarians, and Transylvanians. Mansions, palaces, and churches were looted. Over 60 percent of the settlement was leveled, and 70 percent of the population was killed. There was an even more terrible fire in 1669, yet still the city did not vanish. In the midst of another attack of plague, the Varsovians rebuilt the Old Town. And the bricks, stones, and tiles of the city came to be perceived as the cultural expression of a stubborn national spirit.

After its reconstruction, the Old Town entered a long period of decline. The city was no longer the capital of a nation. Wealthy families built their fashionable houses in other parts of Warsaw, and the historic core became a district for the middle class. By the 1900s maintenance had slowed, and the number of residents in the Old Town grew as the poor moved in. In comparison with the more modern neighborhoods of Warsaw, the lack of sanitary infrastructure and amenities made the Old Town a slum. Dilapidated, worn, and frayed, the proud old buildings nonetheless retained their inherent beauty under a layer of grime.

Early in the twentieth century, Warsaw was the focal point of a Polish cultural renaissance. Theater, music, and journalism flourished. Poland briefly reassumed nationhood. Universities were established and the city became a sophisticated continental capital, frequently referred to by Poles as the "Paris of the East." The Varsovians were justly proud, for the modern industrial city that had grown up around the historic core of the Old and New Towns was an integrated artistic assemblage of traditional and classically inspired architecture, adorned with fountains, public sculptures, parks, pleasure gardens, cobbled streets, decorative ironwork, and elegant kiosks and streetlamps. In 1927 the city hosted the International Chopin Competition for Young Pianists. By the eve of the Blitzkrieg, Warsaw was one of the most beautiful cities of Europe and held about 1.3 million people, for whom freedom was a precious and infrequent commodity.

OCCUPATION BY THE THIRD REICH

On September 1, 1939, when the first bombs were dropped on Warsaw by the Luftwaffe, Poland had a multiethnic population of about 30 million people. Over the next five years, one-fifth of these would be killed: about 6 million Poles, including virtually all of the more than 3 million Jews. Of these many victims, it is estimated that only 600,000, or 10 percent, were combatants killed in fighting. The vast majority were executed, starved, or exterminated. There were seven German concentration camps in Poland, two of which—Auschwitz and Treblinka—were to become particularly infamous. In addition, millions of Russian prisoners were jammed into camps and left to starve. And at over four hundred other places a minimum of one hundred Polish civilians were executed at a time, without trial.

Most of these ad hoc murder locations are little known, but investigators have found that when the authorities have failed to document the position of such sites, rural neighbors have done so. Across Poland, there are unused open fields where farmers do not plow, for they know that to do so would disturb the remains of the murdered. Hidden in woodlands, there are simple homemade monuments where the anonymous living remember the anonymous dead. In Poland in World War II, the Germans perpetrated a Polish genocide, a Jewish genocide, and a Russian genocide. They reduced the country to a vast killing field and made Warsaw a city of death.

Between 1939 and 1944 some 800,000 people, or 60 percent of Warsaw's population, were killed and most of the town destroyed. The intent of this carnage was chilling. The Nazis had decided to depopulate Poland and reconfigure Warsaw to hold 130,000 German inhabitants occupying an area about 5 percent of the size of the prewar city. In Würzburg, in Bavaria, town planners of the Third Reich drafted precise drawings identifying a historic area of "Germanic" architectural character in which select old buildings would be saved (including a historic castle to serve as Hitler's state residence), and a modern provincial city would be built up around them. The Pabst Plan, composed of fifteen drawings and a miniature architectural model, established that the new German agricultural center would be located in the sector around the Old and New Towns of Warsaw. (The Pabst Plan is named for the German army architect Friedrich Pabst, who refined the idea of destroying an enemy's national cultural identity by destroying its physical manifestations: architecture, art, and historic archives. The actual design for the new German city to be located in the former site of Warsaw was created by another German army architect, Hubert Gross.)

The first siege of Warsaw was a bitter struggle that lasted three weeks. The Polish toll was 10,000 dead and 50,000 wounded. About 12 percent of the city's buildings were extensively damaged. On September 17, the Russians advanced across the eastern border of Poland, and Stalin and Hitler partitioned the country according to a prearranged plan. Although the Soviets would not remain allied to Germany, it is estimated that during this brief period they were responsible for the death of about 1.2 million Poles.

In Warsaw, the Germans were soon creating cities within the city: a German sector, a Polish sector, and what the Nazis officially referred to as the Jewish Quarter (*Judenviertel*), which came to be known as the Warsaw Ghetto. Prior to the war, the Jewish community in Warsaw had been a thriving society of successful merchants, bankers, teachers, and professionals, with the largest urban population of Jews in Europe. The community had its own Yiddish theater, a Jewish press, and separate schools. Now the Nazis ordered that a particularly dense area of tenements be isolated, occupying about 760 acres, and that all of the city's Jews be crowded inside. A 10-foot wall was built all around the sector and guards posted on the perimeter.

The Warsaw Ghetto became a holding tank for Jews collected from the surrounding countryside. As more and more people were crowded together, more and more of the inhabitants died from lack of food and from diseases caused by the severely congested and unsanitary living conditions. It is not known exactly how many Jews died in Warsaw. Estimates of the resident population of the ghetto taken at different moments in its short but traumatic history vary from 300,000 to 600,000 people. To some extent, the inhabitants were dying as quickly as new victims could be found and packed inside. Life in the ghetto had achieved a virulent stasis with death.

For six centuries, Jewish life in Warsaw had persisted and often thrived, but in the summer of 1942, it came to an end. A message was sent to the German governor of Warsaw by Heinrich Himmler: "A general plan for the destruction of the city ghetto should be submitted to me. In any case, we must arrive at the stage in which the residential area, which exists at present for 500,000 subhumans [Jews] and which has never been suitable for Germans, will disappear from the face of the area, and the city of Warsaw, with its million inhabitants, which has always been a center of agitation and rebellion, should be reduced in size."

The "final solution" had emerged. At the rate of about 5,000 people a day, an estimated 350,000 ghetto residents were loaded onto cattle cars and shipped to the gas chambers. Some 60,000 Jews, weakened and primitively armed, chose another fate: at dawn on April 19, 1943, the Warsaw Ghetto uprising commenced. They fought against insurmountable odds for twenty-eight days.

The German solution to the urban guerrilla tactics of the Jewish resistance, the ZOB (Jewish Combat Organization), was to quell the rebellion one building at a time. With armed troops in attendance to act as execution squads, the ghetto was razed structure by structure. Afterward, bulldozers pulverized and leveled the broken pieces. The Germans had in effect erased an urban area of about one square mile. No buildings remained, no sidewalks, no streets, no green—just a field of shards.

Outside the ghetto, the harshness of the occupation resulted in a determined Polish underground whose activities were in turn met by further German brutalities. Ad hoc executions began to occur throughout the metropolis. After the war, 220 commemorative markers would be erected in the city in remembrance of the thousands of victims killed out of hand. The price for resistance was death, but it also became clear that ultimately the price for submission would be the same.

Early in the occupation, the German governor of the city had received an order from Berlin requiring him to "do everything possible to strip the city of its traditional character as the focal point of the Polish Republic." Because the Pabst Plan had initially left in place select historic structures contributing to a contrived Germanic townscape, a team of town planning and architectural experts had been required to evaluate which old buildings might be saved as part of the new city. (The elimination of the Jewish ghetto had always been a constituent of this scheme.) Now the Germans used the scholarship of their experts to perpetrate an intellectual obscenity. People who had been trained to revere the beauty of architecture and of cities lent their knowledge to the destruction of the very achievements to which they aspired. In order to subdue the fighting spirit of the Poles, the Germans attempted to eradicate their culture by destroying the most profoundly meaningful aspects of Warsaw's cityscape. This is one of the most revealing moments in the history of architectural conservation, a juncture of extreme inversion of values. Perceiving the Germans' intent, the Varsovians began a cultural counteroffensive.

One of the unexpected phenomena of World War II was that in cities subject to bombardment, planners recognized the inadvertent opening of a unique possibility for advantageously restructuring the metropolis. With the Industrial Revolution, modern cities had developed complex public and private vested interests in buildings and infrastructure that made change difficult. Each alteration of the city required the simultaneous reconciliation of the needs of multiple constituencies. But during the Second World War, with the introduction of indiscriminate strategic bombardment, many explosions unintentionally eliminated this tangle of vested interests. Unbeknownst to one another, in war-torn cities across Europe, local planners were surveying the damage and developing ideas for the reconstruction. Because this work had been done while the war progressed, postwar rebuilding in many cities was substantially advanced immediately upon the cessation of hostilities.

As Varsovian town planners anticipated the damage to come, they too began a covert operation to remake the city. Compared with their counterparts in France, England, and Germany, however, the planners in German-occupied Warsaw drew up such designs at risk of their lives, for the occupational authorities had declared such activities illegal.

A covert Studio for Architecture and Town Planning was secretly located in the Cooperative Building Enterprise to study postwar needs for housing and industrialization. (Its first director, prior to his deportation to Auschwitz, was Szymon Syrkus, one of the noted pioneers of modern Polish architecture.) The planning department of the municipal council, in association with the Studio for Regional Planning, created a secret commission of town planning experts to study the redevelopment of Warsaw's traffic circulation routes. Other illegal groups of architects were formed spontaneously across the city. One of their documents, a directive for Warsaw reconstruction, was written by the light of the flames of the burning city and hidden in POW camps until the end of the war, when it became a seminal reference for the reconstruction.

The most extraordinary clandestine operation occurred among members of the faculty of architecture of Warsaw Technical University. At the beginning of the century, Polish architects had begun to document the landmarks of Warsaw through measured drawings and analytical studies. Once Poland became an independent nation, its conservation bureaucracy assembled surveys of the city's historic assets. Additionally, approximately a hundred photographic studios had come to exist in Warsaw prior to World War II; many of these had captured the cityscape in pictures. Now such documentation would be critical if historic Warsaw was to be rebuilt. In some instances, old paintings would also be quite useful, especially a few highly detailed portraits of the city made in the eighteenth century by the Venetian painter Bernardo Bellotto, the nephew and student of Antonio Canaletto.

By command of the German occupational force, the university had been reduced to a secondary school for training in the building trades. In an act of moral resistance, the professors and students of the defunct Department of Town Planning, while pretending to do mechanical drafting exercises, continued the education of the next generation of Polish professional planners and architects. Over 150 students participated. In direct violation of the German prohibition on planning, pupils developed studies for the rebuilding of Warsaw. They predated their works so that, if they were discovered, the drawings would appear to have been created before the invasion. The documents were hidden in the monastery of Piotrków, outside the city. After the war, Warsaw Technical University would retroactively accredit twenty-three graduate papers, nine doctoral dissertations, and eight postdoctoral studies.

And in response to the waves of destruction that enveloped the city, members of the faculty undertook the task of assembling photographs, sketches, and drafted representations of Warsaw's historic structures. In a climate of frequent arrests, deportations, and public executions, and before the eyes of the gestapo, the studies continued. Methodically, the legacy of Warsaw was recorded so that the past would not be stolen from the children of the future. It is hard to imagine that ever again will such important conservation scholarship be done under such dangerous conditions.

On August 1, 1944, a second Warsaw Uprising began, this led by a contingent from the Polish Home Army. By this stage of World War II, two Polish governments-in-exile now existed. One was located in London, the other in the Soviet Union, and each claimed sovereignty over the embattled city.

By September 17, Soviet forces had reinvaded Poland from the east, this time as an ally to the West and enemy of the Third Reich. The Soviets advanced to within 75 miles of Warsaw and stopped. Fighting in the city was furious and bloody, and the Varsovians were close to victory over the Germans. But since the Polish Home Army was associated with the London government-in-exile, the Soviets would not intercede and help. They let the Germans prevail.

Much of the fighting had occurred in the medieval cityscape of the Old and New Towns, which was decimated by hundreds of thousands of explosions. The continued insubordination by the Poles of Warsaw had caused the Germans to reconsider whether they might refashion parts of the historic city to their own uses after the war. With the Old and New Towns in ruins, Hitler issued a final punitive order to completely raze the city.

The Germans divided Warsaw into zones and began a systematic eradication of the metropolis. They had already ascertained which structures represented the most significant parts of the Polish heritage. Selected buildings and statues were officially marked for the "demolition and annihilation squads." If blockfronts had an architectural unity, they were fractured by destroying those buildings that most contributed to the artistic whole. Corner buildings—which are often more architecturally dramatic and original—were especially targeted.

As this was occurring, a professor from the Technical University, Stanislaw Lorenz, obtained a special pass allowing him and a handful of other faculty members to reenter the deserted and devastated city. Hidden in the architectural school was the amassed documentation of the historic structures of Warsaw. It required several trips in an old truck to bring the material out. This too was hidden in the Piotrków monastery, in the ancient stone coffins of dead monks.

Of 957 buildings which the Poles had classified before the war as individual monuments or structures contributing to the special ambience of historic districts, 782 were totally destroyed and 141 partly demolished. The Nazis had reduced to rubble 96.5 percent of the city's historical and architectural legacy.

Germany was not the only nation that intentionally targeted culture as a tactic. British bombing was commonly referred to by the German populace as "Baedeker bombing," in reference to the famous cultural guidebooks, and the infamous firebombing of Dresden was a deliberate act of cultural desecration in response to the German bombing of Coventry. In contrast, for much of the war in Europe, low-altitude daylight bombing missions by the United States were ten to twenty times more precise than their British counterparts and often were surgically exact with the aim of avoiding damage to cultural resources. In Japan, however, the Americans had no such scruples. Mock wooden cities were constructed in the United States to perfect the impact of incendiary bombs, and the medieval building culture of historic urban Japan was largely eradicated.

In terms of the number of explosives directed at a single city, Berlin was subject to more bombardment than any other metropolis. In all, about 100 million pounds of explosive devices were dropped on the German capital in more than three hundred Allied bombing missions in which vast armadas of planes—as many as a thousand bombers in twelve hours—passed over the target area and emptied their payloads. Additionally, some 80 million pounds of hand grenades and artillery shells were fired by Soviet ground forces during the final battle for the metropolis.

In comparision, the Germans used a relatively small volume of high explosives on Warsaw: about 12,000 pounds were dropped in the initial aerial bombardment. Yet the calculated, building-by-building destruction rendered by the German occupational force was extraordinarily more potent in its effect. In Berlin, which was about four times bigger than Warsaw, at the war's end, 70 percent of the city's buildings were lightly damaged, 9 percent were salvageable, 8 percent heavily damaged, and 11 percent totally destroyed. In Warsaw, however, 80 percent of the buildings were entirely eradicated. Large parts of the German capital, many of them quite beautiful, remained intact; in Warsaw virtually all of the beautiful aspects of the city were erased from the earth. When General Dwight Eisenhower visited Warsaw, he was appalled: "I have seen many towns destroyed during the war, but nowhere have I been faced with such extent of destruction executed with such bestiality."

For many Varsovians, there was one more hammer blow to come. With victory in hand, the Allies yielded Poland to the Soviet sphere of influence.

Each of the two governments-in-exile had adherents among the Polish population. Generally, communism found more support in agrarian areas, while opposition tended to be strongest in cities. As documented in oral interviews with surviving administrators, planners, and architects engaged in rebuilding Warsaw (collected in 1994 by Anna Naruszewicz for her doctoral thesis at the Warsaw Technical University), more than 90 percent of those who worked on the reconstruction were initially opposed to communism and experienced widely shared profound grief at the end of the war. Forsaken by the Allies, much of the population of Warsaw found that one form of foreign occupation had been bartered for another—and to the very government that had recently killed over a million Poles and then stood by, withholding its aid, as the city was obliterated.

Wounded and betrayed, the Varsovians returned to a traumatized landscape. Few people in history had been so grievously pounded by an unkind fate, yet they were not broken. From out of the ruins, they would build one of world's most remarkable urban architectural legacies.

THE NEW WARSAW

Across Europe, and wherever the new destructive technology of modern warfare had been visited on urban areas, an extraordinary phenomenon occurred. People came back to their beloved cities, which had seemingly become wastelands hostile to human life. It is an amazing fact that, no matter how devastated by the Second World War, no city of substantial size was abandoned. All were rebuilt.

In Warsaw, the first task was to defuse the urban landscape. Sappers combed the ruins searching for mines and unexploded shells. When they were finished probing a building, they would scratch a message somewhere on the wreckage—on the remnants of a wall, on a door, or on a window frame: "Cleared of Mines." In the first three months of 1945, more than 100,000 armed explosives were dismantled and removed from the city.

Warsaw had no water for drinking and cleaning, no sewage system, no electricity, no telephones or telegraph, and no means of public transport. The city's hospitals were crippled, and the railroad bridges that once connected the metropolis to a trans-European network had been destroyed. The settlement was cut off from the world and offered little shelter from the elements. In many ways, it had been set back seven hundred years.

Yet from distant points across Poland and Europe, from internment and forced-labor camps, out of hiding places and released from military service in the Allied armies, on bicycles and carts, walking or by hitching a ride, the survivors found their way back. On the day of its liberation the city had a population of 164,000 people; eight months later the number of inhabitants had more than doubled, to 366,000.

The war-damaged cities of Europe would now require novel answers to a host of uncommon urban problems: How is a damaged city rebuilt? Who owns the property in ruins? Who will own the new properties to be constructed? Who finances the rebuilding? Where do materials come from when there no longer is a construction industry? Where does the money come from when manufacturing is devastated, business cannot function, there are no stores for shopkeepers, government is penniless, and no one has cash to buy anything? What branches of government are responsible for clearing rubble, feeding homeless people, providing water when there is no plumbing? Such practical considerations are answerable only if fundamental spiritual considerations are first resolved.

In Warsaw, three principles of unlikely aspiration were immediately determined by broad consensus among the Polish population. For Communists, the rebuilding of Warsaw would be a tool for propaganda, the creation of a model city of social justice. For non-Communists living under Communist rule, re-creating the historic core would be an act of symbolic moral resistance. Through a fusion of disparate motives, the new metropolis would be a symbol of national pride, a city of accumulated memory, and a city of dreams.

First, Poland decided that the seat of the national government would continue to be located in the city that was no more. With few buildings of value still existing in the torn landscape, under communism, the shard-covered land of Warsaw was nationalized. This enabled the state to afford the cost of the properties for the many large office buildings required by an extensive modern bureaucracy. Also, elimination of the constraint of private ownership of property freed planners to consider substantial alterations to parts of the cityscape that survived from the industrial era. (In most of Poland, however, land was otherwise allowed to be privately held, particularly commercial and residential lots in older urban areas where prewar ownership could be established.)

Second, Polish sociologists urged that the lost historic monuments of Warsaw, particularly the Old and New Towns, be re-created in their exact original locations. One of the country's most respected social scientists, Stanislaw Ossowski, strongly advanced this idea: "If the Warsaw community is to be reborn, if its core is to be constituted by former Varsovians, then they have to be given back their old rebuilt Warsaw so that they can see in it the same city and not a different town in the same spot"—nor the same town moved to another site. Thus the significant buildings, streets, squares, and parks of the past would be remade in the same location they had occupied for centuries. The Germans would not be allowed to steal from Warsaw that specialness of place which constitutes the essence of collective urban memory.

Traditional burgher houses set in the old cityscape would look exactly as they once had been. The sun in its seasonal journey across the sky would illuminate and cast shadows in the town's plazas and courtyards just as it had for several hundred years. Cold winter winds would howl down the same alleys and cooling summer breezes would waft through open windows consistent with the recollections of older Varsovians. The continuum of urban experience would not be broken.

The decision to rebuild the street pattern exactly was reinforced by the critical consideration of cost. In many other war-torn cities, historic street patterns were re-created because investigation of costly substreet infrastructures revealed that most of these networks, although disrupted in many places, were still functional and needed only to be reconnected. In Warsaw's historic core, where there was a greater prevalence of landmarks, the historic street pattern would be reproduced with few modifications. Farther from the center—in areas developed during the eighteenth, nineteenth, and twentieth centuries— significant landmarks were spaced farther apart, and the street pattern could be modified to better accommodate modern traffic flow.

And the city of dreams? City planners would have a second chance to build a metropolis that realized their ideals. The plan for the new city would not repeat the mistakes and speculative excesses incurred during the modernization of industrial Warsaw. The new capital city would have vast amounts of higher-quality housing for the general populace, and more public parks and open green expanses. And although the facades and basic building envelope of the structures of the Old and New Towns would be remade, new interiors would have the amenities that the original historic buildings had lacked—modern plumbing, heating, electricity, bathrooms, kitchens, and open yards in the rear.

The ultimate symbol of the merging of preservation with the needs of the contemporary metropolis was the building of a highway bypass beneath the brick burgher houses of the Old Town. Before the destruction of the city, this underground tunnel would have been difficult to construct, because ancient masonry buildings are easily damaged by undermining. Yet the flow of traffic in prewar Warsaw suffered by having to circumvent the zone of narrow winding streets that constituted the historic core. In the new Warsaw, a solution was readily achieved: the underpass was constructed before the masonry buildings of the Old Town were re-created, and as a result history and modernity were served at the same time.

Once a general plan was agreed upon, a Capital Reconstruction Bureau (Buiro Odbudowy Stolicy) was formed, and more than a thousand architects, planners, engineers, economists, sociologists, and lawyers applied to work on the reconstruction. One of the planners, Stanislaw Jankowski, described the spirit of the moment: "In those days the bureau's employees were the happiest of all Varsovians. They were given a loaf of bread, a coupon to get a pair of shoes, and a chance to fulfill their most magnificent dreams! Some drew up plans, others were sent to do fieldwork—depending on what shoes each of them had." Undaunted by the Herculean dimensions of the task before them, one of every six Varsovians worked on the reconstruction, ensuring that their city would continue to defy the storm.

In the beginning, the rebuilding was accomplished by the most primitive of means, by hands sifting through the wreckage. Warsaw had been transformed into an enormous jigsaw puzzle, and pieces of buildings had been blasted randomly in all directions. Before the historic zones were cleared, conservation experts, with the voluntary assistance of hundreds of ordinary citizens, endeavored to piece together as much of the urban architectural puzzle as possible.

The deconstruction of the city revealed layers of history formerly hidden under the finished facades of Warsaw's buildings. In one structure it was discovered that a Baroque doorway had been set within the stone arch of a medieval entry and covered over with stucco. In instances like this, architects decided to expose the underskin of the reconstructed building so the historic stylistic accretion would be perceptible as a matter of public architectural education. Lost medieval frescoes were uncovered; forgotten arrangements of streets and buildings were reinstated. When an older building condition was discovered beneath a nineteenth-century accretion, the Varsovians chose to rebuild the structure in its earlier historic form.

Just as the Germans had tried to identify what was most characteristically Polish about the city's architectural legacy, the Varsovians now decided to return buildings to a prior architectural incarnation rather than re-create forms that had been derived during a political period when Poland was occupied by foreign powers. Nineteenth-century buildings from the period of Polish partition were not likely to be reconstructed at all. Similar ideological bias was also reflected in the initial decision of the Communist government not to rebuild Zamkowsky Castle because it was a symbol of the aristocracy. Later administrations, however, reversed this position and reconstructed the castle meticulously, both inside and out, as a symbol of Polish national independence.

As workers examined the wreckage, they made a wonderful archaeological discovery: it turned out that the historic fortifications which had once encircled the Old Town had not been entirely demolished in the centuries after their military usefulness passed. Rather, they had been assimilated into the construction of adjacent buildings. As a result, they had been shielded from the devastation incurred during the Warsaw Uprising by the outer skin of the buildings that surrounded them. It was also found that, in the past, parts of the old defensive walls had been cannibalized for reuse in other structures. This material could now be put back in place. Together, these findings presented an unexpected opportunity to re-create the city as it had existed during an earlier manifestation. A decision was made to fill in the gaps and reconstruct the fortifications so that the Old Town was once again enveloped by a moat, a double line of defensive walls, and a barbican and Gothic bridge.

By December 31, 1947, more than a million cubic meters of debris had been cleared from the city. Voluntary contributions had begun to flow in from across Poland to the Civic Fund for Warsaw's Reconstruction (Spoleczny

Fundusz Odbudowy Stolicy). The rebuilding of historic Warsaw became a national mission. Across the country, Poles deferred bettering their personal quality of life so that the stream of funds from the nationalized economy would continue to feed the work. During the next two decades, 50,000 local committees would raise 4.5 million zlotys—the equivalent of the cost of constructing over 100,000 rooms of new housing.

At the Capital Reconstruction Bureau, the pace of work quickened. A rule was adopted: "Answers are to be given the same day to questions that are asked." Draftsmen worked through the night, and design decisions were made on site in the midst of the commotion of construction.

A complex new problem emerged. The reconstruction had to be as precise a copy as possible, down to the finest detail. But buildings that truly looked old could not be created using modern construction technology, because different methods of fabrication result in a different finished aesthetic character. Old handmade glass is uneven and refracts eccentric glimmers of light, whereas modern manufactured glass is a uniform flat plane. Old wrought iron has less strict geometric perfection, but is more artfully shaped in curves, volutes, and decorations than machine-made ironwork. Traditional masonry is often laid in thin, even lines of mortar, while modern brickwork tends toward thicker, clumsier joints due to a loss of craftsmanship.

Even at a glance, the eye sees all these slight differences in material, texture, color, and workmanship. Old buildings look old because of an aura of "handmadeness" exuded by historic architecture in many dimensions and facets. If the copies of Warsaw's architecture were to have verisimilitude, to look right in the eyes of those who remembered, lost skills of handcraftsmanship would have to be revived and secrets of traditional workmanship rediscovered. The technology of the past would have to be re-created and relearned.

A particular advantage of socialism was now revealed. The Communist government of Poland would create an official state enterprise dedicated to the revival of lost construction arts and the preservation of material culture: the Pracownie Konservacji Zabytkow (Ateliers for the Conservation of Cultural Property). Organized in 1945 as a unit of the Ministry of Culture and Arts, the PKZ would eventually employ eight thousand individuals in branch offices in twenty-five cities. Specialized ateliers would study the following subjects:

- old wood-building construction
- historical methods of fabricating bricks, ceramics, and terra-cotta
- the conservation problems of murals, frescoes, polychrome sculpture, and painted architectural interiors

- the manufacture of artistic furniture, inlaid wood veneers, and elaborate parquet floors
- the preservation of all sculpture in all media
- the preservation of paintings
- the decorative use of exotic materials such as mother-of-pearl, tortoise-shell, inlaid and gilt precious metals, ivory, horn, lacquer, shells, and feathers
- the restoration of historic clocks and old furniture fittings
- the conservation of papers and books
- the re-creation of historic textiles
- the replication of historic and stained glass
- the reconstruction of wooden church-interior details such as pulpits, pews, and confessionals
- historical fabrication methods of ferrous metals, copper, bronze, zinc, lead, silver, and gold for roofs, bells, wrought-iron doors, gates, fences, firearms, chandeliers, and locks
- the restoration of historic organs
- the reproduction of ethnographic rural architecture and folk art

In a country that had been robbed of its heritage, what was likely the world's most comprehensive and extensive preservation bureaucracy per capita was established to reconstitute centuries of culture. Eventually Poland would spend 7 percent of its yearly national budget on historic conservation; compare this to the 0.7 percent that France spends on a preservation program widely admired for its thoroughness.

The initial reaction from foreign conservation experts to the reconstruction of Warsaw's historic center was occasionally skeptical. To some, the remaking of the Old and New Towns was the contrivance of a false history. Foreign scholars pointed out that the re-created buildings were not exact replicas either inside or out, where many late nineteenth- and early-twentieth-century accretions had not been reproduced. But as the PKZ workshops carefully created a virtual lost world out of exquisite handmade replicas, another reality became overwhelmingly obvious: the reproduction of the landmarks of Poland was a triumph of the human spirit and one of history's most poignant affirmations of the value of urban architectural culture. In 1980 the meticulous reconstruction of the historic center of Warsaw was added by UNESCO to the list of sites protected by the World Heritage Convention, and took a place of equal standing with the other great landmarks of architectural history "which need to be preserved as part of the world heritage of mankind as a whole."

This is not to say that the landmarks of Warsaw are endangered to any degree. The re-created patrimony of the city is protected assiduously by the heritage-conservation statute of Poland, adopted in 1962, which might very well be the most comprehensive single statute ever conceived for the preservation of a nation's material legacy. The Polish statute protects both immovable properties (structures such as buildings and bridges that are permanently rooted to a physical site) and movable properties (fine art, decorative art, historical and archaeological artifacts), prohibiting their "destruction, deterioration, devastation, loss, or transfer outside of Poland." (In this phrase, one is struck by the inclusion of the word "devastation," which is perhaps unique to the conservation law of a country that had been devastated so many times.)

The 1962 law then goes on to establish a national register of monuments, and includes within its protective umbrella the conservation of large-scale urban environments such as historic towns and settlements, parks, public gardens, cemeteries, groups of buildings (ensembles) of architectural value, as well as individual buildings—their interiors and their surrounding exterior environments. In short, any aspect of the city that is beautifully made or of historical meaning may be protected. All of this is within the oversight of a minister for culture and arts who heads a national Department of Museums, Historic Monuments, and Sites. The director of the department is the conservator-general of Poland, who oversees the work of the forty-nine conservators for the forty-nine *voivodships* (administrative districts) of the country. Warsaw is a complete *voivodship* unto itself, with its own conservator.

Having re-created their lost heritage and devised a bureaucratic system to protect it, the Varsovians now focused on a problem endemic to all historic centers encapsulated by modern conglomerations: the often abrasive juncture of the new city with the old. As in other Eastern European nations within the Soviet sphere of influence after World War II, such questions often became issues of ideology, and the physical expansion of modern Warsaw to its current population of more than 2 million was much affected by the architectural ideas of the so-called Architect of the Communist State, Joseph Stalin.

COMMUNIST WARSAW

For the "people's democracies" of the Communist bloc, the Iron Curtain abruptly changed the evolution of architectural culture. Nationalization of building and town planning expedited the transformation. Architects were organized into state planning offices and were forbidden to maintain private offices on private commissions. All buildings were required to comply with the official six-year plan. State-run architectural schools adopted the new curricula, noncomplying professors were fired or relegated to lesser positions, and

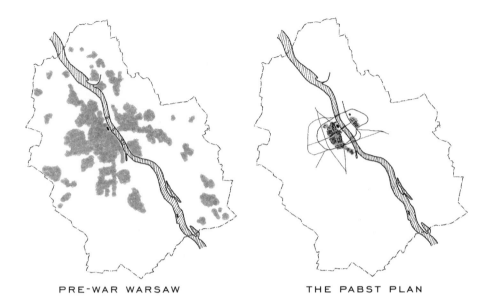

PRE-WAR WARSAW   THE PABST PLAN

The saga of Warsaw · The pre-war built-up area of cosmopolitan Warsaw held about 1.3 million people (dotted line indicates pre-war municipal boundary and small black dot marks the Old Town). · Under the Pabst Plan, the Old Town was to be surrounded by a new "Germanic" townscape, aligned to select existing streets and urban infrastructure, but serving a greatly reduced number of inhabitants. · After the devastation, only outer fragments of the pre-war conurbation survived. Historic Warsaw had been erased. · After the reconstruction, the re-created Old Town (small black dot), while but an infinitesimal zone in the extended modern conglomeration, nonetheless, has become the spiritual representation of the city's continuity. *(All drawings at the same scale.)*

public exhibitions, periodicals, and books all propagated the "proper" architecture. In one fell swoop, all the Iron Curtain countries underwent a severe change of architectural aesthetics.

In Warsaw, the architectural edicts from Moscow would have a more extreme effect on the urban environment than in other places, because Warsaw was more seriously damaged than any other city in Europe and because the creation of the modern nation of Poland established a need within the capital city for numerous governmental buildings. Immediately after the war, during the first phase of the rebuilding, Stalin's assertion of Socialist Realism as the appropriate architectural style for eastern bloc Communist nations altered the look of all new construction in downtown Warsaw.

Buildings designed in the style of Socialist Realism were overscaled hybrids: with historical decoration applied to modern functionalist structures. They were aesthetically half new and half old and, in contemporary architectural terms, might be described as "contextual." The architecture of Socialist Realism honored the traditional European concept of having a principal

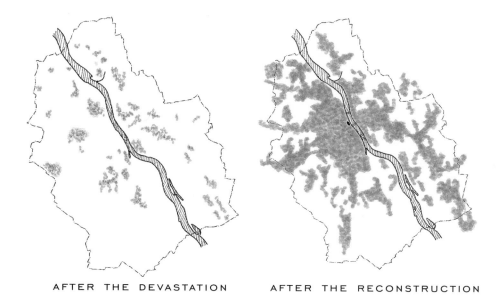

AFTER THE DEVASTATION   AFTER THE RECONSTRUCTION

facade facing the street, forming a street wall and framing public spaces, but generally the buildings were much larger than historic structures. Since the rebuilding of Warsaw had begun at the center and spread progressively outward, the first stage of the construction of the Communist city was a somewhat monolithic but natural continuance of the general urban character of downtown historic areas—except for one extremely gigantic building, a final gift from Stalin: the much hated Palace of Culture in Warsaw.

As a symbol of political unity with Poland, the Communists decided that a Moscow-style skyscraper would be erected in downtown Warsaw, near the main train terminal. A team of Soviet architects, fresh from designing the megalithic Moscow University, descended on the Polish capital to construct a 230-meter, thirty-story tower with ten elevators. It was a high-rise Russian version of a Roman Bath, equipped with a winter garden, museums, youth facilities, theaters, cinemas, auditoriums, restaurants, swimming pools, a gymnasium, and a congress hall, which altogether would serve 12,000 people. It was ostentatious and out of scale, dominating the skyline of a city that revered the low-scale character of its historic past. As is commonly said in Poland, "The gift was bad and expensive."

After the death of Stalin in 1953, the architectural prejudice of the Soviet leadership against modernism as the architectural style of the intelligentsia, particularly Western intelligentsia, gave way to the importance of solving the principal urban problem of all postindustrial societies: the rapid growth of metropolitan areas and the lack of facilities to accommodate that growth. In the Soviet Union and its satellites, this meant the mass construction of giant prefabricated, formularized housing blocks set in green parklands. The new marching order was "House the people," all the many millions of them.

As the state prohibition against modernism was lifted, the idealism associated with providing modern housing for whole urban populations caused numerous architects to adopt as a model for such projects the work of Le Corbusier. Since before World War II, the French architectural master had been one of modernism's most influential propagandists. In numerous compelling drawings he envisioned vast landscapes of elegant modern apartment blocks set in idyllic parklands, even proposing that large parts of the center of historic Paris be demolished in order to accommodate such towers.

Similar illusions were soon created by the first photographs of the acres of new housing blocks in Communist cities. Had a socioeconomic miracle occurred? While mammoth populations were being housed in rows of gleaming new structures, the new buildings were cheaply built and poorly engineered. (Few of these matched the architectural refinement of Le Corbusier's proposals, which, as it turned out, required upper-middle-class tenants in order to offset the costs of their construction.) Within several decades, the miracle had become a giant urban eyesore—cracked, stained, and peeling. Vast regiments of these decaying buildings would now mar the cityscapes of all the Communist nations. In Moscow such structures would constitute a travesty, not only because they uprooted significant historic areas and fractured the scale of the historic cityscape, but also because they would soon need to be extensively repaired. The Communist version of Le Corbusier's concepts for city design would be one of the most damaging urban-planning follies of the twentieth century.

In Warsaw, interest in the work of Le Corbusier had first been planted by Szymon Syrkus, a founding member of the International Congresses of Modern Architecture and one of the authors of the Athens Charter—two early attempts to promote modern architectural design philosophy. Partly because they are better constructed, maintained, and landscaped by the Poles, the extensive Corbusian city of public apartment buildings that surrounds old Warsaw would be decidedly superior in quality to its Moscow prototypes, though many architectural critics find such areas vacuous and oppressive. The dream city of Polish modern architects would be but partly realized.

One aspect of the building of the modern Communist Warsaw was undeniably superior, however. Unique among many of the cities of the world, Warsaw would devise a way to mediate the architectural juncture of the historic city with the contemporary urban conglomeration.

Throughout Poland, the reconstruction and rehabilitation of historic centers had been an important matter of national pride and identity. The

Poles were trying to create a beautiful urban legacy to replace the legacy lost. Therefore, they did not find acceptable the abrasive discontinuity that resulted when modern prefabricated large-scale constructions were placed next to traditional, handmade, low-scale landmarks. Over time, a simple but effective solution was created: Polish architects began to design transitional buildings that bridged the gap in scale and style between modern and historic zones. Transitional buildings were slightly larger than traditional structures but less modernistic and plain than the new housing blocks. In some places this matter was considered so important that relatively new buildings were torn down to erect structures that more effectively reconciled the old with the new by fine-tuning the colors, proportional rhythms, and patterns of building fenestration.

THE WARSAW CONGLOMERATION

Today's Warsaw is an extensive contemporary conglomeration of somewhat shabby mass-produced Communist housing, spreading over the countryside, row upon row, set in broad tracts of patchy parkland and encircling the remnants of a traditional European cityscape that carefully embraces the small re-created historic core perched on a grassy embankment above the river Vistula. Warsaw carries its scars proudly, for it does not wish to forget its history. The 220 commemorative plaques marking wartime execution sites surprise the visiting pedestrian. One tablet is mounted on an old foundation; another is set on a rock rising up out of the sidewalk; and yet another is bolted to an old garden wall. Such markers remind us of a violence that seems out of place in the city of today.

Run-down red-and-white municipal trolleys clatter past a stark masonry container marking the site of the loading dock for trains to Auschwitz. In the midst of a quiet residential district a long, low wall frames a sun-drenched rectangle of gravel—the gestapo prison yard at Pawiak. An unpretentious public park holds the monument for those who fought in the Warsaw Ghetto Uprising. In a downtown plaza, bronze warriors frozen in combat commemorate the soldiers of the Polish Home Army. An old burgher house is forever pockmarked by unpatched bullet holes. A remnant of the ghetto wall is sandwiched between two buildings. These many dark testimonials make Warsaw seem fixated on death, until one understands the choice made by the survivors of World War II to never forget the sacrifices of their neighbors.

Landmarks appear in almost every neighborhood. Amid rushing automobiles a decorative iron fence surrounds a flower-filled traffic island. The ironwork is adorned with finely shaped metallic leaves, intertwined metal vines, and fanciful wrought cornucopias. Such elaborate hand-fashioned objects are usually a product of the past, but in Warsaw one cannot read the cityscape so easily.

A contrast of preservation extremes · The 999
structures of the Forbidden City (within the vertical
rectangle surrounded by a moat), many of great size
and opulence, require an enormous ongoing
investment in conservation—testing the resolve of the
Communist Chinese government. · In Warsaw, the
will of the Polish people to reclaim their stolen
patrimony has created a new heritage for humanity—
protected by stringent conservation laws. Re-created
historic structures are shown as black solids. A
highway crosses the Vistula River and tunnels beneath
the central historic zone. An arc of medieval
fortifications surround the restored Old Town (A).
· In Jerusalem, the monuments and vernacular urban
texture of the ancient walled city (shown as gray
tone), a focal point for three of the world's great
religions, continue to be threatened by a history of
discord and intolerance. *(All drawings at the same scale.)*

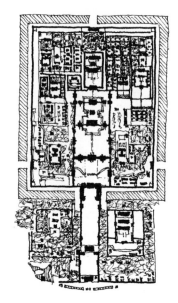

BEIJING: THE FORBIDDEN CITY

Is this a reproduction or a true fragment of another era? The extensive exterior detail and craftsmanship of a handsome brick church seem beyond the ability of copyists, yet its stark unadorned interior reveals that it is a facsimile of one more place that was dynamited by German demolition squads.

"The entire nation builds its capital city," reads the motto etched on a building at the entrance to the re-created historic zone. Farther along are the patched brick battlements, the moat that has become a park, and, hovering above the parapets, the picturesque roofscape of orange tile roofs, dormers, chimneys, and decorative church spires of the Old Town. In its winding cobbled byways, surrounded by this complex reprise of the past, one realizes that the entire historic district is a memorial to those who died because the Poles would not be subjugated.

Twenty years after its completion, peeling and slightly worn, historic Warsaw looks less artificial than when every feature was brand-new. As such imperfections accrue with time, a patina of wear will refine the job of replication, giving it verisimilitude—the appearance of plausibility. But the copy will never be identical to the original. Living cityscapes record the changes that occur with the progression of history. In Warsaw that historical record was erased when the Old and New Towns were leveled. In the reconstruction, the Varsovians have edited the unvarnished truth—and some of its occasional ugliness, stupidity, and imperfection—out of the cityscape. Perhaps they

HISTORIC JERUSALEM

WARSAW: THE RESTORED HISTORIC CORE

understood the ultimate futility of trying to put all such idiosyncrasies back. Historic Warsaw, the achievement of a more recent generation, is an evocation of selected parts of the past. The particular character of six hundred years of evolution has been stolen away forever. The Warsaw of today is a new tale.

On Sundays and holidays in the historic city, one can watch Polish grandparents show their children and grandchildren the product of their labors from the proudest days of their lives, the days of privation, the days of the rebuilding, the days when ordinary people became heroes. Their sadness and pride are tangible. Other civilizations, in other places, have erected great pyramids, great walls, vast palaces, giant cathedrals, and structures that reach to the clouds. The reestablished modest historic townscape of Warsaw is a message to the world that human dignity is beyond price, a value that survives all tyrants. That is what the architecture of the city tells us when we see the triumph of Warsaw with our hearts as well as our eyes.

CHAPTER FIVE
THE TRAGEDY OF THE MEGACITY

CAIRO

Mother of cities, mistress of broad provinces and fruitful lands, boundless in multitudes of buildings, peerless in beauty and splendor, she surges like the sea with her throngs of folk.

—IBN BATTUTAH, *The Travels of Ibn Battutah*, 1340

The taxi ride from the airport to downtown Cairo passes the City of the Dead, a vast Muslim cemetery filled with the extravagant monuments that link age-old traditions to an uncertain future. One of the characteristics of Islamic architecture is its adaptation of the building traditions of the peoples conquered by the Muslims. In Cairo—where history's supreme monuments to death, the Great Pyramids of Giza, were erected by the Egyptians some 4,500 years ago—Islamic culture also produced a singular burial tradition. The Muslim City of the Dead is meant to house the living as they take up temporary residence in ornate tomb-dwellings in graveyards and make seasonal obeisance to the ancient founders of their families.

Today, through the windows of the taxi one sees that the renowned cemetery has become a permanent domicile for the impoverished of Cairo, an illegal squatters' city of 100,000 inhabitants. Nearby, the largest medieval Muslim city extant, an apogee of human social enlightenment during the Middle Ages, is now a scene of destitution, disease, and premature death, as shoeless children play in garbage-strewn streets stained with leaking sewage.

As the population of the earth moves to cities unprepared to house such vast numbers with the basic elements of decent habitation, hundreds of millions of children will be born to similar conditions—frequent illness, stunted growth, and a shortened life span. In Cairo, we may see the approaching global tragedy, in which numerous cities of the dead will house the victims of the human-wrought apocalypse, and the monuments of civilizations will be subsumed in the enveloping chaos.

⚶

I was told by international conservation authorities to go to Giza, on the outskirts of Cairo, to see the plight of the pyramids. So I went and was shocked by their condition. But what I discovered inside the city of Cairo itself was an equally deplorable loss of irreplaceable cultural substance.

In the capital city of modern Egypt are located two of the world's most fabulous architectural treasures: the 4,500-year-old burial grounds of the pharaohs of the Old Kingdom, and the 1,000-year-old Muslim city of mosques, bazaars, and minarets. Today, both of these are in imminent danger of degradation from the environmental and social anarchy within the modern metropolis, whose sufferings are the by-product of an uncontrolled population explosion, a culture of illegal settlement, and an insufficiency of resources to provide for its inhabitants.

I will tell the story of Cairo, the largest city in Africa, in three related stages. One is set in medieval Islamic Cairo and traces its ascent to a city of unsurpassed majesty. The second is set in the vast, illegally built contemporary metropolis and is a social parable that reflects on an impending global future. The third recounts the fate of the Pyramids of ancient Egypt.

Many dimensions of the current urban dilemma of Cairo are not unique; they are the problems of the marginalized megacity, problems that are found in other underdeveloped nations and that raise troubling questions about the imbalance between our human-made environments and those of nature, about the inequitable distribution of wealth among people and nations, and about who should pay for the conservation of humankind's architectural patrimony. Until some answer is found to these dilemmas, many of the world's most significant monuments will remain imperiled.

ANCIENT ISLAMIC CAIRO

Although the Egyptians, Greeks, and Romans all established settlements in the general area of the modern metropolis, Cairo is a quintessentially Muslim city in its official state religion, its historic architectural character, its medieval urban configuration, and its contemporary sociology. The genesis of Cairo occurred near the end of the sixth century, when from out of a neighboring Arabian desert came a prophet whose visions would alter the world.

The sacred revelations of Muhammad (570–632) would consolidate the tribes of Arabia into a unified culture and military juggernaut, and Muslims would attain a thousand years of dominion over a geographic area larger than that of Alexander or Imperial Rome. Their empire at one point stretched from Spain across North Africa, from Turkey through the Middle East, to Pakistan, India, and down into Southeast Asia. Shortly after the death of Muhammad, his disciples had conquered Damascus (635), Syria (636), Jerusalem (637), Tunisia (670), and Spain (711). In 641, as they overran Byzantine Egypt, the Arab armies made straight for the location where the course of the Nile fans out from a single stream into the several tributaries that constitute the delta, a complex of interwoven waterways connecting the great river with the Mediterranean Sea.

At this strategic point, the first inland site from which one could control the passage of river traffic, they established a town on the eastern side of the Nile, across from the Pyramids and the site of the ancient Egyptian river port, in order to maintain land contact with the Arabian Peninsula and not be cut off from the rest of the Muslim Empire during the flooding of the lowlands near the river. Here, on the high ground above the floodplain, several generations of various Muslim dynasties would gradually build one of the largest and most beautiful cities in the world.

Many historians have noted that although Islamic culture and the Muslim religion were founded in the desert and first took root among nomadic peoples, to most completely live a Muslim life required the urban institution of the mosque. The need for the city and for the mosque was based on two of the five tenets of Islam: fasting in the month of Ramadan, making a pilgrimage to Mecca, the reciting and belief in the shahada ("There is but one god and Muhammad is his prophet"), almsgiving, and praying toward Mecca five times a day. Both almsgiving and praying were best carried out in a communal environment, and Muslims worshiped as a community whenever possible, particularly for the Friday noon prayer.

As the nation of Islam spread, the form and functions of the mosque evolved. Since the earliest cultural roots of the Muslims were founded in a wandering desert life and they had no architectural tradition of permanent structures, they adopted, mastered, and reinterpreted the architectural forms of the cultures that they encountered. The first mosques were based on the shapes and methods of Roman buildings, since the foreign regions initially conquered by the Muslims had been part of the Byzantine Empire. Eventually architectural influences from Spain, Istanbul, Jerusalem, India, and wherever Muslim military architects were stationed were mixed together.

The fundamental function of the mosque is to shelter Muslims joined in common prayer. However, the mosque gradually became a center of community life, with secondary functions. Some mosques took the role of schools or universities, hospitals, mental asylums, public baths, or libraries. Mosques were often set in extensive walled grounds to create a zone of peacefulness amid the constant daytime commotion of the crowded city. Within this zone there were gardens, shaded walkways, cool waters for bathing, and serene internal spaces funded by the generosity of citizens and princes. Since the Muslim religion forbade figurative representation in art, the internal and external walls of important buildings were often decorated with calligraphic excerpts from Muslim scripture. The mosque became the physical manifestation of prayer, an act of almsgiving, and a sanctuary of meditation, learning, and social compassion.

The configuration of Muslim cities was much affected by the age-old rivalries of the wandering bedouin tribes. This continuing ebb and flow of political power within the nation of Islam had two direct effects on urban form. First, throughout Muslim history, Islamic cities tended to be broken up into segregated zones according to groups or religious sects. These separate quarters, or wards, maintained distinctive tribal identities. Different Muslim groups would generally refrain from destroying a mosque even when it was not built by their own faction. Yet they would still feel the need to build a mosque of their own as a form of individual almsgiving and worship. So cities such as Cairo gradually accumulated an extensive collection of such civic building types. Second, when a particular faction achieved political supremacy, it would often construct a separate fortified seat of power as an expression of princely benevolence and as protection against being overthrown by a competing tribe. This need for a defensive wall between the rulers and the society they governed resulted in two kinds of Muslim cities: an idealized princely city and a living commercial city, separate but in close juxtaposition. The princely city was a planned artistic environment in which open public spaces were maintained as amenities. Such were the luxurious cities of Scheherazade and the fabled *Thousand and One Nights*.

In the commercial city, the rights of property ownership reigned supreme, and public spaces and roads were infiltrated by encroaching private interests until streets became narrow twisting passageways. These were the cities of the fabulous grand bazaars.

Over the course of Cairo's history, several different princely and commercial cities would be built on a gradually expanding site, as the tides of political power shifted. The medieval Muslim city, which remains at the heart of the metropolis today, contains within it the intermeshed remnants of those earlier incarnations of separate origin.

The first of these distinct settlements was a military encampment called Fustāt (the Entrenchment), established around A.D. 640. By 750, the 'Abbāsids had replaced the Umayyads as the ruling family of the Islamic empire, and they created a princely city just north of Fustāt. Their new municipality, al-'Askar (the Cantonment), gradually fused with the older commercial center of Fustāt to form a single urban entity.

By 876, during a period of decline in the fortunes of the 'Abbāsids, another princely city had been created one step farther north. The new city was constructed by the son of a former slave, Ahmad ibn Tulun, an 'Abbāsid governor of Turkish descent who instituted his own autonomous dynasty. He called his capital al-Qatā'i (the Wards), for its separation into several ethnic neighborhoods. In the heart of the new metropolis he raised a palace, a hospital, parade grounds, an aqueduct, baths, public markets, gardens, and an extraordinary place of worship.

THE MOSQUE OF IBN TULUN

Unlike Christian worship, which focuses on a single point of ceremony, the Muslim religion requires no priestly or ritualistic intermediary between the worshiper and the object of worship. The space inside a mosque serves a community of peers and theoretically has no hierarchical architectural element other than the mihrab, a niche located on a peripheral wall and serving as a compass so that worshipers can be sure they face Mecca as they pray. Since all supplicants and all prayers within the mosque are conceptually equal, all architectural locations and spaces within the mosque are conceptually equal as well. Early mosques were organized as rectangular grids, with fields of vertical columns supporting the roof. Spatially, such three-dimensional checkerboards of interconnected voids were somewhat like the shaded spaces beneath a canopy of trees.

Early Muslim architects adopted the architectural form and structural logic of Roman aqueducts, which were supported by rows of equal and repetitive arches sitting atop of rows of equally spaced vertical piers. This created buildings whose internal spaces comprised many smaller quadrants opening one upon another, in all directions, through archways. In the earliest mosques, it was the custom of the Arabs to take columns from other buildings, often Christian churches, to serve as supports for the arches and roof.

The Mosque of Ibn Tulun was to have 300 points of vertical support, but the emir hesitated to destroy so many places of worship in order to acquire the necessary columns. He asked his architect to find another solution. And the architect proposed that 156 broad piers of equal design and dimension be constructed to support the 328 identical arches above. So it was in the great mosque that a perfect unity was achieved between the form and spiritual function of the building. Words from the Koran were inscribed in golden letters above the arcades. Geometric patterns were carved in the stone archways and in long horizontal bands that encircled the building's interior. Decorative bronze lamps lit the many recurring spaces, and at dusk the Mosque of Ibn Tulun shimmered in a cloud of incense. The multitude of piers, supporting a multitude of peaked arches and defining a multitude of spaces, housed a multitude of the faithful as they sang to the one God and his singular prophet.

Just as the Gothic cathedrals were both a symbolic focus for European medieval society and architectural markers in the townscape, so too were the domes and minarets of mosques both important symbols and indispensable guides for urban navigation. As the bells of the great cathedral signaled the passage of time for the Christian city, so the calls of the muezzins set the hour for prayer for all Muslims. And in both Europe and Islam, the roofs, towers, and steeples of places of worship were the highest and most elaborate architectural elements in the cityscape, defining the artistic character of the skyline and declaring the primacy of religion.

While the streets of both European and Muslim medieval cities were of unequal and narrow widths, with numerous angular turns, the mosque, much more than the cathedral, was to offer a contrasting urban environment of simplicity amid complicated surroundings. The reasons for this difference are fundamental and, over the centuries, would cause Christian and Islamic cities to develop substantially dissimilar physical, social, legal, and governmental forms.

In Europe, a long tradition of civic consciousness rooted in democratic Athens and republican Rome would result in the formation of independent chartered cities during the Middle Ages and the rise of the city-state during the Renaissance. In such places as Venice, Florence, and Amsterdam, a tradition of autonomous municipal governance would flourish. When purer water was needed, a citywide system of aqueducts and reservoirs was designed. When improved sanitation was required, a city-wide sewer system was conceived. Cities gradually came to be perceived as complex constructions whose problems demanded holistic planning by responsible civic authorities.

In Islam, cities were not chartered as separate political entities but were governed by regional military rulers whose first responsibility was to the larger empire. In such political circumstances, the city was not administered by its inhabitants for its own purposes. Many Muslim cities would not produce independent municipal governments until the twentieth century.

The aspect of city design that would most clearly demonstrate the importance of such differences was the evolution of the urban street pattern. While both Islamic and Christian medieval street layouts would be similarly angular and organic in plan, the European metropolis would gradually develop straighter streets, wide main avenues, and rationalized geometric plans to facilitate inner-city vehicular movement as the city's form and conception evolved from the Renaissance city to the Baroque city and then to the modern industrialized city with mass transit. During the same thousand-year span, the streetscape of the Islamic city would grow more tangled and narrow, restricting access primarily to pedestrians.

Islamic laws defining the rights of private property owners exacerbated the situation. In Europe, the street was owned by the municipality, and passage was kept clear by statute. In Islam, the air rights over the street and to some extent the privilege of occupying the street itself were possessed by the owners of contiguous private lots. As a result, Muslim streets were encroached upon by cantilevered structures overhead, which gradually blotted out the sun, or by stalls and shop extensions at ground level, which made the public thoroughfare further twisted and compressed. When it was first created, a princely city might have a plan that provided open public spaces, but whenever it was allowed to merge with the commercial city, the clarity of the original street layout would gradually be eroded.

One encumbrance to the creation of a central autonomous authority to solve municipal problems was the very efficacy of the mosque. During the Middle Ages, as its social functions expanded, the mosque became so deeply embedded in Muslim culture as a house of worship, a social center, an urban landmark, a proud expression of Islamic artistry, a form of almsgiving, and a focal point for different ethnic neighborhoods, its vitality diminished the necessity for other urban institutions. Also, the physical characteristics of the mosque deliberately alleviated the compressed character of the encircling city.

The Mosque of Ibn Tulun was one of the earliest and most significant models for the building type. Its precinct measured 530 feet by 533 feet and covered 6.5 acres (about half the area of the base of the Pyramid Cheops or a footprint about 1.3 times as large as that of the Piazza and Cathedral of San Marco in Venice). It had a place for ablutions (cleanliness is part of the religious discipline), a covered space for congregational worship, and an adjoining courtyard—300 feet by 302 feet—to accommodate the overflow of worshipers on Fridays and special holy days. A symbolic fountain stood in the center of this open area, and a 130-foot-high corkscrew minaret hovered above the complex. Surrounding the mosque and its environs was a pair of brick walls adorned with fanciful crenellations. The walls were separated by 67 feet of buffer space—to further preserve the serenity of the internal environment and to isolate the building from fires in the city.

All the elements of this architectural composition were organized on a rectilinear grid of proportionally related geometric shapes. In plan, the fountain was composed of a circle within a square within a rectangle, and located in the center of a square courtyard. The courtyard was set along the central axis of the rectangle of the inner wall, which was placed along the center axis of the square of the outer wall. These elementary geometric relationships achieved a simple composition of universal forms and understated majesty.

The emir's mosque evoked order and harmony, whereas the city tended toward cacophony. The configuration of the mosque observed an obvious visual logic, whereas many streets within the commercial city were winding alleys terminating in dead ends. The open spaces of the mosque remained inviolate for centuries on end, whereas the public spaces of the city were constantly being eroded.

A peculiar equilibrium had been achieved in the Muslim cityscape: the mosque had become an alternative city within the city. Just as the Islamic city would be segregated into tribal quarters for centuries after the bedouins had left the desert, the geographic origins of Islam would long affect the sensibilities of Muslim culture. The princely city, with its flowing waters, bubbling fountains, shaded palaces, aromatic gardens, and fruit-bearing orchards—whether in Baghdad, Cordova, Cairo, Istanbul, or Delhi—was an evocation of paradise for a people whose culture was rooted in unforgiving arid environs. And as one stands within the cool eternal geometries of the Mosque of Ibn Tulun, another simple analogy is obvious: the Muslim mosque is an oasis, a refuge of geometric order surrounded by an ever-shifting organic medieval cityscape.

THE BIRTH OF AL-QĀHIRAH

Four generations of successors followed Ibn Tulun before the ʿAbbāsids regained ascendancy. In reprisal, they obliterated the Tulunid city of al-Qaṭāʾi; only the great mosque survived. By 969, the Fāṭamids had risen to power and undertaken the construction of a new princely city to rival Baghdad in its grandeur and which would be called upon its completion Al-Qāhirah (the Victorious, or Cairo). Travelers of the period would describe this location of the two cities, the Fāṭamid princely court of Al-Qāhirah and the commercial city of Fustāt, as one of the most lavish cityscapes in the Mediterranean—until a plague in 1063, an earthquake in 1138, and the destruction of Fustāt by fire and war in 1168 reduced to ruin all but a handful of the architectural landmarks that have come down to us today.

Nonetheless, the greatest glory of Al-Qāhirah still lay before it in a sustained era of city building during which successive generations of finely crafted

structures would be accumulated across three hundred years of Islamic dominion. At the dawn of the thirteenth century, a fortuitous shift in the geopolitical
fortunes of the city would result in an enormous surplus of wealth to be spent
on opulent architecture. The general cause of this change was the emerging
military threat of the Mongols under Genghis Khan (1167–1227) and, a century later, under Tamerlane, or Timur (1336–1405), which disrupted the reli-
ability of the northern caravan routes of the spice trade and imperiled Islam's
hold on Baghdad and Damascus. Thus both the political capital and the spice
trade route were moved south to Cairo, which had long been one of the
region's major cities as well as an important river port but which now would be
the chief commercial and political center of the Muslim Empire. It was a
metropolis unrivaled in wealth in either Europe or the Middle East, until
Vasco da Gama found a route by sea to India and the monopoly of Asian trade
held by Venice and Islam was broken by the Portuguese, Dutch, and English.

The rise of Cairo's fortunes coincides with the arrival of its most renowned
prince and warlord, Sultan Salāh al-Din (Saladin). In an era of warfare before
gunpowder and artillery, Saladin would long ensure the security of Cairo by
wrapping it in mighty fortifications. Although his military duties allowed him
to stay in the city for only eleven years, he opened the existing princely city to
development by the general populace, introduced a *mãristãn* (hospital) mosque
and a *madrasah* (university) mosque to the cityscape, and built his own
entrenched palace, called the Citadel, on a bluff overlooking the Nile and the
Pyramids beyond. In a few short years, he laid out the basic configuration and
components of the city for hundreds of years to come.

Strangely, Saladin is also charged with using the Pyramids as a quarry,
removing the limestone shells of the monuments. Since the sultan is known in
history for his vision, restraint, and cultural sophistication and since the
Citadel is built on top of a potential quarry, his initiation of this practice is
surprising. That was the beginning of the end. For 3,500 years the Pyramids
had remained intact as pure white geometric forms; but now, in the building
of Islamic Cairo, they would slowly be stripped, much as the monuments of
Imperial Rome were leveled in the making of the Renaissance city of the popes.
As Cairo grew more extensive and beautiful, the Pyramids became progressively
less perfect.

In 1260 a former Turkish slave named Baybar became general of the
Muslim forces, defeated the Mongols after their destruction of Baghdad, and
made Cairo the undisputed capital of Islam. The victory of Baybar signals the
beginning of the Mamluk reign and the pinnacle of the building of architectural monuments in the city. One of the significant reasons for the construction of so many beautiful buildings was the unending rivalry among the
Mamluk ruling classes for political supremacy. Such constant competition

caused this era of Islamic history to be fraught with intrigue and brutality, but those vying for hegemony also erected numerous noteworthy buildings as a sign of their rising distinction.

Houses grew to five, seven, nine, and eleven stories to accommodate a fast-growing populace. Enormous palaces were built for the luxury of the ruling classes. Bazaars overflowed with exotic treasures and often were made into extended indoor shopping malls as the streets were roofed so that traders from around the world could bargain for precious goods undisturbed by the vicissitudes of weather. Mosques were constructed for the personal aggrandizement of their sponsors as well as for all kinds of social needs, but, in particular, Al-Qāhirah would be noted for the princely burial mosques of its nobility and, on the outskirts of the city, two extended burial grounds—cities of the dead—would be filled with hundreds of fantastic constructions. (At various points in Cairo's history, when its economy languished, and poverty and homelessness occurred, the great cemeteries would be inhabited by squatters.)

The splendor of Cairo was constituted not merely by its size and grandeur but by the particular aesthetic qualities of the city's architecture. Several decorative devices were singularly Islamic. First, there was the use of alternating rows of different-colored masonry, often cream and red, to create horizontal bands around a building. This striped effect, called *abalq,* had been imported from Andalusian Spain and caused the eye to apprehend the complex combinations of forms from which Muslim mosques were constituted as the many courses of stripes undulated over a building's surface.

Another masonry device was a masonry corbeling technique using stalactites *(muqarna)*—small overlapped geometric coves used to create honeycomb-like structures under domes and cantilevers. The use of *muqarna* introduces an organic decorative richness to both interior and exterior architectural compositions. Roofs, cornices, balconies, and arches supported by the crystalline formations of stalactites appear to have grown naturally from out of the building's mass.

The determinant that most accounted for Cairo's unique appearance was the adaptivity of the metropolis to its climate. In a part of the world where the sun was intense and nearly vertical, one of the few forms of relief was shade. Thus as the density, height, and population of the city increased, the streets were not widened, since deep, narrow canyons resulted in an environment of cool shadows. Structures cantilevered from the street facades of buildings further blocked the sunlight. Here, an unusual and beautiful architectural innovation evolved in Muslim houses, which on the outside were mostly plain stuccoed structures. In order to ventilate houses while also ensuring privacy and the modesty required of Muslim women, windows that opened to the street were covered with decoratively carved wooden lattices *(mushrabiyyah),* sometimes fitted into window openings but often configured as enclosed wraparound balconies. A typical Cairo street had many such finely crafted projections adorning the public way so that buildings on either side of the street nearly touched.

The intricate patterns created in this woodwork were part of a tradition of ornamentation particularly associated with Islamic culture. Since figurative representation of the real world was forbidden by the Koran, Muslim artists and artisans developed elaborate interlaced patterns as a decorative motif. Such designs (in tile work as well) could be composed of pure geometric shapes or abstracted shapes of such natural forms as leaves, fruits, and flowers. The interest of Muslims in advanced geometry caused such patterns to become mathematically complex, utilizing the overlapping forms of polygons and circles to create the fantastic interwoven and repetitive designs that we call arabesque. The compositions are often nearly hypnotic. Both the positive object and the negative space are designed so that figure and ground are interchangeable. Thus, two patterns exist simultaneously, but the mind can focus on only one pattern at a time. It is a perceptual paradox: both designs are before us at all moments, but the perception of one pattern obscures the perception of the other.

The intricacy and extent of the use of these decorations—*abalq, muqarna,* and arabesque—flourished in Cairo as in no other Muslim city. Particularly during the Mamluk reign, the exterior surfaces of all important public buildings were embellished by meticulous craftsmanship. Wooden screens, doors, boxes, and furniture were finely carved with arabesque designs. Tile walls and band courses were glazed with colorful abstract patterns. Geometric designs were etched into stone walls and minarets, and across the curving surfaces of domes.

In 1362, these Cairene architectural traditions gave expression to one of the most renowned works of Islamic architecture, the *madrasah* (university) Mosque of Sultan Hassan. As compared to the Mosque of Ibn Tulun, the Mosque of Sultan Hassan is a far more vertical mass, reflecting the general increase in the scale and density of the growing city. The structure is a large, multistory urban fortress, 113 feet high, into which an open courtyard 100 feet square has been carved. Facing this central space are four floor-to-ceiling, barrel-vaulted alcoves making a giant cruciform public area. A vast projecting cornice decorated by a thick layering of *muqarna* wraps all the way around the building's exterior, which is over 500 feet long and articulated by tall niches culminating in half-domes and stalactite pendentives, as if such features were carved into the building's limestone bulk. The entrance to the mosque is through a giant arched opening 66 feet high. A huge dome and two tall minarets bring the composition to a crescendo. It is a majestic, simple building with controlled use of decoration and large gestures of scale whose architecture reflects a peak of refinement. Just as the Mosque of Ibn Tulun is an architectonic expression of the basic functions of the early mosques, the Mosque of Sultan Hassan takes the shape of a complex urban institution rooted in established Muslim culture.

From the thirteenth to the fifteenth century, the metropolis would grow to a populace of 500,000 people. Many European travelers during that period were awestruck by Cairo's cosmopolitan culture and extensive physical beauty. In 1481, one of these, a traveling Jewish merchant named Meshullam Menahem, wrote in his notebook: "If it were possible to place the cities of Rome, Milan, Padua, and Florence together with four other cities, they would not contain the wealth and population of the half of Al-Qâhirah." More precisely, it would still be twenty years or more before London reached 250,000, before Paris exceeded 200,000, and before Renaissance Rome, Lisbon, Seville, or Amsterdam held as many as 100,000 inhabitants.

By 1517, medieval Muslim Cairo—an area about three-fourths the size of historic Venice—would be endowed with almost a thousand distinguished works of architecture. The quality of these structures in terms of their design and craftsmanship would make Cairo a singular architectural accomplishment of Islamic civilization. In the medieval era, it was a city where philosophy, physics, mathematics, and the arts flourished. Its mosques were designed to precise arithmetic proportions and served a variety of urban social purposes. Its cosmopolitan streetscape held as many as 12,000 shops jammed with commercial activity from around the world. The city contained a Christian quarter, a Jewish quarter, a Greek quarter, an Egyptian quarter, a Turkish quarter, and bedouin quarters. The sculptural opulence of its important buildings made the city's skyline a panorama of varying architectural shapes.

Al-Qâhirah was centuries ahead of its time in many respects, but the seeds of its dissolution were already planted in its sociopolitical framework. Its inflexible military governance often produced capricious autocratic rulers. Just outside its affluent civic center were the shantytowns of the poor. Unregulated encroachments so thoroughly blocked the sun in the city's many blind alleys and dead-end streets that lanterns were required around the clock to illuminate an otherwise endless darkness.

In 1501 Pedro Álvares brought the first transoceanic spices from Asia to Lisbon. By 1517, Ottoman rule had begun a centuries-long era of decline under foreign domination. Four hundred years later, the medieval Islamic city of Cairo—with many of it social and political problems intact, and its architecture crumbling and faded—would emerge again into the light of the world's consciousness as an extraordinary landmark and piece of living history in imminent danger of being irrevocably lost.

THE DILEMMA OF THE MARGINALIZED MEGACITY

While cities in Europe and North America underwent a gradual physical, social, and economic metamorphosis that transformed them into extended modern urban conglomerations, Cairo remained stagnant. Not having evolved into an industrialized society by the first half of the twentieth century was common among nations of the African continent.

Because Egypt had been assimilated into the Ottoman Empire, many of its socioeconomic characteristics were a continuation of the centuries-old medieval model of Muslim military authority. From 1517 to 1798, Cairo became a backwater in the new empire. Its intellectual talent and wealth were siphoned off to Istanbul, its population declined, and its buildings began to decay. While European cities came to be paved, Cairo's streets were still made of compacted dirt. Travelers soon noted the rising piles of refuse that polluted the environs of the city, and as the standards of sanitation were raised in other urban areas, Cairo became known as one of the dirtiest large cities in the world.

In 1798, the French under the command of Napoleon I began an era of European dominance, and with the building of the Suez Canal (1859–69), Cairo once again became an important strategic location in global politics. For the next three-quarters of a century, England and France dictated the foreign affairs of Egypt, as the African continent was divided into a patchwork of colonial possessions to be exploited by the industrialized powers of Europe.

Although the French occupied Cairo for only three years, they left a permanent cultural stamp on the city, whose population had declined to approximately 250,000 people—one-half the size of medieval Al-Qāhirah. A detailed social and physical survey of the metropolis was undertaken during the French occupation, and Cairo's great Islamic landmarks were identified. Street cleaning was reintroduced to the city to reduce the threat of disease from unsanitary conditions. A long straight roadway was extended out to the Pyramids. Aesthetically, Paris became the model for the expansion of colonial Cairo.

But neither the French nor the British, who followed them, could change one of Cairo's most immutable facts: the narrowness and organic logic of the city's historic center, which made the introduction of modern infrastructure and circulation extremely costly and sometimes impossible. Most of the great landmarks of the historic center were inextricably woven into the twisting street pattern, and the core area could not be altered without a corresponding alteration of innumerable significant buildings. It became evident that in order to conserve the landmarks of Al-Qāhirah, the street pattern would have to be retained and the modern infrastructure compromised. Since during this period, European travelers were drawn to Cairo as much for the exotic orientalism of the Islamic core as by the Pyramids, the preservation of Al-Qāhirah became a basic assumption for colonial town planners. Thus, the British laid out brand-new Parisian-type boulevards *outside* the historic area. New cosmopolitan neighborhoods were created, surrounding older traditional zones. Trolley lines skirted the medieval center. At the turn of the century, gaslights were introduced to the modern parts of Cairo, while in the core, people continued to carry lanterns at night.

A sanitary service was established to protect the British occupying army. Old dumps were leveled, garbage was used for landfill, and swampy areas were drained. Smallpox vaccinations were made mandatory. Nile water was filtered. Deep aquifer wells were dug. Infant digestive disorders, diarrhea, tuberculosis, pneumonia, dysentery, typhoid, cholera, and measles were contained. And the city grew. By 1930 a million people lived in greater Cairo; by 1950 there were two million.

In 1952, for the first time since the fifth century B.C., Egyptian sovereignty was reestablished with the formation of the Republic of Egypt; its first president (taking office in 1956) was a colonel in the rebellion, Gamal Abdel Nasser. The metropolis inherited by Nasser had changed dramatically since the rise of the Ottomans. Al-Qāhirah was now three intertwined cities. Although much deteriorated, medieval Islamic Cairo—with its fortified gates, its Citadel of Saladin, and the domes and minarets of its mosques—was still basically in place. Enveloping the historic city was an extended modern Egyptian version of Paris, with broad avenues and Europeanized apartment buildings, universities, offices, schools, hospitals, museums, and hotels. At the fringes of the modern and historic cities were the fantastic Mamluk cemeteries, the shantytown cities of the dead, which housed the dislocated poor. European Cairo had a modern infrastructure; medieval Cairo was hardly penetrated by these advances; and life in the cemeteries was primitive.

As in other colonized cities in the Middle East, much of the shift to modernism in Cairo was superficial. Behind the European-like facade, broad swaths of Muslim society retained many centuries-old traditions. One such medieval practice was the cause of extensive degeneration of historic buildings. For several centuries, as a protection against the recurring threat of economic reprisals due to the ever changing fates of various ruling factions, it had been the practice of Muslim landowners to place their properties in trusts, called *waqfs,* rather than hold them outright. As a result, much of the city's property had been administered by *waqf* managers trying to assure their clients an uninterrupted flow of maximum earnings. As the general fortunes of Cairo declined, many *waqf* managers failed to invest in the repair and long-term upkeep of buildings. During the Ottoman era, as commercial activity waned, population decreased, and the demand for residential space diminished, large numbers of *waqf* properties, particularly housing, fell into ruin. The upper residential stories of many buildings gradually collapsed and were removed, over many decades, story by story, until just the ground-floor retail, commercial, and manufacturing uses continued. Throughout the medieval core, weeds sprouted on deteriorated roofs, upper brick walls crumbled and turned to dust, wooden balconies sagged, stucco surfaces became scabbed, arabesque details disintegrated, ad hoc roofs were created at lower heights. The residential aspect of the historic city became progressively less lofty, less beautiful, and less adorned.

Numerous *waqf* properties became eyesores—unmaintained sites, or vacant lots, or the homes of squatters. Since most medieval mosques had been endowed and managed through philanthropic *waqfs,* as such bequests declined in their relative value, many religious buildings grew decrepit and tattered. During the colonial period, as various administrations attempted to modernize the city, *waqf* ownership was a major impediment. The construction of contemporary public buildings and infrastructure requires assembling many smaller plots or arranging for continuous right-of-ways, but *waqf* properties were extremely difficult to assemble, even when such properties had been abandoned, because the original legal knots of the medieval *waqf* could not be untied.

When Nasser assumed power, it was evident that Cairo needed to be freed from the strictures of *waqf* ownership and the abandoned plots nationalized, and so at last many of these legal tangles were unraveled. (This was only a partial remedy; *waqf* ownership of mosques continues to be an impediment to the conservation of some of Cairo's landmarks.) Yet this was a minor alteration when compared to the larger social engineering that was needed for Egypt as a whole.

MARGINALIZATION

A second wave of industrialization occurred prior to and after the Second World War, and the speed of developmental transformation quickened. Components of this evolution were increased agricultural productivity, urbanization, modern infrastructure, political stability, legal continuity of the rights of property, universal education, and widespread access to health care. After the war, as colonialism gave way to national self-determination in Asia, the Middle East, and Africa, many new governments of fledgling nations attempted to initiate a similar developmental metamorphosis.

Several decades later, globalization was the issue. A twenty-four-hour world economy emerged in which multinational corporations shifted production centers to the most economically favorable locations for manufacturing. The industrial revolution had become globally mobile, and much of the world was becoming a single interconnected marketplace.

At first it was thought that the best places for this new industrial growth would be the places where labor was least expensive. Nations and cities competed to become locations for multinational economic expansion. For underdeveloped nations the potential benefits were many. Multinational firms infused local economies with employment opportunities and training for local citizens, and the new firms often needed services that local businesses might be able to provide.

But the general experience of internationalized manufacturing corporations, in the sixties, seventies, and eighties, showed that the existing infrastructure, social benefits, and advanced general education of the more developed nations were prerequisites for a competitive work location in a world of rapidly changing technology. Several Asian societies readily adapted to such conditions and quickly became part of the extended modern realm and linked to the global economy. Many other developing countries, in South America and Africa, were unable to achieve the interrelated package of social and physical changes that would allow them to become players in the new global marketplace. Such nations were bypassed by opportunity and, today, have become marginalized.

In Egypt, the formulas for the future hadn't worked as hoped. To the contrary, in many dimensions an even greater disparity had evolved between the quality of local life and the standard of living in the leading modern nations. And the socioeconomic liabilities that made the modernization of Egypt difficult to achieve would also result in a complex and pressing environmental threat to the Islamic landmarks of Cairo.

THE EXPLOSION OF POVERTY

Enormous urban population growth is one of the by-products of industrialization. The mechanization of agriculture, subsequent migration from rural areas to cities, the decline of infant mortality, and increased life expectancy as a result of modern sanitation and wider access to health care—all of these forces contribute to the swelling of cities. Yet in the first generation of industrialized nations, along with this increase in urban population came a dramatic economic expansion that raised the general standard of living, created a vast and more prosperous middle class, and reduced urban poverty.

After World War II, as marginalized cities in South America, the Middle East, and Africa became urbanized, economic expansion did occur, but it was not proportionate to the increase in population. Moreover, the degree and speed of population growth were escalating. Cairo grew twentyfold, from 600,000 to 12,000,000 inhabitants, in the twentieth century, compared to a similar twentyfold increase in the size of the New York conurbation, from

900,000 to 18,000,000 over a 150-year period. And there was an obvious critical difference between the two cities. New York grew from a prosperous city of regional importance to an enormous rich urban conglomeration of world-wide significance. In Cairo, the relative wealth of the city declined and the general standard of living degenerated as the population multiplied.

The leaders of Egypt were faced with a paradox. The average Egyptian saw that the best chance for a better life was in cities. This perception was justified by the fact that with each passing year the increased number of people in Cairo required that the city receive an increased proportion of the strained national budget. This fact, in turn, drew even more people to the already clogged metropolis, where the increase in population far exceeded the increase in public services. The result was that each year there was less money per person in Cairo. The economic growth of the country was falling even further behind the rate of the growth of population. Inadvertently, a self-perpetuating downward socioeconomic spiral had been induced.

A MASSIVE, CRIPPLED GOVERNMENT BUREAUCRACY

These negative trends would be exacerbated by a major strategic misjudgment in policy made by the Socialist government of the Nasser era. In an effort to encourage more young people to acquire a college education, Nasser dramatically expanded the university system and promised a job in the Egyptian bureaucracy to every college graduate. At the time, this policy seemed to serve two purposes: to expand the bureaucracy and to raise the general level of education in the country.

But the program was not well implemented, and frequently the graduates were not trained to serve in the public sector and not placed in jobs relating to their areas of expertise. Year after year, floods of alumni from the growing university system were subsumed into the growing bureaucracy. As the size of government grew, bureaucratic authority at every level became more compartmentalized and diffuse. Soon large numbers of approvals from numerous departments were required in order to get anything done. And since the new bureaucrats were often not knowledgeable in their new positions, more and more inefficiency was created.

As the national budget decreased in proportion to the ever-increasing bureaucratic population, the bureaucrats were paid less each year. Eventually, many employees could not support their families on their government pay. A second source of income became necessary. Regulatory powers were systemically abused to generate payoffs. Large numbers of bureaucrats were absent from their positions while working at other jobs. (One study has estimated that a typical Egyptian bureaucrat worked, on average, from twenty minutes to two hours a day.) Low salaries and red tape deterred the brightest university students from entering government employment. In these conditions, few branches of the bureaucracy could sustain a sense of social mission.

The bureaucracy had become, de facto, a welfare system. And because of its size and complexity, individual accountability was extremely difficult to measure. Yet as irrational and destructive as this phenomenon became, the system could not be amended because a vast voting bloc of bureaucrats and students obstructed reform. An extensive, corrupt, and inefficient organization had been put into place, which held the future of Egypt and Cairo hostage, since major social reforms required implementation by the governmental apparatus and a huge amount of the nation's budget was commanded by a sector that produced little while obstructing the efforts of others.

THE UNAUTHORIZED METROPOLIS

A far wider climate of illegality soon was bred. With each passing year, as more and more people came to a city that had proportionately less money per inhabitant, the municipal government hesitated to assume the responsibility to provide social and physical services for the now unwanted influx of people. Cairo could not afford to build the new housing, schools, hospitals, roads, and sewers that were needed. Yet people must live. So families without places to dwell co-opted land and built their own homes. Here is a phenomenon seen throughout the developing world. The current politically correct term for such communities is "informal settlements," but this does an injustice to the human reality.

The illegal settlements in Cairo and many other places do not comprise only shanties, but also include substantial middle-class residences made of durable materials. These are extensive communities built outside the lawful framework of established cities, and several million people in Cairo were to be housed by this process. Illegal settlements are built without an official street plan, without properly engineered infrastructure, and without compliance to building, health, and safety codes. The land on which such settlements are built is taken or bartered for in an underground property market. No studies are undertaken to see if it is wise to expand into such areas, because illegal settlements occur under governments that have abdicated the responsibility to plan the growth of the city.

Residents of such areas were not part of the official city and therefore did not have the right to health, education, and social services. In these illegal communities drinkable water was carried in, in barrels borne by donkeys; human sludge was carried out in the same way. Electricity was pirated by tapping into nearby power lines. Emergency vehicles often could not penetrate

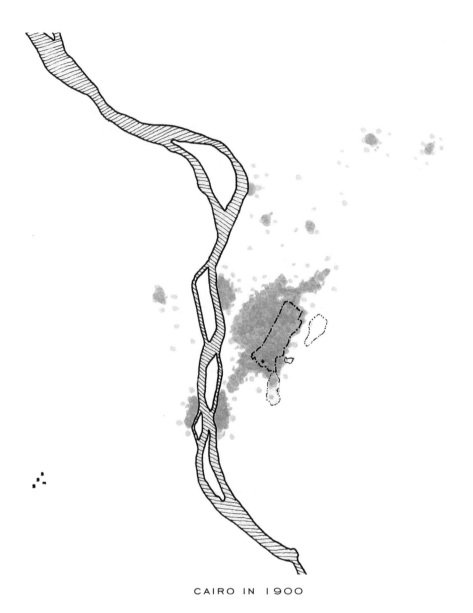

CAIRO IN 1900

The tragedy of the illegal megacity · By the beginning of the twentieth century, medieval Islamic Cairo was composed of the remnants of various cities built by different Muslim dynasties, over hundred of years, in the same general geographic location. The historic zone outlined in thick dotted line is the Unesco study area of today. Thin dotted lines mark the medieval Cities of the Dead. The four small shapes to the west of the Nile are the Great Pyramids and Sphinx at Giza.

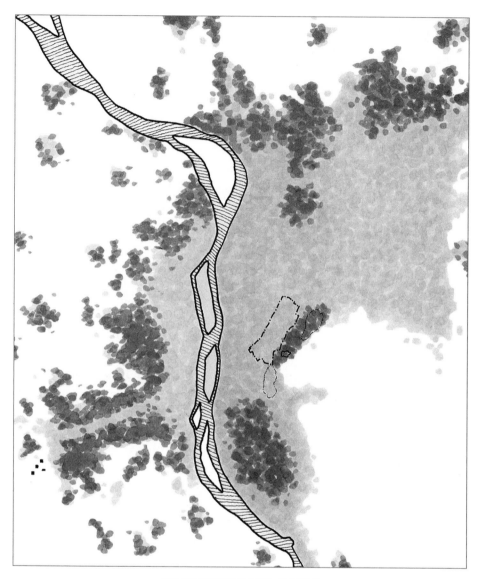

CONTEMPORARY CAIRO

· By the end of the twentieth century these extraordinary historic sites have been subsumed in a vast modern conglomeration whose true dimensions can only be approximated. Dark gray tone indicates illegal settlements built between 1947 and 1986, as estimated in a study by the American University in Cairo. Pale gray tone indicates the built-up urban area prior to 1947, a substantial part of which was also settled illegally. (*Both drawings at the same scale.*)

the unauthorized narrow roads, and there were no hydrants to provide pressurized water to fight fires. Barefoot children played next to unlicensed community garbage dumps on unpaved dirt streets where sewage leaked to the surface. Many vanished illnesses reappeared. Rates of infant mortality were reversed, and youngsters who survived often had their growth stunted due to the constant exposure to such conditions. And because illegal settlements frequently occurred in less desirable locations next to industrial areas and dumps, their residents often were exposed to the most toxic of modern pollutants as well.

As unhealthy as these conditions were, they were still an improvement over other options. For despite the poor quality of life, conditions in these illegal settlements are frequently far superior to those in depressed agricultural areas where modern infrastructure and social services are totally unavailable. Moreover, in those few places where Egypt attempted to erect low-income housing it was so cheaply built that virtually overnight such complexes became more environmentally repugnant than the shantytowns. How, then, to stop people from helping themselves after the government has failed?

Sixty-two percent of all the housing built in Cairo since 1950, and 80 percent of all the housing since 1980, was built illegally. About two-thirds of the total mass of the contemporary urban conglomeration was constructed outside the established minimal standards for public safety. A vast unauthorized metropolis had emerged in which an environment of unprecedented virulence had been created for the marginalized urban poor whose businesses and homes existed outside the city's legal structure.

THE ASSAULT ON THE CITY'S HERITAGE

The human settlement that was Cairo had become an environmental catastrophe. For decades, in the absence of sewers, several million people were draining wastewater directly into the ground. In those parts of the city served by the municipal water supply system, every day at least half of Cairo's treated water was lost to leakage in aged pipes. This, too, was absorbed into the ground. As a result, the water table below Cairo became greatly expanded and exceedingly toxic, rising to levels that once had not seemed possible and enveloping the foundations of the centuries-old landmarks of Islamic Al-Qāhirah. Here the social dilemmas of the city intersected with the physical fabric of the historic metropolis to bring about an architectural conservation predicament of extraordinary complexity.

Just beneath the surface of the ground is an upper zone of permeable soil which absorbs the natural precipitation from the atmosphere. Once atmospheric water enters this zone, it flows through the permeable material following the general contours of the earth. This flow of water in the earth is called the groundwater table. Although the groundwater system of soil, gravel, and sand, along with plant and insect life, acts to some extent as a natural filter and purifier, the capacity of this natural system to cleanse polluted water is limited. Thus, dense cohabitation in a fixed location has always posed the problem of how to dispose of mankind's excretions. During the later parts of the Middle Ages, pollution of the groundwater table by disease-carrying microbes resulted in cities that were frequently ravaged by plagues and other epidemics. Finally, in the nineteenth and twentieth centuries, as medical scientists established the causes for the spread of disease, sanitary commissions were formed in industrialized cities to ensure a separation of wastewater from drinking water and to eliminate locations in the urban environment where polluted groundwater came to the surface.

In Europe, the historic centers of many major cities were not made fully sanitary until well after World War II. In the newly industrialized cities of Asia, this standard has only recently, and only partly, been achieved. In the cities of developing nations, the proliferation of illegal settlements has resulted in an unprecedented number of human beings living outside the benefits of contemporary public health practice. Presently, many experts estimate that 50 percent of the world's urban population, or about 2 billion people (about 25 percent of all of the planet's inhabitants), live in such terrible conditions. In spite of our civilization's technical capacity to ensure a healthful living environment, paradoxically, never before in history have so many people existed in such extremely unhealthy circumstances.

Centuries ago the medieval Islamic architects of Cairo understood that an interaction of the materials of their buildings with the groundwater table was potentially damaging. Today, through chemical analysis, we know that polluted groundwater in human settlements has a heightened salinity that causes several kinds of stone to disintegrate. In historic Cairo, the stone most easily available for building was the limestone of the Nile River basin. Used to make the white outer skin of the Pyramids, this stone, readily carved, long-lasting, and beautiful, was also particularly vulnerable to damage from heavily salted water.

As the foundations of such structures come into contact with the groundwater table, porous limestone acts like a sponge. Moisture is pulled upward, by capillary suction, within the walls of buildings, from one stone block to another, several feet above the level of the water table. As the water table of Cairo rose to just below the surface of the ground, parts of buildings permeated with moisture were also exposed to the air. When the salinated water evaporates, a dense salt deposit is left behind, on and in the stone. A repetitive process of saturation and parching, saturation and parching, results in a buildup of salts. This phenomenon is exacerbated by the extreme dryness of Cairo's climate. With time, such salt deposits grow to an extent that when the walls are made wet again, and the salts recrystallize and expand, the limestone is torn apart from inside. Further, the cement that holds together masonry structures is also subject to injury, as moisture from within masonry walls causes lime to be leached out of mortar, reducing it to a condition that loosens the bonds between one brick or stone and another. Under siege by heavily salinated groundwater, both the stonework and the mortar of the landmarks of Al-Qāhirah became so soft, they crumbled at the touch of a finger.

In order to guard their buildings from such damage, Muslim architects did two things: they built their foundations where the water table was well below the surface, and, when this was not possible, they built a horizontal barrier of impervious granite within the foundations to stop groundwater from wicking up into the walls of structures. In other words, medieval Cairo was deliberately protected from the very problem the city's buildings would eventually fall prey to. In order to circumvent the safeguards of medieval architects, the natural conditions of the region would have to be dramatically altered and the water table of the city raised by several feet. In the midst of a desert, this was improbable. Yet it was, of course, exactly what occurred.

Estimates of the number of surviving landmarks in historic Al-Qāhihar vary. A large number of residential structures decayed and were lost throughout the period of Ottoman rule. During the Nasser era, residential rent controls were instituted in the historic zone and the owners of numerous structures were unable to keep their buildings in good repair, resulting in the loss of several hundred more historic buildings. Of a thousand buildings indexed at the beginning of the twentieth century, more than half have been ruined. Since less opulent residential structures were generally not included in this count, it must be assumed that at the very least half of these have been lost as well, especially since the collapse of the roofs of residential structures is a common phenomenon throughout the area. Nonetheless, by all estimates, both European and Arab experts agree that no other city of the Muslim world presently holds anywhere near the wealth and number of beautiful historic buildings as Cairo. But what remains is threatened today as never before.

The damage caused by the rising groundwater table was exacerbated by other sources of environmental toxicity. Air pollution due to industrial waste and the exhaust of automobiles is ten times greater in the city than the world average. When rising damp on the outer surface of limestone walls combines with the chemical constituents of air pollution, nitric and sulfuric acids are formed, further corroding the outer surface of old landmarks. Simultaneously, the accumulation of polluted dust on roofs and other horizontal architectural features, when made wet by rain, causes such acids to leak down into the inner structure of buildings. At ground level, the high microorganism count of Cairo's groundwater causes bacteria, fungi, and spores to flourish and produce carbonic, oxalic, sulfuric, and nitric acids, which additionally threaten the limestone.

The result of this multifaceted assault is visible to anyone walking in the historic zone. Casual observation reveals innumerable instances of the chemical decomposition of beautiful buildings at various heights and levels. As the illegal settlements proliferated, particularly since the end of World War II, the treasures of Al-Qāhirah began to be assailed unremittingly, every hour of every day, of every month, of every year, for decades.

The socioeconomic problems of the city have aggravated the onslaught. Failure to control the spread of illegal settlements has undermined both the resources and the moral integrity of the bureaucracies empowered to enforce building and zoning codes. A general culture of lawlessness arose in the management of the physical environment. In the historic core, regardless of the listing of buildings as monuments and the requirement that changes to listed buildings meet proper standards of conservation practice, new buildings went up, old buildings were altered or leveled, and inadvisable conservation methods were widely used—all without official overview.

Within a few years, more than 60 percent of the structures of the authorized city were in violation of the law in some respect. The intractable and mammoth Egyptian bureaucracy engendered a thicket of rules without also designing a reasonable mechanism for enforcement. In 1956, 1966, 1981, and 1984, the national legislature was forced to grant general amnesties for illegalities—which further undermined the possibility of compliance. (Why assume the burden of obeying the law when violations were forgiven?) Worst of all, even the work of official agencies often failed to adhere to established conservation regulations. The government itself was openly violating its own standards.

Meanwhile, as the residential structures of the area decayed, the number of homeless people living in Cairo increased. As the historic core became less and less desirable as an area of habitation, land values went down, rents diminished, the upper and middle classes moved out, and the poor moved in. Services and maintenance declined, garbage piled up, more of the poor moved in, and, even as residential space decreased, the residential density mushroomed. Since the infrastructure for water supply and sewage removal were either decrepit or nonexistent, the historic core itself became a major source of the pollution and raising of the water table.

A further impediment to saving Al-Qāhirah is the lack of support in Muslim society for the conservation of the Muslim heritage. International conservation authorities have noted this problem in many places in the Muslim world, whose cities have suffered the destruction of an enormous number of historic buildings. (A similar absence of urban conservation initiative would occur in Japan and China.) The phenomenon is somewhat inexplicable, although widespread poverty in Muslim society does focus governments on more pressing and primary social problems. Also, the historic tendency in Muslim administration toward a central military authority had not inculcated the civic traditions of local self-governance seen in the European city-state. In most other places in the world, the impetus for historic preservation is civic pride and identity, but a similar sense of *civitas* had not developed in Cairo. Perhaps this is not surprising in a metropolis where so many inhabitants lived outside the civic social contract.

In 1984, a UNESCO report estimated the cost of restoring Islamic Cairo as 350 million pounds. The total yearly budget of the Egyptian Antiquities Organization for saving all the monuments of Egypt was only 3.5 million pounds. All of these circumstances contributed to the fact that the main force for the preservation of Islamic Cairo came from abroad—from other cultures, often not Islamic.

THE INTERNATIONAL EFFORT TO SAVE AL-QĀHIRAH

The sociological and physical survey of Cairo done under Napoleon I was the first step toward developing an empirical understanding of the metropolis. In 1880, a nongovernmental group, the Comité des Monuments de l'Art Arabe, was formed to save the Islamic heritage of the city and to introduce the general principles of European preservation practice. The committee surveyed the city, identified significant structures, and undertook a number of meticulous and well-documented restorations. This standard of practice became the model for the official Cairene and Egyptian bureaucracies that followed. But more importantly, given the limited financial resources of Egypt, the efforts of foreigners attracted international attention to the pressing need to conserve endangered historical assets.

The dramatic expansion in the population of Cairo after World War II, followed by the proliferation of illegal settlements and the raising of the water table, drew worldwide concern to the pressing and complex problems of the preservation of Al-Qāhirah. By 1972, several foreign conservation missions had been activated, and eventually Italy, France, Germany, Poland, Denmark, India, and the United States all joined in the effort to save the historic cityscape. In the 1980s UNESCO named Islamic Cairo to the World Heritage List, giving it official recognition as one of humanity's most precious cultural assets, and several international conferences were held to analyze the problems of conservation. The attention of the world's expertise had been focused on the dilemma.

Initial efforts of the foreign missions to save specific buildings revealed daunting complications. Experience showed that each mission needed to maintain hands-on control of conservation projects; otherwise significant amounts of funds would disappear into the maze of the Egyptian bureaucracy via corruption or bureaucratic misappropriation. Once a building was restored, the continuing attack by groundwater and the growing toxicity of the environment immediately began to corrode the restoration. Eventually, the foreign missions began to explore methods of isolating structures from the water table. Trenches were dug around restored landmarks, and pumps were installed. Sophisticated procedures were devised for making a complete horizontal slice through endangered buildings and inserting a synthetic polymer barrier to prevent the dampness from rising up into the monument. The costs of conservation in this complex situation were extraordinarily high.

Then, in 1992, Cairo was struck by an earthquake. Many minarets were endangered, and innumerable historic structures were weakened with cracks. Earthquake damage in combination with the continuing environmental attack and decades of deferred maintenance put a large number of structures in immediate and serious peril. All of the existing problems were made worse. Moreover, it became evident that the combined endeavors of the foreign missions would secure only a sampling of Islamic monuments for the future unless Cairo and Egypt first solved the problem of providing infrastructure for all the neighborhoods that were illegally draining human waste into the groundwater.

This would be an enormous task. By the late 1980s Cairo's overworked sewage treatment plants were partially treating only half of the city's sewage. The other half—the waste generated by 6 million people—was clogging the main sewage lines and causing about five hundred surface floods a day. A sanitation problem unprecedented in human history had been created. Numerous advisory reports from foreign experts called for the installation of sewers in the historic core as a first priority. For years, this had been ignored by the Egyptian government. The initial sewer and water-supply program was focused on the illegal settlements just outside historic Al-Qāhirah.

Throughout the developing world, wherever illegal settlements proliferate, eventually both the permanence of such settlements and their need to be regulated are recognized by government. Then begins a difficult and excessively costly process of interjecting a rational infrastructure network into an ad hoc pattern of settlement. In Cairo, one of the initial programs to put in water lines and sewers encountered unforeseen and surprising complexities after the infrastructure was installed.

Many of the newly urbanized residents from agricultural villages were unfamiliar with modern plumbing and did not understand the physical principles that governed the use and maintenance of water lines and drainage. After several months, two phenomena began to occur throughout the settlement. Numerous residents were disposing solid garbage in kitchen sinks,

A Mosque of Ibn Tulin
B Mosque of Sultan Hassan
C Citadel of Saladin
D Walls of Saladin

THE UNESCO STUDY AREA OF ISLAMIC CAIRO

inadvertently clogging the drains of the building. Simultaneously, when faucets developed drips, few people understood that this could be remedied by replacing a washer. Throughout the settlement the combined misuse of the drainage system and the failure to fix leaks resulted in a slow but continuous and growing pattern of flooding. Clogged sinks would spill over and drip water onto the floor. Gradually this unending drippage would find its way downward

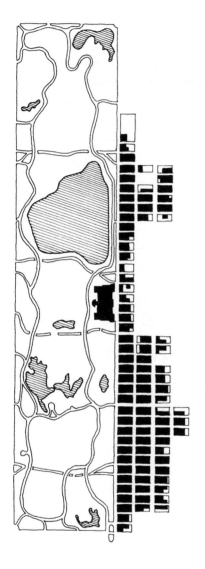

Contrasting urban zones of historic value
• The UNESCO Study Area of Islamic Cairo is densely filled with great architecture. (Monuments are shown as small white shapes with a black dot, or cross-hatched with lines.) In its street pattern and the relationship of its urban components the sector is a unique cultural expression of world civilization. But how much of it will survive? And for how long?
• The adjacent Upper East Side, Metropolitan Museum, and Carnegie Hill Historic Districts and the scenic landmark of Central Park in Manhattan—though not as old as Islamic Cairo—are protected at the request of their inhabitants, who actively participate in the ongoing administrative process by which New York's patrimony is conserved. (*Both drawings at the same scale.*)

FOUR CONSERVATION AREAS
IN MANHATTAN

through the structure. Over months, continuing exposure to water damage would cause decay inside walls, to floorboards, and to ceilings. The most unfortunate victim, of course, would be the tenant on the bottom floor.

The tenants' solution to the problem was to break open with a sledgehammer the main drain pipe to the sewer—at a point before the blockage—and reactivate the flow of water through the upper part of the system. This became a widespread spontaneous phenomenon throughout the settlement, and the new infrastructure was destroyed by residents unfamiliar with a technology that required ongoing maintenance. After an expenditure of millions of dollars, the wastewater of the settlement continued to run into the groundwater table.

The government had not foreseen the need to explain the rudiments of modern plumbing to people who had never lived with it before. Nor had officials capitalized on an opportunity to expand the local economy by training plumbers, selling plumbing parts in hardware stores, and manufacturing such materials locally. What at first glance seemed like a simple problem—the introduction of domestic plumbing—had unforseen cultural ramifications. And the landmarks of Al-Qâhirah continued to decay.

THE ABUSE OF THE PYRAMIDS

The problems of conserving Islamic Cairo demonstrate the interconnectedness of the social and physical realities of the city. New technologies alone can solve only finite aspects of the problem. The goodwill and help of outsiders have but a partial impact. Long-term preservation of Cairo's heritage requires gaining control of the physical environment of the city, and that in turn requires some degree of solution to the socioeconomic dilemmas of the country. But the problem to be solved before all others is the reformation of the culture of governance in the Egyptian bureaucracy. Without such reform, even when opportunities for an improved future can be identified, Egypt's own government constitutes a blockade to betterment. The abuse of the Pyramids is just such an example.

For a country with a rich and unique cultural history, international tourism represents a critical commercial sphere with potential for growth. In the United States, for example, tourism and travel are the nation's chief export (when revenue from abroad is considered as export income) and the country's second-largest employer after health services. Even for capitals of the global financial market—Singapore, London, Paris, New York—tourism is a primary component of successful urban economies. And relatedly, if cities are to become centers for international tourism, they must have the amenities that make visits by foreigners a comfortable experience.

In the jet age, although historic Al-Qâhirah has attracted worldwide interest among Islamic scholars and architectural historians, the most popular tourist attractions have been the ruins of pharaonic Egypt. Of several preeminent locations, perhaps no other site symbolizes the unique achievement of ancient Egypt as clearly as do the Great Pyramids and the Sphinx at Giza. Few other monuments in the world are as ancient or as universally recognized.

THE FIRST LANDMARKS

The evolution of the civilized settlement of Cairo began several millennia ago, before there was any city at all. There was just the sun, the desert, and the life-giving river, which made human habitation possible in an otherwise desolate environment. Once a year the river overflowed and deposited a layer of rich black soil across its floodplains. Because of the persistent warmth of the climate, several growing seasons could be sustained in these naturally rejuvenated and fertile fields; and eventually, from the Mediterranean to the Sahara, villages sprang up along the river's shores. The political and social integration of these many small communities, linked by the highway of the great river, eventually became the civilization of ancient Egypt—a civilization tuned to the cyclical cadence of renewal brought by the Nile.

Once human society consolidated along the 500-mile length of the river, this slender corridor of fertile land allowed Egypt to sustain an elevated civilized state for well over two thousand years. The Egyptians developed advanced methods of irrigation, horticulture, and animal husbandry. They wrote the first histories and literature. They produced elegant visual and decorative arts. And they refined the use of stone in public buildings and in sculpture, erecting numerous monuments, and giving definition to the concept of landmarks as human marks upon the land.

Regardless of our continued study of their genesis, the Great Pyramids—of Cheops, Chephren, and Mykerinos—remain an enigma in many ways. They were erected in the earliest days of recorded history, and only part of their story has reached us in the form of written documents. We do not know exactly how it evolved that the pharaohs should have such elaborate tombs whose construction was a hands-on national undertaking. Most historians now believe the Pyramids were built by the Egyptians themselves rather than by slaves, and that the annual period of mass labor occurred during the months when the Nile was flooded, when farmland was inundated and the river was at its widest for transporting stones by water. The science by which the Egyptians positioned the Pyramids accurately on a north-south axis of the globe can only be hypothesized, although we realize that Egypt had a sophisticated knowledge of astronomy and surveying. Nor, finally, have we managed to comprehend how a people with primitive metal tools could fashion such mammoth hard-stone monuments with machine-like modern technical precision—one of the heroic feats of world architectural history.

Their incontrovertible physical reality speaks to us directly from out of the past. First and foremost, the Pyramids are mountains in a terrain that grinds the peaks of nature down to sand. The Pyramid of Cheops, the largest of the three, comprises over 2.3 million stone blocks weighing about 3,000 pounds apiece. In contrast to the gentle curves of the perpetually shifting mounds of light brown sand that surround the monuments, the four triangular sides of the three Great Pyramids at Giza were perfectly white and flat before their outer limestone skin was stripped away.

The Pyramids were built more than three thousand years before the giant constructions of the Aztecs, Mayans, and Incas; two thousand years before the Great Wall of China; and five hundred years before the ziggurat of Ur. This early evidence of intelligent life on earth, were it seen from outer space, was a bit of mathematical precision on an otherwise untouched sphere of natural greens, browns, and blues. In the most primary sense, this is of course what the Egyptians intended: to produce a distinctly human mark large enough to make their existence seem of consequence. The Pyramids were meant to be visible traces on the cosmos, and to assert the significance of human affairs even when measured against the vast size of natural formations and the endless expanse of time.

For 4,400 years the Great Pyramids stood on a plateau about 5 miles into the desert. In the time of the Egyptians, Giza was just a small river port. During the months of flooding, the waters of the Nile extended across the river's flat-lands to the base of the Pyramids' plateau. But in the latter half of the twentieth century the urban conglomeration of Cairo subsumed the stretch of seasonal floodland between the Nile and the plateau, and today the Pyramids are situated on the edge of the sprawling capital city.

This is unfortunate for two reasons. First, because Egypt is 95 percent desert, it suffers from a lack of arable land. Since virtually all of the land between the monuments and the river has supported farming for many thousands of years, the settlement of this area decreases the amount of productive farming acreage even as the city grows and suffers periodic food shortages. From the days of the pharaohs until the 1970s, Egypt was an exporter of grain. Today, it must import food to feed its people. Second, the chaotic architectural forms of the troubled contemporary city contrast poorly with the dignity of the timeless monuments that were meant to be juxtaposed against the emptiness of the surrounding desert. Given both the sanctity of the monuments and the need for arable farmland, there was good reason to retain much of the centuries-old natural buffer zone of the river's floodplain and to direct the growth of the metropolis elsewhere.

A further attack on the Pyramids was demonstrated recently when the international conservation community discovered that construction was under way for a highway on the Pyramid plateau within clear view of the monuments. This was in violation of several international agreements that Egypt had signed in order to be eligible to receive foreign aid for architectural conservation. Most developed countries will not offer financial assistance for preservation unless the receiving nation is a signatory to such accords as the Athens (1931) and Venice Charters (1964), which establish universally recognized standards for monument conservation. Egypt signed both of these agreements, and it also nominated the Pyramids for inclusion on the World Heritage List, which was initiated by multinational agreement in 1972. In return for the recognition and status that comes with placement on the list, Egypt pledged to preserve not only the landmarks themselves but the desert environment surrounding them. The location and design of the new highway were in blatant contravention of all these commitments.

Once the threat of the highway became known, UNESCO rushed in a team of experts to encourage the Egyptian government to adhere to the documents it had signed. After an initial period of resistance, the government declared the location of the highway on the Pyramid plateau to be an oversight by the bureaucracy, and the roadway was rerouted. Subsequently, UNESCO consultants discovered that during the two years prior to the beginning of construction, eighty-five separate approvals for the location of the thoroughfare had been granted at various levels of the Egyptian bureaucracy. Perhaps the only people in the world who did not know that the Great Pyramids at Giza were under the protection of national and international conservation statutes were the officials of the government of Egypt.

The shortsightedness of Egypt's planning is only part of the problem. Other forms of chaos are allowed to reign on the site of the Pyramids. For some time, the Egyptian government has failed to adequately police the monument precinct. Most international guidebooks to Egypt offer some kind of warning that the experience at the Pyramids can be unpleasant: "Every visit to the Great Pyramids includes a stroll, or sometimes a run, through a veritable obstacle course." "You will still need to beware of con men; call the tourist police if necessary." "Be prepared for the hordes of touts, the numberless 'guides' and 'watchmen' who gather about you like mosquitoes." "Nowhere else is Egypt's ravenous tourist industry so, well, ravenous." "Do not let the incredible hassles of every description spoil the experience."

Under the gaze of the official tourist police, bedouin camel drivers invite tourists for a ride and, once the victim is mounted, whip the camel to a gallop in order to charge the victim for stopping the beast. Pony drivers offer to hold tourists' cameras as they mount and then extort payment for returning the cameras. Con men posing as officials demand to examine tickets to the Pyramid site, which they then steal. At intervals, the uniformed tourist police drive the omnipresent throngs away, but this is done as much to receive payoffs from the con men and touts as to protect the tourists. Meanwhile, the monuments themselves are frequently left unmonitored, and visitors climb the lower levels of the Pyramids, picnic on the giant blocks, and write graffiti on the millennia-old stones.

These things go on with the knowledge and tacit complicity of the government of Egypt, which also mounts a yearly advertising campaign to lure visitors from around the world to come to see the monuments and to spend their money in Egypt. The government's failure to provide reasonable social order at the Pyramids violates an unwritten but universally understood compact between foreign tourists and their host countries, which are expected to maintain basic civility so that visitors can have fair access to historical sites.

The tourists most vulnerable to the abuse of the con men are those who have come to Egypt on their own rather than as part of a packaged tour. In modern travel parlance these are known as the cultural tourists as opposed to mass tourists. It is precisely the tourists who are rebuffed, the cultural tourists, who are most valuable for Egypt's future. Across the world, mass tourism has a more negative effect on a nation's environment and the least positive effect on a nation's economy. Mass tourists on packaged tours benefit a few large hotels, restaurants, and tour operators, and the profits from mass tourism often go into the pockets of overseas operators. Cultural tourists, however, often eat at local restaurants, stay in a wide variety of lodgings, and spend their money in local businesses. Mass tourists overcrowd the major sites and jam surrounding highways, while cultural tourists disperse across a much wider variety of experiences and often make use of existing mass transit. At the Pyramids, the lack of protection for independent cultural tourists makes enjoying the monuments far more difficult for the very people whose presence in the country provides the greatest benefit for the local economy. Once again, the phenomenon supported by official policy retards the advancement of Egypt's welfare.

THE FUTURE OF CAIRO'S ARCHITECTURAL PAST

At the dawn of the twenty-first century, a new period of urban revitalization and redefinition is unfolding. Some cities that feared they were starting on a long road of decline have found new meaning as centers in a global marketplace. Other cities, whose plans to participate in the international economy have gone awry, must respond to the new rules as they emerge. Marginalized nations and cities face the most severe obstacles. Their disadvantages are many, their opportunities for success are fewer, and they must solve their problems while engulfed in abject and heartbreaking poverty.

In Cairo, the modern conglomeration is beset with what appears to be a problem without solution. A vast unlawful and poisoned metropolis has emerged out of official despair and abdication of responsibility. The process by which the illegal settlements take shape often does not draw upon the knowledge of city planning that has been developed over the centuries. Thus as Cairo's poor improve their lot in one dimension, inadvertently, terrible conditions are made several degrees more intolerable in other ways.

Twice in history the shape of Cairo's architectural landscape bespoke an important advance in human civilization. In each instance eternal values were given expression in built form. The Great Pyramids rose up out of the shifting desert sands to become icons of our ability to construct a meaningful existence. The minarets and domes of Al-Qāhirah were the material expression of a collective prayer. Today the skyline of the modern city is seen in a polluted purple-brown haze. The Pyramids rise above shantytowns; the domes and minarets of mosques crumble in the shadow of the exclusive modern hotels that dominate the city's skyline. This inversion of cultural values need not prevail.

Inexplicably, the greatest obstacle to saving historic Cairo is the broad lack of sympathy among Muslims and Egyptians for the careful preservation of their own remarkable architectural legacy. Here the future and the past are caught in an unyielding knot. Ultimately, the patrimony of Cairo must be maintained by Cairenes. Can preserving the heritage of the city become a priority in a situation where so many children are born to lives of such forbidding hardship and privation?

Perhaps part of the answer involves an elementary fact: no matter how hard they have labored, or what extraordinary obstacles have been overcome to build their livelihoods and homes, the majority of poorer Cairenes do not possess official recognition of ownership of their assets. As described by Hernando de Soto in his pioneering book on Third World economics, *The Mystery of Capital*, "They have houses but not titles; crops but not deeds; businesses but not statutes of incorporation." They have hard-earned wealth that cannot be activated as capital in a world where capitalism has become the primary mechanism by which individuals may raise the condition of their lives. In this regard, the

city has been divided into two societies: those who live within the social contract and those who live outside it. For how long can an alienated urban populace remain productive under such unfair conditions?

Two other facts pointed out by de Soto are crucial: "In Egypt, for instance, the wealth that the poor have accumulated is worth fifty-five times as much as the sum of all direct foreign investment ever recorded here, including the Suez Canal and the Aswan Dam." Yet registering ownership of illegally built assets can require the approval of more than thirty branches of the bureaucracy and take as long as ten years.

As governments in Asia, Africa, the Middle East, and Latin America explore the potential of de Soto's recommendations we may hope that he has identified a means to stop the dreadful downward and self-perpetuating dilemma of the massive, impoverished, illegal megacity. If marginalized Cairenes gain ownership of their properties, their stake in their own metropolis will be actualized. They will have taken ownership of hope as well as of their city. Upon having been embraced by the social contract, will they in turn embrace the obligations of the stewardship of their architectural patrimony?

Until such a time, if the world values the legacy of Cairo, then it must help. If we wish to share the benefits of knowing the diverse history of our species, we must share the responsibility for conserving the products of that remarkable and unfinished story. This requires a multinational act of conscience. Otherwise, until the conditions that exist in Cairo are changed, the greater part of an extraordinary heritage will be lost forever amid a scale of human suffering that may dwarf the Pyramids themselves. Perhaps the lesson of Cairo can be reduced to this: urban architectural preservation cannot be isolated from urban issues of human justice.

CHAPTER SIX

IDEOLOGICAL CONFLICT WITH THE PAST

MOSCOW AND BEIJING

We had such suggestions too—i.e., to turn the old city of Moscow into a museum and to build a new city by its side. We turned them down and reconstructed Moscow. The result is not bad at all. The demolition of old buildings in Beijing is a task that must be done somewhere in time.

—SOVIET PLANNING ADVISERS IN COMMUNIST-GOVERNED BEIJING

No other nation in the twentieth century has destroyed the historic nucleus of its capital to the extent that we have managed to do.

—S. HAN MAGOMEDOV, RUSSIAN HISTORIAN, 1988

Possibly the greatest single work of man on the face of the earth is Peking.

—EDMUND N. BACON, *The Design of Cities*

Sadness is evident on the streets of Moscow. The pavement is cracked, curbs are crumbling, the streets are riddled with potholes. Doors to apartment buildings hang off their hinges, locks are broken, and wooden slats cover shattered windows. Faucets throughout the city drip in an epidemic of unrepaired plumbing. Officials estimate that half of the hot water of Moscow is lost through leakage; half of the fuel expended to heat the water is thus also wasted.

An omnipresent dust blankets the metropolis. Babushkas (old women) with brooms made of twigs and straw sweep the dirt from one spot to another, only to watch the wind redeposit it somewhere else. This is the same dirt to be found on the streets of Mexico City, Cairo, and the large cities of other under-developed nations. It is the dirt of privation, of places too poor to patch the paving, fill the cracks, and stop the crumbling. Moscow will not be rid of it until Russia solves the larger problems of its struggling economy.

Depression hangs in the air, as if the city has fallen into a deep hole—notwithstanding the elegantly dressed privileged few who skip over breaches in the sidewalk as they hurry to opening night at the Bolshoi. Perhaps it is daunting for Muscovites to know that so many of their society's wounds are self-inflicted. In this same place, a vast illiterate society has been provided with universal education and institutions of higher learning that enabled Russian scientists to put cosmonauts in space. Meanwhile, many great artists continue to leave, and the deteriorating and fractured cityscape will not be quickly healed.

Beijing, too, is plagued by the dirt of poverty, many of its residential neighborhoods are also decrepit, and yet the city exudes the positive energy of a people embarked on a collective upward path. Nowhere is this feeling greater than in the mornings in Tiananmen Square, as Chinese from across the People's Republic await the opening of the Forbidden City. Since 1989 access to the Palace Museum has been limited to 30,000 visitors a day. They arrive on foot and by bicycle, bus, car, and the city's first modern subway. Not very far away, high-rise hotels and office buildings form a ragged new skyline. Traffic clogs the roads and industrial pollution muddies the air.

At the beginning of the twentieth century, the bulk of China remained a medieval agrarian culture, and the last emperor still sat on the Dragon Throne. Today a portrait of Mao marks the entry to the processional route to what was once the palace of the Son of Heaven, much as the Tomb of Lenin commands Red Square. People of many different dialects and facial types spanning the empire gather in the giant public plaza. By Western standards, the majority of these visitors are quite poor; they have packed their lunches because they cannot afford to purchase refreshments. Once the doors open, a steady stream of humanity flows through the arched entrances cut in the thick red walls, eager to explore the 980 buildings, the countless courtyards, and the passages and gardens.

Around noon they break to have lunch. Families find a corner in which to gather together and eat. Children are allowed to play, but no one litters. Not too long ago, none of the forebears of today's visitors could see these hidden wonders—the ultimate achievement of their own civilization. But now the wheel of human history has turned, and a broader justice has arrived for the thousands of Chinese who each day visit the no-longer-forbidden city.

⚛

Twentieth-century rulers of Communist states in Russia and China inherited a rich patrimony of historic buildings in their capital cities. However, since in both nations Communist revolutionary movements represented an attempt to correct deeply rooted social inequities in which large agrarian populations were exploited by elite consumer cities, Communist policies often had an anti-urban and anti-intellectual bias. At various intervals, the architectural achievements of past generations were associated with rejected historical values. The fundamental role of the city as the incubator of creative innovation frequently went unrecognized. Artists and the urban intelligentsia were intermittently perceived as potential critics of Communist policies, and artistic expression was suppressed as nonconforming intellectuals were purged.

In Moscow, postrevolutionary policies eventually became remarkable for their open hostility to the city's architectural heritage. In Beijing, Soviet advisers on city planning proposed that a similar anticonservation policy be applied to the oldest intact capital city of imperial China, causing the Chinese to be caught between dogma, a dramatic need to modernize their country, and a centuries-old reverence for their own history. Moreover, since the historical period during which Communism came to ascendancy was also the era when cities across the world were undergoing dramatic reconfiguration and population growth due to industrialization, the effect of Communist thinking on the physical fabric of the metropolis was magnified, the complexity of urban planning was increased, the speed of change was accelerated, opportunities for retrospection were briefer, and the potenial for the destruction of historic assets was heightened. In this context, solutions to complex urban problems were sought from a conceptual point of view skewed recurrently by dogma and propagandistic priorities, while the civic spirit of each city was shattered by terrible repressions visited on inhabitants by their governments.

Architecturally, and prior to their similar destiny as capitals of the two great Communist superpowers of the twentieth century, historic Moscow and Beijing were more unalike than similar. Moscow was a city built in the European town planning tradition and had a Baroque pattern of radial concentric avenues superimposed over a narrow and irregular medieval street pattern. Beijing was built on a giant orthogonal grid. The form of Moscow evolved over many centuries and represented the reconciliation of urban ideas from various historical periods. Beijing was conceived as an integrated artistic whole, and although its design was extended and enriched, its basic formulation was little changed over time.

Yet despite these differences, in the context of human social development and prior to the era of Communist rule, the two historic capitals shared an important characteristic. More than that of any other city in Russia, the physical form of Moscow articulated the singular attributes of Russian architectural history. And more than any other city in China, Beijing was the ultimate expression of Chinese civilization. Each city was a unique manifestation of its national culture.

HISTORIC MOSCOW: THE THIRD ROME

Situated between the political poles of Constantinople and the Mongol Empire founded by Genghis Khan, medieval Moscow blended two different cultural strains. A city of Greek Orthodox, and eventually Russian Orthodox Christianity, it rose to prominence as an administrative center for the gathering of Mongol tribute.

In a climate with long, cold winters, wood buildings were warmer than those constructed of stone. And because wood was plentiful in the surrounding geography, the growth of the city throughout its history, and in fact to some degree even into the twentieth century, was more readily accommodated by the simpler, faster, and less costly construction of wooden structures. The fires that warmed Moscow's buildings, however, also dried their wooden parts, making them highly flammable. Over the centuries, the closely packed city would be repeatedly consumed in conflagrations as a result of accidents, internal civic discord, and warfare.

As the Greek Orthodox religion gained primacy, numerous houses of worship were erected. Based upon protoypes established in the Byzantine Empire, as the building type evolved in Russia, it developed distinctive characteristics. Like the Cathedral of Saint Mark in Venice, medieval Russian Orthodox churches, though much smaller, were often composed of several interconnected interior spaces crowned by separate domes. But in Russia the multiple peaks of churches assumed a greater verticality and a surprising degree of compositional variety.

In part this artistic diversity evolved because much of the visible exterior construction of these early canopies was decorative and not constrained by the structural necessity of supporting heavy loads across wide spans. However, the fanciful tops of Moscow's churches also were consistent with regional wooden building traditions which, throughout Russia's history, have exhibited an astounding eclectic plasticity, rising upward in implausible and intricate combinations of architectural form.

Thus the churches of Moscow, even as they gradually came to be built of masonry, endowed the city with many different decorative crowns. Its roofs were steeply pitched because of the thick blanket of snow that covered the city in winter. And since the empire that came to be centered in the city long retained active commercial, cultural, and political relations with its Asian neighbors, Moscow's church rooftops were often described by latter-day historians and early European visitors as reflecting the patterns of Oriental rugs, as being reminiscent of the shape of Mongol tents, or as having the profiles of Tartar helmets—all in unusual combination with the Eastern Mediterranean forms of traditional Greek Orthodox architecture.

Monastic chronicles of the twelfth century contain the earliest written records of the settlement, situated on the slopes above the Moskva River. In 1236, it was leveled by the Mongols and was rebuilt by the Muscovites in the same place. In 1293 it was razed again and subsequently rebuilt yet again.

By the time of Czar Ivan IV (1530–1584), Russia had been consolidated into a sovereign kingdom, and a great citadel called the Kremlin had been built in the city's center. (This first czar, also known as Ivan the Terrible, was one of harshest of Moscow's rulers in a highly autocratic political culture.) Decorative swallowtail crenellations adorned tall battlements of dark red brick, and numerous high towers protected the fortress at critical approaches. The architects, imported from Italy, introduced more advanced construction techniques to the city. This is reflected in the great Uspensky (Assumption) Cathedral, which is far larger than previous religious structures built in masonry, and is the earliest surviving church of many that were assembled in the Kremlin and filled with highly refined frescoes and icons. (The city became a center for Russian medieval religious art, particularly in the work of Andrei Rublyev, who lived in Moscow for the last twenty years of his life.)

The towers of the Kremlin were capped with ornate peaks in the shape of tent roofs. Five beautiful gilded cupolas adorned the Assumption Cathedral. During this period, as Moscow struggled to free itself of Mongol hegemony, a ring of fortified monasteries had been built in the countryside around the city. Minature cities unto themselves, the monasteries were the first line of defense, housing troops when the city was threatened, and similarly constructed with wondrous masonry towers, bulwarks, tall gateways, and numerous churches within their walls.

A central public space serving the communal and commercial life of the city had long existed at Moscow's center. Situated just outside the eastern walls of the Kremlin, it was known as Kransky, or the Beautiful Red Square ("Kransky" means "beautiful" as well as "red"). When Ivan IV defeated the Tartars and conquered Kazan in 1552 (generally ending Mongol political influence), yet another magnificent cathedral, the Cathedral of the Intercession on the Moat, also known as Saint Basil's, was constructed to commemorate the victory and enclose the southern side of the city's main plaza.

In 1382 and 1445, the misery of Moscow's poor led to riots. In 1547, similar uprisings and two fires destroyed much of the town. In 1571, the Crimean

Tartars leveled Moscow. In 1583, after one more calamitous fire, the ten domes of Saint Basil's were topped with ten differently decorated crowns, and the signature onion-shaped dome turban of Russian architecture achieved its ultimate expression. In a culture of ornately configured church roofscapes, this was one of the most fantastic, composed of dense layers of decorative features and covered with bright multichromatic and gold-leaf patterning. An enduring symbol of the city, beloved by Moscovites, and the epitome of a particularly Russian architectural aesthetic, had been consummated.

In 1589, the Russian Orthodox church broke free of Constantinople, and Moscow subsequently became known as the Third Rome, the home of an independent patriarchate. Moreover, as Moscow's surrounding wooden townscape was many times lost and reinstated over the centuries, its masonry citadels, towers, and churches came to embody not just its piety and urban architectural character, but the continuity of the city's culture.

Under the Romanov dynasty oppressive conditions fueled more social unrest, followed by harsh reprisals throughout the second half of the seventeenth century. During the reigns of Peter the Great (1682–1725) and Catherine the Great (1762–1796), a second capital—Saint Petersburg—housed one of the most brilliant courts in Europe, as Russian monarchs made a sustained effort to introduce ideas from the Enlightenment to a country that for centuries had been cut off from West.

The two capitals were dramatically different in physical form. Since Saint Petersburg was built in a largely underdeveloped area, like the city of Washington in the United States, it was one of a select number of cities that put into practice the sweeping organizational ideas in city planning that had evolved during the Renaissance and the Baroque eras. Long axial boulevards and giant public spaces shaped by elaborate classical architectural constructions could be created without first deconstructing a previously existing cityscape. Much of the design of the city was the work of architects from abroad—from Italy in particular—and the second capital brilliantly fulfilled the latent potential of European urban planning concepts.

Serious fires afflicted Moscow in 1737, 1748, and 1752, but the city was rebuilt each time. A terrible outbreak of the plague occurred, and the city was repopulated. While Peter the Great had reduced Moscow's status to that of a provincial center, Catherine the Great allowed the life of the court to oscillate between Russia's older and newer capitals. Saint Petersburg represented the new Europeanized face of Russia, whereas Moscow embodied ancient traditions and the old, and sometimes regressive, social order. Hence, under Catherine, plans were initiated to reformulate the compacted medieval city with wide boulevards and classical architectural vistas. And in many of its outer parts, Moscow soon assimilated European architectural planning culture. Yet the labyrinthine pattern of medieval property ownership made other, more central areas difficult to change.

On September 15, 1812, an officer in the army of Napoleon Bonaparte wrote, "On entering Moscow I was seized with astonishment and delight. Although I had expected to see a wooden city, as many had said, I found, on the contrary, almost all the houses to be of brick and in the most elegant modern style." The French also found that a city of 275,000 people had been deserted and set aflame as the Russian army burned buildings of supplies that could not be emptied. The city was dry, the wind blew for four days, and looting by the invading French exacerbated the condition. By the time the rains came, two-thirds of Moscow was lost.

churches
monasteries

Moscow in 1836 •The city has been built after the French invasion. A customs toll wall encircles the conurbation. The ring roads are established. The Kremlin remains a fortress at Moscow's center. There are 175 individual churches shown, and numerous other churches exist within the walled compounds of monasteries.

Once more, the city rose from the ashes. And to an even greater degree, the classical town planning ideas initiated by Catherine the Great were realized. Lost handsome buildings were reinstated, while others were added to the cityscape. A town plan of radial-concentric boulevards was merged with the old medieval core, and a map of the city drawn in 1836 shows that over two hundred churches were in place, having survived the fire or been newly created. Though much changed as an urban landscape, the tradition of the city's numerous eclectic roofscapes persisted.

The effort to achieve modernization begun by Peter the Great had altered Russia fundamentally, introducing essential social, economic, administrative, and religious reforms. Opportunities for education were greatly widened for many classes of people, particularly in cities where the leading universities and academies were located. These changes had a profound effect on the nation's cultural life. Prior to these improvements, Russian cultural development was predominantly associated with the Orthodox church and its ceremonies. There was little secular literature, art, or theater. Just over a century later, however, in Moscow and Saint Petersburg, a remarkable florescence occurred. Pushkin, Tolstoy, Dostoevsky, Chekhov, Gorky, and other writers emerged onto the world stage. The music of Rimsky-Korsakov, Moussorgsky, Borodin, Tchaikovsky, Rachmaninoff, and Stravinsky was celebrated around the globe. The Moscow Art Theater, led by director Constantine Stanislavsky, altered the shape of modern theater. And a renaissance in dance, fostered in the Russian Imperial School and the Bolshoi Ballet, set new standards for classical ballet far into the twentieth century. Russian adaptations of European culture had resulted in an explosion of enduring and widely esteemed artworks.

Moscow and Saint Petersburg had become two of the world's most significant cultural centers, attracting artists and intellects from across Europe. While the architecture of Saint Petersburg reflected how Russia refined ideas from the West, Moscow reflected how such ideas could be modified by a culture that had assimilated Slavic, Greek Orthodox, and Asian influences. Accordingly, as new European architectural styles infiltrated the city, Muscovite architects would often freely add modifications. As in other Western capital cities of the period, this eclectic response also grew out of the fact that the new building types of the industrial city, such as department stores, hotels, and apartment buildings, had few immediate precedents in architectural form. Particularly at the city's center, where the presence and symbolic meaning of historic architecture was strongest, the new architectural ideas and technology from abroad underwent many curious adaptations.

In 1884–1885, the old string of commercial buildings that framed the eastern side of Red Square was replaced by one of the world's earliest and largest interior retail arcades, lit by vast skylights supported by an ingenious use of arched metal and glass. The facades of the building—called the Upper Trading Rows and later known as the GUM State Department Store—were designed in an Italian Renaissance style, but its roofscape echoed the indigenous towers and peaks of the Kremlin.

Completing the enclosure of the square, a massive historical museum had been erected to the north in 1873. Constructed of dark red bricks and incorporating traditional decorative features, it culminated in a whimsical profile of spires and tent roofs in a deliberate Russian national style. The culture of the city was alive with new ideas and the "Beautiful Red Square" at the core of Moscow had become one of the most distinctive urban spaces in the world.

The serfs were emancipated in 1861, but they were not freed from their debilitating poverty. Although railroads now crisscrossed the nation and factories were constructed in cities, the former agricultural workers who labored in them found they had exchanged one form of exploitation for another. Government grew more corrupt and repressive. The seeds of insurrection had been sown. In 1905 the first stages of what would become the Russian Revolution begun. By 1918, Lenin had installed the new Soviet government in Moscow.

During the prolonged civil war that followed, atrocities occurred on both sides and Bolsheviks often assaulted places of worship. Priests were killed or sent into exile; churches were pillaged; and with the establishment of the Soviet state, all religious institutions were banned. Long after the madness of war abated and the nation assumed the normalcy of peacetime, the planning of the new society was periodically affected by an antireligious bias in which the architectural achievements of religious institutions were associated with a rejected past. Having triumphed over the obstacles of history, the historic metropolis whose unique architectural identity was founded on the myriad pinnacles of its houses of worship now came under the assault of it rulers.

HISTORIC BEIJING:
THE METROPOLIS AS A WORK OF ART

In contrast to the evolving form of Moscow, historic Beijing may be the most totally integrated aesthetic whole of any great city ever built. It represents the architectural culmination of a continuous ancient culture, dating back to about 2000 B.C. and supplanted in 1911, when the last imperial Chinese dynasty was overthrown.

Unlike other large historic cities—Rome, Cairo, and Paris, which increased in physical dimension as the number of inhabitants grew and political power and wealth were accrued—Beijing was conceived from the outset as a giant city and a complete urban composition. Two circumstances contributed to this phenomenon. First, although the Chinese realm fluctuated in size across its history, the ruling families who utilized Beijing as their administrative center—the Yuan (Mongols), the Ming, and the Qing (Manchurians)—were all able to consolidate large parts of the kingdom and each of these dynasties commanded the resources of one of the largest empires in the world, thereby acquiring the wealth to build and maintain a majestic capital on an immense scale. (The geographic extent of the kingdom was, in several eras, greater than that of the Roman Empire or the Ottoman Empire at their peaks.) Second, the unique ceremonial significance of the capital city and its many prescribed institutions and functions had already been established centuries before the rise of the Yuan, Ming, and Qing by a legacy of Chinese town planning, which spelled out in great detail the requirements for that place on earth where the emperor, the Son of Heaven, mediated the relationship of Chinese society to the forces of the wider universe. Compliance with these formulas, by definition, resulted in one of the largest and most opulent cities in the world.

The characteristics of traditional Chinese architecture and city building were governed by an abstract conception of the cosmos in which the landmass of the earth was geometrically aligned along north-south and east-west axis lines. The Chinese imagined the universe as a vast spheroid, and the earth as a series of idealized squares, somewhat like a cube. In this conception, benevolent blessings on the agrarian kingdom of the Chinese emanated from the south and the sun.

Although, like the capitals of European city-states, Chinese cities served to mix in creative ferment the most talented intellects and artists of the empire, they did not evolve into industrial centers. The primary role of the imperial Chinese metropolis was to manage an agricultural society. Central bureaucracies located in cities planned large public works such as irrigation systems and canals to disperse farm products. And in the capital, the emperor exercised the "mandate of heaven," performing those vital ceremonies that established annual harmony with the forces of nature. From the seat of the "virtuous prince," *yin* forces (negative and passive) and *yang* forces (positive and aggressive) were maintained in equilibrium: rain balanced sunshine, cold followed warmth, barrenness was offset by fertility, the constancy of the four seasons was ensured, and human affairs, theoretically, were administered with justice and morality.

One of the most striking characteristics of Chinese civilization was a long tradition of government by scholar-officials steeped in the wisdom of Confucianism. As the system evolved, nationwide examinations, culminating with the most rarefied tests taking place within the imperial palace—the Forbidden City—and under the auspices of the emperor produced a vast meritocracy by which the widespread empire was administered in harmony with the "great unity." Often in Chinese history, this system of appointments made upward social mobility possible for brilliant individuals of the lower classes, and when a talented student was identified, an entire village might support the educational efforts that would end in the placement of a fellow peasant in a high official position.

In determining the design of the imperial capital, the emperors and scholar-officials of the Yuan and Ming were guided by the Confucian classic the *Zhou Li*, from what was called the Late Spring and Autumn Period (770–476 B.C.) in which the following specifications for the layout of the capital metropolis are listed: the size of the capital should reflect its significance in the hierarchy of authority; the city should face toward the brightness of the south; it should be laid out in squares and rectangles aligned with the four directions of earth; its internal organization should reflect the orderliness of the universe; each social function should have its appropriate place, meaning that higher uses such as imperial palaces, temples, and the mansions of princes should be positioned in more important locations, and lesser activities such as markets and mercantile shops should be situated at secondary sites; the imperial palace should be placed at the heart of the settlement; the ancestral temple should be to the right of the central axis, the altar to heaven to the left; a great wall symbolizing the power of the emperor should enclose the whole metropolis. And the list continues, at great length, specifying innumerable aspects of the city's shape and life.

Thus, in 1260, Emperor Kublai Khan—having completed the Mongol conquest of China begun under his grandfather, Genghis Khan—would create a new imperial city called Da Du in the general location once occupied by several earlier northern capitals. Foreign visitors, such as Marco Polo, described the Yuan metropolis as one of the grandest and most cosmopolitan cities in the world: "The whole city is laid out in squares like a chessboard, and arranged in so perfect and masterly a fashion that no description can possibly do justice to its beauty." Yet the glories of Da Du were short lived. In 1368, much of the city would be destroyed in the fighting that preceded the founding of the Ming dynasty. The Ming capital—called Beiping Fu, and known to us today as Beijing—was equally magnificent. It had a similar plan and was constructed atop the old Mongol city, but nonetheless it was virtually an entirely new urban structure. The following dynasty, the Qing, elaborated and added its own stylistic touches, but otherwise Beijing retained under the Qing the basic elements of the Ming metropolis.

The first phase of Beiping Fu, a vast construction built within a rectangular framework of walls, was created in the fifteenth century. The city was almost three times the size of Imperial Rome, at the time when historians estimate that Rome had become the first city to hold a million people. While the forums of

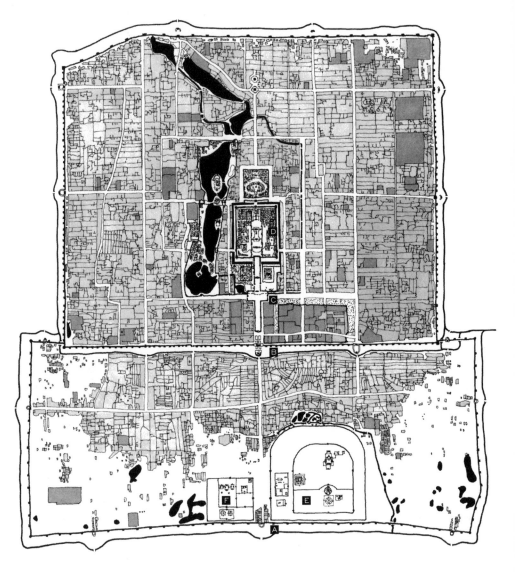

A Yungtingmen Gate
B Zhengyangmen Barbican
C Tiananmen Courtyard

D Forbidden City
E Temple of Heaven
F Altar of Agriculture

The Inner (or Imperial) and Outer (or Chinese) Cities of Beijing (Based on a map compiled in the 1930s by L.C. Arlington, an American Customs and Postal official, and William Lewisohn, a British army officer and journalist.) · The feudal city is almost entirely intact. Western trolleys and a railroad (not shown) have penetrated the cityscape and several foreign legations have been constructed in a large compound located just inside the Inner City and east of the central spine. Moats encircle every wall of fortification.

Rome would grow erratically and fail to establish a greater prevailing spatial order for the city, the Chinese metropolis was organized from the outset around a long central axis that ran north-south, bisecting the settlement and extending into the surrounding suburb, where the Temple of Heaven and Altar of Agriculture were eventually constructed. The length of this spine, around which were arranged the most significant structures of the city, was comparable to and somewhat greater than the length of the axial line in modern Paris that runs from La Défense through the Place de l'Étoile to the Louvre.

All major roads in Beiping Fu ran either north-south or east-west, dividing the city into a great rectilinear grid. The rest of the passageways through the settlement, called *hutongs,* were far narrower and of varying width, but were also predominantly aligned on the north-south, east-west axes. Almost every building in Beijing was rectilinear in plan and one or two stories high, with few tall or multistory constructions. Major residences, monuments, and significant institutions consisted of multiple buildings grouped so that they formed private rectangular courtyards, which were also in alignment with the great grid of the city. Important buildings and complexes were generally entered from the south.

Beijing was composed of walls within walls within walls: every residence was enclosed, every temple and institution was surrounded, and the metropolis as a whole was fortified. Only in commercial zones did the fronts of buildings commonly face and frame the street. Gateways, arches, and doorways existed in all sizes and degrees of elaborateness, each observing a strict architectural hierarchy of detail that signified the status and social rank of the occupants or institution within. Avenues, streets, and lanes were marked with decorative three-bay memorial arches *(pailou)* made of painted wood, stone, or brightly glazed bricks; these arches alerted the passerby to the prominence of the families and institutions associated with the thoroughfare. The repeated presence of memorial arches throughout the street pattern, each one unique in its details, gave the city a celebratory character that is distinctly Chinese.

Three mammoth walls established the geometry of the plan of Beijing, and their great towers and gateways were major points of orientation within the urban environment. The Ming walls of the original Beiping Fu, known in later years as the Inner City, were 20 kilometers long, with nine barbican-fortified gates. These massive portals generated the major avenues of Beijing's grid and thus marked the principal vectors of the city's geometry. While the walls of Da Du had been made of rammed earth, the walls of Beiping Fu were constructed of masonry; they were about 35 feet high, 55 feet wide at the bottom, and 37 feet wide at the top. Every 90 yards, a bastion projected outward. The summit of the ramparts was paved, and the battlements were crenellated. In 1533 Beijing was expanded, and another imposing line of fortifications was built,

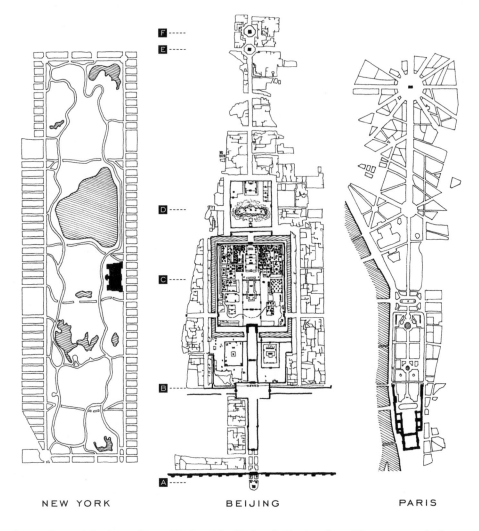

NEW YORK   BEIJING   PARIS

Long urban axial spines · Central Park in New York. · In Beijing: from Zhengyangmen barbican (**A**) to Tiananmen courtyard (**B**), to the Forbidden City (**C**), to Jingshan hill (**D**), to the Drum Tower (**E**), to the Bell Tower (**F**) · In Paris: from the Louvre through the garden of the Tuileries, to the Place de la Concorde, to the Arc de Triomphe. *(All at the same scale.)*

enclosing a rectangle of land to the south which came to be called the Outer City. This wall was 14 kilometers long and 7.7 meters high and boasted seven additional barbicans and watchtowers. The third monumental wall of the settlement was the interior one that surrounded the Forbidden City; it was 9.9 meters high and 3.5 kilometers long. All of these major walls were encircled by wide moats.

The great city walls of Beijing had several levels of significance. They established the harmonious geometric alignment of the capital with the poles of the Chinese cosmos. Their size and extent proclaimed the authority of the emperor and the kingdom. They symbolized the orderliness of Chinese society, in which every inhabitant's house, courtyard, and daily life—whether that of a prince or a peasant—was also aligned with the giant grid of the capital city and the earth. And like the Great Walls of China—the thousands of miles of fortifications that surmounted the tortuous landscape of steeply rolling mountains to the north—the mammoth fortifications of Beijing proclaimed the permanence of Chinese civilization in the face of the uncertainties of history.

Protected within these great fortifications were the many institutions of the city—its markets and commercial zones, theaters, brothels, teahouses, military compounds, temples, universities, government offices, and, most important, the Temple of Agriculture, the Temple of Heaven, and the Forbidden City. Each of the imperial compounds was immense. The Forbidden City is similar in size to historic Jerusalem as we know it today, while the outer wall of the Temple of Heaven is large enough to enclose the entire site of the three Pyramids at Giza. Each compound was made up of numerous structures and elaborate landmarks arranged in configurations that were in accord with the cosmological geometries of the Chinese universe. And all were designed to take the viewer through a deliberate sequence of impressive architectural spaces and structures. In these locations, the Chinese believed they were establishing the center of the world.

Time and size were two important design components. By constructing an experience that was vast not only spatially but also temporally—requiring a substantial amount of time to traverse each segment of the urban composition—the scholar-bureaucrats who designed Beijing heightened the viewer's sense of drama. By making huge constructions that obviously required vast amounts of human labor and skill, they increased the impression of power and wealth for inhabitants and visitors alike.

The long sequence of entry to the Forbidden City of the Son of Heaven began at the Yungtingmen gate, the southern starting point of the great center axis of Beijing. Here, a mammoth 5-mile-long moat and wall commanded the wide plain. Once through this barrier and within the teeming streets of the Lower City, a central avenue pointed straight to another distant watchtower, moat, and prodigious wall almost 2 kilometers away. In 1601, a Jesuit missionary described the scene: "These walls are far higher than those we are used to in Europe. Soldiers always stand guard as if it were wartime, and eunuchs are posted at the gates to collect duties." Beyond this point, the axis continued across a 200-meter-wide plaza to another barrier wall and elaborate gate structure.

Here the main ceremonial pathway commenced. An exterior colonnaded corridor, 400 meters long, led to a large open courtyard where five ornate marble bridges spanned yet another moat, beyond which five arched gateways penetrated another high thick wall—the Tiananmen gateway (to which the giant portrait of Mao Tse-tung is currently affixed, facing out to the modern square created by the Communists by demolishing the great colonnaded corridor). The next length of passageway, the Thousand Paces Gallery, ended in front of the entrance to the Forbidden City.

At Wumen, or South Gate, the red stucco walls of the imperial city turned inward to form a three-sided plaza, 200 meters on each side. A large two-story pavilion was perched above the entry wall, and four towers looked down from the corners of the square. All these structures were capped by multitiered tile roofs in imperial yellow—a color reserved for the exclusive use of the emperor—as was the center archway of the three doors to the Forbidden City and *all* the central pathways that bisected the entire complex.

Early in the twentieth century, at the conclusion of the Boxer Rebellion, a French naval officer would express a universal first reaction to the architectural experience that lay beyond the portals at Wumen: "No one of our European capitals has been conceived and laid out with such unity and audacity. It is easy to understand why the Chinese ambassadors who came to visit our kings in the times when their immense country was flourishing were not particularly dazzled by the sight of the Louvre or of Versailles."

In comparison with the palace and gardens of Versailles, which is situated in the countryside outside Paris and actually occupies a somewhat greater expanse of ground, the Forbidden City is an urban architectural expression: a city unto itself set in the midst of a metropolis. While Versailles is dominated by a single great edifice, with a supporting cast of lesser buildings, the Forbidden City is an assemblage of almost a thousand structures. These varied in magnificence from great imperial palaces for the various generations and branches of the imperial family, to numerous ceremonial halls and buildings of state, several temples, the dwellings of concubines, the apartments of eunuchs, government offices, theaters, libraries, workshops, stables, school-rooms for the imperial offspring, kitchens, an apothecary, a chapel for shamanistic rites, a hall for composing poetry, a garden for reciting poetry, a printshop, the barracks of the imperial guard, and innumerable private court-yards and gardens.

The principal design device of the imperial city was repetition. Basic elements would be used over and again in different combinations, and structures of greater significance were distinguished by architectural compositions of greater elaboration. Important buildings were raised up on paved terraces—the number of terraces increasing with the building's importance—faced with gray brick and intermittently bordered by white marble balustrades. In the most exclusive areas, the balustrades were further decorated with intricately carved phoenix and dragon designs, while at the bottom of each post large dragon-head drainage spouts cantilevered outward. About six hundred bollards and spouts would embellish the terraces surrounding the Hall of Supreme Harmony—one of three great halls devoted to ritual state purposes.

The structures of the Forbidden City were mainly of wooden post-and-beam construction, with distinctively Chinese sloped-roof trusses that curved upward and were covered with imperial yellow tiles. More important buildings had double-hipped roofs. Decorative glazed ceramic dragons embellished the ends of roof peaks. A parade of identical ceramic figurines marched down the lower end of every roof eave. An elaborate system of interlocked brackets allowed the roofs to cantilever outward, so that the whole roof assembly seemed suspended in air.

The many walls within the Forbidden City were stuccoed and painted flat red. The wooden parts of all buildings were generally covered with a layer of deep red reflective lacquer, except where where more elaborate multichromatic decorations were applied. Windows and doors were made of wooden screens carved in intricate geometric designs. Beautifully crafted molded-tile decorations and panels encrusted the entrances to royal palaces and adorned the numerous archways. And throughout the city, gold leaf was used to highlight the geometric and symbolic design motifs as if it were ordinary paint. In particular, the ceilings, beams, and columns in principal rooms were often thickly coated with gold that shimmered even in the shadows.

The designers of the Forbidden City would use this palette of architectural elements to create endless variations on the central theme of imperial grandeur. By increasing and decreasing the density of decoration, by composing building masses with greater and lesser complexity, by shrinking and expanding distances and volumes, they designed each piece of the city's composition to signal its social significance. Here was one of the singular urban landmarks in human history.

Like the architects of the Italian Renaissance, who perceived that urban structures played a dual role—the exteriors defining a city's street patterns, the interiors serving private functions—the scholar-planners of the center of the Forbidden City also advanced two design purposes at the same time. Particularly in its principal ceremonial zones, structures were massed in long lines that defined the boundaries of a sequence of majestic spaces; and they were also arranged to punctuate significant vistas, with particular emphasis on the four cardinal points. In this duality lay the ultimate refinement of the composition of the Forbidden City: its vistas, spaces, and architectural masses were composed to be experienced simultaneously. The city was a complex composition of mass and emptiness, of sound and silence, unfolding in all directions. The ceiling of its grand exterior urban rooms was the sky itself.

The greatness of Rome, Constantinople, Tenochtitlán, Baghdad, Alexandria, Babylon, and Cordova would disappear with time, becoming mere memories of distant and fabled places. Few of the legendary imperial capitals would survive into the era of photography, to face the challenge of the modernization of the historic metropolis. Cairo and Kyoto are two such places, but the foremost is Beijing.

THE FALL OF THE SON OF HEAVEN AND
THE RISE OF THE COMMUNIST STATE

An inevitable consequence of Western industrialization was the shrinking of the globe, as communication and transportation technology eliminated the insulation of distance and time. In Europe and America, industrialized societies emerged in gradual stages over hundreds of years. Asian countries, however, modernized abruptly after the forced commercial penetration of their markets by modern military nations. This threat to their right to self-determination compelled the civilizations of Asia to adapt quickly to Western knowledge and foreign ways of thinking. Particularly in cities, centuries of tradition were hastily overturned.

In 1842, under the Treaty of Nanking, China was required to accept opium from colonial India in order to produce a favorable balance of trade for Great Britain. This was the beginning of a period of colonial exploitation by foreign industrialized powers that undermined China's ability to command its domestic and foreign affairs, making the ancient civilization unable to isolate itself from the broad currents of a changing world.

By 1911 the Manchu dynasty had fallen under the weight of its own corruption, and traditional civil service examinations had been ended. By 1915 there were as many as 130,000 schools teaching a modern curriculum in China's cities. For four decades no single political group was able to consolidate power. Foreign intervention continued. Regional warlords gained power, and numerous nationalist movements developed in support of Chinese sovereignty. In Hong Kong, Taiwan, Siberia, Korea, Outer Mongolia, Tibet, Vietnam, and Burma, Chinese dominion was dislodged. And the shrinking empire was consumed by civil, factional, and foreign wars, even as it endeavored to make the transition to modernity.

Centralized government existed only for short periods of time, because no single group could long command authority. When modern reforms and advances were initiated by various temporary regimes, they usually benefited the inhabitants of urban areas. When drought or floods caused famine in the countryside, there was little relief for the starving. Warlords and other military forces struggled to control geographic areas in order to exploit them. Peasants were conscripted and taxed. Highly favorable commercial concessions to foreign powers were bartered for Western armaments. The Sino-Japanese Wars began. China was invaded and occupied. World War II followed.

After decades of fighting, the two most successful groups to mount a resistance to the Japanese were the People's Nationalist Party, or Kuomintang, and the Chinese Communists. By the end of World War II, both sides were armed—the Kuomintang by the United States and the other Allied powers; the Communists by the Soviet Union. A final civil war for ultimate control of a vast geographic area ensued. Of the hundreds of factions that had struggled to gain political power since the fall of the Manchus, one group—the Communists—had focused on relieving the plight of China's rural population. Over decades, the Communists had slowly built a wide base of support by forming an alliance with unlettered and impoverished farmers. Once a village or region was consolidated, agrarian reforms were instituted. The civil war had become, literally, a peasant revolution.

In 1949, decades of fighting ended with the establishment of the People's Republic of China. The Kuomintang retreated to Taiwan, taking with them a trainload of priceless artifacts from the Forbidden City. The party that had come to power had an antiurban bias. From the Communist historical perspective, many of China's cities had been consumer cities—elite societies that produced few actual commodities but nonetheless consumed great amounts of agricultural products. Beijing was a prime example of this phenomenon, so long as the administration of the empire, or the wealth accrued from innovative thinking, or the products of cultural refinement were not taken into account as having social value—an evaluation that defies the facts of the history of civilizations. An immediate ideological objective of the Communist rulers became the changing of the consumer cities of China into producer cities. In this conceptual political equation, the industrialization of consumer cities morally justified their expenditure of food and made them Socialist cities whose workers would be equal partners with their agricultural counterparts. The largest consumer city, the capital, was an anachronism, a metropolis designed by scholar-officials and the reflection of an agrarian feudal civilization reaching back two milennia. Imperial Beijing would be ideologically remade into a symbol of the Socialist state.

A TIME OF TERROR

Two very different but extraordinary and fragile historic cities would now be subject to Communist management. Although the culture and history of the

Soviet Union and the People's Republic of China were substantially different—their evolution under communism would have a traumatic parallel. In both nations, decades of internal political struggle and foreign conflicts (World War I in Russia, and World War II in China) had resulted in extended periods of social instability and economic degeneration. Consequently, as Soviet and Chinese Communist governments came to power, they faced immense developmental problems on multiple fronts. Nor could they rest assured that their ascendancy would be permanent if they failed to fulfill their promise of widespread economic improvement. To accomplish such extensive changes required time. But outside Russia and China, foreign capitalist nations supported rival counterrevolutionary movements. Internally, significant segments of the domestic populace had not been avid supporters of communism.

Thus to ensure the perpetuation of their authority, and in response to foreign threats, ideological purges were instituted by the Communists to secure domestic political hegemony. This recurring facet of Communist totalitarian rule produced eras of terror that not only silenced opposition, but also suppressed common dissent and open discussions of policy. (With the fall of communism in Russia, it is now known that about 20 million people died in purges during the regimes of Lenin and Stalin. In China, equivalent figures cannot be determined, but the 1999 edition of *The Black Book of Communism* estimates that 65 million civilians have died of state-instituted repressive policies, including the Cultural Revolution—perhaps the worst of many ideological campaigns—which resulted in anarchy, terror, and the breakdown of productive accomplishment and rational social planning.) For the subject populaces, nightmares became reality. Without warning, periods of apparent openness were followed by years of oppression. Relatives, neighbors, and colleagues might suddenly become informants or disappear to be "cleansed" or "reeducated"—euphemisms for execution and deportation to forced labor camps.

For thousands of years, cities had been engines for the advancement of civilization. Their positive chemistry was based on the free flow of ideas stimulated by face-to-face exchanges that occur when people of different talents live and work in close proximity. Having decimated the urban intelligentsia, would Communist cities flourish in a climate that made civic dialogue perilous? Could societies once subjected to purging soon forget the horror? Although postrevolutionary life in Moscow and Beijing would often be characterized by noble intentions and heroic accomplishments in the face of daunting obstacles—making the benefits of modern economic development available to vast impoverished populations—the urban history of these decades must also be viewed against the backdrop of intermittent, harsh, and often capricious political terror.

A Gothic gateway in Prague. Many remarkable artifacts have been handed down from earlier generations of urban societies which, in their own time, decided to save vestiges of the past as part of the continuing life of the city. The Powder Tower, or Saint Ambrose's Gate, in Prague marks the old line of the city's otherwise vanished fortifications.

Heritage devoured. The Pantheon (1) is one of the foremost achievements in structural engineering in the history of architecture; it, like many large public monuments in ancient Rome, was built to last for ages. And indeed it has—in large part because of its conversion to a church. Most other imperial landmarks—equally astounding as architectural accomplishments—were over the centuries cannabilized for their materials. Today, only a few skeletal ruins remain, such as the massive arches of the Baths of Diocletian (2).

Adaptive reuse. Across two thousand years, the fortifications of the ancient city have been adapted in numerous instances by different generations of Romans to changing architectural tastes and vehicular circulation needs. At the Porta Pia, facing into the city center, an entry in the Mannerist style (3) was added by Michelangelo to a gateway from the imperial era.

Michelangelo's Piazza del Campidoglio. Looking up the main stairway (4) one sees a conscious fusion of Imperial-Roman and Christian-Renaissance culture. Giant sculptures from antiquity frame the entry to the piazza. A pair of buildings with matching facades flank the square. The Senator's Palace, with its campanile, has also been refashioned in a Renaissance style. Looking at the Capitoline Hill from behind (5), in the Roman Forum, the rear wall of the Senator's Palace sits upon the Imperial Roman Tablarium, which serves as the foundation for Michelangelo's masterpiece of contextual urban design.

Resurrecting the stolen cityscape. In response to the erasure of their historic capital city by the Germans during World War II, the government of Poland created one of the most comprehensive conservation bureaucracies of any nation in the world. And the Varsovians re-created Warsaw consistent with the image in their memories. Old squares were put back, lost landmarks were rebuilt to the finest detail, the ancient fortifications of Warsaw, lost for many centuries, were made to once more encircle the medieval center (1), and modern urban improvements were introduced, such as the construction of a highway underpass—built beneath the historic zone before fragile masonry streetscapes were reinstated (2).

A museum of urban change. As old buildings were reassembled, previously invisible evidence of their architectural evolution was discovered. Restorers left such conditions revealed, as a matter of public education. Thus, a smaller Gothic masonry profile is expressed along the side wall of a building enlarged in the seventeenth century, heavily damaged in World War II, and today restored (3).

Communist Warsaw. The re-created Old Town was surrounded by a modern conglomeration of mass-produced housing blocks common to cities behind the Iron Curtain (4).

Monuments of conscience. Memorials to the victims of German repression haunt the urban landscape, as in a sculpture commemorating the Warsaw Ghetto Uprising (5).

Treasures of civilization under assault. The modern megacity of Cairo holds two peerless architectural patrimonies: at its periphery, the Great Pyramids and Sphinx of Giza (1), and at its center, a medieval Muslim cityscape (2) of numerous wondrous monuments such as the Mosque of Ibn Tulun (3), a pinnacle of accomplishment in world architectural history. Uncontrolled population growth, pollution, poverty, and a culture of illegal settlement expose both of these legacies to continuous hostile environmental siege.

A conservation dilemma of daunting complexity. Less than half of the city's sewage is treated; it flows directly into the ground water table, producing acids and microbes that devour the stone foundations of monuments. Automotive and industrial air pollution render the rain caustic, thus attacking the upper parts of buildings as well. Extended poverty depletes building maintenance. Heightened population density increases the wear on structures. Deteriorated masonry eventually crumbles to the touch (5). A recent earthquake has exacerbated the damage (4).

A legacy of celebratory pinnacles.
For centuries, Moscow's architectural crown of myriad eclectic
churchtops and towers made it
distinct. The city's tradition of
architectural creativity had deep
vernacular roots, in the hundreds
of churches (2), constructed and
reconstructed as Moscow was several times destroyed and rebuilt. At
the heart of the settlement, in Red
Square, this broad cultural expression reached its formal culmination. The fantastic onion dome
turbans of Saint Basil's and the tent
roofs of commercial structures like
the Lower Trading Rows (1), as well
as the towers of the Kremlin (3),
were the epitome of a joyful and
particularly Russian architectural
accomplishment.

In 1918, with the establishment
of the Communist state, all religious institutions were banned.

Urban planning via ideology. Communist propaganda required that Moscow be modernized as a symbol of Soviet progress, and waves of prefabricated housing blocks inundated the urban landscape (4). The ambience and scale of the old city was fractured, thousands of historic structures were demolished, and surviving churches were dwarfed (5).

Shoddily constructed, the new residential towers soon deteriorated, while historic buildings decayed from decades of neglect. As Communist rule came to an end, Moscow was left with a mammoth bill of deferred repair.

Deconstruction of an unparalleled patrimony. As the Communists assumed power in 1949, they inherited one of civilization's singular urban artifacts: the vast, intact medieval cityscape of Beijing—an integrated object of environmental art whose architectural parts, such as the Forbidden City (1), were set in alignment with the poles of the Chinese cosmos.

Modernization, dogma, and the influence of anti-conservation Soviet planning advisors would cause numerous historic assets of the Chinese capital, as in Moscow, to be torn down. The broad avenues of the old city were zoned for ad hoc high-rise development (2) and the historic milieu was fractured.

The dawn of preservation? After the Cultural Revolution, and with the fall of the Gang of Four, government was reformed and a policy of architectural conservation was adopted. Off the main thoroughfares, along the city's narrow byways, dilapidated residential compounds, when restored (3), reflected the subtle and mysterious beauty of millennia of Chinese cultural development.

In commercial areas, old streetscapes of intricately carved wooden shopfronts awaited reclamation (4). In those few areas where the authorities established historic districts, the transformation was astounding (5).

The mutability of Communist governmental policy presents an uncertain future. Will the remaining vernacular beauty of historic Beijing be saved or erased in the twenty-first century?

Conservation and economic equity. In the age of wind-driven ships, the exotic tropical city of Singapore commanded a lion's share of the Asian-European trade. Yet by the end of World War II, the city's commercial vitality had faded, and poverty, illegal settlement, and economic underdevelopment cast a pall over its future.

Remarkably, by the 1990s, the island city-state had achieved one of the highest standards of living in the world and 80 percent of Singapore's families owned the place where they lived. But this single-minded effort to create economic justice for its inhabitants also resulted in unrestrained development that replaced the city's colonial commercial center with a ubiquitous contemporary urban environment (1, 2).

Saving a heritage of intercultural synergy. In response to a decline in tourism, as well as the outcry of its citizens, Singapore's highly professional and authoritarian government enacted a comprehensive program of conservation. In several undeveloped areas, surviving architecture reflected a fertile cross-cultural exchange among Chinese, European, Indian, and Malay neighbors. Blocks of godowns (2) and shophouses (4) were an amalgam of the various architectural traditions embodied in a diversity of religious structures (3, 5). Today, these districts and landmarks are disconnected islands of history in the urban landscape.

The sculptural cityscape. For hundreds of years the buildings of Vienna were beautifully designed, handsomely carved, and thickly embellished with sculpture. In the Altstadt (2), throughout the Ringstrasse (1), and as Vienna expanded during its industrialization, the amassed structures of the city constituted a remarkable collection of fine art.

3

The art of public housing. The residential projects of Red Vienna were some of the finest public housing built in the twentieth century—conceived in a modern architectural style, yet contextual in their siting, character, and details—and a continuation of Vienna's tradition of architectural excellence. 3: Karl Marx Hof by Karl Ehn, 1926–1930.

4

After the bombing of World War II. During the recovery the most significant damaged buildings in the Altstadt were rebuilt, but many others were reconstructed with plain stucco facades (4). Plaques recorded the date of destruction and the date of repair (as to the right of the doorway). Set within profusely adorned streetscapes, these bare elevations were permanent testimonials to the desolation of war.

Denuding the continuum of beauty. Further reduction of the loveliness of the cityscape occurred in the postwar era due to municipal housing policies that, while supporting the interior rehabilitation of historic structures, often sanctioned the stripping of their facades. Recent enactment of conservation protection zones will, to some degree, forestall the continuation of such practices. Yet many richly articulated buildings and whole blockfronts (5) remain unprotected.

5

Historic Amsterdam. Over centuries, a diverse environmental harmony has been achieved with a simple palette of repetitive urban elements (1, 2). Canals, bridges, trees, bricks, and a multitude of narrow buildings with eclectic roofs are interwoven in a uniquely beautiful urban milieu.

Customs of social equity.
The city's long tradition of constructing socially assisted housing reached a pinnacle of creative architectural achievement in the period prior to World War II. Amsterdam School housing, like the residential complexes of Red Vienna, were an early form of contextual modernism—a reconciliation of contemporary design with the building culture of the historic city. 3: P. L. Takstraat complex by P. L. Kramer, 1919–1923.

Stadsherstel. A unique feature of contemporary conservation in Amsterdam, preservation-minded social housing societies have restored hundreds of historic structures. One of the foremost of these is Stadsherstel, whose mission is to reclaim old areas of modest buildings as subsidized residences. The restoration of corner buildings and pairs of structures (4, 5) has a magnified impact in renewing urban areas.

ATHENS

The beautiful city lost. When first built up after the founding of the Greek nation-state in the mid-1800s, modern Athens was a graceful low-scale environment of classically inspired vernacular architecture set in tune with the stylistic traditions of ancient Greek buildings (1).

The lovely city soon was subsumed by a vast agglomeration of shoddy speculative development, urban sprawl, illegal settlement, and industrial and automotive pollution (2). In the midst of this disorder, the Acropolis ruins (3) and archaeological zones of the classical city became isolated islands of enlightenment.

The Eternal Hill. Today, after 2,500 years, the remnants of the Acropolis (4: east elevation of the Parthenon), though recently rehabilitated to the highest modern conservation standards, will inevitably continue to suffer hastened deterioration due to the city's highly acidic atmospheric pollution.

The question to be posed when the rain in Athens no longer melts stone involves the repatriation of the Parthenon sculptures from museums in foreign countries. Most of the surviving sculpture from the east pediment (5: detail), as well as parts of the Panathenaic frieze, are currently in the British Museum.

The city of beautiful parts. Often described as a collection of villages, across its history London was built up and governed as numerous separate parts, frequently of great architectural beauty and cohesion unto themselves. This was especially true in its numerous speculative housing estates (2, 3), which were models of urban civility and graceful design. Although the organization of its street plan was somewhat chaotic, the city was an extended lovely maze, and distinctly recognizable in its spirit of place and architectural culture. 1: St. Paul's Cathedral.

The fractured milieu. Damage from bombing in World War II generally occurred in the area of London east of St. Paul's—thus leaving intact the mass of the city's beauty. But postwar development fractured the urban environment. Numerous blocky modern towers were built throughout the cityscape (4, 5), looming over graceful old squares, blockfronts, and landmarks.

The evolution of the artistic cityscape. Over centuries, French rulers would attempt to refashion their capital in accordance with Renaissance urban planning ideals. Numerous institutions would be created to advance classical architectural thinking. Various monarchs would create models of Renaissance urbanism through speculative real estate development (2: the Place Dauphine, 1606). A central state bureacracy, the Royal Building Administration, would establish a new method of urban organization in several large projects at the heart of the growing city (1: the Place de la Concorde).

A palace of the people.
As the city expanded due
to industrialization, a
refined vernacular archi-
tecture was inculcated in
building codes and cul-
tural institutions such as
the Ecole des Beaux Arts.
    The physical elements
of Paris were stylistically
knit together in an extensive environmental sculp-
ture of creative visual
variation (3, 4).

**Halting the erosion of
beauty.** Postwar modern-
ization eroded the outer
neighborhoods of the
urban sculpture, and tall
buildings threatened to
rupture the city's mag-
nificent vistas. Even
when new development
was built at a lower scale,
it often disrupted the
existing milieu (5: the
mall and rail hub of Les
Halles). Thus, the center
of Paris was designated as
one of the largest urban
conservation zones in
the world.

VENICE

The artifact in ecological balance. The beauty of Venice is inextricably tied to the natural environment that surrounds it.

With the demise of the Republic, environmental vigilance faltered and eventually stopped. Floods in 1966 awakened the world to Venice's peril. Today, as a result of an international conservation campaign, and at great cost and effort, the city's ecological balance with its natural setting has been reestablished.

The architecture of the Piazza San Marco (1) and typical canalscapes (2) embody an unusual fusion of Arabic, Byzantine, and Italian Romanesque, Medieval, and Renaissance architectural traditions.

1

2

The threat of social disequilibrium. The massing of buildings on its islands also reflected Venice's social organization around the campos of parish churches. Such plazas, with their communal wells (3), also functioned as cisterns for collecting rainwater. But the traditional social life of the city is quickly eroding, as a tourist economy displaces the services that sustain residential life. Venice has always required constant building upkeep due to the continuous assault of heavily salinated atmospheric moisture (4: the reestablished municipal program of canal drainage and foundation repair). But who will maintain the city's buildings if Venetians no longer live in Venice? 5: Typical condition of accrued facade decay.

Preserving the city of change. In the nineteenth and twentieth centuries, New York emerged as a world capital of commerce and culture and it quickly expanded in its horizontal and vertical dimensions. The city became a behemoth of urban infrastructure and a dense conglomeration of tall buildings.

As skyscraper technology developed, huge multi-story structures sprouted up within the old urban fabric. Today, conservation of the city's diverse architectural heritage involves a conflict with development potential, as inhabitants seek to protect a quality of life inherent to environments of a lower scale (2: Upper East Side Historic District).

Preservation groups have proliferated in neighborhoods across the metropolis, and numerous older areas have been designated historic districts (1: SoHo Cast Iron Historic District). In several cases, the continuance of historic structures was enabled by the transfer of development rights, increasing the disparity of size between old landmarks and adjacent new towers (3: South Street Seaport Historic District).

4

The evolving patrimony. While the practice of conservation has increasingly become part of the cultural ethos of the city, saving its most significant architectural achievement, its legacy of great skyscrapers, requires a reconciliation with visions of the future. Several great skyscrapers have been listed as individual monuments (5: The Chrysler Building in midtown Manhattan). Numerous others have been demolished. Meanwhile, the cityscape continues to ascend en masse, largely the aesthetic product of the vagaries of the commercial real estate market (4: Downtown Manhattan and the twin towers of the World Trade Center).

5

The city of aesthetic extremes. As one of the few Japanese cities spared the fire-bombing of World War II, historic Kyoto holds a precious legacy of delicately constructed, medieval wooden urban culture. As in Beijing, postwar modernization has fractured the cityscape and caused the demolition of numerous old buildings along its main avenues (2). In recent decades, a chaotic contemporary environmental aesthetic has emerged, typical of modern Japanese cities (3). Yet numerous serene old monuments (1: Temple of Higashi Hogan-ji in downtown Kyoto) and several largely intact historic neighborhoods—with building parts of bamboo, paper, straw, and clay—continue to survive in a splintered milieu.

3

Saving the vanishing historic ambience? While the landmarks of Kyoto have for some time been protected by law and custom, only since 1995 has an effort been made to save old neighborhoods of vernacular building construction. Several small preservation areas have been created (4: the Kamigamo Shakémachi District; 5: the Sagano Toriimoto District), evidence of a highly refined architectural culture, which, until the second half of the twentieth century, was still multivarious in its beauty and knit together as a coherent urban whole, unique to world civilization.

4

5

Landmarks of conscience. In the second half of the twentieth century a new kind of urban monument began to appear: sites whose history raised questions of social morality, sometimes of implicit communal self-criticism. The architectural shapes and spatial characteristics of such places are frequently atypical and sometimes shocking in the cityscape. 1: The Kaiser Wilhelm Memorial Church incorporates the bombed ruins of one of Berlin's former major landmarks with a minimal modern structure to create a permanent reminder of the horror of war. 2: The vacant lot of the *Topography of Terror* marks the location during the Third Reich of the offices of the Gestapo and Secret State Police. The emptiness of the lot, situated in the center of a major European capital, implies that the cruelties inflicted by these institutions have rendered the land unsuitable for normal use.

Symbols of social values. While setting aside tracts of archaeological value is one of the earliest types of conservation actions in cities, the recent recovery of the Aztec Pyramid Site in Mexico City (2) has more complex connotations. The great temple had been leveled by the Conquistadors as an act of cultural repression, stones from the Aztec structures were cannibalized in constructing the colonial capital, and several important new architectural symbols were raised within the immediate vicinity of the old center (1: The Cathedral of Mexico). With the discovery of the Coyolxauhqui stone (below) in the late 1970s, old colonial structures were removed in order to let the pyramid site reassume a central space in the life of the city. An ancient Indian heritage had been recognized by modern Mexican society as having primacy over the colonial patrimony.

The layers of history revealed. Monuments from across the turbulent history of Jerusalem are allowed to exist at their original ground levels in the restored Old Jewish Quarter. The tops of columns from the old Roman Cardo rise up out of a depression whose bottom marks the approximate street grade in A.D. 300. Once below, the Byzantine marketplace continues as a subterranean shopping mall and museum. New modern housing is constructed on platforms that leave the archaeological material undisturbed and is designed to reflect historic vernacular architectural forms. The city has become a living museum.

COMMUNIST MOSCOW: THE CITY
DESTROYED BY DOGMA

An extraordinary period of societal invention had arrived. As the newly instituted Communist regime strove to correct the centuries-old dehumanizing exploitation inflicted on Russia's underclass of factory workers and farmers, it would make sweeping reconfigurations to the physical, economic, and social identity of one of the world's largest nations—and attempt to achieve this transformation overnight.

First, the seat of government was established in the Kremlin, in the center of old Moscow, as a symbol of historical continuity. And in 1918, in the midst of changes in many other spheres, a remarkable landmarks restoration program was instituted by Vladimir Ilyich Lenin.

In the decades prior to the revolution, as in the industrial nations of Europe, a movement had begun among Russian architects, historians, and artists to enact national legal protections for ancient monuments. As the Communists took residence in the Kremlin, Lenin was approached with this idea. Some historians interpret his embrace of preservation as purely pragmatic, a desire to avoid unnecessary destruction of badly needed material assets. As the program unfolded, however, the architects and historians in charge used their mandate not just to stop unwarranted demolition of serviceable structures but to painstakingly reclaim numerous badly deteriorated important landmarks of the city.

The directive issued under Lenin by the Executive Committee of the Council of Workers' and Soldiers' Deputies is a call to arms to save the past: "Citizens, the old masters have gone, leaving behind a vast heritage. Now it belongs to all the people! Citizens, take care of this inheritance . . . do not even touch one stone, protect the monuments, the old buildings, articles, documents—all this is your history, your pride. Remember, all this is the soil from which will grow your new people's art."

Indeed it was a revolution. No systematized government effort had before existed to reclaim the landmarks of the cityscape, which had been destroyed and rebuilt, destroyed and rebuilt, numerous times across its history. As modern conservationists now attempted to recover the most ancient buildings of Moscow, they discovered that their hasty and unscientific reconstruction in earlier periods had often been several times erroneous, piling mistake upon mistake. Dilapidated crumbling monuments frequently were a puzzle of misaligned parts. In order to reassemble such buildings correctly, extensive research was required and the Department on Museums and Preservation of Ancient and Artistic Monuments established a notably high standard of investigative scholarship, sometimes studying for more than a decade before reconstructing the most antiquated of important structures.

During this era about 10,000 buildings were registered, and 3,000 were restored and rehabilitated. Many of these were churches, which, as some of the oldest masonry structures in the city, were of great significance to the architectural history of Moscow. It was a painstaking and heroic effort, much of which was soon to be undone. For over the decades of Communist rule after Lenin's death, seasons of destruction randomly followed seasons of adaptive reuse and conservation. And bite by bite, large parts of the heritage of the city were devoured.

This pattern unfolded gradually. At the dawn of the Communist era, the country was burning with new and idealistic thinking for the great postrevolutionary experiment, and extraordinary things seemed possible. First, basic needs such as restarting the process of industrialization, redistributing agricultural land, stabilizing social institutions, and erecting nationwide infrastructure had immediate priority. Over several decades, with single-minded effort and working with minimal resources, Russia was gradually transformed, sometimes at a terrible price: the collectivization of agriculture, for instance, when obstructed by the peasants themselves, was compelled by the use of political repression, at a cost of 8 to 10 million lives. By the later years of Lenin's rule, as the quality of basic living was raised throughout the nation, the means became available for urban reconstruction, and a small number of extraordinary buildings were built.

Moscow had become the crucible for numerous intellectual factions espousing different architectural visions for the new Socialist society. One group in particular had come to international attention: the Russian Constructivists, whose drawings had been exhibited in several European cities and in New York. The Constructivists, along with a handful of other modern architects, would develop a minimal architectural aesthetic of primary forms and sparse decoration composed in expressive angular compositions. The results, for the international avant-garde, were riveting. From the outside, it appeared that the social revolution had fostered a new era in architecture.

But the built reality did not fulfill the theoretical promise. Like early modern masterworks in other countries, the unusual forms of the Constructivists were not readily adaptable to mass construction; often they were highly labor-intensive and costly to fabricate. In Russia, mastery of the technologies of industrialized construction lagged behind that of more developed societies, hence these problems were greater. Built with meager budgets and poorly maintained, Constructivist buildings soon deteriorated. And there was a further problem. While the Russian modernists hoped to create an emancipated architecture for their comrades in the new Socialist state, the newly urbanized peasants longed for housing that looked like palaces. Constructivism was most appreciated by the Russian intelligentsia. This association would contribute to the demise of this remarkable advance in architectural creativity. An aesthetic that might have given a revolutionary face to the new society was abandoned, and came to exist primarily on paper.

In the months preceding his death, Lenin had written a testament recommending that Joseph Stalin be removed from his post as general secretary of the central committee because of his capricious exercise of power. This testament was suppressed and never acted upon. The ultimate goal of many Communist revolutionaries had been to create a classless international society in which property was owned in common by a stateless proletariat, a social structure aspiring to ultimate freedom for all individuals. The development of a powerful centralized government was meant to be a necessary but temporary step in a process of evolution. With the ascent of Stalin to the dictatorship of the Soviet Union, the coalescence of power that had begun under Lenin would now become a period of totalitarianism, extreme nationalism, and ideological suppression, enveloping all facets of Russian life. The forced-labor camps soon were filled, the Great Terror commenced, and restoration of monuments ceased.

The collectivization of Soviet architecture began with the abolition of all factional groups and the creation of the Union of Soviet Architects. An official state architectural style called Socialist Realism was declared, and throughout the Soviet Union and the nations of the Iron Curtain, architects and buildings were to conform. Like Hitler and Mussolini, Stalin had selected a modernist-historical architectural aesthetic, characterized by massive scale and classical Roman antecedents, to express the omnipotence of the totalitarian state.

Until this moment, Moscow had been only partially transformed under Communism. Yet as Leon Trotsky observed: "The capital plays as dominating a role in the revolution as though it concentrated in itself the will of the nation, because the capital expresses most clearly and thoroughly the fundamental tendencies of the new society." As a result, the master plan of 1935 called for Moscow to industrialize, expand, modernize. It would increase its population from 2 million to more than 11 million inhabitants, and would be altered from a low-scale historic townscape to a metropolis dominated by multistory constructions. While the basic historical layout of radial streets connecting to intermittent concentric avenues would be honored, the old routes would be greatly widened. In several areas, this would result in extensive destruction of the historic urban fabric. Furthermore, the new boulevards and public spaces would be lined with mammoth structures in the Socialist Realism style. This abrupt increase in scale would cleave the remnants of the old neighborhoods. A propaganda pamphlet of the period declared: "An army of architects has conquered the city. They demolish the one-story slums over which those who dreamed of 'originality' had shed tears."

Meanwhile, the Communist regime was confronted with the affection that much of the existing population felt for the familiar historic landmarks of the city. Although the peak of the Russian renaissance had passed and numerous artists and intellectuals would be sanctioned, be expelled, or leave during the Communist era, Moscow still continued to be a major center of ballet, opera, and symphonic music, and the old cityscape contained proud memories of a faded glory. Yet one particular intellectual group condoned an erasure of the city's architectural legacy. Like many of their counterparts in the industrialized world, modernist architects, including the Constructivists—engulfed in a theoretical war with traditionalists, and in their idealistic fervor to create a new architecture for the emerging society of broader social equity—argued that the old cityscape should be swept away. In the ideological gamesmanship of the time, the Communists used this implicit sanction to justify their desire to transform Moscow. Ironically, the modern avant-garde did not benefit from their tacit approval of the government's plans. The Communists rejected Russia's architectural achievements, both the new and the old, and thereby ensured that a vast amount of ugliness would blight contemporary Moscow.

Although the country had been chilled by Stalin's purges and political terrorism, a handful of architect-planners spoke out in opposition. Given an

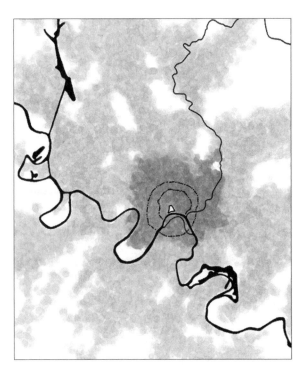

The contemporary Moscow conurbation · Dark gray tone shows the built-up area by 1900. Pale gray tone shows the approximate built-up area by 2000. Dotted lines indicate the ring roads and small white triangle indicates the Kremlin.

absence of the protections of due process and the unpredictable harshness of the authorities, to criticize the Party line was to brave incalculable jeopardy. Nonetheless, the dissenting architects advised selective road widening to avoid the eradication of precious historical assets; they also recommended locating the bulk of new development outside the old core, which was in any case too small to absorb the increased population of the modern city. They deplored the damage to historic properties. "Reconstruction demands decisive measures. Surgery is required; but when you need a surgeon, you do not call for the executioner." (This was a reference to planners like the French architect Le Corbusier, who espoused the total destruction of historic Moscow: "Everything in Moscow must be redone after everything first has been destroyed.") The dissent of this small group of native architect-planners made it clear for the historical record that the path to destruction was a deliberate choice, disregarding options that could still achieve the city's modernization in a reasonable way.

Throughout Europe, many of the beautiful historic capitals had already seen the need for compromise to preserve centuries of culture. Separation of the modern and ancient aspects of the city allowed the integrity of each to be respected. In Moscow, however, political ideology coalesced in support of the obliteration of Russian cultural accomplishment. The cityscape was to be purged.

A study by the Russian Academy of Architecture has estimated that between 1924 and 1940, about 50 percent of the historically significant buildings of Moscow—including more than two hundred notable churches and several principal streetscapes, holding a rich accrual of major buildings—were demolished by the Soviet government. Ponderous Socialist Realist structures replaced the landmarks that had been lost. Then, in midprocess, World War II commenced and drained the nation of resources for new construction.

Afterward, although recovery from the war further strained national assets (over 1,700 Soviet cities and towns had been destroyed), Stalin soon proposed that eight towers of unprecedented size be erected to dominate the Moscow skyline. Dispersed throughout the city, these symbols of the Communist state—known stylistically as Stalinist Gothic—oddly, assumed a form reminiscent of the set-back, historicized, corporate skyscrapers of capitalist New York. The Soviet towers were luxurious, with rich appointments and costly finishes, and they were gigantic: the complex for Lomonosov State University, for example, held all the teaching facilities for a complete institution of higher education. It was more than one hundred times greater in mass than Saint Basil's—seven times higher at its pinnacle, and fifteen times wider across its base. Ironically, like the czars before them, the Communists were building bastions of imperial luxury, largely for the use of the Party elite, among whom influential architects often lived opulently. All this in a nation afflicted by widespread privation and political repression.

The great towers further splintered the cityscape and introduced an extreme disparity of scale. So far as the aesthetic relationship of its parts was concerned, the metropolis had ceased to exist as a whole. A chaotic disorder had been introduced, and saving the continuity of the historic city would no longer be a restraint to disconnected development.

Nevertheless, the buildings of the Stalinist era were well constructed and their historicized styles bore some relationship to the architectural continuum that had preceded the advent of communism. And beneath the chaos of the city, the stations of an extraordinary new subway system, adorned with heroic sculptures, crystal chandeliers, marble floors, and high-speed wooden escalators, were palaces for the people. The subway was perhaps Stalin's most useful legacy to the metropolis. The next generation of Communist structures would have fewer compensations.

By the time of Stalin's death in 1953 the eighth great tower—the Palace of the Soviets—had progressed only as far as its foundations. It was never completed. Nikita Khrushchev would renounce the cruelty of Stalin's regime— although he himself had been a zealous participant at the time—dissolve the Union of Soviet Architects, abandon Socialist Realism and Stalinist Gothic, and convert the concrete basement of the Palace of the Soviets into the world's largest outdoor heated swimming pool. Khrushchev's reforms also redefined architecture as a technocratic tool to advance the production goals of the ministries of the enormous Soviet bureaucracy. A government document outlining the new direction was titled "Measures for the Further Industrialization, Improvement in Quality and Cost Reduction of Construction." Architecture would still serve propagandistic purposes, but not through aesthetic design. New buildings would showcase the capabilities of Soviet industrialization, as legions of state apartment blocks were constructed to alleviate the massive housing shortage.

As the new social housing program commenced, preservationists hoped that Khrushchev, if in discrediting Stalin, might reestablish the conservation program of Lenin. It was not to be. During the Khrushchev era, an estimated 10,000 churches were closed in the Soviet Union. Many of them were subsequently eradicated.

Throughout this latest period of dramatic urban change, Moscow had little voice in determining its fate. Cities in the Soviet Union were not allowed either to establish or to coordinate developmental priorities. The administrative structure of the Communist government delegated authority for different sectors—such as housing, public health, mass transportation, and education— to separate national ministries. Production quotas were established by the

Central Committee. In urban planning, local city councils were responsible for the integration of sectoral initiatives, but their role was advisory. Individual ministries, even when they were located in Moscow, were powerful fiefdoms of autonomous power that determined the destiny of cities from a narrow perspective.

The nationwide goal of providing decent housing for all citizens was admirable, but the task was colossal. The single-minded resolve to speedily erect large amounts of housing resulted in a lowering of construction standards. In an effort to reduce site-specific labor, state housing was prefabricated in factories and assembled on location. Inside, standardized minimal amenities were cheaply built. Outside, the hand craftsmanship needed to fuse together the factory parts was insufficient. When they were first raised, the long rows of radiant new blocks appeared to be a miracle. The seeming accomplishment of such a vast harvest of good under Khrushchev's premiership raised expectations of similar productivity from the leaders to follow, and further waves of mass housing ensued. In the 1990s, as whole generations of state apartment buildings began to disintegrate, the calamity was revealed. A huge percentage of the homes of Moscow would require massive interior reconditioning, extensive exterior rehabilitation, and in some cases total gutting. Some experts estimate that as much as 50 percent of the city's current housing will require total interior reconstruction by the year 2010.

In the inner city, it became the policy to fill in empty lots with large modern housing blocks, regardless of where the lots were located or whether the new buildings related to the scale and ambience of existing neighborhoods. When such disparities occurred, no attempt was made to moderate the resulting disproportionate relationships. The ministries that built the housing were filling production quotas; the larger environmental character of the city was not their responsibility. The cityscape of Moscow was fractured to a degree rarely matched across the world.

Meanwhile, the prerevolutionary housing stock of the city, some of which had been of excellent quality when first built, was not being adequately preserved. Throughout Moscow, for decades, proper maintenance was deferred from one regime to another. Although many landmarks had been adapted for new uses during the Communist period, many others, including surviving places of worship, had been abandoned and these were experiencing severe decay.

As the Soviet Union was dismantled and Communist rule came to an end, systemic economic failures were revealed. Today the cities and urban landmarks of Russia languish under the load of a mammoth unpaid maintenance deficit. Rampant organized crime attacks the very fiber of the city's well-being. Widely felt economic failures make government vulnerable to corruption.

People still must stand in line to buy scarce commodities. A massive state apparatus remains a labyrinth defying public accountability. Can an urban planning and conservation bureaucracy—the recently created Administration for Defending Monuments of History and Culture—be effective in such a climate?

Outside the hidden rooms of government, preservation has become a grassroots populist movement, and the very church that was destroyed to make way for the construction of Stalin's unrealized Palace of the Soviets is being raised anew. The rebuilding of the Cathedral of Christ the Savior is a symbol of Moscow's desire to reclaim its past. But all across the metropolis, the volume of urban injury and desperately needed repair is appalling. The city of wondrous church pinnacles had been brutalized by its rulers.

COMMUNIST BEIJING: THE CITY DENUDED BY DOGMA

In 1949, as the Communists assumed authority in Beijing, China was even less developed as an industrialized society than Russia had been in 1918. For more than a decade, the foreign power that had most reliably supported the Chinese Communists was the Soviet Union. As the Cold War began, a substantial flow of financial aid and teams of Russian experts were sent to the newly formed People's Republic. By 1960, the year of their recall, more than 1,200 technical advisers were involved in charting policy within the ministries of China's government. Especially in the early life of the new nation, when Chinese technical capability was at a minimum, the influence of Soviet experts was considerable. In the area of city planning, members of the same Soviet system that had developed the anticonservation plan that was destroying historic Moscow helped plan the future of Beijing. At that time in the city, there were only fifteen Chinese architects—educated professionals who could speak with authority about Chinese architectural culture and the planning of modern cities, and who could offer a vision different from that of their foreign advisers.

After a period in which conditions were stabilized, longer-range strategic thinking began. In 1953 the first master plan for Beijing, as well as the first five-year plan for the country's development, was unveiled. The slogan for the five-year plan was "Learn Everything from the Soviet Union." The "Draft on Reconstructing and Expanding Beijing Municipality" had six major points: Beijing should be a socialist city; it should be the center of national government; it should be a major industrial hub; new water resources to support industrial expansion should be developed; its new modern road system should follow the existing road network; and "the major danger is an extreme respect for old architecture, such that it constricts our perspective of development." Another planning group, which included the most widely respected local architects, argued that the governmental and industrial expansion of Beijing should occur outside the historic city, which should be preserved as a major artifact of Chinese civilization. But the technical expertise of the Soviet advisers prevailed.

Over the next thirty years, although several other plans would be developed and no single plan would be implemented in its entirety, the basic goals of the Soviet-influenced Draft on Reconstructing Beijing would shape the destiny of the metropolis. The city had few water resources, yet it would develop industries requiring heavy water use and expand residential water demand as the population grew tenfold. Increased traffic brought about by this expansion in population produced heavy levels of automotive pollution, which combined with high levels of industrial pollution to create an acid rain that melted the stone carvings of the landmarks of the city. (The resulting degree of air pollution in Beijing is extreme. In 1996, and even after the government had initiated a program to lessen pollution, the industrialized outskirts of the city presented an eerie landscape: factories spewed forth billowing clouds of smog; the leaves of trees, blades of grass, every building and object in the the surrounding landscape was covered by a blanket of gray dust; bicyclists pulling heavily loaded carts wore cloth masks as protection from the shroud of contaminants.)

In order to open a network of roadways, the hundreds of memorial arches, or pailou, which had invested the city's thoroughfares with a distinctive character, were removed. Ancient bridges were widened and their carved marble railings destroyed. The great gateways to the city were torn down. While the grid of the historic streetscape would be honored, thus saving an important element of the city's character, the low-scale profile of the traditional city was disrupted as major avenues were zoned for multiple-story modern buildings. The result of this policy was to create a schizophrenic center where major roads were lined ad hoc by myriad bulky contemporary structures towering over neighboring low-scale historic environments. These vectors of commercial jumble and undistinguished buildings cut wide swaths across the cityscape. In a historic environment that was the ultimate example of a metropolis governed by aesthetic rules, the environmental cacophony of contemporary development unregulated in terms of urban design was a harsh intrusion of alien values. While the Forbidden City, the Temple of Heaven, and many other landmarks would be restored, like Moscow, modern Beijing became a fractured environment of unrelated elements.

Also as in Russia, individual ministries became separate fiefdoms competing for power. In areas such as the development of housing, transportation, and industry, the objectives set by the central government were pursued as isolated agendas. The municipal officers of Beijing were not authorized to integrate the actions of these more powerful national ministries. As a result, housing was commonly built with inadequate support services for the inhabitants—for example, people were moved to areas without mass-transit connections to their workplaces, without sufficient schools and day-care centers, and without medical facilities.

During the Cultural Revolution (1966–1969) and the reign of the Gang of Four (ending in 1976), professionals working in planning and land-use regulation were removed. Comprehensive city-planning was disavowed. Arbitrary rules—for example, that no existing building could be replaced by new construction—led to the siting of industrial plants wherever open lots occurred, even in the middle of residential districts. Over a thousand of such factories were erected. New construction had to be carried out at the lowest possible cost, and established building standards were abandoned. Protection of historic assets was considered ideologically incorrect. Temples in particular were looted and many of China's movable artworks and artifacts were destroyed. The Cultural Revolution became an indiscriminate purge of culture itself.

THE DESTRUCTION OF THE WALLS OF BEIJING

Perhaps most damaging to the singular character of the ancient city was the gradual erasure, across the 1950s, of the mammoth walls that once surrounded it. In no other instance in urban history had such giant fortifications been constructed as an integral part of the design of an immense metropolis. In themselves, like the great pyramids at Giza and Teotihuacan, the walls of Beijing were an extraordinary monument of world civilization. As an integrated component of a vast urban composition, they were unparalleled.

When the age-old enframement of walls and gateways was destroyed in order to build a ring of highways and a subway (completed in 1985), Beijing lost a singular opportunity to reconcile the ancient city and the contemporary metropolis. The old fortifications not only established the basic geometry of the urban composition of Beijing but were of such a giant scale and massive presence that they might have served as a strong counterpoint to the larger buildings of the modern city. In these great bastions, built in confluence with the enduring geometries of the planet, had existed the possibility of a compelling symbiosis between the historic capital and the modern structures of Beijing's future.

In the early days of Communist rule, the city's local architects had foreseen this possibility and argued on its behalf before the walls were replaced in order to expand the city's transport infrastructure. Because of the nationalization of property, the same upgrading of the city's movement system would have been possible, had the land bordering the walls been allocated for this purpose instead. It is telling that in the 1980s the official policy of the Communist

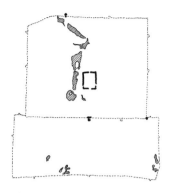

BEIJING: MING AND
CHING DYNASTIES

IMPERIAL ROME

BYZANTINE
CONSTANTINOPLE

Preserving the great walls of urban civilization · The ancient cities of Beijing, Rome, and Constantinople, with thin dotted lines showing the extent of the destruction of walls, and heavy dotted lines marking segments of the fortifications preserved as part of the continuing contemporary metropolis. · In Beijing, the walls surrounding the Forbidden City have been saved, but only three small fragments have been preserved of the city's outer bulwarks. (*All drawn at the same scale.*)

regime was to admit how grievous and unnecessary the destruction of this critical element of the old city's fabric had been—particularly because the advent of Communism had given the government control of all the properties of the city. In the reformulation of Tiananmen Square we see in microcosm what might have been achieved across the whole metropolis.

Early in the reconstruction of Beijing a new governmental center was created at the heart of the city (1954–1960). Here planners revised the progression leading to the Forbidden City, removing several historic buildings and expanding a wide public plaza that still observed the ancient compositional rule of symmetry around the central axis. Large modern governmental buildings frame three sides of the large space, which on its northern border continues to be defined by five marble bridges spanning a stream and leading to five arched openings in a thick historic wall crowned by an ornate Qing pavilion. The new architecture is clumsy, and scarcely comparable in refinement to the ancient structures. But the new space is dynamic and charged with historical meaning. A giant portrait of Mao hangs on the ancient fortifications overlooking the square and embodying the intersection of China's past and future.

In its formal and symbolic reconciliation of old and the new, Communist Tiananmen Square shows what the cityscape might have become had its perimeter walls been conserved and the area around them zoned for modern development. As in Rome, the life of the city would have pulsed through numerous breaches in the thick stone barriers. Tall modern towers manifesting the industrial empowerment of the contemporary nation-state would have been juxtaposed by the equally massive bulwarks of the ancient civilization.

Beijing could have become one of the few modern-historic conglomerations to generate a comprehensible spatial and psychological topology, allowing the new settlement and the old one to coexist with integrity. Sadly, however, instead of embodying a unique rapprochement of the past and future cities, much of the fabric of contemporary Beijing has become a place too familar in the current world, a place that has embraced mediocrity and exemplifies a widespread failure in modern urban development. As the stones of the ancient walls fell, a special opportunity was lost forever.

SAVING THE HUTONGS AND COURTYARD HOUSES

Prior to the Cultural Revolution, the Chinese Communist Party had begun to rethink its culture of governance. In the 1960s, a political break with the Soviet Union led to the withdrawal of Russian technical aid. Unfortunately, before reforms could be implemented, the Cultural Revolution produced an era of havoc. Afterward, in the 1980s, planning was reinstituted, and the work of national ministries was finally coordinated. Officials realized that the policies that had built Beijing into an industrial center were in conflict with the tolerances of the natural environment, so a long-range plan to reduce heavy industry and industrial pollution was initiated. The future of the metropolis was

The contemporary conurbation of Beijing · In 1950 the historic feudal city was essentially intact, holding a population of about 4 million people. · By 1995, the built-up area (gray tone) had expanded to accommodate about 12.4 million inhabitants. Except for the partial remains of three gateways, the great city walls (dotted lines) were demolished. Many extraordinary monuments survived, but the historic urban fabric of Beijing's courtyard houses and commercial structures remained imperiled. Ultimately, will this singular artifact of civilization largely be erased? (*Both drawings at the same scale.*)

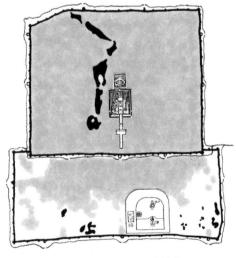

BEIJING IN 1950

reconsidered from a less ideological perspective. The isolation of China from non-Communist developmental trends was ended. Internationally, the new global economy had demonstrated the vital function of cities as the birthplaces of innovation. Beijing's role as a national center of administration and culture, as a magnet for world tourism, and as an inculcator of creative thinking was recognized as the new goal for the metropolis. Preservation of the heritage of the city was integral to these functions, and sophisticated landmark conservation laws were instituted on paper.

These new planning and conservation regulations were, implicitly, a correction of the mistakes of the past. In 1982, under a Cultural-Asset Protection Law, landmarks were established at different levels of importance. Beijing had 35 assets of national significance, 174 of municipal significance, and 854 of value at the county level. The government instituted 187 developmental control zones around national and municipal landmarks. Two other statutes were

BEIJING IN 1995

aimed at protecting the character of historic environments: the 1985 Regulation on Building Heights and the 1987 Land-Use and Height Controls for the Old City. The combined effect of these overlapping regulations was to control the character and quality of all development in the Old City of Beijing.

The Cultural-Asset Protection Areas conserved the style and exact form of designated areas like the Forbidden City, so that nothing new could be built in such places. In areas of Beijing where the general historic character of a neighborhood was intact, the government proposed to regulate the spatial density of settlement and the architectural style, height, volume, and design of new buildings, so that the ambience of such historic districts would be maintained. In parts of the metropolis where numerous historic landmarks existed but were scattered, the design of new construction would be controlled according to its proximity to important historic buildings; this would ensure that the surrounding urban context related sympathetically to historic assets. Finally, areas immediately adjacent to these historic zones were zoned so that an architectural transition might be established between lower-scale historic areas and multi-story modern structures.

This assemblage of regulations mirrored conceptually the laws that Paris and Warsaw applied to new development in or near their historic districts. The institution of such policies in Beijing would be timely. In several locations, low-scale vernacular neighborhoods which retained the character of the imperial city were under threat of invasion by modern development. Through the new laws these vestiges of old Beijing could be saved.

The low-scale historic districts of Beijing were not found on the major avenues, which had already been redeveloped. But off the bustling boulevards of the old grid, giant midblock areas were broken down by small lanes and narrow passageways called *hutongs*. Many of these less-frequented side streets could hardly accommodate a single motor vehicle. Along the hutongs, in both the residential areas of the old Inner City and in the commercial zones of the old Outer City, a world of handcrafted architecture still existed, the product of the centuries-old Chinese building tradition. That these neighborhoods had survived, nestled in corners of the fast-developing contemporary capital, was attributable to the fact that these old shops, and particularly the old residences of princes, court officials, and affluent merchants, had been adapted to the needs of the Communist proletariat.

According to the traditions of the ancient capital, residences were composed of several single-story structures organized around quadrangular courtyards and aligned on the compass points, with privacy secured by a frame of walls. The modest house of a merchant or physician, for instance, might be composed of a single quadrangle and three or four structures. The house of a prince could incorporate seven or nine quadrangles, with buildings along the sides of each courtyard linked by canopied passageways. In the homes of princes and former emperors, sizable gardens with pavilions and ponds were constructed within the walls. This was a private world in which rooms could safely open up to interior gardens for sunlight and air, and the sounds, sights, and fragrances of nature. Covered verandas lined the quadrangles, making a transition between inside and outside. During inclement weather, elaborately carved screen walls sheathed with oiled paper let in light to interior spaces. In warmer seasons, doors and windows were opened so that interior spaces flowed into the garden. Like the Forbidden City and Beijing as a whole, each house observed the rules of Chinese geomancy and balanced the forces of yin and yang to attain a compositional serenity.

During the Communist era, although some courtyard houses had been converted to schools, kindergartens, restaurants, day-care centers, museums, workshops, and bureaucratic offices, most were used for mass housing. A residence that formerly sheltered the family of a single prince might be adapted as the communal abode of numerous families. Initially, one household might occupy all the buildings surrounding a single quadrangle. But with the growth of Beijing's population, it became common for a different family to occupy each structure so that four households shared a courtyard. In recent decades, the open space of the quadrangles sometimes came to be filled with freestanding structures that housed even more people. Since the courtyard houses had not historically been served by plumbing and running water, communal bathrooms were constructed along the hutongs, as modern infrastructure gradually reached the various neighborhoods of the city. The world inside these residences evolved into dense communities of people living in close proximity, with twisting communal passageways winding through each maze-like unit.

Meanwhile, in the old commercial areas of the city, elaborately carved and decorated street facades of shops, sometimes two or three stories high, also had survived the vicissitudes of the changing city. Although battered and diminished, the character and details of these historic environments persisted—particularly in their rear elevations—waiting to be reclaimed if China's economic growth ever made it possible to restore and adapt them. To a Western preservationist, the loss of original architectural features in the old residential quadrangles and in commercial areas was daunting. But for a Chinese preservationist, ancient traditions in wood construction lent a profoundly different perspective to the problem.

Unlike the major historic cities of Europe, which evolved to be largely constructed of stone and masonry, the historic cities of the Far East were built mainly of wood, and consequently were far more vulnerable to fires. In China, capital cities were particularly exposed because of the conflagrations resulting from warfare, as new dynasties toppled old ones. Frequent destruction by fire required that damaged parts of the cityscape be reinstated if cultural continuity was not to be lost. Because the actual fabric of a wooden city might inevitably perish, emphasis was placed on the continuation of form and usage. This led to a particularly Asian attitude toward conservation.

In Asia, it was a matter of periodic maintenance to replace failing parts of wooden monuments with replicated pieces. By contrast, in Europe, an effort was made to protect the exact pieces of material of important historic buildings. As a consequence, European landmarks showed their age; they looked old. In Asia, wooden landmarks in good repair might very well look recently built, since their actual materials could be brand-new.

Because Asian cities made the transformation to industrialization far later than European cities, ancient traditions of craftsmanship survived into the modern era. As a result, the historic city in Asia had the potential to be reclaimed. In Beijing, this meant that as long as representative pieces of battered historic buildings still survived to serve as templates, the wooden architecture of the traditional city could be reestablished. But does the government of China have the will to renew the Chinese architectural heritage? Will the preservation program of the municipal government of Beijing be honored by powerful national ministries? Or will some future regime abandon the city's current conservation guidelines?

Unwavering continuity of law is the prerequisite that gives preservation statutes their meaning. This is a lesson taught innumerable times in the past. Particularly in Rome, the example is stark. Countless times, various popes abandoned the policies of their predecessors and destroyed ancient artifacts that others had striven to save. Conservation was followed by destruction followed by conservation followed by destruction, and so on, over centuries, until 90 percent of the imperial city had been devoured.

Many of China's citizens recall the period of openness inviting honest criticism of government policies ("Let a hundred flowers blossom, a hundred schools contend") that preceded the Cultural Revolution, and the revisionism that then condemned those who had spoken out in good faith. In the temporal grip of such fervor, much of the damage to human lives and historic material artifacts was not reversible. It is insufficient to describe such a period as merely a temporary aberration, for in a broader sense the Cultural Revolution demonstrated the vulnerability of authoritarian government when sufficient checks and balances do not prohibit power from being seized by extreme factions with extreme policies.

These wounds may be healed, and it is only with the passage of time that we will learn whether the statutory conservation consciousness of the People's Republic will actually bear fruit in reality. The new mandate of heaven claimed by the reformed government may very well be a fresh page in the Communist version of the *Zhou Li*. The half of historic Beijing that still survives is a wonder beyond compare. In the words of Marco Polo, it is "altogether so vast, so rich, and so beautiful, that no man on earth could design anything superior to it." The half of Beijing that was destroyed, in the three decades from 1950 to 1980, constituted one of the single greatest losses of urban architectural culture in the twentieth century.

❧

The tale of the conservation of cities under communism is a far more complex and varied story than the histories of Moscow and Beijing. In Saint Petersburg—known as Petrograd and Leningrad before reassuming its historic name—a heroic effort was made after World War II to reconstruct the monuments of the city's imperial past. Behind the Iron Curtain, Warsaw also recreated its historic center, lost in the same war. In Prague, one of the world's singular architectural environments was not maintained and was allowed to decay as Soviet authorities drained the city of economic resources. After the fall of communism, the Czech government cloaked the historic city in construction netting and restored the bulk of it in less than a decade. Similarly, large parts of the Communist-governed half of historic Berlin were allowed to slowly decompose—until the reunification of the city. In Romania, during the dictatorship of Nicolae Ceauşecu, cultural destruction was systematized, large numbers of ancient villages were bulldozed, and wide swaths of devastation were cut through historic Bucharest. Old Havana has suffered but has also indirectly benefited from the privation of Cuba. New development has not torn the city apart, but neither are there adequate funds for its maintenance, and Cuban conservationists stretch their imaginations to invent low-cost preservation techniques. Will historic Havana be rescued as was historic Prague?

Ultimately, regardless of the distinct attributes of Communist urban planning and regulation, the central urban dilemma of the twentieth century was encountered in Communist cities just as it was in most other places: the conflict between the historic metropolis and modern development. In this regard, Moscow and Beijing were no different from numerous capitalist cities where a different ideological prejudice—the belief that market forces should not be fettered by government regulation—allowed real estate speculators to have free rein and many old cityscapes were fractured by mammoth buildings disproportionate in size and style to historic neighborhoods. Here, too, ideological bias compromised holistic planning.

Sadly, also replicated during the century in many cities was the institutionalized terrorism that the Russian and Chinese governments inflicted upon their own people. Urban centers under the authority of Hitler, Mussolini, Franco, Idi Amin, the Khmer Rouge, and the leaders of numerous other military states in South America, Africa, and Southeast Asia, have suffered this fate, as have places of deeply rooted racial prejudice such as the cities of South Africa and the United States. Why is this tragic history relevant to historic conservation? Because cities are much more than the physical containers we invent to hold our lives; they are also the living social culture of their inhabitants. Thus we must ask, can a spirit of *civitas* exist in cities where civil dialogue is perilous? And, what are the effects of such tragedies on the collective urban soul?

CHAPTER SEVEN

PRESERVATION AND ECONOMIC JUSTICE

SINGAPORE

East and West must seek my aid.
Ere the spent hull may dare the ports afar
The second doorway of the wide world's trade
Is mine to loose or bar.

—RUDYARD KIPLING, "SINGAPORE," FROM *The Song of Cities*

At the end of World War II, Singapore was an underdeveloped city whose once legendary commercial vitality had faded. It was a place with daunting obstacles and limited opportunities for betterment. Some 250,000 squatters lived in shacks on the outskirts of the metropolis, while in the slums of Chinatown, block after block of decrepit two-, three-, and four-story shop-houses were divided into small dark cubicles, jammed together like compartments in a beehive. As many as a hundred people lived in each shop-house. Toilets were primitive and drinking water contaminated. Scraps of cloth served as doors. Many inhabitants hardly had space to lie down. There was no place to cook, no room to bathe, no sinks in which to wash clothes, and often no window for ventilation in the sweltering tropical heat. These were the notorious black holes of Singapore.

Today orchids grow in the city's subway stations. Sleek modern trains carrying one of the better-educated urban societies in the world glide into immaculate air-conditioned platforms. Aboveground, a high-tech modern city has been erected where once there was destitution. But in fashioning this economic miracle, Singapore almost became a city without a past. It destroyed much of a unique colonial architectural heritage that shed light on how this particular society succeeded in alleviating the sort of economic injustice that induces despair for millions of people across the globe. In the effort to secure a better future, Singapore cut out the heart of the historic city, eviscerating the cultural ambience from which its success had sprung.

colonial?

❧

Discussions of Singapore often involve a complex moral dilemma. Its authoritarian government regularly violates the civil liberties of its citizens while fashioning one of the healthiest and most advanced urban societies in the world. The record of political abuse is long and thoroughly documented by such organizations as Amnesty International, Asia Watch, the U.S. State Department, and the Committee on International Human Rights of the New York City Bar Association. Yet the reality of Singapore's economic success is equally well established.

For the visitor, Singapore's elevated quality of life is instantly apparent in the prevailing aura of pride among its people and in the obvious positive qualities of the physical environment. Singapore is cleaner, more efficient, and healthier than almost any other city in the world.

After I had witnessed the destitution in marginalized megacities—Cairo in particular—the dilemma of understanding Singapore forced me to confront a basic human truth: that political repression does not weigh any more heavily on the scale of injustice than economic and social deprivation. Is infringement on democratic rights more terrible than the oppression of poverty and the premature death of the children of the poor?

Those who, like me, were born and raised in a democratic society may find it surprising that citizens of Southeast Asia regard Singapore's intolerant but honest bureaucracy as a relative blessing. Moreover, for citizens of impoverished societies, the ascent of Singapore, regardless of the city's flaws, is a beacon of hope. For citizens of developed democracies, the culture of Singapore must give us pause before we automatically condemn it. We need to recognize that the meaning of Singapore is much affected by the point of view and cultural bias of those who are writing the story.

A JEWEL IN THE EMPIRE'S CROWN

Singapore does not immediately come to mind when one makes an inventory of the great buildings of the world. The city does not hold a singular architectural work of transcending value like Katsura Villa, Saint Peter's, or the Mosque of Ibn Tulun. Nor is there an extraordinary assemblage of constructions framing a great urban space like Red Square, Rockefeller Center, or the

Piazza San Marco. Neither does the texture of the city constitute a peerless aesthetic environment of interrelated structures, as in Amsterdam, Venice, or Prague. In such places, over extended periods of time, powerful civilizations have accumulated wealth, fostered a sophisticated cultural milieu, developed a refined architectural taste, and accrued unsurpassed artistic value in the built environment. Such is not the legacy of Singapore.

Yet buildings embody more than the aesthetic flowering of civilization, and in the cityscape of Singapore are recorded several important lessons of history. The commingling of different ethnic building traditions in the city's neighborhoods manifests a strikingly positive cultural pluralism that evolved in Singaporean society. The story of how a widely destitute populace was provided, in a remarkably short time, with the amenities of modern housing shows how abstract social ideals become tangible realities and offers a clue to why some governments succeed in overcoming poverty while others do not. Here also is a significant chapter in the evolution of our contemporary global world; a conjunction of Asian and European cultures, of preindustrialized and industrialized civilizations. Finally, the parable of the city's initial impulse to destroy its architectural legacy, and the change of heart that occurred as Singaporeans contemplated living in a metropolis without visible evidence of their particular history, is testimony to the significance of architectural culture even when it may not be aesthetically unsurpassed, but is beautiful nonetheless in the eyes of the children of its builders.

THE TROPICAL ISLAND ENTREPÔT

The facts of the island's early history make for a simple tale. It is a story of the wind, the sea, a diversity of people learning to work with one another, and the special place they built to live in. And it is a relatively recent story. This is because the island has never been a particularly hospitable natural environment for sustaining human life through agriculture. Singapore's soil has always been too poor in nutrients to support rice farming, and it was steadily leached of even this minimal fertile value by the frequent downpours in the equatorial oceanic climate.

The earliest chronicles to mention human habitation on the island record that in the fourteenth century the natural harbors of Singapura and its strategic location along important sea routes made the otherwise inhospitable island a backwater port for a transient population of trader-brigands. These were the infamous Malay pirates—the Illanun, Balanini, and others of the Malay Archipelago, who in squadrons of oar-driven galleys would attack heavily laden Chinese junks and native trading ships caught in the doldrums.

The history of Singapore as a continuous permanent urban settlement and a place with a civic identity begins, more precisely, in January 1819, when a British

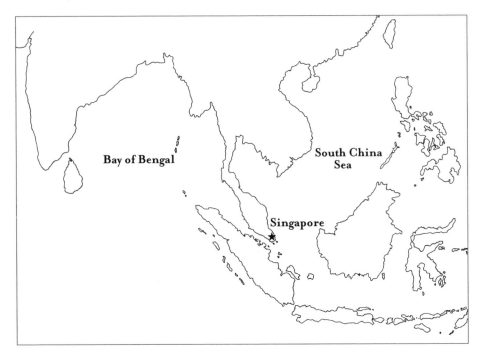

THE FORTUITOUS GEOGRAPHIC LOCATION
OF THE ENTREPÔT OF SINGAPORE

colonial administrator, Sir Thomas Stamford Bingley Raffles (who was at the time Lieutenant-Governor of Bencoolen), sailed into the harbor formed where the Singapore River joins the Straits of Malacca. Great Britain required a deep-water port along the route between the Indian Ocean and the South China Sea to compete with other European naval powers, in particular the French and Dutch, for dominance of a global commercial market connected by ship. Sir Thomas had identified Singapore as a site for the consolidation of British colonial operations in Asia. In an age of wind-driven ships, the crucial determinant of the location for the new port city was the need for a safe haven from the seasonal monsoons prevalent in the Southeast Asian seas and, in particular, in the Bay of Bengal. Singapore would provide the British military and commercial fleets with sanctuary from these storms at a critical juncture in the passage between China and India. If Britain could maintain a military presence in the area, the commercial investments of British businesses in the Far East would be more secure. Thus the choice of Singapore harbor as the location for a new commercial city was decided by the island's fortuitous relationship to the prevailing winds.

At first, the British authorities failed to recognize the value of the new settlement. There seemed to be many other potential locations that could serve the empire's strategic needs equally well. But Raffles had a broader vision: "This is by far the most important station in the East; and, as far as naval superiority and commercial interests are concerned, of much higher value than whole continents of territory." He had perceived that Singapore's precise geographic position within a maze of islands, archipelagoes, peninsulas, seas, straits, oceans, gulfs, and bays made it a perfect hub for several different regional trading markets as well as the transcontinental commerce of the Europeans. He had envisioned a self-sustaining network for the dispersal of imported manufactured goods and the gathering of regional raw materials.

From many different points on the compass, the prevailing winds were favorable. For the Bugi traders from Borneo, Celebes, and Bali, the southwest monsoons would speed them to Singapore. They would collect local produce on the way and carry European manufactures homeward when the northwest winds began to blow. Similarly, the junks that traversed the South China Sea, exchanging Chinese silks and teas for opium from British India, rode the monsoons' winds back and forth with the change of seasons. For the Western maritime traders in their square-rigged ships, the deepwater harbor of Singapore had access to such a variety of routes that no matter the direction of the seasonal gales, there was almost always a sea-lane open to distant destinations. Later, in the age of steam-powered ships, Singapore lay directly on the route required for coal refueling depots between Europe and Asia.

With the defeat of Napoleon, Britain quickly became the world's major colonial industrial power. The navigational skills of the British navy were peerless, and penetrated all locations on the globe. British mechanical inventions and commercial acumen forged an urban industrial revolution that supplied a profusion of manufactured goods for trade with an extended network of overseas markets. British colonial rule instituted a framework of law and political stability for the prosperity of private enterprise. Sheltered by this Pax Britannica, Singapore was made a free trade port in which preindustrial Eastern cultures engaged in commercial exchange with the industrialized West. The city was an intermediary center for transshipment, an entrepôt.

From across Southeast Asia, people were drawn by the commercial opportunities and the chance to make a new life: Indian merchants, indentured laborers, and convicts from the British Raj, Bugi traders, Arab Malay merchants, and most of all, immigrants from the far-ranging empire of China populated the quickly expanding town. By 1824 the original Malay fishing village of about 150 tribespeople had grown to 10,683 inhabitants. By 1849 it comprised 52,891 people, and by 1901 there were 226,842.

The river was both the heart and the major artery of the new settlement. The deepwater port for the sleek, tall-masted clipper ships lay offshore where the river's mouth met the coastline. A flotilla of sampans and junks—with families often living on board, and moored year-round at night in mid-stream—plied the inland waterway. Every dry piece of land along the banks was occupied, and swampy areas were filled in to be built upon. Like Amsterdam, Singapore became a depository for stockpiles of trading goods, and quays (wharves) and godowns (warehouses) lined the river's shores. European traders would unload their cargo of manufactures, which would later be dispersed to Asian markets with the seasonal change in the winds. Bugi traders would do likewise, depositing cargoes of pepper, spices, and copra to be stashed, sold, and eventually carried swiftly back to Europe or India. The waters of Singapore's streams ran to the river, which ran to the straits; these led to the oceans, which in turn connected to the wide seas. From its earliest conception, the vitality of the metropolis was rooted in its linkage to a global economy.

After a number of years, Raffles returned to the city and was distressed at the chaotic pattern of urban growth. To remedy this, he formed a committee that laid out the plan of 1828 and gave an enduring structure to the settlement. The river's shores were zoned for mercantile activity and formed the central dividing line of the settlement. To the south was located a commercial quadrangle, an Indian district, and an extended Chinese kampong (trading community). To the north stood a square for government buildings, a European town, an Arab kampong, a Bugi kampong, and a military cantonment. Sir Thomas, who was the founding president of the London Zoological Society, also provided for a hospital and an experimental botanical garden.

Year round, the temperature and humidity were in the high 80s. Frequently, violent equatorial storms unleashed tropical downpours. Singapore was unrelievedly wet, hot, and humid, and among the earliest colonists, a practical approach to the climate led to a commonsense architectural solution. For hundreds of years, resident Malays had constructed wooden buildings that provided shade, shed water, were safe from local predators, resisted termites, survived the great winds, breathed, and were made of materials indigenous to the island. Now, the first European settlers likewise used Malay plank-and-atap (palm leaf) construction with wide verandas, built by local laborers with traditional native tools.

As Chinese, Indians, Arabs, and other nearby islanders immigrated to the settlement, each group from a different building tradition, no one architectural culture supplanted the others, but all were subsumed into a collective whole. In many ways, Singapore was to develop a culture of the plurality. The early colonial history of the city benefited from the efforts of several broad-minded individuals from different races who respected the community's diversity. Enlightened British colonial governors, successful Chinese businessmen, leading Indian merchants—all shared an interdependent economic interest and found that cooperation made their city flourish. Within just a few decades, a lion's share of the Asian trade flowed through Singapore's waterways, and many in the city prospered and could afford to build permanently and well.

British colonials constructed Europeanized versions of Indian stucco buildings whose airy, cool designs had been transplanted from the British Raj. Immigrants from the Portuguese trading settlement of Macao brought a Mediterranean color palette from the Iberian Peninsula. From the Chinese building tradition came Minangkabau-style upturned roofs, fan-shaped air vents, ceramic balusters, decorative tile treatments with dragons, phoenixes, and flowers, and bamboo-shaped roof tiles *(tong wa)*, which were a deterrent to the spread of fire among the closely packed shop-houses of Chinatown. To adapt such roofs to the sweltering climate of Singapore, vented rooftop additions called jack roofs were created to relieve the buildup of hot and humid air inside the houses.

Europeans, Chinese, and Indians all utilized traditional Malay concepts for making buildings breathe. Malayan verandas, fretted eaves, decorative ventilation openings, and hand-carved swinging doors, called *pintu pagar,* provided for privacy and the circulation of air. And every culture adopted French colonial louvered shutters, or jalousies, which offered shade, kept out the rain, and admitted cooling breezes.

Both the Chinese and the Indians admired the classical details of European architecture. Using imported architectural pattern books, they reconfigured and embellished various classical elements with multicolored stucco ornamentation. Indians introduced a traditional technique for fabricating this external plaster work, called Madras *chunam*—water, egg white, lime, shell, sugar, and coconut husks mixed into a smooth paste that could be polished to a fine finish when hardened.

Places of worship—including Chinese Buddhist and Indian Hindu temples, Arab mosques, and English churches—tended to retain established traditional architectural styles as a symbol of deeply embedded historic values. To achieve authenticity in the sculptural decoration of Hindu shrines, craftsmen were frequently brought from India. Such buildings would often be so stylistically distinct that they told the educated viewer not just their national origin, but what precise religious sect or region they represented. For similar symbolic reasons, government buildings adopted a European classicism as a reminder of the established British colonial social and legal order.

The Raffles plan had designated a segregated district for each ethnic group; but in reality the zones of the city merged with one another, and there was much cross-fertilization in the compact cityscape. The buildings of the immigrant city re-created a little piece of home, while also assimilating the attractive aspects of the architecture of their new neighbors. Although a few shop-houses, terrace houses (rows of shop-houses with walled patios in front along the street), and godowns were designed by architects, most were composed by builders, craftsmen, and their clients. These peculiar multicultural buildings were native to the island and constituted a Singaporean vernacular: a common language of tropical architectural form.

With the opening of the Suez Canal and the advent of steamships, Singapore's already dominant commercial position was enhanced. Rubber and tin became the principal exports. More business and more wealth generated larger trading houses, banks, and insurance companies. In 1870, a transcontinental telegraph linked the island city to the larger world. Department stores, hotels, schools, hospitals, and colleges were constructed. Gradually, formally trained European architects took up residence in the city and received commissions to design the more substantial and structurally complex buildings (eventually some of these architects would be native Singaporeans, trained in Europe and returned home to practice). Many large institutional and commercial structures were composed by designers who, as part of an intellectually self-conscious discipline, consciously borrowed from Singapore's varied palette of ethnic forms. Through this process, European styles were reinterpreted and renamed: Chinese Georgian, Chinese Corinthian, Chinese Baroque, Chinese Eclectic. The shapes of these formally designed structures then became part of the culture of the city. It was as if the buildings of the metropolis were conversing, and this exchange of architectural ideas mirrored the larger collaboration among the peoples of the city. With time, straits-born (locally born) Chinese were referred to by the Malays as *pernanakan,* and Singaporean-style buildings would be referred to as *pernanakan* architecture.

Set among tropical plants and jungle flowers, the cross-cultural pastel architecture of Singapore would make the city one of the world's most exotic destinations. Victorian roofscapes were edged with Malayan fretting. European godowns were decorated with Chinese embellishments. Spectacles of intertwined sculptural figures crowned the roofs of Hindu temples. The minarets and domes of mosques punctured the skyline. In Little India, Palladian cornices, capitals, and brackets were painted in a riot of vibrant colors. A transcontinental bouquet of flower tiles from around the world adorned the exteriors of immigrant buildings. A copy of an imperial nine-dragon wall announced the entrance to the Chinese Chamber of Commerce. A staid British bank was roofed in ceramic bamboo tiles. Flotillas of sampans and junks crowded the teeming river. Sophisticated travelers disembarked from elegant transoceanic steamships. Rickshaws and automobiles jammed the streets. Hawkers hollered in dozens of dialects. And Rudyard Kipling, Joseph Conrad, Somerset Maugham, and Noël Coward sat on the veranda of the Raffles Hotel sipping Singapore Slings and looking out on a city vista unlike anyplace anywhere else before. But all too soon, the special allure and mystery would be erased.

THE MODERN ISLAND CITY-STATE

World events altered the balance of power in Asia. As China evolved into modern nationhood, it refused to continue its compliance with Western pressure to maintain a market for opium, and Britain's favorable balance of trade in Asia was diminished. Two new industrialized competitors, the United States and Japan, gained commercial footholds in the Pacific rim. Japan emerged as a military power in the Russo-Japanese War of 1904–1905. World War I cost Britain millions in wealth and manpower. Mao Tse-tung led the Red Army on the Long March. The Second World War in Europe commenced.

On December 7, 1941, in a multifront military campaign that spanned the Pacific Ocean, Japan successfully attacked Hong Kong, Malaya, Hawaii, the Philippines, and Singapore. Manchuria was already occupied. Many of the major cities of China were embattled or taken by Japanese forces, and within months Burma and the Dutch East Indies would be subjugated. Europe's grip on a vast colonial empire had been wrenched loose in a single astonishing outburst.

Asian peoples were transfixed by the demonstration that the combined might of the European powers was insufficient to stop a single Eastern nation acting alone. The fiction of Western invincibility was shattered. Further undermining the hold of colonialism, at the outset of the war, Japanese conquerors spoke of "Greater East Asia co-prosperity spheres" and bequeathed token independence in conquered regions. This made it morally unfeasible for real liberty to be denied by former colonial masters after the war ended. The map of the world was about to be redrawn.

Conditions in Singapore had grown adverse in the years before and during the war. With the suppression of piracy, the advent of steamships, the opening of the Suez Canal, and the development of many Asian societies, other ports began competing for shares of Singapore's entrepôt trade. The city's advantages in the global economy were eroding.

Simultaneously, Singapore itself began to change. One of the most significant transformations was sociological. Historically, a majority of the city's people had been laborers working for minimal wages. Many of these workers were brought to the city as needed and shipped out when the demand lessened. Most were Chinese coolies who received only a part of their pay directly, while the rest was sent home by their employers to their families in China. This predominantly male population lived meagerly, either with relatives in Singapore or in rooms within an employer's shop-house. The end of the nineteenth century was an era of dramatic political upheaval in China. Increasingly, Singapore's coolies took up permanent residence in the city and brought their families from the mainland. By now the Chinese represented a decided majority of Singapore's inhabitants. As the number of coolies increased, the living spaces within the shop-houses became smaller and smaller, eventually being reduced to the cubicles that came to be known as the black holes. Without access to kitchens to prepare food, coolies and their families purchased their meals from hawkers who cooked on the streets. Water taps and bathing facilities were scarce. Human waste was collected in night-soil buckets. Garbage collection was inadequate. Sanitary conditions worsened with each additional inhabitant.

As this permanent population of underprivileged laborers grew and the entrepôt trade began to falter, unemployment rose and buildings and infrastructure became increasingly worn out and overburdened. To some degree these conditions were a direct result of the colonial equation in which the ruling elite exploited the colony for cheap raw materials and labor. During World War I, the high cost and scarcity of materials exacerbated the problem. In the Depression, there was a shortage of capital for new construction, and even more severe joblessness among the poor. World War II brought new development to a halt and decreased the basic maintenance of buildings. By the war's end, one-third of the population was crammed into dilapidated slums.

Squatter settlements grew up on the fringes of the metropolis. In 1946 a rent-control statute fixed payments at affordable rates for tenants, but the reduction in income for landlords made it uneconomic to maintain properties already badly in need of repair. The city's rate of decay increased. Infectious diseases began to take a greater toll. By 1962 some 750,000 of the city's 1.6 million residents—that is, 48 percent of the populace—lived in conditions that did not meet modern standards for hygiene and building safety. At a time when Singapore was called upon to dramatically reinvent itself, extended poverty was straining diminishing resources and throngs of underprivileged workers were already on the march.

Throughout Southeast Asia, Communist parties had gained widespread recognition for their active participation in resisting the Japanese. Conscious of such sympathies, and with the advent of the Cold War, the British government hesitated to grant political independence in countries where the outcome of the struggle with communism was uncertain. In Singapore, Britain's recalcitrance in conceding political self-determination inflamed anticolonialist feelings and enhanced the standing of the Communists, who were in the forefront of those calling for independence.

Making the situation more complex was the fact that the departure of the British and the closing of the British military base would cause 20 percent more of the city's workers to become unemployed. Together, underemployment, limited educational opportunities, declining trade, an inadequate industrial base, widespread political unrest, and the lack of housing, sanitation, and other social services, might readily have pulled Singapore into a downward spiral. In this volatile context, the most potent of Singapore's people—the wealthy Chinese trading and commercial families—began to assert themselves.

As a general principle, the more successful Chinese in Singapore were those who had adapted to and mastered the British colonial system of laws and business. This group of people embodied a blend of Eastern and Western cultures. Children of such families were often bilingual, and some had been educated in Britain. Many had been inculcated with Western principles of administrative management and scientific thought. The main concern of the Chinese elite was to reestablish a favorable climate for business. Historically, in Singapore, this had meant social stability via enlightened bureaucratic administration, continuity of international law, and unrestricted commerce, or free port status.

A remarkable societal transformation was about to occur. In 1959, Singapore was granted political autonomy in its domestic affairs. In parliamentary elections, the first majority and ruling party was the People's Action Party, and the first prime minister was a straits-born Chinese, Lee Kwan Yew, whose father was the supervisor of an oil depot. Lee had graduated with honors from Cambridge University and served as a lawyer for Singapore's labor unions. Under his leadership, the predominantly Asian population of Singapore would adopt the civil service traditions of their former colonial masters as the means to attack the myriad problems besetting the decolonized city. The social mechanisms once used for the control and exploitation of the Chinese, Indian, and Malayan underclasses would now be the tool to create a wider economic equity and social justice.

The new government of Singapore identified three fundamental objectives. First, there would be no bureaucratic corruption. Monies meant for social progress would not be stolen for private gain. The bureaucracy would be held to the highest standards, for it was to be the mechanism for societal betterment. Exceptional bureaucratic achievement would be rewarded at levels of compensation more commonly found in the private sector, and Singapore's bureaucracy would compete with business in attracting the best of the city's talent.

Second, although each environmental enhancement would improve health, reduce mortality rates, and increase life expectancy, the government would nonetheless try to keep overwhelming population growth from sabotaging economic progress. They would initiate a voluntary program of birth control by way of economic incentives. Via these policies, from the very outset, the new government of Singapore would reduce corruption and over-population—two of the most common and discouraging obstacles to advancement in underdeveloped nations in the postindustrial age.

And third, the development of Singapore would be planned rationally. This might seem a simple matter of common sense, but in reality it is very unusual. It is extremely rare for government policies to reflect the best thinking of the most educated minds. In almost all societies, the integrity of expert thinking is compromised by special interests and politics. In Singapore, much for the better but sometimes for the worse, and especially in regard to economic development and social engineering, multiyear plans were rationally implemented with single-minded focus. (Such plans should not be confused with those that were devised under Communist regimes in China and the Soviet Union, which were often capricious in their logic and ruthless in implementation, causing the death of many millions of people.)

The People's Action Party began by getting specialist advice from outsiders and then following it. Studies by private consultants and the World Bank suggested that Singapore could expand its industrial base by offering financial incentives, improving infrastructure, and aggressively pursuing foreign investment. Thus the tax code was rewritten to stimulate foreign investment and the expansion of manufacturing. Special industrial zones were founded and provided with infrastructure. The city reestablished its free port status. And an Economic Development Board opened promotional offices in every major industrialized nation. By 1976 about 71 percent of Singapore's exports were being produced by companies with overseas affiliations. By 1989 local manufacturing had grown from 12 percent to 30 percent of the gross national product.

Singapore expanded its deepwater harbor and, within a decade, became the second busiest port in the world. As the natural-rubber trade declined, the country began processing oil. Using modern agricultural techniques, the island was able to reduce the amount of land dedicated to farming while dramatically increasing total agricultural output. Entrepreneurs accustomed to short-term risks and profits learned to make a wider range of longer-term investments, and banks and financial institutions proliferated. Mass transit was made modern, clean, and reliable. Hospitals provided the highest-quality health care. In 1987 the island-wide sewer system was completed. In 1996, in international comparative testing, the performance of its primary and secondary school children placed the Singapore school system first in the world.

Most important of all, Singapore built housing. When the People's Action Party assumed power, fewer than 9 percent of the city's 1.5 million people lived in public apartments. By 1970, the Housing and Development Board had provided the poorest one-third of Singapore's people with modern quality dwellings. By 1994 the board had constructed 740,384 apartments and sheltered close to 90 percent of the population, which had climbed to 2.8 million. But the most amazing statistic of all was that by the 1990s some 80 percent of Singaporean families owned their own residence, due to a government program mandating personal saving. Few societies in the world have created such broadly shared economic prosperity.

A relatively small city-state of 3 million people had become the twelfth-largest exporter and thirteenth-biggest importer in the world, with one of the highest standards of living among industrialized nations. Its diversified economy had vital interests in trade, communications, manufacturing, banking, transport, and finance. It had joined an elite group of cities—New York, Tokyo, London, Frankfurt, Paris, Zurich, Toronto, Amsterdam, Milan, Hong Kong, Taipei, and Seoul—as a center of the new global economy.

This extraordinary socioeconomic change radically transformed the physical landscape of the island. Rivers were dammed to form reservoirs. Mountains were leveled to create infill. New towns and extended housing suburbs had

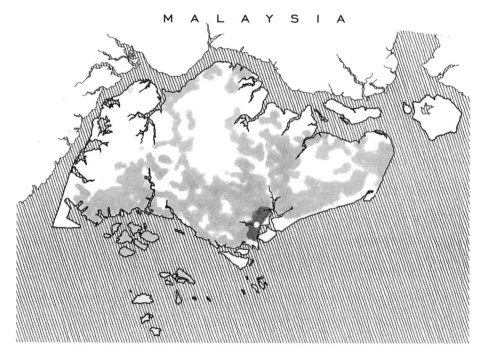

The contemporary conurbation of the island city-state of Singapore · Dark gray tone indicates the size of the original British colonial settlement of 1830–1840. Pale gray tone indicates the built-up area by 1990. White dot indicates the lost historical center. All islands drawn with heavy black line are part of the city-state.

spread development out of the city and across the island. The natural acreage of Singapore declined from 38 percent to 14 percent. A network of broad highways had been constructed. Industrial land use tripled. Multistory shopping malls, parking lots, and condominiums proliferated. The central business district grew skyward in the shape of numerous modern towers. In the process, myriad historical properties were leveled by the deluge of growth and improvement.

LOSS OF THE SPECIALNESS OF PLACE

A number of circumstances had combined to put older structures in the city's heart at the greatest jeopardy. As part of a strategy to create an international center for banking and finance, the People's Action Party had decided to revitalize Singapore in its historical topographic position. The old central business district had been zoned to allow buildings of a far greater height, and highway access and mass transit service had been dramatically upgraded. Tax abatements for new buildings in the center had been offered by the government. Since the historic lot size in these downtown areas was often too small to accommodate the footprint of an economically viable modern office structure, the government of Singapore compelled small-property owners to sell so that larger plots could be assembled. Such decisions greatly enhanced the potential profitability of developing downtown properties, and it became inevitable that many old downtown buildings would be leveled to make way for large modern structures. Unfortunately, also in this area were numerous historic buildings of significant design playing an important role in the composition of the colonial cityscape. Three nongovernment reports—a 1958 master plan by the Singapore Improvement Trust and two reports by United Nations consultants from the early 1960s—had called for the conservation of this historic area. People's Action Party planners had rejected this advice.

Situated on either side of the spot where the Singapore River connected to the harbor were two architecturally dramatic zones. To the north of the river, as stipulated in the original Raffles plan, was a governmental center of handsome civic buildings designed in European Classical Revival style and symbolizing the power of British colonial rule and Singapore's status as a jewel in the empire's crown. Across the river to the south, on a tract of land that jutted out into the harbor, rose a cluster of eclectic commercial structures representing the mercantile wealth of the city. During the late nineteenth and early twentieth centuries, the commercial hub had become a lively compilation of ornately detailed buildings in a variety of European styles touched by Asian and tropical influences. This distinctive architectural sector, with its greater height and embellishment, culminated the massing of the historic cityscape. The rest of

Singapore, built at a lower scale and composed of the vernacular multiethnic architecture of various immigrant populations, fanned out from around these two central areas. Low-scale immigrant neighborhoods reflected the spontaneous process of creative cross-cultural association and adaptation of form. The architecture of the commercial center demonstrated how the harnessing of that multicultural inventiveness as urban entrepreneurial power had gradually lifted Singapore from a Malay village to a colonial trading post, then to an entrepôt for transcontinental trade, and ultimately to one of the world's most vibrant commercial emporiums.

The commercial buildings of the mercantile center were, unfortunately, outmoded and without up-to-date environmental technologies, especially air-conditioning. Many of the neighboring shop-houses of Chinatown had become decrepit and filthy during their decline into overcrowded slums. Hence, at the outset of the revitalization of the city, numerous buildings in the historic core were widely seen as an environmental blight. At a moment of heightened desire for change, historic Singapore had become a symbol of the social and economic deficiencies of the past.

Here was a tale of urban renewal already well known in Europe, where in the period before and after World War II, various historic inner-city areas had become badly dilapidated and perceived as targets for clearance. The cities of Europe eventually learned it was a mistake to tear down such areas rather than to renew them. Older areas at the city's center, even when they have become slums, often include significant early historic structures capable of being revived. Singapore did not understand this lesson.

Equally important, the preservation of historic zones near the city's center preserves not only old landmarks and their history but often their scale as well. In the modern era, this is critical because the size of many contemporary building types is disproportionate to that of the historic metropolis. In Cairo and Istanbul, skylines whose pinnacles were once the domes and delicate minarets of mosques are now dominated by looming and massive modern hotels. In London, a policy of allowing intermittent oversize contemporary apartment and office blocks throughout the city has disrupted the ambience of many of the most beautiful residential squares, parks, and neighborhoods in the world. In Novy Arbat, in Moscow, a once lovely old community has been displaced by long rows of giant gray residential slabs, which overwhelm remaining parts of the historic city. Here in particular, the metropolis has been rudely fractured with no accommodation between the old and new, as if the aesthetics and visual coherence of the urban environment are of little consequence to the daily lives of the millions of people who reside in the Russian capital.

Thus Singapore destroyed the ambience and most of the buildings of the colonial emporium that marked the entry to the Singapore River and the historic architectural visage of the city as it looked out to the sea. A dramatic urban panorama had been cut out from the center of Singapore and, in the process, the organic architectural logic of the historic cityscape was annulled. In its place was constructed a new business district of generic modern skyscrapers, many of which were three, four, and five times the height of typical historic buildings and ten to fifteen times as large in mass. The once coherent cityscape had become a jumble of disparate parts. In the official book describing the evolution of the new financial district, the agency in charge, the Urban Redevelopment Authority, would evaluate the aesthetic results of its own policies: "Any 'unity' of the central area that might have been apparent during colonial days has become increasingly elusive." Many of the same mistakes, already regretted in other places, were repeated once again.

Was the destruction of the old mercantile center a rejection of repugnant symbols of European imperialism? The preservation of the former British governmental complex indicates that Singapore felt no need to expunge this aspect of the past. In fact, unlike other former colonial cities in Southeast Asia, such as Hong Kong, Singapore has protected buildings illustrative of its years as a colony. Instead, the fragmentation of the cityscape seems to reflect the widespread contemporary urban policy that the form of the city is best determined by the speculative forces of the marketplace. In this equation, short-term profitability often dominates features that might otherwise enhance the long-term livability of the metropolis.

The story of Singapore reflects a recurring modern conservation paradox. Throughout the developing world—in the face of the harsh realities of high infant mortality, malnutrition, illiteracy, unemployment, lawlessness, and homelessness—economic revitalization must be given priority; architectural preservation seems, by comparison, a secondary matter. But even after having attracted much-needed new investment, governments often hesitate to apply restraints to growth and, again, preservation is deferred. Finally, when crucial economic goals are secured, too late society focuses on the significance of its past.

So it was in Singapore, which held no architectural masterpieces of broad acclaim but was a city known for its singularity of place. Great societal advancement had been achieved, but had a substantial loss of historical fabric been necessary in order to accomplish that good? Midway through the process of urban evolution, citizens began to decry the injury. Eventually, a group advocating conservation of Singapore's historical assets was formed. (Generally such advocacy groups have not flourished under the People's Action Party, except where the government has made official provision for public criticism in preapproved forums.) But the concerns of preservationists were not the primary motive in the alteration of government policy. An economic concern,

the decline of income from tourism, caused a reevaluation of the city's planning priorities.

TOURISM, CULTURE, AND CONSERVATION

Early in its elaboration of a multifaceted strategy for balanced economic
growth, Singapore planned to expand tourism in order to stimulate local
employment and heighten export income in its balance of trade. Several initiatives were undertaken. A national airline of the first quality was developed—
Singapore Air, to this day annually rated one of the finest lines in the world.
Numerous modern hotels were constructed. A beautiful and highly efficient
airport, Changi International Airopolis, was built just outside the city, and
2,800 weekly flights connected Singapore to 124 cities around the globe by
1994.

As the city's transformation progressed, Singapore's tourist industry grew
rapidly. By the early 1980s, tourism was the third-most-productive sector in
foreign exchange earnings and constituted about 5 percent of the country's
gross national product. As a result, another plan was instituted to further
expand the number of hotel rooms in the city. But by 1986, although many
more hotels had been constructed, occupancy rates had fallen to 55 percent
and tourism's rate of growth had been declining for several years. While
tourism is affected by many unpredictable outside forces, Singapore's planners
began to suspect something was fundamentally wrong with their approach.
Otherwise, a successful tourism industry might have represented about 10 percent of the GNP, a difference of many billions of dollars a year more.

The bureaucracy responded in its typical thorough way. Visitors were
polled and outside experts were brought in. It was discovered that 70 percent
of the tourists were coming from within Asia to celebrate the economic miracle
of Singapore. These were not disappointed at the city's transfiguration. But
the tourists coming from outside Asia, representing the other 30 percent of
the city's visitors and the group from whom future growth in tourism might be
attracted, had been lured to the island by its romantic historical image. But
what the non-Asian tourists found was a modern metropolis not unlike the
contemporary cities they had left back home. Why travel halfway around the
world to find comparable shopping malls and snack on the same fast foods?
Where were the sampans, the color, and the history? Where was the Singapore
of legend? The official report of the Tourism Task Force found that "in our
effort to build up a modern metropolis, we have removed aspects of our
Oriental mystique and charm best symbolized in old buildings."

The government had in fact created a Preservation of Monuments Board
as early as 1971. But in the board's first decade of existence, barely twenty

individual structures and no historic districts had been registered. This left several thousand historically and architecturally meritorious buildings exposed to demolition. Now the question was this: what was left to preserve?

Notwithstanding the absence of conservation protections, an important part of Singapore's unique architectural legacy was still intact. In several separate areas near the city's center and hidden in the shadows of tall new constructions, whole communities of shop-houses, terrace houses, and godowns, although greatly decayed, were nonetheless still standing. In these neighborhoods, the curious interplay of architectural forms from different places recorded the story of how the peoples of Singapore came together to create an unusual urban culture. But if such neighborhoods were to be conserved, Singapore would have to learn a new ethic of urban development in which saving the past becomes an integral part of planning for the future.

Once more, the efficient bureaucracy was mobilized. Teams of officials were sent abroad to study preservation legislation and its implementation in cities in Australia, the United States, and France. Soon the city was empowered to set aside historic districts, and by 1993 some 5,200 buildings in significant neighborhoods were protected. A professional conservation department was established within the Urban Development Authority. In 1986 a Tourism Product Development Plan, budgeted for over U.S. $200 million, included substantial sums of money to revitalize historic areas. A program to upgrade infrastructure in historic districts was instituted. Financial incentives were offered to property owners of historic buildings. Together, such initiatives were aimed at stimulating further investment by the private sector in architectural conservation through gentrification—a strategy that had been successful in Amsterdam, Paris, and other European cities. Perhaps the world's most thorough package of government publications on preservation was printed as part of an extensive public education process. Overnight, Singapore had enacted a comprehensive conservation agenda, and 18 percent of the city's protected buildings had been rehabilitated by 1993. In 1994 about 6.9 million tourists spent $10.9 billion, representing 10.3 percent of the gross national product. Historic preservation had proved to be an economically sound investment.

THE EMERGING GLOBAL MONOCULTURE

The loss of Singapore's historic center foreshadows a disturbing global phenomenon. It is sad enough when a people and a city expunge their own cultural achievements, but in the twentieth century, throughout the world, where historic architecture in old cities is lost, it is frequently replaced with the new architecture of an international modern monoculture. Whether in northern or southern climates, in Asian, African, European, or American cultures, the generic buildings of modern development change little in response to their geographic and social surroundings. Just as American fast-food chains offer identical dishes, with the same names, in the same wrappers, by waiters in matching uniforms, so most of the new architecture of Singapore primarily reflects the economic formulas of modern speculative development.

In the old commercial center of the city, now replaced by a modern high-rise steel, glass, and concrete central business district, one can distinguish two important elements of this trend that breed international cultural uniformity. First one notes a simple fact of wide design implication—that modern structures with sealed windows and interior climatic controls do not respond in their forms to local environmental conditions. In the old commercial core, much of the aesthetic character of Singapore's buildings was derived from such distinctive elements as covered walkways, French colonial jalousie windows, Chinese jack roof vents, overhanging Minangkabau roofs, Malaysian hand-carved swinging doors, fretted roof eaves, and decorative air screens—building components that created shade, allowed the flow of cooling breezes, and provided protection from frequent downpours. These features not only caused Singapore's cityscape to look tropical, but also reflected its links to other regional architectural cultures facing similar climatic problems.

International architectural uniformity is further propagated by the express desire of underdeveloped client-nations and client-cities to achieve symbols of social, economic, technological, and cultural parity. In such places the meta-phorical value of new modern buildings cannot be overestimated. For poten-tial outside investors, the ubiquitous contemporary office tower represents the effort of underdeveloped nations to create a secure harbor in which to do busi-ness. In addition, for local citizens, prototypical modern structures can be symbols of their nation's progress toward ending marginalization and achiev-ing membership in the global economy.

Thus, even when major international architects—Kenzo Tange, I.M. Pei, Helmut Jahn, Paul Rudolph, John Portman, and Kevin Roche—were imported to Singapore to construct signature buildings, their designs, some-times quite distinguished as objects in themselves, nonetheless produced a contemporary urban visage matching the look of major commercial centers in other places. The unique regional legacy of Singapore was replaced with for-eign brand-name buildings. Of course, this is exactly what the architects were asked to accomplish. In this regard it is interesting to remember buildings of Kenzo Tange and I.M. Pei where they attempted to assimilate and reinterpret local architectural culture in contemporary form. Pei's recent hotel outside Beijing embodies the spirit of historic Chinese buildings. It looks Chinese. His new museum buildings in Japan are an evocation of ancient Japanese temple forms. Similarly, Kenzo Tange's work in the country of his origin, done early in his career, is an express attempt to reconcile Western modernism with historic Japanese building traditions, producing several masterful designs widely admired as some of the finest contemporary architecture of the postwar period, including his culturally evocative yet technologically advanced venues for the Tokyo Olympics. But in Singapore it seems apparent that neither Pei or Tange was asked to direct his considerable design talent to create a modern expression of the city's unique historic architectural culture. Thus a cityscape that in its colors, materials, configuration, and details once responded to the particular tropical climate of Singapore and a century of cultural exchange between its European and Asian inhabitants was replaced with an architecture whose forms belong to no particular geography.

While the speed and thoroughness of Singapore's current conservation efforts would seem to ensure the protection of any important remaining historical assets, in the end, the most important benefit of preservation was not attained. The People's Action Party waited too long before listening to those who lamented the loss of the city's past, and the particular exotic visage of Singapore at its center was lost. This is, in part, a weakness of authoritarian governance: when voices are stifled, they are difficult to hear.

In its years in power, the People's Action Party had restrained political dissent in a number of ways. The content of local newspapers was controlled. The dissemination of foreign publications was restricted. Periodically, those in political opposition were incarcerated indefinitely under emergency national security acts. Districts that voted for opposition candidates were the last to receive infrastructure improvements. In other instances, the party used its control over the bureaucracy to damage the professional careers of critics of government policy. A climate of political intimidation does not promote open critical discussion.

It is worth noting that in recent years sociologists in Singapore have increasingly focused on the multicultural community dynamics that underlie the modern city's ascension—a history recorded in physical form in surviving shophouse neighborhoods. Now, having achieved economic parity, Singapore is focusing on its cultural uniqueness—on what makes its society different.

Could both the new and the old Singapore have been accommodated in the same general location? With the advantage of hindsight, I believe the answer is yes. The economic success of the planning produced such a greatly expanded demand for office space that not only had the historic commercial center been extended farther out into the old city, but large areas of the harbor were filled in to create tracts of new land for future expansion. In other words, the central business district eventually became so large it was unable to fit in the historic center in any case. The conservation of a mere dozen blocks downtown—in the area around the old commercial core, Raffles Place, which bordered on the river and faced out to the harbor—would have saved that identifiable sculptural amassing of urban culture that made Singapore unique and a magnet for ships from across the world. Then all the pieces of the historic city would have been linked together in a comprehensible totality for Singaporeans and visitors alike. Preserved residential quarters would not have become scattered anomalies, and old Singapore would still be there, where it all happened, surrounded by the second miracle of the modern metropolis. What Singapore acted too late to save was the piece of the urban puzzle that tied the cityscape together: the material architectural product of a creative cultural explosion that once had made it a place unlike anyplace else.

CHAPTER EIGHT

PRESERVATION AND SOCIAL CONSCIENCE

AMSTERDAM AND VIENNA

Long ago it was said that "one half of the world does not know how the other half lives." That was true then. It did not know because it did not care. The half that was on top cared little for the struggles, and less for the fate of those who were underneath, so long as it was able to hold them there and keep its own seat. There came a time when the discomfort and crowding below were so great, and the consequent upheavals so violent, that it was no longer an easy thing to do, and then the upper half fell to inquiring what was the matter. Information on the subject has been accumulating rapidly since, and the whole world has had its hands full answering for its old ignorance.

—Jacob A. Riis, *How the Other Half Lives*, 1890

Housing manifests in physical form the unfolding of a city's social conscience. In the modern era, a critical stage occurred as industrialization and the mechanization of agriculture drove agrarian populations from the countryside to urban centers. The poorer parts of the populations of cities—60 percent in New York in 1894, for example—were densely packed together in debilitating conditions. The average London tenement dweller had less living space than prisoners in the city's jail cells.

Descriptions of such slums, in various cultures—of how the other half lived—are tragically similar. Buildings were poorly constructed, unmaintained, and vulnerable to fires. Contagious diseases were rampant. Inhabitants went unwashed, in dirty clothes, amid squalor and crime, as unscrupulous landlords capitalized on human misery. In 1900 in Manhattan one of the worst tenement blocks housed 2,781 people in 605 apartments, with 264 toilets and not a single bath. Exacerbating the situation was the fact that the capital for developers to erect tenements often required a higher rate of interest from banks, due to a greater degree of risk, due to the terrible conditions such buildings inculcated.

For many residents, a self-perpetuating and vicious cycle existed. Increasing demand for space drove rents higher still. Impoverished families were often compelled to lease parts of their meager allotment of space for income. Informal home industries (craft work) took up further space and introduced noxious substances into the home. In cities where rent controls were instituted, new construction became unprofitable, and the maintenance and building of rental apartments declined. Since the poor could not afford to purchase costlier dwellings in new neighborhoods, frequently they were unable to move. As urban employment opportunities changed and manufacturing relocated in the outskirts of the city, long commutes were required of those with the least available means of transport.

In many industrializing cities, shantytowns grew up in unoccupied open spaces. In New York, the low swampy areas of inner Manhattan that were reclaimed to make Central Park had first to be cleared of squatters' huts. On the outskirts of Vienna, similar illegal housing had been built on government lands, on abandoned estates, and in the vineyards of old monasteries. This phenomenon was not new to cities; the medieval cemeteries of Cairo, for example, the Cities of the Dead, had often been occupied by the homeless. But in the expanding cities of the industrial era, shantytowns became more and more common. Indeed, today they have reached such epic proportions that close to a quarter of the earth's people live in such illegal communities. In these dire circumstances, the slightest bad luck—illness, accident, fire, unexpected loss of employment— could lead to sudden destitution. The combination of these many negative factors caused large numbers of people to live on the edge of despair.

A paradox had evolved. Life in the city, though miserable in many ways, was still a substantial improvement over life in the countryside. New jobs in manufacturing, government, and a growing service sector offered greater opportunities for employment. The cultural assets of the city—its social institutions, cafés, restaurants, and shops—enriched the quality of daily living. Moreover, although services such as education and medical care were unevenly distributed and available mostly to those who could afford them (in 1887, in London, infant mortality in poor neighborhoods was double that in more affluent sections; and the average age of death among the upper classes was fifty-five, as compared to twenty-nine among the lower classes), nonetheless, the limited access in the city was preferable to the utter lack of services in rural areas. Most important, in the city, opportunities for self-improvement were far greater. No matter how remote, the chance of achieving a better life was compelling to those on the lower rungs of the socioeconomic ladder.

Such glaring disparities in the quality of life raised fundamental questions of social justice. The proximity of city neighborhoods put the poor in direct daily contrast to the middle classes and wealthy. Contagious diseases spawned by slum conditions showed that the fates of the city's inhabitants were inexorably intertwined. Street crime claimed victims of all classes. Social upheaval threatened, and in 1917, throughout Europe, the Russian Revolution raised the specter of violent changes in the established order.

Simultaneously, other strands of social development produced a moral response. Traditions of charity in Christian Europe date back to the Middle Ages. The church and various workers' organizations such as guilds, confraternities, and trade associations had all historically made efforts to help the destitute and less fortunate. Writers such as Charles Dickens, Victor Hugo, Émile Zola, James Joyce, George Bernard Shaw, Karl Marx, and Friedrich Engels described the plight of *les misérables*. Universal suffrage, unionization, and the rise of socialism made the interests of the lower classes a permanent part of the political landscape.

Together, all these factors engendered the building of subsidized housing throughout the industrialized world. Especially in northern Europe, governments began to take direct responsibility for ameliorating the inequities of market economies. Two new ideas had emerged: that society should establish minimal standards of decent living for the urban poor, and that opportunities for individual growth and advancement should be made universal.

As urban populations mushroomed, it became clear that the provision of adequate housing would require a huge, highly organized, and costly effort. The metropolis would be expanded and transformed in a quantum leap to a new size. Yet many of the European cities that were most aggressive in building low-cost blocks of apartments were also places of great historic charm. Since housing is the most prevalent building form in cities and determines in great part the aesthetic character of the metropolis, the very beauty of the city itself was at stake.

Three aesthetic issues emerged. First, public housing constituted a somewhat new building type. What architectural configuration should such buildings be given? Would the new housing be traditional in design, or would the new technologies and uses of these buildings be expressed in a more modern architectural language?

Second, tracts of new housing located both within and outside traditional centers did not just add a few more buildings to the city; they were major extensions of the metropolis and complete urban environments unto themselves.

How were these new parts of the growing city to relate to the existing urban context? Should the city as whole be subject to aesthetic planning?

Third, over a period of about one hundred years, as cities around the world entered similar stages of development, urban conservation laws were enacted. Extended civic disputes took place over which parts of the historic city were to be saved and what architectural form modern buildings should take when built in the midst of historic areas.

In many places, some of the oldest neighborhoods had become ghettos and suffered from decades of deterioration. Here, wretched living conditions made old districts a symbol of misery. The clearance of slums to make way for new and more sanitary housing seemed an obvious improvement. But beneath the layers of grime irreplaceable evidence of unique urban cultures was embedded in complex historical matrices of dilapidated structures.

At the edges of the nineteenth-century city, block upon block of tenement housing had been built. These first responses of the private market to the need for housing were often poorly constructed, with minimal interior amenities. However, their exterior design was frequently semitraditional (much of this building was designed by contractors freely copying stylistic elements from architectural pattern books) and melded aesthetically with the older city core; the result was an extended cityscape of stylistic continuity. As housing standards improved, should these buildings be upgraded or torn down and replaced? Did structures of such relatively recent construction, which were not examples of sophisticated architectural achievement, have artistic value as a broad cultural expression? Particularly in Europe, where the history of cities often extended back thousands of years, the question was perplexing and involved other recently outmoded building types such as early factories, warehouses, sanitariums, terminals, and hospitals. How old did buildings have to be to deserve the label "historic"?

When would urban populations stabilize? How big would the metropolis ultimately become? At the time, few places were able to foresee the many interconnected consequences. The city was being reshaped without a clear perspective of the final result. Thus, in an era of uncertainty, as different groups claimed their right to various aspects of the city—in the name of economics, efficiency, health, aesthetics, and social equity—the future was molded by the fleeting passions of the urban debate.

AMSTERDAM AND VIENNA

In Amsterdam and Vienna, in the first part of the twentieth century, two of the world's most beautiful and intact historic environments, were the site of progressive attempts to develop social housing. Each of these advanced housing

does not have / be sacrificed

initiatives was a massive physical and economic endeavor that transformed its cityscape. Each also gave birth to architecturally significant transitions from traditional to modern architecture, resulting in some of the most splendid public housing of the industrial era. The forms of this architecture assumed a palpable connection to the architectural traditions of each city's history. Early Viennese modern would look singularly Viennese, just as the architectural character of early modernism in Amsterdam was distinctly associated with the city from which it sprang.

Later, in the period of hardship after World War II, the historic patrimony of each city came into conflict with modern developmental goals. In Amsterdam, a marvelous resolution of social equity, modernization, and architectural preservation would evolve in one of the world's most sophisticated urban conservation initiatives. In Vienna, an exemplary housing program would clash with architectural conservation, and the historic architectural elegance of the city would be diminished.

Historically, Amsterdam had been the capital of a vast mercantile empire whereas Vienna was the capital of an extended political empire. Amsterdam had been governed by a stable municipal oligarchy and had largely determined its own fate. Vienna had been ruled by an autocratic monarch. As a city constructed in water, Amsterdam had invented a unique architectural vocabulary and method of building to suit a geographic location where the weight of structures was difficult to support. The buildings of Vienna had been built with thick, heavy walls, richly encrusted with decoration. Amsterdam avoided architectural ostentation; Vienna flaunted it.

Each city had a period of florescence as a focal point of European civilization during which time a remarkable physical reconceptualization occurred, surrounding each ancient core with a marvelous assemblage of urban and architectural parts. The transformation of Amsterdam led to a beautiful arc of canals. The transformation of Vienna led to a beautiful arc of boulevards.

HISTORIC VIENNA: THE CAPITAL OF THE ENLIGHTENED AUTOCRATIC STATE

The metamorphosis of Vienna from a medieval town into an elegant industrialized cityscape is one of the most celebrated urban transformations in history and a component of one of the golden ages of urban civilization. This reorganization created a continuum of architectural form whose visual and conceptual coherence disguised a complex social reality fraught with contradictions and destined for tragedy during World War II. While all cities encompass degrees of darkness and light, the extremes of Vienna during this period of urban architectural accomplishment are startling. During a short span of time—before, during, and immediately after its florescence—it combined cultural achievement, vivaciousness, and humanism with barbaric intolerance.

For six hundred years the evolution of Vienna was linked to the fortunes of the Hapsburgs, Austria's dominant monarchial family and the longest-ruling house in European history (1276–1918). At the zenith of their power, Hapsburg monarchs were recognized as emperors of the Holy Roman Empire, a Catholic and largely Germanic dominion commanding large parts of central Europe and the successor state to the empire founded by Charlemagne. Once the rise of the Hapsburgs had been achieved, the prominence of Vienna was inversely related to the geographic extent of their domains. Over centuries, as the scope of their sovereignty decreased (and the modern nations of Europe gradually emerged), Vienna's significance as the major Hapsburg capital was heightened.

Vienna's territorial position at a crossroads of trade, where the Alps meet the Carpathians, on the border between Europe and the Ottoman Empire, caused the city to be highly fortified and compressed within its walls. For centuries it was commonly known as the strongest citadel in Christendom. The Turks made two major attempts to expand into Europe, with serious sieges of Vienna, in 1528 and 1683. After the second assault was repulsed, the Ottomans were pushed down the Danube and lost control of Hungary. This geopolitical change repositioned Vienna at the center of the empire, rather than on an imperiled frontier.

During this period, the Hapsburgs reestablished Vienna as their principal administrative seat, and the city became densely packed with migrants from across a wide territory. Situated between the Germanic and Slavic regions of Europe, the city assumed a cosmopolitan international character. After the second siege, with wealth pouring into it from across an extended empire, Vienna was refashioned. The city's angular medieval street pattern persisted, but virtually all of its structures were recast in the Baroque architectural style. Timber construction ceased, and the city became a beautiful ensemble of thickly sculpted stone and masonry facades.

A particular social-architectural characteristic was also established. Except for the most affluent residents, apartment-house living became a custom for people of all economic levels. While the wealthiest members of the court endowed Vienna with splendid urban mansions known as *Adelspalais*, or aristocratic palaces, the lesser nobility rented apartments in grand multistory buildings. These *Mietpalais*, or rent palaces, and *Zinspalais*, or interest-bearing palaces, imitated the appearance of the great mansions. Although different classes often lived in the same structure (with the poor occupying smaller apartments on the upper floors), lower foyers, stairways, and entrances were imposing and frequently opulent. However, the beautiful outer shells of the buildings of

Vienna, especially those built exclusively for the lower classes (known as *Mietkaserne,* or rent barracks), often disguised very spare interiors. Vienna became a city in which outward style was crucial.

This preoccupation with architectural ostentation eventually led to the creation of an imperial commission to regulate the exterior designs of new residential structures, so that a hierarchy of architectural ornamentation came to distinguish the dwellings of different classes. Nonetheless, to the end of the nineteeth century, the architectural quality of tenement facades continued to contradict the poor conditions within. As a result, the city was knit into an architectural whole, and residents spent much of their time outside their homes, in Vienna's public spaces.

Liberated from the immediate threat of hostile siege, Vienna expanded into its surrounding rural districts (the faubourgs), and a second defensive barrier called the *Linienwall* was built. The reign of Empress Maria Theresa and her son Joseph II (1765–1790) was a period of humanistically informed despotism. As in other European monarchies influenced by the Enlightenment, numerous social, political, and religious traditions were overthrown in an effort to construct a more widely productive and equitable society. Serfdom was abolished, government censorship curtailed, torture was done away with, a modern penal code was instituted, primary school education was expanded, universities were secularized, and the power of the church was reduced. In 1783 an Edict of Religious Tolerance fostered the establishment of an emancipated Jewish community within the city. Eventually this community would be closely associated with a period of advanced intellectual accomplishment.

In the meantime, a renaissance in music was occurring. The initial florescence of Vienna, a musical flowering, contributed to the development of the modern symphony, especially in the works of Haydn, Mozart, Beethoven, and Schubert. Hapsburg monarchs assembled distinguished orchestras, opera companies, and music academies. Their cultivated patronage was expanded by the higher nobility. People of all classes went to the opera and concert halls. The most gifted composers, teachers, musicians, and singers from across the empire were attracted to Vienna, where they worked in a stimulating environment that recognized and rewarded high achievement. With the passage of time it would be widely perceived that, in those years, the city became the birthplace of modern music.

In the early nineteenth century, Napoleon's conquest of Vienna confirmed the inadequacy of the fixed fortifications of the city under the assault of modern artillery. The inner walls surrounding the old city core became particularly redundant. In 1806, the Holy Roman Empire was dissolved, and by 1867 the territory under Hapsburg rule had been further reduced to the Austro-Hungarian dual monarchy. Although the government was losing hegemony in other places, Vienna was becoming more important as a symbol of power, thereby requiring an expansion of the buildings of its public realm at the exact moment when a large area of redundant space became available at the city's center. The city would now become one of the richest, largest, and most culturally advanced in Europe, as the concept of the Ringstrasse (ring road) was invoked, cloaking the metropolis in an imperial cosmopolitan splendor belying the fact that it was also a power in decline.

THE MASTERSTROKE OF THE RINGSTRASSE

In the initial stages of industrialization, as cities grew more crowded and their functions expanded, three types of historic urban space, inherent to many capital cities, had been subsumed into the fabric of the growing metropolis and had the potential to yield some breathing room: outmoded military installations, former royal estates, and former large religious complexes. The adaptation of traditional green space often was a simple matter of making it available to the populace at large. Much of the public parkland in London, Berlin, and Paris consists of former royal preserves, while public green spaces in Beijing and Kyoto are largely composed of the historic gardens associated with great temples and imperial compounds.

The obsolescence of military fortifications presented a different chance to reformulate the urban environment through adaptation of wide long tracts winding through the metropolis. An important conservation matter and several city planning issues are common to this situation. In terms of historic conservation, the removal of ancient walls takes out of the cityscape a major physical element that determined the character of the urban environment. The tall walls of ancient fortifications mark different periods of urban growth and explain why the inner core of a historic city is so compressed. The barbicans and gateways of old citadels distinguish significant ancient roadways, and once a city grows outward, they also denote the crucial connections between old and new circulation systems. Retention of such structures makes the topography of the cityscape comprehensible.

Although in most cities the removal of old defensive walls was first addressed long before the enactment of modern preservation laws, the resolution of this question sometimes reflected a desire to retain the historic character of the city. In both Istanbul and Rome, for example, changing societies continued to preserve the walls of ancient Roman fortifications over many centuries, passing these artifacts on to us today. In Prague, the ornate pinnacles of surviving medieval tower gateways have remained a part of the living city for over six hundred years, marking an earlier stage of urban growth and serving as symbols of a singular architectural tradition.

Such instances are unusual. In the modern era—although planners around the world cite the Ringstrasse as an example of productive urban change—the demolition of fortifications frequently led to development plans that had negative side effects. The boulevards of Beijing that replaced the mammoth historic walls of the city and were lined with an ad hoc array of bulky modern buildings, and the outer ring of freeways and contemporary housing towers that follow the course of Paris's Baroque entrenchments, alienate the traditional centers of these cities from the modern metropolis surrounding them. Cityscapes severed by walls became cityscapes severed by highways, polluted with excessive noise and noxious gases and fractured into unrelated zones.

In contrast, although built before the advent of the automobile, the removal of old perimeter walls in Vienna was an act of creative destruction. The new buildings and spaces of the Ringstrasse project were intentionally conceived to meld with the fabric of the traditional cityscape. Instead of forming an alien zone superimposed in the midst of Vienna, the Ringstrasse integrated the parts of the city to make a new urban whole. Pieces of the past were lost, but cultural continuity was achieved in the attainment of a new magnificence.

At the heart of the expanding metropolis—which had grown from 247,000 people in 1800 to 444,000 in 1850—and encircling the medieval core, the inner zone of Vienna's old fortifications occupied an arc of land varying in width from 200 yards to 600 yards. In 1857, Emperor Franz Joseph ordered that this defensive zone be reallocated to meet the needs of the modern capital. The imperial decree was systematic and farsighted. It declared that the old and the new city be linked together; that a traffic belt be created of parallel ring roads on either side of the Ringstrasse zone; that a competition be held to elicit ideas on how best to design the scheme; that a planning commission be formed to evaluate the proposals; that more than half of the parcels within this belt be sold to private builders to relieve an acute housing shortage; and that the resulting sales revenues be reserved to fund the public buildings and infrastructure of the project.

The resulting Ringstrasse plan provided wide boulevards for vehicles, trams, and pedestrians to circumnavigate the medieval core. Between its roadways, numerous structures were constructed to serve the needs of a developing modern society: new apartment houses, a city hall (Rathaus), a national parliament, museums of art and history, an opera house, several theaters and concert halls, and a university. Public gardens and parks were interspersed among public buildings to form a new civic center near the historic palaces of the Hapsburgs.

Although the project had been initiated by imperial decree, the design of the Ringstrasse reflected a political shift in the city's governance. In response to a revolutionary action led by the ascendant middle class and the urban intelligentsia in 1848, the Hapburgs instituted a constitutional monarchy and granted the right of self-governance to the city. By the time of the Ringstrasse project, the new city council was dominated by the Liberal Party. This group had already embarked on a program of urban improvements, which included rerouting the Danube and securing the city from seasonal floods, providing new infrastructure for clean drinking water, and constructing 150 elementary and secondary schools, as well as public baths, gas and electric works, and the first municipal hospital. As the Ringstrasse evolved, the Liberals were also able to influence both the general composition of the project and the particular form of several important buildings.

Since most of the Ringstrasse was conceived and built in a single continuous effort within a decade and on open land without existing structures as constraints, its designers were working on an unpainted canvas. It is thus telling that the major public buildings were not stylistically uniform or arranged in a single complex. Instead each institution had an autonomous presence, assuming an architectural form symbolic of its meaning in an increasingly pluralistic society, but nonetheless was also situated in alignment with the wide inner ring road that unified the project and was the major public promenade of the reformulated metropolis.

The university adopted forms from the Italian Renaissance to symbolize the rebirth of the classical pursuit of knowledge. The Rathaus was composed in a German Gothic style associated with the rise and empowerment of the medieval burghers. The museums of art and natural history were aligned to the great palace complex of the Hapsburgs and made to look like palaces for the people, bequeathed by a benevolent enlightened monarchy. And the most important symbol of all, the building to house the new national parliament, was done in a Greek Revival style. Three classical temple facades dominated the front elevation as it faced the Ringstrasse, statues of ancient Greek historians lined the ramps that led to the entry portico, and the figure of Athena, the patron goddess of Athens, rose up out of a fountain in front of the building—a design meant to convey the aspiration that the governance of Vienna be as participatory and democratic as that of the legendary Greek city-state. The separate buildings of the various institutions that lined the ring road articulated both the political empowerment of a wider portion of society and the greater breadth of social concerns embraced by the modernized government.

At the same time, in order to achieve continuity in the cityscape, the major radial avenues—which sprang from the Alstadt, crossed through the arc of the city's former walls, and extended out to the expanded metropolis—were retained. Within the ring road belt, between these cross avenues, blocks and streets were laid out in orthogonal grids. The organic street pattern of the old medieval center was thus reconciled with the rationalized contemporary geometries of the Ringstrasse zone. And in new residential neighborhoods, new

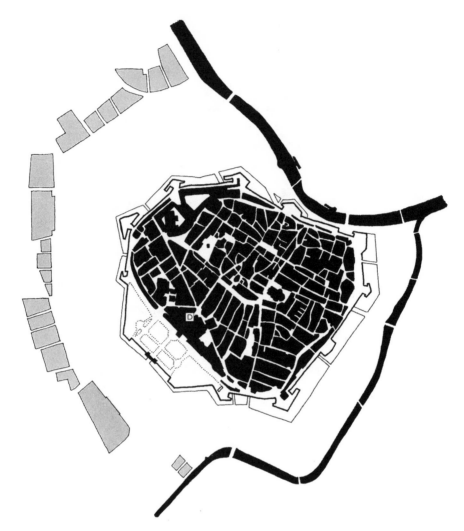

THE FORTIFIED ALTSTADT

The Ringstrasse · Vienna prior to its metamorphosis: The historic buildings of the Altstadt are shown in black. Buildings in light gray represent existing structures of the surrounding metropolis, which extends for a kilometer farther in all directions. A black line indicates the course of the fortifications, which are surrounded by an open ring-of-fire. · The plan of the Ringstrasse development: New buildings are indicated in dark gray. Their arrangement, as shown, is approximate, since the final form of this central zone of Vienna would change as various structures were constructed and other buildings were demolished. (Derived from a drawing published in 1888 by the Royal Institute of British Architects.) *(Both drawings at the same scale.)*

A Rathaus
B Museums of
  Art and History
C Parliament
D Palace

THE ALTSTADT ENVELOPED BY THE RINGSTRASSE

apartment blocks (comprising 590 new flats) were designed in reference to historic styles, and followed the Viennese tradition of adhering to street walls and looking like urban palaces. In both the public areas and the residential zones of the Ringstrasse, the new parts of the city spoke with an architectural vocabulary rooted in either the medieval or the classical building traditions of Vienna.

The forms of the public sphere of the city were purposely educational. As with the construction of beautifully landscaped public parks and art museums in other capitals of the world, the Liberals believed that exposure to such cultural refinement was ennobling. Thus the institutional zone was conceived as an extended urban museum through its integration of landscape design, architecture, and (in the principal interior spaces of its public buildings) of sculpture, painting, and the decorative arts. This synthesis of art and architecture was also a continuation of the city's custom of richly articulated facades.

Over the centuries, Vienna's architecture had become rife with sculpture of the highest quality. Dramatic pairs of figures arched over doorways, muscular Atlases bore the weight of lintels, noble knights stood guard over building corners, delicate nymphs pointed to roof peaks, allegorical figures—permanently frozen in action—greeted visitors at entryways, noble busts decorated long rows of decorative panels beneath window openings, prides of lions roared to the sky from cornices, patterns of vines and flowers were finely etched across facades. With the construction of the Ringstrasse, across a greatly expanded area, everywhere the eye turned, art had been integrated into the built environment.

The Ringstrasse had given the architectural composition of Vienna a theme and a crescendo, an expanded public realm, a new civic center, and a new urban identity. Yet the past had been connected to the present. The Ringstrasse was the embodiment of a cultural and political evolution, and the cityscape as a whole had been elevated to a high work of urban art consistent with old traditions but as modern in its time as any place in the world.

From out of this society now came a second period of cultural florescence whose ideas would once again reach beyond the city and change the world. Economic factors were crucial. Like ancient Athens, Vienna was a consumer city at the center of an extended empire, and the expendable wealth of the aristocrats of the Hapsburg court produced a large market for consumer goods. Simultaneously, the creation of a modern government bureaucracy generated a vast professional civil service. Manufacturing, trade, and printing expanded. Numerous craftsmen and small entrepreneurs flourished. Speculative banking expanded. Butchers, bakers, grocers, tailors, boot makers, hatters, and household servants were needed. An expanded middle class emerged. Vienna became a place of conspicuous consumption.

As Athenians had gathered in the agora, the Viennese strolled along the Ringstrasse and congregated in the city's cafés. (Most Viennese, except for the very poor, ate out at least once a day.) All classes rubbed elbows at the theater and the opera. Dance halls and private balls could attract more than a quarter of the city's population in an evening. Social discussion was elevated by the growing number of inhabitants educated at the city's universities. The quality of Vienna's journalism contributed to a more discriminating reception of art, music, and literature. The city's conservatories were some of the finest in Europe, attracting painters, architects, musicians, and students from across the continent.

The ensuing florescence, in fin de siècle Vienna, was more diverse than the first, which had been primarily musical. Achievements in music were also a part of this flowering—in the works of Johannes Brahms, Gustav Mahler, Arnold Schoenberg, and Anton Bruckner—but they were accompanied by advancements in medicine, in the work of Sigmund Freud and Alfred Adler; in literature, in the work of Hugo von Hofmannsthal and Karl Kraus; in architecture, in the work of Otto Wagner and Adolf Loos; and in the Secessionist movement in the visual arts, in the work of Gustav Klimt and Oskar Kokoschka—to name but the best known of a wide gathering of creative personalities.

Significant to this flowering was the engagement of Jewish society in the cultural life of the city. Not only were Mahler, Schoenberg, Freud, Hofmann-sthal, and many other notable Viennese figures of Jewish lineage, but since the Edict of Toleration Jews had assumed a prominent position in most intellec-tual spheres. While they represented only 8.6 percent of the total population in 1910, they accounted for 32 percent of the gymnasium students, 33 percent of the university students, 39 percent of the faculty in the medical school, 61 percent of the doctors, 58 percent of the lawyers, and 60 percent of the jour-nalists. Jews were principal participants in all aspects of the city's intellectual creativity—as patrons, critics, producers, and audience.

Yet in a society that had kept Jews apart for centuries, Jewish participation in the creative milieu of the city bred mistrust in many quarters. In addition, Jewish intellectuals played an active role in the political movements centered in Vienna, which pressed for social reform. The Ringstrasse symbolized the tri-umph of liberal ideology and the flowering of a city whose politics would grow increasingly divisive and become marred by anti-Semitism in the decades prior to the Second World War.

THE FALL OF THE HAPSBURGS AND THE POLITICIZATION OF THE CITYSCAPE

As the century turned, Vienna became an ideological battlefield. Just as the Liberals had remade the metropolis in their own image, the two principal metropolitan administrations to follow each represented different constituencies and enacted different sets of improvements when coming to power. Consequently, the physical and social modernization of Vienna occurred in pieces, as various parts of society gained the franchise and voted into municipal control parties sympathetic to their interests. The policies of each administration, while it was in power, became the justification for a particular ideological and class bias, producing periods of extremes.

The physical cityscape became politicized as well. Many aristocrats and members of the ascendant middle class (bourgeoisie) resided in the old city and near the Ringstrasse. Thus many of the civic improvements implemented by the Liberals had focused on the center of the city and enhanced bourgeois life. As the legal boundaries of the metropolis expanded outward, subsuming zones where the lower middle class resided, the balance of voting power shifted, and in 1895, the Liberals lost control of City Hall to the Christian Socialists, who represented the concerns of newly enfranchised lower-class artisans and shopkeepers. Their agenda continued the geographic relationship in Vienna between various classes, their politics, and where they lived.

The new regime resumed the work of building up the municipal hospital system and constructing more schools; they also enacted a farsighted city plan that protected a ring of green territory surrounding the city (the Wienerwald, or Vienna Woods). In the direct interest of their constituents, they created a municipal savings bank and insurance company to serve as a social safety net that benefited the poor but not the impoverished. Finally, the Christian Socialists developed a beautifully designed mass transit system linking the parts of the expanded metropolis—first by trams, and then by a modern metro system, which particularly helped those without the means for private transport to move about the cityscape. The Christian Socialists also institutionalized anti-Semitism as an official element of their party platform.

Economic conditions suddenly changed. Defeat in World War I marked the end of the reign of the Hapsburgs, the dissolution of the Austro-Hungarian dual monarchy (redistribution of the population into successor states took the following form: Austria, 6.5 million; Hungary, 8 million; Czechoslovakia, 13.6 million; Poland, 7.7 million; Romania, 8.8 million; Yugoslavia, 7.5 million), the demise of the city as a major center of European political power, and the establishment of the republic of Austria, a nation with greatly diminished resources from the very moment of its creation.

The collapse of the empire devastated the city's economy and produced a period of extended and general hardship. The nobility lost their wealth. The army and civil service were reduced. Businesses, banks, and manufacturing, dependent on the conspicuous consumption of the court, failed. The affluence that had built the Ringstrasse and paid for the luxuries of the aristocratic class had been based on the geopolitical advantages of a declining power. Meanwhile the industrialization of Vienna and Austria had lagged behind that of other European societies. Vienna was a consumer city whose productive capabilities could not compete in an open market.

Widespread unemployment in Vienna had led to a severe housing shortage as the city's laissez-faire policy of letting speculative development meet the need for new residential construction failed to produce affordable residences for an increasingly destitute lower class. Poorer inhabitants frequently rented sleeping space in an alcove or hallway. In the city as a whole, 22 percent of dwellings had indoor lavatories; but in the poorer districts: 90 percent of households were without toilets or faucets, and more than 75 percent were without electric or gas service as well. On the outskirts of the metropolis, illegal settlements sprang up, as about 150,000 people built shacks and planted subsistence gardens. The opulence of fin de siècle Vienna and the beautiful outer shell of the city's architecture had masked a society in which people living with minimal means were vulnerable to the unpredictable cataclysms of life. And with the fall of the Hapsburgs, just such a cataclysm had struck.

In 1919 the new republic made Vienna an independent province, expanding the boundaries of the municipality to include a large urban proletariat. Initially this population had been drawn to the city by the abundant opportunities of a great capital but now they were unemployed and living in wretched conditions. As this mass of people attained the right to vote, the political schism in Austria deepened.

Austria's pattern of geographically formulated politics now isolated the city from the rest of the country. On a national level, the Christian Socialists consolidated power among agrarian, lower-middle-class, and conservative interests, capturing the national assembly. Social Democrats found much of their support in Vienna among urban intellectuals, Marxists, Socialists, and factory workers, thus controlling the municipal government of the capital, which as the only major metropolis of a small nation, occupied a position of urban primacy and represented about one-third of the population of Austria.

Surrounded by an alienated countryside, Socialist Vienna would now attempt to redress the problems of its poorest inhabitants. From out of Vienna's widely respected university system, and with an important contribution from the Jewish intelligentsia, a body of critical thought had evolved on how to correct the injustices of modern industrial life. An extraordinary program of civic reforms, recognized internationally as one of the most significant precursors of the social welfare state, was quickly put into action by the

Socialist-controlled city government. Once again the city would be remade. The new era would be known as "Red Vienna."

RED VIENNA

The municipally funded housing program of Red Vienna provided living quarters for about one-tenth of Vienna's inhabitants (200,000 people), in four hundred housing blocks constructed during a fifteen-year period. Support facilities such as health clinics, dental offices, libraries, retail stores, nursery schools, theaters, playgrounds, and public green space were integrated into the projects. Average rent cost less than 5 percent of an inhabitant's income. For its day, the program was one of the largest and most progressive urban housing efforts in the world, absorbing 25 to 30 percent of the city's annual budget.

For these projects the municipal authorities required extensive tracts of land and the money to pay for them. In this regard, a program by the previous municipal administration, the Christian Socialists, was crucial.

The Federal Rent Control Act in 1922 was designed to reduce the labor costs of industrialists by decreasing the cost of living for industrial workers. This allowed the manufacturing sector to keep salaries low and helped the struggling Austrian economy to compete more effectively with the new nation-states that surrounded the republic after the breakup of the Austro-Hungarian Empire. While rent control made apartments cheaper, however, it did not increase their number.

Freezing rents at low levels had made the development of speculative housing unprofitable, decreasing the cost of land throughout Vienna. As a result, the city could afford to purchase property competitively on the open market and within a few years doubled its holdings from 17 percent to 34 percent of the municipal area. Red Vienna then added a graduated tenant rental tax, heavily weighted in relation to luxury apartments, and a payroll tax levied on employers. This kept the cost of apartments low for the poor, while generating 40 percent of the construction costs of public housing. Together, rent controls, tenant and payroll taxes, and a depressed speculative housing market were the economic underpinnings of the social housing program.

As a matter of ideological propagation, the Socialists conceived of the housing complexes as both private dwellings and public buildings—as communes that supported a collective life. In this regard the program had the purpose of politically indoctrinating the proletariat class and consolidating their support, just as the Ringstrasse had been a symbolic device to propagate the ideals of the Liberal party. Yet the inclusion of residential support services within each complex also made the new housing convenient for its inhabitants

*not
shared
ident*

without placing the burden for providing these services on the existing communities where the housing was built. Since these lands were not acquired through right of eminent domain, they were scattered about the cityscape due to the vagaries of the real estate market. Because the municipal government was required to build within the city's legal perimeters, the communes were located in neighborhoods near existing mass transit services.

All these contingencies affected the architectural forms of Red Vienna housing, which were site specific, with different designs and layouts tailored for different locations. While no basic repetitive model was created, a distinctive type of architectural solution evolved, one that mediated between historic and modern forms. The Socialists wanted buildings that looked different, as symbols of the new and better world they were creating—but the proletariat desired buildings whose architecture had traditional overtones, reflecting their assimilation into established society. Similar conflicting goals also existed for the architects. The large scale of the housing projects, the integration of support services into the buildings, and the quasi-public nature of the gardens made Red Vienna housing a new building type—even though large courtyard apartment blocks were an architectural tradition in the metropolis, with a distinct formal language embedded throughout the built environment.

Such conceptual dilemmas had already been addressed in the work of two of the city's most preeminent urban theorists: architect Otto Wagner and urban historian Camillo Sitte. Each had examined the conflict between tradition and modernity; each would eventually gain international recognition for his ideas. And although neither would actually design a Red Vienna project, the imprint of their thinking was part of the architectural culture of the city.

In his groundbreaking 1889 study *City Building According to Its Artistic Principles,* Camillo Sitte had anticipated the conflict in modern city planning between the technocrat-engineer and the artistic architect, the conflict between a city designed for circulation efficiency and a cityscape whose architecture was artfully arranged to make beautiful public spaces for its inhabitants. Over the next century, as modern planning frequently produced sterile geometric urban configurations, Sitte's analysis of the organic evolution of irregular and much-loved old European plazas would make architects conscious of the humanist tradition in historic city building that modernism often failed to understand and assimilate. His influence would be indirect, but nonetheless would help to make each Red Vienna housing complex a unique artistic composition that responded to the eccentric conditions of the different plots of municipally owned property.

The influence of Otto Wagner was more immediate. Not only was he widely recognized as one of Vienna's greatest architects, but many of the most important designers of Red Vienna housing had studied with him in the Special

School for Architecture at the Academy of Fine Arts. Although in the early years of his practice Wagner had designed apartment blocks in historical styles on the Ringstrasse, in midcareer his design for Vienna's first subway system, the Stadtbahn, crystallized his ideas on how modern urban functions and technology might be reconciled with existing architectural traditions. Over eight years, he designed thirty-six stations as well as the viaducts, tunnels, and bridges that facilitated the laying of track through the cityscape. His work was a fusion of modern engineering with historic and contemporary design forms inspired by the Vienna Secession visual arts movement. While each train station incorporated architectural traditions from its neighborhood, Wagner also developed a palette of generic design elements that were used throughout the system. He made the Stadtbahn a visually distinctive continuous integrated structure for the whole city, while simultaneously responding to the specific characteristics of different locations in Vienna.

His approach to teaching was derived from his personal design method. All the student projects in his studio were concurrent exercises in urban composition and individual building design. Wagner believed that architecture should be conceived with regard not only for contemporary functions and technologies, which would cause buildings to become more modern, but also for the compositional continuum of the city as a whole, causing the social face of new buildings to act in concert with existing historic structures and spaces to make the city more beautiful. Unlike most other twentieth-century architects, Wagner required his students to draw each building proposal in its urban surroundings, a practice he followed himself. This simple discipline had significant effect on the designer's state of consciousness. Reconstructing the immediate cityscape on paper focused the architect on the visual characteristics of the urban environment. The geographic points from which pedestrians could view a building were a decisive consideration. Due to the irregularity of narrow historic street patterns, each urban site had particular vistas within which an architectural design could be seen. Wagner required that the forms of new buildings be compositionally reconciled in each of these contextual vistas. His architecture thereby established artful relationships, from critical urban vantage points, with the spaces and buildings around it.

In addition, since pedestrians also experience structures up close, in partial views, Wagner demanded that details and individual building elements—doorways, windows, shopfronts—be consistent in their design with the larger conception for the whole building. After weighing all these considerations, Wagner made buildings that were coherent and contemporary yet also part of the larger cultural continuum of Vienna.

Typecast as the historicist versus the modernist, Sitte and Wagner were set in opposition to each other during their lifetimes, but their mutually reinforcing ideas on contextualism were a legacy of insightful urban thinking. Both had advocated looking carefully at the city before changing it.

Into this thickly embroidered urban fabric Red Vienna architects now inserted structures whose modernism established a new scale and character but whose reinterpretation of historic building traditions ensured that the new housing looked particularly Viennese. Since 190 architects—33 of them trained by Wagner—worked on the project, the structures varied from site to site, but in general, Red Vienna housing was larger than traditional rent palaces but not overpoweringly so. The projects continued the historical convention of locating the facades of buildings on the perimeter street walls of blocks. Each building retained the tradition of architectural ornamentation, but more minimally and in the modernist style. Construction was largely done by hand in order to employ large numbers of workers, craftsmen, and artists.

The planners of Red Vienna identified four basic urban conditions in the municipally owned properties scattered across the cityscape: new housing that filled the space between existing buildings; new housing that occupied a complete city block in the historic city; new housing that occupied several adjacent blocks in the historic city; and housing complexes built outside the existing urban fabric, which could become complete urban worlds unto themselves. This act of conceptual differentiation reveals both a state of mind and a process of design consistent with the work of Sitte and Wagner: a commitment to build in response to the character of the existing urban landscape.

As works of building art, particularly in the finest complexes such as Karl-Marx-Hof, designed by Karl Ehn, the projects sometimes were among the most creative modern architecture to be built anywhere in the world. Simple contemporary forms with precise proportions and elementary geometries were highlighted with surprising decorative details and touches of modern art. Doorways were frequently articulated in minimal but arresting compositions. Touches of sculpture or surface modulation enriched select architectural elements. Historic building massing was sometimes recast in a reductive interpretation of traditional form. Major entrances were marked by powerful design gestures: a giant arched opening, a clock tower, a startling cantilever. Small circular windows or other eye-catching features punctuated the rhythms of rows of repetitive rectangular openings. Setbacks might modulate a building mass as it turned a corner. Odd angles were introduced into prevailingly orthogonal compositions in response to the eccentric configurations of existing urban plots.

Such gestures were more than just welcome investments in aesthetics. They conveyed the importance that the municipal authorities placed on sustaining more than the basic physical needs of the inhabitants. The tradition of urban housing in Vienna emphasized external appearance; the new public housing continued that custom. Just as the Baroque rent palaces had been invested with sculpture and artwork, so hundreds of artists were employed by Red Vienna to embellish municipal apartment blocks. The poor were not being asked to reside in buildings whose visual sparseness advertised a minimal economic investment. Nor were they asked to live in housing whose character was divorced from the city's proud architectural heritage.

Because the housing was well built and not designed by repetitive aesthetic formula, because it conformed with tradition yet embodied a modern way of life, and because it looked Viennese, its inhabitants bore no social stigma. Thoughtful urban design had served thoughtful social reform. Moreover, the city was not fractured as it was modernized. (Compare this to public housing in the United States, where municipal housing was often a stark departure from all previous building traditions and constituted an alien zone separated from the norms of the cityscape). Once again, Vienna had extended itself with reason and artistic sensitivity.

This era of accomplishment, however, ended with violence and negation. The polarized political climate of Austria, which had empowered the Socialists to unilaterally construct a powerful vision of a more equitable society, now took a sudden and extreme turn. Politicization of the housing program had made the communes into bastions of socialist ideology. And it is not surprising that the inhabitants of Red Vienna apartments largely supported the party that had housed them, further strengthening the Socialists' hold on the city.

The Russian Revolution and the establishment, in 1919, of a Soviet republic in Hungary had raised concern about armed insurrection in Austria. The urban social programs of Red Vienna were perhaps the most progressive in Europe, but they occurred in a nation whose rural populace supported the more conservative agenda of an opposition party. Moreover, the anti-Semitic platform of the Christian Socialists further ostracized the Social Democrats, many of whose leaders were Jewish.

With both sides fearing a putsch, the Social Democrats formed an armed guard. In 1927 political demonstrations ignited several days of street fighting during which more than one hundred people were killed and the Ministry of Justice was burned. The worldwide depression further destabilized Austria's economy. The Nazis rose to power in Germany and pressed for unification with Austria.

In 1934 civil war broke out and the social housing blocks of Red Vienna became fortresses as government troops assaulted the communes. After four days the Christian Socialists had prevailed, the Social Democratic party was declared illegal, the republic was abolished, and democracy was replaced by an authoritarian Fascist state. In 1938, Hitler entered the weakened and divided country at the head of his armies. The Anschluss was proclaimed, and Austria joined the Third Reich.

Of the 200,000 Austrian Jews, 150,000 were forced to emigrate and 50,000 were exterminated. The liberal and progressive urban society that had evolved out of the Enlightenment—making Vienna an international center of culture, producing two remarkable eras of intellectual florescence, and resulting in two notable masterstrokes of advanced urban planning (the creation of the Ringstrasse and the housing of Red Vienna)—was denuded of its wealth of human capital. The country had become the foe of the city, and the brilliant creative flowering of Vienna was extinguished, in part as a consequence of a deep-seated religious intolerance that cannot be disassociated from the violence that erupted within the city itself and the violence that would now be unleashed against its beautiful assemblage of architectural parts.

HISTORIC AMSTERDAM:
THE BEAUTIFUL CITY OF PROFIT

Perhaps it is obvious that a people who perfected the construction of seawalls and windmills as a way of reclaiming a massive geographic land area from the water would build itself a novel city. Nonetheless, Amsterdam is a surprising human creation. Although it was once the center of a wide commercial empire that monopolized much of the riches of the world, it is a capital without grand imperial buildings to proclaim its majesty. Nor are the streets of Amsterdam paved with gold, although there was gold enough to do so. Instead, the city is composed of a network of utilitarian canals, lined by neat files of trees. Behind this canopy of greenery, and likewise running parallel to the canals, are lines of narrow brick houses forming an eccentric but unified street wall crowned by fanciful peaked roofs of endless variety. The pinnacles of these structures— block after block of them numbering in the thousands across the cityscape— form a composition of myriad singular architectonic expressions, all woven together in a greater urban hierarchy.

For centuries, Amsterdammers have loved brick, using elegant long, rectangular bricks with straight, narrow lines of mortar. They curved, angled, coffered, corbeled, cantilevered, and arched the bricks, and set them in herringbone patterns. They constructed the front elevations of their brick buildings with a slight forward pitch, to protect the facades from the rain. They used bricks of different hues, or stained them black with water-repelling oils yielding a glowing and deeply colored surface. With a modest palette of elements— water, bridges, trees, and bricks—through its social coherence and perpetual imagination, Amsterdam weaves a singular urban music. It is not the grand, imposing symphony of Vienna but the song of a cityscape where many different individuals artfully knit together their separate existences into a useful harmony of life.

In contrast to the expressive and varied architectural crowns of the city, Amsterdam's governance was carefully measured and conservative. Unlike the administration of modern Vienna, with its shifts between extremes, Amsterdam was a city noted for its stability. Its ascent to become a major center of world trade and European culture was due in large part to its ability to minimalize factionalism. Had the Netherlands not practiced inclusiveness over the centuries, much of it might not have existed at all.

Whereas Venice is a city whose existence depends on an artificially induced environmental state within its immediate natural surroundings, Amsterdam occupies but a small part of an immense territory reclaimed from nature by human devices (an area that has grown to approximately 2,500 square miles, which is larger than Delaware and about half the size of Northern Ireland). The process of recovering arable land from the fens of the Netherlands began in the Middle Ages. It not only changed the geographic character of the area, but had far-reaching social and political effects as well.

Beneath the surface of the low-lying marshlands of the Netherlands is a thick layer of peat on top of a substratum of sand. Sometime in the Middle Ages, the inhabitants of this area learned that by digging drainage ditches around an isolated plot, they could lower the water table, and the dried layer of peat would support farming and cattle grazing. But as the layer of peat dehydrated, it compressed and sank, and the resulting farmable acreage was below sea level and subject to flooding. Thus the Hollanders found it necessary to build a wall of dikes to protect these low areas from the higher tides of storms and the seasonal inundations of rivers.

Since the integrity of the whole system was vulnerable to compromise by a single breach—indeed, early in this history several large areas were lost to the sea through flooding—the people of this low-lying area formed cooperative organizations to maintain the extended wall of dikes. As early as the twelfth century, local communes were established. By the thirteenth century, regional water boards were regulating new construction and maintenance and levying taxes over wide areas, with large landholders bearing a proportionately greater tax burden. Each farmer understood that the protection of everyone's livelihood was only as secure as the weakest link in the community. Geographic necessity had inculcated awareness among the Dutch people of a common interest that transcended other differences: the benefits of centralized administration, cooperation, and tolerance.

With the adaptation of the windmill to help drainage, even larger land areas could be reclaimed, and the resulting agricultural surplus made possible the creation of cities devoted to other commercial activities. Situated on the floodplains of large rivers that reached far into central Europe (the Meuse and the Rhine), and having access to the Atlantic, the North Sea, and the Baltic, the

Hollanders were well positioned to become both saltwater and inland traders. Furthermore, their unique and extensive network of man-made and natural waterways constituted a highly efficient transport system for the collection and dispersal of trade goods.

Fishing had long thrived, and the people of the Netherlands were already accomplished boatbuilders and sailors. As transglobal sea routes to Asia reduced the importance of overland routes to the Mediterranean, the balance of European commercial power shifted to the seafaring nations of the Atlantic: Britain, France, Spain, Portugal, and Holland. Of several Dutch cities, Amsterdam was particularly well situated, with a deepwater port located at the mouth of the inland waterway network. Even more important, its administrators gradually created a physical and social structure that greatly enhanced the city's commercial growth.

Although cities in the medieval Netherlands had developed late compared to those in other parts of Europe, they quickly gained municipal freedom in the management of their affairs. This was partly due to the experience of Holland in delegating administration of the dike system to local authorities. Unlike Vienna, which as an imperial capital did not become a self-governing city until late in its history, Amsterdam soon came to be directed by a council of its more prominent merchants and burgomasters, who made economic growth their first priority. As the city's increasing mercantile success produced greater riches and political influence, the governing oligarchy became commensurably more powerful, gaining a greater degree of control. By 1480 the destiny of the city was completely in its own hands. Amsterdam became an environment designed by commercial interests to support commercial ends.

The trade practices that resulted in Amsterdam's rise often were not innovative in themselves but were adapted from those of other places and systematized through centuries of diligent governmental management. This single-minded perfection and integration of elements affecting business created a multidimensional commercial advantage. The cost of shipbuilding was lower in Holland than anywhere else in Europe because builders could buy raw materials in bulk and control the wages of laborers. (It has been estimated that in the seventeenth century, Dutch ships cost 40 percent less than those made in England.) The expense of freighting was minimized to reduce the price of trade goods. Amsterdam's merchant exchange was better organized, its banking was quick and reliable, access to capital and insurance was easier, and interest rates were low.

Large corporations were developed to exploit monopolies. This spread out the risk of speculative business investment and created economic advantages of scale. An example was the East India Company, which built an extensive trade network in Asia and established colonies throughout the Far East, at its height sending out more than 300 ships and 80,000 people a year. A similar network

of Amsterdam-linked trading offices and banks facilitated commercial trans-
actions throughout Europe. By the seventh century, more than 800 shipping
companies were delivering goods to 180 destinations.

It became a practice of the city's government to underwrite commercial
immigration and thereby generate a stream of new capital, technical knowledge, business expertise, and trans-European trading contacts. When Antwerp
fell to the Spanish in 1585, Amsterdam opened its guilds to newcomers, made
citizenship readily available, compensated merchants for moving costs, and
found relocation sites for manufacturers. In response, former Portuguese Jews
from Antwerp expanded Amsterdam's business in diamonds and textile production, while the resettlement of Antwerp's numerous printing businesses,
coupled with Amsterdam's tolerant liberalism, which allowed the production
of books that were banned in other places, made the city one of the major publishing centers in Europe.

Just as the burgomasters shaped the institutions of Amsterdam to foster
economic progress, so was the physical environment constructed to provide
commercial advantages. Medieval Amsterdam had been built up on both sides
of the river Amstel where a dam separated the river from a harbor (the Ij),
which connected to an inland bay (the Zuider Zee), which opened out to the
North Sea. The form of the metropolis evolved in response to careful control
of the flow of these waters.

Due to the weight of its buildings, the layer of peat on which Amsterdam
was constructed suffered even more from sinking than the open agricultural
fields around it. In the city's early days (from sometime in the thirteenth century), buildings were made of wood. But the frequent need to heat interiors,
due to a cold, wet climate, plus the closeness of structures in the settlement—
compacted within the city's defensive walls and pushed together because dry
land was so laborious to create—made fire an omnipresent danger. (In 1452,
two-thirds of the city was destroyed.) As a result, building regulations enacted
by the town council mandated construction in brick with slate or tile roofs, and
subsidies were available to help those unable to afford such costly imported
materials and more elaborate construction methods.

Supporting the weight of these structures was a problem that Amsterdam
would struggle for centuries to solve. Ultimately, the construction of solid
foundations demanded the driving of long wooden piles through the layer of
compacted peat to an impenetrable stratum of hard sand, which generally lay
about 13 meters (or about 43 English feet or 46 Amsterdam feet) below the
surface. Depending on the size and design of the building, hundreds or thousands of piles might be required (the great Exchange Building on the Dam, one
of the largest public buildings in Europe at the time of its construction,
needed 13,659 piles).

Driven by hand with heavy wooden mallets, the piles in Amsterdam's earliest masonry structures (usually only 5 to 7 meters long) invariably failed to reach the sand substratum. Moreover, the crowns of piles and the wooden structures built on top of them to distribute the load of upper masonry walls were subject to rot if not constructed below the level of the city's groundwater table. With time, many of these buildings shifted unevenly, cracked, or collapsed, requiring painstaking efforts to stabilize and mend.

In the 1400s, the city introduced strict standards for pile driving. By the 1500s, all foundations required municipal approval. During the 1600s, it became technically feasible to drive down to the solid layer of sand, as heavy pile-driving frames were developed, which required the strength of forty or more men to operate. Yet if the piles were not perfectly vertical, the buildings' foundations were in danger of settling unevenly. Due to the variable and hidden conditions of the subsurface, the construction of foundations in Amsterdam would remain a costly art, subject to error, until the latter half of the twentieth century. (Today, after the passage of centuries, it is rare that the conservation of historic architecture in Amsterdam does not require the rehabilitation of piles, their crowns, the wooden structure that rests on them, and subsurface parts of masonry walls—all of which must be achieved while not destabilizing ancient neighboring edifices.)

As the city prospered and grew, the scarcity of land drove property values higher. Buildings became tall, narrow, and deep, and were built out to the street wall, with high-pitched roofs and steep internal stairs that economized on interior space. In order to further maximize the room within buildings while still preserving the width of the public way, the front facades of structures were inclined forward so that the upper floors tilted outward and were slightly larger in floor area (a condition that Amsterdammers refer to as "in flight"). As in other medieval cities, most houses accommodated businesses as well as residential functions. In order to bring goods and furniture into the upper floors—stairways being too steep to allow passage—hoists were cantilevered outward at the top of each building's canal facade. Merchandise could thereby be unloaded directly from barges into the storage areas in buildings. The forward cant of front elevations facilitated this process, allowing loads to swing free and not bump or drag against the building front.

Although over the centuries Amsterdam would gradually adopt classical architectural styles from other parts of Europe, the wetness of the climate led to singular building designs. The forward cant of facades enabled structures to shed rainwater on more exposed brick street-elevations, and roofs had to maintain a pitch of 50 to 60 degrees to prevent wind-driven rain from penetrating beneath the overlapping roof tiles. The extreme angle of these gable roofs posed an aesthetic condition for which classically inspired architecture had no conventions. Resolution of classical styles with the steep triangular shape at the pinnacle of the facade (each with a protruding hoist beam) produced an endless variety of solutions, none of which came to be adopted as a universal standard. Whether inspired by classical or medieval design traditions, buildings developed an individual expressiveness in the way they reached to the sky, and many were elaborate compositional concoctions. Local conditions had bred a unique and picturesque architectural culture.

By the fifteenth century, Amsterdam had refined the design and size of its shipping fleet and greatly expanded trade. Widespread population growth throughout Europe had greatly increased the demand for grains from the north, particularly from Poland. In response to unpredictable fluctuations of supply, the city greatly increased its storage capacity, thereby being able to provide grain even when crops were poor. This expansion of the city's warehouse potential became one of Amsterdam's most important commercial attributes, making a wide range of trade goods accessible to any purchaser at any time. Each of these buildings bordered on a canal and was readily approachable, often by the very seacraft used for transport.

In the first stage of its evolution Amsterdam flanked the Amstel and was surrounded by fortifications and a moat. In order to protect both the neighboring fields and the city from flooding, both sides of the moat were, in effect, a pair of high dams. In the city's second stage of growth (in the fifteenth century), another wall and moat were constructed farther outward, parallel to the Amstel and to the first moat, which was retained as an inner-city canal. In this way, the ground plane was raised above sea level (the area bordering the Amstel would eventually be 100 feet higher than the original grade), and the islands of the city—although covered by buildings—were actually the bulwarks of elevated protective seawalls.

Entry to each canal from the harbor was controlled by a pair of locks. At high tide, strategic locks were opened, allowing the tides to flush water through the city's canals inland up the Amstel. At low tide, another set of locks was opened, to allow sewage to flow out of the Amstel, through the canals, and into the bay. The power of this outward surge scoured the harbor's bottom and kept it from filling in with sediment. In a geographic location in which every building and square foot of land required inordinate effort to construct, a remarkable urban environment had been conceived. Where once there were but marshlands and bogs, the Dutch had slowly assembled a long waterway, bordered by storage and wrapping around itself in a single compact configuration. The urban environment had become a technological feat—a complex and extensive dam linked to both inland waters and the sea—extending the reach of the city out across the world.

THE TRANSFORMATION OF THE RING CANALS

By the 1600s, Amsterdam had become Europe's leading financial and trading center, with a fleet greater than those of the English, French, and Spanish combined. Its commercial and cultural life had been enriched by immigrants from across the Continent; its warehouses held the largest store of grain in Europe. This extraordinary wealth made possible a cultured cosmopolitan life among its rich, and Dutch painting became world renowned, reaching a pinnacle in the works of Rembrandt van Rijn. The moderate character of Amsterdam's Protestant governance—stressing social stability, productivity, and an openness to new ideas—had given the city a reputation for tolerance. No ghetto had been zoned for its Jewish inhabitants; charitable organizations abounded; and through its printers of maps and books the city became a leading disseminator of the new ideas of the European Enlightenment.

During the century of Amsterdam's Golden Age, waves of immigration (largely Protestant) increased the city's population from 60,000 in 1600 to 200,000 by 1660, making it the third-largest city in Europe. A period of dramatic physical extension began. Once again old ramparts would be raised, new fortifications constructed, and an existing moat would become yet another canal, but the expansion in the seventeenth century, like the transformative gesture of the Ringstrasse in Vienna, would dramatically redefine Amsterdam as an urban construction.

Amsterdam's initial islands formed a sequence of canals roughly parallel to the Amstel River. The shape of the medieval city was geomorphic, its forms reflecting the contours of its natural surroundings. The compilation of its parts was organic, a gradual accrual in which each new island resulted from compliance with an evolving formula for dikes, canals, and commercial efficiency. In contrast, the additions of the Golden Age would be geometric and would introduce an idealized mathematical configuration.

This change in mind-set reflected a different self-awareness on the part of the city. Amsterdam now saw itself as an important focal point of the world. Over the centuries, the Dutch experiment in urbanism had gradually become an alternative to the autocratic governments in Catholic Spain, Catholic France, and the Papal States. The Protestant cities of the republic of the seven united provinces of the Netherlands were self-governing and free of any all-powerful central authority. More than one-half of the population of the Netherlands lived in cities, compared to 25 percent in England and France. Amsterdam was resolutely independent in a country whose vitality relied on autonomous centers of urban prosperity. Thus, while Rome and Paris were remade with grand avenues and boulevards focusing on imposing monuments

THE RING CANALS OF HISTORIC AMSTERDAM

A comparison in urban texture · Amsterdam in 1835: The intricate dike, dam, bridge, street, and canal system of Amsterdam—surrounded by fortifications and linked by water to the cities of the Netherlands and the sea—represents a pinnacle of urban engineering. · Venice in 1838: The paths, bridges, and island campos of the city—separated by a network of canals—are closely woven together in a complex organic urban structure tuned to the rhythms of the surrounding natural environment. Each cityscape is a singular object of evolving environmental artistry. (*Both drawings at the same scale.*)

THE CENTER OF HISTORIC VENICE

to the power of a central church and state, the new plan for Amsterdam symbolized an alternative urban hierarchy.

The expansion was influenced nonetheless by the broad currents of European cultural development. In particular, the urban designs of the Italian Renaissance and the reconstruction of Rome under the popes had instilled an intellectual recognition of the city as an object of design. But instead of creating awe-inspiring roadways and public plazas that focused on prominent structures, Amsterdam built a geometric matrix consisting of a spacious belt of three parallel canals (the Prisengracht, the Keizersgracht, and the Herengracht), which flowed around the existing city in an irregular and unclosed polygon, segmented and linked to the historic center by radial circulation routes. The configuration looked much like the pattern of straight threads in a spiderweb.

An arc of outer fortifications with twenty-six bastions, each crowned by a windmill, enclosed the expanded metropolis, which quadrupled in area. Different sectors were zoned for different uses, a trend that had already been developing in the historic center of the city. The three principal canal belts were set aside for upper-class homes, while an area to the west was laid out in an orthogonal grid of canals, blocks, and streets to serve a mixed-use community of residential, commercial, and manufacturing—with the aim of segregating noxious activities from prime residential neighborhoods.

Each canal was bordered on either side by a quay, a row of trees, and a roadway. Bridges interconnected the ground circulation system at canal crossways. The new islands were subdivided into lots whose proportions were deep and narrow, as in the historic core. No building could occupy more than 56 percent of its site, and it was stipulated that a minimum distance of 160 feet be kept between the rear walls of structures to ensure a sufficiency of light and air in backyards. While some of the new mansions on the ring canals occupied adjacent properties and were twice the size of their neighbors, their overall dimensions were based on the repetitive module of the city's lots. Similarly, as classical styles became part of the city's architectural vocabulary, classical facades were composed to the dimensions of the universal lot size and remained in proportion with the rest of the cityscape, while often culminating in picturesque rooftops.

In 1648, at the traditional center of the city, at the Dam, a great Exchange Building was constructed in a classical style. It was enormous and opulent, in keeping with the transglobal commercial dominance of the city, but the elements of the cityscape were not arranged to focus upon it from afar. The Exchange was an understated moment of high drama. Throughout the cityscape, the wealth of Amsterdam was expressed with reserve, and this lack of ostentation was a basic part of the city's aesthetic character.

In contrast to Venice, whose island blockfronts along the Grand Canal usually consisted of only a handful of buildings, the blockfronts on Amsterdam's three ring canals comprised a dozen or more buildings, aligned in long street walls. This difference was significant. In Venice, as in Renaissance Rome and Florence, a single palazzo could dominate its immediate urban mass. In Amsterdam, the houses of the wealthy were closer in size and magnificence to other facades, and each mansion, no matter how luxurious, remained aesthetically secondary to the greater urban volume of the block. The visual message was that the whole was greater than its individual parts.

Whereas in Rome and Paris long, straight boulevards magnified the effect of major urban architectural events terminating such vistas, in Amsterdam wide tree-lined canals took a different angle at each axis, and straight lines did not extend far across the cityscape. Instead of focusing the eye on an ultimate end, the city enclosed the viewer in its continuum of form. Yet this was also a continuum of diversity. Paris, particularly in the era of Haussmann, would develop street walls of elegant architectural unity, but Amsterdam erected street walls composed of a mélange of buildings with imaginative roof configurations. As a general comparison, Paris subsumed individuality to serve a grand design, while Amsterdam accommodated diversity within a unifying structure.

The concept for the enlargement of the city had given physical shape to Amsterdam's success in providing a useful social structure that supported individual commercial innovation. Like the Ringstrasse, built a century later in Vienna, the forms of Amsterdam became a symbol of the ideas that made it. The ring canals of one of first cities devoted to capitalism were a coordinated matrix that synthesized individual architectural invention, oddly similar in concept to the future matrix of the giant grid of New York, which was also a city of tolerance, immigrants, and free enterprise. Quite naturally, when first established by the Dutch, the American colonial city was given the name New Amsterdam.

THE SOCIAL HOUSING OF THE AMSTERDAM SCHOOL

The modernization of Amsterdam during the Golden Age was a sophisticated act of urban conservation in its time. The old city core had been preserved, and its urban elements and organization had been brought to a new level of refinement in the arc of the ring canals. As in the cities of the twentieth century, the population growth of Amsterdam during the seventeenth century was unprecedented, the volume of new construction was unparalleled, and the size of the expansion called for a new system of urban organization. Yet the technology and aesthetics of architectural construction by hand continued. The new social uses of structures had not necessitated a dramatic increase in their size, nor had technological advances in intercity movement and communication caused a dramatic revision of infrastructure. The next major period of urban expansion involved a far greater complexity. By then, almost two centuries later, Amsterdam's commercial preeminence had faded and the city had become a beautiful anachronism in an emerging modern world.

The modern social housing movement that occurred in Amsterdam prior to the Second World War—virtually concurrent with the public housing program of Red Vienna—was born of a long tradition of philanthropy. Of particular historical significance is the era that began in 1579, at the end of the Reformation, when Amsterdammers converted to Protestantism, when the Netherlands won its independence from Catholic Spain, and when a new generation of Calvinist burgomasters took power. As in other areas of Europe evolving out of a medieval agrarian economy, in the Netherlands Calvinist concepts of thrift, hard work, and individual responsibility supported the successful development of urban mercantile economies. Moreover, Calvinist concern over the economic exploitation of lower-paid workers had entered the general social consciousness, and the new burgomasters of Amsterdam took an immediate interest in the system by which the city aided the poor.

Rapid population growth during the city's commercial expansion provided Amsterdam with a much-needed pool of unskilled laborers; at the same time, fluctuations in the economy, wars, plagues, and the inherent dangers of sea traffic (the loss of life among East India Company seamen varied from 6 percent to 15 percent and up to 23 percent in the worst years) exposed a substantial part of Amsterdam's population to the hardships of poverty. Large numbers of unemployed, impoverished elderly, orphans, and widows became a permanent part of the city's social composition.

With the shift from Catholicism to Protestantism, establishments of the Catholic church lost their privileges in the city. After being given the authority by the states of Holland to divest Catholic monasteries, orphanages, and poorhouses, and as they assumed responsibility for such institutional services, the burgomasters were confronted with the larger task of evaluating whether existing programs met the needs of the city's marginalized inhabitants. This practical assessment of the reality of human suffering and the resulting attempt to alleviate it were quite unusual for their time.

The Burgher's Orphanage was expanded and re-endowed, so that the number of residents doubled to a thousand by 1660. Two existing hospitals were allocated new facilities in vacated convents. An additional home for sick soldiers was opened. Aid to the housebound sick, old, and orphaned was expanded by building warehouses for grain, cheese, peat, and wood, and by constructing new municipal centers for the distribution of relief. A central administration for alms coordinated a program for boarding out homeless young people. In 1662 a second municipal orphanage, the Almoner's Orphanage, provided a dwelling for 1,300 more children.

In addition to the direct involvement of the municipal government, independent religious organizations helped unfortunate members of their particular faith. By 1695 the Reformed Dutch church had founded an old men's and women's home and an orphanage that housed a thousand children. The Catholics maintained four almshouses, a virgins' home, a boys' orphanage, and a poor office to aid the housebound destitute. Similarly, the Mennonites and Lutherans established almshouses and orphanages of their own.

With time, the burgomasters grew to expect each religious faith to help in providing a network of social aid for the inhabitants of Amsterdam. While the interest of the ruling elite in providing relief for the poor was somewhat motivated by a practical concern for quelling social unrest and indoctrinating recipients to various religious tenets, the extent of the city's combined effort elicited the wonder of many contemporary Europeans. As in the administration of the dike system, the organization of the social safety net was a partnership that integrated governmental and private efforts, allowing different groups to respond to the problem, each according to its religious or social values. As Amsterdam emerged into the industrial age, this deeply embedded tradition of pluralism led to a unique and remarkable solution to the dilemma of social housing.

By the second half of the nineteenth century, although dwarfed by the great industrial capitals of Europe and no longer one of the major cities of the world, Amsterdam had emerged from a period of decline. Its port was dredged, a new cross-country canal linked it directly to the sea, and railway connections to the Continent were established. These improvements in infrastructure stimulated a revival in shipping, banking, insurance, and finance, which in turn attracted a new influx of immigrants, many of whom earned modest incomes as factory workers and unskilled laborers. At the same time, the gradual depression of agriculture in the Netherlands further increased the city's economically marginalized inhabitants.

As the poor moved into the city's center, the rich departed to dormitory suburbs. Vacant houses became crammed. Wet, uninhabitable basements were overoccupied. Empty backyards were filled with flimsy shacks. The city's canals were open sewers that ebbed and flowed with the tide. Disease and misery became widespread. The problems of the industrial city grew, and with each step forward, as opportunity expanded, population increased and poverty worsened. Changing economic and social conditions had combined with a quantum leap in size to fundamentally alter the nature of urban life.

As in most other places, the full complexity and nature of the change was not initially recognized. Thus, in an effort to provide more affordable housing, Amsterdam increased the availability of credit for construction, hoping that the commercial real estate sector would erect the many new buildings needed. The result was block upon block of substandard housing and several poorly built new neighborhoods of dismal living quality. Rents were exploitative; apartments were too small; light, air, and sanitation were inadequate; and in the worst instances construction was unsafe, causing buildings to collapse. (The sheer monotony of these environments, shaped by the formulas of speculative development, provoked concern at the Board of Health that their occupants might suffer negative psychological effects. On the other hand, some of this housing, designed by developers and builders, constituted a rich evocation of popular architectural culture and was aesthetically superior to similar tenements built in other places during the same period.) While many developers were unscrupulous in their search for profits, and the municipal bureaucracy was understaffed and ill prepared to administer building regulations, the larger problem was that construction of decent low-rent housing was unprofitable within the cost structure of the open market.

As parts of the inner city became slums and were threatened with clearance, and as picturesque canals were filled in to create new roads and better circulation, elements of the historic environment began to be eliminated. Growing numbers of citizens became alarmed and called for preservation of the historic center. In addition, a new ring of speculative housing began to surround the old metropolis. Numerous Amsterdammers began to ask that the expansion of the city meet a reasonable standard of beauty.

Appreciation of the aesthetic accomplishment of previous generations had yielded a critical perspective. In Amsterdam at the turn of the century, the positive qualities of the historic architectural legacy, particularly the area of the ring canals, became a standard of measurement for the future growth of the metropolis. The new city should be well constructed, thoughtfully arranged, and aesthetically pleasing, and should relate to the urban conglomeration that had preceded it. As these concepts gained wider popular support, the government was compelled to find a solution, but it also hoped to minimize intrusion on the prerogatives of private real estate ownership and development. The resulting approach would unfold in gradual steps, eventually activating the transformation of society on several levels.

By 1900, Amsterdam's population had increased to 500,000 people, and public health conventions were enacted. The municipality stopped selling its properties outright to private developers and initiated a practice of offering long-term leases in order to control the growth of the city and the quality of new construction on public lands. In 1905 a new municipal building ordinance established more rigorous standards for light and ventilation, regulated building heights in proportion to street widths, outlawed the filling in of courtyards, ended the use of cellars as dwellings, and restricted the height of new buildings to five stories. Most important, in 1901 the Netherlands passed a farsighted housing act that sponsored low-cost housing to be built by the city and nonprofit societies. Every municipality with a population greater than 10,000 was required to develop a master plan for its expansion.

The traditional collaboration between government and civic groups in managing urban life became further institutionalized. In addition to empowering private organizations to construct housing, during this era the authorities also provided subsidies to charitable groups to build schools and construct and manage hospitals. This pluralistic approach allowed scope for debate and gave different ideologies an active voice in the management of the city. (Such autonomous subcommunities within the greater whole of Amsterdam were called *zuil*, or "pillars," by the Dutch.)

Upon passage of the Housing Act, numerous groups organized nonprofit housing societies and applied for government certification. Employees in the city's gasworks formed a Socialist housing society and a Catholic housing society. Jewish diamond workers were represented by three societies: Liberal, Socialist, and religious. The Technical Society of Democratic Engineers and Architects offered rent subsidies for the "financially weak." Socialist municipal transit workers, teachers, firemen, and the police formed separate organizations. Workers' mutual aid societies and labor unions participated, as did Christian workers, Protestants, and Catholics. By 1920 more than twenty such groups and ninety building projects had been officially approved.

As each subgroup of society struggled with the dilemma of how to build affordable housing that met a reasoned measure of health, safety, aesthetics, and urban planning, a substantive civic dialogue began, and extended over several decades, on how to modernize the metropolis. This was exactly the hope of the statute's authors, who intended that charitable societies establish thoughtful and higher standards for all those who built in the city.

The key to elevating the quality of housing was knowledge. Social scientists were needed to study the living conditions of the poor and the family dynamics of their households. Doctors and other medical personnel undertook an examination of how environmental conditions affected health and the spread of disease. As the complexity of these questions was revealed, training became a prerequisite for the municipal administrators who regulated the housing program, as well as for the professional consultants who advised the private societies. In response to pragmatic social and physical problems, the study of such disciplines was formalized and to some extent invented, as university programs expanded understanding and educated the necessary experts.

The practice of architecture was revolutionized. Road patterns and infrastructure in the initial expansion of the city had been designed by civil engineers, while speculative apartment houses were predominantly designed by developers, builders, and draftsmen. Once the aesthetic character of this work was judged to be inadequate, the obvious solution was to employ architects—with their understanding of structural engineering , construction, history, and visual design—to plan the city and to shape social housing. This represented a historical shift for the profession, which was being asked to utilize its talents on behalf of people of all classes, not just the wealthy and powerful. New schools of architecture were opened and old curriculas were extended to address issues of city planning, public health, and social reform.

In Amsterdam—as in Vienna, where the influence of Otto Wagner would expand architectural thinking—one of the city's earliest and most revered modern architects, H. P. Berlage, would enrich the public discourse through his personal intellectual exploration. Like Wagner, Berlage recognized the inevitability of change due to industrialization and developed an aesthetic in which contemporary forms expressed the new functions, construction methods, materials, and advanced structural techniques of modern architecture. The excellence of his buildings and society's acceptance of them paved the way for others to further explore new architectural expressions. Moreover, and again like Wagner, Berlage foresaw the need for a rapprochement between the emerging modern metropolis and the historic milieu of the existing city. Here he was influenced by the work of another Viennese, Camillo Sitte.

In 1892, Berlage produced a condensed translation of *City Building According to Its Artistic Principles,* making Sitte's thinking more widely available to Dutch architects. He found that two of Sitte's basic contentions were profoundly germane to the building of housing in Amsterdam: that buildings in the cityscape should be artfully arranged to create amenable public spaces, and that such artistic effects could not be achieved unless the design of individual structures supported the larger urban plan.

Both of these principles informed the beauty of the ring canals, where buildings were aligned in a street wall that followed the geometric configuration of the circulation system and where over hundreds of years, the rules of architectural style had caused many separate structures, designed by different individuals, to be integrated into a coherent totality. Thus, in 1908, as Berlage introduced the subjects of city planning and urban design to students at the recently established architecture academy in Amsterdam, he argued that contemporary architects of modern mass housing were required to mold large segments of the city into harmonious environments. In order to achieve this result, not only would each housing project require a thoughtful urban plan, but another method of artistic coordination would have to be devised to replace the defunct aesthetic rules of abandoned historic styles. The theoretical objective was clear, but its achievement in the real world would require many years of public debate as well as trial and error.

Berlage himself addressed the problems of layout in 1904 in his influential proposal for a new district of housing in the south of Amsterdam. The architect's scheme, known as the Plan Zuid, demonstrated an alternative to the unrelenting and efficient orthogonal grids of developers by introducing angular street patterns interrupted by diversely shaped public spaces around which blocks of housing were massed in dramatic configurations. The design followed Sitte's ideas in creating many small communities within a larger cityscape. Yet much of the civil engineer's regularity was also kept. Berlage had found a compromise between the need for efficient circulation and the creation of distinctive neighborhoods of individual character.

Several times in the years that followed, members of Amsterdam's City Council would reject the street-pattern proposals of real estate developers because the plans were unaesthetic: "The public way serves not only those living along it, but the entire city, and the municipality must not give permission to something that is in conflict with the universal laws of beauty." Berlage would then be asked to redesign such areas. When one of these failed plans was the responsibility of a particular branch of the city government, pressure was applied to hire more artistically skilled professionals. Indeed, in 1910, the public works department created the post of aesthetic adviser and retained one of Amsterdam's more prominent young architects, J. M. Van der Mey (later in his career the designer of one of the city's prominent modern office buildings, the Scheepuaathuis).

As more housing was erected it became clear to a larger proportion of people across the political spectrum that unless whole building blocks were orchestrated to support a central design theme, the result could be cacophonous. (In an early effort to raise the quality of one such project, the task of design was restricted to formally trained architects rather than to builders, draftsmen, or developers, but this arbitrary gathering of talent resulted in an arbitrarily compiled streetscape of competing forms.) For many in the city's governance, restricting property rights for aesthetic purposes was anathema, as was the regulation of artistic standards. Yet the unregulated process had proved deficient in meeting the growing popular desire for architectural coherence. How else was the unity of the city to be achieved?

A host of politically difficult questions were raised: Who were to be the architects? Who was to choose them? On the basis of what criteria were they to be picked? And who would evaluate their work? Particularly in an era when the field of architecture was divided between traditionalists and modernists, the selection of architects was confusing to the laypeople in government and housing societies. Even the architects themselves could not agree.

A critical citywide discussion on the merits of design was engendered by institutionalizing formal and informal regulatory forums. Two architectural societies were created. One—of which Berlarge was a member—included craftsmen, builders, developers, draftsmen, and architects and focused on establishing standards of professionalism. A rival, second society, the Genootschap Architectura et Amica, restricted its membership to architects with demonstrable talent in design and was committed to advancing the artistic aspect of building. An advisory jury of architects, the Committee on Aesthetics (Schoonheidscommissie), carefully reviewed proposals for projects on publicly leased land, which included all construction under the Housing Act. The City Council issued final approvals and debated the aesthetic issues as well. The Board of Health, the Department of Public Works, and the Ministry of Housing each experimented with different regulatory stratagems to raise the level of artistic success. A Committee on Urban Beauty reviewed proposals for alterations to historic structures and made detailed suggestions for design revisions. Meanwhile, within the housing societies (there were fifty-eight officially recognized corporations by 1925), people from all walks of life, both benefactors and beneficiaries of the housing initiative, joined the greater discussion. Amsterdam's participatory, transparent, and pluralistic approach to governance had given the metropolis a social voice in which the high arts of architecture and city building became issues of popular concern.

The particular architectural style that grew to be more widely accepted in the city came to be known as the Amsterdam School and was largely advanced by young architects associated with the Genootschap Architectura et Amica. Ironically, since Berlage was not a member of this group, it was in his plan for Amsterdam South that buildings by Amsterdam School architects found broad support among the city's populace. The construction of apartment blocks for the Plan Zuid, designed by various Amsterdam School architects, and representing several housing societies, was a tour de force.

Since the concerns of social workers and housing experts largely determined the layout of interior plans, the primary focus of the architects of the Plan Zuid was on the public environment, on the design of facades. Projects of the Amsterdam School were particularly successful in this regard. The buildings were dramatic and rose to eye-catching compositional climaxes at crucial urban points in plan. The style synthesized modernism and traditionalism, with allusions to indigenous buildings of the Dutch countryside and, oddly, shapes adopted from the native ships and the village huts of Dutch Colonial Indonesia. These vernacular forms were combined with modern block-long horizontal massing and highlighted with sleek curving lines and complex twisting volumes of abstract geometry. The buildings celebrated the expressive use of brick, which rooted the housing in the traditions of Amsterdam's architectural history. Entries, steps, windows, and other special features were enriched by elaborate handcrafted, modernesque details, in a style commonly referred to by historians as Arts and Crafts. This was an affirmation in the face of modern industrial standardization that the work of the artisan still had value. The joy of human creativity was not relinquished to the machine, yet modern machine shapes were part of the architecture's expressive visual vocabulary.

Berlage and the Amsterdam School indirectly collaborated in accomplishing the lessons of Sitte. Within a few years, singular communities of Amsterdam School housing formed a circle of architecture of uncommon quality around the historic city. It was an urban ring of greater scale and a contemporary milieu of less individualized expression than the circle of ring canals; nonetheless these new neighborhoods retained an association with Amsterdam's past. This cultural linkage was most clearly seen when buildings of Amsterdam School design were inserted within the historic core and rested compatibly with the traditional forms of the city.

The premature death of the Amsterdam School's most brilliant designer—architect Michael de Klerk, who died at age twenty-three—the dissipation of the style's expressiveness in its evolution to a more extreme modernism, changes in the government's housing policy, which shifted back in favor of private development, worldwide economic depression, and World War II brought this special era to an end. Nevertheless, when contrasted with the armadas of repetitive, mass-produced urban housing that were to be built in the decades to come—in Communist and democratic societies—the social housing experiment of Amsterdam in the early twentieth century conveyed an enduring message: that people of all classes deserved good design.

In comparison to inhabitants of cities where the aesthetic parsimony of public housing socially brands its recipients, as if in punishment for their need, residents of social housing in Amsterdam and Vienna could point with pride to the beautiful visual features of their buildings. In both places, modernism had adapted to existing urban traditions of city building, and the homes of the economically less fortunate were linked to a common heritage shared by all the people of the city. The aesthetic concerns of conservation had found confluence with issues of social equity.

THE END OF THE ERA OF BUILDINGS MADE BY HAND

In the second half of the twentieth century, particularly in the developed nations of the world, modernization of the city, society, and architecture assumed a greater velocity and all-encompassing effect.

Modern building budgets were subsumed by interior improvements in plumbing, climatic control, lighting, and communication technology that upgraded private and public spaces at home, at work, and in recreation, with the result that smaller proportions of the construction effort were directed toward the elaboration of facades. These changes dramatically improved interior living conditions, and it became the norm, among governments, to attempt to share such benefits with as wide a proportion of society as possible. Even in cities whose population had stabilized, commercial competition, issues of social equity, and the desire of all classes of people to live better continued to drive expansion of the modern sphere.

Meanwhile, on the exteriors of buildings, modern architects had developed expressions that further departed from the forms of traditional architecture. Expanded use of large sheets of glass, concrete, metals, and synthetic materials presented the viewer with a different visual atmosphere and a new vocabulary of architectural elements, and most contemporary structures looked out of place when juxtaposed with older parts of the city.

In the majority of modern buildings, in the thousands upon thousands of structures that serve the needs of everyday life, resolution of details and connections between different materials were not as finely crafted as in the past. Especially in Communist countries, and everywhere in the construction of low-cost housing, modern facades of prefabricated building elements often were shoddy in comparison to historic facades previously worked by hand. Such aesthetic differences were multiplied infinitely across the public face of the modern city.

The very ethic of construction was altered. Traditional craftsmen had measured their work by the standard of the critical eye and had asked themselves, Does the result look right? Now, under pressure to construct or adapt large numbers of buildings, nonvisual craft criteria of speed and economy gained greater emphasis. Old skills died out from lack of use. Even when contemporary architects called for traditional building methods, the results often failed to meet the visual standards of old. Moreover, in developed societies, more equitable compensation for the costs of craftsmanship made extensive exterior handwork prohibitively expensive.

Together, changes in scale, craftsmanship, materials, function, building economics, and basic architectonic language caused a sharp aesthetic separation between contemporary and historic architecture. The age-old continuum of building by hand was fast dying out, and the reserve of handcrafted historic structures was becoming an unrenewable and finite resource. Historic conservation laws, already enacted in many places, became universal and were made more restrictive and more widely encompassing.

Although Amsterdam and Vienna were no longer subject to the bursts of population growth they had experienced in the first stages of industrialization, the upgrading of housing for inhabitants of all economic levels caused waves of renewal and expansion. (Vienna reached a population peak of 2 million in 1910, shrank to 1.3 million by the end of World War II, then increased to its current size of about 1.5 million. In the golden age of the seventeenth century, Amsterdam's population was 200,000; after industrialization and World War II it numbered about 850,000, and it has since decreased to about 700,000.) At the same time, as in most of the cities of Europe, the historic environment of each metropolis was in desperate need of restoration. The era of economic depression prior to World War II, damage from the war itself—from deferred maintenance and from bombing—and shortage of resources during the recovery period resulted in widespread accumulated disrepair. All these factors required both cities to confront the increasingly more difficult problem of adapting the historic environment to contemporary functions—of reconciling what often appeared to be irreconcilable differences—without destroying the beauty accrued by hand, across the centuries of their assemblage.

MODERN VIENNA: SOCIAL EQUITY AND THE LOSS OF BEAUTY

Fifty-two Allied bombing raids and a final ten-day battle for the city during World War II caused nearly a quarter of the buildings of Vienna to be harmed or destroyed. Some 8 percent of all its residential buildings were severely damaged and another 12 percent were leveled. This was the first phase in a gradual reduction of the city's beauty, which would continue in the postwar years as a by-product of a complicated weave of municipal policies to improve the quality of housing.

The wartime destruction was scattered across the cityscape, with less harm in the old historic center (the Altstadt) and more at the periphery, where industry and rail yards were located. Unlike Warsaw, whose ancient core was lost completely and then re-created in full detail—Vienna chose a more complex solution to a more widely dispersed problem. Some of the city's most important damaged landmarks, particularly those located in the Altstadt and on the Ringstrasse, were totally duplicated, but many other injured buildings were remade with plain stucco fronts, minus their exterior decorative features. The city administration filled midblock holes in historic neighborhoods, reestablishing the continuity of traditional street walls, but allowed the symphonic flow of decorative ornamentation and beautifully articulated architectonic elements to be forever broken by blank facades.

While this approach to reconstruction may be partly ascribed to the economic necessities of a severe postwar housing shortage, and the development of a spare modern style by Viennese architects such as Adolf Loos, a notable feature of these alterations speaks to another consideration. In structures *another way to remember history*

redeemed during the recovery, bronze plaques at street level recorded the fact of each building's demise and partial resurrection. Not only had a choice been made to leave the cityscape wounded, but public testimonials to the diminution of Vienna's loveliness became a permanent presence in the city's living urban culture. Whereas the reconstruction of Warsaw expressed an unwillingness by the Poles to accede to a reality imposed by their enemies, the plaques of Vienna articulated several ideas: the resilience of the Viennese in recovering from the war's brutality, Austria's determination to remember the horror of armed conflict, and an acceptance of the aesthetic price incurred during the country's allegiance to the Germans. Vienna's approach to restoration was wonderful, terrible, and thought-provoking (an issue discussed in greater detail in Chapter 14, "The City Redeemed").

Beyond this specific cultural act lay a larger question: Would the architectural assemblage of the city be otherwise protected in the coming years of economic revival and eventual prosperity? The conservation laws of Austria left the matter in doubt.

As in most other places in Europe, the first legal protections of the architectural heritage of Vienna focused on the most important individual landmarks (when initiated in 1850, with the Hapsburgs' establishment of the Imperial and Royal Central Commission for the Investigation and Preservation of Built Monuments). Upon formation of the Republic of Austria, the responsibilities of the royal commission were transferred to a Federal Monument Office. A national Law for the Protection of Monuments was enacted in 1923 and remained unchanged for fifty-five years. The statute protected buildings, ruins, and archaeological sites, as well as such movable artifacts as paintings, sculptures, and prehistoric objects. It failed to safeguard architectural ensembles, however, unless every building in the group was an individual monument.

This was a severe liability in preserving one of the most significant aspects of Vienna's architectural accomplishment. Although numerous structures would be listed within the Altstadt and along the Ringstrasse, much of the growth of Vienna in the nineteenth and early twentieth centuries—an era known by the Viennese as the *Gründerzeit*—was left exposed to diminishment. The beautiful rent palaces were a prime example. Extending block after block around the outside of the Ringstrasse, they were fashioned in the last era when Vienna's buildings were classically styled and facades were richly articulated.

A musical metaphor is especially telling in describing the meaning of these areas. In the city that bequeathed to the world an extraordinary musical legacy, music was embraced by all society, and the beautiful architectural adornments of Vienna's cityscape were as interrelated as notes in a musical composition. In the era of the Ringstrasse, in fin de siècle Vienna, visitors flocked to the city for its operas, symphonies, dances, and beautiful buildings, but also to experience a unique cosmopolitan lifestyle of multicultural richness. Vienna gave birth to the symphony and was a symphony of life, a melding of many elements into a dynamic living whole.

Under Austrian conservation law, the lesser architectural notes—which were of substantial aesthetic, urban, cultural, and historic significance and a vast extension of the handcrafted beauty of Vienna—were vulnerable to deletion from the greater totality. The area not protected was also the sector most subject to the city's rent-control laws, and the combination of these two circumstances led to a further stripping of the city's architectural ornamentation.

The Austrian rent-control law of 1917 gave tenants the right to pass on to children, grandchildren, and other close relatives the opportunity to lease apartments at controlled prices. The law also recognized permanent improvements made by tenants to their lodgings as real property, and it allowed them to merge adjacent apartments into one dwelling. Such protections led tenants to remain in flats for generations.

As the quality of housing improved with new construction, these older, largely rent-controlled residences, constituting more than half of the city's apartments, became by comparison the most substandard living units in Vienna. Most of the apartments had originally been constructed without central heating and individual bathrooms, and some even lacked indoor toilets. By the late 1950s and early 1960s, the hardships of postwar recovery had abated, yet the interior and exterior conditions of Vienna's rent palaces had worsened, since their owners had neither the funds nor the incentive to renovate them. Ending rent controls was a possible solution, but it had several potential negative consequences.

Privatizing the housing market would have produced gentrification—geographically segregating different economic and political groups within the city—and at the same time depriving a huge percentage of the population of affordable places to live. Furthermore, opening the city to speculative development would have driven property values higher and undermined Vienna's continuing production of social housing, based on the acquisition of land at low prices. In order to avoid such circumstances, Vienna enacted a highly unusual practice of granting subsidies to tenants for restoring rental apartments. This program of municipal loans was very successful, and large numbers of flats throughout the city were renewed. Tenants and rent controls were kept in place. But there was one significant drawback: the exteriors of these structures were not being similarly revived. The beautiful molded stucco facades of the *Gründerzeit* rent palaces were being allowed to waste away as a result of decades of deferred maintenance, while their interiors were elevated to new and higher standards.

Comparison with the housing market in New York—where rent controls have been reduced so that smaller subsidies are offered to fewer people—is telling. In historic areas where market forces have total to partial command, gentrification and economic segregation occur, but the preservation of architectural beauty is valued as a positive feature in renting or selling renewed apartments in old buildings. In New York, numerous historic districts have been designated at the request of upper- and middle-class inhabitants to protect the positive aesthetic ambience of such neighborhoods, which are recognized as the sum of their many parts, requiring the defense of lesser contributing structures as well as individual landmarks. This was accomplished in 1965 through the enactment of a landmarks law, which immediately assumed the legal obligation to protect the city's historic districts. At the same time, lower-income groups are not well served in many regards. In their neighborhoods the age-old tale of economic exploitation continues, and the city is marked by numerous and extensive slums where human misery is heightened by environmental decay and blight. In these communities, landmarks preservation often seems a superficial and academic concern to inhabitants only partly served by the social contract.

The socialization of Vienna's housing market had avoided a comparable degree of social ostracization. The municipality became the largest landowner in Austria through the construction of almost half of Vienna's living quarters, in addition to being the major partner in renewing the bulk of the city's private rental apartments. Social justice was far better dispersed in Vienna than in New York, but at the price of allowing the reduction of the architectural patrimony.

Vienna endeavored to revise its approach with several overlapping legislative initiatives. In 1972 an amendment to its building code provided for the designation of historic areas, and a fund for the preservation of historic facades was established (the *Stadterhaltungsfonds*). A national Urban Renewal Act (1974) and a Housing Subsidy and Improvement Act (1984) called for comprehensive urban revitalization and created subsidized loans to the owners of such buildings for the improvement of rent palaces. The city also established a Land Procurement and Urban Renewal Fund (1984) to purchase property, which was then made available to private developers to build subsidized apartments.

The underlying intent of these laws was to increase the quality of housing while still maintaining subsidies, shifting the burden of exterior renovation costs to the municipality and the better-off tenants. Landlords were allowed controlled increases in rents to pay for improvements to both the interiors and the exteriors of buildings, while poorer tenants received greater financial assistance to offset higher rents. On paper this matrix of legal instruments seemed to solve the problem of the deterioration of *Gründerzeit* apartment buildings, but in reality it was only a partial success.

Renewing the rent palaces was an extremely complex process due to the stipulation that no existing tenants be displaced and that apartments remain affordable after their modernization; such prerequisites are part of Vienna's "gentle urban renewal." This process avoided disrupting the social composition of the community and the friendships of neighbors. At the same time, however, increased light and air were needed, and rear yard accretions from early in the industrial era had to be removed. Upgrading bathrooms required new rooms in each living unit. Thus, as the total amount of interior space diminished, the demand for interior space increased. The solution to this problem was found in the conversion of attics into habitable apartments, but this was a costly and elaborate undertaking. The huge number of structures requiring such extensive renovation made the initiative vastly expensive. Rather than absorb the additional cost of restoring ornate stucco and stone embellishment—by now in terrible condition from decades of deterioration—many rent palaces were stripped of their decoration and given plain plaster fronts, much like the blank street fronts of war-damaged buildings.

In 1995, municipal authorities acknowledged that although Vienna's laws did not support the denuding of buildings that contributed to the city's aesthetic and cultural significance, by now numerous beautiful structures had been stripped. (Vienna's conservation statutes otherwise constitute a complete and thoughtful program of preservation—if they are adhered to.) Professionals in the government were attempting to eliminate this contradiction, in which public moneys were awarded to projects that reduced Vienna's heritage.

Conservation protection reached a new level of professionalism with the publication of a careful, block-by-block survey of the city's architectural assets. Ninety-eight protection zones were created, with the intent of preserving about 6 percent of the city's total building stock and almost all buildings more than one hundred years old. Simultaneously, housing administrators amended their policies so that one department was not reducing patrimony while another was registering it for protection.

Yet the city agency responsible for compliance with conservation standards—Municipal Department 19, Vienna Architecture and City Planning—which oversees ten thousand buildings dispersed across a wide area, is dramatically understaffed, with a professional staff in 1995 of only about ten. A direct comparison with New York is impossible because in Vienna individual monuments are administered by another agency at the federal level. However, since much of the work in New York involves supervising historic districts (about 20,000 properties), it is instructive to note that the professional staff of the New York City Landmarks Preservation Commission fluctuates from forty to sixty people and is hard-pressed to regulate all the changes proposed each year to so many buildings. Vienna must accomplish a similarly complicated task with a staff that is far smaller in size. A thorough job is impossible with so few people.

In Vienna after World War II, an admirable effort to create social equity gave people of all classes affordable housing of increasingly higher quality, but

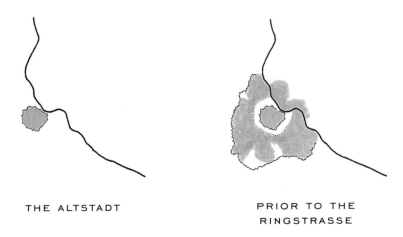

THE ALTSTADT

PRIOR TO THE
RINGSTRASSE

The growth of the Vienna conurbation · The contemporary metropolis is shown within its
municipal boundaries (dotted exterior line), beyond which lie the Vienna Woods. Light gray tone
indicates the extent of the built-up area. Dark gray tone marks the municipal Protection Zones.
Numerous other individual monuments (not shown), from various eras, are scattered across the
cityscape. The course of the Danube River is controlled via modern engineering. *(All drawings at the
same scale.)*

prior to an authentic and uncompromised commitment to preservation in the
mid-1990s, four decades of deterioration were allowed among a group of
beautiful buildings that would have been highly prized in many other places.

The results are sad to behold. Not because the *Gründerzeit* environment is
any more schizophrenic than other insensitively modernized historic neighborhoods in other cities—alternating erratically from handsome older buildings to modern insertions and numerous stripped facades—but because the
beauty of the surviving rent palaces is so extraordinary. Historic building
facades in Vienna have a voluptuous quality, a degree of sculptural refinement,
that few places in the world can match. In places in the *Gründerzeit* ring where
several blocks of such structures are still intact, the cumulative effect of richly
molded architectural elements is arresting—deep shadows of intricate form
dance across the length of cumulative street walls.

Unfortunately, as in other places in Europe, Vienna was slow to recognize
the significance of its large masses of late-nineteenth-century architecture. A

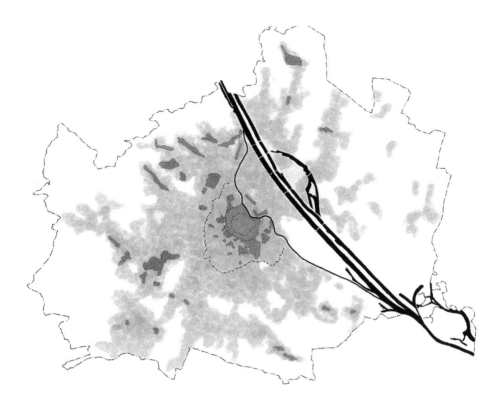

THE PROTECTION ZONES OF CONTEMPORARY VIENNA

choice was made in favor of social equity at the price of aesthetic continuity. But was the choice necessary? Were preservation and better housing truly at odds? Were there other possible options in a Socialist-governed municipality, which had at its disposal numerous potential controls to influence the quality of the built environment? (Remember that the municipality owned half of Vienna's land and a third of its apartments.) In the end, the compassionate planners of Vienna failed to recognize the city's most obvious asset: the great symphony of form that surrounded them every working day during the years of its gradual erosion. They came to see their error only after the damage was done.

MODERN AMSTERDAM: SOCIAL EQUITY AND THE PRESERVATION OF BEAUTY

By the end of World War II, although damage from bombing had been limited, the historic center of Amsterdam had reached a perilous state of decay. Unlike the Altstadt of Vienna—whose grand palaces, beautiful apartment houses, and imposing buildings of state supported the continuing vitality and prominence of the traditional core—the medieval structures of old Amsterdam, which were far more utilitarian when first constructed, were fast deteriorating from decades of obsolescence and neglect. In Vienna, residence in the Altstadt in a host of exceptional individual landmarks remained fashionable. In Amsterdam, however, a unique townscape of numerous modest buildings was being abandoned.

As early as the end of the nineteenth century, residents were vacating canal houses for modern accommodations in districts located outside the last moat of the city's demolished defenses. Prior to the construction of modern sewers, several canals had been filled to eliminate the reek from sewage, a step that merely transferred noxious odors to different locations within the same general environment. Other canals were converted to streets, allowing greater access to the city center but making traffic congestion worse within the ancient center's medieval labyrinth.

Modernization of the city conflicted directly with its preservation, for the simple reason that making Amsterdam truly accessible to automobiles meant converting its sunken waterways into street-level roads. This would dramatically alter the traditional cityscape and eliminate its unique picturesque quality. Typically, canals and the street walls of buildings were separated by a sidewalk of modest width, a single-lane road, and a narrow quay lined with intermittent trees and limited spaces for parking. Boats navigated on waters below street level, slipping under the thousand gently arching spans that connected the city's ninety islands. If the canals were converted to streets, the rhythms of life in Amsterdam would be inexorably altered. Flowing currents would be replaced by hot exhaust fumes and the clamor of inner-city vehicular traffic. Many hundreds of bridges would have to be eliminated and, with them, the uninterrupted pedestrian vistas down the center of canalways. The beautiful metropolis would no longer be reflected in its own waters. Not only would the urban object itself change, but the vantage points from which its loveliness had long been contemplated would be destroyed as well.

The narrow width, steep stairs, and ancient construction of Amsterdam's medieval buildings made it difficult and costly to adapt them to new housing standards. Hand-driven piles from the earliest years of the city's construction were often inadequate and unstable. Shifting foundations caused structural degeneration, which extended upward, causing building facades to misalign, window and door openings to become crooked and less tightly sealed, and masonry and plaster to crack. Temperature extremes and pervasive dampness aggravated such defects; old dwellings and warehouses needed constant repair to avoid accrued decay from the infiltration of excessive salts and moisture. In addition, the repair of foundations was a delicate operation, since buildings were closely packed together and neighboring structures often suffered from similar problems. As edifices in the historic core lost their desirability in the open real estate market, maintenance inevitably declined and many damaged places were left exposed to the elements. (It had become common practice in the deteriorated homes of former patricians to dismantle, remove, and sell beautiful old custom-fitted interiors.) Inside the shells of these degenerating structures, poorer occupants were jammed, in miserable conditions, with no place else to go. Together, the problems of structural decay, social inequity, and the inefficiency of the city's configuration made Amsterdam an especially fragile and difficult historic resource to save.

Notwithstanding, during the first half of the twentieth century, Amster-dammers struggled to solve various aspects of the dilemma. In 1900 the filling-in of one canal too many inspired a popular pamphlet entitled "Violation of the City," and launched the community's modern conservation movement, with the creation of the Amstelodamum Society—the first historical organiza-tion in Amsterdam devoted to saving the old metropolis as an integrated urban environment. In 1918, the Hendrick de Keyser Society began restoring the exteriors and interiors of selected important historic structures, to retain a record of life in earlier periods. By the 1990s the society had saved 250 build-ings nationwide, eighty of them in Amsterdam. Modern business facilities and new social institutions such as schools, hospitals, and government offices were erected to revive the city's center. A provision in Amsterdam's Building Code of 1921 stipulated that new development in the historic core be reviewed by a Committee of Urban Beauty to avoid aesthetically intrusive modern additions. Mammoth amounts of beautiful Amsterdam School housing were constructed outside the historic core at the city's fringes. And by 1933, a detailed inventory of the historic architectural patrimony of the Netherlands had been made, identifying 4,200 individual monuments of national significance in old Amsterdam. Yet regardless of these and many other efforts, even before the dawn of the Second World War many important listed structures had already been demolished—a thousand would eventually be lost—and numerous other unlisted historic structures had been abandoned. The virtual cessation of maintenance efforts during the war made conditions substantially worse.

In the first stages of the postwar recovery, as Amsterdam revitalized its port and industries, the syndrome of outward migration continued. Numerous old houses were left half empty or occupied by squatters. With each passing year of accumulated neglect, the cost of restoring such buildings rose. As contem-porary housing standards continued to improve in Amsterdam and across Europe, the demand for better, more spacious, and more affordable living quarters increased. And when additional low-cost modern housing was built on the city's periphery, the antiquated dwellings of the old city became, by comparison, even less desirable.

A paradox was emerging in the minds of the city's planners. The modernization of Amsterdam logically required completing its sewage system, extending the availability of utilities, creating more social housing, building a modern airport, upgrading regional rail links, expanding inner-city mass transit, and improving vehicular flow in the center and outward to the suburbs. Together, these acts would connect the old city with the rest of the Netherlands and with Europe and the world. It would enhance the city's desirability as a place of residence and business, stimulating a process of gentrification by which Amsterdam's many thousands of historic buildings might be renewed through investments of the speculative real estate market. But improving the efficiency of the vehicular circulation system required severe disruptions in the very canals that made the city unique, and gentrification would drive out the poor and the middle classes. Harnessing market forces to preserve the historic city would eliminate its social diversity and reduce its physical distinctiveness.

Although a royal decree of 1945 had forbidden the demolition of buildings listed in the national inventory of significant historic structures, the preservation laws of Amsterdam still did not protect the majority of more humble constructions that comprised the harmonious cityscape—the very buildings that were most endangered and subject to loss. The authorities were slow to protect the old town center because designation as "historic" entailed two obvious repercussions. First, if the extraordinary sums needed to rehabilitate Amsterdam's architectural legacy were not to come from gentrification, they would have to come from the government. Second, designating the townscape as historic would theoretically eliminate the possibility of adapting the city to cars. In an increasingly faster-paced and competitive modern era, how were people to get around? On bicycles?

In the years that followed, initiatives to modernize surface circulation met with mounting public opposition from conservationists and neighborhood residents of all classes, who feared that gentrification would either force them to leave their homes or make the center an inhospitable place to live—crawling with tourists and swarming with cars. Would Amsterdam suffer the fate of Venice, where residential services would eventually so decline that normal life was insupportable? A 1952 letter to municipal officials articulated the counterargument to the logic of government planners who, in making the city competitive with other places, were making it more like other places and less the special place that Amsterdammers loved. Cosigned by several preservation groups, including the Amstelodamum and Hendrick de Keyser Societies, the letter suggested that "the approach to historical building conservation based on protecting individual properties is unsatisfactory. Amsterdam's townscape, which is one of the loveliest in the world, does not derive its beauty from the relatively small number of buildings important to the history of art. The beauty of her townscape springs from the totality of her facades, their coloring, their proportions and their interplay with the street-canal environment—including its cobbling and greenery. Preserving remarkable buildings alone will inevitably result in the erosion of the townscape as a whole."

Unconvinced that this goal was achievable, but recognizing that somehow as much of old Amsterdam as possible should be saved, the government met citizens halfway. In 1953 a Municipal Department for the Conservation and Restoration of Historic Buildings and Properties was created to inculcate higher professional standards and guide a recently instituted policy of providing government funds to save a limited number of important endangered monuments. In 1957 a new city ordinance established specific aesthetic rules to limit the disruptions caused by modern additions. It was required on streets of seventeenth- and eighteenth-century buildings, where facades leaned forward, "in flight," that new structures assume a similar cant. New contemporary buildings were to reflect the floor heights of their historic neighbors, most of which were graduated, with higher ceilings at the bottom and lower ceilings in the upper-floor units. The total building stature was also to be similar.

Step by step, the people and government of Amsterdam were creating a net of legal restraints to protect the built historic heritage. But the larger economic and social problem of saving the historic city still remained unresolved, particularly in the case of run-down neighborhoods of vernacular structures. These older parts of the city remained in greatest jeopardy from extensive modernization, for in the minds of officials such buildings symbolized the very obsolescence and decay that needed to be removed in order for contemporary Amsterdam to prosper. An act of imagination was needed to change the way the problem was being framed.

"STADSHERSTEL IS RESTORING THE CITY"

The Company for City Restoration (Stadsherstel) inverted the problem and found a solution. Incorporated in 1957 as an authorized organization under the Housing Act, the purpose of Stadsherstel was "to be solely engaged in the interests of public housing in the Netherlands, particularly where residential space, which is characteristic of the appearance of the city, is in danger of being lost through urban development and which, when modernized to present-day requirements, can be preserved."

The company led by example, restoring the most unwanted and endangered buildings of the historic milieu, which were not monuments, and converting them to subsidized housing of modern interior quality. Stadsherstel went where others would not and saved buildings that recorded the history of the lives of everyday people. The company strove to keep original tenants and the existing mixed economic character of neighborhoods, and reclaimed dilapidated areas to demonstrate their inherent beauty. After renovation, Stadsherstel stayed on as a landlord and kept its buildings in excellent repair, so its good works would accumulate across the old cityscape. It accomplished these goals while turning a profit for its investors (shareholders received a tax-exempt return of 5 percent per annum) and steadily enlarged its capital base so that an increasing number of structures were saved with each passing year. (Beginning with a value of 1.1 million guilders, or about U.S. $500,000, Stadsherstel's 400 properties—of which 350 have been restored—were worth about 120 million guilders, or about U.S. $540,000,000, by the mid-1990s.)

Frequently the buildings Stadsherstel selected were almost beyond redemption and, in proportion to their potential income, far too costly for their owners to renew. In 1995, I saw one such edifice, which was tenuously braced, crooked, worn, and perilously close to collapse. When I revisited the city three years later, a reassembled handsome house miraculously graced a neighborhood now under revival—and a broken streetscape had been made whole.

As Stadsherstel's ability to undertake such projects increased, it developed a tactic of identifying those buildings whose rehabilitation would most con-tribute to uplifting whole city blocks. Highly endangered structures of historic character had first claim. Corner buildings, when revived, provided a positive culmination to two street fronts and were highly visible from other places in the street pattern. (Here one might recall how the Germans especially targeted corner buildings in their destruction of the beauty of Warsaw.) By restoring adjacent structures, the precarious work of foundation correction was simpli-fied, and pairs of brightly renewed facades constituted a greater aesthetic criti-cal mass. Neighboring buildings which were not owned by the company, but which merely needed a new coat of paint or other minor repairs, were also given subsidies, so that they too might contribute to the upward environmental evolution. By planning the most advantageous sequence of actions, Stadsherstel provided a countermomentum to the decline of the historic cen-ter. The renewal of a few critical parts made whole neighborhoods look sub-stantially improved.

As recognition of the company grew, the mere purchase of a building by Stadsherstel raised the hopes of residents in marginalized communities. Before restoration began, a large white sign with red lettering would be stretched across decrepit facades: "Here too Stadsherstel is restoring the city." Afterward a discreet hexagonal bronze plaque would record the company's *gentrification~ NOT detrimental*

presence as a landlord, assuring neighbors that the renewed building would be well maintained for years to come. Savvy speculators and property owners came to know that non-Stadsherstel structures in the immediate area were likely to gain in value. And over the decades of the company's continuing work, gentrification—much desired by government officials—was stimulated through the unforeseen route of carefully preserving the city's humblest historic houses. The company taught Amsterdammers to see their city through optimistic eyes—to recognize the physical environment's latent potential.

Stadsherstel's sound management and sustained commitment—as well as the inclusion on its board of leading businessmen from finance and industry and experts in preservation, city planning, and architecture—impressed those in government and business circles who often dismissed the goals of preservationists as well meaning but narrowly focused and impractical. Moreover, by linking preservation and subsidized housing, Stadsherstel counterbalanced the negative social effects of the economic gentrification that its own efforts set in motion. The company had given Amsterdam a precious gift: a realistic strategy for urban renewal proven to work in practice.

Working in close collaboration with governmental agencies, by today, 30 percent of the funding for Stadsherstel's projects are derived through national, provincial, and city grants (a sum that in the 1970s was as high as 75 percent). As in Vienna, original residents are encouraged to move back once renovation is done. Each year, forty to fifty apartments become available to the two thousand applicants on Stadsherstel's waiting list. Those tenants with limited means are eligible for rent subsidies, established and paid by the government to offset rising open-market rates.

Stadsherstel's example also influenced the city's preservationists, and other societies devoted to conservation and social housing were established. One such group, the Diogenes Foundation, provided residential studio accommodations for artists in renewed historic buildings, completing ninety-six restorations by 1985. The foundation purposely selected nonmonuments in neighborhoods whose environmental critical mass did not satisfy the requirements for intervention by Stadsherstel. Diogenes, in other words, went where Stadsherstel would not. In cases where the costs of refurbishment were especially prohibitive, the Aristoteles Foundation helped artists assume ownership of apartments, once the structures had been modernized. This group saved fifty-one derelict buildings by 1980. To meet musicians' need for dwellings in which they could practice without disturbing their neighbors, the Jan Pietersz House Foundation renewed historic buildings and added special noise-abatement features. In all, about sixty such groups, each in its own way, helped to revitalize the city's historic legacy by directly undertaking the restoration of endangered structures.

The work of these organizations linked conservation to Amsterdam's tradition of social housing construction, which dates back before the Housing Act of 1901. Like the general housing societies that throughout the postwar period were constructing huge amounts of contemporary housing at the modern city's expanding periphery, the housing-preservation foundations facilitated dialogue between the authorities and the people who required living accommodations. The city was talking with itself. An important planning idea had been established: that restoring old buildings as subsidized residences solved several social problems simultaneously. Moreover, since the government had long before assumed responsibility for underwriting affordable housing that speculative real estate development was unable to provide (and by 1992, the City Housing Department co-owned more than half of Amsterdam's housing stock), the new housing-preservation societies came to be perceived as allies rather than outside critics. Like the general housing societies before them, the preservation foundations established new methods and higher standards for the city in matters of conservation and urban planning. Their work provided models of excellence. Most significant, by actively helping to shoulder the economic burden of conservation, preservationists came to command a higher moral position, enhancing their empowerment in the citywide political dialogue.

THE FINAL DEBATE: NEW DESIGN IN THE OLD CITY

There would be one last attempt by planners to restructure a large area of the historic city: the Nieuwmarkt Reconstruction Plan. In 1953, during construction of a subway (the Metro), officials proposed to demolish major portions of the old city and alter its pattern of canalways for a new complex of office buildings. Parts of the area targeted for destruction had once been occupied by the old Jewish quarter, which had deteriorated after Amsterdam's 100,000 Jews, about 12 percent of the city's population, were deported during the German occupation. (Many Amsterdammers resisted the Nazi effort, as in the heroic but ultimately unsuccessful attempt to hide Anne Frank and her family. Here also, was the studio-home in which Rembrandt had created several of his celebrated images of scenes from the Old Testament.)

In the center of this area sat a handsome house, constructed in 1671 and located atop one of the city's early seawalls. The fight to save De Pinto House (Pintohuis) mobilized a wide constituency in favor of Amsterdam's preservation. A foundation was created to restore the building as an office for conservation organizations and to rehabilitate three neighboring historic houses as apartments for the elderly.

Architects, neighborhood residents, and citywide urban activists asked officials to alter their basic approach from urban restructuring to urban renewal. And the government was forced to listen. Whole sections of the Nieuwmarkt Reconstruction area initially targeted for demolition were retained and restored. The historic street-canal pattern was kept. Plans to build offices were modified to include housing as well as facilities for small businesses and shops. Buildings were redesigned at a scale sympathetic to that of the historic city, with heights and architectural massing that recalled the rhythms of old street walls. As a result, by its completion in the early 1970s, although several historic blocks had been demolished, the area had retained its mix of social uses and income groups, as well as its general scale and street layout.

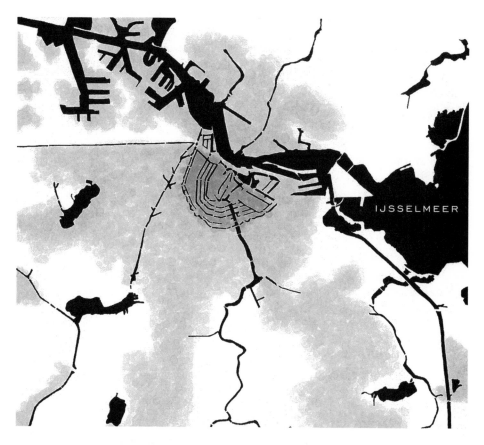

The contemporary conurbation of Amsterdam · Dark gray tone indicates the historic core once enclosed by fortifications. Light gray tone shows the extent of the immediate built-up area. Black indicates the major waterways and waterbodies of an extended system which is far more complex than shown.

During the construction process, a landmark of legislation was enacted. In 1961 the Netherlands passed a definitive Historic Buildings Conservation Act, causing nine thousand of Amsterdam's buildings eventually to be listed as monuments. A system of conservation subsidies was created. At its height in the 1960s and 1970s, eligible owners were provided with as much as 70 percent of the costs of restoration: 30 percent from federal, 10 percent from provincial, and 30 percent from municipal sources. Under the new law, seventy to eighty restorations a year (reaching a peak of 103 in 1967) were accomplished by the Restoration Office. And special provisions were enacted to help historic neighborhoods in a severe state of decay. Upon approval of a master plan for renewal, rehabilitation areas became eligible for federal subsidies.

The federal law also enabled municipalities to protect whole historic environments by invoking the status of Protected Town Views, and the historic cores of most cities in the Netherlands were thus designated. Yet the most significant ancient center of all was not officially registered. Amsterdam, while holding 17 percent of the nation's monuments, was conserved by virtue of a gentlemen's agreement between the municipality and the national government. A new approach to urban renewal had been developed on paper, but officials still questioned whether it would work in reality.

By the early 1970s the Nieuwmarkt Reconstruction Plan was completed. The redeveloped area was an awkward compromise between contemporary design and historic building traditions, shaped by hard-won political concessions. It was not nearly as compatible with the rest of Amsterdam as the buildings it replaced. On several neighboring blocks in the erased Jewish quarter, unsympathetic large modern structures constituted the worst major disruption of the traditional city in the twentieth century. The price of dramatic urban surgery had been made evident.

Thus began the era of renewal and conservation. By the 1990s some 6,000 registered historic monuments and 140,000 nonregistered historic structures had been saved, restored, or renewed. The cost of this work was approximately 2,500 million guilders (about U.S. $1.4 billion), about 45 percent of which was contributed by the government.

In 1971, when another worn-down quarter of modest structures (the Jordan) was subject to reclamation, under the new conservation law it was declared an official rehabilitation area. Instead of sweeping away whole blocks, the planners integrated modern architecture into the historic texture of the Jordan, on smaller building sites occupied by imaginative small-scale designs. As in the era of Amsterdam Housing, the city's many levels of public design review and the participation of people and organizations across the political spectrum produced a continuing exploration of architectural aesthetics.

In recent decades, Amsterdam has become one of the world's most interesting environments where architects attempt to design contemporary structures within the historic context. The general policy shift to less radical urban renewal has helped mediate the design problem. Designers are rarely asked to impose a huge modern element into an environment of many small historic parts. Municipal restrictions on total building height, the spacing between floor levels, and the alignment of facades when adjacent buildings are in flight (canted forward) compel developers to ensure that new buildings are of the same general scale and character as their neighbors.

As the city is gentrified and as property values rise, individual modern infill canal houses will likely be built more often. Where such buildings already exist, a wonderful sense of cultural continuity arises when well-designed contemporary houses become but one more individual facade flanked by neighbors in an extended street wall. As new architects in a new era, with new materials and a new vocabulary of form, make new cultural statements within the restraints of the historic context, the aesthetic dialogue continues among the thousands of individual canal houses across Amsterdam's history.

In Amsterdam and Vienna, after World War II, different societies with different patrimonies faced an uncertain future. Both places were driven by a concern for social equity, both places eventually enacted comprehensive conservation statutes protecting the historic milieu, but one place, Amsterdam, stopped the culture of destruction via modernization at an earlier date.

Stadsherstel had introduced a more inventive way to think about the renewal of the city. Problems of urban conservation, urban revitalization, and urban social housing were reconciled by being solved simultaneously. The historic city was largely saved. New architecture was asked to engage in the collective urban aesthetic colloquy. Amsterdammers learned to live with the liabilities of the historic environment in order to retain its other cherished attributes. And in the early twenty-first century, on every work day, 30 percent of those employed in the old city travel to their jobs on bicycles.

CHAPTER NINE

THE CITY OF THE GODS BESIEGED

ATHENS

Such is the bloom of perpetual newness, as it were, upon these works of Pericles, which makes them ever to look untouched by time, as though the unfaltering breath of an ageless spirit had been infused in them.

—PLUTARCH, GREEK HISTORIAN, SPEAKING OF THE ACROPOLIS, IN A BIOGRAPHY OF PERICLES, A.D. 100

Athens is dry and ill-supplied with water. The streets are nothing but miserable old lanes, the houses mean, with a few better ones among them. On first arrival, a stranger would hardly believe that this is the Athens of which he has heard so much.

—DICAEARCHUS, A VISITOR TO ATHENS IN THE SECOND CENTURY B.C.

Perhaps in no other place in the world is the urban conflict of old versus new as conspicuous as it is in Athens. The topography of the vast and many-faceted modern metropolis presents an elementary and powerful visage. Amid a broad sea of somewhat shabby low-rise urban sprawl, stretching for miles in all directions, rises a massive and time-honored promontory, one of the singular rock outcroppings on the planet: the Athenian Acropolis, a site of unsurpassed artistic and architectural brilliance.

In this spot, 2,500 years ago, humankind discovered that the city, the polis, could be the mechanism by which civilization was advanced.

Half a millennium later, Athens was razed by the Romans and lost its independence. It remained under foreign domination until the founding of an independent Greek state in 1833. By the beginning of the twentieth century, the Athenians had constructed a beautiful and balanced townscape, which briefly flourished and then was lost in a tidal wave of unrestrained urban development and illegal settlement. Today the ancient ruins on the hill, bleached white by the centuries, slowly decay from an ongoing assault by unchecked automotive and industrial emissions. Covering the contemporary metropolis in a purple haze, this blanket of polluted air, when wet, turns to acid. Thus, though recently restored, the precious remaining stones of one of civilization's most irreplaceable landmarks continue to deteriorate.

⚜

The story of the evolution of modern Athens is, like that of Cairo, a tragic tale of uncontrolled urban growth and an absence of effective municipal governance eventually coming to attack the spiritual heart of a city. In addition, in the recent effort to save the Acropolis, the global significance of historic urban architectural preservation is uniquely crystallized, raising challenging questions for the future. While the great central hill of the city is deeply beloved by Athenians, and as an urban icon is still considered sacred, the fate of the buildings on the Acropolis is more than a local matter.

As individual monuments, the Pyramids at Giza are two thousand years older. As a city, the Jerusalem of David and Solomon preceded Periclean Athens by half a millennium. Yet on the Acropolis are several structures whose aesthetic subtlety reflects the awakening of society to the expressive power of the art of architecture. In ancient Athens, great buildings became the means by which an urban community expressed its most deeply held and intangible beliefs. Moreover, for much of the world, the Athenian Acropolis is where common roots touch the bedrock of Western urban civilization. In Athens we celebrate the flowering of genius in a society that nurtured the integrity of the individual mind.

THE LANDMARKS ON THE SACRED HILL

To appreciate the ruins of classical Athens we must understand how basic the accomplishments of the original builders were. As with the Pyramids of Egypt and other structures from the first civilizations possessing written records, the creation of the Athenian Acropolis required, to some degree, the invention of the art of architecture itself. For example, when we study the system of proportions by which a classical Greek temple was composed, we are witnessing the birth of the idea that the human mind and eye are affected by the mathematical balance of aesthetic elements in a visual composition. We behold not just the specific way in which the proportions of the building are determined, but the invention of the very concept that there is such a thing as proportional balance. Many of our most fundamental intellectual formulations can be traced back to the ancient city some 2,500 years ago.

Here one of the first experiments in democracy became a model for numerous other societies across history and still remains a vital idea today. Here were constructed some of the most widely admired structures of all time, whose architectural aesthetics were so influential in Western civilization that virtually every major city of size or institutional importance has some building whose form alludes to the ruins on the Acropolis. And here the capacity of the city to nourish creative thinking resulted in one of civilization's most remarkable outbursts of intellectual invention, causing subsequent urban societies to ponder for thousands of years afterward how such sociocultural alchemy ever was sparked.

Yet here also, on the slopes below the Acropolis, even at the moment of its creation, was a remarkably ugly, disorganized, and unsanitary city. Similar incongruities would be shared by the Roman Empire some five hundred years later. In both cases, advances in the planning and building of cities were applied erratically, if at all, in the capital cities of Athens and Rome, while the colonial cities spawned by these civilizations embodied the most highly developed urban thinking of their times. Athens was a dirty, disorganized sprawl whose sanitary deficiencies would cause more than a quarter of its inhabitants to die of the plague at the outset of the Peloponnesian War, whereas the Hellenistic cities of the Middle East were mapped out with elegant geometric planning. Likewise, large parts of Rome were polluted, cacophonous, and overcrowded, while its colonial towns would be designed with aqueducts, sewage systems, orthogonal grids, sidewalks, and prescribed population limits.

Also the same was the fact that it was nearly impossible to update either capital city due to the obstacle of vested interests resulting from the private ownership of property. Rome could not untangle the unsanitary maze of cheap tenements that formed the larger part of the city, and Athens could not bring cleanliness, order, and adequate open public spaces into the heart of an urban area whose pattern of ownership was planted in its arbitrary and unplanned form.

Like the buildings of other early civilizations, the architecture of Greece is inextricably linked to the country's natural environment. In contrast to the long horizontal of the Egyptian desert, Greece is a turbulent landscape of rolling rocky hills. The Pyramids use giant mathematically derived forms, set in contrast to the organic shapes of nature, to make an obviously human mark on the land. Constructions like the Pyramids and the Sphinx employ the power of hugeness. In Greece, the buildings were smaller, and it was the intricate intellectual formulation of the architecture which made a distinctly human imprint on the landscape. Greek landmarks stressed the subtlety of human thinking.

The hilltop site upon which were constructed the buildings of the Acropolis evolved over time, having been associated with the gods of ancient Greece far into the past. The complex of buildings that we know today through their remains, was the ultimate architectural expression to occur at this location. Many other structures had been situated here before these were built, and early modern conservation interventions have removed most of the evidence of the numerous buildings and changes that occurred after the decline of Athens. The accomplishment embodied in the classical ruins of the Periclean Acropolis have come to freeze the hilltop forever at a particular moment in history.

The final composition of the classical Acropolis was formalized during the age of Pericles and evolved not just in relation to the history of the structures on the hill but also from the traditions of Greek architecture. The Parthenon in particular is linked to a heritage of earlier Greek temples built in numerous other locations. These structures have great commonality of form. To some degree they are meant to look the same. The purpose of temples was to mark places in Greece that were associated with the gods, and their similarity of form expressed the cultural unity of a geographic area divided into separate self-governing cities. These divisions were so numerous that when Aristotle undertook a study of Greek urban governance, he found 158 separate political entities. The presence of temples, with their similar look, proclaimed the oneness of the larger civilization of Greece.

Historians believe the first temples were constructed of wood, but during the period of the ascendancy and dominance of ancient Greece, temples were largely made of limestone and eventually marble. The proportions, composition, and construction of these buildings were calculated by means of slowly evolving aesthetic formulas that determined the size and shape of each architectural element and its exact placement in the larger temple configuration. Eventually these formulas came to be differentiated as three distinct styles: Doric, Ionic, and Corinthian.

The elements of the temple were constructed on a rectilinear stone platform. This horizontal terrace established a level and clearly human-made geometric zone amid the varying contours of nature. With the exception of the sloping pitch of the rooftop, all the component pieces of the temple were arranged at right angles to, or parallel to, the stone terrace. At the core of the temple, a series of straight walls parallel to the outer edge of the platform enclosed the sanctuary of the god. Surrounding this long rectilinear construction were exterior rows of round columns. Atop the columns sat a framework of heavy rectangular stone beams that supported a pitched roof running the length of the temple and culminating in two vertical triangular endpieces, or pediments. The rock outcroppings in the natural environment were massed and shaped organically; the precisely carved stone elements of primary forms that sat upon the rectilinear stone terrace were an expression of the abstract mathematics and artistic conceptions of the human mind.

Except for its much smaller size and defensive walls, the historic city from which the Acropolis buildings emerged had the same basic topography as the Athens of today. There was the massive knoll on which was constructed a high sacred place, and there was a disorganized urban sprawl composed of low mud-brick courtyard houses with thatched roofs and narrow, unpaved, twisting lanes that spread out from the bottom slopes of the mound onto the plain below.

In Greek, the words *acron* and *polis* combine to mean "upper city." For as long as the Acropolis was inhabited, it served two purposes: as a place of natural fortification by virtue of its steep slopes and water supply, and as a place dedicated to the gods, in particular to Athena, the patron goddess of the city. As Athens became larger and of greater political and economic consequence, the Acropolis was strengthened as a final defensible bastion, and its temples gained in their architectural and sculptural splendor.

In 480 B.C., in a war in which Greece defeated invading forces from Persia, the buildings on the Athenian Acropolis were badly damaged. Later, during the forty-one years from 447 to 406 B.C., when Athens was at the height of its cultural and political power, the Acropolis was rebuilt. The reconstruction used the surviving stone from former temples on the hill as a symbolic act of cultural continuity. At the same time, an innovative approach in design yielded a complex that quickly became recognized throughout Greece as the new standard for public architecture.

In earlier schemes, the hilltop precinct had been laid out with a pair of typical temples, each six columns wide. The Periclean solution was quite different. Its structures, in combination with stairs, walkways, ramps, and numerous sculptures—both freestanding and integrated into the mass of buildings—constituted an environment of primal power and mystery. The new Parthenon had an eight-column front, was unusually large, and was opulently adorned with sculpture. Furthermore, all the architectural elements of the building were subtly angled and curved to correct for optical distortions when viewed in perspective. No other temple building in Hellenistic civilization would assume the singular expense and complexity of construction incurred through these superhuman fine adjustments, through which the Parthenon achieved an ultimate serene aesthetic balance and perfect architectural harmony (a matter discussed in greater detail later in this chapter).

Across from the Parthenon was the Erechtheion named for the Greek king Erechtheus, the second major temple of the revitalized Acropolis complex. The new Erechtheion provided an understated and asymmetrical counterpoint: it was much smaller, all four of its elevations were different, and the facade that faced the Parthenon was largely a blank wall from which projected a small porch surrounded by a low balcony. Supporting the roof of the porch were six caryatids, or columns in the shape of Greek maidens. Like those of the Parthenon, the quality of these carvings and the unity of this simple composition would influence architecture for many centuries. If the Parthenon was a grand masterpiece, the Erechtheion was a delicate and refined one.

The ceremonial ramps to the Acropolis led straight through the center of yet another structure: the Propylaea. The Propylaea was a building of many messages and parts. Built into the top edge of the Acropolis, its two truncated temple fronts, one facing in to the sacred precinct, and the other facing out to the city, appeared as if they had grown out of the rock itself. It was a majestic formal entry point; it made an awe-inspiring transition from the outside world to a sanctified place; it was the fortified gateway to the upper city; it channeled the flow of people and stone.

Above the entryway, to one side and projecting outward into space, was a small platform upon which sat a jewel-like temple. As one ascends the Acropolis, the steep sides of the hill hide the architecture above, except for the temple of Athena Nike, whose image appears and disappears between the trees and around the bends in the pathway, beckoning the climber upward to the place of the gods.

Yet another of the innovative features of the new Parthenon was particularly striking. On the vertical face of the framework of beams above an interior ring of columns, a long bas-relief sculpture wrapped around the structure. Depicted on this frieze was the Panathenaic Festival, in which, every four years, the citizens of Athens marched in long procession up the hill from the lower city to the higher sanctuary. This was the first time in Greek history that the citizens of a city were depicted along with gods, goddesses, and heroes in the sculpture of a temple, and the creation of this frieze marks a significant moment in the development of human society.

The rise of Athens is one of the most revealing examples of the role of the city in civilization. The first cities were the means for early societies to gather talented individual specialists, in one place, to stimulate the exchange and growth of ideas. Cities were the vehicle by which the intellectual power of human society was originally marshaled. In classical Athens, this potential was harnessed in an extremely effective way as, over the centuries, the city's participatory form of democracy brought its residents into constant and stimulating critical dialogue at the heart of the living lower city, at its agora.

The agora was a public square and marketplace and the central location for many of the collective activities of Athens. While the Acropolis was the symbol of Athens, the agora was where the cooperative life of the community actually occurred. Compared to the random development of the rest of the lower city, the agora of Athens became carefully defined as its significance evolved, and similar public squares would be positioned at the heart of all later Hellenistic cities. In classical Athens, the agora gradually became the lower city's largest and most formal plaza, framed by many of the important buildings of civic life. At various moments in the history of Athens a visitor might find Socrates teaching philosophy in a corner of this open common space, or one could witness a law court in session, hear a political debate of one of the city's official assemblies, view a theatrical presentation, observe a religious ceremony, or survey the varied commercial wares from the far-flung Athenian empire. If we were to name an exact location in history as the birthplace of democracy, the agora of Athens would have a compelling claim.

It has been estimated that, at its height, perhaps one-seventh to one-tenth of the inhabitants of Athens were citizens: about 40,000 males out of a total of 150,000 free people, served by around 100,000 slaves. The very inequity of this situation—a select few individuals being supported by the work of women, foreigners, and bond servants—is precisely what made possible the wide involvement of male citizens in the life of the city. These conflicting facts reveal yet another basic reality: from its earliest conception, Athens was complex and contradictory, holding within itself, simultaneously, the dark and the ennobling dimensions of human character. Nevertheless, those who were fortunate enough to hold citizenship could afford to devote all their time to public activities.

The obligations of the citizen were manifold. They formed the volunteer army, served as civil administrators and judges, participated in theatrical and athletic competitions, made laws, and voted in the general meetings that determined public policy. In order to fulfill such responsibilities a citizen had to be physically fit, literate, and learned.

Modern historians calculate that the law courts required about 6,000 jurors annually, each of whom knew the basic concepts of Athenian law and were chosen by lot. There was an executive council of 500 members called the Boule, and since no citizen was allowed to serve for more than one year, a considerable proportion of the citizenry of Athens had legislative experience. Every citizen could speak and vote in the assembly, where the quorum was sometimes as large as 6,000. Studies of the Athenian theater have projected that each year about 2,000 inhabitants competed in thirty new dramatic presentations as members of the chorus, a role requiring each participant to master both the dances and the oral recitations. At a moment in human history when, elsewhere, emperors, pharaohs, kings, tyrants, and warlords had absolute authority, the Athenian democratic city-state constituted a radical new idea.

These freedoms were at their height in the period from 510 to 404 B.C., when a series of ordinances enabled the widest participation of Athenians in the life of their city. Across about five generations, this interval of political and social liberation spawned a remarkable achievement in intellectual and artistic spheres. In successive order, each studying with his predecessor, Socrates (468–399), Plato (427–347), and Aristotle (384–322) produced works that would form the foundation of Western philosophical thinking. A legacy of tragic and comedic theater was created and passed on to the present in the still-performed plays of Aeschylus (525–456), Sophocles (496–406), Euripides (480–406), and Aristophanes (448–388). One of the earliest important examples of written history was devised by Thucydides (460–400) in his history of the Peloponnesian War. Traditions of farsighted civic service were actualized in the lives of such statesmen as Themistocles (525–460), Aristides (d. 468), and Pericles (495–428). And works of art and architecture whose impact would endure for millennia were created by numerous anonymous artists and by two whose names have reached us: the painter Polygnotus (d. 447) and the sculptor Phidias (500–432), widely credited with the general composition of the Acropolis and the major sculptures of the Parthenon. With the exception of Renaissance Florence, nowhere else in history has so much far-reaching accomplishment come from such a small human assembly.

As Athenian philosophers and playwrights examined the possibilities of the fully realized individual, Athenian artists elevated figurative sculpture to unsurpassed heights of refinement. Their works endeavored to make manifest in idealized form the accomplished intellect dwelling within the accomplished body aspiring to moral behavior. The quality and abundance of carving that adorned the Parthenon—in its pediments, its metopes (the sculptural zones of its exterior frieze), and its illustrious inner frieze depicting the Panathenaic Festival—constituted one of the most impressive integrations of sculpture and architecture in history.

Poised over the city, the perfect temple riveted the eye from faraway places in the surrounding geography. It was the pride of Athens. Its Panathenaic frieze showed a cross section of the city's people giving thanks for the gift of the gods, which was the very idea of the city itself—a place where individual talents were recognized, fostered, and utilized for the public benefit. In Athens, for a short and glorious time, a society had taken to itself the freedom to let its unrestrained creativity determine its destiny.

For thousands of years thereafter, the social symbolism and the architectural aesthetics of the Acropolis were invoked often in the important buildings of Western civilization, in a long line of cultural evolution. Greek architecture would be reinterpreted and expanded, for instance, by the Romans—establishing what we now call the classical tradition. This would be enriched and revived once again during the Italian Renaissance, would mutate to become the Baroque, would be imported to England through the works of Andrea Palladio, and would be utilized by Napoleon for the grand monuments of his Empire. European colonization would transplant the classical tradition to North and South America, Africa, Asia, and Australia. It would be brought to the United States by Thomas Jefferson to metamorphose many times more as the Georgian, Federal, Greek Revival, Italianate, French Second Empire, Neo-Grec, Beaux Arts, Neo–Italian Renaissance, Neo-Georgian, Neo-Federal, and Neo-American classical styles. Mussolini, Hitler, and Stalin would propose classically inspired monoliths for the buildings of their totalitarian states. And near the end of the twentieth century, on a hilltop in Los Angeles, American architect Richard Meier would invoke the Acropolis in the white stone–clad buildings of the Getty Museum complex. The achievements on this one small Greek promontory would influence the human-built environment throughout the world and across time.

Yet as revered as the Parthenon has been, only its ruins have come down to us today. Modern examinations of the temple's original construction have found it to be so basically sound that it could have survived earthquakes, weather, and aging over the two and a half millennia since its erection. What the Parthenon could not survive was human history. Should contemporary visitors to the Acropolis wish to comprehend the full glory of the building, they must reconstruct it in their imaginations. With the passage of time, much of the Parthenon's fabric was needlessly destroyed or taken away to foreign places, while the bulk of the ancient city of Athens was soon erased by war.

THE CITY BESIEGED BY HISTORY

In the centuries after the completion of the Periclean Acropolis, Hellenistic culture continued to spread via the conquests of Alexander the Great, the general admiration for Greek civilization by the Romans, and the continuation of Greek influence in the Byzantine Empire. Yet for the living city of Athens, the zenith had passed.

In 88–85 B.C., the Roman general Sulla made a punitive example of the rebellious metropolis, leveling most of the houses of Athens and its fortifications but leaving intact its civic buildings and monuments. Otherwise, under the empire, Athens was often granted imperial favor and the status of a free city because of its widely admired schools. Various emperors constructed new public buildings: a concert hall, a law court, the temple of Olympian Zeus, an aqueduct, which is still in use today, a library, a gymnasium, and a small temple on the Acropolis. Around A.D.250, the old defensive walls of the city were rebuilt. By 267, they had been breached.

The sack of Athens by the Heruli, a Germanic tribe from the north of Europe, resulted in the burning of nearly all the city's public buildings. The lower city was plundered, the agora was totally destroyed, and the stones of the Parthenon and the Erechtheion suffered substantial thermal damage. Except for the buildings of the Acropolis and a few random structures of the lower city, the Roman and Germanic invasions obliterated the metropolis of Socrates, Plato, and Aristotle. In the years that followed, the devastated monuments of the lower town were cannibalized for their materials by the Athenians themselves, as they constructed a new line of fortifications encircling an area less than a tenth the size of the former city. In the age of Pericles an official city architect had been responsible for the timely maintenance of public buildings; now the reduced city was unable to preserve even its most sacred monuments. For several decades the Parthenon remained intact but unroofed, wounded.

The schools of Athens sustained the city's cultural preeminence in the Greek world under the early Byzantine emperors, and within a century the city had grown back to its former perimeters. But by A.D. 529, paganism had been banned by the emperor Justinian, the philosophy schools had been closed, and the Parthenon and Erechtheion had been converted into churches. Athens was, in effect, reduced to a small provincial backwater outside the main currents of history.

At the Parthenon, an unfortunate tradition was initiated: theft. A large number of the sculptures of the east pediment were removed to Constantinople and the sculptural decorations of the metopes were disfigured. Thus began the practice by which foreign powers looted the Acropolis for its extraordinary carvings.

In 1204, the city fell to French crusaders and a bell tower was added to the Parthenon. In 1311, Athens was taken by Catalan traders from Spain. In 1388, Florentines occupied the city, followed by Venetians, Florentines, and Venetians once again. In 1456, the Ottoman Turks captured Athens and transformed the Parthenon into a mosque. They added a minaret to the top of the Christian campanile.

In the fourteenth century, gunpowder became widely used in European warfare. Eventually, the Turks strengthened the fortifications of the Acropolis and stored explosives in the Propylaea and the Parthenon. In 1640, a bolt of lightning caused an explosion in the Propylaea. In 1687, Athens was besieged by the Venetians. The temple of Athena Nike was dismantled by the Turks to reinforce the Acropolis bastion, but an artillery barrage eventually hit the Parthenon and shattered the middle sections of the building. Until this moment the mass of the building had remained intact for over two millennia. Pieces of the structure would now remain scattered across the plateau for another 150 years.

The occupation of the Acropolis lasted six months. Before relinquishing the site back to the Turks, the Venetians attempted to loot carvings from the west pediment of the Parthenon, causing parts of one of the incomparable sculptural groupings of European civilization to fall and break.

Early Ottoman rulers had long respected the site, but in the declining years of their empire corruption developed at many levels. In the years following the Venetian siege, the Turks utilized fallen marble blocks on the Acropolis to reinforce their defensive installations. Then, in 1803, a British expedition under the leadership of Lord Elgin purchased permission from the Ottomans to take sculptural pieces from the plateau. The lion's share of the remaining parts of the Panathenaic frieze and major surviving pieces of the west pediment were removed. One of the six caryatids of the Erechtheion was extracted and replaced with a plaster cast. In all, fifty sculptural pieces were carried away. Three other fragments were purchased by the French ambassador. The Greeks, now in servitude, were powerless as their ancient heritage was bartered by one foreign power to another.

The Greek War of Independence against the Turks resulted in two sieges of Athens (1822–1827 and 1827–1833). The military encampment that had grown up within the fortifications on the Acropolis had become a village unto itself, with small houses and alleys built in the shadows of the stately and towering Parthenon. The lower town of Athens occupied the same general area as in the days of Pericles. Here, too, vernacular residential structures of the resident Turks, Albanians, and Greeks were casually intermingled with the surviving monuments of classical Athens, Rome, and Byzantium. Although much had been destroyed in various sieges, the cityscape that had evolved of remnants from different eras constituted a rich amalgam of historical evidence. Now once again Athens would suffer the devastation of war. After the fighting had stopped, a Bavarian officer described the scene: "I entered the Acropolis and witnessed the pell-mell of scattered marbles. In the midst of that confusion, between capitals, broken pillars, small and large marble blocks, lay cannonballs, shell fragments, human skulls and bones, many of which were piled close to the comely caryatids of the Erechtheion."

The trials of history had fractured the Acropolis monuments and scattered their pieces across continents. What remained of the lower city of classical Athens lay beneath the scorched earth. The birthplace of democracy was no more; but where the sacred mound met the sky, the skeletal remains of the

Parthenon still shimmered in the sunlight. After more than two thousand years of subjugation, what city would the Greeks now build with their newly won freedom?

THE BIRTH OF THE CITY BEAUTIFUL

Creating a Greek state free of the Ottoman Empire required substantial foreign involvement, and this development occurred in an era when European powers were vying for colonial hegemony across the globe as a result of an increasing need for inexpensive raw materials and new markets for the manufactured goods of the Industrial Revolution. In addition, a significant cultural influence was involved in the widespread support of Europeans for Greek independence: this was a love of ancient Greek civilization. Many philhellenes—admirers of ancient Greece, like the English poet Lord Byron—fought and died in the revolution.

Although the Ottoman Empire was in decline at the beginning of the nineteenth century, its military superiority to the rebel forces required the countervailing threat of European intervention if Greek autonomy was to be achieved. Consequently, in 1832, in the Treaty of London, which declared Greece an independent kingdom, Great Britain, France, and Russia were declared protectors of the sovereignty of the new nation, and seventeen-year-old Otto I of Bavaria, himself an avid philhellene, was named the first king of the Greeks.

The new monarch enthusiastically assumed the Greek spelling of his name, Othon, adopted Greek national dress, and pressured the Regency Council of Greece to name Athens as his capital. Wider historical events had set in place an ironic cultural confluence for the planning of the new metropolis that would rise above the ashes of the old city.

The transformation of Athens would be astounding. The prerevolutionary city had been a medieval military outpost with little infrastructure and a circulation system that accommodated only pedestrians and horses. The postrevolutionary city, however, would mirror the form of the industrialized capitals of the developed nations of Europe and America. The prerevolutionary town of several thousand inhabitants had evolved organically over many centuries; the postrevolutionary metropolis would accommodate a modern urban society and be planned by professional engineers and architects trained in Germany. Through the European-trained professionals serving the Bavarian-born king, the classical influence would be rerouted in its journey from ancient Greece to Imperial Rome, to Italy during the Renaissance, to Bavaria, and back to the capital of the aspiring modern nation. The Greeks themselves hadn't built like their ancient forebears for nearly two millennia. It would be through the

Germans that classical buildings would once again be constructed in the city from which their inspiration had originated.

The first step was to make a detailed archaeological and topographical survey of the surrounding area. To accomplish this, two young architects were appointed: Gustav Eduard Schaubert from Silesia, in central Europe where modern Poland meets the Czech Republic, and Stamatios Kleanthes from Thessaly. Both had been trained at the Berliner Bauakademie and were former pupils of the internationally renowned German classicist architect Karl Friedrich Schinkel.

The architects and a team of archaeologists examined the wreckage and mapped out the existing conditions. In the lower city, about eighty of an original twelve hundred one-story houses had survived the fighting (the king had taken up residence in the only two-story stone structure). Except for the Acropolis, the Temple of Theseus, and a handful of Roman, Christian, and Muslim monuments, little of historic Athens remained.

The destruction of war had created a unique opportunity. For a brief time, planners and architects could accomplish in Athens what had proven extremely difficult to achieve throughout the historic capitals of Europe: they could build a major city according to a larger conceptual plan. Throughout the late eighteenth, the nineteenth, and the early twentieth centuries, as historic cities expanded due to industrialization and as the demands of vehicular transportation required street plans with broader and straighter roads, the knot of private property ownership and the numerous historic buildings constructed in compliance with ancient street patterns made it inordinately complex to revamp old city configurations in favor of new ones.

In Athens, it was now possible to plan a new metropolis on a grand scale. Although the city had only 4,000 inhabitants when the Greeks regained their independence, it was anticipated that the population might grow to be ten times as great. For miles in all directions around the Acropolis, an extended agricultural plain provided ample room to build. One major question remained: exactly where would the modern capital be located? And here the new city came into conflict with the old.

Historical circumstances had created a climate in which there was wide agreement that the ruins of ancient Athens were sacrosanct. For the Europeans, their very involvement in Greek affairs arose from a desire to see the cradle of Western civilization back within the Western sphere of influence. For the Greeks, who for centuries had been hobbled by foreign domination, the classical era was a heritage with which the new nation could feel proud to identify. Thus, it was generally settled that the ancient ruins on the Acropolis would not only be preserved but would to some extent be reclaimed and reconstituted.

The lower city of Athens had always occupied the bottom slopes of the Acropolis. Each time it was decimated by war, it had been reconstructed in generally the same location. As a result, somewhere underneath the remnants of the existing townscape lay the toppled remains of the agora of the classical period. Surviving monuments aboveground were few in number, often small in size, and scattered. Should the new city be built in the same location, or should an area surrounding the Acropolis be set aside as empty parkland to be excavated by future generations?

The concept of an archaeological park located at the very heart of the city was already a long-contemplated idea in Rome and therefore an idea well known among European architects. Since the Renaissance and the reconfiguration of Rome by the popes, an area to the west of the Capitoline Hill had been left open where the center of ancient Rome had once existed. Throughout this period, numerous excavations occurred. Some were the work of early archaeologists and architectural historians; others were treasure hunts for lost statuary; but most were the work of quarriers who mined the ancient buildings for the marble with which to construct a capital for Christianity.

By the Age of Enlightenment, a more rational and carefully disciplined approach to archaeology and to the study of antiquities had begun to prevail, and an archaeological zone around the Roman Forum was secured. With the establishment of Italian nationhood in 1873 (and the end of papal rule) a more lasting legal status was achieved in the first master plan for Rome in 1887. The function of the city as a living museum of its own past had been recognized.

In Athens, the youthful architects developing the city's master plan—themselves products of an education steeped in the revival of classicism, and aware that their work would be watched carefully by professionals across Europe—trained their vision upon the object for which many foreign philhellenes had given their lives: the preservation of the remnants of the classical city. In 1833, one year after they had begun work, their visionary plan was ratified. It consisted of two basic components: an area laid out with a rational street pattern and an archaeological park.

On the plain to the north of the Acropolis, a street configuration reminiscent of the palace town of Versailles was proposed as the location of the new capital. Here major urban monuments and public spaces were to be located at the junctures of important boulevards and straight, wide avenues. This street pattern, in the Baroque planning style, was devised so that both the central boulevard of Athens and numerous other thoroughfares were aligned to focus on the Acropolis. Thereby were achieved vistas of the hilltop from numerous vantage points throughout the cityscape, ensuring the primacy of its symbolic presence.

The southern edge of the area designated for building was adjacent to an extended archaeological park, which included the Acropolis itself and an area of land wrapping around the whole hill. Within this sector the ancient agora and many other important historical remains were located. While at the time the fledgling government of Greece could not afford the expense of a careful excavation of the archaeological zone, the architects foresaw that "future generations will certainly reproach us for our lack of foresight in not allowing for this at some time in the future." The archaeological park in Athens was one of the earliest of such zones given legal status at the core of a major city.

Setting aside a tract of parkland in the center of a large city is a difficult and costly endeavor requiring substantial farsightedness. As historic European cities mushroomed due to the urbanization of industrialized societies, many such large parks—such as the Jardin des Tuileries and the Luxembourg Gardens in Paris and Kensington Gardens and St. James's Park in London—were made economically and politically feasible through the fortuitous reappropriation of former royal properties. In 1856 in New York, when the land for Central Park was acquired, the park was situated beyond the extent of dense urban growth, which helped to make the price less prohibitive. As soon as the park was created, nearby property values began to rise and a stream of proposals commenced for ways to reallocate various parts of the parkland for other uses. A recent study has shown that if every one of these ideas had been constructed over the years, Central Park would by now have vanished.

In Athens the Acropolis was considered a state-controlled military fortification, but other parts of the archaeological zone were not state-owned. When the new plan was adopted, the idea of securing this area for public use came under attack. Speculators had begun purchasing property in the old town from former Turkish owners as soon as it had been determined that the capital of the new nation would be situated in Athens. This had driven up the cost of real estate, and the government of Greece had limited funds for expropriation. As a result, a part of the lower hillside of the Acropolis continued to be inhabited rather than be set aside.

Today this area is known as the Plaka. Over the decades it has evolved from a low-rise residential neighborhood to a tourist-oriented zone of shops, restaurants, and hotels. A recent architectural survey has revealed that fewer than a dozen small houses in the district date back to the Ottoman period. Meanwhile, an abundance of unexamined significant archaeological material exists below ground. In other words, had the Schaubert-Kleanthes proposal been followed and the Plaka appropriated, the remnants of one of civilization's most significant and earliest cityscapes would have become part of the living metropolis and the heritage of all humankind. The current cost of reclaiming the built-up parts of this area for public purposes is astronomical.

Soon after the Schaubert-Kleanthes plan was adopted, a third German-trained architect-planner, Leo von Klenze, was consulted by the king. Klenze recommended a series of modifications to the street pattern of the Schaubert-Kleanthes plan, including leaving more of the circulation plan of old Athens intact. This helped to maintain a sense of the original urban context of several early Christian churches dating back to the eleventh and twelfth centuries. Also on the advice of Klenze, the Acropolis was demilitarized. No longer would there be a strategic benefit to bombing the sacred precinct, and restoration efforts were begun to return the plateau to its classical elements only. Finally, Klenze recommended that a government agency be created to protect the antiquities of the city, and in 1834 the Greek Archaeological Service was instituted. On the Acropolis, the accretions of several centuries were gradually removed and the primacy of the classical monuments was restored. Ground level was lowered until bedrock was reestablished, while fallen parts of the monuments were set back up, resurrecting their profile against the sky.

From 1839 to 1892, a number of significant public buildings in the Neoclassical style were constructed in the city: the University of Athens, the Academy of Science, and the National Library. Although they would not achieve the pure aesthetic integrity of their ancient Greek predecessors, these new structures made a conceptual bridge between the past and the future. They were built in stone and derived their outward form from classical Greek temples. Inside, they adopted contemporary interiors for the publicly instituted educational functions of a modern society. As industrialization began, new infrastructure was introduced to Athens to provide clean water, remove sewage, light the streets at night, and transport the growing masses of the city. Between 1870 and 1896, the population grew from 44,500 to 123,000, and in 1896 the transformation of Greece was given international recognition when the first revival of the modern Olympic Games was staged in Athens.

Throughout the metropolis, in old and new neighborhoods, developers constructed vernacular residential and commercial buildings influenced by the notable structures of both the ancient and the contemporary city. Hundreds of buildings rose up, and even those of modest size and expense were articulated with classically influenced architectural elements and details. The endless variety of these vernacular structures—rarely designed by architects, and often taking their forms from architectural style books and catalogs—expressed a broad cultural connection with the architectural values of the past. Athenians of today recall their parents' and grandparents' descriptions of what the city was like when it first blossomed after Greek independence. The predominant low scale of urban construction in those early days allowed the streets to be bathed in sunlight; flowering citrus trees and vegetation were abundant, and the buildings of Athens—those high up on the Acropolis, the civic buildings in

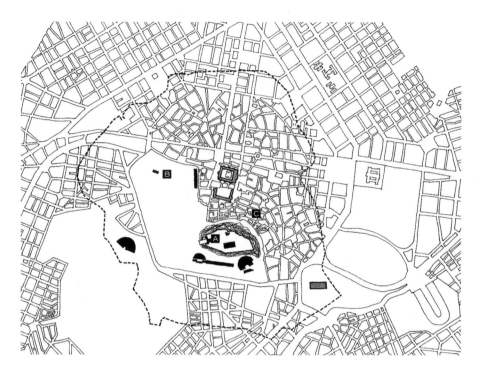

The center of Athens in 1960 · The Acropolis (A) sits in an archaeological park that also holds the ruins of the Periclean Agora (B). The Plaka (C) covers other early parts of the ancient city. Surviving remnants of major monuments from classical Athens are shown in black. Surviving remnants of major Roman monuments are shown in dark gray. The course of the walls from Periclean Athens is indicated by a dotted line. The street layout reflects in part the plans of Schaubert, Kleanthes, and Klenze, as well as later additions by speculative developers.

important public squares, and the more modest structures of everyday life— drew their forms from a common architectural source rooted in the very land itself. A beautiful and coherent metropolis, unified aesthetically on several levels and crowned by one of the most conspicuous architectural symbols in Western civilization, had emerged from the chaos of war.

THE LOSS OF THE CITY BEAUTIFUL

Yet the fair metropolis would not endure for long. The commitment by government to make an orderly arrangement of the city's parts in anticipation of the future ended with the Schaubert-Kleanthes-Klenze planning effort. In the following decades, the municipal administration of modern Athens was characterized instead by a lack of planning and a reluctance to moderate private development. Under the Ottomans, the Greeks were not allowed to own land in their own country, so once they won independence, restrictions on the use of private property may have seemed onerous, particularly when imposed initially by foreign (German) administrators. Instead of either adopting a new design or adhering to the old one—except for requiring straight streets to facilitate the expansion of the infrastructure—administrators simply made a catalog of the schemes of private real estate investors and the built area of the city was allowed to grow ad hoc. Between 1,878 and 1,900 permits for 173 alterations to the municipal plan were granted to various private developers without public review or oversight.

After World War I and the fall of the Ottoman Empire, a second development exacerbated the unplanned growth of Athens. In 1921, Greece and Turkey exchanged alien ethnic minority populations; approximately 1.5 million repatriated Greeks from former Ottoman territories were resettled in Greece. In Athens the population jumped overnight from 473,000 to 718,000, and because neither the city itself nor the nation as a whole had the financial resources to construct adequate housing, squatter settlements appeared on the outskirts of the metropolis. From this moment forward, dramatic increases in population growth and haphazard illegal development shaped the expansion of the urban agglomeration.

Recent UNESCO studies have indicated that since the founding of the modern nation-state, although the population of Greece as a whole has increased 12-fold, the population of Athens has increased 150-fold. Current estimates place the population of the metropolis at around 4 million people, but this figure is just an approximation. Like other large cities in countries where the pace of urbanization outstripped the development of an industrialized economy—Cairo, Mexico City, and Istanbul, for example—a ring of illegal settlements gradually surrounded the metropolis.

Since Greek independence, continuity in the administration of Athens has been undermined by the recurring political instability caused by fourteen revolutions—including the abolition of the monarchy, its subsequent restoration, and its final abolition in 1973—as well as a number of military coups d'état, a brutal period of German occupation followed by a savage civil war, and numerous dissolutions of various parliamentary governments. Of particular significance here is the civil war, which lasted until 1949. During this time the city's governance was conspicuous for its corruption and laxity in regard to land-use regulation. When the fighting had stopped, widespread deferred maintenance of buildings, shortages of housing for an expanding population, and unchecked speculative development caused Athens to be almost totally rebuilt several stories higher. From that moment to today, at least 50 percent of the new construction in the city has been through illegal development. Existing houses were expanded without permits, and large areas of the city were

bartered in a black market in property, and squatters built whole neighborhoods without complying with official regulations.

Over the course of this widespread reconstruction, much of the classically
inspired vernacular architecture of the beautiful city disappeared. Developers
constructed acre upon acre of ugly, poorly made, generic modern buildings.
The general increase in the height of the city reduced the amount of sunlight
that reached the streets. As the population grew, the number of private motor
vehicles proliferated until traffic clogged the city. Since Athens sits in a plain
surrounded by higher mountains, it experiences inversions similar to those of
Mexico City and Los Angeles. This geographic characteristic, coupled with the
historical failure of the Greek government to control industrial pollution in
the Athenian basin, and further combined with the dramatic increase in automotive emissions, made Athens one of the more polluted cities in the world.

The introduction of preservation laws had begun with the archaeological
statutes whose purpose was to save the remains of antiquity. After World War II,
numerous other conservation initiatives were undertaken by various national
regimes, but discontinuity from one administration to another often meant
that programs of previous governments were abandoned by the governments
that followed. Because the power of taxation was controlled at the national
level, city officials had few resources with which to continue local conservation
programs on their own. Further, the frequent change of national administrations removed from the political equation a degree of accountability in regard
to conservation programs that require years of sustained work in order to have
an effect. The end result is that, although in theory, Athens is protected by a
wide variety of preservation laws at national and local levels, the effect of these
statutes is erratic and unreliable. Nor would any national or municipal administration attempt to designate as a historic district the graceful vernacular of the
modern capital. Once the beautiful city was lost, the most critical issue, and a
matter of worldwide concern, was to what degree the remains of the Propylaea,
the Erechtheion, the Temple of Athena Nike, and the Parthenon would be
safeguarded.

RECLAIMING THE VISION OF THE ACROPOLIS

Early efforts to restore the landmarks of the Acropolis had begun soon after
Greece won its independence. Over the centuries, damage from several bom-
bardments and explosions and numerous changes to the complex had caused
various parts of the original monuments to be broken, removed, or
rearranged. The ruins of the Ottoman garrison town, as well as various additions to the fortifications that ringed the hilltop, had in part been built with
material from the classical buildings themselves. In addition, myriad other

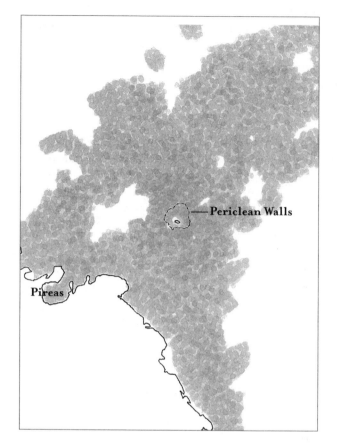

Periclean Walls

Pireas

THE CONTEMPORARY CONURBATION OF ATHENS

fallen pieces lay scattered across the plateau. Together, this volume of dislocated marble constituted an enormously complex puzzle.

Unfortunately, the conservation work of the new Greek government did not meet the standards of more scientific reconstructions in other cities during the same period. In Rome, in 1821, years of careful research had informed the restoration of monuments such as the Arch of Titus, where marble of slightly different color was used to distinguish new material from original stonework so that the parts of the monument that had been carved and constructed in antiquity would not be confused with the work of modern conservationists. In Athens a different philosophy prevailed. The archaeological remains were considered romantic ruins, and the arbitrary re-creation of the basic forms of the classical masterpieces was sanctioned. This resulted in a great deal of damage. Stone pieces of various monuments were reassembled incorrectly, without anyone having determined their original position in masonry walls. In order to fit misaligned parts together, original 2,000-year-old broken blocks of marble were recut to create smooth new joints. This left for future generations an even more complex puzzle of misplaced and mutilated pieces. And the lead-coated iron ties, which the ancient Greeks had used to reinforce the structures in the event of seismic activity, were replaced with uncoated iron fittings. Over several decades, these would rust and rupture innumerable original stones that had otherwise survived for millennia. Mounting air pollution in Athens made such damage worse and attacked many other parts of the buildings. And an uncontrolled stream of tourists further wore down the monuments simply by passing through the site.

In 1971 a report by UNESCO alerted the world to the fact that the Acropolis monuments were in extreme and immediate jeopardy. Once this situation came to international attention, the government of Greece quickly assembled a qualified team of local specialists, the Committee for the Conservation of the Acropolis Monuments, to analyze and correct the problem. Given the significance of the monuments, a question must be asked: Why hadn't such a well-qualified team been assigned before?

The UNESCO intervention demonstrates one of the principal means by which the effort to save the built heritage of humankind is accomplished. UNESCO and three of its subsidiary programs—the World Heritage List, an official listing of the most significant cultural and natural sites in the world; ICOMOS, an international network of conservation specialists; and ICROM, a center for the advancement of preservation technology—are the means by which the most advanced conservation practices are disseminated across the globe. In Athens, as in many other places, the UNESCO critique brought to the local government's attention its responsibility to conserve a Greek patrimony that is also the heritage of all the peoples of the world.

Today, funded by Greece and other European nations, the Acropolis monuments are being restored to the highest standard made possible by sophisticated construction methods and modern chemical and computer analysis. Old iron rods and fittings are being replaced with non-rusting titanium parts attached to the old stone with a special reversible cement. Damaged marble is repaired and then impregnated with a chemical sealant to impede further decay. And through the use of detailed computer analysis of the surfaces of the ancient stones, it is now possible to identify matching broken pieces of marble, and to determine their original placement in various monuments. This capability has resulted in the identification of numerous scattered fragments of the ancient buildings and facilitated the deconstruction and subsequent reconstruction of the landmarks to a degree of accuracy heretofore not possible. The complicated jigsaw puzzle is finally being solved.

The result of this scientific renewal of the monuments confirms a fact that architects and historians have postulated for many hundreds of years. The

Acropolis buildings and particularly the Parthenon attain a height of perfection in their design and construction to some degree unparalleled in architectural history. In this regard, the new reconstruction has further advanced our knowledge of such refinements, and recapturing this state of perfection became the standard for the monuments' conservation. The myriad heavy, perfectly matched pieces of these sublime compilations of ancient marble had to be shifted back to their faultless balanced state.

The perfection of the Parthenon is in part a reflection of its remarkable fine adjustments to offset the visual distortions of human perception. Ancient designers had observed in earlier temples that when vertical columns were placed in a long line, equidistant from one another and at right angles to a perfectly flat base, several visual illusions occurred. The horizontal line of the base appeared to drop in the center, the end columns appeared to be farther apart than the inner columns, and the weight of the roof and pediments appeared to be pushing outward, as if to knock the columns off-balance. Regardless of its actual structural stability, in terms of visual perception, a completely aligned temple seemed to be reacting to the forces generated by the weight of its upper structure. The architects of the Parthenon made a series of corrections that would set the architectural elements of the new temple into a state of visual equilibrium, or rest.

Their solution was rational and astounding. They made fine adjustments to all the massive marble pieces that constituted the vertical and horizontal elements of the architectural composition. (Some of these corrections had been attempted before in earlier Greek temples, but never to the degree and extent consummated in the Parthenon.) First, the platform of the temple became an imperceptible and gentle curve, slightly raised in the center instead of being perfectly level, so it no longer appeared to sag. This required the cornice and beams above to be slightly arched as well. In the long colonnade wrapping around the building, each column was slightly tilted inward toward a conceptual focal point almost a mile above in the sky so that the vertical supports appeared to be more stable. The columns themselves and the spaces between them were made to diminish in thickness toward the center of each elevation of the colonnade, making all these elements appear to be of exactly equal dimensions. Given it had become customary for the profile of columns in a Greek temple to be slightly bowed and tapered so they looked properly thick enough to support the temple's roof—an architectural effect known as *entasis*—the combination of all these modulations produced an elevation that was minutely curved in almost all of its lines while appearing to be perfectly straight and aligned at right angles. The result of these many small and subtle compensations for visual distortion was a building that looked serenely in balance.

In making such minute and specific alignments to the huge marble blocks, a structure that seemed to be made of identical parts was in fact composed of numerous pieces with infinitesimal differences in measurement and shape. Since the common standard of construction in temple buildings was to make a building look seamless, the Parthenon would be constructed to tolerances so small that a modern jeweler could hardly accomplish them, and the recent scientific restoration of the structure has established that its joints are commonly crafted to a closeness of one thousandth of a millimeter. Even the most exacting construction technologies available today rarely match these standards, which the ancient Greeks achieved by hand.

The decision to make imperceptible adjustments in accord with the subtleties of human perception had made the construction of the building into a heroic task of fine craftsmanship, which would not be duplicated in any Hellenistic edifice thereafter. It dramatically increased the work involved in a temple already of unprecedented cost, and it required that the architects convince those in control of the building's budget of the value of such discriminating modifications. Since the cost of rebuilding the Acropolis was a major economic undertaking for the city, since accounts of public works in Athens were often inscribed in stone and placed in conspicuous locations for the public to see, and since it was common practice to question officials in regard to their administrative judgment, it is unlikely that the decision to make such elaborate refinements was not subject to public approval. This means that a broad segment of the citizenry of Athens appreciated the need for such sophisticated architectural adjustments. Rarely in the entire history of Western architecture would a society have enough confidence in its judgment to make such a costly investment in so refined and abstract a concept.

Yet all of these architectural refinements represent but part of the artistic achievement of the final structure. For as construction proceeded, and the potential ethereal perfection of the Parthenon emerged, the sculptural aspirations of the project were elevated as well. And the great Panathenaic frieze was created. And the spaces in the metopes, which had traditionally been left blank, were carved. Much of this, and the work in the pediments as well, was designed, directed, or carved by Phidias, one of the great figurative sculptors in history. And the sculpture itself, which would be seen at extreme angles from below on the ground, was also adjusted in its proportions for the distortions of perspective. Thus by craft, artistry, science, and sheer will, the Athenians made supple the stone of the Parthenon. The plasticity achieved in the ultimate assemblage of marble was as if poured from their minds as a single unified conception.

The modern restoration of the Parthenon made a degree more visible that which had not been seen for centuries. And the wonder of the building's perfection is that as much as we gain knowledge of its many subtle attributes, the sum of all these separate aspects never quite accounts for their combined effect. It has always seemed that the whole would be more than the tally of its parts. But we cannot know for certain, since we cannot see it.

The reconstruction raised once again the question of reassembling all the building's dispersed and celebrated surviving sculptural pieces, primarily the material taken from the Acropolis by Lord Elgin and currently exhibited in the British Museum. Should the pillaged art of the world be returned to the cultures from which it was taken? Such was the case after the defeat of Napoleon, when the French returned to the Italians the numerous treasures stolen from the Vatican. Similarly, Germany has given back most of the artwork looted by the Third Reich in World War II.

Yet it is also true that to return the Parthenon sculptures to their place in the building would doom them to destruction by the air pollution of Athens. Already the Committee for the Conservation of the Acropolis Monuments has removed to museological environments several important carvings and replaced the originals on the building with copies. The surviving caryatids of the Erechtheion have recently been replaced in the same way. Plans are currently being developed to construct a museum to house the original sculptures of the classical buildings until a day when the acid rain of Athens no longer threatens them.

But the larger question of the reassembly of the Parthenon involves our understanding of history and the nature of human accomplishment. Putting the Parthenon back together would present the viewer with an astounding assemblage whose artistic affect can at present only be hypothesized. As much as the florescence of Athens is celebrated, we still may not know its glory. In this regard, the ultimate restoration of the Parthenon and of the spirit of classical Athens is only partly within the control of Athenians. It is a moral and ethical question that cannot be resolved until the city's environmental pollution and wavering integrity of governance have been corrected. One can only hope that someday this unsurpassed sculptural and architectural achievement will once more be seen, comprehended, and felt by future generations and that the surviving artistic components of the Parthenon will eventually stand together in the particular sunlight of the city that gave them birth.

CHAPTER TEN
THE COMPREHENSIBLE
URBAN VISAGE

LONDON AND PARIS

Do cities make sense? Paris certainly does! As for modern American cities, mechanical agglomerations of attached rectangles, I have my doubts.

—RENÉ HUYGHE, MEMBER OF THE ACADÉMIE FRANÇAISE

One hardly knows whether to laugh or cry on seeing a modernistic architecture imported into London.

—STEEN EILER RASMUSSEN, *London: The Unique City*

Prior to World War II, in different and similar ways, Paris and London were two of the world's most beautiful cities. Both were capital cities and the pride of powerful nations with wide colonial interests. Both were leading industrial centers and, as such, two of the earliest cities to begin the process of urban modernization. Both cities were very large, wealthy, and filled with extraordinary amounts of beautiful architecture, great urban palaces, extensive royal gardens, handsome residential neighborhoods, several grand railway terminals, and world-famous commercial and cultural institutions. Each city had a celebrated subway: the Metro in Paris and the Underground, or the Tube, in London.

Yet Paris and London were made and governed by substantially different means. Paris was an artistic urban sculpture whose various parts were carefully knit together by a centralized national authority over approximately four hundred years since the importation of the Italian Renaissance to France. During the same general length of time, London was built up and governed as a gradually expanding patchwork of numerous artistically composed urban pieces, but its beautiful parts were frequently autonomous, and unjoined with one another. Nonetheless, both cities were recognized internationally as symbols of their nations' ideals and as unique cultural expressions.

After World War II, drained by their involvement in two great armed conflicts, badly in need of massive amounts of new housing, and struggling to maintain their vitality in the global economy, London and Paris sought to renew themselves. As important world centers of commerce they could not ignore the growing economic hegemony of New York and the glittering skyscrapers closely associated with its empowerment. Thus Paris and London began to build within their respective historic environments large modern towers of alien design, materials, and scale. While Great Britain and France were two of the first nations to enact historic conservation laws, neither country had extended such protections to safeguard the milieu of urban townscapes. In London and Paris, the historic urban visage—the singular visual character of both places and particularly their skylines—came under assault.

THE HISTORIC EUROPEAN CITY AS AN ARTISTIC CONSTRUCTION

London and Paris reflected in their historic beauty two discernibly different phenomena in the making of urban environments. In part, their brilliance was produced by the will of their rulers in the palaces, public edifices, and urban design initiatives of powerful monarchs and nobles. At the same time, the extended aesthetic continuity of their urban fabric reflected the native architectural culture of their inhabitants—in the thousands of handsome residential and commercial buildings that constitute the bulk of their built conglomerations.

Making the city coherent and beautiful had long concerned numerous European urban societies. In the Middle Ages, as commercially successful towns gained greater degrees of autonomy, and as wealth was spread more widely among the populace, a larger number of the buildings of cities were handsomely made of increasingly more permanent materials. Several variants caused constructions in medieval towns to be shaped in complementary ways. Builders tended to use the most readily available materials derived from common sources. Workers were adept in proven traditional construction methods. Local environmental conditions made particular building features more suitable and therefore widely repeated. Established functional norms in the use of interior rooms and the way that exteriors addressed the street, as well as in plot shapes and building sizes, made the configuration of numerous structures similar.

Together such phenomena caused cities in different geographic and political regions to develop particular languages of vernacular architectural form.

The design of different types of buildings also expressed the relative social hierarchy and lent to cityscapes a larger sculptural order. Principal religious structures established a city's peaks, piety, and symbolic center. Fortifications represented military power and provided a visual frame for the urban conglomeration. Civic buildings and palaces of the nobility symbolized wealth, privilege, and authority and embellished the cityscape with high architectural art. And the merchant houses, often clustered around a central market square, not only spoke of their owners' growing political and economic empowerment but also imitated design elements from buildings of the upper classes. In such structures, the formal architecture of the rulers of medieval society became part of the vernacular building tradition.

Medieval Muslim cities and those in feudal Japan and China attained a similar vernacular cohesion with their own particular palette of building types and visual design traditions. Yet much of the architectural beauty of Beijing and Kyoto, and Cairo as well, was turned inward in private religious, governmental, and residential compounds, while the principal facades of buildings in medieval European townscapes came to face outward to the street, to the circulating and gathering spaces of the public realm. Moreover, as the merchant class of European cities increased in size and power, and distinct cultures evolved in different European urban centers, the self-identification of inhabitants was linked to the place in which they were born and invested their lives. Accumulated architectural beauty in the public realm of European medieval cities became a consciously pursued societal objective and a matter of civic pride, producing cityscapes as widely distinct as those of medieval Amsterdam, Venice, and Prague.

From the Renaissance came a heightened awareness of the aesthetic potential of architecture to define the public realm. Cities became more rational in their street layouts and more purposely integrated as architectural environments. Building codes were instituted for reasons of health and fire safety as well as to instill architectural aesthetic conformity. Street widths were regularized for efficiency of vehicular movement, and also in relation to the angle of the sun, to ensure its penetration into streets and squares. In many places, the coordinated architecture of whole street walls—of whole blocks of buildings—supported the hierarchy of major avenues linking major urban focal points in a greater urban plan.

With industrialization, physical change was further driven by social reform. A steadily enlarging middle class not only empowered cities economically but altered the political equations of governance. Universal education, medical care, suffrage, and the sanitation and safety of the urban environment came to be seen as entitlements and materialized in architectural form in the building of universities, schools, museums, libraries, hospitals, and better-quality housing. Artistic embellishment of the public realm of cities reflected both real social progress and communally shared aspirations. The physical forms of the cityscape articulated the social values of its inhabitants.

In large industrial and national capitals like London and Paris, handsome neighborhoods of housing and myriad commercial structures emerged. Initially designed by builders using architectural pattern books, and eventually requiring the legal stamp of registered engineers and architects, these were the new vernacular buildings of the industrial age. Long traditions of design, construction, the use of materials, their colors and detailing, and building regulation, civic self-respect, and the penetration of sunlight had produced cityscapes composed of complementary architecture focused on and organized around a continuous public realm. And although arrived at in remarkably dissimilar ways, the vast industrial cityscapes of London and Paris had come to manifest an extent of environmental beauty never before seen. Moreover, in particular aspects, the architectural artistry of each metropolis was unmatched across the history of cities. But differences in how their urban splendor accrued would have a telling effect on the degree to which their beauty would later be denuded.

HISTORIC LONDON: A CITY OF MYRIAD PARTIAL PLANS

Nomenclature is important in discussing the evolution of London, both because it can be so confusing and because confusion about where the city ends and begins has long been a part if its story. In London, there is a self-governing area known as "the City." This is not the whole city of London, nor does it include many of the places most identified with the spirit of London, such as Trafalgar Square, Westminster Abbey, Piccadilly Circus, Hyde Park, Covent Garden, 10 Downing Street, Parliament, Big Ben, the Royal Albert Hall, the British Museum, or Buckingham Palace. All these special places, and a hundred others as well, lie outside the City but inside the area that all foreign visitors recognize as the unique continuum of place that evolved along the river Thames. (For purposes of clarity, what Londoners colloquially call the City, or the Square Mile, will here be referred to as the City Corporation, the old incorporated city, or the old commercial core.)

Nor is the question of what constitutes the city merely an exercise in terminology. It is a matter of ongoing dispute. Administratively, the metropolitan area of London today comprises thirty-two boroughs and the City Corporation— thirty-three somewhat independently governed areas. In terms of its physical reality, it is even more fragmented, composed of hundreds of beautiful small autonomous parts. Yet it is a giant metropolis which, although requiring integrated coordination and planning, rarely over its history empowered a central municipal authority to undertake such tasks.

THE CITY CORPORATION

Throughout architectural and city planning history, some of the most influential ideas have taken the form of unbuilt drawings. Many innovative concepts for buildings have not been realized, but as drawn representations of structures they have widely affected the thinking of architects. In the field of city planning, one of the better-known drawings was Christopher Wren's unrealized plan to rebuild London after the Great Fire of 1666.

Prior to the fire, London had emerged as one of Europe's most important commercial centers and during an era of remarkable cultural flowering had produced a treasure of enduring poetry, drama, and literature, particularly in the works of Christopher Marlowe and William Shakespeare. Yet it was also a place with an underlying division. For centuries, two urban centers had existed in increasingly intertwined proximity along the north side of the Thames. To the east lay the incorporated City of London, a mercantile center of chartered independence since the Middle Ages and the hub of Britain's economic vitality. The old incorporated city still retained an outer defensive wall, tollgates, and a closely packed, irregular medieval street pattern. To the west lay Westminster, the seat of the monarchy and the national government. By 1661, greater London had expanded beyond these centers and was still continuing to grow. Throughout this densely built urban environment, most structures were made of timber. In the ensuing conflagration, 89 churches, 13,200 houses, and 400 streets—80 percent of the area within the walls of the old commercial core—were destroyed.

Like other notable disasters in urban history, the Great Fire of 1666 provided an unusual chance to reformulate a large city at its center—where the vested interests of property ownership would otherwise have made substantial change difficult to achieve. In his proposal to reshape greater London, including the incorporated city, Wren was influenced by developments seen in Paris, where the French kings were employing urban design ideas developed during the Italian Renaissance and used by the popes in the creation of Christian Rome. As both Paris and Rome expanded in size, winding medieval mazes were replaced by straight avenues, culminating in large public spaces and punctuated by grand buildings in classical architectural styles at the ends of urban perspectives. In Rome in particular, street patterns had been rationalized and the architectural design of individual buildings was consciously interrelated to create larger urban compositions—an approach to city building eventually referred to as "the grand manner." The organic growth of medieval towns had been superseded by a new concept: that the form of large and growing capitals could be planned. Wren proposed a similar restructuring for all of the expanding area of London. It was not to be.

For centuries, the lucidity of Wren's drawing has captivated urbanists, haunted Londoners, and been cited in the history of city planning as a classic example of a rare opportunity lost—an opportunity to improve circulation, increase the general coherence of the town's layout, and create the dramatic central public spaces of a great city. Historians list several pragmatic reasons in the aftermath of the fire for the old incorporated city, and Greater London along with it, not being refashioned. Among these are a shortage of labor, lost records of property ownership, anxiety in regard to the potential delays and equity of real estate redistribution, and concern that an extended process of reconstruction would cause the mercantile center to lose its commercial advantage in competition with other British and Dutch cities.

And there was another reason. The rebuilding of Rome and Paris, in the grand manner of the Baroque, was being achieved through the centralized administrative authority of the popes and the French monarchs. Therefore, the general concept of comprehensive city planning was associated with the exercise of absolute and autocratic power as well as with Catholicism or "popery." Yet the Great Fire of 1666 had occurred in a period of political turmoil in Britain, as a broad proportion of English subjects contested whether the king's right to rule was either unbounded or divine.

The English Civil War (1642–1648), also known as the Puritan Revolution, culminated in the execution of Charles I, the creation of a commonwealth, and the dictatorship of Oliver Cromwell. The Restoration (1660) reestablished the rule of Parliament and, in turn, that of the monarchy (Charles II assumed the throne vacated at his father's death). The Glorious Revolution (1688) permanently confirmed the sovereign powers of Parliament. In this struggle to widen the participation of the British in their governance, the economic and political support of the merchant class of London was crucial. As noted by English political philosopher Thomas Hobbes, "But for the City the Parliament never could have made the war, nor the Rump [the incomplete parliament convened during the Civil War] ever have murdered the King."

The Great Fire had raged for three days and was still out of control when Charles II commanded that large numbers of buildings be torn down and whole streets leveled through blasting by the Royal Navy in order to create fire lanes in the burning city. History records that the king saved the metropolis, and that had the officials of the incorporated city taken similar decisive action earlier, far less of the trading center might have been lost. Regardless, in a politically

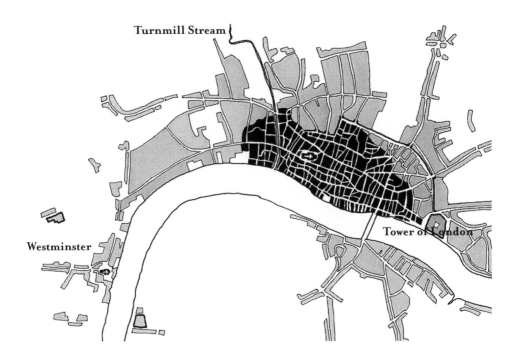

Turnmill Stream

Tower of London

Westminster

DAMAGE WROUGHT BY THE GREAT FIRE

volatile situation, the continued economic power of the City Corporation was threatened by the damage due to the fire itself and to the extinguishing of it. Thus with the question of Parliament's sovereignty still to be finally resolved, and with the merchants and businessmen of the incorporated city wary of infringements on their autonomy, London would not be remade in the architectural symbols recently employed by all-powerful Catholic autocrats.

It is interesting to compare this situation with the creation of the Ringstrasse in Vienna, whose plan embodies many elements of the grand manner, although it was constructed two hundred years later. In Vienna, both the medieval commercial core and the Hapsburg palaces had shared the defensive security provided by the old walls of the city, and the physical visage of Vienna was a fusion of all these elements. In London, three separate areas of fortification existed: the walls of the Incorporated City, the walls of the king's palaces at Westminster, and the walls of the Tower of London—directly adjoining the old commercial core and, to its inhabitants, the symbol of a sometimes hostile authority.

The remaking of Vienna—a collaborative venture involving commercial, parliamentary, municipal, and imperial interests—occurred as the Austro-

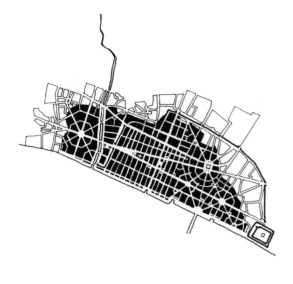

The plan not implemented
· The area of built-up London in 1661 is shown in gray tone. The area destroyed by fire is shown in black (in both drawings). Old St. Paul's is marked with a small white cross. · The plan by Christopher Wren extends beyond the western toll wall of the Incorporated City (outlined in heavy black line), and across Turnmill Stream, where an octagonal traffic round is intended. A straight embankment is proposed for the Thames River. The new St. Paul's is marked with a small white cross. (*Both drawings at the same scale.*)

WREN'S PLAN

Hungarian government evolved into a constitutional monarchy and the capital city was ceded the right to self-government. It was a self-generated initiative, at a politically opportune moment. The timing of the Wren plan for remaking London occurred by accident, while contention existed among the City, the Parliament, and the King.

There was also a crucial difference in how the two plans affected their respective urban cores. The design for Vienna's Ringstrasse circumscribed the historic commercial center, and the medieval street pattern and separate identity of the old city were kept intact. In London, the proposal of Christopher Wren would have reformulated the burned and leveled old commercial center, which would have lost much of its historic distinctiveness and, to some degree, been subsumed into a larger urban construction. The Ringstrasse was built on land available for redistribution, while every square foot of the old Incorporated City of London was already claimed.

To some extent like Amsterdam—which also retained its medieval core as a symbol of historical continuity, and whose seventeenth-century enlargement in three great ring canals forgoes the application of the grand manner—the rejection of Wren's plan by the incorporated city was a deliberate act of conservation,

Ideology in design

at a historical moment when preserving symbols of political autonomy was significant. Yet it can also be said that while the separate historic identity of the old commercial city was preserved, the City Corporation's commercial self-interest had compromised the possibility of making greater London into an integrated whole. At the time, both London and Amsterdam had outgrown their old line of fortifications and a question emerged as to how they should be extended. But unlike Amsterdam—which, while preserving the character of its old center, also initiated a concept for rationalizing future expansion—the City Corporation made no similar contribution to the growth of greater London. (In Wren's proposal the area of the incorporated city would have been rationally linked by broad vectors with the greater growing conurbation.) Moreover, in the decades and centuries to come, the self-interested parochialism of the City Corporation would frequently impede the efforts of others to govern Greater London as a single urban entity.

Nonetheless, in the period surrounding the Great Fire, several positive countervailing urban design efforts came into being. One grew out of the fire itself. Charles II's Act for the Rebuilding of the City of London established controls that dramatically upgraded the standards for building and regularized street widths. Individual structures were required to comply with universal rules for heights, the alignment of cornice lines, fire safety, interior materials, structural soundness, exterior materials and their coloration, and the continuity of building fronts. These simple guidelines had the immediate effect of regularizing the heroic and rapid reconstruction of the old incorporated city itself—turning a ramshackle maze into a handsome cobblestoned assemblage of well-built masonry architecture. Between about 1669 and 1672, over 12,000 houses and numerous public buildings were raised. By requiring houses to be built in three standard elevation types, the building code also promulgated a far-reaching urban artistic concept, that the street walls of London would be composed of architectural elements of simple repetitive harmony. In the long term, for hundreds of years thereafter, the building code ensured that streetscapes throughout London were consolidated as visual compositions. Across London's history, this was perhaps the single greatest contribution to the architectural integration of the metropolis.

Meanwhile, the work of two of the city's greatest architects, Inigo Jones and Christopher Wren, set an enduring artistic standard for subsequent generations, introducing to Britain the Italian Renaissance style and its concepts of urban organization. For several centuries, the dominant pinnacles of the skyline of London were largely those created by Wren. He designed fifty-one classically inspired and beautifully proportioned churches in the decades after the fire, culminating in one of London's finest architectural achievements—the towering Cathedral of St. Paul, which was the latest widely admired building in a clear line of architectural excellence linking the domed structures of Brunelleschi to Bramante to Michelangelo to Palladio to Wren. The English master designer also provided London with its finest ensemble of classical architecture, planned in the grand manner, at the Royal Naval Hospital and College at Greenwich—a symbol of intellectual and artistic refinement to house the symbol of Britain's growing colonial power through its mastery of naval science and technology. Few architects in history have so widely embellished a single city in so many important ways.

Inigo Jones provided another kind of model for London's future. In addition to his several remarkable buildings, and the introduction to England of a highly influential classical architectural style patterned after the works of Andrea Palladio, in 1631, prior to the Great Fire, he collaborated with the fourth Earl of Bedford to create the innovative residential development of Covent Garden, located in an area that remained undamaged between the old commercial core and Westminster. Here was made manifest the Italian Renaissance concept of the city organized as a stage set for living, wherein the buildings that framed the open square were designed as integrated works of architecture, working together to create a dramatic sense of place. While Wren's more comprehensive plan for the city would not be adopted, Jones's concept of creating a zone of unified beautiful architecture around an open public space would long abide. In applying this idea broadly in the years to come, London erected some of the finest residential neighborhoods in urban history.

THE GREAT ESTATES OF THE GREAT LANDLORDS

As Amsterdam School social housing and the apartment blocks of Red Vienna exemplify the high architectural achievement possible in the construction of subsidized municipal housing, the great estates of London are an example of enlightened residential real estate development whose methodology offers enduring lessons in the art of city building.

Several features contributed to the high environmental quality accomplished in the building of the great estates, but most important was the degree of architectural and urban design control exercised by the great landlords—a group of about thirty-five aristocrats—as they capitalized on the value of their properties. Over much of the two centuries after the Great Fire, as the Industrial Revolution gradually unfolded and Britain extended its commercial empire, London was subject to an increasing rate of population growth and physical expansion. During this period, the bulk of the terrain accommodating the expansion of the conurbation was owned and developed by these great landlords who, instead of selling properties outright for development, leased the right to build upon their lands.

Although these developments owed part of their architectural cohesion to the building code created for the City Corporation by the king, extended to Westminster in 1700 and adopted for London as a whole in 1774, the great landlords further required that aesthetically coherent blocks of houses be arranged in pleasing order around central urban terraces, crescents, rectangles, circles, and squares. In practice, the holders of the great estates—often restricted by deeds of trust that forbade their unreserved sale—would create a master plan for the development of an area, divide their properties into lots, and lease them to builders or individuals. The houses themselves were constructed by speculative contractors and leaseholders, at their own expense, for future ground rents. At the end of the lease, varying up to ninety-nine years, ownership of the houses returned to the landlord, who might then extend the lease or redevelop the lot.

Thus the great landlords had a long-term interest in the financial performance of their properties. Architectural and urban planning excellence added palpable value to their holdings. By requiring sound building construction, disciplined exercise of architectural aesthetics, stylistic continuity (particularly in such understated English classical styles as the Georgian), and an orderly arrangement of building fronts around streets and gardens, they achieved a special sense of place in each estate. By building at a low scale, with generous allocations of open space, they endowed the estates with sunlight and greenery. By requiring compliance with a master plan, they harmonized the separate efforts of numerous builders, often working from architectural pattern books and, in the growing stages of industrialization, using mass-produced windows, doors, moldings, and other building parts. And by diligently maintaining their properties thereafter, aristocratic landowners further secured the highest possible long-term returns.

As this phenomenon progressed, the great landlords found themselves competing to create neighborhoods of lasting beauty in such places as Leicester, Grosvenor, Berkeley, Manchester, and Bedford Squares, to name but a few. Old London was surrounded with splendid residential enclaves of attached town houses.

Although largely designed in a stark and understated neoclassical style, with long rows of simple repetitive facades using common architectural elements, the great estates were diverse and eclectic in their ground plans and architectural drama. Each complex was laid out in a simple geometric plan in which blocks of buildings surrounded open green spaces configured in different primary geometric shapes. The architecture orchestrated the rhythm of its elements to create long harmonious lines highlighted at the corners and in the centers with unusual dramatic massing, and the introduction of special eye-catching features such as balconies, bay windows, and classical pediments over

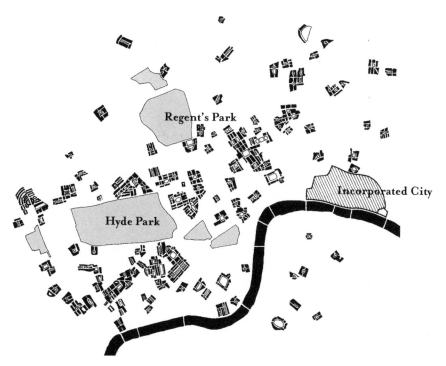

Some of the circles, squares, and crescents of the great estates · Blocks of buildings (shown in black) frame open public spaces (small outlined shapes) dispersed across the cityscape. (Derived from a drawing in Edward Jones and Christopher Woodward, *A Guide to the Architecture of London.* London: Orion, 1997.)

windows or atop whole buildings. While the grand manner was used in Paris to produce awe-inspiring vistas of national power, Renaissance urban design principles in the organization of the great estates conveyed domestic tranquillity and the sense of a well-ordered pluralistic society. The great avenues of Paris terminated in impressive public edifices. The geometric street plans of London's great estates led to central gardens of trees, pruned lawns, and beautiful plantings. In Paris, grand urban design themes celebrated human intellectual conceptions cast in enduring materials. In London, grand urban design brought nature into the city and softened the harshness of environments of cobblestone, slate, cast iron, and masonry.

Yet because one of the underlying commercial motives was to provide secluded class-segregated communities, the great estates were purposely located off the main streets of the city, with access through gateways. (In 1879 it was estimated that there were over 150 such barriers in the city.) Beneath their outward beauty, they made manifest social divisions of privilege and wealth. Nor were the street plans of the estates designed to connect in a logical way to neighboring areas; they were focused inward, making sense in their internal organization but not in their outward connections. In this regard, the great estates constituted an arc of autonomous urban islands surrounding the angular medieval street pattern of London's core. Strangely, the city as a whole much resembled in its organization the conglomeration of the islands of Venice. As each Venetian island was a block of buildings surrounding a central campo (piazza), so too were the great estates walled-in enclaves. As the ground circulation system of Venice was a labyrinth of eccentrically joined passageways and bridges, so too did the great estates result in a winding disconnected greater urban street pattern. And as the canals of Venice flowed between its separate islands, so did the main thoroughfares of London weave around the great estates.

These semipublic estates filled the city with enclaves of unified architecture, but they did not unify London itself. They were a continuum of environmental character but resulted in an impractical larger plan for the organization of what was soon to become a vast industrial metropolis. They were but one more way that the greater agglomeration was increasingly an aggregation of autonomous centers—handsomely built, well designed, architecturally cohesive, green, and of great beauty in themselves, but randomly amassed.

THE MASSIVE BEAUTIFUL MAZE

Although the social and economic changes due to industrialization would eventually affect nations on every inhabited continent, the term "Industrial Revolution" initially applied to innovations primarily occurring in Great Britain. More than in any other major city, the impact of this phenomenon of urban life would first be felt in London. Between 1800 and 1900 its population growth was prodigious, increasing from 1 million people to 6.5 million, at which point it was the largest city the world had ever seen.

In many other European capitals, a rationalized superstructure of major transportation routes would be adopted for the industrial city's expansion. In London, an assortment of individual communities would be added in installments—and the highway pattern of the greater city was almost as eccentric as the medieval labyrinth of the old commercial center had been. (Acquiring a taxicab license eventually required perhaps the most arduous test of navigational skill of any city in the world.) Moreover, with the City Corporation's refusal to restructure its street pattern after the Great Fire, and once the great estates were completed, large areas of the center of London were permanently segregated and untouchable. With each passing year, as the metropolis grew, as population increased, and as the number of vehicles multiplied, movement through the local road network became increasingly difficult.

In 1812 the Prince Regent and the architect John Nash had been successful in creating a long axial ensemble of streets, buildings, and squares that curved across London from St. James's Park and Carlton House Terrace to Piccadilly Circus, Regent Street, Portland Place, and Regent's Park—in an effort to give the city a more comprehensible urban structure. Long white stone facades of coordinated classical architecture framed the streets and open spaces along the route. Throughout this angling vector, London assumed an urban character similar to that of the orchestrated grandeur of Haussmann's Paris. Had other similar projects occurred, the metropolis would have been dramatically altered. But such large-scale change was difficult to achieve without a central municipal authority.

In 1837, 1839, 1856, and 1858, the City Corporation successfully blocked efforts to merge it with Westminster. In 1829 Greater London was consolidated into a single police district, but the City Corporation established its own constabulary unit. In 1847 a Metropolitan Commission of Sewers was created, yet the City Corporation resisted inclusion. In 1855 the incorporated City excluded itself from the managerial authority of the newly instituted Metropolitan Board of Works.

Meanwhile, as the capital of the world's greatest commercial empire, London continued to amass enormous wealth and to adorn itself handsomely. Numerous spacious parks were created by making former royal preserves available to the public. Imposing monuments, great museums, libraries, churches, and other institutional and commercial structures of sophisticated design were wedged into the greater agglomeration. At the time, few cities in the world could match its quantity and quality of public buildings or the general richness of detail, construction, and expressiveness of design of its architecture. Particularly in the central area of the great estates, Westminster, and the City Corporation, the streetscapes of London were filled with substantial and often glorious buildings. The chimneys, domes, spires, steeples, crests, and turrets of the new generation of structures—while somewhat diluting the supremacy of churches in the older skyline—also enriched it with a cornucopia of inventive sculptural expression.

Several magnificent train terminals were built. In the era of the great estates, London had been a walking city. The advent of regional rail lines in the 1830s opened the surrounding countryside to development and gave birth to the modern middle-class suburb. A wave of speculative building projects, consisting of rows of attached cottages with yards, sprouted up at the fringes of the expanding city. The metropolis was expanding its boundaries. But while the English could now travel more easily across rural distances, few of London's several train terminals were located directly in the city's center, and changing from one train line to another often required traversing the inner urban core, a slow and seemingly interminable journey. If London could not be tied together aboveground, it would have to be interconnected and rationalized by tunneling beneath the confusion.

In 1863, London's subway, or Tube, conveyed 9 million passengers swiftly across the cityscape and offered an alternative transportation system, alleviating the crowding of vehicles in the streets. In 1883, Parliament enacted a Cheap Trains Act, making the interconnected regional train and subway system an affordable mass-transit network. It was a practical planning conception of brilliance, creating an underlying structural skeleton to a city that otherwise defied attempts to give it a greater physical order. In other places, like New York, the subway network would often reflect the general circulation system above ground; the Lexington Avenue Line would follow the course of a thoroughfare bearing the same name, as would the Broadway–Seventh Avenue Line. In London, to a far greater degree, the path of the Underground achieved direct links not possible in the city above. The plan of the Underground was the plan of important urban locations, not the plan of important existing streets. Nonetheless, it offered to London's inhabitants an abstracted yet comprehensible expression of the city's configuration that could be held in the mind as a single idea.

Also in 1883, *The Bitter Cry of Outcast London,* by Andrew Mearn, was published. Like *How the Other Half Lives* by Jacob Riis, published in 1890 in New York, *The Bitter Cry* focused the city's attention on the misery of its outcast poor, constituting about one-third of London's population at that time. As a result, another surge of suburban building was initiated, beyond the first wave of speculative housing. These early examples of municipal social housing, comely attached cottages designed in the Arts and Crafts style (whose construction extended into the early twentieth century), were built by philanthropic societies and the city's newly formed central administration.

In order to plan and coordinate these and other large-scale municipal projects, in 1898 the County of London, consisting of twenty-eight separate municipal districts, and its governmental apparatus, the London County Council, were created. Finally the political, administrative, and physical boundaries of the city were made to correspond with one another—with, of course, one important exception: The twenty-ninth element of the greater metropolis, the City Corporation, remained an autonomously governed island situated at the center of the agglomeration—a permanent, wealthy, and powerful obstacle to true unification. As London continued to grow outward, it would subsume those villages at its expanding periphery. Once those former rural towns and their distinctive street patterns were assimilated into the giant beautiful maze, they eventually achieved representation in the central municipal administration.

The jumbled urban construction contained a wealth of riches. While London had only partly adopted the unifying principles of Renaissance urban design, and the city as a whole was not a coordinated set piece, its diversity was a celebration of architectural invention. Particularly at its center, numerous small parts of the metropolis were models of thoughtful urban organization. Though plotting a course through the greater maze could be confusing, it was also a journey of visual delight and surprise. Made widely recognizable through photography and motion pictures, it was a place known around the world, a city of awe-inspiring public structures, of blocks of eclectic, well-constructed, and handsome commercial buildings, instantly recognizable central urban sights, beautiful parks, and countless graceful tree-lined enclaves of attached houses. Equally familiar were its small domestic icons: its numerous cheery pubs and bright red telephone booths, post boxes, and double-decker buses. Most of all, it was a symbol of a particularly British version of cosmopolitan civility, with a long horizontal silhouette graced by myriad fanciful peaks, punctuated by more than a hundred church steeples, and crowned by the towers of Parliament and the dome of St. Paul's. It was the heart of England.

In the months before World War II some 600,000 city schoolchildren were relocated to the countryside in anticipation of German bombing.

HISTORIC PARIS: THE CITY THAT BECAME A PALACE

As Oliver Wendell Holmes observed: "Good Americans, when they die, go to Paris." This is especially true for Americans who love the study of cities. Paris confirms our potential to make the built metropolis a conscious work of art. Like Beijing, it is a massive historic environmental sculpture. But though much of the beauty of Beijing is often hidden from view behind great walls and gateways, the loveliness of Paris was designed to be experienced from its streets. One discovers the notes of its architectural symphony simply by walking—in virtually any direction—and letting its handsomeness unfold.

While both Paris and Beijing required strong centralized administration in order to orchestrate their copious and competing urban parts, they were made in strikingly different ways. When first envisioned by the scholar officials of Kublai Khan in A.D. 1260, Beijing was the product of a two-thousand-year tradition dictating the formation of medieval Chinese capitals: it was designed to be a giant artistic whole, housing about a half million inhabitants in a fixed geometric street pattern, with numerous major monuments, thousands of supporting structures, and a great rectangular perimeter of mammoth fortifications. In contrast, Paris developed over several centuries as it grew from a medieval town to the cultural and political center of Europe in the Age of Enlightenment and, finally, in the era of industrialization, a city of tree-lined boulevards, unified streetscapes, and magnificent vistas illuminated by thousands of elegant streetlamps. Much of the splendor of Beijing was preconceived, while the splendor of Paris evolved and accumulated.

THE NATIONALIZATION OF CLASSICAL ARCHITECTURE IN FRANCE

At the beginning of the seventeenth century Paris was poised for change and expansion. Like other medieval townscapes, it was an angular organic compilation of vernacular structures accrued over several centuries. Its street pattern consisted of the space left over after buildings had been crammed within the area protected by its fortifications. While not as commercially vital and innovative as Italy, the Netherlands, and Great Britain, France was the largest country in Europe, with a population of about 20 million people and an internal stability that exploited the economic and political advantages of its size. To enhance their prestige in the contemporary international sphere, the French rulers made their capital city a physical manifestation of the most progressive architectural thinking of the time—ideas from the Renaissance in Italy. Achieving this goal required a revolution in French architecture.

During the Middle Ages, many aspects of the formulation and construction of Gothic architecture had been kept secret by building guilds. Architects for the most part were former master builders well versed in this veiled process. Even today, historians continue to search for information on how the elevations of great cathedrals were derived from their floor plans. In contrast, the rebirth of the classical architectural tradition during the Italian Renaissance made the building design process less secretive, allowing the participation of a wider spectrum of society. In order to learn the new architecture, many architects and potential patrons flocked to the ruins and new constructions in Rome. But it was easier to disseminate ideas by printing books. The seminal source to circulate across Europe was the only text to survive from antiquity. *Ten Books on Architecture*, written around 25 B.C. by the Roman architect Vitruvius, included measured drawings of ancient buildings, an explanation of the classical system of proportioning, and advice on the practice of architecture and the training of architects. The first major treatise of the Renaissance, written in 1452 by Leon Battista Alberti, and also entitled *Ten Books on Architecture*, was directed toward the enlightenment of patrons so they might better sponsor the new style. *Four Books of Architecture*, written by Andrea Palladio in 1570, included drawings of contemporary building designs by its author and was especially instrumental in the spread of Renaissance architecture in England.

Thus in 1540–1541, Francis I of France invited the Bolognese architect Sebastiano Serlio to become the official royal adviser on architecture and painting. During his life, Serlio wrote eight illustrated handbooks on classical theory and application directed principally to the practicing architect. Several of these were published in France, with French translations. His *Sixth Book of Architecture,* though unreleased as a complete manuscript, included etchings of designs that adapted the new style to French building traditions.

In the following decades, the French kings built several large public complexes, monuments, and grand palaces in the new style. The ceremonial center of Paris came to be arranged according to Renaissance urban design concepts and set the architectural trends for fashionable society. Various monarchs became involved in commercial real estate development. And a central state bureaucracy evolved to oversee such constructions, establish building regulations in the city, and institute schools and academies to direct the training and practice of professionals in the building process.

In an absolutist state, efforts to remodel Paris began with the most important architectural symbol in the city, the Louvre, the fortified medieval tower castle of the king at the heart of Paris along the banks of the Seine. In 1546, the royal residence was transformed into an urban palace in the Italian style. This was the first step in assembling a vast new ensemble, a process that continued across several centuries. The most significant change occurred during the reign of Louis XIV (1643–1715) when a mammoth classical facade was added to the front of the complex. The design was academic and restrained, and through its long horizontal composition of repetitive architectural elements, it exploited the perspective effects inherent in the Renaissance style. The new front elevation also organized the whole complex around a central axis, which resumed on the other side of the building in an extended garden called the Tuileries, designed by the great French landscape architect Le Nôtre.

Like the vast garden complex Le Nôtre designed for Louis XIV's country palace at Versailles, the Tuileries was laid out in a giant geometric pattern. Although the elements of these two compositions were trees, plants, paths, plazas, lawns, sculpture, balustrades, pools, and fountains, the huge dimensions of the gardens showed what might be achieved when similar organizing principles were applied to a cityscape of buildings, streets, and open public spaces. So compelling in its time was this urban planning conception that drawings of Le Nôtre's designs soon circulated throughout Western civilization, eventually becoming the basis for the layout of such cities as Washington, D.C.

The meaning to Paris was more immediate, for Le Nôtre continued the central axis line of the palace and gardens outward in a long tree-lined roadway, the Champs-Élysées, linking the city to the open countryside. Eventually, the avenue would be lined with handsome buildings as it was subsumed into the widening urban agglomeration. As in the extended central organizing spine of

Beijing that ran through the Forbidden City, Paris now had a dominant axis around which the new cityscape might be arranged.

From 1663 to 1691, the Crown created the Collège des Quatre-Nations (later renamed the Institut de France), an imposing building of handsome classical design, which, although located on the opposite side of the Seine, was amassed so that its curving front facade embraced a cross-axis to the main spine of the Louvre and Tuileries. In 1671 a massive government hospital complex for wounded war veterans, Les Invalides, was also constructed on the Left Bank. With a central tree-lined boulevard directed to the north across the river, Les Invalides utilized both the perspective methods of Le Nôtre's gardens and dramatic architectural massing to create another powerful urban vista focusing on the city's principal ceremonial route. Situated in what were then the fringes of the city, the Collège des Quatre-Nations and Les Invalides were both crowned with Renaissance-inspired domes, portents of an unfolding architectural transformation. Like the great estates of London, both of these projects were isolated enclaves of Renaissance order. But unlike the great estates, each project also supported the larger organizational transformation of the city as a whole.

In 1748–1753, a huge traffic circle and plaza at the juncture of the Tuileries and the Champs-Élysées called the place de Louis XV, and later known as the place de la Concorde, was created as a central point where several streets converged. Decades later, under Napoleon Bonaparte the inherent architectural drama of this radiating center was heightened. The dominant axis of the city was emphasized by two triumphal arches: the Carrousel, between the Louvre and the Tuileries, and the Arc de Triomphe, which culminated the perspective up the Champs-Élysées, and was the largest triumphal arch in history. South of the place de la Concorde a wide bridge spanned the Seine, providing a graceful sight line to the imposing Roman portico that had been added to the Palais Bourbon. Napoleon accentuated the northern cross-axis out of the plaza by creating a visual terminus in the form of a massive Roman temple— the Church of La Madeleine—and he framed the street leading to the church (the rue Royale) with identical architectural facades on the northern side of the place de la Concorde.

Here was the masterstroke in a moment of grand urban design, for Napoleon extended the line of these classical structures all the way down the side of the Tuileries—along rue de Rivoli, the street running parallel to the main axis—in a long, graceful architectural ensemble. The design featured continuous cornices, lines of balconies, and a ground-level arcade of archways. The peaks of this wall of buildings, rising above the treetops of the Tuileries, formed a refined backdrop to the magnificent formal gardens.

As this new center of cream-colored stone evolved, Paris continued to grow. In order to influence the character of the remainder of the metropolis, several French monarchs became involved in what we would describe today as commercial real estate projects, with the idea that they might establish models for residential growth. Historians commonly regard such efforts as pioneering examples of the integrated residential piazza. The first of these, the place Dauphine, constructed by Henry IV in 1606 on the Île de la Cité, consisted of walls of continuous classical facades framing a triangular common ground, introducing stylish urban homes to a revitalized commercial district. Also initiated by Henry IV, the elegant place Royale, known today as the place des Vosges, constructed in 1612, was a large rectangular public park surrounded by attached uniform mansions, stimulating higher-quality development in a new area of the city. In both projects, private owners were compelled to follow official elevations designed by the royal architects.

By 1687, the urban design concept had become more refined. In the Place des Victoires interlinked classical stone facades were arranged in a wide circle in a project financed by independent businessmen with the Crown's support. Again, the contrast with the secluded great estates of London is telling. The great estates were situated off the main streets of the English capital, and major thoroughfares were required to wind around them. The place des Victoires was located at the crossing point of several Parisian streets and designed to elevate the quality of the larger public realm.

Similarly bisected by a prominent transportation vector was the place Vendôme, completed in the early 1700s. The uniform street walls of this eight-sided piazza—with its ground-floor arcade of rusticated stone, steep blue-slate roofs punctuated by rows of dormers, and a continuous cornice—were constructed simply as facades; many of the buildings behind this architectural screen were filled in later by the purchasers of various segments. Financed by a consortium of speculative developers with the Crown, under Louis XIV, as one of the partners, the place Vendôme was an unusually explicit effort focused on the beautification of the city's architectural mass and at the same time of its streetscape.

As well known as these many projects soon became in the capitals of Europe, they were but initial evidence of a much larger transformation. Two cityscapes had come to coexist in Paris. One was a medieval townscape of wooden construction and irregular streets, largely composed of burgher houses with outwardly canted exterior walls and steeply pitched gable roofs—the site of one of the most notable European universities of the Middle Ages, whose historic spiritual center was the Cathedral of Notre Dame on the Île de la Cité. The monuments and history associated with medieval Paris were a source of French identity and pride. The other cityscape was the emerging Renaissance town of elegant structures made of stone, with buildings arranged in street walls. These two were fundamentally at odds with each other.

To generate a transition to classicism, basic rules for construction were gradually altered through the enactment of ever more stringent building codes. And as the city expanded, legions of classically trained architects provided form for the thousands of new structures that would be built. The sustained effort necessary to accomplish these objectives was exerted by a central state architectural and town planning bureaucracy, organized during the reign of Charles V (1364–1380) and initially known as the Administration des Bâtiments Royaux (Royal Building Administration), whose very existence as a social institution became a tradition itself. Since the Middle Ages, various French kings had utilized the Royal Building Administration to better organize construction trades, establish higher standards of practice among artisans, and refine the architectural design of their palaces, estates, and castles. (One of the purposes of translating Serlio's books into French had been to help educate French building administrators.)

In order to contain fires, improve vehicular circulation, and change the aesthetic of the city, a ban was enacted in 1607 on the construction of new houses in wood. Buildings were no longer allowed to project out into the public way, and the street facades of all new structures were required to be in alignment. In 1667, after the Great Fire of London, the French authorities further prohibited exposed timber structural elements in the exteriors of existing old buildings. Thus a layer of external stucco was commonly applied to such structures, utilizing powder from indigenous stone and closely matching the color of modern classical buildings. This muted the aesthetic clash of old and new.

Simultaneously, French monarchs and their ministers strove to establish a new national cultural identity for the contemporary political state. In 1635, Louis XIII and Cardinal Richelieu instituted the Académie Française for the refinement of the French language. In 1648, Louis XIV and Mazarin founded the Académie Royale de Peinture et de Sculpture. Royal workshops were organized for the manufacture of furniture, tapestries, and other decorative appointments. And in 1671, Louis XIV's Minister of Finance, Jean-Baptiste Colbert, brought into existence the Académie Royale de l'Architecture, a tuition-free learning institution whose prominent graduates, upon winning the Rome Prize, were sent by the king to study at the Académie de France in Rome.

The Académie Royale de l'Architecture developed a systematic curriculum encompassing artistic draftsmanship, technical engineering, theoretical design, and classical scholarship. Completion of this course of study became a requirement for careers in the growing bureaucracy and a prerequisite for

Crown commissions. In 1771–1777 an instructor at the academy, Jacques-François Blondel, published his lectures on the application of classical design theory in the modern milieu. Blondel's book was one of the earliest of numerous influential publications, attesting to the excellence of French architectural practice and the breadth of society's interest in architectural matters.

Suspended during the Revolution, the Royal Academy was reinstituted under Napoleon Bonaparte as the École des Beaux-Arts. For more than two centuries, the Académie Royale–École des Beaux-Arts would be a model for, and in the judgment of many historians the birthplace of, modern architectural education in Europe. Few institutions have achieved such a high level of excellence and sustained it for so long.

In 1783, a new building code coordinated the height of structures in relation to the width of streets, ensuring the penetration of sunlight into the public way. Developers were required to submit building plans for official review, and a cadre of municipal inspectors ensured compliance. These more demanding building requirements enlarged the proportion of residential structures directly designed by architects, producing greater aesthetic refinement in buildings of all types. The general standard of construction in the city was elevated. Apartment houses began to appear, and throughout the 1830s their numbers increased as a new wave of urban growth ensued, due to the effects of industrialization.

Several great terminals were constructed for a national railway system centered on Paris. As in London, the efficiency of this faster means of regional transport suffered when travelers attempted to cross the city from one terminal to another in order to change lines. The streets had become exceedingly crowded. Like London, Berlin, and New York, the industrial expansion of Paris resulted in several giant leaps in population, from 550,000 in 1800, to 1.3 million in 1850, to 2 million in 1870, to 3.3 million by 1900. And also like London, Berlin, and New York, cramped overpopulated neighborhoods of poverty, dirt, crime, and illness grew up in a city unprepared for the size, density, and social needs of the modern metropolis.

The cityscape and urban culture of Paris were ripe for artistic completion. Dispersed across the agglomeration, its numerous sophisticated urban ensembles had yet to be truly unified. It had a host of well-trained architects, a corps of professional civil administrators, a widely shared communal pride in the beauty of French classical architecture, an established vocabulary of urban design that required individual buildings to serve the enhancement of the public realm—and a citywide dilemma that demanded immediate resolution. At this historical moment, in 1853, Georges-Eugène Haussmann, a brilliant career administrator in the French governmental bureaucracy, was appointed by Napoleon III as the Prefect of the Seine. As Sir Peter Hall in *Cities in*

Civilization would observe in regard to Haussmann's achievements: "No one in the entire history of urbanism, neither Pericles nor the Roman emperors nor the Renaissance popes, ever transformed a city so profoundly during such a short space of time."

INDUSTRIAL PARIS: THE CITY OF LIGHT

As Haussmann began his tenure, the human misery in industrial cities was of a scale unforeseen, shocking, and threatening to civic stability. When judged against the broader equity achieved half a century later in social housing programs in Amsterdam (from 1900 to 1920) and Red Vienna (from 1919 to 1934), the refashioning of Paris would ameliorate these conditions only in part. While failing to provide better living accommodations for the poor, industrial Paris was nonetheless a model of progressive urban design. Greater cleanliness, health, safety, efficiency of movement, and sheer environmental beauty were its accomplishments. As the first industrial metropolis to solve such problems holistically, its cityscape was much emulated but not quite matched—in the extent of its physical grace—anywhere else to this day.

Developments prior to Haussmann's appointment set the stage for his program of sweeping urban improvements. As the hub of rail transportation in France, Paris had become a major industrial and financial center, a city of enormous accumulated wealth. In 1852, by plebiscite, the Second Empire was created with Louis Napoleon Bonaparte as its emperor. Determined to refashion Paris, Napoleon III appointed Haussmann. The ensuing building campaign fostered a construction boom, employed one of every five Parisian workers, further enriched the wealthy through real estate investment, and provided a handsome city for the middle class. All the strata of society benefited to some degree.

Haussmann's plan was direct, rational, and audacious in its scope. In order to eliminate filth in the city, he paved 400 miles of streets and built more than 260 miles of sewers. So that Paris might have clean drinking water, he quadrupled the water supply and laid a delivery system of aqueducts, water mains, and pipes that increased almost sixfold the number of buildings served. He expanded the public parks from 47 acres to 4,000 acres and doubled the number of trees adorning the city's roadways. He built bridges, markets, theaters, schools, churches, synagogues, and public meeting halls. But most of all, he created the boulevards of Paris, lined them with houses, and called upon the architects of the École des Beaux-Arts to make them beautiful.

One of the most important precedents for the city's aesthetic completion had occurred during the reign of Louis XIV, when a ring of boulevards was created along the right of way of outmoded medieval fortifications. The zone between this circle of avenues and the following outward loop of external defensive walls was annexed by Haussmann in 1860, doubling the physical extent of metropolitan Paris. (The area of the city became approximately the size of historic Beijing.) The perimeter of outer fortifications defined Paris as an object. Grand tree-lined boulevards with wide sidewalks and broad roadbeds were the structural tool for modernizing the city.

According to an enormous and highly accurate plan, 71 miles of wide new roads were to be cut through the tangle of the city's spontaneous growth. The new street pattern of major thoroughfares linked important points across the city in an eccentric spiderweb of crisscrossing diagonals. More than 27,000 houses would require demolition, but more than 100,000 would be built or reconstructed in correspondence with these lines.

As in the making of Vienna's Ringstrasse, these acts of destruction removed from Paris significant historical material from an earlier, preclassical incarnation. The destruction of old neighborhoods, although often rationalized as a necessity for making or widening roadways (Haussmann was ruthless in this regard, in several instances destroying medieval churches in the name of transportation efficiency), was also part of a policy of slum clearance. Several of the oldest historic quarters of Paris were among the most crime-ridden and dilapidated, and were therefore erased. No provision was made for those displaced and the poor were forced to move out to the city's perimeter, replaced by the middle class in new, higher-priced, upgraded, market-driven housing. The most blatant example of slum clearance occurred on the Île de la Cité, where a medieval townscape surrounding two of the city's most significant Gothic monuments—the Cathedral of Notre Dame and the Sainte-Chapelle— was largely expunged.

Although there was much criticism of these policies, the laws meant to inhibit the destruction of historic assets were weak. The minister of the interior had begun listing the monuments of France in 1837, but the nation's first preservation law was not enacted until 1887, after Haussmann's tenure, and it required the consent of owners before private property could be protected. Meanwhile, in Haussmann's era, under the system of compulsory purchase and compensation utilized by the state, many of these buildings would probably have been lost whether or not the 1887 law had already been in existence. Nevertheless, destruction of the medieval fabric of the Île de la Cité would be one of the city's most significant historic losses, eventually inducing the creation of conservation statutes (and foreshadowing a similar ideological historical bias in Mussolini's eradication of medieval structures in Fascist Rome).

In evaluating Haussmann's policies from a contemporary perspective, another aspect of preservation is relevant. The making of the roadways of Paris was much more than a mammoth act of civil engineering; it was also an achievement in urban artistry. Haussmann comprehended the historic classical legacy of the city—in which public squares, streets, and architecture had been woven into unified ensembles—and applied this model to the entire built environment. Whole sections of Paris were designed to bind together the geographically separated monuments of the city's past. The modern context was shaped to harmonize with the character of existing landmarks. As a result, that beautiful public realm envisioned over the centuries by the rulers of France finally became a reality.

Haussmann mandated that the architecture of the new boulevards be unified, so that each facade aligned with the street wall and combined with its neighbors to make continuous elevational compositions—as in Napoleon's rue de Rivoli. Like the Renaissance piazzas of the kings, every boulevard became an integrated public space in addition to offering a long urban perspective. When major historic buildings did not exist at the juncture of avenues, new monuments were created in association with traffic rounds, to provide a dramatic architectural culmination to each urban vista.

Enforcement of building codes caused roofs and cornices to be aligned, since new structures were invariably built to the maximum allowable height, and developers furthermore were encouraged by Haussmann's administrators to assemble contiguous lots. In this way individual buildings could be constructed as part of larger, integrated compositions. This *architecture d'accompagnement* had long been a regulatory goal. Now, with so much construction occurring at one time, a further degree of consistency of style, proportion, material, and massing was mandated by the authorities—from one block to another, down the length of streets, across squares, and into adjacent neighborhoods. Particular attention was paid to the design of those corner buildings that formed a transition from great boulevards to the more intimate byways of old Paris. When new areas were opened for development, the first buildings constructed were purposely made to serve as examples for those that followed.

Like imperial Beijing, materials and colors were repetitive, as if the whole city had been painted from a single palette of cream-colored limestone, slate-blue roofs, and gray paving blocks and curbstones. Paris was one of the foremost centers of iron manufacturing; hence, ornate black iron balconies, tree grilles, lampposts, benches, kiosks, bollards, fences, gratings, and even sidewalk urinals were all conceived as part of a complementary layer of adornment. Every element in the urban environment was sculpted by designers and architects trained to make subtle aesthetic variations within the classical mode. Enormous aesthetic diversity was exercised within the exacting restraints imposed by French administrators.

In 1861 the competition for a national opera house, terminating a vista of one of the new boulevards, was won by Charles Garnier. His drawings ushered in an era of richly expressive design, the Second Empire style, of molded classical architecture combined with sculpture, painting, and the decorative arts. This synthesis of visual aesthetic disciplines had been cultivated in the École des Beaux-Arts for decades, and now the great school reached a pinnacle of impact. Architects came from around the world to study in its programs, as its graduates enriched the physical form of Paris with countless beautiful designs.

Completion of the magnificent Paris Opera House in 1870 also marked the end of Haussmann's tenure. France was defeated in the Franco-Prussian War, Napoleon III was ousted, parliamentary power was reinstated, and the Paris Commune—a civil revolt of workers and Communards—seized control of the city's governance in 1871. Several major Parisian monuments—symbols of the failure of the establishment to rectify social inequities—were assaulted by the revolutionaries: the Tuileries Palace (lost and not replaced), the Hôtel de Ville (rebuilt), the Palais Royal (restored), and the column of Napoleon Bonaparte in the place Vendôme (re-created). In an act of brutal suppression, government troops killed or executed 17,000 Communards.

Yet even in the face of such bloodshed, the redevelopment plan soon resumed. Many of the improvements on Haussmann's map were half completed, in a deconstructed and conflict-scarred city. And despite continuing unrest among workers and the poor, officials discovered wide public sentiment, especially among the middle and upper classes, in favor of completing the process of urban modernization.

With the construction of some of the earliest, largest, and most elaborate department stores, Paris became a mecca for shopping. Renowned hotels provided luxury and comfort for visitors to international expositions in 1855, 1867, 1878, 1889, and 1900. Street cafés abounded. A new generation of exuberantly designed apartment buildings was constructed with slate-covered and steeply pitched roofs with dormer windows, sometimes referred to as mansard roofs. Although the degree of administrative design control was lessened, regulation of building heights in proportion to street widths, and general concurrence among architects, developers, builders, and clients on the appropriateness of French classical design, continued to ensure environmental coherence in street walls, if now with greater aesthetic variation.

Foreign visitors to the city's expositions marveled at what had been accomplished. French citizens' pride in their capital became a palpable phenomenon. A decades-long political impasse in regard to the construction of a subway system, the Metro, was quickly resolved, in order to provide visitors to the 1900 exposition a further example of the trendsetting prominence of the city.

Between the end of the Second Empire and the First World War—a period known as the Belle Epoque—a renaissance in painting unfolded. French academies and the great public art museum of the Louvre had for some time made

The beautiful sculpted cityscape · The streetplan of Paris in 1937 incorporates several immense idealized Renaissance vistas such as from the Louvre (A) to the the the Arc de Triomphe (B) and back across the Seine to Les Invalides (C). A spiderweb of broad straight avenues, lined by an elegant *architecture d' accompagnement* has been carved out of the city's mass by Haussman. Many of these vectors are designed to link the city's train terminals (shown as black masses with white dots). Penetrating the city along the periphery formed by its last line of fortifications are several massive and haphazardly shaped rail yards (rendered with parallel black lines), a harbinger of the emerging conflict with modernization.

Paris a preeminent center in the training of visual artists. But the social and technological changes of industrialization caused a sweeping reappraisal of aesthetics in all spheres of art, and the modernization of painting largely took place in the studios, cafés, salons, and galleries of Paris. The array of creative personalities contributing to this transformation was astounding: Manet, Monet, Degas, Renoir, Pissarro, Seurat, Cézanne, Picasso, Braque, Juan Gris, and Matisse, among others.

The city had become the cultural center of the Western world and a won-drous place in which to walk, to sit, or to watch the parade of strollers. It was a singular urban stage set, amassed for the infiltration of sunlight, embellished with trees and flower beds, and offering perspectives of beauty in all directions. It was the most modern of cities, with wide distribution of electricity, gas, pneumatic postal services, and telephones. And while the elegant facades of its housing often hid poor living conditions, while poverty was pervasive in many less frequented byways, and while the fundamental problems of industrializa-tion would not be resolved for decades, a remarkable social evolution had occurred.

The boulevards of the City of Light were an urban environment conceived by kings, yet accessible to all. The public realm of Paris had become a palace for the people, its streetlamps and illuminated windows offering infinite glittering vistas, as in the Hall of Mirrors at Versailles. It was the fulfillment of urban design thinking from the Italian Renaissance and the epitome of the Baroque city of absolute monarchs, but it was also an environment made possible by the vernacular embrace of French Renaissance architectural aesthetics by the mass of the city's inhabitants.

SAVING THE LEGIBLE URBAN VISAGE

Can the environmental legibility—the architectural and cultural cohesion—of traditional urban agglomerations be maintained in societies that have adopted new values, symbols, building forms, construction technologies, and modern urban infrastructure? Can the visage and spirit of the old city be saved while simultaneously being revived both physically and economically as but one discrete part of a far more massive urban aggregation? Can the old and mod-ern parts of the metropolis be combined in a new environmental synthesis with a comprehensible relationship of parts? Or does the vastness and complexity of the modern city doom it to fracturing and incoherence?

As World War II came to an end, London and Paris each contained a remarkable accrual of architectural culture. Each had made numerous major contributions to Western civilization during several periods of florescence and thereby had implanted within their social traditions some special and intangible urban chemistry. Each was a capital city and primary urban center of major economic and symbolic importance. And as such, each would be subject to enormous pressure to modernize in order to compete in a changing global economy, while at the same time retaining traditional aspects of form important to national identity. At the core of both cities, the past and the future were thrown into perpetual conflict for decades.

MODERN LONDON: FRACTURING THE SPIRIT OF THE SKYLINE

Since the end of World War I and especially after the hardships of World War II, many parts of historic London had fallen into disrepair. Housing conditions for the working class often were dismal. Shrinkage of the nation's vast commercial empire due to geopolitical change, loss of manpower from the fighting, and damage inflicted on urban areas in the Battle of Britain had led to an extended financial crisis. The city itself had been bombed for five years. Most of the physical damage had occurred around and to the east of St. Paul's, encompassing parts of the old City Corporation but focusing largely on warehouse and industrial areas, which included a number of poorer residential neighborhoods. Although nineteen of Wren's surviving churches were lost—twenty-three remain today of the original fifty-one—the mass of Greater London, including its great estates and major urban monuments, had survived intact. But retention of London's position as a major global financial center was crucial to the nation's recovery. Did the new postwar world order not also require a new kind of modern city?

Once again, with a third of the City Corporation reduced to rubble, came the call to redesign London as a whole. In 1943, Sir Patrick Abercrombie's Greater London Plan proposed that the growth of the metropolis be contained within an enveloping greenbelt (an initiative widely embraced and quickly established), that a network of concentric and arterial highways be created to alleviate vehicular traffic jams, and that blitz-leveled and obsolete, run-down properties be subject to comprehensive urban redevelopment. It was a sweeping conception enveloping all the parts of the now massive conurbation.

Just as Christopher Wren's plan after the Great Fire embodied a new approach to urbanism by restructuring the medieval city in the grand manner, so did Abercrombie's proposal open the door to rebuilding London using the ideas of Le Corbusier (widely admired by architects and planners in Great Britain), who in 1925, in his Voisin Plan, had advocated raising mammoth modern towers, set back in green parklands, in the midst of historic Paris. In order to achieve the conversion to large complexes of freestanding residential towers, requirements in the old building code of London would have to be set aside, particularly those that restricted height and ensured that building fronts were aligned along street walls. The city's building traditions would have to be abandoned.

The City Corporation protested the call. Ironically, after centuries of posing an obstacle to unification, the Corporation's approach to reconstruction endeavored to preserve the environmental unity that had been accomplished in a cityscape composed of diverse elements. They proposed the alternative of maintaining the existing urban anatomy: keeping the old relationship of buildings to streets and preserving the height limits that allowed church steeples to crown the city's silhouette: "We suggest the conservation wherever possible of features which are of traditional and archaeological significance and add to the architectural dignity of the City. Can it seriously be thought that we, proud to have had a part in promoting its welfare, are unconscious of the romance and history which the very street names breathe? Whatever the surface destruction, the City can in no circumstances be regarded as virgin land, a blank plan upon which the pencil of a planner can freely or fancifully travel."

Although the situation after the war was in many ways different from that of the city after the Great Fire, the City Corporation had pointed out one of the most important distinctions: London had become one of the greatest collections of beautiful buildings in the world. But this time its political leverage was not sufficient to forestall a plan that many hoped would finally bring the disparate pieces of London together.

Therefore, in 1947, with the support of the London County Council, Parliament passed the Town and Country Act, empowering the urban areas of Britain to initiate plans for comprehensive redevelopment. The bill had an inherent policy contradiction that would become apparent over time. On the surface, it cleared the way for London to adopt the Abercrombie plan. A city made up of houses was now to become a city with many large apartment towers. The legislation simultaneously increased governmental authority to protect the nation's architectural heritage, allowing the preservation of inhabited dwellings for the first time. Eventually, popular support for the protection of distinctive urban neighborhoods brought about a wide extension of these powers. In other words, the 1947 Town and Country Act allowed the old building code and the character of the historic cityscape to be substantially violated in some areas while planting the seeds in other places for retaining vast amounts of London's traditional fabric. Potential for both the fracturing and the protection of London's historic ambience had been inculcated.

More than a decade later, with the recovery of Britain's economy, enthusiastic application of the ideas of Le Corbusier led to the construction of about 350 residential towers in the County of London between 1964 and 1975. Much of the new housing was poorly constructed and poorly managed. It shattered the ambience of the historic city and today has begun to be torn down in several areas, as have some large postwar housing complexes in the United States. Yet even when these complexes were well built and sensitively designed, the larger result was in many ways disastrous. Since the general height of London's towers was modest compared to skyscrapers in places like New York, the new housing complexes often failed to increase the number of living accommodations per acre when compared to traditional lower-scale development. They were shaped as long horizontal blocks rather than vertical shafts, but they were still sufficiently tall and bulky to be alien in the historic context. So while disrupting the cityscape, they often failed to improve either the quality or the quantity of the city's residential stock.

Moreover, the division of London into semiautonomous governmental units made each borough responsible for the social and economic revitalization of its own area. Caught in the fervor of what was perceived to be progressive change, many local authorities felt the need for a new housing complex of their own. Large squat buildings ruptured the skyline of the metropolis. Once the character of London was breached in numerous locations, the issue of protecting the low-scale ambience of the historic center became somewhat moot. Similarly large hotels and office structures materialized across the city. Here is a critical point in the psychology of preserving historic cities: When the object is to preserve a unity of ambience, a few violations of that aesthetic harmony can undermine a hundred successful efforts to preserve it. Once such wholeness is destroyed, it is difficult to argue that the disrupted unity must be saved. One violation leads to another and another.

Damage to the city's historic character was not confined to its urban silhouette. From innumerable locations on the ground, taller modern structures—frequently of marginal architectural quality and disturbingly different design and materials—violated the street pattern and intruded upon the low-scale character of integrated old neighborhoods and squares. Meanwhile, as the intermittent stubby towers went up and the economy improved, so did broad appreciation of London's historic patrimony. A movement to reclaim its dimmed splendor spread across the metropolis. Large numbers of old houses—whole rows, terraces, circles, crescents, blocks, and neighborhoods—began to be restored.

While conservation in Britain dates back to the Ancient Monuments Act of 1882, the ability of preservation bodies to make binding designations evolved in gradual steps over a century. Initially only the most ancient archaeological sites and landmarks—medieval castles and Stonehenge, for instance—were saved. With time, great palaces, manors, and major architectural works became protected. The process was implemented by national authorities, and was slow to develop because Great Britain established the principle in law that owners should be justly compensated for their properties if they did not wish to continue to own them as monuments.

After the loss of numerous historic assets in World War II, and in anticipation of sweeping urban redevelopment, the 1947 Town and Country Act not only provided for the protection of inhabited houses but also shifted part of the responsibility for conservation to local authorities. This was the initial step in dealing with the fact that large sections of Britain's historic cities merited conservation. But the precedent of providing just compensation made the application of binding preservation statutes a potentially giant economic hurdle. The government simply couldn't afford to purchase all the buildings that deserved to be saved.

Since much of the loveliness of London was achieved through a host of modest structures gathered together in unified streetscapes, designation of only the most important individual landmarks failed to safeguard the distinctive quality of many urban districts. Two legal steps were required to make the

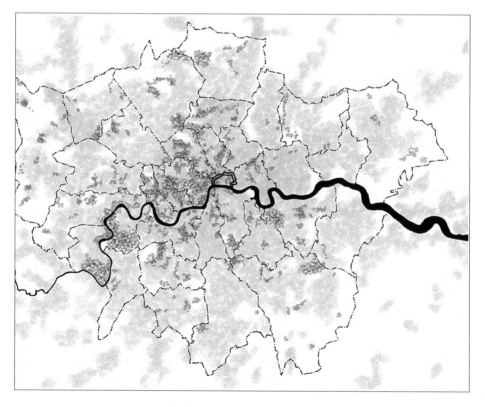

The conservation areas of the contemporary conglomeration of London · The boundaries of London's 32 boroughs are shown in dotted line. The 33rd administrative unit: the Incorporated City is located at the center. The built-up area of the metropolis is indicated in light gray tone. Conservation Areas are shown in dark gray tone.

preservation of large urban areas feasible. First, the 1967 Civic Amenities Act gave local governments the ability to identify whole Conservation Areas. Second, the Town and Country Amenities Act of 1974 established that the amount of compensation paid to disinclined owners be equal to the value of their property with its historic building on it. This allowed local authorities to find purchasers to restore and maintain endangered historic houses for continued residential use instead of having to pay compensation based on a property's highest value in the open real estate market, which might be for offices or other commercial purposes.

Application of these statutes rested entirely with each community. If a locality could galvanize the support of a historic neighborhood's residents, the restrictions of being listed, or designated, could be applied and, in those cases where individual owners wished to sell their property, the community would find someone to preserve the building as a landmark. Where communities were united in pursuit of conservation, the law had teeth. Where communities were not active in finding alternative purchasers, the law had substantially less effect.

By comparison, the New York City preservation law gave one centralized authority the ability to save historic districts and individual monuments of local and national interest—without requiring compensation. The advantage in New York is that the city can be more aggressive in saving many different types of buildings, including whole residential, commercial, and manufacturing districts. And since the City Planning Commission in New York often acts in concert with the Landmarks Commission by zoning historic areas to reduce the pressure of incompatible development—New York can be more thorough and proactive in its efforts to save the city's patrimony as a whole. In London, maintenance of listed structures is often superior because British conservation laws allow government authorities to compel owners to maintain their properties. In New York, however, more areas can be saved more easily.

While vast amounts of London were protected by the boroughs as Conservation Areas, one of the most significant initiatives in saving the character of historic London was the refusal of the people of the city to adopt the highway proposals of Abercrombie or anyone else. In a story of recurrent administrative illogic, here perhaps is the strangest chapter.

Improving the road network for vehicular movement seemed an indisputably rational goal to the professional planning establishment of the city. But when actual plans were articulated—when particular streets were named for widening and when living neighborhoods were selected to contain the routes for major highways—public resistance became insurmountable. Moreover, with the creation of the greenbelt, a new outer edge for London had been created: the territory of the agglomeration encompassed not only the twenty-eight boroughs of the London County Council and the incorporated City but forty-two noncounty boroughs as well. Many civic leaders believed that as long as London was divided into numerous autonomous authorities, a master plan for highways was not achievable. Thus in 1963, in the London Government Act, Parliament created the Greater London Council, consisting of thirty-two boroughs of less independent authority, the City Corporation, and a professional central planning bureaucracy. After hundreds of years the city's government was finally consolidated—for the purpose of dividing the metropolis with highways.

In 1969 a blueprint for a network of highways was proposed by the council's planning department. During a two-year public inquiry 22,000 objections were heard from the boroughs themselves, from community groups, and from countless individuals. Opponents of the highway scheme raised a basic issue. Traffic experts noted that during rush hours traffic in the inner city moved at the same slow speed as that of the horse-drawn vehicles a century before. It appeared that once a saturation point of traffic was reached, the historic street network could accommodate no higher speed.

Therefore, building highways to provide a greater number of vehicles quicker access to the center would only increase congestion. Truly providing greater efficiency of movement through the inner city required widening the streets of the existing labyrinth. This would have three effects on life in the historic urban environment: it would require the destruction of innumerable lovely streetscapes, raise the level of automotive pollution, and change the character of London from a walking city served by the Underground to a driving city served by motorways. The Greater London Highway Plan was defeated.

By 1986 the Greater London Council was abolished and a system of cooperative planning between the thirty-two boroughs and the incorporated city was instituted; it continues today. (Governmental unification of the city was attempted for the wrong reasons, in the wrong way—although the excellently trained team of professionals that constituted the central planning bureaucracy of the council, as well as the historic research office, have been retained in an advisory role to the boroughs.) To defeat the highway plan, more than a hundred grassroots community groups (referred to in London as amenity societies) had mobilized; they continue to fight to preserve London's buildings, its urban character, and its natural environment. Proactive involvement by the citizenry has resulted in the protection of most of the significant historic parts of London as well as such initiatives as the recent extensive cleansing of the Thames. Similarly, the construction of tall hotels in low-scale neighborhoods has virtually ceased, due to widespread acknowledgment of the inherent contradiction of such buildings: they destroy the ambience of the very places that hotel guests have traveled across the world to see.

London is the only major city in Britain not cleaved by superhighways. A simple reality had become evident: preserving the beautiful maze meant preserving some of its intrinsic liabilities as well. The people of the city would move about on foot and in the Tube. Like those who lived in the medieval historic cores of Rome, Prague, Amsterdam, Vienna, and many other old European town centers, Londoners affirmed that both beauty and its disadvantages were part of a special way of life.

Walking through London today is an extended journey through handsomely preserved places of amazing diversity and richness. Unfortunately, many incongruent modern structures and frequent jarring notes taint the splendid visual symphony in numerous locations. The aesthetic magic of historic London prevails for a moment, is shattered, resumes, is shattered again, and continues once more. From high points in the city, along the Thames or wherever one gains an overview, intrusive mediocre contemporary structures overpower the old skyline. They bully the spirit of historic London as they blot out the sun, and the loveliness of the old buildings often fails to assert itself in the horizon.

In regard to the future, the recent demolition of oversized, poorly made postwar municipal housing is an important initiative. Can mistakes made during the modernization of the metropolis be reversed? Can intrusive structures be removed once they become obsolete? Can fractured cityscapes be healed?

Perhaps too late, a solution for reconciling the historic city and its needs as a contemporary metropolis has evolved, as London starts to concentrate even taller modern office towers in discrete clusters to the east of St. Paul's, in the high-rise structures of the old commercial center and in an area of abandoned warehouses called Canary Wharf. Had such an approach been arrived at immediately after World War II, then the beautiful accumulation of villages and estates, and all their jumbled glory, might still retain a coherent skyline of architectural excellence. Yet such an initiative would have required a coordinated act of planning by a central municipal authority.

In 1934, in a widely read portrait of the metropolis, *London: the Unique City*, Dutch author Steen Eiler Rasmussen observed in regard to the growing infatuation of British architects with of the ideas of Le Corbusier: "One hardly knows whether to laugh or to cry on seeing a modernistic architecture imported into London, which is far less suitable to the spirit of the age than the Georgian houses of about 1800. There is now a quantity of English books on the latest fashions in foreign architecture, but I have yet to find one English book dealing at length with the standardized type of Georgian town house [of the great estates], the sight of which is one of the most remarkable experiences to the foreigner in London."

How could London not have known its own beauty? Perhaps London never was quite well enough defined to determine where it began and where it ended.

While disputing whom the city belonged to and where its outer perimeter should be drawn, and as its various parts defended their autonomy, Londoners failed to recognize a crucial moment—when the loveliness of the heart of their metropolis became endangered. And the comprehensible historic visage of the greater whole of the city was splintered.

MODERN PARIS: THE ALLURE AND EXILE OF TOWERS

Following the surrender of France in 1940, Adolf Hitler observed: "Wasn't Paris beautiful? In the past I often considered whether we would not have to destroy Paris, but when we are finished in Berlin, Paris will be only a shadow. So why should we destroy it?" Four years later, with the Allies advancing and the French capital about to be liberated, he would wonder instead: "Is Paris burning?" Had his orders been followed? Had explosives yet been detonated in the Louvre, Les Invalides, the Eiffel Tower, the Cathedral of Notre Dame, and other major landmarks? But the commander of the German occupation had refused to comply.

Destruction from modern warfare would heighten concern for the preservation of material culture in France, which was already one of the first European nations to pursue a policy of legal protection beyond the mere listing of monuments. As early as 1840, an official nationwide survey of historic assets was completed. In 1882 the Musée des Monuments Français had been established, providing a collection for the study of architectural artifacts and traditional building technology. Protection of state-owned historic buildings was mandated in 1887, and in the same year an accredited degree program in historic preservation was created to train state conservationists in the Department of Historic Monuments.

In 1913, the nation expanded its efforts, requiring preservation of both public and privately held historic landmarks (*monuments classés*), their interior decorative features such as statues, paintings, stained-glass windows, and other artistically fabricated building elements (known as *objets immeubles* when in their original location, and *objets mobiliers* once they had been moved). The statute also safeguarded buildings of lesser but nonetheless substantial distinction (*monuments inscrits*), and required maintenance of the historic context surrounding important buildings. By 1914 an extensive program of financial support for the conservation of French landmarks was instituted by the National Treasury of Historic Monuments (Caisse Nationale des Monuments Historiques), as France became the battlefield upon which mechanized modern warfare was unleashed.

During the First World War, 850 classified historic buildings in France were damaged, 600 of which were churches and 30 of which were major landmarks deemed to be beyond recovery and thus removed from the list of national monuments. Within ten years, through an intensive effort, most of the damage had been repaired.

In anticipation of the destruction of the Second World War, 45,000 *objets immeubles* and *objets mobiliers* were moved from their historic settings to safer places. The initial German onslaught obliterated medieval townscapes in Rouen, Orléans, and Tours. Upon the capitulation of France, Paris was declared an open city. For four years, every day at noon, German troops paraded in review down the Champs-Élysées and though Napoleon's Arc de Triomphe. As Allied forces began their invasion of Europe, the ancient city of Caen lost three-quarters of its buildings due to aerial bombardment. In Le Havre, 172 bombing raids leveled four-fifths of the city. Of 20,000 historic structures listed by France prior to the outbreak of hostilities, 3,000 were damaged or lost by the war's conclusion. And, once again, a national effort commenced to rectify the harm.

The determination of France to save its material culture had yielded a vast and highly sophisticated conservation bureaucracy and a system of liberal public subsidies for maintaining the nation's patrimony. (The French government today allows tax exemptions equal to 50 percent to 100 percent of the sum spent by owners on the maintenance of listed historic properties. Professional consultation from preservation specialists in the French building administration is free to the custodians of historic structures. And it is customary for the government to contribute 50 percent of the costs when major restoration work is undertaken.) Yet statutes to protect whole historic districts, such as the integrated cityscape of Paris, did not exist. Although destruction from warfare had bypassed the French capital, destruction from modernization would not.

Like London, Paris had languished without improvement through two world conflicts and a global depression. It survived, but much of its building stock suffered from more than four decades of deferred maintenance. This problem continued long into the postwar recovery. In the second half of the twentieth century, three major urban planning initiatives jeopardized the degree to which the beauty of the capital was saved: the accommodation of inner-city vehicular movement, the need to upgrade housing, and the construction of modern towers within the city's old line of outer fortifications.

Although the city's mass-transit network was substantially expanded, the number of automobiles in the Paris conurbation increased between 1940 and 1990 from approximately 500,000 to 4.5 million vehicles. Haussmann's wide boulevards were not broad enough to serve this ninefold growth. Moreover, making Paris accessible to a large number of cars was a problem compounded by its historic dimensions.

The evolution of Paris as an artistic whole within the envelope of its fortifications had resulted in an identifiable historic area. Compared to three other European cities whose traditional centers were also clearly defined, Paris has a historic core that is about ten times the geographic size of that of Amsterdam, including its three great ring canals; four times the size of Vienna, inside the line of its nineteenth-century fortifications; and four times as large as Rome, as bounded by its ancient imperial walls.

By the year 2000 the Paris conurbation housed about 10 million people (of which about 2 million lived in the center, with another million commuting into the city to work); the conurbation of Amsterdam housed 1.8 million; Vienna had 1.6 million; and Rome held about 3 million. In all these cities, the historic architecture was close to the public thoroughfares, making it extremely difficult to widen roadbeds. In Paris this problem was compounded by the longer distances across the historic city.

Beginning in the 1950s, promenades in the inner city were narrowed. Sidewalks with two rows of trees were pruned back to one row, increasing the width of roadbeds, removing greenery, and narrowing the pedestrian concourse. Sidewalks with one row of trees had their greenery removed entirely. An expressway was cut though the very heart of the city by eliminating one of the romantic tree-lined quays winding along the banks of the Seine. Due to adverse public opinion, however, construction of a second highway along the remaining quay was deferred. A great highway, the boulevard Périphérique, was built around the periphery of the city in the open field of fire that had surrounded the last ring of fortifications, and the outer edge of historic Paris came to be defined by a barrier of high-speed vehicular traffic. More cars had access to the center, and therefore congestion continued. The generous esplanades of the city, which had long been a defining element in its character, had become decidedly less gracious.

In 1904 the city had identified seventeen of its most overcrowded, disease-prone, and dilapidated slums. At the end of World War II, most of these *îlots insalubres* still existed, while squatter towns of deplorable misery pockmarked the fortification zone. A study in 1954 showed that residential accommodations in historic Paris widely lacked modern amenities achieved in other places: a mere 48 percent of Parisian apartments had toilets, only 19 percent had bathtubs or showers, and only 26 percent were centrally heated.

An aggressive program of housing construction ensued, and outside the boulevard Périphérique several huge complexes of low-cost modern apartment slabs and towers were raised. Made of prefabricated industrial parts, these *grands ensembles* marched along for miles. Frequently dreary, monotonous, and oppressive, they nonetheless increased the city's housing stock. But alien shapes, greater height, increased mass, and the starkly different aesthetic of modern architectural design had been introduced to the greater agglomeration.

As a second wave of industrialization revitalized the French economy in the 1960s, the allure of modernization and the need to finally rehabilitate the city's slums led to a radical change in the building code. Penetration of the low-scale traditional center with tall modern towers was a concept widely familiar to and rejected by Parisians since the Voisin Plan of Le Corbusier in 1925. But while the cultural and aesthetic violence to the existing milieu proposed by Le Corbusier was appalling, in subsequent years, the artistry of his numerous beautiful buildings—the Villa Savoye (1931), the Swiss Pavilion (1932), the Unité d'Habitation in Marseilles (1952), the Chapel of Notre Dame du Haut at Ronchamp (1954)—gave the idea a degree of credibility. Now the historic metropolis was divided into two zones. In its central districts (arrondisse-ments) numbered 1 to 12—within the old ring of grand boulevards created by Louis XIV, where most of the city's monuments were located—the allowable height of buildings was raised slightly above historic norms. In the outer arrondissements, numbered 13 to 20, where most of the îlots insalubres were situ-ated, the general height limitation was increased and allowances were made for taller buildings when set back within property lines. In other words, in the outer zones of the historic city the traditional street wall could be broken and towers would be permitted to penetrate the historic skyline.

Construction of incompatible architectural forms was not just allowed but encouraged; within its old lines of fortification, historic Paris would no longer be aesthetically unified. The transformation was quick, extreme, and far-reaching. Raising the permissible height for new buildings that were set back made it profitable to tear down existing edifices aligned with the street wall in order to erect bigger structures that did not conform to the city's traditional urban geometry. For speculative developers and housing administrators alike, plain rectilinear boxes of factory-made building elements, quickly assembled with a minimal quality of craftsmanship, were less costly to build, and therefore proliferated in the city's outer historic zones. In these areas of late-nineteenth- and early-twentieth-century tenements, whose facades con-formed to historic architectural traditions—the quality of housing was upgraded, sometimes quite marginally, but the city's architectural conformity of style, colors, materials, height, and massing was broken.

Overnight—particularly on its northern, southern, and eastern fringes—the avalanche of medium-height modern towers and slabs changed both the character of the public realm and the architectural perspective of virtually every street and block. Outer historic Paris became a jumbled amalgam of old and new. Several large areas where major thoroughfares intersected with the boule-vard Périphérique were designated for more aggressive redevelopment. Here major buildings of even greater verticality and bulk would be allowed.

While a general consensus seemed to exist in Paris that residential slabs of moderately greater size were necessary for improving housing conditions in the outer arrondissements, and that outside the boulevard Périphérique even taller skyscrapers might be erected, each new inner-city development initiative brought larger towers closer and closer to the beautiful low-scale historic center.

In old industrial areas, like the Port d'Italie and Bercy, whole environments of modern curtain-wall towers were created—removing slums, old buildings, and the poor. At the Font de Seine, the magnificent urban vista created by the formal alignment of the Jardins de Trocadéro, the Pont d'Iéna, the Eiffel Tower, and the Champ-de-Mars was encroached upon by a cluster of tall hotels, luxury apartment buildings, and prestigious offices, gentrifying yet another part of the city.

Three particularly egregious projects caused a reversal in direction. First, in 1973, on a hillside overlooking the traditional center and at the location of *îlot insalubre* number 17, the Tour Montparnasse was erected. At 210 meters tall (680 feet)—about six times greater than the general height allowed in outer arrondissements, and the largest skyscraper in Europe at the time—the building hovered above the beautiful peaks of the historic milieu and altered forever the profile of Paris when looking to the south.

Second was the bewildering jumble of office buildings at La Defénse, one of the strangest chapters in postwar urbanism in Europe. Erecting a district of skyscrapers as the distant culmination of the great axial line of Paris, running through the Louvre and the place de la Concorde, was an idea long contemplated by the city. Competitions had been held in 1929 and 1931 to envision the effect. Hence in 1964 construction was approved for about thirty 100-meter-tall buildings, arranged in a coordinated ensemble (assimilating one of the few positive features of the Voisin Plan), and outside the boulevard Périphérique.

By the 1970s the greater latitude in the building code and increased public overruns in underwriting the cost of the project's infrastructure led to both a loosening of planning controls and a relaxation of architectural coordination at La Defénse. The result was an increase in market-driven buildings of greater height, arbitrary interrelationship, and disassociated expression, not an aesthetically unified arrangement of parts as called for by Le Corbusier. That a city renowned in the history of formal urban planning had failed to coordinate the aesthetics of such a significant development is inexplicable. In the eyes of many Parisians, unforgivable damage had been done to the city's visage. Looking up the Champs-Élysées, a visual scramble of speculative development had become the permanent backdrop to the beloved vista of Napoleon's Arc de Triomphe.

The third project, a proposal for another large development of giant office towers—a "world center of commerce"—located deep inside the historic core at the old market district of Les Halles, capped the argument. The public outcry was vehement. The visage of Europe's most beautiful city would not remain beautiful for long if its historic urban profile was not protected. The construction of towers in the center of Paris was blocked. Yet surrounding Les Halles, and having festered for decades, was the city's most infamous slum, *îlot insalubre 1*. A new strategy for urban adaptation and renewal would have to be devised.

One of the notable elements stimulating a shift in policy was a 1973 report to the City Council that documented the decline of the capital's reputation as a major international center of the arts; this would strike a primal chord of Parisian identity. Erosion of the city's unique physical character was one element contributing to the fall. Gentrification was another, making it impossible for artists to afford studio space in the city's center and reducing the vibrancy of a socially diverse urban population. Initial plans to redevelop the area of Les Halles would continue in this negative vein.

Not only would the proposed towers intrude upon several major urban vistas of the classical cityscape (hovering above the rue de Rivoli and the Jardin des Tuileries and dwarfing the Cathedral of Notre Dame), and remove a popular Parisian historical landmark (the marketplace itself), but the quaint streets, cafés, and shops of one of the city's oldest neighborhoods would be erased. In opposition to this, public awareness of the aesthetic, historic, and cultural significance of the old working-class neighborhood was raised by articles, speeches by conservation activists, and even tour guides. Defense of the vulnerable area showed that the city's protective net of conservation statutes was defective.

The great landmarks, major buildings, and prominent vistas in historic Paris were generally well protected, but no binding legal commitment had been made to save the interwoven fabric of more modest old buildings and narrow byways that lay between the vectors of the city's principal thoroughfares. In these places—often dilapidated, frequently slums, yet also holding some of the most ancient structures of the capital—the history of the evolution of Paris was recorded and a special environmental aesthetic flourished. Here was a visually sensitive pluralism of creative architectural expression, a charm that Parisians and visitors alike experienced as essential and unique. Urban modernization was not simply pushing out the poor. In removing the manifestations of their existence, it was also eliminating evidence of their contribution to the distinct character of Parisian life.

In neighborhoods across Paris, the beautiful charcuteries (delicatessens), pastry shops, restaurants, cafés, and boutiques to be found on every other block had storefronts, awnings, and lighting fixtures whose design harmonized with the milieu. Often, the elegant lettering and graphic proportions of the signage were as visually discriminating as the architectural design of the buildings on which they were posted. Even the displays in shop windows—rows of colorful pastries, carefully arranged trays of prepared foods, displays of clothes, antiques—were part of a living, changing, and extended visual sensibility that was the essence of existence in Paris.

SAFEGUARDING THE CORE

An alternative yet untried development methodology was already in place in the Commission Nationale des Secteurs Sauvegardés, created in 1962 during the tenure of André Malraux as minister of cultural affairs. Under the new law, comprehensive preservation plans were designed for the physical, economic, and social evolution of important historic towns and cities in France, with financial provisions for their implementation. As the fate of Les Halles was debated, reclamation was progressing in the first protected neighborhood to be designated in Paris and the largest of such districts in the nation—an area neighboring Les Halles called the Marais, which shared a major part of *îlot insalubre 1* and all of *îlot insalubre 16* as well.

In the secteurs sauvegardés historic assets were evaluated, restoration priorities set, housing conditions upgraded, and strategies for economic revitalization created with attention to the employment of existing resident populations. Subsidies were offered to owners unable to afford the expense of building rehabilitation (up to 80 percent of the costs of restoration were paid for by the state). Temporary or alternative housing was provided for tenants as work progressed, and original inhabitants were given priority to resume residence afterward. This could be achieved only in part, since raising living accommodations to modern standards inevitably involved increasing the amount of space per person, providing living quarters with separate rooms, and removing backyard shacks and building accretions with insufficient light and air. By definition, the amelioration of slum conditions resulted in a reduction in their density. Nonetheless, it was hoped that the *secteurs sauvegardés* would result in socially responsive gentrification, retaining the special diversity of different communities, saving the texture of modest historic architecture, and revitalizing local economies to ensure the continued maintenance of old districts once they were restored.

On paper, the integrated approach of *secteurs sauvegardés* was a leading example of comprehensive urban conservation—which occurred in differently structured formats in places like Amsterdam and Bologna as well. In reality, even as the controversy over Les Halles continued, the government's inclination toward gentrification seemed excessive. Public criticism pushed the authorities to make greater provision for a mixed social occupancy and the retention of local businesses. With trial, error, and dispute, the first application

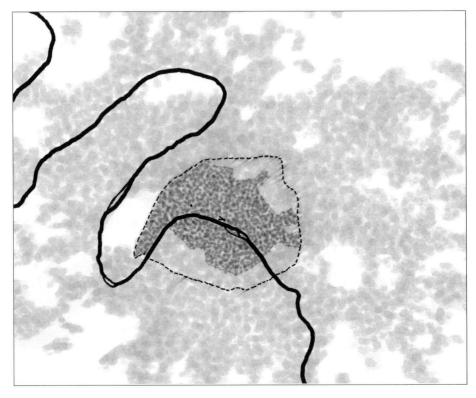

THE MODERN CONURBATION OF PARIS

of the new urban renewal strategy to the Paris neighborhood of the Marais would ultimately prove quite successful, causing a second *secteur sauvegardé* to be created in the 7th arrondissement, adjacent to the Hôtel des Invalides. The markets of Les Halles were ultimately demolished, however, and replaced by a multilevel shopping mall of uncommon ugliness but nonetheless somewhat in scale with the surrounding cityscape.

In 1974 a New Land Use Plan, created in collaboration with the Atelier Parisien d'Urbanisme, finally protected all the surviving parts of the historic center, an area encompassing the inner arrondissements and extending outward to the western side of Paris to the boulevard Périphérique and the Bois de Boulogne. Allowable building heights were lowered to historic norms. In Montmartre, in fact, permissible heights were even lower than historic standards, thus especially encouraging the retention of old buildings. As a result land values deflated and new development was discouraged. All new construction in these areas was subject to governmental design review, requiring that old street walls be honored and that new facades be compatible with the

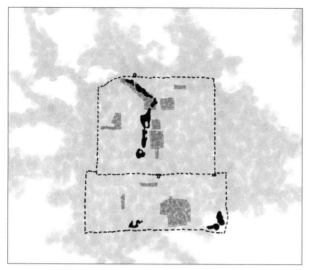

THE MODERN CONURBATION OF BEIJING

Central preservation areas in Paris and Beijing • Perhaps the two largest and artistically integrated cityscapes ever achieved, historic Paris and historic Beijing are surprising similar in size (as indicated by the dotted lines demarking the extent of old fortifications). In each place the modern agglomeration has greatly expanded (pale gray tone). • In Paris, by the close of the twentieth century, an overlay of several conservation initiatives have resulted in a large protected historic zone (dotted dark gray tone). • In Beijing, conservation zones are smaller and more dispersed, are largely focused on major monuments, and safeguard far less of the vernacular character of the ancient metropolis. (*Both drawings at the same scale.*)

historic environment surrounding them—a modern reimposition of the old regulatory concept of *architecture d'accompagnement.* State-sponsored subsidized housing initiatives, built by the private sector, were required to comply with similar design guidelines. Although not every structure in these areas was officially designated as a monument, in essence the center had been made into a vast historic district covering about 60 percent of the area surrounded by the boulevard Périphérique. The zone would include about 300 *monuments classés* and 900 *monuments inscrits,* each also protected in regard to its relationship with surrounding buildings within 500 meters of sight. This may well be the largest single continuous conservation area in any city in the world.

Today, approaching Paris by car requires transversing the familiar postwar modern environmental confusion of multilane highways, dreary large housing compounds, and ubiquitous commercial and industrial complexes. Once across the boulevard Périphérique, along the Avenue de la Grande Armee, however, rows of trees line the street and buildings start to look distinctly French. Suddenly, upon arriving at the Étoile, visions of classical elegance and breathtaking Baroque grandeur extend to distant horizons. In many places the old city bears scars from its struggle with modernization; the historic center is somewhat sanitized—the poor having been displaced through gentrification encouraged by their own government—and the elegant promenades are less green than once they were, but the artistry of the great sculptured cityscape endures.

There is never enough time to see Paris. The city is like some favorite long, beautifully written novel, which the reader hopes will never end. It is a place always wonderful to revisit because it is conceived to be beautiful from infinite perspectives. It is designed for the sunlight, but after dark it turns into a glittering palace. The orchestrated architectural drama of its main boulevards, if traced from one great culmination point to another, seems unending. Yet off its principal avenues, unexpected medieval angles and surprising intersections produce a vast eccentric charm. From this place an unparalleled outpouring of visual fine art bursts forth. And in this place the visual artistry of city building was cultivated, refined, and raised to an extended collective sphere that marks a height of human social attainment. Here is one of the fundamental scales against which the potential beauty of cities is measured.

The contrast with Beijing seems relevant, not simply because of a similarity of geographic extent, but by virtue of a similarity of architectural accomplishment. At the beginning of the twentieth century, the capitals of France and China were the two largest works of unified urban artistry in the world. Today Paris is still largely intact, while Beijing is fractured and continuing to lose more of its unique character with every passing day. No direct comparison can truly be made, the culture and history of each place being so different. But was the consensus that made Paris beautiful more inclusive? Did more contemporary Parisians share a sense of ownership of the beautiful construction because its loveliness was focused on the public realm and was therefore more widely experienced by a greater proportion of its populace? Did more of the beauty of Paris affect the daily of life of more Parisians? And did more Parisians therefore feel the wound deeply and cry out when the visage of their lovely city began to be eroded?

Like London, historic Paris succumbed to the allure of modern towers, but once the consequence of their presence in the center was recognized, the building of skyscrapers was restricted. In part this must be attributed to the concentration of the cityscape in an identifiable aesthetic mass that allows it to be perceived and administered as a totality, just as its governance as a totality over the centuries has allowed it to be constructed as an orchestrated whole. London, conversely, was built in many separate parts, managed as many separate parts, and interrupted in many different places.

Yet the larger question involved in the modernization of these two splen did capital cities is ultimately a global issue. During the twentieth century, throughout the world, the culture of architecture and city building changed so dramatically that centuries of accrual of stylistically unique urban environ mental value was ended. The historic city has become a finite resource, and urban preservation has become a matter of saving not just important individual structures but of saving the special character of whole cityscapes, of the way their parts were woven together in a comprehensible visage that marked the distinctiveness of old urban cultures in a world that in many aspects began to evolve toward global cultural conformity.

CHAPTER ELEVEN

TOURISM VERSUS THE HABITABLE CITY

VENICE

So we advanced into this ghostly city, continuing to hold our course through the narrow streets and lanes, all filled and flowing with water. On we went, floating towards the heart of this strange place—with water all about us where water never was elsewhere—clusters of houses, churches, heaps of stately buildings growing out of it—and everywhere the same extraordinary silence.

—CHARLES DICKENS, *Pictures from Italy*

The visitor approaching by train cannot see Venice from the causeway that reaches out into the lagoon surrounding the historic metropolis. The only things visible are blue-green water, sea grass, and finally train yards. Inside the Stazione Ferrovie dello Stato Santa Lucia is a rush of activity. But take just one step beyond the doors of the terminal and you are engulfed by Venice, transported back in time. A pastel-colored medieval townscape capped with orange tile roofs extends in all directions. Vaporettos, gondolas, and motorboats weave through turquoise channels. Mysterious alleys, bridges, and byways lead to undiscovered treasures. Waves splash upon sidewalks at high tide. Gulls perch on candy-striped gondola poles. Stately classical buildings of white marble celebrate the flowering of the Renaissance. Beautiful palazzi with trefoil Byzantine Gothic windows speak in an architectural language unique to this special place.

From here, across many centuries, the trade goods of Asia were dispersed throughout Europe, and an often enlightened government ruled with restraint and tolerance, constructing a jewel among cities. Yet tomorrow, where will the children of the metropolis find playmates? As the higher economic rewards from tourism drive real estate values upward, and drugstores, hardware shops, butchers, and cobblers are replaced by hotels, gift shops, and restaurants, how will ordinary Venetians—teachers, shopkeepers, nurses, gondoliers, the elderly, and young married couples—afford to live here? As school classes grow smaller, will youngsters have to traverse the whole city to find companions? If Venetians do not live in Venice, who will keep up the ancient buildings, fix the leaks when they first begin to drip, and patch the plaster before it corrodes across whole facades? Can Venice survive the success of its tourist economy? Is a city still a city when it no longer is a home to its people?

⚜

Saving Venice is one of the most complex urban conservation problems in the world. As in other great cities, historic architectural preservation in Venice is not separable from the larger and intertwined issues of the whole metropolis—economic, social, political, and environmental. Nor are the quandaries of any city divorced from the broader developmental dilemmas of its nation and region. Yet Venice is more complicated. Its singularity as a historic built environment and the way these special characteristics clash with the forces that determine the vitality of modern cities is the reason. Its problems are extraordinary because there really is no other place—and has never been any other place—quite like it.

Venice is unique among the great historic cities in several ways. First and most obviously, it is a city built in water, in the Venetian lagoon. And, like Amsterdam and Aztec Tenochtitlán—two other cities built in watery environs which were also the capitals of great empires—its creation required the development of special local technologies in order to construct buildings and to reconcile the human-made settlement with the forces of the surrounding natural environment.

Second, Venice is unique among great historic capitals in that so much of the city's fabric survives from such an early date in its evolution. It is one of the largest, most complete, and architecturally most significant medieval urban constructions in the world, whose history stretches back more than a millennium. It is more intact than Kyoto or Beijing. It is older than Prague or Cairo.

Third, Venice is unique in that it survives in its geographic context. Unlike historic cities situated on land, the Venetian conurbation in the nineteenth and twentieth centuries did not spread over the immediate natural terrain—a wide, shallow sound that might have been more aggressively filled to accommodate modern expansion. Instead, contemporary Venice encroached on mainland areas bordering the lagoon. (Tenochtitlán and its macro-environment of managed wetlands were destroyed by the Spanish during the construction of colonial Mexico City, and the development of Amsterdam in the nineteenth and twentieth centuries obliterated the marshes and agricultural fields that once surrounded it.) So Venice is one of the few medieval urban environments that can still be seen as it once existed in nature. And because it continues to exist in the same setting, Venetians must maintain the lagoon that encircles the city, as did their forefathers in centuries past. Here is a paradigm of how the cities of our quickly expanding urban world may yet be required to find a rapprochement with the natural environment—a reconciliation that has been widely ignored. It is a delicate relationship that, until recently, Venice was gradually losing, thereby imperiling its existence.

THE CITY IN ENVIRONMENTAL BALANCE

Venice's rise to world power, its social and cultural achievements, its beauty and architectural singularity sprang from its relationship to the body of water in which it was constructed. It was a city built in a setting where large cities usually had not existed.

Although it would eventually become a great maritime power, Venice was at first a refuge from the political instability that plagued Italy after the fall of the Roman Empire around A.D. 570. It was a rare enclave of civility in a prolonged era of turbulence when Italy was frequently invaded by Germanic (Gothic) tribes vying with the Byzantines for hegemony in Europe. The lagoon itself was the city's defense. As Venice evolved, it gradually learned that although the construction of a permanent cityscape in a wetland environment would require laborious construction methods, such a setting had several advantages.

The lagoon that surrounds Venice is wide and shallow, and more than fifty times larger than the area that would eventually be occupied by the city itself. A lagoon is a form of estuary: a partly enclosed coastal body of water in which saltwater and freshwater are mixed by the sea's tides. The Venetian lagoon has a specific mix of characteristics that allowed it to serve as a defensive barrier to both land and sea attack, as a deepwater port, as a center of commercial fishing, as a site for salt- and glass-making, and as a natural mechanism for eliminating the human waste produced by a large urban settlement.

As a defensive barrier from assault by land, the tidal marshlands and bogs that border the Venetian lagoon are a treacherous maze impassable to soldiers on foot. Inside the bay, an irregular network of navigable channels weave between numerous shallow areas and sandbars. The eccentricity of this shifting natural pattern put hostile naval forces at a severe disadvantage when maneuvering against native Venetian seamen during a sea battle. In the heat of fighting, enemy forces might easily run aground.

Although most of the lagoon is shallow, a curving deepwater channel runs through its center and penetrates the long chain of barrier islands that isolate the estuary from the Adriatic Sea. Venice was built in the heart of the bay on the islands that constitute the Rivo Alto (high bank) that embraces the deepwater passageway where it forms a sweeping and sinuous curve, later called the Grand Canal. This positioned the city where seagoing ships could find safe harbor and anchorage.

When first occupied, the lagoon was also fed by freshwater from several rivers and streams. This produced wetlands rich with aquatic plants and the microorganisms—fish, mammals, birds, and insects—associated with such natural systems. Here was another advantage to building a city in what seemed an unnatural location.

Until the nineteenth century and the identification of the role of bacteria in the transmission of infectious diseases, the sanitation of urban areas was achieved by a process of trial and observation. Unknown to the Venetians, who believed that the tides flushed away the city's waste, a far more complex chemical and biological process was at work—a process that today is recognized as a highly effective method of wastewater treatment. When human waste enters the estuary, it is broken down, and its components become part of the food chain. The action of the tides within the lagoon reduces solid waste into small particles, which become food for microscopic animals and insects. Plants absorb nitrogen, phosphorus, and other compounds from the water. The oxygen released by submerged plant roots supports the activity of bacteria and fungi, which further break down organic waste particles. (Artificial wetlands with an ecological dynamic similar to that of the lagoon of Venice have become a means of sanitation in many smaller contemporary urban communities.)

Moreover, the barrier islands that protect the Venetian lagoon restrict the waves that wash through the estuary with the changing of the tides. A specific balance is achieved. The tides are sufficient to flush the waste out of the city and disperse it into the broad lagoon, but not so active that polluted water moves too quickly for the natural cleansing processes to take effect. Given sufficient time, nature will eventually sanitize human waste, but dense urban settlements overburden most natural systems. The ratio of Venice's size to the extent of its lagoon and the unusual effectiveness of the estuary as processor of organic waste made the location of the city very propitious in this regard.

The microscopic animals and insects that thrive in this environment become food for larger creatures, eventually supporting an abundance of edible fish, fowl, and mollusks. Shallower areas of the estuary also produce heavily salinated water due to an increased rate of evaporation, yielding large amounts of table salt—a vital product in the Middle Ages for preserving meat, and the main commercial export of the city for several hundred years. Salt from the lagoon is also absorbed by seaweed, which when reduced to ashes forms sodium carbonate—a primary component (along with the fine sand to be found in nearby riverbeds) in the making of glass. And Venice for many centuries was one of Europe's major suppliers of glass.

Much as the physical characteristics of the lagoon were particularly felicitous for Venice, the ascent of Venice as an independent city-state and a great maritime power was affected by its geographic location between Constantinople and Europe.

In A.D. 330, when the Roman Empire was divided into Eastern (eventually Greek Orthodox) and Western (eventually Latin Roman Catholic) spheres, Venice was located between two strong geopolitical poles. During the early Middle Ages, as various Gothic tribes conquered different parts of Europe, the original community of fishermen and salt makers gradually became a colony of traders; their skills at shipbuilding and navigation grew, and Venice became a self-sufficient outpost at the far reaches of the Byzantine Empire. By the time Charlemagne consolidated Gothic Europe and was crowned emperor of the Holy Roman Empire, Venice was a trading and diplomatic intermediary between different civilizations. The Venetians' position was further strengthened as the Muslim Empire expanded in the Middle East (occupying Jerusalem in 637), the southern Mediterranean (taking Alexandria in 642), and parts of Continental Europe through Spain (claiming Cordova in 711), for Christian Europe became landlocked from Asia. Italian maritime cities—Venice in particular—became the major commercial link between East and West.

The life of the city as a global trader and intermediary exposed Venetians to the cultures of different places and inculcated in them a cosmopolitan consciousness. Venice became a Gothic metropolis assimilating cultural strains from Byzantium, the Muslim Empire, and the Italian mainland. Simultaneously, the practical limitations and unusual freedoms of building in the center of a lagoon would combine with the multicultural orientation of the city to produce architecture unlike that found anyplace else.

The construction of buildings on the low-lying islands of Venice required the sinking of wooden piles into a compact substratum of sand and clay, the *caranto*, upon which was built a wooden raft that served as a platform for stone foundations. This allowed Venetian buildings to "float" in shifting geological strata. Since the piles were driven to a depth below sea level, the wood was constantly submerged and gradually mineralized in the saltwater. Posts could thus last almost indefinitely. The current piles of the Ducal Palace, or Doges' Palace, were last examined in 1874, at which time they were 530 years old and entirely sound. In other cases, however, mineralized piles would splinter when subjected to lateral pressure.

Because the sinking of piles was an expensive, labor-intensive process and the *caranto* substratum could shift over time, it was necessary to make the buildings of the permanent city as flexible and light as possible. The exterior walls were accordingly made of a light brick and soft mortar, and were highly plastic. Inside, wooden construction was carefully integrated with the masonry to distribute the weight of the building evenly should the foundations move. In larger structures the supporting walls were thinner in the upper stories. But while the lightness of Venetian buildings was necessary, what made it possible was the security of the city from outside attack. In Gothic cities on the mainland, urban structures were designed as fortresses in case of invasion. The impenetrability of Venice's natural defenses allowed its buildings to be constructed of less heavy materials, with numerous openings for light and air, which further reduced the amount of solid masonry in exterior walls.

In an era when the use of glass in windows was considered a luxury, the numerous glass furnaces situated on the nearby island of Murano made it feasible for Venice to become a city sparkling with glazed fenestration. At first, the shape of window openings in the residences of the city was based on Byzantine architectural models with shallow arches. With time, a Muslim-influenced residential building type evolved (called a *fondaco* in Venetian, from the original Arabic *funduk*). These buildings combined trading offices and warehouse facilities on the lowest floor with residences in the upper stories. Thus, Arabic horseshoe-shaped and inflected arched windows became part of the city's formal vocabulary. Eventually, a distinctly Venetian-style window evolved, with ornate tracery carved in stone and synthesizing Byzantine and Arabic forms with those of Gothic Europe. The architecture of the city assumed an effervescent quality punctuated by the reflected light of its many glazed windows.

As the population grew, the central islands became densely settled. Each island was a separate parish, with a community church situated next to an open square known in Venice as a *campo*. In order to supply fresh drinking water, the *campo* was designed to work as a rainwater cistern and well. Beneath the paved walking area of each plaza the Venetians constructed a large cavity sealed by an impermeable shell that prohibited the penetration of saltwater. This underground tank was filled with sand, which acted as a filter, and a well reached from the bottom of the cistern up to the plaza, where a decorative wellhead was placed. Neighboring buildings had steeply pitched roofs with gutters and spouts that collected and delivered rainwater to the *campo* cistern, where the liquid seeped downward through the sand to the well bottom. Each parish island (sixty-eight would eventually be developed), with its church, *campo*, and cistern, was a self-sufficient unit of the larger city.

As more and more of the central higher areas of the lagoon bed were recovered and the number of islands increased, the Venetians were careful to maintain the flow of major navigable channels. While most medieval cities have an eccentric circulation pattern that is often described as organic, the irregular configuration of the islands of Venice and its network of canals grew in direct response to the natural flow of water within the estuary. Gradually a second independent movement system was developed on the land. For commercial purposes, warehouse-residences had doors that opened to a canal for the loading and unloading of trade goods, and another doorway that led to the winding network of medieval pedestrian pathways (calle) of the city's neighborhoods. Eventually 350 to 400 bridges (ponti) crossed more than 200 original channels, linking 118 separate islands in a vast patchwork.

Until the fall of the Venetian Republic in 1797, a special branch of government—called the Piovego in the medieval period and, later, as it became more specialized, the Savii alle Acque—strictly monitored development to ensure that the natural flushing action of the lagoon continued to clean the city. Over the centuries, the Venetians had learned that silt gradually accumulated and the canals grew shallower, reducing the flow of the tides. Therefore, they devised a laborious system of constant canal maintenance, which has been documented back to the fifteenth century. Areas of the city were isolated and drained through the use of temporary dams. The canals were then dredged, foundations and embankments were repaired, and the temporary dams were removed and installed in another area. The process of rehabilitating all the city's canals took about twenty years, by which time it was necessary to begin the cycle once more.

As the city assumed its ultimate form (the population reached about 130,000 by 1500, when Venice was one of the largest and wealthiest cities in Europe), the Venetians gradually gained a deeper understanding of the living lagoon upon which their lives depended. Lagoons are an unstable evolutionary state of estuaries. They are either in the process of filling up with the sediments deposited by rivers, or emptying out to become deep bays through the tidal action of the sea. Both of these extreme conditions were undesirable for Venice—the silting of the lagoon would expose the city to attack by land, while the deepening of the estuary would make the harbor navigable by hostile forces from the sea—so the city decided to interrupt the natural process. Although their scientific knowledge was rudimentary compared to our understanding today, studies at the University of Padua and within the Venetian bureaucracy had uncovered a fundamental environmental concept, which by 1718 was expressed concisely as "Element opposes element."

If the Venetian lagoon was to remain to be shallow and wide with periodic navigable channels, its evolution toward either a bay or a wetland would have to be permanently arrested. Neither the sea nor the rivers could be allowed to dominate. An artificial state of environmental equilibrium, or stasis, had to be created in which the movements of the sea and the rivers were controlled so that they perpetually counterbalanced each other. Given the variables of weather and the changing conditions of the land and sea, this was a problem of enormous complexity that Venice would gradually solve over a period of several centuries through a sophisticated program of regulation, monitoring, maintenance, and the construction of public works.

The Venetian lagoon is approximately 40 kilometers long, varying in breadth from 5 to 10 kilometers. It is protected from the sea by several narrow barrier islands and peninsulas, with three major openings through which the tides flow in and out of the estuary. Historically, a dozen rivers and streams debouched into the lagoon, including three major rivers: the Sile, the Piave, and the Brenta, which flow out of the mainland a distance of approximately 50 to 75 kilometers. None of these water sources could be simply blocked; each had to be allowed to continue to flow in order for the Venetians to achieve a balance of opposites responding to varying climatic conditions.

Between 1300 and 1800, more than 160 kilometers of canals and several large dikes would be dug on the landward side of the lagoon, creating a complicated system of diversions that would allow the city either to redirect floodwaters around the lagoon and out into the Adriatic or, at other times, let a

Historic environmental interventions in the Venetian lagoon · Maintaining environmental stasis in its lagoon was crucial to Venice (the inhabited core of central islands are shown in black). These large civil engineering projects required a commitment founded in knowledge. Over centuries, the Venetian Republic gradually came to know that constructing massive seawalls (solid black lines), lengthy dikes (dotted line to the east of the lagoon), and more than a hundred miles of river diversions (dot-dash lines) would preserve a delicate balance of opposing environmental elements in the surrounding natural terrain.

controlled amount of freshwater enter the lagoon at specific locations. Correspondingly, numerous sea barriers, eventually protecting a length of around 20 kilometers, would be constructed along the edge of the Adriatic to protect the narrow strip of barrier islands from being either swept away by violent storms or slowly devoured by the tides.

Commercial activities—such as the construction of salt pans and fish farming, which involved the artificial isolation of parts of the lagoon—were closely regulated. Continuous dredging was required, both in the city's canals and in the lagoon itself. And between 1610 and 1792, an official area encompassing the whole lagoon environment was mapped out and monitored at 102 datum points.

All this activity stabilized the natural conditions that had so decisively determined the shape of the city and its architecture. The action of the Venetians in preserving the character of the lagoon also perpetuated the character of the urban agglomeration. Radical alterations in the defensive characteristics of the lagoon would have precipitated radical changes in the configuration of the cityscape. A fundamental principle had been revealed: the conservation of the built environment of Venice would always involve the conservation of its natural environment as well.

The ability of Venice to sustain an effective environmental program within the lagoon over many centuries was made possible by the continuity of the city's government. Venice had not been conquered or ruled by a foreign power since recognition of its independence by Constantinople in 814. Nor was it torn by the frequent internal political upheavals that had afflicted Italian cities on the mainland. From 1140 to 1160, it was run by a continuous form of republican government in which administrative and legislative powers were vested in assemblies constituted of members of the patrician class. The highest official of the republic was the doge, who was elected for life but could be removed for high crimes against the state. This oligarchic government was, in effect, a commune devoted to the continued mercantile success of the city. It consciously fostered the political stability that, at the dawn of the Renaissance, made Venice one of the world's great commercial and political powers, with diplomatic ambassadors at every major court in Europe.

THE CITY AS AN ARTISTIC CONSTRUCTION

At its height, the maritime empire of Venice included a substantial portion of adjacent mainland Italy, as well as a string of cities, islands, and territories on both sides of the Adriatic, around Greece and east to Istanbul and beyond. This extensive network offered safe harbor for the Venetian republic's ships, controlled piracy in the sea-lanes to the Middle East, provided food and basic necessities that the city did not produce, and offered new commodities and markets for trade. Over the centuries, the flow of wealth through the metropolis generated a cityscape filled with extraordinary buildings.

The Grand Canal had become one of the most remarkable urban thoroughfares in the world, a broad curving passageway lined by imposing warehouse-residences and ornate palazzi. The many parishes and monasteries of the city had built numerous large and splendid churches that were often a distinct blend of Byzantine and Italian medieval architecture. At the heart of the city, where the Grand Canal merged with the deepwater harbor that connected to the sea beyond, the major public plaza of the city was bordered by its most important symbolic buildings.

Like Saint Basil's in Moscow or the Duomo in Florence, the singular form of the Basilica of Saint Mark—inspired by the Christian Roman architecture of Constantinople—is an architectural expression unique to the city and its culture. The basic plan was a Greek cross composed of five squares, over which were constructed five domes perched on spherical pendentives, a structural advance of the Byzantines. And like the great church of Saint Sophia, the interior surfaces of the domes, barrel vaults, and pendentives of Saint Mark were richly adorned with exquisite gold mosaics. Although the original structure took only thirty years to complete, its embellishment required centuries of refinement and additions. The completed building was a dense, sumptuous treasure box embroidered by the site-specific artworks of generations of Venetian artists and the most precious plunder from hundreds of years of foreign conquest.

Immediately adjacent is the Doges' Palace, whose unusual eclectic design integrates Gothic, Arabic, Byzantine, and Renaissance architectural elements. Here, in the ducal residence, the Palace of Justice, and the great hall of the city's legislature, were housed the principal administrative functions of the empire. The first two floors of the structure are wrapped by a Byzantine portico and Gothic loggia of elaborately carved white Istrian stone. The floors above are enclosed by a screen wall with an inlaid geometric pattern of pink and white stone. Arabic crenellations marched along the crest of the facade. Like that of Saint Mark's, the aesthetic elaboration of the Doges' Palace eventually came to reflect centuries of accumulated endeavor by Venice's artists and architects, who filled the interior with masterworks of furniture, painting, and sculpture.

In parallel with the other city-states of Italy, a heightened civic self-consciousness had evolved in the metropolis. The majority of the city's adult males participated in public and civic life. All male nobles—who numbered from 1,000 to 2,500 in different eras—were eligible to vote in the Great Council, the Maggior Consiglio. Many non-nobles belonged to guilds or *scuole,* religious fraternities devoted to mutual assistance and public philanthropy. The largest of these, the Scuole Grandi, of which there were eventually seven, was composed of 500 to 600 prominent upper-class Venetians. Participants in the minor guilds varied from about fifty to seventy-five members, and there were Scuole Piccole for goldsmiths, cabinetmakers, carpenters, builders, stonemasons, clothmakers, spice dealers, rope makers, boatbuilders, vintners, and bakers.

By the eighteenth century, over 400 *scuole* provided aid for widows and orphans, the aged, the destitute, lepers, and former prostitutes; they also supported public health care, promoted education, and sometimes built subsidized housing for the poor. In the eighteenth century, four orphanages dedicated to music—the choirmaster of one of these was Antonio Vivaldi— became famous throughout the Continent, making significant contributions to the development of classical symphonic music. Although the Venetians could be tyrannical in the pursuit of commercial interests abroad, and power and its privileges were enjoyed by an elite minority within the city, civil unrest among the lower classes erupted infrequently. The culture of Venice had evolved to the point where most families had a male member directly involved in the workings of Venetian society.

As the Renaissance widened interest in learning, Venice housed over 125 publishing houses and became the most prominent printing center in Europe. The city's churches, government, *scuole,* and nobility became important patrons of the arts. Throughout Venice extraordinary artistic creations—often integrated into the decorative fabric of interior walls and ceilings—by the Bellinis, Carpaccio, Giorgione, Titian, Bassano, Tintoretto, Veronese, and eventually Tiepolo, Longhi, and Canaletto, adorned palaces, churches, and public buildings. The living city constituted one of the major art collections of the world and, from across Italy, leading intellectuals, architects, artists, and craftsmen were drawn to the islands in the lagoon. The city's inhabitants' pride in the prosperity and social advances of the metropolis fostered the realization that Venice was unique. The splendid physical agglomeration of the city also reflected the power of the republic, the contributions of its citizenry, and the cultural milieu that blossomed in this urban setting. Thus, as the development of perspective drawing and city planning during the Renaissance engendered consideration of the metropolis as an object subject to design, Venice looked at itself and, with its extensive wealth, began to add a number of carefully orchestrated architectural effects that would transform its built environment into an artistic construction.

Due in part to the laborious efforts required to build in the estuary, the medieval city was highly compressed, with structures crowded close together. Because most buildings were low, the cityscape took the form of a homogeneous horizontal aggregation of cellular clusters. From within the maze of its pedestrian pathways, facades were seen partially or at extreme angles. Only across the periodic open spaces of its campos or along its broader waterways could architecture be seen from afar and whole designs be appreciated.

In contrast, the major buildings of the Renaissance were designed as the culmination of dramatic vistas or as the sculptural climax of the city's urban massing. The fact that the new architecture constituted a radical aesthetic departure from the medieval fabric of the existing city heightened the effect of creating a visual counterpoint. The colors of the Gothic city were predominantly earthen hues of orange, brown, and ochre. The same clay from which bricks were made was often used for roof tiles, and the stucco that covered many facades was routinely mixed with dust from the bricks to color it. The tints of the medieval city, literally, came from the same earth. Against this palette, the classical white stone facades of Renaissance buildings were a blaze of light, and the organic rhythms of the Venetian city were punctuated with the distinctive bright notes of the new architectural aesthetic.

As classically designed churches and *scuole* (most *scuole* had their own building, symbols of their piety and good works, sometimes of grandiose design) rose in prominent places in numerous campos, the city became a place of visual surprise. During the Renaissance, architects came to be valued as artist-intellectuals. As a result, the new buildings, responding to the eccentric angles and massing of the city, embodied a heightened degree of compositional invention. Around a blind corner the mass of the city would unexpectedly open up and white Renaissance structures would come into view, conspicuous and in sharp contrast to the vernacular medieval context.

The decisive transformation would occur at the center of the city, in the piazza and piazzetta of San Marco and the Doges' Palace. The basin of San Marco was the geographic location in the configuration of Venice where several islands were separated by wide expanses of water. (The distances between islands ranged from a quarter-mile to a mile.) Looking out across the basin from the center, one saw an urban panorama of water, ships, and islands. Looking back toward Saint Mark's, one saw the formal entrance to the heart of Venice.

Over a period of about two hundred years, from the late fifteenth century to the late seventeenth century, some of Italy's greatest architects designed masterworks that captured both ends of these vistas. On the outward islands opposite Saint Mark's, three major buildings—beacons of elevated architectural conception—punctuated the horizon: the churches of San Giorgio Maggiore and the Redentore (the Redeemer), both by Palladio, and the church of Santa Maria della Salute by Baldassare Longhena. Large and arresting, the great churches spoke of the wealth, reverence, and enlightened patronage of the city-state. The eye was riveted by the sophistication and majesty of their proportions. Next to Santa Maria della Salute, the government erected a Customs House whose design united with the sculptural shapes of the church

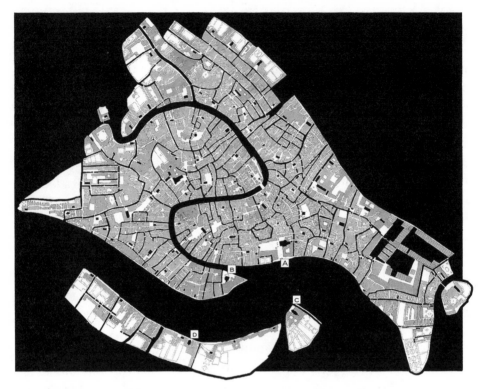

The canals, islands, and churches of Venice · When canals and other water bodies are drawn in black, the urban structure of the settlement becomes evident. Initially each island was a parish unto itself, with a church facing a central campo with a cistern and well (religious buildings—churches, monasteries, and *scuole*—are shown as small black shapes). As Venice prospered and grew, its cityscape became more densely compacted and varied in its organization. During the Renaissance, the settlement's organic medieval order was embellished by long orchestrated architectural vistas—not cut through the urban fabric as in Paris, but seen across bodies of water. (For greater detail see illustration, page 219.) A: The Piazza, Piazzetta, and Church of Saint Mark's. B: Church of Maria della Salute. C: Church of San Giorgio Maggiore. D: Church of the Redentore.

to dramatically terminate the architectural massing of the island of Zattere. The combined effect of these important monumental constructions transformed the city into a stage set for its own pageantry.

At the heart of Venice was created one of the most subtle and compelling public spaces in urban history. For several centuries an eccentrically configured L-shaped plaza had existed in front of Saint Mark's (the Piazza San Marco) and along the side of the Doges' Palace (the Piazzetta San Marco) facing out to the Grand Canal and the harbor. A large and beautiful campanile had been built where these two plazas merged. This was by far the tallest structure in the city, marking the central significance of the plazas to the ceremonial and public life of the metropolis. (Its striking design would influence the shape of urban towers throughout history.) The lines of the piazza and piazzetta were not precisely parallel or perpendicular; nor were the major structures geometrically centered. The arrangement was organic, having developed in response to both the geomorphic lines of the city's canals and a medieval architectural conception of space.

But during the Renaissance, the piazza and piazzetta were rationalized through the construction of classically inspired structures along the perimeter of the plaza—except to the east, where the church and palace were situated. Although the new structures were actually separate buildings, they all adopted a similar architectural approach: the new walls of the plaza were knit into a continuous horizontal perimeter of repetitive bays in white Istrian stone, with arched openings, rows of equidistant columns, and an open arcade along the ground floor. A simple shift in plan was also accomplished. The piazza and piazzetta were both widened so that the campanile stood apart as an independent structure and the facade of San Marco was situated more on center to the piazza. A mysterious but powerful contrast had been achieved. For centuries afterward, visitors from around the world would be seduced by the unquantifiable magic of the space. The irregular angles of the organic city had been reconciled with the rationalized Renaissance stage set, and the intersection of the several different architectural traditions of the cosmopolitan city, accrued over the centuries of the city's life, were brought together in a potent artistic totality. Standing at the juncture of the piazza and piazzetta, in the shadow of the golden facade of San Marco, with the distant image of San Giorgio Maggiore suspended above the lagoon, one could see the evidence of an uncommon moment of cultural achievement in the history of cities and civilizations.

THE CITY IMPERILED BY WATER

By the end of the sixteenth century, Vasco da Gama had encircled Africa, Magellan had sailed around the tip of South America, and Sir Francis Drake had circumnavigated the globe—establishing new routes to the trade of Asia. Maritime dominance began to shift to such Atlantic seafaring nations as Portugal, Spain, Holland, and Great Britain. The seeds of Venice's decline had been sown, but it would take centuries to deplete the city's extensive wealth and wide holdings.

In 1797, after a thousand years of continuous self-government and many decades of economic stagnation, Napoleon terminated the republic. Under the French, the Austrians, the kingdom of Italy (through World War I and a worldwide depression), and the Fascists (before and during World War II), and then as subject to the complex and overly bureaucratic administrative apparatus of the modern nation of Italy (which between 1949 and 1974 had thirty-six parliamentary governments), the ability of the city to determine its own destiny and rationally plan its modernization was compromised. The continuous program of dredging the canals and monitoring the lagoon faltered and broke down.

Napoleon closed many of the republic's institutions, as well as numerous churches and monasteries, often abandoning such buildings to decades of neglect. The emperor also had the west side of the Piazza San Marco rebuilt as a more integrated part of the enclosure around the public space, which he is reputed to have called "the finest drawing room in Europe." The French, Austrians, and Italians all endeavored to widen the medieval pedestrian-circulation network by filling in numerous canals. Meanwhile, the economic marginality of both Italy and Venice made it impossible to maintain the city's extensive public and private architectural and artistic holdings. For more than a century, the city was exposed to unchecked deterioration.

In 1850 a causeway was constructed across the lagoon, and the metropolis was linked by train to the rest of industrialized Europe. Venice had long been an important stop on the grand continental tour and the direct railway connection further increased the number of visitors. More hotels were constructed, and tourism gradually became the most vital growth sector of the struggling urban economy. In 1932 an automotive causeway was built adjacent to the train line, but the enormously complex task of creating a circulation system for cars within the historic city was not attempted.

The Gothic city resisted modernization. The expense of building in the lagoon was one reason. Architecturally, the much larger scale of contemporary industrialized development and its corresponding need for modernized urban infrastructure were extremely difficult to reconcile with the delicate and intertwined fabric of the small-scale historic city. As income from tourism increased, the economic motive for conservation became evident, and the city was faced with a vicious circle: Without a revitalized economy, Venice could not afford to maintain its precious body. Tourism in itself would not rejuvenate the city. Yet the introduction of industrialized architecture would mar the beautiful object that visitors traveled from afar to admire.

After World War II, the rapid transformation of modern Italy into a major industrial power expanded the Venetian agglomeration in its mainland boroughs of Mestre and Maghera. The port of Venice was renovated, and deep cuts were made in the bed of the lagoon to accommodate contemporary transoceanic shipping. The expansion of heavy industry also brought higher pollution levels, a rising regional population, and a suburban residential ring. In 1966 the floods came.

Disastrous high tides resulting from torrential storms that inundated northern Italy focused the world's attention on the peril of both Florence and Venice. The national government called for the help of UNESCO. An emergency team of international experts found much more than the damage caused by a fleeting natural disaster: a treasure of civilization was on the verge of extinction. The makeshift modernization and poverty of Venice had brought about a complex and interwoven set of social, economic, environmental, political, and ecological problems. These were being propelled to a crisis by an alarming physical fact: Venice was sinking.

The city whose unique significance had developed from its favorable relationship to an aquatic environment was now being destroyed by the water that surrounded it. Since its creation, the historic city had been slowly descending into the lagoon, due to the pressure its urban constructions exerted on the layer of clay beneath its foundations. Careful examination after the floods revealed that the rate of sinking had drastically escalated in the modern era. UNESCO scientists located the cause.

Deep below the *caranto,* in the geological formation beneath the city, was a pressurized water aquifer. Modern manufacturing in Mestre had been withdrawing large amounts of water from artesian wells, which decreased the internal pressure within the formation. As this geological structure compressed, Venice was being pulled downward. Residential artesian wells among the expanded mainland population added to the problem. Since the edges of the city's islands had been built close to water level in order to facilitate the transfer of goods between ships and warehouses, slight variations in the elevation of the islands had dire consequences, allowing high tides to sweep inland across piazzas and into buildings. Scientists also feared that global warming would intensify the problem.

As the lower portions of buildings became more regularly exposed to the waters of the lagoon, moisture rose upward within masonry walls via capillary action. At the same time, factories were emitting airborne pollutants that coated the exteriors of buildings and turned to acid when wet. Bricks and stonework throughout the city were corroding. Inside buildings, rising moisture was damaging priceless artworks integrated into interior surfaces. Prevalent saltwater had always been a threat to the preservation of the city. Now modern atmospheric pollution and centuries of lack of maintenance quickened the damage (modern pollution, deferred maintenance, and environmental imbalance in a desert similarly constitute an omnipresent attack on the historic buildings of Islamic Cairo). UNESCO's initial study identified over a thousand artworks and hundreds of major and minor historic structures in immediate jeopardy.

Intensified wave action caused by motorboats in the lagoon was accelerating the physical deterioration of stone foundations bordering the canals. Exhaust from residential heating was worsening the air pollution. Droppings from Venice's vast flocks of pigeons contributed to the erosion of stone architectural features. Agricultural pollution was draining into the rivers that emptied into the lagoon. Industrial waste added more contamination to the estuary, as did oil spills from tankers. Many canals had silted up, causing septic systems to malfunction and substantial levels of raw human waste to leak into the lagoon.

During the summer months algae and scum proliferated in the city's narrower canals, due to the increased density of nutrients in the water. This process, known as eutrophication, depleted the canals of the oxygen that supports aquatic life and caused them to fill with decomposing matter. The streets filled with noxious gases during the height of tourist season. Eventually the fumes became so intense that, in extreme conditions, many residents and visitors had to be hospitalized.

Out in the harbor, deepened channels for modern sea traffic had heightened tidal action. This had speeded erosion, and shallow areas in the middle of the lagoon were being swept away. The roots of sea grass growing in these shoals had helped retain the soil; the removal of sea grass though the washing away of shoals further hastened underwater erosion. Meanwhile, large areas of saltwater marshland on the edges of the lagoon had been filled in for industrial purposes. Now toxic industrial and agricultural waste was further attacking the animal and plant life of the natural marshland cycle that cleaned the water. Fish farming was inhibiting the tidal flow that was part of the purification process. As the volume of waste increased, the estuary was becoming less and less effective at processing it. The lagoon was becoming both too deep and too shallow. While the city's canals were choking, the center of the lagoon was evolving into a bay in which waves increased in strength, further jeopardizing the city. Centuries earlier, the features of the natural environment had favored Venice. In the modern era, the human settlement was attacking nature, and nature was attacking back. A negative downward spiral had been activated, and the ecological balance of the city had been lost.

Because these problems were interrelated, they all had to be dealt with. Every one of them either required very expensive solution, such as overhauling the heating systems of the city, or would levy a substantial toll on emerging industries—forcing manufacturers to find new water sources, for example. And extensive action had to be taken without delay or an extraordinary heritage would be lost. But Venice could not generate the astronomical amounts of money that were needed. Nor could the city or the Italian government command the army of scientists and technicians that were required.

As has often happened, the help of UNESCO was indispensable. The marshaling of international aid to save the heritage of humankind may seem a commonplace occurrence in the world we now inhabit, but this is a recent phenomenon. To name but the major operations, between 1960 and 1990, the UNESCO Cultural Heritage Division mounted international campaigns to save the following:

· the monuments of Nubia (Egypt)
· the city of Venice
· the archaeological site of Carthage (Tunisia)
· the temple of Borobodur (Indonesia)
· the archaeological site of Moenjodaro (Pakistan)
· the Acropolis of Athens
· the cultural heritage of Katmandu (Nepal)
· the cultural heritage of Montenegro (Yugoslavia)
· the city of Fez (Morocco)
· the historic buildings of Malta
· the cultural heritage of Sri Lanka
· the historic sites of the island of Goree (Senegal)
· the historic city of Sukhothai (Thailand)
· the city of Hue (Vietnam)
· the ancient cities of Mauritania
· the historic monuments of Istanbul
· the site of Goreme (Turkey)
· the old city of Havana
· the historic cities of Sana'a and Shibam (Yemen)
· the monuments of Paharpur Vihara (Bangladesh)
· the historic sites of Guatemala
· the historic city of San Francisco de Lima (Peru)
· the Jesuit missions of Argentina, Brazil, and Paraguay
· the artistic heritage of Ethiopia
· the historic sites of Haiti

The existence of an institution that constantly amasses the most current technical expertise to alleviate threats to the world's heritage, and that has the political credibility to call for public assistance from many countries, is an invention of the twentieth century. That the people of wealthier nations contribute to the preservation of cultures foreign to their own marks a major step in the evolution of civilization. The saving of Venice was one of the earliest and has been among the greatest of these campaigns, perhaps because the glory of the city and the tragedy of its loss were so indisputably apparent.

Once UNESCO declared a state of emergency, spontaneous offers of help quickly came from around the world. Thirty-five separate organizations participated in the campaign: they came from Australia, Belgium, Canada, Denmark, France, Germany, Iran, Luxembourg, the Netherlands, Sweden, Switzerland, the United Kingdom, and the United States. Twenty private groups within Italy also collected and channeled contributions to the work.

Galvanizing worldwide public support was crucial to overcoming the single greatest obstacle to the preservation of the city: the administrative perversity of the Italian bureaucracy. The giant governmental machine of the modern Italian nation was legendary for its labyrinthine complexity and for the culture of illegality bred by this lack of transparency. A web of bureaucratic rules concealed the actions of politicians and administrators whose kickbacks and siphoning of public funds have been estimated at $6 billion to $12 billion a year. The public was defrauded and victimized, as were the many dedicated Italian civil servants who were frustrated in their endeavors to make their government productive. Saving Venice would require long-range planning at national and regional levels as well as the enactment of special laws and appropriations, and the coordinated action of numerous branches of government. As a result, the untangling of Italy's bureaucracy was a fundamental and requisite first step.

UNESCO's mobilization of worldwide public opinion demonstrated that the Italian government would be widely condemned if it did not act quickly. Thus, early in the campaign to save the city, an official International Advisory Committee ensured public accountability in Venice, in Italy, and around the world. Eventually UNESCO would also be given the statutory right to participate in pertinent planning bodies. Responsible Italians collaborated with UNESCO in using moral force as a lever to effect prompt action. The process was not perfect, however. Foreign participants often marveled at the degree of interdepartmental wrangling and the intractability of different administrative organs.

A cumbersome process was activated to attempt a heroic task: the complete reconception of the city's environmental structure. A bureaucracy infamous for making simple problems complicated would now be compelled to find sophisticated solutions to a dilemma of infinite complexity. Once the analysis of the puzzle was finished and the needed actions were identified, between 1984 and 1988 more than 2.7 trillion lire (2.2 billion $U.S.) was appropriated at national, regional, provincial, and metropolitan levels. By the campaign's end, miraculous results had been achieved.

As a prominent official in the Italian government put it: "UNESCO has been both our good and our bad conscience. Our good conscience when both the highest institutions and ordinary citizens have engaged in battles that have brought significant victories. Our bad conscience, on the other hand, if we call to mind the delays, the neglect, the broken promises, the violations in the name of consumerism. Our conscience, but not ours alone: any problem or proposal that affects Venice mobilizes public opinion the world over; alliances are formed and decision-making processes become of necessity more transparent, with the involvement of experts, public figures, and the world's press."

As a result of in-depth studies by teams of international and Italian experts, regional planning was instituted to reduce industrial and agricultural air and water pollution at their sources. A prohibition was enacted that stopped industry from drawing water from the artesian system. Aqueducts were constructed to provide new sources of water. Domestic heating plants throughout the city were converted from oil to gas fuel. The citywide infrastructure of septic tanks and sewers was expanded and rehabilitated. Higher standards for the maintenance of historic buildings were mandated. Movable works of art were placed in the controlled climatic environments of museums.

The continuous program of cleaning the canals was reinstituted, and a sophisticated monitoring effort was launched to deal with the complex environmental determinants affecting the modern lagoon. Fish farming and other commercial operations in the estuary were once again controlled by the city. In areas where the lagoon had been filled to create dry ground for industrial uses, channels were cut through the landmasses to reinstate a more natural pattern of tidal flow. More effective saltwater barriers were constructed along the Adriatic coastline. The flow of water from the mainland via rivers was carefully managed. Deepwater shipping was restricted. The shorelines of Venice's islands were refurbished to limit the penetration of normal high tides (*aqua alta*) onto pavements and into the ground floors of buildings.

New environmental programs were activated. The interdependent qualities of the natural ecosystem had been recognized. Marshlands and shallow areas of sea grass were reestablished in the lagoon. Large parts of the estuary were designated as wildlife sanctuaries in order to protect the variety of creatures linked by the natural food chain. As had been first recognized by the city's early inhabitants, "element" was made to oppose "element" and environmental equilibrium was achieved once more. When internal pressure was regained in the aquifer, Venice actually rose.

With this wide expanse of problems attended to, international congresses of conservation specialists were held to determine how best to restore the city's artifacts. Since the environmental conditions of Venice were unique, special techniques had to be developed. Each painting, mural, fresco, sculpture, mosaic, and architectural detail had to be treated with meticulous care: these artifacts were priceless, irreplaceable, and often frail. Specialized workshops, schools, and laboratories with the most sophisticated equipment were set up. The artistic wealth of the city represented the accumulated endeavors, across many centuries, of numerous artists, architects, and craftsmen. In the same way, the threatened physical material of the modern city would be saved by the accumulated endeavors, across millions of hours, of a legion of dedicated conservators.

By 1992 foreign cash donations for the restoration of art and architecture totaled around $16 million. About $64 million was directly spent on the conservation of art and architecture by the Italian government. Over 80 monuments and more than 800 works of art were saved by the international committees, yet the greater significance of international participation was much more than monetary. The science, techniques, and standards established as groups from around the world adopted Venetian monuments and lovingly restored them, were a model for how to proceed. They were also a manifestation of the belief that the culture of Venice was the culture of all humankind.

THE THREAT OF TOURISM

From the beginning of the international campaign, a long-range problem occupied the mind of everyone involved. The most egregious conditions of deterioration could be stabilized; negative environmental conditions could be reversed. But a careful program of ongoing maintenance was necessary if the historic cityscape was to be preserved for generations to come. Venice had to be able to maintain itself. And here was the dilemma. The most viable economy of the modern metropolis, the economy of tourism, was making Venice unlivable for residents. Who would maintain the city if no one lived in it?

An astonishingly complex maintenance effort was needed, requiring close coordination between the municipal government and building owners. Deferred maintenance was endangering virtually every building in the city, and would continue to do so for as long as Venice was subject to salt, water, and waves. Since rising dampness and the decay in foundations and lower stories was the principal problem, the upkeep of buildings was tied to the continuous cycle of maintaining the canals. As parts of the city were isolated by temporary dams and canals were drained for dredging, it was possible to rehabilitate foundations. At that moment, several important operations could be performed: Damaged piles could be restored. New stone or masonry could be inserted in areas of extreme decay that were normally below water level. Shifting foundations and sections of uneven settlement could be corrected. And once a building's substructure was stabilized, damage due to uneven sinking could be rectified in upper stories. As a preventive measure, an imper-meable sill of silicone could be implanted into and all the way around a build-ing's base, to block the rising of dampness in walls. This was difficult and costly but highly effective. Afterward, plaster could be removed from masonry walls for the first three feet above the protective sill (the zone of highest exposure to saltwater infiltration), allowing the structure to breathe and dry out. And while the canals were drained, corrections to septic tanks and sewage systems could be introduced.

Since most of the buildings in the historic city had at least one elevation facing a canal, and because it was otherwise costly to isolate a single building for repairs to its foundation, timing a building's rehabilitation to coincide with the draining of canals was an important cost-saving economy. Under the republic, a single cycle of dredging the lagoons had taken twenty years. It was the hope of the modern municipality that the contemporary cycle could be achieved in eight to nine years. The city would pay for canal maintenance, but the owners of buildings were responsible for the costs of building conservation and upkeep. Yet even when this complex program of repairs was achieved, across Venice further severe injury to buildings was nonetheless accumulating because of a lack of normal residential building maintenance.

For many years, numerous buildings had been neglected. Because the structures of the historic city had been engineered to be highly flexible and light in weight, and to resist uneven settlement, Venetian buildings could sus-tain substantial damage without failing. Rarely had these buildings collapsed, even from the tremors of earthquakes, and Venetians well understood that their buildings could tolerate much abuse. After the campaign to rectify the major environmental problems, however, numerous small injuries to struc-tures had been left unfixed throughout the city, and major damage either had already occurred or was in progress. Substantial parts of the city were on their way to falling apart. The magnitude of deferred maintenance was astronomical and rising.

Why was Venice not being maintained? The answer was not simply a matter of money.

Cities cannot be sustained if they do not have a constituency to support the quality of life. The environment of the city is complex and dependent on many circumstances that are constantly changing and acting simultane-ously. Ultimately, life in a city is too complicated to be objectively defined or engineered: it has to be experienced holistically. When people live in a city and experience its quality of life day and night, across seasons, years, and decades, the populace makes the urban environment a fit place in which to exist. When a city is inhabited, its residents have a stake in the character of the urban continuum.

In Venice, tourism was attacking many of the qualities that make a city habitable, and residents were being pushed out. So many people fled that soon there would not be enough inhabitants to protect many of the pleasant details of life in the city. The widespread failure to maintain buildings was a reflection of this social phenomenon. The historic city was not being repaired because too few Venetians actually lived in Venice and were subject to its conditions.

For decades the city's residential population had been decreasing—from 178,000 in 1945, to 145,000 in 1960, to 92,000 in 1981. Because there was little space in which to erect new buildings in the historic center, most contemporary public housing was constructed on the nearby islands of Guidecca and Murano and in mainland areas such as Mestre. By 1995, about 70,000 people lived on the islands of historic Venice, as compared to 300,000 people living in other areas of the municipality. Venetians living in Venice no longer constituted a voting majority in their city government.

Like the interconnected problems of the lagoon's ecology, the reasons for the decline in residential population were many and interrelated. Because of Venice's long economic stagnation, the quality of housing in much of the historic city was poor. In 1975, of the 39,400 residential buildings in the city, some 12,400, or 31 percent, urgently required repairs. Especially on ground-level floors, the increasingly high tides escalated the amount of rising damp and heightened the degree of discomfort within dwellings until 15.5 percent of dwellings suffered from extreme dampness. As residents began to compare their lot to that of residents in more modern housing, the lack of daylight resulting from the city's closely packed buildings came to be considered a liability (13.5 percent of the city's apartments needed electric lighting in nearly every room for many hours of the day).

The success and volume of tourism in proportion to the size of the city raised the value of real estate so that only the wealthy and the subsidized poor could afford to live in historic Venice. By 1995 some 7 million tourists a year, or about 20,000 visitors a day, came to the city. The nonsubsidized middle class was being squeezed out by the higher property prices and rents paid by hotels, restaurants, gift shops, and other stores that catered to visitors. In addition, as a greater percentage of career opportunities were located outside the historic center through the construction of industrial complexes in mainland areas, hard-pressed middle-class families moved to cheaper but more modern housing situated closer to their workplaces.

With fewer and fewer families living in the city center, the demand lessened for shops providing groceries, hardware, housewares, dry cleaning, and toiletries, and the income of such businesses declined, making it difficult for them to compete with the rising real estate prices produced by tourism. A vicious circle was created. As the businesses that catered to residential needs decreased, the quality of life for residents grew worse. More residents left. More shops serving residents closed. Soon, in many neighborhoods, schools closed, and children had to travel farther across the city to go to class and to find friends to play with. More people moved, and residential amenities declined further.

Many of those who still lived in the city were elderly with fixed incomes. As real estate prices rose, they couldn't afford to stay in their apartments. The municipal authorities banned evictions, endeavoring to protect the poor and elderly living in private rental dwellings. As a result, the owners of such buildings were unable to benefit from rising property values by either leasing at higher prices or selling. The economic incentive to rehabilitate such restricted properties was lost. A black market in housing developed. Students from the two universities in Venice were willing to rent without a lease, and about 10,000 apartments were occupied illegally. In other cases, landlords sought tenants who were not residents of Venice and therefore not protected by the city's ban on evictions. Currently, authorities estimate that 70 percent of the available private rental housing of the city is occupied by nonresidents. Many of the city's wealthier real estate owners used their lodgings part-time, or simply bought properties as investments and purposely kept them vacant. By 1995 about 14 percent of the dwellings in the central city were unoccupied, and 75 percent of these were being warehoused until real estate prices rose higher.

At the height of the tourist season, visitors to Venice sometimes outnumbered the inhabitants (as many as 100,000 tourists, as compared to 70,000 permanent residents). Tourists jammed the city's vaporettos, clogged its alleyways, and filled its restaurants. Many Venetians working in the city were inconvenienced. A substantial percentage of inhabitants could not afford the entertainment that foreigners enjoyed.

Meanwhile, with the end of the campaign and the resolution of the immediate threats to Venice, the habitual byzantine machinations of the bureaucracy commenced once again. Major amounts of the funds allocated for the conservation of historic properties and their conversion to modern subsidized housing are not being released. A system of much-needed dikes to protect the lagoon from the higher tides due to global warming and the greenhouse effect is not being constructed, after years of careful research and successful testing.

That governments left to their own devices can become counterproductive is not unusual. But how can a municipal government be pushed to act responsibly, when there are no constituents to pressure it? The current administration continues to be subject to undue influence from the tourist lobby and from those who benefit from the existing conditions. Today the UNESCO Liaison Office for the Safeguarding of Venice continues to coordinate the twenty-four member bodies that are still striving to conserve the city's cultural treasures. Yet the volume of necessary work far exceeds the goodwill of people from abroad.

The inhabitants of the great city at the center of a vast empire were once proud to identify themselves as Venetians. They were Venice, and Venice was they. Until the modern governments of Italy and Venice direct their whole-hearted energies to increasing the number of Venetians who live in the historic city, it will not be truly saved. But when Venetians once again have an immediate stake in the character of the historic urban environment, at all times of night and day, during every season, over decades, then the innumerable positive acts that inhabitants devise to make a city livable will be unleashed. Only the same degree of creativity that produced Venice can save it, and no city can be saved unless it is loved. It can be cherished from afar and helped from afar, but it can be preserved only by people who love it from inside.

CHAPTER TWELVE

POLITICS AND PRESERVATION IN THE MODERN METROPOLIS

NEW YORK

Overturn, overturn, overturn! is the maxim of New York. The very bones of our ancestors are not permitted to be quiet a quarter of a century, and one generation of men seem studious to remove all relics of those which preceded them.

—EDITORIAL, *Harper's Weekly*, 1869

When people list the wonders of modern New York, they are usually referring to the glittering towers of the island of Manhattan, where the Empire State Building, the United Nations, the World Trade Center, the Metropolitan Museum of Art, the Guggenheim Museum, the Broadway theaters, Wall Street, SoHo, Chinatown, Greenwich Village, and Central Park are located. Even among its inhabitants, New York is commonly divided into "the city" and "the outer boroughs"— Brooklyn, Queens, the Bronx, and Staten Island, which together with Manhattan constitute the official metropolitan area.

When I was growing up in the outer borough of Staten Island, going into the city meant taking a ferryboat across the harbor, past the Statue of Liberty, to the tip of Lower Manhattan—a journey from quiet and greenery to densely packed tall steel and concrete, flashing neon lights, speeding yellow cabs, honking horns, rumbling subways, hurry, excitement, anonymity, high culture, honky-tonk, jostle, grit, glamour, and worldly sophistication. When neighbors returned from a visit to "the city," lengthy descriptions were needed to account for the many astonishing recent transformations of the metropolis. It seemed we could never quite establish an image of Manhattan in our minds, before it was overturned yet again.

For residents and visitors alike, New York is a place of unending change—moving faster, growing taller, altering fashion, exploding with ideas, perpetually in pursuit of new ways to make more money, and attracting successive waves of international immigrants that enrich the city's social alchemy. It is the speculative developer's dream; a place of conspicuous consumption and enormous wealth, whose geological substructure, liberal zoning, and modern construction industry will sustain buildings of almost any height imaginable. And because in the minds of New Yorkers there is no end in sight, the city knows few limits; it habitually grows on top of itself, tearing down old buildings to erect new and higher ones. This primal urge to expand upward causes many sudden changes of elevation, with the result that New York has perhaps more exposed, undeveloped building sidewalls than any other city in the world. On these masonry surfaces, decades-old commercial advertising is a fading chronicle of changing habits of consumption, speculation, and mercantile invention. Some lots of the metropolis, particularly those in the center of lower Manhattan, have been built up, reduced, and reconstituted at a greater height three, four, five times and more in the past three hundred years.

New York was a major center of the modern world for much of the twentieth century. Its enormous wealth, considerable architectural talent, lofty dreams, and the unapologetic ambitions of a surging American civilization produced thousands of noteworthy buildings and numerous gracious neighborhoods. Many of these have been victims of the speed of transformation. For most of the city's history, few architectural accomplishments have been considered so illustrious that New York would avert its gaze from the opportunity yet to be realized by building something newer.

FROM COLONY TO MEGALOPOLIS

Since its founding in 1624 by the Dutch West India Company (the city was called Nieuw Amsterdam before being given its current name by the English), on the southern square mile at the tip of the island of Manhattan that faces out to the harbor, New York had avidly pursued commercial growth, securing a singular geographic advantage in 1825 with the construction of an inland water route connecting the city to the Great Lakes region. The Erie Canal, industrialization, and cheap immigrant labor enabled New York to become a major manufacturing, financial, and trading center. And as the city grew, it became architecturally ingenious as well—erecting in the late nineteenth and early twentieth centuries increasingly higher structures that freely adapted European building styles in gradually more advanced construction technologies.

With the advent of the skyscraper, building after building staked its claim as the world's tallest edifice, yet the city's low districts and high peaks retained a binding visual relationship through their shared architectural roots. The pinnacles of tall office buildings—utilizing advances in structural steel skeletons, elevators, fireproofing, heating and ventilation, plumbing, lighting, machine-powered construction equipment, and mass-manufactured building parts—were imaginatively crowned like Gothic cathedrals, Florentine palazzi, Venetian campaniles, Byzantine churches, French châteaux, Parisian department stores, and Greek and Roman temples. Lofty new apartment buildings similarly borrowed a wide variety of forms from historic architectural sources. Cast-iron manufacturing buildings—precursors to rolled-steel, metal-frame, curtain-wall towers—were commonly in the Italianate style. The giant department stores of Ladies Mile showcased the French Second Empire. Quiet low-scale residential enclaves derived their appearance from styles like the French Beaux-Arts, English Tudor, Gothic Revival, Georgian, Spanish Mission, Anglo-Italianate, Queen Anne, Neo-Grec, Renaissance Revival, Romanesque Revival, and Greek Revival. A particular American architecture had developed from large new building types, advanced construction technology, and the eclectic artistic fusion of modern and foreign historic styles. New York became as diverse in its forms as its multiethnic population. The exploding high-rise industrial city—although often ragged in its abrupt changes of height—nonetheless appeared to be evolving toward an implausible urban coherence aided by a continuity of materials (being predominantly built of masonry and glass), a marriage of styles (because the design of the vast majority of buildings referred to some degree to historic architectural antecedents), and most significantly, by adherence to the sculptural framework of the giant grid of Manhattan, which seemed to have the potential of melding unrestrained leaps of architectural creativity into a new urban order.

It was a place not seen before in civilization, where human inventiveness appeared to have broken free of earthbound limitations. As exuberant American industrial cities vaulted to unprecedented heights in the history of urban environments—limited for millennia to the four, five, six, or seven stories it was feasible to climb by stairs—places like New York and Chicago became packed at their centers with twelve-, sixteen-, and twenty-story buildings. And when Chicago set a limit to the height of its skyscrapers, the unimpeded corporations and speculators of New York lifted their skyline to fifty and sixty stories and more. The Empire State Building reached eighty-five stories, and the twin towers of the World Trade Center rose to 110 stories. And at a one point there were more sixty-story buildings in Manhattan than in the rest of the world's great cities put together.

The resulting density required New York to be in the forefront of advances in urban infrastructure, a pioneer in the construction of modern transportation and communication systems, and in the regional planning of large metropolitan areas. In the central business districts of Manhattan, armies of workers labored among the clouds, and when the day's exertions were done, at rush hour, a vast network of subways (the largest system in the world), highways (the largest network prior to Los Angeles in the 1970s), bridges (three of which were at the time of their construction the longest ever constructed), tunnels, and commuter trains—linked to a host of elevators—helped to speed astonishing masses of people through jammed and ever more deeply shadowed canyon avenues. By the end of the twentieth century, the city itself had grown to 8 million inhabitants, while the agglomeration around it held about 18 million.

The greatest American modern metropolis became a world center of culture, commerce, and government. In its numerous handsomely endowed institutions—a vast public library system, preeminent hospitals, museums, theaters, concert halls, and universities—and a broad offering of social services unequaled by any other municipality in the United States, the city was a showcase of American democracy and a beacon of opportunity. Millions of people were drawn from foreign shores and, as described by Peter Hall in *Cities of Tomorrow,* New York became "the greatest city of immigrants in the world, with half as many Italians as Naples, as many Germans as Hamburg, twice as many Irish as Dublin, and two and a half times as many Jews as Warsaw."

FROM FRACTURING TO CONSERVATION

Modern architecture, modern planning, and post–World War II expansion would alter the aesthetic evolution of the human-made agglomeration. Steel and glass office buildings with spare rectilinear curtain walls—set in plazas and no longer aligned with traditional street walls—introduced a new and disquieting urban geometry. As the economic formulas of speculative builders minimized exterior architectural investment in large modern buildings, with the rare exception of such marvelous works as the Seagram Building and Lever House, a legion of aesthetically impoverished structures infiltrated the cityscape. Poorly designed in their exterior skin, they were clumsily massed as volumes, and crudely situated in relation to neighboring buildings. Slum clearance in poorer residential neighborhoods of Manhattan—on the Lower

East Side and in Harlem, for example—led to massive tracts of modern housing that also disregarded the old urban pattern and, when subsidized for the poor, was cheaply made and of empty monotonous design. The next wave of ostensibly bigger and better replacement structures, abruptly dropped into place as if by a less imaginative civilization, began to render cacophonous a cityscape whose potential for unity had been only partly realized.

Two negative trends were occurring simultaneously—a generation of urbanistically jarring and dissociated architecture was being erected across the cityscape, and handsome historic buildings that complied with old traditions were being removed. In many parts of New York, the possibility of urban architectural coherence now seemed beyond attainment. Social incoherence became manifest in racially divisive slums that looked as if they'd been battered by aerial bombardment. Crime rates and environmental pollution increased. Numerous areas on the fringes of the metropolis—where highways, train tracks, industry, and commercial strips were jammed ad hoc between spurts of cheap postwar speculative residential development—acquired a numbing disorder and ugliness. The municipal government declared bankruptcy. Demographic trends shifted, and increasing numbers of people deserted the city for its suburbs, fearing that the giant metropolis had become too large to be managed.

In 1965, New York instituted a Landmarks Preservation Commission with broad powers to save some of the beauty under threat of erasure by a loosely reined speculative real estate market. The new commission was given comprehensive authority to designate and regulate individual landmarks, historic districts, interiors, and parklands—a far more complete degree of oversight than had been granted to similar bodies in many major European cities that had long ago begun the effort to conserve their patrimony. A cultural awareness counter to the heritage of perpetual change was introduced.

Building by building, in a typical participatory American democratic forum, the conservation effort unfolded. Anyone could have a say in open public hearings on every important issue, and these meetings sometimes lasted fourteen or fifteen hours. From across the metropolis, people from all walks of life came to City Hall to join in the conversation: millionaires, socialites, celebrities, and immigrant shopkeepers; mothers, fathers, grandparents, and schoolchildren; respected academics, amateur experts, realtors, politicians, contractors, lawyers, laborers, and world-renowned architects.

Would the city's culture of constant change accommodate the saving of beauty and history as unchangeable fixtures of the future? Again and again, opponents to heritage conservation raised the most damning criticism known to New Yorkers: "Preservationists are freezing the city in time, making it a museum, and stifling economic growth!" Could the unrestrained metropolis learn restraint? Could grace, harmony, and meaning, once achieved, be allowed to accrue?

THE POLITICS OF DEFINING CULTURAL VALUE

As the official process of preservation began, New Yorkers commonly recognized many of the human-made marks on the land that gave the city pride and cultural individuality. They knew the built environment from living in it, across the span of their lives, in the different seasons of the year, and by the changing light of each day. In addition, among educated experts, there was wide agreement as to which structures deserved to be officially designated as landmarks and protected forever. Purely as a matter of architectural and historic knowledge, designating properties for protection would have been an uncomplicated formality. Yet in practice, application of the conservation statute was fraught with political and legal complexities.

Difficulty arose out of an elementary fact: heritage cannot be saved if it is torn down. Hence the primary task of conservation is to restrict the right of property owners to dispose of notable buildings in ways that damage or destroy them. But in a city that had constantly grown upward, where many structures were not built to their full allowable height, numerous owners—while making good use of historic properties at their current size—dreamed of a financial windfall at some future date. At that point, a historic building was often altered, enlarged, or demolished in order to create a bigger structure in its place. This too was part of the culture of the city and a prevalent way of investing money on the part of both business owners and residents: buy a building, improve it, live in it, and sell it at a profit. In addition, many businesses periodically required extensive interior and exterior renovations in response to changing technological, social, and design trends. As a result, many owners, even when sympathetic to the general idea of landmarks conservation, vigorously opposed designation of their own properties.

Since landmarks are often valuable or located in expensive parts of the city's center, their owners are often wealthy, wielding potent political influence on behalf of their interests. Whereas members of the Landmarks Commission were appointed for fixed terms of three years, like judges, all were subject to reappointment and confirmation by the mayor and popularly elected members of the City Council. The chair of the commission served at the discretion of the city's chief executive. And although the commission's power to regulate changes to historic structures could be overturned only by the courts—an extremely rare occurrence—such authority came to apply only after the designation of landmarks and historic districts had been confirmed by other bodies of elected officials, a function first undertaken by the Board of

Estimate and, in recent years, by the City Council. While this system of checks and balances protected against abuses of power by the commission, the involvement of career politicians introduced the possibility of public office-holders wielding their authority for the benefit of private interests.

In 1988 an investigation by the New York State Commission on Government Integrity substantiated that all important elected municipal officials receive contributions to their campaigns from major developers, landowners, and businesses in the city. When asked about the effect of such donations, one of New York's most forthright chief administrators, Mayor Edward I. Koch, replied: "I'll take their calls; they won't get anything from me, but they get access." His chief political consultant added, "It's a way of saying, 'Hey waiter!' with a loud voice." The practice of purchasing special access to public officials was part of the broad political culture.

Behind closed doors and carefully hidden from scrutiny, the conservation process was recurrently subverted on behalf of private interests. During the period when the city's Board of Estimate was authorized to ratify designations, the fate of buildings in the outer boroughs was considered a parochial matter by borough presidents, who would rarely vote for confirmation in opposition to another borough president. In effect, this gave each outer-borough president a veto over the preservation procedure in his or her part of the city. Hence, the Landmarks Commission screened potential designations for clearance, commonly doing so in private rather than having a landmark officially rejected in the public record. Protected from general knowledge of their actions, outer-borough presidents could block designations in concealed negotiations where select property owners were less subject to the law than the general majority. Similarly, few generations of the Landmarks Commission would advance the designation of a structure in the face of mayoral objections, particularly when the preservation of a historic building interfered with public development initiatives supported by the mayor's office.

While obviously susceptible to the kind of influence whose special access Mayor Koch publicly acknowledged, his administration was also particularly effective at upholding important citywide designations when opposed by the borough presidents en masse. One ludicrous case that should be mentioned here involved the Broadway theaters, several of which had already been destroyed. These were situated in the center of New York, and were of extraordinary property value; their owners had lobbied vigorously in opposition to designation. At three o'clock in the morning, confirmation was deadlocked, when one of the borough presidents offered to change sides if an unusual stipulation could be met. It was required of the pro-designation alliance that a particular national television star, who had been associated with the effort to save the theaters, promise to attend the annual fund-raising event of the official's favorite local charity. Called in the middle of the night, the star agreed to the request, and the theater designations were approved. Protection of the nation's cultural legacy had been suspended by a thread of personal caprice. Upon disbandment of the Board of Estimate in 1981, comparable political dynamics would occur in the City Council as it assumed the authority to ratify designations.

Regardless of the questionable nature of such practices, enactment of the Landmarks Preservation Law had raised fundamental questions of financial equity. Who would pay for the conservation of designated structures? And should owners be compensated when the saving of a landmark forestalled the erection of a profitable new building? These issues were new to New York and constituted a dilemma that many cities have struggled to solve. In Europe, early efforts to list monuments were often accompanied by substantial financial relief from the government in the form of generous tax exemptions, low-interest loans, grants, or the outright purchase of monuments. But such policies eventually led to insurmountable problems when conservation efforts expanded beyond the protection of rarefied individual landmarks to whole historic environments, like the core of old Amsterdam, all of central Paris, or the numerous extensive great residential estates of London. No municipality in the world can afford to fully compensate the owners of every property of cultural significance. This is one of the reasons preservation of historic zones in Amsterdam, Paris, and London is currently achieved under urban planning laws rather than conservation statutes, in an effort to divorce European governments from the precedent of providing liberal subsidies.

New York solved the problem more simply and directly: it didn't offer significant financial compensation to the owners of designated properties. Justification of this approach was based on the idea that the value of urban property is not inherent in the land itself but is a function of the collective positive attributes of the human-made environment. Property value in cities is created by public investment in infrastructure—water supply, sewage removal, electrical power, telephone systems, and the vehicular circulation network—in the maintenance of mass transport, and in the provision of police and fire protection, sanitation, schools, cultural institutions, hospitals, and public parks. Value is further accrued through an infinite number of acts of environmental husbandry by the city's inhabitants: by every homeowner who maintains his or her house, by people who tend their front gardens and sweep their sidewalks, by landlords who upgrade their buildings, and by companies that maintain their properties well. Collectively, these myriad separate contributions increase the value of land in the city. In this context, the framers of New York's preservation statute considered the conservation of value bequeathed from the past—

by individuals, institutions, and developers who built with pride, by workers who fashioned buildings with skill, by architects who endowed their designs with beauty—as yet another means of expanding the cumulative worth of the metropolis. The landmarks law would "stabilize and improve property values, foster civic pride, protect the city's attractions to tourists, strengthen the economy, and promote the education, pleasure, and welfare of the people."

Nonetheless, a legal struggle loomed, threatening to undermine New York's attempt to save the beauty of the built environment. The matter was a function of the balance of governmental power in the United States. In Europe, national preservation authorities have often played a decisive role in preserving the heritage of cities, but in the United States the power to implement urban architectural preservation has predominantly rested with local governance. Federal authority to protect historic properties does conserve important archaeological and natural sites like the Grand Canyon and the pre-Columbian Indian ruins of the Southwest, monuments of great national significance, such as the Statue of Liberty and Ellis Island in New York, but national laws can safeguard only an infinitesimal portion of the total heritage of the nation, with an especially limited effect on cities. In fact, fewer than 1 percent of New York's significant properties would be protected under federal mandate.

Once the city acted to preserve its heritage, however, the legality of its effort was ultimately decided at the federal level, in the U.S. Supreme Court. Those who opposed the conservation endeavor contended that the designation of landmarks was an unjust deprivation of property value, unfairly distributed, and arbitrarily imposed on the basis of imprecise and unquantifiable standards—since in the United States, as in most societies, owners are entitled to fair compensation when a government "takes" their property to build a highway, dam, or other public work. On the other hand, when a community institutes citywide height restrictions, fire codes, or zoning regulations to protect the quality of life for all inhabitants, governments are not required to compensate every owner who is adversely affected. To varying degrees, and depending on the circumstances, landmarks preservation involved both these legal distinctions. Resolution of these issues was not clearly established by legal precedents.

Thus, as the New York commission set about the task of identifying and regulating the city's historic patrimony, it needed to achieve a difficult balance between politics and law. The metropolis was not unique in this regard. Political manipulation on behalf of private interests has affected the shape of cityscapes throughout urban history, as in the repeated failure of Roman emperors to improve their capital's vast, poorly built, and unhealthy patrician-owned tenements. Although such pressure was habitually exerted on the New York preservation process, it ultimately caused the loss of only a small portion of important historic properties, because the persistence of the public and of later administrations of the commission eventually saved many structures whose designation had initially been blocked. The greater danger lay in the degree to which it undermined rational implementation of the landmarks statute.

Consistent and fair determination of designations by a single set of objective standards was crucial in upholding the law's validity, as well as the public's confidence. And due to the serious economic consequences of restricting major properties at the center of Manhattan, and the clear legal construction of the city's statute in empowering the commission to take such action when appropriate, many authorities considered it likely that the very constitutionality of municipal landmarks preservation in the United States would be tested in the Supreme Court via a New York case.

All these circumstances made the otherwise basic scholarly task of designating significant properties ("listing" and "registering" in cities in Europe and Asia) a matter of daunting complexity. In the heat of sometimes impassioned debate, in the weighing of matters with immediate repercussions on the lives of real people, while outside officials exerted pressure on behalf of private interests, as activists ardently defended their neighborhoods, and where each decision was subject to review by both newspaper editorial boards and the courts, it was crucial that commissioners not lose sight of the ultimate goal. Though the motivations of some players might be questionable and their views narrowly defined, many of their concerns were legitimate. And if one listened carefully, through the tempest of the democratic forum, the voice of the metropolis could be heard searching to understand how certain structures embodied beauty and meaning of such enduring value that they should be protected forever. The landmarks law had caused New York to critically reexamine itself from a new perspective.

HISTORIC DISTRICTS: ARTICULATE KNOWLEDGE BECOMES POWER

A month before his death in 1963, President John Kennedy spoke of the importance of heritage conservation in the United States: "I look forward to an America which will not be afraid of grace and beauty, which will preserve the great old American houses and squares and parks of our national past, and which will build handsome and balanced cities for our future." Two years later, Jacqueline Kennedy helped lead the effort to enact the New York landmarks conservation law.

Just as the designation of medieval monuments embodied the roots of cultural identity in France in 1840, in New York in 1965 many of the first buildings to be officially protected were those from the era of the founding of the United States. Such structures were historic house museums whose preservation was already ensured, churches, or structures located at the city's outer perimeter, where property was less valuable, and their designation was popularly, legally, and politically incontestable. For Americans, this heritage represented a sacred trust that morally justified the application of the law.

But as the commission moved beyond such uniquely beloved buildings, conflicts with property rights were inevitable. Broad-based political support for conservation was needed, and it came from within the historic neighborhoods of New York. Here large numbers of residents saw the landmarks law as a mechanism by which they might protect the ambience of areas of harmoniously related historic buildings, an ambience under threat of disruption by indiscriminate speculative development and the alien architectural aesthetics that had become prevalent in the era after World War II.

Across New York, in areas that varied in size from a dozen to more than 3,000 buildings, communities began to ask for official recognition. The extent of these areas was often considerable. The Greenwich Village Historic District, for example, is comparable in size to the Altstadt of Vienna; the Upper East Side Historic District to the historic Old and New Towns of Warsaw, the Upper West Side Historic District to the Old City of Jerusalem, and the Brooklyn Heights Historic District to the Old Town of Edinburgh. Politically, the Landmarks Commission could not have designated these areas if their inhabitants were opposed—since the elected officials of the Board of Estimate would not have confirmed such wide restrictions of property against the will of their constituents. But when organizations of conservation activists sought designation of their communities, the task of convincing reluctant property owners of the benefits of preservation status was undertaken by their neighbors.

All decisions by the commission were subject to challenge and review in local, state, and federal courts. While there were few such legal actions, the results were significant. Written opinions by the courts often expanded and clarified provisions of the landmarks law that, when applied to reality, were imprecise. One of the principal concerns of judges was that the designation and regulation of landmarks and historic districts be justified in concepts comprehensible to the general community as well as to affected property owners. The commission's criteria thus became more specific and concisely applied, yielding elaborate reports for each official decision. A rational scale for measuring architectural and historical significance was being refined.

Specific buildings were designated when they were significant examples of one or more of the following:

- architectural style, such as a particularly beautiful Greek Revival house, an Italianate factory, or a Beaux-Arts museum
- architectural type, perhaps a singular example of a schoolhouse, department store, or office building

- a specific method of construction, such as an early structure framed in cast iron, or one of the first noteworthy curtain-wall buildings
- the work of a master, like the Guggenheim Museum by Frank Lloyd Wright or the Seagram Building by Ludwig Mies van der Rohe
- high artistic value, such as the U.S. Customs House, with its large exterior sculptures by Daniel Chester French, who also carved the giant statue in the Lincoln Memorial in Washington, D.C.
- unique historic aspects of the nation or city, like the Statue of Liberty and the Brooklyn Bridge

Whole historic districts were designated when they constituted, according to the law, a "distinct section" of New York, with a "special character or historical or aesthetic interest or value," and represented "one or more periods or styles of architecture typical to the city." Such measures are not unique to New York, the United States, or any society that has enacted conservation statutes. They are simply the intellectual framework within which scholars in all places have studied architectural and urban history.

Yet in a strangely counterproductive policy decision (still sustained as of this writing), the Landmarks Commission in New York has never officially released its list of guidelines for individual designations—a result of excessive legal defensiveness in a litigious society. Nevertheless, since every designation reflected these criteria, neighborhood conservation activists soon deciphered them. In order to enhance the possibility of official protection, New Yorkers were learning the architectural history of cherished buildings, of their neighborhoods, and of the city as a whole. By showing a consolidation of community interests and substantial historical evidence to support designation, many communities expedited the safeguarding of local landmarks or the endowment of status as historic districts.

Once an area was named a historic district, all new construction and exterior modifications to buildings were regulated by the Landmarks Commission. Significant alterations required a public hearing. This included the construction of new apartment houses, town houses, office buildings, museums, and commercial structures. The design of a storefront, the addition of a new rooftop, the refurbishing of a decorative iron fence, and even the installation of new windows in an old facade could require a public hearing in order to clarify the commission's policy in a particular neighborhood or situation, when a normally small matter had unusually large effect on other important buildings, or when an owner objected to the commission's standards. (With experience, the commission established guidelines, enforced by its staff, for the regulation of most minor projects.) The hearings gave residents a voice in how their neighborhoods changed, and they protected the owners of well-kept historic structures against those who would detract from environmental beauty, while profiting from building in its midst. Since the law stipulated that within the eleven-member commission there be at least three architects, one historian, one city planner or landscape architect, and one realtor, the review of proposals for new construction was done on a professional level. To participate fully, community groups quickly became conversant in issues of contemporary architectural aesthetics and urban design. Often they sent representatives to public hearings unrelated to their communities simply to learn the process. Subsequently they often used concepts elucidated by commissioners and professional staff members to argue on behalf of their neighborhoods.

The advocacy and knowledge of preservation groups made it increasingly difficult for politicians to intercede on behalf of narrowly focused private interests. As public testimony became more substantive and probing, the level of analysis among commissioners was also raised. Depending on the skills of various chairmen and commissioners, an elevated urban discourse was engendered. Open debate on the future of the cityscape attracted the press. Newspaper coverage gave exposure to the arguments of all parties, providing another counterbalance to narrowly oriented political influence.

In historic neighborhoods across the city, restoration of old buildings became a broad cultural phenomenon. When undertaken en masse, whole areas were physically and economically revived, an evolution now known as gentrification. This process often has negative connotations in the United States, because it forces poorer residents out. Among European conservation planners, however, gentrification is a much-desired goal, stimulating private investment in preservation and lessening the need for governments to underwrite the restoration of old buildings. In order to ameliorate the negative social repercussions, European cities commonly offer rent subsidies to preserve the mix of social classes and economic uses—a balance of social equity rarely practiced in the United States, except in places like Charleston, which is discussed in Chapter 15, "The City Redeemed."

In New York, the designation of historic areas undergoing gentrification assured broad application of professional preservation standards as regulated by the Landmarks Commission, solidifying the improvement of such districts and stabilizing property values at an accrued higher value. Local conservation construction industries were generated. Homeowners, who in many cases had directly undertaken the restoration of their buildings, acquired knowledge of conservation techniques. Thus armed by the press, their willingness to engage politically, their growing understanding of urban architectural history, and hands-on conservation experience, community preservation groups then pressed the commission to apply even higher standards of architectural design and professional practice on behalf of their neighborhoods. In turn, this

THE ALTSTADT IN VIENNA

A comparison in urban size and texture · The heritage of New York represents a more recent stage of urban evolution then, for instance, the Altstadt of Vienna. · Although similar in size at ground level, the Upper West Side Historic District is composed of buildings of lesser vintage and of much greater height—especially along its eastern spine of Central Park West. · Whereas the angular street plan of the Altstadt reflects its medieval genesis, the grid of Manhattan is designed to accommodate vehicular circulation and other modern urban infrastructure. · The plan of Greenwich Village is a hybrid, a place in Manhattan where earlier more organic urban growth ends and the great rectangular grid begins. *(All drawings at the same scale.)*

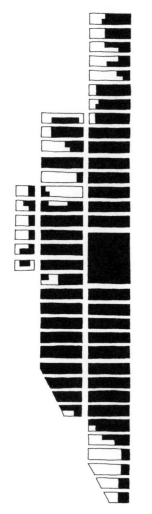

THE UPPER WEST SIDE HISTORIC DISTRICT

raised the general regulatory vigor of the Landmarks Commission across the city. The increased involvement in conservation of a wide body of citizens, on a substantive basis, propelled the preservation process forward.

Many specific examples might be cited of the impact of such groups on the cityscape, but the single most effective neighborhood advocacy organization may also be the city's smallest: the Society for the Architecture of the City, Inc. Composed of three to five people, none of whom hold degrees in architecture or urban planning, the society began monitoring the commission when an unsympathetic modern storefront was proposed for a historic structure in the Greenwich Village Historic District. Afterward the society's representative

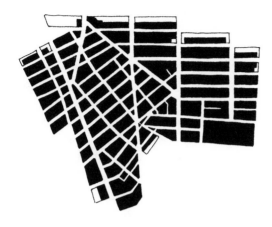

THE GREEWICH VILLAGE
HISTORIC DISTRICT

began appearing at all public meetings, staying for hours on end, taking copious notes, and learning the policies of the Landmarks Commission in all associated matters. One year later, another storefront was proposed for an
important old building in Greenwich Village. Since neither the architect nor
the commission's staff could find evidence of the original historic design, it
was recommended that a fairly contemporary storefront be approved—until a
representative of the Society for the Architecture of the City uncovered an old
photograph in a dusty municipal archive. This information changed the commission's decision and altered the design of the new storefront. Through
scrupulous research and carefully reasoned positions, the society began to
affect a growing number of commission decisions. A periodic scholarly journal
called *Village Views* was initiated and sent for free to about a hundred individuals
working in city government or highly positioned in civic matters. The journal
was collected in the library of Columbia University.

In 1987, during a period when designation activity had slowed significantly, a meticulous statistical study documenting the rate of decline was
printed in *Village Views.* This study received front-page coverage in the
Metropolitan Section of the *New York Times,* much to the embarrassment of the
commission, and motivated the city to rekindle its efforts. At every important
public discussion involving the preservation of the physical environment—at
the Board of Estimate, the City Council, the City Planning Commission, and
the Landmarks Commission—the Society for the Architecture of the City has
offered thoughtful and technically detailed reports, frequently so voluminous
that they dwarf the efforts of the largest preservation groups. Recently yet

another careful analysis by the Society—of plans to revitalize Rockefeller Center—decisively improved the conservation of a preeminent architectural accomplishment of twentieth-century urbanism.

In the open public forum of the Landmarks Commission, articulate knowledge had become power. Attention to the industrial buildings of SoHo was directed by a study by the Friends of Cast-Iron Architecture. This group's widely read report, *Cast-Iron Architecture in New York,* expanded scholarly comprehension of the city's building history and led to the creation of the SoHo Historic District. As in the era of the creation of Amsterdam School social housing, the landmarks law inspired a broad civic dialogue that critically assessed architectural design and planning. Informed public involvement, inculcated in historic districts and preservation societies, altered the balance of conservation politics. This encouraged the Landmarks Commission to take action in difficult-to-save areas in mid-Manhattan, where conflicts with non-residential landowners occurred.

Landmarks preservation became the most proactive urban planning initiative in New York, compelling the City Planning Commission to set height restrictions that complied with the prevailing size of buildings in historic districts, which came to include more than 19,000 structures. Public structures in every borough—schools, firehouses, museums, churches, and libraries—were renewed to a higher standard. Designation of the beautiful tile and terra-cotta decorations in select old subway stations led to the refurbishment of all original stations on the transit system. Public review of the work of the Parks Department established higher design standards and more careful preservation practices, empowering private conservation groups to reclaim the lost glories of the city's most beautiful green sanctuaries.

THE RIGHT TO DEVELOP THE AIR

As popular political support for conservation increased, residential enclaves and other low-rise areas gradually became protected across the five boroughs, with the designation of over a thousand individual monuments and more than seventy historic districts. But in the central business districts of Manhattan—downtown in the Wall Street Financial District and in the Midtown area south of Central Park, where an exuberant urban environment of great skyscrapers mingled with many of the city's most important monuments—conflict between preservation and economics reached an intensity perhaps unequaled in urban conservation history. In no other place that had adopted preservation laws was it possible to build such high buildings in such an enormously valuable urban context, at the very location where the built environment most embodied the unique cultural achievement of the city.

Historic districts and scenic landmarks in Manhattan · The combined land area of protected historic properties in Manhattan, although discontinuous and but one of the five boroughs of New York, is about one half the size of historic Rome. (Note: In making such statistical comparisions, the approximate area of Manhattan's 752 individual landmarks has been calculated, although they are not shown in this drawing. Also, several early historic districts, now subsumed in later and larger historic districts, are not identified in the map.)

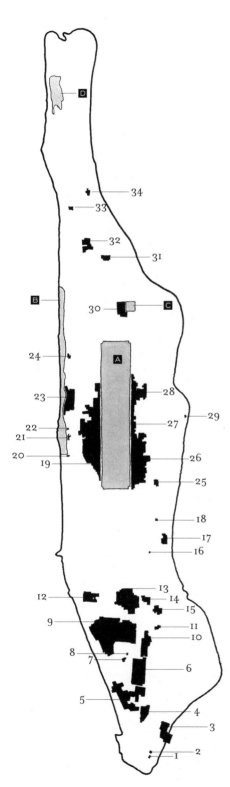

1.   Fraunces Tavern H.D.
2.   Stone Street H.D.
3.   South Street Seaport H.D.
4.   African Burial Ground and the Commons H.D.
5.   Tribeca South, East, West, and North H.D.'s
6.   SoHo–Cast Iron H.D.
7.   Charlton-King-Vandam H.D.
8.   MacDougal-Sullivan Gardens H.D.
9.   Greenwich Village H.D.
10. NoHo H.D.
11. Saint Mark's H.D.
12. Chelsea H.D.
13. Ladies' Mile H.D.
14. Gramercy Park H.D.
15. Stuyvesant Square H.D.
16. Sniffen Court H.D.
17. Tudor City H.D.
18. Turtle Bay Gardens H.D.
19. Upper West Side/Central Park West H.D.
20. West 71st Street H.D.
21. West End–Collegiate H.D.
22. Riverside Drive–West 80th–81st Street H.D.
23. Riverside Drive–West End H.D.
24. Riverside Drive–West 105th Street H.D.
25. Treadwell Farm H.D.
26. Upper East Side H.D.
27. Metropolitan Museum H.D.
28. Carnegie Hill H.D.
29. Henderson Place H.D.
30. Mount Morris Park H.D.
31. Saint Nicholas H.D.
32. Hamilton Heights H.D.
33. Audubon Terrace H.D.
34. Jumel Terrace H.D.

A. Central Park S.L.
B. Riverside Park S.L.
C. Mount Morris Park S.L.
D. Fort Tryon Park S.L.

It was this precise dilemma that had inspired the conservation statute. The trigger was an extreme act of cultural self-negation: the demolition in the early 1960s of Pennsylvania Station, a steel and glass evocation of the vaulted public monuments of ancient Rome. The terminal was one of the city's finest individual works of architecture, a symbol of its pride, and a principal ceremonial entry to New York. Across the street from Penn Station, another popular landmark, the U.S. General Post Office, established a facing Roman Revival classical facade along Eighth Avenue across the width of two blocks, from Thirty-first to Thirty-third Streets. This was one of the most potent architectural relationships between two great buildings that existed in the city. As the *New York Times* editorialized, "Until the first blows fell, no one was convinced that New York would permit this monumental act of vandalism. Even when we had Penn Station we couldn't afford to keep it clean. We want and deserve tincan architecture in a tinhorn culture. Any city gets what it admires, will pay for, and ultimately deserves." The prophecy was fulfilled. Once leveled, the magnificent Roman Revival train station was replaced by a modern office and sports complex of pedestrian architectural quality. A building that complied with the grid was replaced by a building that violated the grid. A beautiful dialogue between two important structures was ended. Greatness had been traded for the mundane. "One entered the city like a god," architectural historian Vincent Scully would write. "One scuttles in now like a rat."

The city's own aspirations, expressed in its zoning laws, made such exchanges virtually inevitable. The industrialized, mass-movement, densely populated towering capitalist metropolis had invested the air above the land with enticing profitability. In the city's first zoning law of 1916 (based on a projected ultimate urban population of 66 million people), no limit had been set on building heights on many properties in business districts. The new zoning law of 1960 was devised to serve a smaller conceptual population of 12.3 million; nonetheless, it made the conflict between low landmarks and high development still worse.

Not only was it no longer required that tall structures adhere to the street walls of the city's rectangular grid, but the new regulations encouraged such deviations. In fact, they made it more profitable to build skyscrapers that were set back in plazas, inside property lines, and at a greater average height and bulk. The typical height of towers in the 1950s was thirty to forty stories. After the change in zoning, buildings of fifty to sixty stories proliferated. In abandoning compliance with the street wall, the simple system of architectural organization that had aesthetically married the buildings of cities for more than a thousand years was eliminated. (It has been estimated that by 1973, under the new zoning provision, the total extra financial benefit realized by office towers in return for not complying with the street wall amounted to about $186 million.) At the same time, the increased interior construction costs and new minimal aesthetics of modernism led to less investment by builders in the exteriors of contemporary buildings. Extensive amounts of tin-can architecture became the norm in a cityscape randomly fractured by large structures that ignored the existing urban geometry.

New York adopted opposing environmental regulations at practically the same moment in time: the 1965 landmarks law was intended to preserve the city's historic urban beauty, and the 1960 zoning law encouraged aesthetic violation of the existing milieu. This was to some degree generally symptomatic of the growing schism between modern development and historic townscapes, something that would trouble all great cities in the second half of the twentieth century. In New York, the new zoning laws forsook the communal and interactive life of the city's streets, resulting in social and architectural alienation. Yet was the world's most modern city suddenly to stop advancing with technology into the future? This dispute would continue for decades. In the meantime, in central business areas the new zoning provisions instituted compelling economic incentives for tearing down underdeveloped old buildings—regardless of their historic and architectural significance.

As the inherent conflict became apparent, the metropolis contrived an economic counterbalance by making the air rights of designated historic structures transferable. In theory, this allowed low historic buildings to realize their potential for development by selling to a neighboring site the right to build higher or to move the allowable building bulk to a different location on the same property where new construction would not require the destruction of a landmark. In reality, while the practice ameliorated financial grievances, it compounded the aesthetic difficulty of conserving beauty and historic meaning.

In both the Midtown and Downtown business districts, low historic properties already dwarfed by surrounding high-rise structures were rendered microscopic by the extreme bulk of new adjacent buildings made even taller, thanks to the preservation transfer mechanism. Disparities of height and bulk were aggravated by a regulation which ensured that giant structures would be built not only in close proximity to but in some instances actually on top of landmarks of modest size. One such example is the fifty-one-story hotel now perched on the roof of the three-story Renaissance palazzo known as the Villard Houses. In such instances, beautiful structures were saved but made to look ridiculous, and tin-can construction clashed with the more refined patina of traditional handcraftsmanship in historic buildings.

Even if such cases were few, the visual common sense of conservation was being subverted. Implementation of the transfer process required the Landmarks Commission to certify that tall new buildings in receipt of relocated development rights achieve a "harmonious" or "appropriate" design relationship with the historic structures from which the air rights originated. Repeatedly—as at the John Street United Methodist Church, where a diminutive Georgian chapel sat in the shadow of a crudely constructed twenty-six-story office structure, or at 100 Old Slip, where a miniature Renaissance palace (eventually the home of the Landmarks Commission itself) sat across a narrow street from a massive thirty-six-story tower of banal and clumsy design—the commission would sanction blatant architectural disharmony, made worse by greater height and bulk added in the name of conservation.

Such decisions were not just perfunctory legalisms. The Landmarks Law required that the commission deal in palpable truths that the courts, the general populace, and government officials could verify. Many thousands of buildings were designated because their conformity with the words and spirit of the landmarks statute was manifest. Billions of dollars of new construction would be regulated on the basis of visual judgments found to be in reasonable compliance with elementary universal factors outlined in the statute: "The commission shall consider aesthetic, historical, and architectural values and significance, architectural style, design, arrangement, texture, material, and color."

Sometimes the commission deviated from aesthetic common sense—in complying with mayoral pressure to approve the construction of projects that obviously failed to meet standards applied in all other instances, in failing to initiate the designation process on behalf of noteworthy structures in the outer boroughs because of the private objections of local officials, or in calling "harmonious" designs that were conspicuously hostile. In such cases not only was the intellectual integrity of the commission compromised, but the validity of the landmarks process itself was undermined. The zoning laws of the city were an arcane and convoluted matrix, impenetrable by the general populace. But the legality of the concisely worded landmarks law was based on a simple proposition: that the architectural beauty and historic meaning of the city were accessible to all.

The conflict over unused development rights in the center of the city required that a threshold of reasonability be established. The Landmarks Commission eventually had to say no in the face of massive development potential—on behalf of the values it was instructed to uphold. This occurred in 1969, when the commission was confronted with a colossal absurdity: the New York Central and New Haven railroads requested authorization to construct a fifty-five-story office building over the roof of Grand Central Terminal. Granting permission to construct the giant tower would have memorialized in the cityscape a failure of moral authority. How then, in good faith, could the commission ask thousands of other owners of historic properties in New York to comply with its regulations? The time to say no had arrived, and the right of

New York to preserve its heritage would be challenged in the U.S. Supreme Court.

The possession of grand railroad terminals had once been a measure of greatness for cities in America, and two of the nation's preeminent stations were situated in New York. But in the 1950s and 1960s, as railroad ridership declined across the country, the owners of Manhattan's two great terminals sought to capitalize on the extraordinary real estate value of their properties at the city's core. This caused the demise of Pennsylvania Station. Grand Central Terminal occupied an even more central position in the cityscape. Below-ground, regional commuter rail lines connected with the city's subway system. On street level, the terminal was located at the crossing of two of the major axes of New York's grid. Built along the north side of 42nd Street and culminating the view up Park Avenue, the dignified Beaux-Arts facade of Grand Central, crowned by a large clock and a dramatic assemblage of sculpture, was one of the few major structures in the city to provide an architectural climax to a long urban vista. Inside, the terminal's main concourse was one of the largest and most impressive interior public spaces in the metropolis.

In 1963, a $100 million office structure (then known as the Pan Am Building), one of the largest in New York's history, had been built on railroad property just to the north of the terminal itself. In 1967, Grand Central was made an individual landmark. Afterward, the City Planning Commission designated eight sites in the immediate area to which the terminal's air rights could be transferred. Regardless, the railroad's owners planned to build on top of the terminal building itself.

Their first application for permission to build the tower requested a Certificate of No Exterior Effect, since the railway owners maintained that suspending the proposed fifty-five-story office building above the terminal did not damage the landmark's exterior features. This request was denied by the Landmarks Commission on the grounds that a mammoth structure hovering above a landmark was "nothing more than an aesthetic joke." The second application, for a Certificate of Appropriateness, proposed to demolish the terminal before constructing the new building. This was denied on the grounds that "to protect a landmark, one does not tear it down." The railroad now appealed to the courts, claiming that landmarks designation had resulted in an uncompensated "taking" or seizure of their property and that the endowment of landmark status was the result of arbitrary aesthetic judgments. After a decade of dispute in the lower courts, the legal battle reached its climax.

On June 26, 1978, the U.S. Supreme Court found the railroad's contentions to be unsupported by the evidence. Furthermore they deemed legitimate the efforts of New York citizens to preserve their architectural heritage:

Over the past 50 years, all 50 States and over 500 municipalities have enacted laws to encourage or require the preservation of buildings and areas with historic or aesthetic importance. These nationwide legislative efforts have been precipitated by two concerns. The first is recognition that in recent years, large numbers of historic structures, landmarks, and areas have been destroyed without adequate consideration of either the values represented therein or the possibility of preserving the destroyed properties for use in economically productive ways. The second is a widely shared belief that structures with special historic, cultural, or architectural significance enhance the quality of life for all. Not only do these buildings and their workmanship represent the lessons of the past and embody precious features of our heritage, they serve as examples of quality for today. Historic conservation is but one aspect of a much larger problem, basically an environmental one, of enhancing—or perhaps developing for the first time—the quality of life for people.

Thereby was maintained the right of cities and towns in the United States to preserve their architectural heritage.

While the transfer of air rights would continue to test the commission on rare occasions, by the year 2000, more than 20,000 properties in New York, constituting about 2 percent of the city's almost one million tax lots, had been designated. In addition, several thousand public debates had been held, well over a hundred preservation societies had been formed, upwards of a million applications for changes to protected structures had been processed, and many billions of dollars of new construction had been regulated. Between 15 and 20 percent of the land area of Manhattan had been deemed of historic and architectural value: 41 historic districts and 752 individual landmarks, including Central Park. Most of the city's important architecture was guarded. But the most essential legacy of all largely defied protection.

SAVING THE CATHEDRALS OF COMMERCE

Difficult as designation of low-rise landmarks in the central business district may be, tall buildings present even more problems. Simply, they cannot be saved against the will of their owners. First of all, the corporations and realtors who own office towers have enormous political clout. And, second, the importance of such enterprises to the city's economy makes the designation of skyscrapers a matter of serious consequence to New York's financial well-being. The decades after World War II were particularly sobering in this regard. Many major business organizations moved their office functions to the suburbs or to other cities, heightening the competition to retain the presence of such institutions. This changeable balance in the city's economic vitality has made wide application of the restrictions inherent to the designation of skyscrapers a matter contemplated with considerable caution by the body politic. Yet here is exactly the problem, for retention of skyscrapers—office towers, hotels, and apartment buildings—involves a considerable number of structures located in the center of Manhattan whose value as real estate amounts to many billions of dollars.

As a class of buildings, the great towers are the most distinct achievement of the city in regard to world architectural history. However, this patrimony is embodied not just in the most significant individual skyscrapers but also in several areas in the city where a majestic and remarkably dense, tall environment has been accomplished. Particularly in Midtown locations less disturbed by the 1960 zoning resolution, where the sculptural massing of the cityscape still adhered to New York's street grid, such assemblages of tall buildings from various stages of the upward architectural evolution are perhaps the most successfully organized agglomeration of large vertical structures in any great metropolis. Here, clearly defined canyons amid blocks of giant buildings, aligned in unison at their bases, framing long views across the cityscape, and often culminating in exuberant acts of architectural creativity at their peaks, impart a soaring cosmopolitan vitality.

Surveying the city's panorama from up high, from the upper stories of tall buildings, one sees the eclectic architectural energy of the city erupting in hundreds of varying summits and innumerable forms of individual expression, yet all conforming with a common geometric and social restraint—the great grid whose long avenues extend to distant horizons. This is of course the material expression of the hopes of the American democracy: to harness the myriad energies of a diverse immigrant people in a vast collective enterprise of unlimited opportunity. As prophesied by Walt Whitman in *Leaves of Grass*, in the modern era, the architectural, historical, and cultural essence of the city became

> As of the building of some varied, vast, perpetual edifice,
> Whence to arise inevitable in time, the towering roofs,
> The lamps, the solid-planted spires, tall, shooting to the stars.

New York's impulse to grow upward is not a matter reserved to the past; it is the continuing saga of the city. While several discernible developments, such as changing real estate values, alterations in zoning provisions, advances in skyscraper technology, and political influence of immeasurable potency, all affect the fate of tall historic buildings, the preservation dilemma cannot be reduced to the sum of these parts. New skyscrapers continue to be erected every day in an ever more densely packed tall environment that is still in the act of becoming itself.

Thus, saving the skyscraper environment is a problem of different dimensions from the conservation of cities whose legacy was realized in relatively distant historic periods and now is largely fixed—for example, the conservation of historic Amsterdam, Paris, Rome, Vienna, Venice, Jerusalem, or Florence. Moreover, because the glory of New York sprang from the Industrial Revolution, the historic constraints of preindustrial building technologies that made ancient cities relatively homogeneous in height were merely a passing phase in the early growth of the American high-rise metropolis. Once the skyscraper phenomenon began, abrupt changes in height became common in the center of the city—a disunity that in many places will be remedied only by the city's continued upward evolution. This makes the potential regulation of such areas as conventional historic districts a difficult prospect.

In the tin-can tinhorn years after the destruction of Pennsylvania Station and the 1960 change in zoning, as the unity achieved in select parts of the tall urban environment was destroyed, many in the metropolis wondered if higher architectural attainment had been permanently left behind. But the creation of the Landmarks Law signaled more than merely the protection of the 2 percent of the city (or the 15 to 20 percent of Manhattan) that was eventually designated. Saving the most important accomplishments of the past was part of a larger effort to effect an accrual of environmental value and coherence. In the regulation of modern additions to historic districts at the public hearings of the Landmarks Commission, as New Yorkers from all walks of life weighed different aspects of the urban aesthetic design problem, a parallel debate occurred among practitioners in the field of architecture. Nor was this discussion limited to New York. It was part of a global reevaluation of the impact of modern design and ideology on treasured historic environments.

The answer that is evolving from these examinations is the same over much of the world. It is the same answer learned by those cities across history that eventually rose to be integrated urban compositions. Buildings in the metropolis, regardless of their individual expressiveness, must also embrace some common visual idea that binds them together as a totality.

Thus, saving the skyscraper legacy ultimately involves a rapprochement between landmarks conservation and zoning, a reconciliation between beauty already achieved and visions of the city of the future. Such planning would require coordination between the Landmarks Commission and other city agencies. In the past, the effect of zoning has been to design the city by default, by the vagaries of the real estate market. In the future, if the zoning law reinstates mandatory adherence to the street wall, the historic city and new construction will no longer be so disparate in character. The process of accrual of integrated environmental value might resume.

Another needed initiative is equally simple as a basic governing concept. One of the few positive attributes of the 1960 zoning resolution in regard to conserving the splendor of the urban environment was the reduction of permissible bulk on a select number of properties in the city's center. As a result, several of the very tallest of the old skyscrapers, which now exceed the allowable building mass, have more value restored than they would have had if demolished. This is, of course, a type of action that should be exerted widely. When the incentive for destruction is removed, many parts of the skyscraper legacy can be saved. (In somewhat different form, both of these actions are currently being contemplated by the city.)

While the most preeminent individual skyscrapers have by now been designated as landmarks, hundreds more merit protection. Another hundred equally beautiful towers have already been demolished.

Will the Landmarks Preservation Commission, in a coordinated effort with other agencies, be able to protect the most important cultural legacy of the metropolis? Will New York learn to mandate cohesion in the tall environments at its center? Will the city of constant change learn to orchestrate its advance into the future, so that the price of growth is not loss of architectural excellence?

CHAPTER THIRTEEN

REVERSING THE CULTURE OF DESTRUCTION

KYOTO

Because Kyoto was spared the bombings of World War II, the preservation of the traditional cityscape here has taken on special historical significance. The wooden dwellings that remain in Kyoto are nearly all that is left of prewar urban Japan.

—DIANE DURSTON, *Kyoto: Seven Paths to the Heart of the City*

Of course there was nothing wrong with wanting to "modernize" the environment in which people lived, in the sense of making it more hygienic, more comfortable, more practical. But the question is, was it really necessary to destroy so much of the traditional environment and culture in the interests of modernization?

—MATSAHUMI YAMASAKI, *Kyoto: Its Cityscape, Traditions, and Heritage*

The wind jostles red paper lanterns in the city's hidden gardens, and the incidental sound seems to be part of a conscious aesthetic plan. Behind the property walls that separate old buildings from the street, each stone, plant, and piece of bamboo is artfully arranged in simple compositional harmony. Even the drip of water from roof eaves is composed. Historic Japan is a state of mind, an exquisite aesthetic balance of the physical components of existence. Outside, in the bustle of the contemporary city, it is numbing to see that so much ancient beauty has been destroyed. Kyoto opens a door to Japan's uniquely glorious architectural past, and just as abruptly shuts it. The city is both a singular compilation of the Japanese built heritage and the victim of rampant modernization. Many serene and glorious fragments of the past are scattered across the urban landscape, but disconnected within a sea of chaotic modern development. To the outsider, one question persists above all others: How could a people who invented such a refined and singular loveliness so completely forsake their own heritage? Why was so much of the beauty of Kyoto abandoned by the Japanese?

HISTORIC JAPAN: EMBRACE OF THE EPHEMERAL

The unique medieval architectural culture that evolved in Japan over many centuries has had an enormous impact on the thinking of modern architects and artists. Medieval Japanese architecture employed a formal minimalism, clarity of structural expression, heightened sensitivity to the character of materials, and repetition of modular architectonic elements—aesthetic devices that would be adopted around the world hundreds of years later, with the advent of Western industrialization.

While modularization and minimalism in buildings made of such durable materials as glass, metal, and concrete would be developed in Western architecture in order to secure the economic advantages of machine-manufactured building materials, the architectural aesthetics of handcrafted structures in medieval Japan grew out of a pragmatic response to environmental conditions and a decision by the Japanese to make buildings easily replaceable, to make them temporary rather than permanent. This approach to architecture and city building is, of course, fundamentally different from the goal of Western urban culture, which is to create structures and cities that will be durable. In the West, the vicissitudes of nature are to be resisted, but in medieval Japan it was impractical to defy a violent and unpredictable setting that regularly brought typhoons, earthquakes, volcanic activity, and torrential rainfall. In Japan, buildings and cities needed to bend with the strong natural forces that acted on them. Moreover, the extreme humidity fostered dense rain forests that made for an uncongenial environment for human habitation, and Japanese buildings would have to take this condition into consideration.

Thus the Japanese constructed wood-frame buildings that could flex when subjected to strong winds and seismic tremors, or could be easily reconstructed and repaired if they were severely damaged. To forestall rot from the rain and humidity, buildings were perched on wooden posts raised above the earth; when earthquakes occurred, the violent forces unleashed in the ground were not transmitted upward. Sliding walls made of light wood frames covered by translucent paper, known as shojis, allowed buildings to be opened up to cooling and drying breezes. This also reduced the interconnected and fixed components of buildings to a minimum, heightening the structural flexibility. Floors were covered with tatami—rectilinear straw mats of standardized dimensions. The proportions of rooms were based on the number of tatamis needed to cover the space. (In Kyoto the standard size of a tatami mat was, and is, 94.5 centimeters by 189 centimeters.) Because this basic building component had an established universal size, many other building elements could be mass-produced, at lower cost, with greater efficiency.

When structures were destroyed, parts from one building could be reused in the restoration of another. This was particularly important in cities, whose highly flammable structures were vulnerable to accidental fires as well as to the fires that erupted during historic periods of constant warfare. When fires grew out of control in urban areas, firebreaks to limit the spread of conflagrations could be quickly opened up by deconstructing buildings. Afterward these could be reassembled in their original location or moved to a different site. From the sixteenth to the eighteenth centuries, the form of the Japanese city came to reflect its combustibility. As the great stone castles of the daimyos, or feudal overlords, arose in the middle of urban settlements, the surrounding wooden city was considered expendable and was not protected by walls. And it was a common practice, in times of hostilities, for the defenders of cities to burn their wooden precincts in order to protect the castle.

The interiors of Japanese houses were sparse, rectilinear, and colored by the muted hues of natural materials—the soft cream color of tatami and the enveloping paper-white of shoji. As various interior shojis were opened or closed, the interior spaces were altered in number and dimension. Objects and furniture were kept to a minimum and could be readily stored away out of sight, allowing rooms to change their function as well as their size. When exterior screens were opened, the interior spaces were extended to include the intense greens of the private gardens.

Except in the tenement houses of the very poor, gardens were an integral part of most buildings in the traditional Japanese city. Temples, shrines, and palaces were composed of compounds of buildings engulfed in gardens and surrounded by perimeter walls. Garden houses of samurai retainers were modest versions of the same idea. The shop-houses of merchants and craftsmen (machinami), which made up the largest part of the historic cityscape, commonly had a private garden situated in the center of each plot, which was otherwise totally hidden by buildings.

When the rooms of Japanese buildings were open to gardens, interiors assumed a profoundly different character from that of Western structures. Absence of exterior walls allowed the changeable and unpredictable reality of nature to become a visual and sensory element in the controlled microenvironment fabricated by humans. In the West, walls, doors, and windows were a shield that protected interiors from the uncertainties of the outside world. In Japan, all such barriers to nature could be drawn aside in good weather, and the natural growth of gardens could become part of the interior space.

The response of the Japanese to destruction, from both natural forces and armed conflict, was part of an interwoven material, spiritual, and philosophical culture. Minimalism in the physical environment reflected the depth of meaning that was found in each human-made object. Beauty in a teacup, a robe, a scroll painting, or a door handle represented the efforts to invest life with meaning, even though human appreciation of such beauty, and the objects themselves, were but fleeting moments of grace in an inexorable passage to nonexistence.

HISTORIC KYOTO: THE CAPITAL CITY OF TREASURES

Established in 794 by Emperor Kwammu, the street plan of Kyoto was influenced by the traditions of Chinese capital cities. It was laid out on a vast orthogonal grid of wide principal avenues oriented to the points of the compass, with the walled precinct of the emperor's palace situated at the city's center. Historians estimate that soon after its founding, the former capital had half a million inhabitants. From 1467 to 1568, during the period of the Sengoku Jidai (Warring States), the beautiful historic buildings that had been constructed in Kyoto were devastated. Under the rule of Toyotomi Hideyoshi, from 1582 to 1598, the city was rebuilt.

From 1603 to 1867, during the Tokugawa shogunate—a military regime that used the wealth accrued from large feudal estates to support massive standing armies—the political capital of Japan was moved to Edo, which was eventually renamed Tokyo. Kyoto remained the residence of the emperor and the center of Japan's traditional culture. In order to curtail the potential political strength of the emperors, the Tokugawa shoguns often compelled new emperors to retire soon after reaching maturity. Thus many former rulers lived in religious communities at the fringes of Kyoto in compounds richly endowed with attractive buildings and gardens. With its palaces for the emperor and shogun, and its numerous shrines, temples, and houses for court officials, Kyoto became an extended treasury of Japanese art and architecture, containing a greater wealth of monuments than any other historic capital city in Japan.

In 1864 the Great Tenmei Fire devastated 80 percent of the city, with particularly terrible effects in closely packed residential and commercial areas. These areas, once again, were rebuilt consistent with historic traditions.

Japan first encountered European traders in the sixteenth century, but these interactions were limited by a policy of national isolationism under the Tokugawa shogunate. As a result, the country's medieval culture was sustained until the Meiji Restoration in 1867, when the government began a concentrated effort to industrialize. In a remarkably brief period of time Japan transformed itself into a modern global power. During the first phase of this metamorphosis, prior to World War II, Western building types and trolleys were introduced along the principal avenues of Kyoto's grid. Since the new buildings were generally consistent in height with the traditional cityscape that surrounded them, the basic hierarchical relationship of Kyoto's parts—of low residential areas to taller monuments to the mountains that enveloped and rose above the city—was retained.

Extensive firebombing during World War II severely damaged all but a handful of important Japanese cities, dramatically reducing the nation's architectural patrimony. Sixty of Japan's largest towns were 40 percent destroyed, and the damage was particularly terrible in areas of wooden structures. This was by design. Incendiary bombing techniques had been refined by the United States military during the test-destruction of mock Japanese wooden residential environments constructed in Florida. Unlike the strategic bombing of industrial, transport, governmental, and military installations, the firebombing of Japanese cities was aimed at the general populace and the places where they lived. Those few cities that were spared, such as Kyoto and Nara (an earlier imperial capital of ancient Japan), though altered by the first stages of modernization, were still largely intact as medieval historic constructions. These former traditional capitals became the last opportunity to save representative manifestations of Japan's unique historic urban culture.

During the postwar era, the country's avid embrace of modernism, the practical need to rebuild decimated urban environments, and a national recovery plan oriented toward rapid urban growth dramatically escalated the pace of urban change. This heightened the conflict between modern development and historic architectural conservation. And historic Kyoto was engulfed by a wave of urban transformations.

THE CLASH WITH PERMANENCE

Sudden modernization of Japanese cities resulted in an extreme clash of cultural, social, economic, and environmental values. As the country's feudal form of authoritarian government evolved into a modern representative democracy, the process of industrialization intensified. Delicate handmade cityscapes of wood, paper, straw, bamboo, bark, clay tile, and mud stucco were abruptly crowded with structures made of concrete, steel, and glass. And although Japan's historic cities were far larger than early European industrial cities (Edo-Tokyo had long housed more than a million people when cities like London, New York, Paris, and Berlin were only a quarter as large), modernization caused the country's urban areas to expand tenfold and more. In a nation where dramatic change was occurring simultaneously in all spheres of social organization and private life, the problem of conserving the urban architectural heritage of Japan became highly complex, requiring a reevaluation of the basic ideas influencing the form and organization of historic cities such as Kyoto, an analysis that would occur only after several decades of destruction had already taken place.

Achieving contemporary standards for fire safety in cities made of wood was difficult. Close proximity of highly flammable structures makes fire hard to contain, and modern interior amenities such as plumbing, heating, and electric systems were difficult to install in old wooden houses. Moreover, as growing numbers of contemporary Japanese adopted Western furniture, tatami mats became impractical. These changes, together with the constant need for maintenance and renewal, made wooden residential structures increasingly less desirable as permanent investments, while the development of reinforced concrete offered an alternative building material that was resistant to fires and earthquakes.

A fundamental historic change was occurring. Prior to industrialization, the Japanese cityscape was a living aesthetic continuum of changing visual sensibilities rooted in traditions from the country's medieval culture. Modernization brought to an end this centuries-long cultural evolution and altered the meaning of old structures. Now they were the material evidence of an abandoned culture of building from a closed period of the past.

Japan began to construct permanent cities in the modern Western mode. Yet almost every concept in the modern Western vocabulary of preservation—permanence; ease of maintenance, replication, and replacement; authenticity—had a fundamentally different philosophical meaning to the Japanese. A primary difference was that continuation of major wooden monuments in Japan was ensured through periodic maintenance. As in China, important buildings were disassembled and rebuilt several times during a century. In general, complete disassembly occurred about once every 300 years, half-dismantling every 150 years, and partial reassembly, particularly of roofs, at more frequent intervals of 50 to 25 years. During reconstruction, stylistic changes were sometimes introduced into historic structures. The Shrines of the Ise Prefecture, whose exact replication has long been held important, were an exception. First constructed in the third century, they have been torn down and renewed every twenty years, or about sixty times. The continuity of the social and general physical presence of landmarks—the perpetuation of their spirit—was the primary objective, rather than exact duplication of the historic object.

To further complicate urban conservation, the Japanese attitude to the public realm of the historic cityscape was different from the West's. In ancient Japanese cities, emphasis was not placed on the development of the street as an environment of symbolic architectural forms. Most historic public ways were meant simply to serve as utilitarian passages. Along the lanes in residential areas of garden houses, walls built along property lines were not designed as major embellishments but as security for buildings with sliding doors made of paper. The most significant elements of architectural assemblages were hidden from public view. In the European city, street facades were the most critical aesthetic side of buildings, making the streetscape a rich accumulation of fixed form. But even in those parts of the Japanese city where structures did have a principal facade facing the public way—in commercial areas—such buildings were not grand architectural statements, whether on wide major avenues or in the numerous smaller streets and alleys that divided the giant quadrants of Kyoto's grid into many smaller blocks. Here, the front facades of buildings were composed of moving architectural elements that opened up to reveal the inside of shops during the day, and that closed down at night. Street walls consisted of elevations in flux rather than fixed facades of constant aesthetic impact.

Yet although historic streetscapes in Japan were not composed with the same goal as public circulation spaces in the European tradition, nonetheless the architectural parts of Japanese streets achieved a singular aesthetic continuity. In garden house residential areas, minimally adorned walls and gateways, with the peaks of houses and trees rising up in the background, produced an environment of sparse tranquillity. In the commercial thoroughfares when shopfronts were open, the streetscape became a colorful bazaar teeming with paper and cloth signage. When shop facades were closed, a rich texture of carefully crafted, minimalist wooden building components lined the public way.

In both these environments, simple elements like drain spouts, doorways, doorknobs, the pattern of rocks in a wall, the joints in a wooden fence, the construction of paper and wood lanterns, the undulating patterns of roof tiles, the arrangement of paving stones in the street, the calligraphy on cloth banners, the contrast of color and texture between the natural irregularities of bamboo, the straight lines of meticulously crafted wooden framing, and the opaque flatness of stucco—all revealed a heightened visual sensibility to the primary relationship of textures, shapes, and materials. Much effect was gained from the accrual of myriad small and subtle aesthetic gestures.

Early European visitors to Japan often considered such traditional streetscapes monotonous and devoid of visual interest. But after industrialization and the emergence of the modern artistic movement, contemporary artists and architects from the West found these same environments filled with discriminating visual meaning. The minimalist beauty created by the Japanese pervaded the human-made environment on multiple levels. In this setting, the uncontrollable aesthetic incidents of nature—the changing pattern of falling snow, the trembling arc of cherry trees bending in the wind, the slow drip of water from a spout—acquired an evanescent loveliness when seen in contrast to the simple and synthesized forms of the human-made world.

In the context of world architectural evolution, historic Kyoto was a unique cultural variation, an extended checkerboard of myriad private open spaces and beautifully made structures of closely interlocking handcrafted parts. The city was endowed profusely with extensive architectural complexes— in all, about two thousand temples, shrines, and villas. These included places of such aesthetic refinement as the Temple of the Golden Pavilion, Nijo Castle, the Imperial Palace, the Katsura Imperial Villa, and the rock garden of the Ryoanji Temple. Its innumerable secluded gardens—in *machinami*, garden houses, palaces, and temples—were of delicate and carefully balanced sensibility. While any building or garden might be lost in a moment, they would be quickly replaced with other equally temporal structures reflecting an aesthetic culture that persisted regardless of the vulnerability of their material products. Five of the forested hills that surrounded the city were illuminated by fires every year on August 16 in a ceremony honoring the souls of departed ancestors. In a low-scale cityscape, this view outward from private gardens was common and prized, a contrast of fragile human-made environmental art with the immutable beauty of nature. Now an era had dawned, when fixed modern Western urban architecture and infrastructure of permanent materials would be inserted into the largely unbroken historic continuum of a city that had embraced its transience.

THE FRACTURING OF KYOTO

As modernization proceeded, the wide main streets of traditional Kyoto, like those of Beijing, readily lent themselves to streetcars and automotive traffic. And the main transportation vectors of the city, also like those of Beijing, became the principal focus of modern development. In this regard, both historic cities were fractured in the same way. Each had pockets of old low-rise architecture set within the areas off principal boulevards. On the main avenues, modern development of strikingly different materials, height, massing, and aesthetic character splintered the traditional milieu.

At different times during this transformation, various nationwide and local policies affecting land use had detrimental repercussions. At one point, for instance, contemporary fire regulations forced the owners of historic buildings to remove traditional wooden architectural elements from street facades and add modern aluminum window sashes. Meanwhile, the introduction of mass transit—first streetcars and later a subway—increased the value of property at the center of the city, where traditional buildings were one and two stories tall. Real estate speculation and zoning laws that allowed dramatically increased building heights drove land prices upward and spawned taller modern structures at arbitrary locations throughout the historic milieu, leaving few blocks of old neighborhoods untouched. The extent to which out-of-scale structures are dispersed across the historic city is staggering even when compared to such chaotic urban landscapes as those of Beijing and Cairo. For many centuries, the peaks of the traditional city had been formed by palaces, temples, and shrines. Now these ancient landmarks were subsumed in a jagged sea of larger modern constructions.

Rising property taxes and values, in combination with excessive national inheritance taxes, made it difficult for the owners of Kyoto's traditional garden houses to pass them on to family members for continued residential use. As a result, many of these houses were demolished to make way for redevelopment, with particularly egregious results in sites that overlooked the enveloping green areas of historic monuments. National conservation laws protected important individual landmarks, but the modern buildings that exploited the views frequently ruined the ambience of historic environments that surrounded shrines and temples and violated the traditional urban skyline as seen from within the compounds of ancient sanctuaries. In the modern era, the widely shared traditional vista of the hills surrounding Kyoto has in most cases been lost.

Unlike Beijing, whose modernization as the symbol of the Chinese Communist state was seen as an ideological necessity and a rejection of the past, the fracturing of Kyoto was in some part due to cultural attitudes deeply embedded in the Japanese urban tradition. Abrupt modernization placed extremely different conceptions of city construction in direct conflict and immediate juxtaposition—Western versus Japanese, permanent versus temporal, traditional architecture oriented to gardens versus contemporary architecture oriented to streets, and handcrafted versus machine-made. Moreover, in a society experimenting with democracy for the first time, traditions of public advocacy were not firmly implanted, and neither individual citizens nor whole neighborhoods spoke out. Reconciliation of these conflicting cultural forces did not occur in time to prevent pervasive visual dissonance.

Although similar aesthetic environmental disorder and fracturing can be seen in contemporary cities in the United States, particularly since World War II, the fracturing of Kyoto was especially intense. A cacophony of suspended aerial utility wiring crisscrossed old streetscapes in central historic areas and was jury-rigged to traditional wooden buildings in visually undiscriminating ways. Highways, pedestrian bridges, and rail lines pierced and hovered above the ancient milieu of handcrafted temples, machinami, and small garden houses at the city's core. A new generation of competing architectural symbols overwhelmed the skyline. Jungles of electronic signs sprouted up in business areas, covering whole neighborhoods with commercial advertisements. Surviving small wooden structures in such areas seemed minuscule when sandwiched between tall, modern blockfronts. Early modern Japanese speculative buildings were often as banal or ugly as their counterparts in the West. One, two, or three of these might invade a historic residential block, each new building jarring in its materials and design and two or three times as tall as the surrounding structures. Later, with the development of a contemporary Japanese architecture whose experimentation in modern composition produced structures of highly expressive but autonomous originality, several parts of Kyoto became a confused mixture of clashing bold designs, flashing with neon, and casting shadows over old neighboring houses that sat beneath the crisscrossing wires.

This cacophony was to some degree symptomatic of postwar Japanese urbanism in general. Traditional culture persisted in the country's new urban context, and most Japanese homes still maintained at least one tatami-mat room, but such manifestations were obviously not perceptible from the public way. The aesthetic realm of ancient Japan lay behind the walls of compounds or in the privacy of people's homes. Meanwhile, in the public domain of the cityscape, Japan created a novel modern environmental order that found meaning in complexity, contradiction, and chaos. While commercial areas such as the Ginza in Tokyo reflected an energy similar to that of Las Vegas or Times Square, the new Japanese urbanism was even more multifaceted and pervasive, reassembling various parts of the modern Western cityscape in new and startling combinations.

Numerous urbanists have contemplated the meaning of these environments. In 1966, Peter Wilson, in The Idea of the City, noted Tokyo's qualities: "Its incomprehensible complexity (each object/event is autonomous, separated from the next by earthquake laws, by scale, by type, and by the time-delay of a fax transmission). Its apparent absence of hierarchy (conditions of downtown, quiet residential, neon zone, artificial landscape, movement corridors, and so on, are folded together, like movie cuts or hologram plates where each fragment contains the whole image). Its overall melancholic grayness (punctuated by neon galaxies and revealing on close inspection an array of infinitely subtle and variable hues). This ordered chaos is today's urban frontier: the sedimentary consequence of media/electronic technology, an endless humming cloud."

In its rush to modernize, Japan imported much from the West. Yet what it did not import was a system of laws to protect the built historic patrimony as a holistic environment. In Europe, as the divergent character of the industrialized city became evident and the threat to integrated old environments was recognized, historic-district conservation laws evolved as a counterbalance and the traditional centers of many cities were saved. In Japan, where so little urban heritage had survived World War II, and where industrialization occurred very rapidly, recognition of the need to protect historic environments lagged.

Hence, even as an urban environment of heightened visual complexity and conflict evolved in Japan, in Western cities an international trend emerged out of the conservation ethic to make contemporary urban development relate harmoniously to its historic context. Similar policies were slow to reach Kyoto. The intense and compacted modern Japanese city—filled with competing architectural forms, commercial messages, and exposed infrastructure—was, although exciting and visually homogeneous in its chaotic density, the antithesis of the serene, handcrafted, paper-and-wood historic milieu of the ancient capital. There were few places in the world where such a contrast of extreme visual opposites coexisted, in equal and disjointed measure, in the same city.

REINSTATING KYOTO'S DISRUPTED HISTORIC DISTRICTS

Although outside observers of the new Japanese urbanism have been cautious in describing the chaos of cities like Tokyo as disorienting and alienating—warning that such value judgments might be the result of Western cultural prejudice—the emergence of a conservation consciousness in Kyoto indicates that many Japanese themselves were dismayed by the fracturing of the city's historic ambience. This dissatisfaction with the character of contemporary urban development is reflected in a series of policy initiatives, gradually enacted in recent years, designed to slow down and even reverse the tide of change.

Kyoto was in the forefront of environmental preservation in Japan. From the time after the Meiji Restoration, from the beginning of industrialization in the nineteenth century, Kyoto's government undertook to save the hilly woodland that surrounded the city and defined its edges. Although traditions of conservation have long existed in Japan—the country's first nationwide statute, the Law for the Preservation of Ancient Shrines and Temples, was created in 1897—such activity primarily involved religious buildings and sites. Both prior to and after World War II, and especially as the second wave of urban modernization intensified, national and local conservation laws were made more comprehensive. They were expanded to protect vernacular structures, individual monuments, and the green areas in and around landmarks. Examples include the Law for the Preservation of Historic Sites, Places of Beauty, and Natural Monuments (1919); the Law for the Preservation of National Treasures (1929); the National

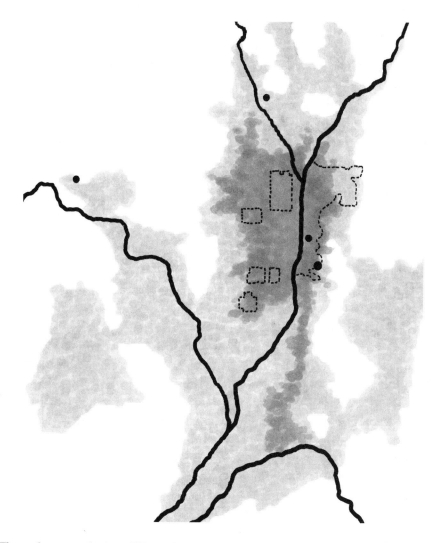

The modern conurbation of Kyoto · Dark gray tone marks the area of settlement by 1911, an approximate measure of the extent of traditional wooden architectural construction. Pale gray tone indicates the expanse of the current agglomeration. The size and location of Aesthetic Areas is shown with a dotted line. Small black circles denote Traditional Building Preservation Districts as of 1996.

Cultural Properties Act (1950); and Kyoto's municipal regulations pertaining to scenic zones (1930) and urban landscapes (1972).

In 1970, an international symposium organized by the Japanese National Commission for UNESCO and the Agency of Cultural Affairs of Japan focused on the need to develop protections for those surviving fragments of the traditional cityscape that existed outside historic complexes. The resulting new laws involved two concepts: more rigorous local zoning controls to preserve the character of areas immediately around historic sites, defined as Aesthetic Areas in the city's land-use regulations, and the creation of a new category of national monuments called Traditional Building Preservation Districts.

The use of the municipal zoning ordinance in Kyoto to create protected zones around landmarks is similar to the effort in Beijing to control the low-scale ambience around its walled monument compounds. In both places, the degree of restriction is greatest in close proximity to landmarks and lessens as the distances from them increases. In Kyoto, these graduated controls require strict supervision of height and materials and the preservation of wood facades within immediate proximity to important historic locations, with greater allowance in secondary zones for taller contemporary buildings of different materials. In addition, inside aesthetic areas, the municipality now requires that the design of new buildings relate appropriately to historic streetscapes. Such rules safeguard environmental coherence—to the degree it still survives—in areas around temples, shrines, and palaces as well as the view outward from within monument sites.

Traditional Building Preservation Districts use a regulatory feature that is in some degree unique to Japan. By 1995, four small areas had been so designated. Each preservation district comprises a surviving urban subcommunity of a different building type and character. The Sanneizaka District, designated in 1972, is made up of garden houses and shops that line the slope up to the Kiyomizu Temple. The Gion Shinbashi District (1974) is a famous and representative old geisha quarter. The Sagano Toriimoto District (1974) is a particularly beautiful thatch-roofed farming village in the mountains outside the city. The Kamigamo Shakémachi District (1988) is composed of rural garden houses built along a stream in a cluster around the Kamigano Shrine. In the late 1990s three other Traditional Building Preservation Districts were being contemplated to save other largely intact neighborhoods: a district comprising the *machinami* of urban cotton weavers; a typical medieval area adjacent to a major temple at Kyoto's core; and a townscape centered around buildings for the production of sake.

This sampling of traditional urban culture, though involving only small areas of the cityscape, reveals the diversity of ancient Japanese building forms and shows how the refined aesthetics of high culture filtered down to grace the lives of people of other classes. Such vernacular examples of beauty, proportion, and graceful simplicity are a significant historical resource for the country as a whole. Moreover, the process for regulating these areas is quite unusual in terms of international urban conservation practice. Rather than attempting to establish the exact architectural composition of each old building facade, as would be done in a typical European conservation district, officials in Kyoto asked the Architecture Department at the University of Kyoto to develop prototypical design solutions for the wood facades of buildings—designs that might have existed—in these neighborhoods. Once historic-district status is officially instated, owners in these areas are required to comply with such prototypes when rehabilitating their property. In typical Western historic districts, in contrast, new buildings of contemporary design are often allowed in vacant lots, or as replacements for intrusive modern structures constructed before official design controls were instituted. Thus, over time, Kyoto's Traditional Building Preservation Districts will evolve toward a greater degree of historic verisimilitude.

This flexible approach to conservation responds to the simple reality that in Kyoto the exposed parts of wood structures rarely last longer than forty years. Thus, few of the buildings that made up such districts when they were first designated were either intact artifacts of great age or facsimiles of centuries-old historic objects. To a far greater degree than facades of masonry and stone in Europe, the highly perishable elements of historic building fronts in Kyoto have been altered many times in the century and a half since the Meiji Restoration. Moreover, the preindustrial streetscape composition of these areas was never entirely fixed, but represented instead the evolving forms of a living culture.

By allowing the owners of properties in Traditional Building Preservation Districts leeway to compose street facades within well-researched historic limits, the city government reinstates a facsimile of the abandoned historic culture. As time passes, particular architectural features in Kyoto's wood historic districts will change, but such revisions will be consistent with the spirit embodied in each traditional neighborhood. The very fact that such districts will continue to evolve represents an important part of their historic character. And it is only through the creation of these districts that Kyoto can recapture its past, because no precise record exists documenting the exact configuration of these changeable historic areas at a particular point in time prior to industrialization.

In this regard, Japan may be uniquely prepared to faithfully re-create its lost patrimony through another means as well. Its Law for the Protection of Cultural Properties has a clause establishing protection for Traditional Techniques for the Conservation of Cultural Properties. This provision empowers the national minister of education to recognize those individuals who have become masters of traditional crafts—such people are designated Living National Treasures—and to make arrangements for passing on such knowledge to future generations. In addition, in Kyoto, because so many of the city's traditional houses continue to be maintained, and classical tatami rooms have been built in many modern homes, old building crafts continue to flourish. With the creation of Traditional Building Preservation Districts, select parts of the cityscape are becoming a living museum as the facades of the city's historic buildings are shaped by the curatorial knowledge of Kyoto's architecture school and by a national effort to maintain Japan's medieval crafts.

Traditional Building Preservation Districts in Kyoto offer a very specific view of history, but a precious view nonetheless. When we walk through such areas we experience an environmental aura different from that of typical conservation districts in Western cities. In the West great effort is expended to save the actual material of old buildings, and a degree of historic eccentricity results. The earliest of the Traditional Building Preservation Districts in Kyoto—those that have been maintained for the longest period of time—share an unnatural stylistic perfection similar to that of the rebuilt Old Town of Warsaw and the historic conservation parks like Colonial Williamsburg in the United States. One notes a loss of the idiosyncrasies of urban evolution; and the material of buildings is all the same age, as if time had stopped. Yet no urban historic conservation district is a perfect window into the past, and all such areas are subject to a continuous process of change in order to accommodate alterations in the life of the city. (To help visitors understand the meaning of such places, the rules by which they are regulated could be posted.)

REVERSING THE CULTURE OF DESTRUCTION

Kyoto's reinstated historic areas represent potential solutions to two continuing urban conservation dilemmas. In the twentieth century, numerous historic environments of wood were severely reduced or erased in cities around the world. Today many surviving vestiges of historic wooden cities are in advanced and possibly irreversible stages of deterioration. Such constructions are often extensions of centuries-old building traditions, and in numerous cases are a continuum of medieval cultures—for example, in China, throughout Asia, and in old Islamic centers along the Silk Road and across the Middle East. The loss of these environments, which endured for many hundreds of years and then began to vanish almost simultaneously in the modern era, is one of the great conservation tragedies of the twentieth century.

The Traditional Building Preservation Districts in Kyoto demonstrate a viable method for reclaiming this jeopardized past. Timeliness of action is critical. Rapidly deteriorating wooden features must be saved or recorded before all trace of original architectural elements disappears. And traditions of craftsmanship must be documented and passed on to future generations if deteriorated or lost building parts are to be accurately replaced. Finally, such areas must continue to be zoned at historic building heights. Otherwise, as in Kyoto, an economic incentive for the development of intrusive larger structures is created, resulting in the destruction and fracturing of old districts.

The importance of these developments can be seen in the struggles of two other cities—Istanbul and Beijing—to save their wooden architectural patrimony. In Istanbul, where the vernacular city of the Ottomans has become an overcrowded and deteriorating slum, conservation authorities have initiated two responses: In some areas, the remains of historic structures are the template for re-creating old wooden buildings in new materials, thereby saving several buildings at a time at moderate cost. In other areas, each surviving element of historic wooden buildings is painstakingly restored so that as much original fabric as possible is saved, preserving buildings one at a time at great cost. Here, the speed of deterioration, driven by poverty, far outstrips the government's efforts to preserve vernacular residential areas in the old Ottoman capital.

In Beijing, the intricately carved wooden facades of mercantile buildings lining the streets in old commercial areas are quickly disappearing, as economic revitalization of the capital increases the speed of destruction. Here, as in Kyoto, economic growth causes old buildings to be torn down on major avenues and old facades on the city's smaller byways to be stripped and updated. Already the lack of resources has caused this patrimony to decay severely. One small area has been restored as a conservation district, however, and along this lane a rich heritage of finely carved facades with decorative wood screens constitutes a stunningly evocative historic setting. Otherwise Beijing, like Singapore and Kyoto, seems fated for broad modernization, inevitably reducing the city's historic character to token examples.

While it is impossible to generalize accurately about such diverse cultural phenomena, a pattern tends to emerge. Economic underdevelopment causes decay of historic assets. The single-minded drive for economic recovery causes demolition of badly deteriorated artifacts. But the attainment of a higher standard of living fosters a desire to keep such properties intact, because they stimulate tourism and because as urban societies gain freedom from economic deprivation, they can focus on issues of cultural self-identification. Thus the means and the will to preserve the past often are gained only after the past has already been destroyed.

But can a city reclaim its heritage after such destruction has occurred? With each passing decade, historic conservation laws in Kyoto have increasingly focused on saving whole environments. The preservation districts, the aesthetic areas, and Kyoto's continuing protection of the city's natural landscape not only forestall recent urban development patterns but to some degree attempt to reverse time, to return remnants of the historic city to a condition that has been lost.

Both Western and Japanese observers of Kyoto's cityscape cannot help asking Kevin Lynch's fundamental question: What time is this place? Or even

What place is this place? The combined effect of Kyoto's speculative real estate market and various conservation laws has been to create confusion between the ancient and the modern city around the historic core. Here the modern and historic buildings make distinct aesthetic claims, but neither type dominates. When looking down at the city from the surrounding hillsides, one sees that the preindustrial and postindustrial landscapes are simply commingled in an arbitrary environmental shuffle in which the garden precincts of major monuments stand out as islands of green. The visage of the city is neither contemporary nor old, neither modern nor traditional, neither Western nor Japanese.

In Europe the preservation of old urban centers often results in an extended area of distinct character whose parts combine to make a critical mass and historical visage. When we think of Paris, Prague, Venice, Amsterdam, or Rome, we tend to remember images of historic spaces and buildings knit together in an environmental sculpture of aesthetically related parts. As preservation districts and aesthetic areas in Kyoto are regulated over the decades, two things will inevitably occur: each district will regain its coherence as a historic ensemble, and out-of-scale unsympathetic modern development will seem more intrusive in contrast. If a greater critical mass of historic ambience is to be achieved at the city's center, Kyoto will have to remove some of the large, intrusive modern structures that fracture its historic areas. This will require creating economic incentives for scaling down such constructions.

While restricting the potential for development is an ordinary feature of historic district designations, removing large structures from low-scale areas is a rare phenomenon. Yet the concept of reversing the mistakes of modernization is gaining acceptance. In London, several large municipal housing projects of unfortunate quality have recently been torn down and replaced by lower-scale buildings. Similarly, in Poland, oversize housing blocks built next to reconstructed historic areas have been replaced by smaller structures. Berlin is contemplating the replacement of out-of-scale municipal buildings from the Communist era and, in some instances, re-creating in these same locations buildings lost in the bombings of World War II. Yet all these examples involve government-owned properties. Reversing private property investments once they have been granted through zoning allowances obviously involves more difficult problems of compensation.

In Toyko, in the midst of Japan's modern urban cacophony, an enormous museum dedicated to preserving the architectural history of the city—a history largely destroyed in the firebombings of World War II—has been created. In giant interior spaces, full-scale replicas of old buildings, fragments of other important traditional structures, and extensive models of historic districts form part of the exhibition. I wandered through this museum, stunned by the beauty of what had once been and, as a citizen of the United States, especially saddened by the passing of a remarkable living culture. Here, buildings are saved as objects, removed from their natural existence as the setting for daily life. In much of Japan, the complex interplay of form and culture captured in living historic cityscapes has been lost forever. That is why Kyoto, as one of the few surviving ancient capitals, is so very important.

With each passing year, more and more of the past is likely to be re-created in Kyoto as part of the living city. This reversal of the development trends of modernization is an idea that could very well influence the future of other places. That such a concept has gestated in Japan may be attributable to the fact that for centuries the Japanese have seen the city as a far more transient and changeable object than has been perceived by builders in the West. In this reversal of time, perhaps the historic visage of Kyoto will once again be legible in the valley within the city's mountains. Perhaps someday we may yet be able to return to the beauty that was Japan. But how much will be done is not clear, nor is the intent of the Japanese. Only time's inexorable passage will bring an answer.

THE WIDENING ETHIC
OF PRESERVATION

"What meaning does your construction have?" he asks. "What is
the aim of a city under construction unless it is a city? Where is
the plan you are following, the blueprint?"

"We will show it to you as soon as the working day is over; we
cannot interrupt our work now," they answer.

Work stops at sunset. Darkness falls over the building site. The
sky is filled with stars. "There is the blueprint," they say.

—ITALO CALVINO, *Invisible Cities*

When we see the vast illegal settlements that today are home to
one-quarter of the earth's population, it is hard not to be
appalled. Is this the blueprint which our modern advances
were intended to fulfill? In the fourteenth century, three-fourths of the
inhabitants of Europe and Asia (about 225 million people) died of the plague
while living in conditions now judged to be primitive—lacking sources of clean
water and proper sewage disposal. Today almost ten times that number (about
2 billion people) live in environments that similarly lack such basic provision.
Yet despite the hardship, inequity, and desperation that spawn such
cityscapes, in Mexico City a vestige of hope can be seen in the gradual evolution
of illegal settlements. In several communities, after the primary goal of acquiring shelter has been achieved by homeless urban colonizers, a second basic
human need is served as individual residents creatively transform their con-
crete-block dwellings by adding layers of colorful paint to their exteriors, often
in the form of exuberant graphic signage.

The proclivity of the wall painters of Mexico City's barrios to invest the
built world with visual meaning and color, however meager such surface treatments might be, is of course similar to the motives of traditional handcraft-
workers whose labor over centuries is manifested in the beautiful historic
cityscapes of the world. Thus it is ironic that in order to create the modern

cityscape, which in its most marginal economic forms is frequently an environment of machine-made sterility, so much of the accrued, life-enhancing craftsmanship inherent to historic environments has been reduced. We suffer from the absence of the very quality we have destroyed.

The conservation of historic cities entails two primary acts of social invention: the initial creation of beautiful old cityscapes and, later, the decision to preserve those environments as part of the expanding contemporary metropolis. The first act of invention marks instances of cultural florescence when urban societies marshal a positive social chemistry in regard to their built surroundings and is sometimes confluent with larger heights of achievement in other spheres. The second act of social creativity, the preservation of cultural patrimony, is in many places simply an act of will—not necessarily reconciling the historic and industrialized cityscape but merely juxtaposing the old and new parts of the metropolis in an unsettled coexistence.

One cannot help wondering if a third act of urban creativity is needed and if this is one of the challenges to be met in the current stage of the construction of cities. Can the modern-historic city, once fractured, be reconceived? Can we envision a different blueprint for the future metropolis? The following chapters focus on several instances when human creativity, born of the widening ethic of conservation, reveals useful possibilities for redefining both the plan and the meaning of the city. Since the disposition of the human-made environment is not inevitable but is subject to our desire, the character of our cities must be viewed as a choice. The question I would raise here—even in the face of complex obstacles and difficult alternatives—is whether other, more positive, options might not be available. In drafting our plans, might we look to the stars, or perhaps more deeply into the human heart?

redefine
plan + meaning
of the city
- creation
- preservation
- redefinition

CHAPTER FOURTEEN
THE CITY REDEEMED

BERLIN, MOSCOW, NEW YORK, AND MEXICO CITY

The inferno of living is not something that will be; if there is one,
it is what is already here, the inferno where we live every day, that
we form by being together.

—ITALO CALVINO, *Invisible Cities*

Progress, far from consisting in change, depends on retentiveness.
Those who cannot remember the past are condemned to repeat it.

—GEORGE SANTAYANA, *The Life of Reason*

As I searched for the beauty of the past in cities across the world,
I also encountered the dark side of the metropolis: the injustice, prejudice, and poverty that exist in all places to varying
degrees. In every city, I was drawn to old neighborhoods bypassed by the
authorities, where preservation was an afterthought. Here, old buildings,
though deteriorated, were less changed. This search frequently took me into
slums—in Istanbul, Cairo, Mexico City, Paris, New York, Jerusalem—and
face-to-face with the human inferno. I learned through my research that questions of social justice were linked inextricably, and in many ways, to the process
of architectural conservation.

Of course, even when landmarks have been preserved primarily because of
their physical greatness or beauty, they cannot be separated from negative
social conditions associated with their creation. The accomplishment of the
Acropolis cannot be divorced from the practice of slavery in the Athenian

city-state any more than antebellum mansions in the southern United States can be separated from the bondage of millions of blacks from Africa. The tyranny of absolute rulers is forever embodied in the opulence of the Louvre, the Forbidden City, Islamic Cairo, and the Stalinist Gothic towers of Moscow.

During the twentieth century, however, as the practice of preservation broadened, the motive for designating historic sites expanded to include a direct focus on questions of social morality. This occurred in stages. First, numerous urban societies found the need to remember the social, economic, and spiritual rectification of class injustices. Some landmarks, such as examples of early subsidized public housing, were designated not only for their physical beauty but also because they embodied social progress. Then, after World War II, several cities commemorated sites linked with the commission of genocide and mass murder. These locations, such as the gestapo headquarters in Berlin and Warsaw, were testimony to the reality of human suffering and raised questions of ethical responsibility. The next step, reflected in a monument to the victims of the Communist gulags in Lubyanka Square in Moscow and in another memorial in Berlin, a Holocaust memorial, demarked the general location from which crimes against humanity had emanated—the cities themselves. Here historic conservation became an instrument for preserving urban moral memory. Finally, another kind of remembrance evolved when several important locations were designated that spoke to the continuance of deeply rooted social problems—such as the African burial ground in New York and the Aztec pyramid site in Mexico City—challenging modern urban communities to address difficult contemporary issues of racial and class inequity.

What does it mean when cities preserve artifacts in the built environment that commemorate their acts of injustice, intolerance, and inhumanity? To what degree do cityscapes reflect the character of the societies that build and inhabit them? Have we endowed the architectural forms of the metropolis with metaphysical meaning? Does the city have a collective soul, a conscience?

THE WIDENING SOCIAL PERSPECTIVE OF ARCHITECTURAL CONSERVATION

Across the world, the focus on social history has increased as modern conservation laws have expanded their purview from preeminent symbols of national identity to structures of the highest artistic accomplishment, then to the most beautiful historic neighborhoods, and finally to environments representative of various periods of urban development.

By preserving modest buildings of less aesthetic distinction within historic townscapes we document the lives of ordinary people. As a result, we keep a record of the social and environmental disparities among different classes, at the least in the distinctions between houses of extraordinary opulence and those of relatively meager amenity. In addition, it has become the preferred practice when saving important buildings to retain the changes and accretions accumulated over their lifetime—to preserve a record of their history—rather than making old monuments look stylistically pure and romanticizing the past. Landmarks have come to be valued as much for what they reveal about life in other eras as for their visual enrichment of the physical environment. Here we have recorded the unvarnished facts of history.

By designating early examples of subsidized housing in London, Amsterdam, New York, Vienna, and Berlin, cities preserved material evidence of the establishment in industrialized societies of minimal living standards of basic decency. Two moral value judgments were implicit in the preservation of social housing. The virtue of rectifying social inequities was given public affirmation. Simultaneously, the existence of social injustice and the debilitating nature of slums were acknowledged. Such designations were an important expansion of the social conscience of preservation.

The positive architectural features of advanced social housing projects spoke explicitly of the negative features they remedied. Progressive housing design provided sunlight where once there had been darkness. Toilets and bathing facilities freed the poor from living in filth. Clean drinking water and provisions for fresh air diminished the spread of disease. Attractive accommodations with reasonable allotments of space recognized the dehumanizing effects of cramming people together in insalubrious conditions. The architectural designation of social housing retained in the cityscape symbols of societal reform that were inherently self-critical, from a stage in urban development when unparalleled numbers of people lived in abject misery.

Linkage of historic conservation with the ills of civilization was not restricted to problems from a vanished past. Preserving outmoded living accommodations in old urban districts was a dilemma that often involved unresolved matters of social equity. Particularly in the decades after World War II, as old cities endeavored to save traditional environments situated at the historic urban core, questions of slum improvement and architectural conservation collided. While overcrowded and dilapidated living quarters were seen by reformers as evidence of a failure to house the poor, among the political establishment such areas were often viewed as tinderboxes of political unrest best removed by slum clearance. Once these districts were officially designated as important containers of architectural history, their preservation and upgrading frequently led to gentrification. The very act of architectural conservation was associated with a process of class segregation, as market economics forced the poor to move, frequently outside the city's center, which then became an exclusive enclave of wealth, business, and tourism. Marginalized populations—

of laborers, artisans, neighborhood shop owners, minorities, the underemployed, and the elderly—were expelled from the historic environments of their own culture.

Conservation of the Marais district in postwar Paris grappled with these trends. Some of the oldest historic material in the cityscape was encompassed within that area in early urban palaces of the nobility and in numerous traditional houses, some dating back to medieval prototypes. Over the centuries, the difficulty of rehabilitating these buildings and the emergence of newer, more fashionable districts turned segments of the Marais into slums.

Legislation in 1962 led to making the Marais a Secteur Sauvegardé, an historic area safeguarded by a program that combined restoration, adaptive reuse, and economic development, yet its rehabilitation threatened to displace many of its poorest inhabitants. Student uprisings in Paris in 1968, denouncing the government's delinquency in amending social problems in France, changed the political climate, and the degree of gentrification first contemplated by urban administrators was tempered. The final program of subsidized restoration helped numerous local residents to stay in the revitalized neighborhood, and today its architectural beauty and, to some degree, its social diversity have been retained. For Parisians, the new Marais is a symbol of complex meaning. It embodies the positive environmental benefits of historic conservation, gives recognition to the architectural history of different classes, affirms the efficacy of social criticism in a democratic government, reflects reform in the city's housing renewal policies, and manifests both the salutary and the negative aspects of gentrification.

The Karl-Marx-Hof public housing estate in Vienna embodies complicated and powerful symbols of social criticism. Constructed in 1930 by a Socialist Party municipal government, Karl-Marx-Hof was one of the most beautiful and progressive subsidized housing projects in the world. This massive multiblock assemblage of large sculptural forms, designed in a premodern style, exemplified Vienna's commitment to social housing of high architectural excellence.

In 1934, civil war between troops of the Austrian national government (dominated by conservative elements with an anti-Semitic political platform) and supporters of the Socialist regime in Vienna turned Karl-Marx-Hof into a fortress and a site of armed conflict. The elected municipal government was overthrown, the Austrian Republic was abolished, and an authoritarian Fascist state was instituted. After World War II, in preserving Karl-Marx-Hof as a national monument, the conservation authorities left unrepaired the bullet holes from the civil war. Already an icon of Viennese architectural design and social reform, the housing complex also became emblematic of the bitter political divisions preceding Austria's unification with Nazi Germany.

REMEMBRANCE AND REGRET AFTER WORLD WAR II

The genocide and brutality of the Second World War were demarcated in a variety of ways in several of the European cities I visited while researching this book. Both those who perceived themselves as perpetrators and those who saw themselves as victims have documented atrocities through physical markers in the cityscape. In particular, remembrance of the Jewish Holocaust has become a phenomenon of singular dimensions—within urban areas and at the concentration camps and ad hoc killing fields—expanding historic preservation's function as a medium for public consideration of questions of societal morality. The extended history of anti-Semitism in Europe lends a particularly complex dimension to these physical symbols.

The horror of aerial bombardment during World War II was memorialized in Vienna in its ancient historic center, the Altstadt, in a decision by the Viennese to replace beautiful old buildings damaged by bombing with structures having plain stucco fronts. Today these unadorned facades stand out in Vienna's old cityscape in two ways. Their simplicity of form contrasts sharply with the richly decorated street elevations typical of the city's historic architecture. And a simple bronze plaque on each reconstructed building records the date it was damaged and the date of its repair. Thus, at numerous points in the Altstadt, the flow of environmental beauty is interrupted by stark recollections of the terror of war. Rather than raising a single abstract memorial or repairing the cityscape to its undamaged state, the Viennese have retained evidence of the consequences of modern warfare as an integral part of the continuing life of their city.

Several questions are intrinsic to these memorials. Since conservative elements in Austria commanded national troops to suppress a Socialist majority in Vienna before leading the country to unification with Nazi Germany and subsequently to war, do the markers allude to the abridgment by violence of the rights of the city? Having willingly entered into alliance with Hitler, do the markers denounce the country's complicity in warmongering? Since the Altstadt held no major manufacturing facilities or rail yards, do the plaques condemn the general practice in World War II of attacking noncombatant civilian populations? Do the plain stucco buildings testify to the resiliency of the Viennese in recovering from terrible devastation? Are these buildings a reminder that the inhumanity and atrocities inherent to war make war itself a state to be considered abhorrent? Or were the plain stucco buildings and plaques created because many such questions needed to be asked?

Physical reminders of barbarism inundate the city of Warsaw, which suffered some of the worst atrocities of World War II. Two instances of premeditated genocide occurred here: a Nazi effort to depopulate the city in order to reconstitute it as a Germanic urban center of about 130,000 people, and an accompanying effort to exterminate all Polish Jews. Of about 1,300,000 Varsovians who inhabited the city before the outbreak of hostilities, 800,000 were killed. The city's Jews and those from the surrounding region were gathered in the infamous Warsaw Ghetto for slaughter. Many were never shipped to death camps; they died in the virulent conditions of the ghetto. Historians estimate the total number of Jews killed at more than 450,000 and up, to about 600,000. Of these, about 60,000 died in the Warsaw Ghetto Uprising, an act of heroic but futile resistance that preceded the razing of the ghetto.

Resistance by non-Jewish Varsovians was remarkable as well, a phenomenon that led Hitler to abandon his original plan to save part of the city for resettlement after the war. Over 200 tablets would later be placed throughout the cityscape commemorating the summary execution of arbitrarily selected victims as a deterrent to continuing acts of civil insurgency. A Nazi program of demolition ensued, an attempt to eliminate the architectural heritage of Warsaw, with the notion that depriving the Varsovians of their cultural identity would undermine their courage to resist. By the war's end, 80 percent of the city's buildings and 96 percent of its monuments were destroyed.

The painstaking and loving re-creation of the ancient city center of Warsaw is a memorial in itself, its reconstituted historic buildings testimony to defiance in the face of oppression. Monuments in memory of the Jewish genocide—a simple rectangular enframement of masonry walls at the site where Jews were loaded onto cattle cars for transport to extermination sites, a small surviving fragment of the ghetto wall, a tall stone-and-bronze sculptural memorial located where Jewish resistance fighters died in the ghetto uprising—all are laden with complex moral connotations.

Anti-Semitism had been prevalent in Poland and throughout Eastern Europe for centuries. Although one of the world's largest urban populations of Jews had established a thriving community within Warsaw prior to the war, their concentration in ghettos was a common historical phenomenon in European cities. While their stories vary from place to place, generally Jews were allowed to live only in restricted areas of cities. Often they were required to wear some mark of identification. Frequently they were punitively taxed. In Eastern Europe in particular, architecturally distinctive synagogues were constructed with great trepidation, since they easily became the targets of pogroms. Few Jewish communities in European cities have been continuously settled. Most endured periods of repression and expulsion. During the European Enlightenment, edicts of religious tolerance gradually made conditions better. Yet by the beginning of World War II, dense populations of poorer Jews still lived in ghetto areas that sometimes were no longer compulsory but nonetheless continued to exist as distinct communities. These long-held prejudices not only fostered the Holocaust, but made the gathering and identification of Jews an easier task for their murderers. The Warsaw Ghetto, an urban concentration camp of the Nazis, lay in an area of the city where Jews were already segregated from the rest of Polish society, where they had already been branded by their neighbors. Remembrance in Warsaw of the Holocaust publicly declares the wrongness of a terrible crime perpetrated by outsiders, but it also memorializes historical attitudes in Polish society that caused Jews to live in ghettos in the first place.

After World War II, the most dilapidated old neighborhoods throughout Europe frequently included depopulated former ghettos. In Amsterdam, the only major modern development project to penetrate the ancient heart of the city, breaking the urban architectural rhythms of traditional canalscapes and street walls, occurs where a Jewish quarter was emptied and left to decay by the Holocaust.

The preserved ancient Jewish ghetto in Venice is beautiful and cloaked in melancholy, a living record of a sad history. In 1516, the Venetian senate had decreed: "Be it determined that, to prevent unseemly occurrences, the following measures shall be adopted, i.e. that all the Jews who are at present living in different parishes within our city shall be obliged to go at once to dwell together in the houses in the court within the Geto [meaning 'metal foundry' in Italian] at San Hieronimo, where there is plenty of room for them to live." And Venice is often cited as the place where the word "Ghetto" was coined.

Like other Venetian parish islands, the ghetto was isolated except for its bridges, which had gates that were closed at night. For centuries, it was forbidden for Jews to break the curfew. Taxes and rents were exorbitant. Residents of the ghetto island were required to wear a badge of identification, which varied over time from a yellow to a red cap, to a letter O sewn on their garments. The community was also compelled to hire Christian sentinels to guard the gateway and patrol the canal that surrounded their islet like a moat.

Yet protected by the city government from more severe forms of persecution, the Venetian ghetto flourished, reaching a population of 5,000 at its height. For hundreds of years, its Hebrew publishing houses made Venice one of Europe's most important centers of Jewish scholarship. Apartment buildings were densely packed and taller—frequently seven or eight stories—than the common four-story height of the rest of Venice, causing the island to assume a fortress-like character, while in other aspects it looked typically Venetian. The synagogues were not architecturally distinguished because it was forbidden in

Venice for non-Christian religious structures to adopt conspicuous facades—a restriction that was gradually relaxed.

In a city of elevated architectural practice, several synagogue interiors of great beauty were constructed, sometimes utilizing the talents of Venice's finest architects—notably Baldassare Longhena, designer of one of the most esteemed landmarks of Catholicism in the city, the church of Santa Maria della Salute—and its most accomplished craftsworkers, including Andrea Brustolon, a master woodcarver of the seventeenth century. Dazzling heights of sophisticated composition were achieved with the help of Christian artists who applied their gifts to the enrichment of Judaic places of worship.

With the unification of modern Italy in the nineteenth century, Jews were legally granted full equality and gradually mixed with the indigenous populations. Prior to World War II, about 750 Jews lived in Venice. Many fled or were hidden by fellow Venetians, but 250 were captured and deported. For these, tolerance in the city became an inadvertent servant of betrayal. Today a plaque in the main piazza reads:

> Men, women, children, masses for the gas chamber
> Advancing toward horror beneath the whip of the executioner
> Your sad holocaust is engraved in history
> And nothing shall purge your deaths from our memory
> For our memories are your only grave.

The Venetian ghetto today is largely bereft of Jews; its magnificently adorned synagogue interiors are hidden jewels in the upper stories of towering old tenements. I wandered through Venice knowing I was in the vicinity of the famous island. Then, rounding a corner, I recognized it from a distance. Every aspect of its historic form—its tallness, separateness, compactness, lack of embellishment—spoke of the life of a people in part assimilated, in part given refuge, yet persistently distinguished by differences of faith. Ultimately, here was the architecture of human tragedy.

THE TOPOGRAPHY OF TERROR IN BERLIN

Berlin is a city haunted by regret and a terrible question. As the capital of a government that practiced genocide as its official policy, Berlin was a scene of unspeakable horrors. Words utterly fail to describe the extermination of millions of Jews, Slavs, Gypsies, and others in the name of racial purification. In the decades since the fall of the Third Reich, while understanding how such atrocities happened has been a painful inquiry for Germans, resolution that they should never occur again has inspired persistent self-examination.

In 1997, in *Hitler's Willing Executioners*—a best-selling and much-debated book that has been broadly confirmed by German readers for its historical accuracy—Daniel Jonah Goldhagen traced strands of cultural development that led to a program of intolerance "willingly acquiesced to by the German people." A 1996 exhibition entitled *Vernichtungskrieg. Verbrachen der Wehrmacht 1941 bis 1944* (Total War: Crimes of the Nazi Army from 1941 to 1944) documented the fervor with which genocide was practiced by the troops of the Third Reich. The exhibit horrified Germans, yet it was verified by veteran soldiers. It was then requested for display in more than a hundred cities and towns across the nation. Two generations after the Second World War, this widening sense that Germany's barbarism should be publicly accounted for has made the rebuilding of Berlin, since its unification after the fall of the Soviet Union, fraught with painful issues in regard to preserving the historic and architectural heritage of the capital.

After the war, Berlin was a shattered city. During 378 Allied bombing missions more than 50,000 tons of explosives were dropped on the city—more than on any other urban center in Europe. About 20 percent of its buildings were beyond salvage, another 70 percent required varying degrees of rehabilitation, and large parts of central Berlin were reduced to skeletal ruins. After the surrender of Germany, the capital was physically partitioned by its occupying forces into four sectors: Soviet, American, French, and British. Berlin as a cohesive entity had ceased to exist.

As detailed descriptions gradually emerged of the horrors committed by the Third Reich, Germany and the world were struck by shock waves of abhorrence—inexorably identified with the former capital. By 1961, with the advent of the Cold War, the East German Communist government had constructed a wall of concrete and barbed wire encircling the part of the metropolis allied with the Western democracies. Berlin became two places, each in ideological opposition to the other. One city was locked in, the other locked out.

The erratic course of the Wall, and its accompanying buffer zone of guarded open land (referred to as the Death Strip by West Germans), wound through Berlin's battered historic center, making it impossible for the physical metropolis to heal. For decades, former central areas on either side of the barrier were characterized by intermittent vacant lots, exposed building sidewalls, dead-end streets, and old bullet holes. Long after other cities in Europe had been reconstructed, and even following the wall's removal in 1989, the scars of war remained in central Berlin.

Yet another distressing memory lingered after reunification. As the capital of the German nation-state since 1871, Berlin had become a major European industrial center, the continent's second most populous city and, during the period after World War I, a preeminent site of modern scientific and artistic invention, particularly in such fields as theoretical science, theater, opera, film, architecture, and design. The rise of fascism and the policies of the Third Reich ended this vibrant flourishing of German culture, to which Berlin's Jews had been major contributors. Many great artists and scientists escaped prior to the war, while others were driven out or became the victims of Nazi repression. To the degree that the city embraced fascism, it embraced the demise of its own florescence. Thus, by 1991, when the seat of national government was reestablished in the city, Berlin had for some time been possessed by forbidding physical and psychological memories.

Although the story of the rebuilding of Berlin is still unfolding, many urban historians have already noted a remarkable aspect of its reconstitution. Repeatedly in the planning process, during the period when the city was divided and after it was made whole, particularly in regard to issues of architectural preservation, Berliners have asked whether the renewed face of their metropolis masked a painful legacy. To what degree should evidence of the victims and perpetrators of Nazism be retained in the cityscape?

Socially self-critical memorials have emerged at numerous locations. Some of these retain physical reminders of Nazi criminality that otherwise would have disappeared as the ruined city was repaired and its occupants and uses evolved with time. Places where Jews were gathered for deportation—such as a synagogue on Levetzowstrasse and a Jewish Retirement Home on Grosse Hamburgerstrasse, both vanished—are today remembered with markers. In the district of Steglitz, a large commemorative wall records the names and addresses of former Jewish residents who became victims. In Neuköln, the history of a forced-labor camp is recorded on a sidewalk at its former location. An explanatory tablet and memorial sculpture by American artist Richard Serra has been placed at the address of Tiergarten 4, to preserve recollection of the building from which an initiative was administered to kill mental patients throughout Germany. A program of eighty small street markers attached to lampposts in the district of Schöneberg, and symbolizing eighty increasingly malicious anti-Semitic regulations of the Third Reich, document the vanished life of neighborhood Jews. Additional signs in two public squares in Schöneberg record the twelve most infamous concentration camps as "Places of Terror We Must Never Forget." Here the people of a community in Berlin recognize the implicit sanction of former residents to acts of barbarism undertaken by their government, in their names, in places both inside and outside their city.

Often, with structures associated with the Third Reich, the commonplace step of preserving old buildings has involved additional efforts to publicly document their history. Conservation of the railroad loading ramp at Grunewald, from which Jews were shipped to extermination camps, required a tablet to explain its significance. Eventually, a memorial wall was created by

Polish sculptor Karol Broniatowski to reinvoke, through the abstraction of art, the suffering that occurred at what otherwise appears to be a mere utilitarian structure.

Similarly, the house at Am Grossen Wannsee 56–58, where the "final solution" to exterminate the Jews of Europe was discussed, has not only been landmarked; it was set aside in 1992 as a Holocaust Memorial Center in yet another effort to create places for public introspection. These acts are especially important to the education of German children, who in many school districts are required to visit former concentration camps, such as the two compounds outside Berlin at Sachsenhausen and Ravensbrück, prior to their graduation.

The most notable monument associated with Nazism to date is an overgrown and largely vacant lot at the crossing of Prinz-Albrecht-Strasse—today known as Niederkirchnerstrasse—Wilhelmstrasse, and Anhalter Strasse. On this block were located the offices of the head of the secret police (the SS), the gestapo, and the Reich Security Main Office—a singular assemblage of agencies sharing official responsibility for repressive police control, racial purification, and genocide.

Targeted for bombing during the war, most of the buildings on the lot had been heavily damaged, and in the following decades they were demolished and cleared away. During the Cold War a segment of the Berlin Wall stretched across the block's northern perimeter. In the 1970s, it was a dumping ground for dirt from construction excavations. The only surviving structure was the former art school that had been coopted as gestapo headquarters, with its basement serving as interrogation rooms. This was reopened as a history museum in 1981.

In 1986, as the city debated whether to build another cultural facility on the site, advocates of its preservation as an undeveloped lot lobbied the municipal government to make exploratory archaeological excavations. Several surviving gestapo jail rooms and a staff kitchen were discovered. As a result, a small building was constructed to house a temporary exhibition entitled *Topography of Terror*, a carefully documented account of the inhumane practices of Germany's legitimate government under Adolf Hitler.

Over 300,000 people viewed this exhibit in the first year, and its duration was twice extended. In 1992, a competition was held for the design of a permanent exhibition hall, with the idea that the lot would remain largely untouched. In 1995, the exhibit was given the status of a permanent memorial, but to date, construction of the permanent hall still has not started.

While the *Topography of Terror*, with its weeds and natural overgrowth, may appear to be a location arrested in a state of urban neglect, it is in fact a monument of very deliberate design. A gravel pathway, a simple viewing platform on top of an overgrown rubble hill, a modest exhibition structure, scattered outcroppings of old masonry walls, and a few discreet signs are spread out amid spontaneous urban greenery. The name of the place is intentionally chilling, a contrast between its current benign appearance and the horror once generated at this location.

Creation of the monument was to some extent happenstance. Several surviving Nazi buildings in Berlin are being reused. Other infamous landmarks, such as Hitler's bunker, were demolished and built over. An apartment complex built during the Soviet period now occupies the site. The *Topography of Terror* exhibit came into existence during a period when German historians were beginning to study the culture of perpetrators and to connect their actions with broad social attitudes. Preservation of the exhibit in what appears to be an abandoned lot symbolizes the criticism that an unpleasant history was being disregarded and buried by the authorities.

When first established, this exhibition existed in an urban backwater created by the presence of the Berlin Wall. With reunification, however, the site assumed a more central location in the city. This is significant in two ways. Historically, the proximity of the exhibit to the ceremonial heart of Berlin reflects the place of such activities in the hierarchy of Nazi government. And its preservation today as an undeveloped but potentially valuable site maintains a visible open wound in the center of one of Europe's major capital cities.

An important message of the *Topography of Terror* is that the city of Berlin has found no other use proper for the site, as if the acts associated with this location have cursed the ground forever. Yet it is not a place that advertises it existence loudly, and many visitors might easily walk by the site, failing to recognize its meaning. This lack of visual prominence involves another controversial issue.

Since 1992, both the federal government of Germany and the municipal government of Berlin have been committed to the creation of a major memorial to the victims of the Holocaust. The site chosen is a block away from the Brandenburg Gate, at the symbolic core of the capital, in an area once occupied by the gardens of Hitler's Reich Chancellery. A major international competition attracted many hundreds of entries when it was held in 1995, but the winning design was vetoed by Germany's chancellor as too strident. Construction of the winner from the second competition—a collaborative design effort by two Americans, architect Peter Eisenman and sculptor Richard Serra—has yet to commence.

While Germany and Berlin have struggled over the apropriateness of its appearance, the resolution to build such a memorial is in itself remarkable. Allowed to be whole once again, the city is quickly changing, and new buildings seem to emerge every day at its center. Many old wounds are being healed; others are being exposed to the light. Berlin's central Holocaust monument and its many self-critical markers will color the very visage of the city in perpetuity, conveying regret and responsibility for terrible deeds that Germans have resolved will not be dissociated from their capital, as if the cityscape is a reflection of its conscience.

THE STONE IN LUBYANKA SQUARE IN MOSCOW

With the breakup of the Union of Soviet Socialist Republics and the gradual opening of government records, historians have been better able to measure the human toll of political repression during the first half of seven decades of Communist rule. With only partial access to sensitive documents, authors of the 1999 edition of *The Black Book of Communism* estimate that by standards of criminality defined in the charter of the International Military Tribunal at Nuremberg, at least 20 million Soviet civilians died, and many millions more were brutalized, at the hands of their own government.

This massive scale of institutionalized terror—largely hidden in its details and magnitude while it occurred, and carried out with capricious finality—produced an environment of fear that shattered the norms of civil society. After the death of Stalin in 1953 and prior to the demise of the Soviet police state in 1991, government records were largely sealed, and evidence of the forced-labor camps was plowed underground. Yet some individuals—including Aleksandr Solzhenitsyn in *The Gulag Archipelago*—dared to openly remember the murder of millions of their fellow citizens during that dangerous period.

Today, while self-critical monuments of conscience are rare in Russia, nonetheless a few hard-won and modest memorials have been raised at important historic locations. On the outskirts of Moscow, several mass burial sites of victims of political terror are now marked with identifying plaques. In the center of the capital, on a traffic island in Lubyanka Square, across the street from the former headquarters of the KGB a simple but remarkable public shrine was created in 1990.

A boulder from an Arctic concentration camp was brought to the city and placed on a large horizontal stone rectangle inscribed with the following message: "This stone from the territory of Solovki, which was a camp of special punishment, has been placed here in memory of the millions of casualties of the totalitarian regime and inaugurated on the 30th of October: which is the date officially recognized by the national government as the Day of Remembrance of the Victims of Political Repression."

In a city of 9 million people, the monument in Lubyanka Square seems minuscule and lost. The stone is small, but its message is chilling. It identifies the otherwise architecturally innocuous former KGB headquarters—today housing a different government agency—as a landmark of horror. It connects the immorality of policies generated by the state to terrible repercussions in the lives of people across the Soviet Union. The reality of the stone insists that the reality of the gulags, though leveled, cannot be wiped away. The stone is small, but it could not occupy a place in the public realm of Moscow without either official consent or official confirmation of the truth of its message.

THE AFRICAN BURIAL GROUND IN NEW YORK

Just as the landscapes of numerous historic cities in Europe are imprinted by anti-Semitism, contemporary cityscapes in the United States are commonly marked by racial intolerance. In virtually every large urban agglomeration, poorer areas—slums and ghettos—are disproportionately inhabited by people of color, in particular by African-Americans. Tangible manifestations of racism in the built environment, in concentrated zones of poverty subject to racial inequity, are a fundamental characteristic of the American metropolis.

Slavery and racial prejudice were a disquieting facet of American life even before the founding of the United States, engendering critical and turbulent moments of social change at different times in history. Across the seventeenth to nineteenth centuries, the enslavement and forced migration of Africans, by the Portuguese, Spanish, English, French, Dutch, and Americans themselves resulted in the arrival of more than 11 million slaves in North and South America and the Caribbean. Historians estimate that the barbarity of this journey into bondage, known as the Middle Passage, caused the death of 1.6 to 2.2 million people—15 to 20 percent of all captives. About a half-million Africans were transported into servitude in the United States.

Because conditions of captivity in the United States were generally less brutal than in other parts of the Americas, when measured by the cruel barometer of natural population increase, by the time of the American Civil War the majority of the country's 4 million slaves, toiling largely on southern plantations, were native-born Americans—generation upon generation, heirs to a life of subjugation. In terms of culture and demography, they were African-Americans.

For several reasons, the bulk of the physical evidence of the lives of slaves has disappeared. Early slave shacks in rural locations were commonly constructed of perishable materials and, like other colonial buildings, unless continuously occupied, were subject to natural deterioration. In urban areas, particularly in the North, where slaves frequently did not have separate lodgings but lived in secondary spaces within the buildings of their owners—in attics, basements, workrooms, and outbuildings—precise records of their places of occupancy are scarce, and the frequent physical transformations characteristic of American industrial centers have erased many layers of history, including those relating to groups other than African-Americans.

In the decades after the American Revolution, when 17 percent of white families in the United States owned slaves, an agreement was framed in the nation's Constitution that the importation of slaves would cease by 1809. This, and the emergence of cotton as the major cash crop of American agriculture, led to large numbers of slaves being sold and moved from Middle Atlantic States like Virginia to rural areas in the Deep South. Many abandoned slave quarters, left untended, would disappear with time.

Nonetheless, in the period prior to the Civil War, 338,637 households possessed slaves, and 2,292 of these owners were large planters holding 100 or more blacks. With the abolition of slavery, the bulk of the slaves' housing was gradually abandoned, torn down, or rebuilt, though it was not uncommon for former slaves temporarily to occupy better-constructed surviving plantation slave quarters. Since the practice of architectural preservation did not become widespread in the United States until the second half of the twentieth century, the significance of saving such sites would not be broadly recognized by society for many decades.

While programs such as the Historic American Buildings Survey, founded in 1933 to create drawings and photographs of important structures across the country, would include documentation of 23,000 plantation buildings from about 300 different locations, most of this material was gathered in the 1930s. By this time, many of the subject buildings were in final stages of deterioration and have subsequently been lost.

To some degree, loss of the sites of slavery also reflects the moral contradiction of the prolonged persecution of African-Americans in a nation ostensibly established upon the principle "that all men are created equal." In the decades after the Emancipation Proclamation and passage of the Thirteenth, Fourteenth, and Fifteenth amendments to the Constitution—abolishing slavery, granting citizenship, and giving the right to vote to former slaves—the majority of African-Americans continued to live in the South, where these newly won rights were abrogated by black codes and Jim Crow laws, epidemics of lynching, and legal and educational discrimination. A vast migration to northern industrial cities ensued. Here the majority of black inhabitants, though less persecuted, were still economically marginalized and compelled to live in racially segregated slums. Institutionalized slavery was replaced by institutionalized racial prejudice—a condition legally addressed but not socially purged by the Civil Rights Movement of the 1960s.

These circumstances all contributed to the fact that, by 1994, of 62,000 sites on the National Register of Historic Places, only 800 were associated with African-American history. Of these, only thirty-three documented former slave quarters, and only eight provided testimony of breeding, imprisonment, and auctioning. Though the National Register does not include all the historic places designated by various states, as of the year 2000, it was the only nation-wide indicator of the relative magnitude of surviving historic slave sites. Meanwhile, public interest in this subject has greatly widened and more buildings are being identified and reclaimed with every passing year. Nonetheless, the preponderance of material evidence involving the sanctioned dehumanization of millions of people, a phenomenon that, at its height, characterized the built culture of the southern United States, had substantially disappeared from the physical environments of American life.

Thus, in the fall of 1991, when an exploratory excavation in preparation for the construction of a federal office building in lower Manhattan unearthed human bones in the reputed vicinity of the colonial-era Negroes Burial Ground, an emotionally charged matter of local landmarks preservation became an issue of nationwide concern.

In compliance with federal, state, and city laws, construction activity was temporarily stopped so that scholars could proceed with a proper archaeological examination. The findings bore witness to the harsh inequities that African-Americans suffered in New York in the 1700s. Although in relative terms New York had not been a major center of slavery, it was still the seventh-largest slave port in U.S. history. By 1790 slavery was still expanding in the state and 10 percent of the city's populace was black, including 2,300 slaves and about 1,000 freedmen and freedwomen. As in several other northern states, manumission occurred in partial steps, and it was not until 1827 that slavery in New York finally ended.

Covered over and built upon as the modern metropolis grew, the Negroes Burial Ground was a former potter's field located outside the city's early walls, where slaves, former slaves, and their progeny were interred during the 1700s because they were not allowed in the sanctified graveyards of the city's churches. Archaeologists soon discovered that bodies had been buried one above the other, sometimes five or six deep, and none with stones to mark their identity or their place in the cemetery.

The federal office building was to occupy about a third of an acre, and even though archaeological excavations did not involve the whole of this area, the number of bodies discovered was startling: 410 were disinterred, out of an estimated total of 500 to 600. To avoid delaying the construction schedule, skeletons were expeditiously but carefully removed by archaeologists to a university for further scientific study. Preliminary investigation of the remains revealed widespread malnutrition. Before the disinterments could be completed, several issues of conscience emerged.

It was soon determined that the Negroes Burial Ground was the largest existing early urban graveyard of slaves in the country, extending underneath many built-up lots in the immediate area. Should these bodies be exhumed, or should they finally be allowed a publicly honored resting place? Should construction of the office building proceed, permitting the burial ground once again to vanish in the cityscape? Furthermore, in a metropolis still plagued by racial inequality—where of more than 20,000 properties designated in the city only a few dozen spoke of the African-American experience and none documented the practice of slavery—wasn't official recognition of the Negroes Burial Ground not just a concern of historic preservation but also a matter of social justice?

The municipality's Landmarks Preservation Commission acknowledged the burial ground's distinction as "one of the most significant finds in the city of New York, if not the country, related to the history of African-Americans" but did not designate it, in part because the commission was not empowered by law to regulate a higher level of government. Regardless of this restriction, the commission's failure to officially recognize a property of such unparalleled historic importance morally sanctioned the effort to cover it over once again. (Had the commission moved to designate the property, its efforts might have been thwarted in the courts, but the ethical importance of the matter would have been trumpeted in the public arena.) Meanwhile, throughout the excavation process, images of the disinterments appeared repeatedly in local newspapers, and the heart and conscience of the city ached, as one skeleton after another was violated.

Reluctant to hinder the construction of a large federal project that promised employment to numerous New Yorkers, the city's elected officials settled on a compromise. At a town meeting in the spring of 1992, it was announced that within the interior of the proposed office building a "significant memorial" would be incorporated. Yet several citizen groups had been formed to try to save the graveyard, and critics proposed an alternative solution. Since the office building was to be composed of two masses—a tall tower and a low pavilion, whose construction might be deferred—a part of the gravesite could be saved, thereby claiming a permanent place in the urban landscape.

By now this was a matter of national prominence. The Black Caucus of the U.S. Congress intervened, threatening to block the federal appropriation for the project, insisting that the burial ground be officially recognized as a historic site, that the pavilion not be constructed, and that untouched graves in this location be left in peace. Their moral position was politically unassailable. Several months later, at a formal public hearing of the city's Landmarks Commission to consider designation of the African Burial Ground, an outpouring of support from across New York was heard.

Today the African Burial Ground is an open plot of grass surrounded by tall buildings, with a chain-link fence and intermittent shrubs along its perimeter. A temporary painted plywood sign indicates its status since 1993 as a city and national historic site. The continuing lack of more respectful fittings, in one of the world's most prosperous large cities, seems sadly inappropriate. This is not a problem particular to New York. While the Holocaust Museum in Washington, D.C., commemorates the victims of anti-Semitism in Europe, Americans have yet to erect in the capital a monument to the millions of casualties of legalized slavery in their own country.

Yet this small parcel of open land in downtown New York has great meaning for many people. While the disinterred skeletons undergoing scientific study will greatly expand understanding of slavery, preservation of a part of the burial ground itself has tangible moral value. African-Americans in New York know that the terrible facts of their history have been officially acknowledged by society as worthy of remembrance. The once invisible historical foundations of racial intolerance in the city have now assumed a physical presence. And after almost two hundred years, some few of slavery's anonymous victims have finally been allowed a resting place in inviolable ground, to be protected in perpetuity, in the name of the welfare of all the citizens of the metropolis.

THE AZTEC PYRAMID SITE IN MEXICO CITY

Located at the core of Mexico City is one of the most beautiful tracts of urban space in the world, although in purely visual terms it is strikingly chaotic: a raw cut in the city's architectural fabric, haphazardly juxtaposed with surrounding buildings and spaces. Its terrain is jagged and confusing, a landscape of truncated angular archaeological remains set in a large depression and traversed by a network of suspended wooden walkways. While the noise, pollution, and teeming life of the city threaten to engulf it, the site persists as an area of contemplation. Its visitors seem to understand that they have entered a place of the spirit, and they behave accordingly, quietly walking among the ruins. Here are remnants of the vanished pyramid complex that once crowned the center of the great Aztec capital of Tenochtitlán. Today, preservation of the spiritual heart of the ancient metropolis is a symbol of hope in a vast, fractured, poverty-stricken modern megalopolis.

Few urban writers fail to mention racism as a fundamental characteristic of contemporary Mexico City, perhaps because racial, economic, and physical segregation are visually palpable in a city partitioned into zones of extreme contrast. Guarded residential, commercial, and business enclaves of conspicuous wealth are predominantly the domain of a small minority of European descent, known as criollos and an elite of mixed European and Indian descent, called mestizos. Mestizos constitute the vast majority of the country's inhabitants. Those who trace their lineage to indigenous Mexicans—that is, Indians—are disproportionately impoverished, largely inhabiting the barrios and immense illegal settlements that stretch to the horizon, swallowing up the surrounding terrain of the capital city.

The zones of privilege are urbane, opulent, gleaming, and largely inaccessible to the poor. The zones of poverty—which most individuals in the upper classes fear to enter—are starkly destitute and haunted by despair. Neither rich nor poor can know the city where they live, for they do not know its many different parts. All inhabitants of the metropolis suffer from its widespread crime and dense air pollution.

At one time, Mexico City was famed for the clarity of light in the valley where it is situated. It was a radiant jewel that awed and delighted its visitors. Like Rome and Istanbul, it occupies a singular place in urban history, having twice risen to become the capital of a great empire. Before its conquest by the Spanish, Tenochtitlán was a vast metropolis with an estimated 150,000 to 200,000 people—more than twice the size of the largest cities in Spain at that time—and unlike any place its European conquerors had ever seen. Bernal Díaz del Castillo, one of the first Europeans to see the valley, wrote,

> When we beheld so many cities and towns on the water, the other large settlements built on firm ground, and that broad causeway running so straight and perfectly level to the city of Tenochtitlán, we were astonished, and said that it was like the things of enchantment in legends, because of the great towers, temples, and buildings that rose up out of the water, and all constructed of stone masonry. Some of our soldiers said that these things seemed to be a dream; and it is no wonder that I write here in this manner, for there is much to ponder in this, and I do not know how to tell it, for there never was seen, or heard, nor even dreamt, anything like that which we observed.

The city that awed the Spanish was a massive feat of environmental engineering, an extended urban settlement of flowing waters and profuse fruit and vegetable gardens created by the Aztecs in what was otherwise an inhospitable natural setting. Subject to fierce regional intertribal rivalries, the Aztecs had established their capital in an arid valley with several large, shallow lakes. Over time, they constructed a nine-mile-long dike and numerous canals to control flooding and, conversely, the drying up and oversalinization of Lake Texcoco, whose center they inhabited. Here an extended network of flourishing green islands, canals, and bridges was created by constructing large rectilinear rafts of interwoven branches called *chinampas,* which were towed into place, covered with mud, and anchored to the lake's bottom by the roots of willow trees planted along the perimeter. Managed equilibrium of the surrounding body of water provided a natural defensive barrier for the city and a local ecosystem to support agriculture.

In the center of the lake was a complex of stone pyramids and palaces, linked to the mainland by several causeways of more than a mile in length. Each of these roads had a fortified gate and massive drawbridge. The formal heart of the city, built upon ground that had been filled and raised, was about half a mile square and organized in a large rectilinear grid oriented to the rising sun of the spring equinox. Important buildings were adorned with brightly painted stucco and fine sculptural figures. This was the latest and last manifestation of a thousand-year-old architectural tradition among the Indian civilizations of Mexico. Its major stepped pyramid was approximately the size of the smallest of the three great Egyptian pyramids at Giza.

When the city is viewed in the context of global urban history, from both an aesthetic and ecological perspective, it is clearly one of the most extraordinary ever built. Yet unlike Bernal Díaz del Castillo, who was able to examine the actual construction, we can see Tenochtitlán only as a place of legend. The city was leveled by the Spanish in 1521, and it is only through historical descriptions and modern archaeology that we have been able to piece together the facts of its former existence—by uncovering various remnants from beneath the modern megalopolis that was eventually built on top of it.

The ferocity of the Aztecs, with their human sacrifices and cannibalism, horrified and frightened the Spaniards. While their commander in chief, Hernán Cortés, was dazzled by Tenochtitlán, he also believed its destruction to be a military necessity, if a small number of Europeans were to subjugate millions of native inhabitants in an immense geographic area.

The capital of New Spain was built by a host of vanquished Indian laborers and craftsmen, within a remarkably brief period of time, reusing stone blocks from Aztec monuments and adopting the old rectilinear grid of Tenochtitlán's ceremonial core. Like the Aztec metropolis, colonial Mexico City was vast, horizontal, and green, with wide streets and large open plazas drenched with sunlight. Its openness and simple geometric order were immediately admired by foreign visitors. Over the ensuing centuries, the empire in Mexico so enriched both Spain and its colonists that in no other place in the colonial Americas were such fabulous fortunes accumulated, and Mexico City was progressively endowed with numerous beautiful structures. Many of these were a fusion of Moorish, Christian, and Islamic building styles from Spain, combined with local architectural traditions, and fashioned by Indian artisans of regional stones and bricks whose coloration was unique to the country's geology. In the eighteenth and nineteenth centuries, the colonial capital became known as the City of Palaces. A great cathedral was constructed on the northern perimeter of Mexico City's large central plaza, the Zócalo, close to the site of the demolished major pyramid of the city that had vanished from sight. The Indians had been slain, exploited, decimated by epidemics of European diseases to which they had no immunity, reduced to poverty, and banished to the outskirts.

As in other Latin American societies, industrialization, modernization, and political reform generated an expanded middle class, especially in Mexico City, where universities and large tracts of modern housing were constructed on their behalf. But underdevelopment of the country's economy as a whole; the control of wealth and capital along self-perpetuating class lines, reflecting the extreme disparities of wealth produced by the colonial economic system; concentration of employment opportunities and social services in a city of unequaled nationwide primacy; massive migrations of people from rural areas; and an explosion of population due to improvements in health care would cause Mexico City to become one of the world's largest urban agglomerations by the second half of the twentieth century. It became a megalopolis of extreme and widespread poverty, without the resources to plan or manage its growth.

Millions of Mexico's poor, upon arriving in a city that had no place for them, built miles of makeshift illegal housing, much of it on land unsuitable for settlement, polluted by industrial waste, and vulnerable to flooding, land-slides, and damage from earthquakes. Unauthorized neighborhoods lacked sewage, garbage collection, utilities, and clean water supply. They had no schools or hospitals. By 1990, in a city of nearly 16 million people, half the population was impoverished, and 60 percent of its built-up area was occupied unlawfully. Violent crime and environmental pollution escalated. The wealthy and middle classes barricaded themselves inside segregated neighborhoods. The poor competed with one another for the smallest opportunity to advance their condition, or merely to survive.

Mexico City has been in a desperate situation for several decades, yet the city endures. In the context of such problems, however, few resources can be directed to preserving the architectural patrimony. Many downtown parts of the beautiful colonial metropolis, deserted by the wealthy and now occupied by the impoverished, have become barrios, decaying from lack of maintenance and overpopulation. Government officials might hope that the private sector would revive such structures for new uses, but preservation in the form of gentrification is strongly opposed by local neighborhood groups. After inheriting the palaces of their oppressors and developing a meaningful contemporary urban culture of their own, the poor see market-driven landmarks conservation as yet another means to marginalize them—to take away their homes, communities, and cultural associations.

Although self-built housing, informal neighborhoods, and ad hoc networks for social assistance are cause for hope in that they demonstrate the impulse of people to work collectively in support of their common welfare, such efforts inadvertently subsidize policies that repress the poor by underwriting services that the upper and middle classes receive automatically. By helping themselves in areas where other citizens of Mexico City receive government assistance, the poor relieve the authorities of their obligation to aid all citizens.

In light of these conditions, governmental efforts to recapture in the cityscape lost remnants of Tenochtitlán represent more than just conservation of the city's built heritage. Preservation of the ruins of Indian civilizations, often a complex and costly endeavor, requires consensus that much-needed resources be allocated for such work. This acknowledges the significance of the pre-Columbian Indian heritage to Mexico's cross-fertilized (mestizo) culture, and gives recognition to a segment of society (Indians) that otherwise is often excluded from the social contract.

Particularly during the twentieth century, as the city expanded into former rural areas and as modern infrastructure and foundations for large buildings were constructed, long-overlooked sites and numerous archaeological remains were rediscovered. Many extraordinary artifacts were transferred to museums, but some larger constructions were saved in situ to become part of the land-scape of the living metropolis. A past that had once been purposely erased was now painstakingly reestablished.

In February 1978, workers laying electric cable in the center of the metropolis, near the Zócalo, discovered an enormous stone monolith. Until that moment, although vestiges of Tenochtitlán had been unearthed at several nearby locations, the exact position of its demolished major pyramid had not been known with certainty. Across four hundred years, successive generations of buildings had been erected above its remains as the cityscape evolved and changed. Recovery of the renowned Coyolxauhqui stone—a horizontal sculp-tural disk about 10 feet (3.25 meters) in diameter and a major feature of the central temple complex referred to in many historic texts—pinpointed the pyramid's position beneath the modern urban settlement.

A special advisory board was established to evaluate the significance of structures erected on top of the temple area. Those with historic material dat-ing from the city's early colonial period were disassembled, their parts num-bered and stored. Over four years, the post-Aztec city was carefully peeled away. When razing the great temple, the conquistadors had simply removed the upper part of the pyramid, before filling in the ceremonial area of Tenochtitlán and building over it. Several centuries later, this horizontal cut through the structure allowed modern archaeologists to see into the inner construction of lower parts of the pre-Columbian building.

It was learned that the great pyramid had been enlarged six times across its history, each of these expansions superimposed on the one before it. Because each incarnation of the structure was sacred, when it was built over, many old sculptural features were left intact. And since Tenochtitlán was erected on a low island in the midst of Lake Texcoco, as the pyramid complex grew larger and heavier, eventually including almost 80 buildings, ground level of the ceremonial center was gradually raised to offset its sinking. Over two hundred years, from 1325 until the Spanish Conquest in 1521, seven progressively bigger incarnations of the building were compiled, with the base of earlier temples starting at lower elevations. Thus, although the conquistadors had demolished the top of the final phase of the great temple, some of the preceding stages of the building, which peaked at lower heights, still survived, encased in the remains of the structure.

The ruins of the great temple provided a wealth of sculptural artifacts and a record of the evolution of Aztec religious and architectural practices. The remains of several neighboring temples were found as well. A museum was built on the site to explain the findings and show its treasures. Yet the most meaningful aspect of the project is the retention of the decimated temple area as a permanent component of modern Mexico City.

Wandering through the plazas surrounding the archaeological dig, I was immersed in impromptu street markets where Indian farmers and craftworkers sold their wares. Demonstrations of dances and music associated with the Aztecs enlivened the marketplace with ancient imagery and sounds. Tamales cooked on primitive outdoor stoves. During lulls in the buying and selling, parents walked with their children among the ruins. Often, I saw whole families quietly discussing the truncated stone remains that surrounded them. Many of these people were obviously of modest means. For hundreds of years their forebears had been banished to the outskirts of Mexican cities. Now at the very heart of the modern capital, at extraordinary expense and by consensus of the society in which they lived, the colonial past had been carved away to reveal the Indian heritage. An act of cultural barbarism leading to centuries of racial persecution had been laid bare. The legacy of the Aztecs, after being removed from sight, had reclaimed a central symbolic position in the city that emerged from the fusion of the culture of its conquerors and the culture of those who were crushed. The market that surrounded the Aztec pyramid site was part of the informal economy of the city, but the archaeological site itself had been officially set aside forever on behalf of all the citizens of Mexico.

CONSCIENCE AND THE CITY

In both developed and underdeveloped nations, the large, fractured cities of the modern era often seem out of control. At various times in their evolution, populations have leaped to sizes far greater than resources would support. Human misery has then been compounded beyond calculation, and problems have assumed a magnitude and complexity that defies apparent solution.

Physical, economic, religious, ethnic, racial, and ideological segregation have undermined—and still undermine—the polity of many urban places. Sheer gigantism makes the metropolis as a whole difficult to see, comprehend, or characterize.

Yet the very act of preserving sites that record injustice and barbarity demonstrates an impulse in city dwellers to hold themselves responsible for conditions that they have caused. If there is no accountability for the human inferno, can we ever hope to constrain it? In this regard, historic preservation involves much more than architectural aesthetics. Conserving the distinctive qualities of old cities makes them identifiable—as places, societies, and cultures—even though anonymous modern agglomerations may build up around them.

Sites such as the *Topography of Terror* in Berlin, the Stone in Lubyanka Square in Moscow, the African Burial Ground in New York, and the Aztec Pyramid Site in Mexico City are all examples of cities' rendering judgment on themselves, as if the metropolis had a collective continuing soul, across history and generations, in which concepts such as guilt and atonement are applicable.

While urban analysts have looked to many kinds of abstract models—mathematical, biological, sociological, economic—in order to understand and predict the phenomena of cities, thinking of the metropolis in intimate human terms, as if it were affected by matters of morality, may be cause for hope in regard to the future. For if the city is subject to human judgment, then it is also subject to human invention, to creating possibilities that may not be predictable, that resist the impenetrable self-perpetuating logic of terrible circumstances, that recognize the wrongs of the past, and, through remembrance and understanding, reveal the prospect of justice and redemption.

CHAPTER FIFTEEN

THE CITY AS A LIVING MUSEUM

CHARLESTON AND JERUSALEM

> But if the big city is largely responsible for the invention and public extension of the museum, there is a sense in which one of its own principal functions is to serve as a museum: in its own right, the historic city retains, by reason of its amplitude and its long past, a larger and more various collection of cultural specimens than can be found elsewhere. Every variety of human function, every experiment in human association, every technological process, every mode of architecture and planning, can be found somewhere within its crowded area.
>
> —LEWIS MUMFORD, *The City in History*

Continuing destruction is the background against which this book was written. If the historic city is a museum of human cultural evolution—helping us to understand why various societies are different, how distinct places fostered singular accomplishments, and what is universal to the human experience—it is a museum whose holdings are rapidly being depleted, frequently without informed consideration of their value to future generations.

The extent of this damage on a global scale cannot be quantified, since few cities have documented the depletion of their historic patrimony—often an embarrassing and inherently self-critical exercise for governments to undertake. The general failure to make such an accounting is, of course, telling in itself. Yet because such destruction persists, gaining some measure of the magnitude of loss on a worldwide scale became an important objective in this study.

CLOSING THE DOOR TO OUR CULTURAL PAST

Judging the value of lost historic buildings in foreign cities required investigating the urban history of each place and applying modern preservation standards retroactively to different architectural cultures. With the benefit of hindsight, what do we regret having lost? Contemporary norms for the practice of conservation have been refined in two widely accepted documents: the Resolution of the Athens Conference of the League of Nations in 1931, and the Venice Charter of the Second International Conference of Architects and Technicians of Historic Monuments in 1964. These evolving standards were consistent with those I had brought to bear during my tenure as a landmarks commissioner in New York.

In all the places I visited, I searched for old photographs of cities. Since photographic records of the metropolis are widely available from the end of the nineteenth century, I was able to gain a sense of how much had been destroyed in the past hundred years due to industrialization. I confirmed these losses by speaking with conservationists in each city. Sometimes I found documents that approximated the destruction that occurred in various periods of urban modernization, as in the stripping of medieval building fabric during the rule of Mussolini. In other instances, earlier inventories of historic structures allow us to measure their eventual eradication, as in a study of Islamic Cairo by the geographers of Napoleon Bonaparte.

Visiting the UNESCO Division of Cultural Heritage and the headquarters of the International Council on Monuments and Sites (ICOMOS), both located in Paris, offered a unique opportunity to expand my perspective. Here I spoke with authorities whose vocation was the conservation of culture around the world. UNESCO specialists on Muslim cities described the wide erosion of built environments linked to medieval Islamic traditions. Asian experts spoke of the depletion by firebombing and subsequent modernization of the bulk of historic cityscapes in Japan and the ongoing reduction of the traditional cityscapes of China. In underdeveloped nations throughout Latin America, old colonial centers were fast disappearing.

In several conversations, I posed this question: "How much significant historic urban material has been lost in the past hundred years?" The difficulty of making such an assessment gave professionals pause, but they understood its importance. I received an estimate from every person asked. The answer was invariably the same and corresponded to my own appraisal: somewhere around 50 percent.

This is a disquieting impression to ponder, even though it is not precise. When experienced as merely a local matter, as just another old building or historic neighborhood removed from the changing cityscape, the destruction around us may not seem excessive, but when viewed across the world over a century, the speed of this global ongoing transformation is alarming. Nor has the damage been limited to structures of recent vintage or lesser significance. Extraordinary losses of ancient and singular architectural value have befallen all the cities discussed in this book.

This occurrence is a tragedy, since it is for the most part avoidable and difficult or impossible to reverse. It is extremely costly to replicate old structures once they are demolished, and it is technically difficult to match historic construction methods. But regardless of cost or challenge, old neighborhoods of modest vernacular buildings have rarely been recorded in sufficient detail to resurrect them once they are lost. Because the destruction continues unabated in many places, and is even escalating in others, I asked myself this: If 40, 50, or 60 percent of the fabric of old cities has been destroyed in the twentieth century, how much will remain after another hundred years of modernization?

As I contemplated this matter, while researching the destruction in city after city, I gradually focused on an unfortunate confluence of general trends in the way we build contemporary urban environments. Several phenomena were linked in a simultaneous and powerful negative equation.

PRESERVATION IN THE FRACTURED MODERN METROPOLIS

With industrialization, world population grew dramatically. When plotted on a graph that begins with the establishment of the city of Jericho at about 7500 B.C., the curve of increase changes from a gradually sloping horizontal to a sharply inclined vertical of almost 90 degrees. Much of this mammoth growth was absorbed in cities, whose population increased by a factor of nearly 19 in

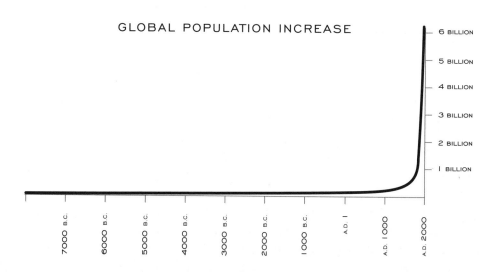

GLOBAL POPULATION INCREASE

the twentieth century: from 220 million to about 4 billion people, from about 14 percent to 50 percent of total global population. Exploding urban populations then spurred a corresponding enlargement of the built environment.

As cities around the world expanded, industrialization also set in motion a basic change in the architectural character of human constructions. After more than 9,000 years of human urban settlement, the making of buildings and cities by hand was rapidly being supplanted by construction with factory-made parts. Particularly during the latter half of the 1900s, this was a striking and widely felt change, evident at a glance in the contrast between the aesthetic aura of historic handcrafted structures and modern constructions of prefabricated materials. In old structures, one feels the quality imparted by the human hand. In modern constructions, the stamp of the machine prevails.

This difference in the character of modern buildings frequently disrupted the ambience of historic environments when new buildings were inserted in their midst. And because modern urban design often disregarded the organization and scale of the historic city, as contemporary agglomerations developed around old urban centers new districts appeared alien in their layout, as well as in their architectural character. Inner-city turnpike systems exacerbated these schisms. The historic city was fractured from within and came to reside in a larger cityscape fractured as a whole.

Furthermore, the fracturing was not just physical; the spirit of the modern metropolis was ruptured as well. In numerous developed and underdeveloped nations, the physically fractured historic metropolis was also divided in terms of social justice. Immaculate suburbs isolated by highways and automobiles, and zones of gleaming modern apartment buildings, offices, and international hotels were not just architecturally distinct but were also enclaves of greater social privilege, sometimes defended by walls and armed guards, as in Mexico City. In contrast, complexes of drab state-funded housing, overcrowded and deteriorated tenement areas in the historic city, and vast illegal shantytowns were both materially and socially underserved by the social contract.

Although the historic metropolis was likewise marked by economic and social inequalities, its form was significantly different. Prior to industrialization, the pinnacles of churches, mosques, and temples—emblematic of a commonality of belief and culture—crowned the profiles of old cityscapes. After industrialization, and especially in cities in poorer nations, a new skyline of modern towers came into being, symbolizing, to varying degrees in different places, segregation on the basis of wealth.

Thus the long evolution of the hand-constructed historic city, which because of its smaller size was discernible as a sculptural totality and whose urban architectural composition had been slowly refined over centuries, came to an end. Architecturally distinct human settlements built in response to variables in climate and surrounding natural terrain—cities like Kyoto, Cairo, and Singapore—were surrounded by highways and landfill that regularized differences in geography, while advanced building technologies insulated the exterior forms of new structures from reflecting local environmental conditions. Urban societies that once produced uniquely acculturated architectural forms were invaded by a tide of buildings unrelated to indigenous traditions.

The industrialization of architecture had led to great advances in the human condition, but with the exception of a very small percentage of structures made by the most talented designers, its economies of scale lent themselves to the mass production of buildings of ubiquitous and mediocre design. Evidence of singular historic urban cultures was being destroyed in the rush to construct a new urban world of global cultural homogeneity and reduced aesthetic value.

I have seen no large city in which the preservation of historic architecture could be divorced from this larger developmental context. Has the fractured metropolis become so commonplace, such an omnipresent state of mind, that we accept its negative environment and psychological consequences as inevitable? Moreover, is it wise when architectural conservation itself becomes a vehicle for social fracturing—when the gentrification of historic areas leads to ostracizing the poor? Is it productive to make the city coherent in one dimension while dividing it in another? Particularly in megacities in underdeveloped nations, where illegal settlement is often as large as, or larger than, the legal metropolis, conservation via unmediated gentrification undermines the already difficult task of building civic common ground. Modern Cairo and Mexico City sadly embody the dilemma: extended poverty, uncontrolled pollution, extreme disparities of wealth, lack of municipal resources, the collapse of regulatory authority, and governmental corruption form physically hostile and socially divided environments, exposing historic structures to unremitting attack.

While continued urban change is both inevitable and desirable, especially to the degree that it expands social opportunity, it also offers us the chance to revise policies that have decimated our cultural patrimony. Here, as a way to complete the journey of this book, I would like to present two of the most progressive conservation projects I discovered in my travels. Each of these initiatives deals with urban fracturing by looking at the city as a physical, social, and spiritual whole and by using architectural conservation as a vehicle to bind the metropolis together. Finding such inventive acts was part of the joy of making this study. Several other remarkable achievements came to light that I was unable to include for lack of space. I bring their existence to the reader's attention, though, because as long as cities continue to harness such creativity, the future has unlimited positive potential.

SCATTERED-SITE PUBLIC HOUSING IN CHARLESTON

In a world where over 320 cities now have a population of over a million people, Charleston is not significant because of its size. Yet although the proportions of the city are those of a provincial metropolitan center, the vibrancy of its urban culture has produced a remarkable commitment to architectural preservation and, in recent years, a unique social housing program, modest in its magnitude, but so thoughtful in conception that it has received numerous awards in America and a certificate of recognition from the United Nations.

Scattered-Site Public Housing in Charleston is consistent with the architectural character of a beautiful and largely intact historic city. It is a conscious alternative to public housing programs in the United States that commonly impose standardized modern buildings of mediocre and alien design in the midst of old cityscapes. Furthermore, Charleston's scattered-site housing speaks to another kind of urban wound as well—a centuries-old injury to the soul of the city, accrued as the beauty of historic Charleston was built with riches earned through the bondage of African-American slaves.

In the eighteenth and nineteenth centuries, Charleston was the major point of entry for Africans kidnapped into a life of servitude on the North American continent. The city was a commercial hub for the agricultural economy of the South, growing wealthy on the trade of plantation products and slave labor and, during this era, becoming for a time the fourth-largest urban center in the United States.

Both prior to and after the Civil War, Charleston was unusual among major American cities, with African-Americans constituting 50 percent or more of its inhabitants. It was a built environment of striking aesthetic coherence, refinement, and beauty—a blend of European and tropical American architectural forms, with numerous substantial buildings of sophisticated quality.

Many of the seasonal urban mansions of plantation owners gradually came to be designed in an architectural configuration called the Charleston single house. Here narrow residential structures, aligned with the city's street walls, were situated to the side of building lots, leaving an open-front patio space. The major long facades of the single houses, with wide and graceful multistory covered balconies, were oriented to this internal formal courtyard, separated from the sidewalk by decorative cast-iron and wrought-iron fences. In neighborhoods of single houses, one saw the narrow side of buildings, often designed and embellished in a classical architectural mode, and intermittent tropical gardens on either side of the street. As the city grew, more modest versions of the single house were built by the middle classes, by immigrants, and by the poor. A common building form had evolved, serving many of the city's inhabitants and giving Charleston a unique urban personality.

African-American life was inexorably intertwined with the city's architectural culture. Not only had slavery provided the wealth to build beautifully, but numerous slaves directly helped construct the landmarks of the city. For centuries a large proportion of black Americans worked as domestic servants and lived in the outbuildings of wealthy homes or in secondary spaces in such mansions. Even before the Emancipation Proclamation, a significant number of freed black tradesmen and private entrepreneurs lived in vernacular variations of the single house. In 1860, five thousand freed people of color constituted about 18 percent of the city's inhabitants. In some instances, free blacks themselves owned slaves—about 190 were slaveholders prior to the Civil War—and built, in the rear of their properties, separate quarters for their bound servants. After the practice of slavery ended and Charleston's economy slowed, African-American churches, schools, workshops, stores, and houses were built across the city, in conjunction with a thriving black community.

Few cityscapes in the United States recorded so thoroughly in physical form the spiritual, economic, and social journey out of slavery and segregation. This is visible in the city's Old Slave Mart; in its jail for runaway slaves; in the Demark Vesey House, home of a successful freedman reputed to have organized an aborted slave uprising; in the house of Sally Johnson, pastry chef, freed person of color, and slave owner herself; in the Freedmen's bank; in the Jenkins orphanage for black children, with its internationally renowned Orphanage Band; in the Mount Zion African-American Episcopal church; and in the more than twenty houses constructed by Richard Holloway, freed black master carpenter and independent builder.

Charleston enacted the first municipal preservation law in the United States in 1931. It was an unusual statute: a zoning ordinance requiring that the design of new construction conform to the character of the old milieu. This was one of the earliest historic district regulations in the chronicle of modern urban architectural conservation. To my knowledge, it was preceded only by the comprehensive preservation statute established by Poland in 1928.

Over the decades, though, Charleston too would be changed. The original area protected by the Zoning Act for Historic Preservation was an early neighborhood of impressive mansions and large houses, constituting only a part of the historic city. This left the municipal and commercial center of Charleston largely unprotected and subject to modernization by mediocre oversize structures common to American cities in the latter half of the twentieth century. Although the area protected by this zoning act would gradually be expanded to include most of historic Charleston, the center of the city was already fractured.

A few modern building types violated the character of residential zones. One of them was federally sponsored public housing, constructed in the 1950s and 1960s, and extensively occupied by black Americans. In a racially segregated society typical of the United States, inhabitants of such buildings were further stigmatized by glaring differences of architectural aesthetics and environmental quality. In the late 1980s, however, under the guidance of Mayor Joseph P. Riley Jr., who was unusually sensitive to issues of race and historic preservation, a different approach to publicly assisted housing was established.

Adopting the form of the Charleston single house, scattered-site housing comprises simple contemporary renditions of Charleston's traditional building forms—in other words, it is an extension of the city's architectural culture. The houses are arranged in small clusters, in different locations throughout Charleston, with the intent of promoting racial and economic diversity. The buildings meld into their surroundings; there are no signs or other physical markers to indicate that the housing is rent-assisted. When possible, scattered-site housing is located on properties that previously held intrusive contemporary structures, thereby reducing environmental dissonance and raising environmental harmony at the same time. Especially in poorer areas, this also helps to preserve property values, community life, and old buildings.

Throughout the United States, because the rise of African-Americans to freedom has frequently involved modest vernacular structures in working-class neighborhoods, over the decades architectural evidence of their story has disappeared through urban renewal or urban decline. But in Charleston, as a result of a farsighted approach to preservation that has embraced the whole historic matrix, and with the positive environmental effects of the city's scattered-site housing program and other intelligent conservation-conscious development policies, the visible evidence of human pain, injustice, courage, and perseverance is being saved for future generations of all Americans.

THE (RESTORED) OLD JEWISH QUARTER IN JERUSALEM

The singular physical metamorphosis achieved in the restoration of the Old Jewish Quarter in Jerusalem offers an alternative vision of the city that could benefit many urban places. This accomplishment is one of the most progressive transformations of a historic cityscape that I found in my travels: a model for the future in terms of architectural conservation and urban planning. Yet the project cannot be divorced from a larger developmental strategy in Israel that results in politically motivated acts of territorial expropriation. The very thoughtfulness of this restoration is also an attempt by the Israeli government to justify its seizure of disputed land. In terms of legitimate civic stewardship, wherein the interests of all citizens are fairly represented, these conflicting impulses are irreconcilable. That such an otherwise extraordinary achievement has been compromised is part of the tragedy of Jerusalem: across the millennia of its existence, it has often been not only a city of revelation and faith but also a city beleaguered by religious intolerance and war. In order to understand the restoration of the Jewish Quarter, a brief account of the city's complex history is necessary.

THE FOUNDATION OF GOD

At sunset, in the fading and oblique rays just before dark, the walls of the city of Jerusalem appear to be made of gold. This illusion results from the coloration and crystalline constituents of the stone from which every building in the ancient city is constructed, a material common to the geology of the region. Jerusalem is built on a mountain of this stone. A number of its buildings are hewn out of bedrock, and some of its outcroppings have come to be considered holy in themselves—points of human connection to the eternal.

Over its history, the city has been built up, reduced by violence, built up again, and reduced again an astonishing number of times. In this process, many cut stones from earlier buildings have been adapted for reuse in later structures. Thus the origins and dates of the stones of Jerusalem are sometimes difficult to determine, and one wonders if particular pieces were touched by David, Solomon, Pompey, Herod, Pontius Pilate, Christ, Hadrian, Empress Helena, Muhammad, Saladin, or Suleiman the Magnificent.

No great city in the world is more visibly rooted in the land that surrounds it, more tangibly a product of the earth, yet so subject to perceptions conditioned by intangible human convictions. The city shimmers and changes before our eyes as if the materiality of rock has been rendered insignificant by optical illusions, the mysteries of history, religious belief, and the immeasurable power of centuries of continuing prayer.

The site itself has always been considered holy. Its earliest known name, of Semitic origin, from before 2000 B.C., was Urasalim, "Foundation of God." Perched on a mountaintop in torturously harsh terrain, Jerusalem has known continuous human settlement for approximately 5,000 years.

Around 1000 B.C., the settlement was captured by David, the Jewish king who made Jerusalem a substantial city and brought to it the Ark of the Covenant. Upon a raised stone terrace called the Temple Mount, the First Great Temple was built by David's son, Solomon, to house that sacred chest containing God's laws and commandments, bequeathed to the Jews by Moses.

In 922 B.C., Jerusalem was conquered by Egypt; in 850, by the Philistines. Jews retook the city in 786, but it was despoiled once more by the Babylonians in 604, and leveled in 586. Having been allowed to return to Jerusalem in 515, the Jews rebuilt in a more modest form the great temple of their forebears. The city was then subsumed, in successive order, within the empires of Alexander the Great, Ptolemaic Egypt, and the Seleucid Syria. In 167, the Syrians desecrated the restored great temple. In 164, the temple was rededicated by the Jews (an event since celebrated in Judaism as Hanukkah).

In 63 B.C., the legions of Pompey captured Jerusalem. In time, a Jew of Idomean descent, Herod the Great, was appointed to rule under the authority of Rome in Judea, the Roman client kingdom situated in the southern part of the area known as Palestine. (The name Palestine is derived from a term meaning "land of the Philistines." Palestine also was the region eventually known by European Christians as the Holy Land. The extent of Palestine has shifted over the centuries, and today is subsumed within Israel, Jordan, and Egypt.)

Herod the Great constructed a capital of surpassing grandeur. An expanded temple mount was established whose western wall would become known in later centuries as the Wailing Wall, the most sacred site of Judaism. Another magnificent Great Temple was built, and a massive fortress was raised, parts of which would serve as the foundation for later bastions built by the Romans, European Crusaders, Mamluks, and Ottomans.

By A.D. 6, Rome ruled Judea via governors, the fifth of which was Pontius Pilate, under whom Jesus of Nazareth was crucified. In 41, the kingdom of the royal family of Herod was reestablished; in 44, the Roman governors returned. In 66, the Jews revolted. In 70, the Romans reconquered the city, leveled it by fire, destroyed the magnificent temple built by Herod The Great, and decimated the population.

On top of these ruins, in A.D. 129, the emperor Hadrian built a Roman town called Aelia Capitolina. The Jews revolted in 132 and held the area for three years. When Hadrian retook the city in 135, he banished all Jews from Jerusalem. Several centuries later, Christianity became the official religion of the Byzantine–Roman Empire, whose capital was situated in Constantinople under the emperor Constantine.

In A.D. 326, while on pilgrimage in Jerusalem, Empress Helena, the mother of Constantine the Great, found the True Cross upon which Jesus of Nazareth died, the rock of Calvary, and the location of Christ's burial. The Church of the Holy Sepulcher, created to mark these sacred sites, was completed in the year 335. During the centuries of Byzantine rule, once again, Jerusalem was made resplendent with numerous religious structures. Most of these, as well as the Holy Sepulcher, were destroyed by the Persians in alliance with the Jews in 614.

Byzantium reconquered Jerusalem in A.D. 630, and the Church of the Holy Sepulcher was rebuilt. By this time, from out of Arabia, another major monotheistic religion had emerged, and in 638 Jerusalem was taken by the

Muslims, who, honoring Adam, Noah, Abraham, Moses, and Jesus as holy prophets, held the city in great esteem.

From 688 to 691, the tenth Muslim caliph, Abd al-Malik, built on the Temple Mount (known by the Muslims as the Haram al-Sharif) a holy sanctuary called the Dome of the Rock, which commemorates the location from which the prophet Muhammad ascended to heaven during his Night Journey. The Jews knew this particular stone outcropping as the rock of Mount Moriah—the site of Adam's creation and death. As it evolved in form and was embellished over the centuries, the Dome of the Rock became recognized as one of the great works of world architectural history, as well as the third major destination of Muslim prilgrimage after Mecca and Medina. An imposing mosque, the Al-Aqsa, was erected on the Haram al-Sharif as well. Within the Al-Aqsa, the minbar of Isa honored the holiness of Jesus.

For several centuries, Muslim rulers in Jerusalem maintained a liberal policy toward Jews and Christians. But in 969, the caliphs of Muslim Egypt gained control of the city and in 1010 decreed the razing of Christian monuments. Once again the Holy Sepulcher was demolished. In 1071, Muslim—Seljuq Turks defeated the Byzantines at Manzikert in Armenia, capturing parts of the Holy Land, and closing the routes of Christian pilgrims.

In 1099 the First Crusade besieged and won the city and established the Latin Kingdom of Jerusalem. Muslims and Jews were massacred and banned from the city. A great fortified wall was built encircling the city. Mosques were converted into Christian churches, and in 1149 the Church of the Holy Sepulcher was rebuilt on its original foundations, with surviving Byzantine building elements fused into the Romanesque structure that we see today.

In 1187, the Egyptian Muslim dynasty founded by Saladin recaptured the city and leveled the walls built by the Crusaders. Jerusalem was regained by the Crusaders in 1229, lost in 1239, regained in 1240, and lost again in 1244 to the Khwãrezmian Turks, who were conquered in turn by the Egyptian Mamluks in 1247. During the 257 years of Mamluk governance, numerous beautiful mosques, minarets, schools, hostels, baths, monasteries, markets, and mausoleums were built. Across this extended period of peace, Jews and Christians were gradually allowed to reestablish residence.

In 1517, Jerusalem was absorbed within the Ottoman Empire. The walls of the city, as we see them today, were constructed from 1536 to 1541 by Suleiman the Magnificent, following the foundation of the toppled ramparts of the crusaders, and utilizing hewn-stone elements dating back to the metropolis of King Herod and perhaps before. The fortifications were not only protection against assault, but a purposeful beautification of the city and an amalgam of stone from across history—a fusion of Jerusalem's many historic incarnations.

Yet once it was firmly within the grasp of the Ottoman sultans, Jerusalem would gradually lessen in significance.

For the next three hundred years the city languished economically, socially, and politically, as a backwater in the Ottoman realm. During the nineteenth and twentieth centuries—and particularly with the emergence of Zionism, an international movement to create an autonomous Jewish state in the Holy Land, Jewish immigration to Palestine and Jerusalem increased. Simultaneously, as the power of the Ottomans waned, nationalistic movements among the Arab societies of the Middle East also gained momentum.

In 1917 British troops occupied Jerusalem, and one year later the Ottoman Empire was dissolved. Throughout the Middle East, European colonial influence encroached upon the sovereignty of emerging Arab nations, and in 1922 the League of Nations upheld the British Mandate to control Palestine. Over the next decades, but principally after World War II, one by one, various Arab states won independence.

In anticipation of the end of the British Mandate, the United Nations resolved in 1947 that a Jewish homeland be established in Palestine and that the city of Jerusalem be placed under U.N. jurisdiction. The region would be partitioned, and no one nation was to have sovereignty over the holy city. War between Arabs and Jews erupted in 1948, and the nation of Israel was founded. In the armistice agreement of 1949, Egypt and Transjordan (later known as Jordan) claimed the remaining parts of Palestine. Millions of Palestinian Muslims became stateless people. Jerusalem itself, situated just outside the border of the new country of Israel, lay within territory claimed by Transjordan. In the Six-Day War of June 1967, Israeli armies captured and assumed control of the ancient metropolis, and Jerusalem was named the capital of Israel. The preponderance of the nations of the world refused to recognize the validity of this action.

DESTRUCTION OF THE OLD JEWISH QUARTER

Over more than six centuries, since the defeat of the crusaders and under the rule of the Mamluks and Ottomans, Jerusalem gradually developed four distinct sections: the Christian Quarter (Protestant and Roman Catholic), the Armenian Quarter (Orthodox Christian), the Muslim Quarter, and the Jewish Quarter, the last being located in proximity to the Wailing Wall of the Temple Mount. To varying degrees, Jewish landmarks within the Quarter traced their lineage back across this span of history. The vernacular texture of the neighborhood—courtyard housing forms, narrow passageways, winding and dead-end streets—was common to Muslim cities of the Middle East. Built.

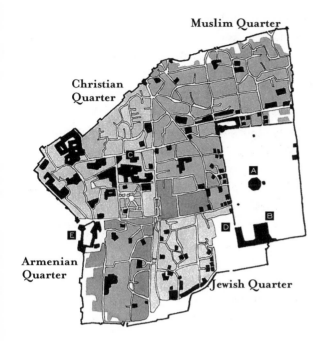

Muslim Quarter

Christian Quarter

Armenian Quarter

Jewish Quarter

The monuments and quarters of historic Jerusalem · The historic city as a whole is an eminent artifact of world civilization. Its major monuments, including its walls and fortifications, are shown in black. Its four quarters are differentiated by dark and light gray tone. Situated on the Temple Mount, or Haram al-Sharif, are the Dome of the Rock (A) and the Al-Aqsa Mosque (B). In other parts of the city are the Church of the Holy Sepulcher (C), the Wailing Wall (D), and the Tower of David Complex (E).

Rebuilt, expanded, and constantly evolving, the exteriors of residential structures in the area reflected 100 to 150 years of change, and centuries more of culturally cross-pollinated architectural tradition.

During the conflict of 1949, the Jewish Quarter was severely bombarded and eventually deserted by its occupants. Afterward, Arab forces further decimated the neighborhood, destroying its synagogues and yeshivas. In violation of the U.N. resolution, Jerusalem was annexed by Jordan for nineteen years and the ruins of the old Jewish Quarter were occupied by homeless Arabs. A plan was adopted by the Jordanians to evict the squatters and level the surviving structures. Before this could be fully enacted, the Six-Day War occurred, and Israel in turn annexed the city and demolished a cluster of Muslim buildings and two historic Islamic structures dating back to the Mamluk era in order to create an open plaza in front of the Wailing Wall.

URBAN MODERNIZATION AND EXPANSION

Israel began to modernize Jerusalem, although surrounded by adversaries who challenged their territorial claims, and subject to civil unrest among a significant segment of its population (Palestinian Muslims)—which had been subsumed within the Jewish state by force. The spoken aim was to restore the ancient city and to reestablish the destroyed Jewish Quarter. During this massive building effort, extending over several decades, there was no true representative governance of the city. Israel's sovereignty was widely repudiated, and Muslim residents of Jerusalem were not free to participate in decisions meant to sanction Israeli expropriation of contended land.

The new Jewish homeland became a miracle in the desert—a garden of modern prosperity. But most Muslims did not share these benefits, and as Israel flourished, it manifested shocking disparities of wealth and opportunity. In precincts surrounding Jerusalem and even within the walls of the Holy City, Muslims often lived in extraordinary poverty. Between 1967 and 1995, although Palestinians represented 25 to 28 percent of Jerusalem's population, 65,000 housing units were built for Jews and a mere 9,000 for Muslims.

The sadness of these differences was inescapable, yet the joy of Israel's accomplishment was also palpable—the unshackling of a people's inventiveness after centuries of prejudicial treatment in foreign societies. Jewish exuberance in creating Israel often was expressed in physical form, in myriad architectural designs of thoughtful and sometimes exciting visual composition. Yet architecture cannot be divorced from the motives that generate it. The construction of modern Jerusalem was both a rush to Jewish betterment and a race to establish economic and physical justification for territorial nationalization. During the twentieth century, and especially after the 1967 war, the population of the metropolis increased tenfold, from approximately 60,000 to 600,000 people. The golden cityscape of Jerusalem, which for several millennia had been a clearly defined object set against a backdrop of natural surrounding terrain, was engulfed in an agglomeration of modern buildings and highways.

Although a national parkland was established around the outer walls of historic Jerusalem, in several places this zone was far too narrow. From several vistas, highways and contemporary structures virtually abutted ancient fortifications. The most egregious of such developments is occurring today at the Jaffa Gate. Tiered parking lots, a hotel, condominiums, and a shopping mall are being built as an approach to one of the city's most ancient portals. Here historic Jerusalem is being treated as a commodity for economic exploitation—a theme park for tourists. Respectful physical planning in regard to one of the most sacred and ancient places of human history has been compromised by overriding political policies initiated in the maelstrom of ongoing territorial conflict.

Yet with few exceptions, Jewish husbandry within the ancient walls of the city was technically sound and aesthetically sensitive. Extensive work needed to be done. The ramparts of Suleiman the Magnificent were decayed from centuries of wear, and battered by the wounds of armed conflict. In many areas they had become a dumping ground for debris. Israel cleared away the base of the city's fortifications, revealing their ancient origins. Once more the Holy

City could be seen to grow out of the rock from which it was constructed. Battlements and gateways were carefully restored. Along the top of the walls a continuous public walkway was established from which visitors might survey the city's historic roofscape. And the ancient citadel of Jerusalem, currently known as the Tower of David complex, was rehabilitated and made into the Museum of the History of Jerusalem.

Overdue improvements such as the introduction of contemporary water supply and sewage removal were achieved, alleviating drainage problems that had damaged historic buildings, and providing modern sanitation for Jerusalem's residents. Myriad ad hoc electrical power connections and a sea of rooftop television antennas were eliminated through the construction of an underground utility network. Unsightly patched asphalt pavement was replaced with new walking surfaces made of Jerusalem stone.

Unfortunately, much of the Muslim Quarter failed to benefit from this program, its residents fearing that other political agendas were being served under the guise of civic improvements. As a result, inhabitants of overcrowded slums hesitated to allot space for modern bathrooms because to do so would have reduced the number of Muslims in the historic center. Similarly, numerous Muslim residents suspected that the motive for inserting new citywide infrastructure was to weaken old buildings and justify their demolition. In 1990, Jerusalem's first Israeli mayor, Teddy Kollek, who served from 1967 to 1993, commented on the civic environment of the period: "Never have we given them a feeling of being equal before the law. They were, and remain, second- and third-class citizens."

THE CITY BECOMES A LIVING MUSEUM

The rebuilding of the old Jewish Quarter would be guided by an advisory council of distinguished philosophers, historians, artists, architects, planners, theologians, and philanthropists called the Jerusalem Committee, established by the mayor immediately upon entering office. While several intrusive oversize modern buildings were constructed on the edge of the area, facing the Wailing Wall, inside the neighborhood a remarkable urban environment was constructed.

Retaining the architectural character of the quarter was a priority, so that the milieu of the greater historic city would not be disrupted. Initial surveys showed that about 50 percent of the sector's damaged historic structures could be rehabilitated. The other half would have to be built anew. In an area subject to earthquakes, proper foundations were a necessity—an extremely complicated procedure in old Jerusalem, which sits on the rubble and ruins accumulated over thousands of years of recurring destruction. Thus, a major portion of the site would first become a painstaking archaeological dig.

Several significant finds were made 20, 30, 40 feet below the surface: a wall from the first temple period of David and Solomon; remnants of a cluster of patrician dwellings from the period of Herod the Great; the architectural remains and furnishings of a Jewish house partially burned down during the Roman conquest of the city in A.D. 70; substantial elements of the Roman-Byzantine settlement; and parts of a Byzantine church constructed during the reign of the emperor Justinian.

In order to provide access to this material and to preserve it in place, it was decided to build the new houses of the Jewish Quarter on platforms suspended above the layers of history that until recently had been invisible. Aboveground, modern dwellings would be constructed of contextual design that knit together surviving fragments of the traditional vernacular townscape. Belowground, and sometimes open to the sky, the city would become a museum. As it had been for centuries, the old Jewish Quarter, with new and old courtyard houses, would continue as a place of secluded residential life, while also becoming an unrestricted civic space dedicated to public education. A three-dimensional network of passageways, stairs, and ramps connected the quarter's different parts.

Having taken two decades to accomplish, the final result is a startling re-definition of the function of the historic city. The modern housing, designed by a number of different architects and all made of Jerusalem stone, is intimate and various in its interpretation of multicultural building traditions. Winding medieval passageways open up to public plazas, where ancient remains are jux-taposed with the structures of contemporary life. From out of a large depres-sion, decoratively carved capitals of the columns of the old Roman marketplace (the cardo) suddenly rise up into view. At their base, one sees the ground plane of the Roman era, which then extends beneath the city into subterranean spaces where the vaulted Byzantine emporium has been restored, with modern shops inserted into centuries-old archways.

Around the corner and up a flight of stone stairs, the visitor arrives at a later era of history: the remnants of the Byzantine Church of Saint Mary. Discreet informative labeling and signage abounds, informing the viewer in several languages of the interwoven incarnations of Jerusalem's past. Ruins of the great Hurvah Synagogue stand near a tall minaret of Mamluk configura-tion. In the underground space beneath a modern yeshiva, a museum of archaeology houses the exterior and interior remnants of Herodian mansions. The cool dim spaces offer respite from the sun. Time and the terrible differ-ences that have divided Jerusalem for most of its history have been suspended.

Distinct architectural elements of different eras are melded together by the commonality of stone. In an era of continuing conflict, the essence of the Holy City has been reaffirmed: it is a place of unending search for self-knowledge. If ever the holiest city on earth achieves peace among its people, the restored Jewish Quarter provides a model for what the metropolis might become.

⚙︎

Wandering through the restored Jewish Quarter, I saw the most complete manifestation that I would find of the city's capacity to tell us of our past. Not only had the physical legacy of the city been given a voice, but old structures had provided the inspiration for a new kind of urban place. Contemporary design, supporting modern life, had taken its forms from an amalgam of several traditions, from an understanding of how the threads of the city's evolution had been woven into a greater whole. Many of the structures of the restored Jewish Quarter were new, of modern building technology and design expression, yet the old city was not fractured and the spirit of historic Jerusalem was as vibrant here as in other, more intact districts.

A basic misconception of architectural preservation was challenged: that once we decide to preserve old structures, the city is frozen in time. This view assumes that the past is a fixed idea, that old areas don't change in meaning as our understanding of history progresses. Born out of tragedy, the new spatial configuration of the Jewish Quarter, with historic buildings from different eras juxtaposed at their various original heights and contemporary structures woven into this matrix, presents the city's history in a new form, a different and thought-provoking perspective of the cultural continuity of Jerusalem.

Revised perceptions of the past have occurred in other places as well, as in Mexico City, where reinstatement of the Aztec pyramid site of Tenochtitlán has changed the balance of symbolic architectural elements at the city's core and the identity of the modern metropolis is now more definitively articulated as a fusion of European and ancient American civilizations. A heritage once repressed became a heritage embraced, visually connecting modern Mexican architecture to ancient forms that have influenced many important contemporary structures.

Similarly, Communist urban planning at the core of Beijing reflects continuing reassessment of the city's identity. In the mid–twentieth century, the conversion of Tiananmen Square into a giant public space—framed by the most important symbolic structures of ancient and modern China, the Forbidden City and modern state memorials to the Communist Revolution—gave material expression to a complex historic shift of values. In the future, should plans proceed to reestablish the nearby massive barbican at Zhengyangmen, a central component of the city's old geometry and the newest major form in the cityscape will be an ancient bulwark destroyed by the government and then revived in the name of progress. A different sense of what constitutes modernization will have emerged.

In Singapore, whole neighborhoods of restored shop-houses, once seen as black holes, are now perceived as an embodiment of the cooperative multiethnic spirit of the current metropolis, and social scientists continue to examine in greater detail how various immigrant groups maintained their cultural autonomy, yet also learned from one another. With modern sociological study, the physical culture of the city has accrued new layers of significance.

In this regard, the presentation of historic information on plaques in the restored Jewish Quarter is much more than a mere embellishment. Such signage transforms the city into a museum, an informed collection of material artifacts. Through such markers, invisible dimensions of meaning, embodied in buildings but not self-evident, assume a physical presence, telling us about the people who built the city, the place of buildings in the economy of the metropolis, the quality and problems of life in other eras, and the aspirations, fears, and beliefs of earlier societies. Sometimes such markers can be moral acts of remembrance, as in the district of Schöneberg, in Berlin, where plaques commemorate Jewish life that once thrived in the neighborhood. With time, the scholarly basis for ideas expressed in such signage will change, as our knowledge of history grows through the development of new analytic tools and the changing focus of research. The living cityscape, having become a living museum, will reflect a continuing and expanding civic discussion. By thinking of the metropolis as an interactive educational experience subject to interpretive presentation, we may enhance our critical grasp of the material culture that surrounds us, alter our collective understanding of the city as a whole, and change the way we see its future.

This raises another issue regarding our understanding of time. While the speed of modern urban change has led to rapid transformation and destruction, it can also lead to rapid reconfiguration of that which we have already built. Having fractured our cities, with time, can we un-fracture them? If we understand that current intrusive structures will eventually become obsolete and subject to replacement, and that vanished historic buildings might be reinstated, an unprescribed palette of urban possibilities is presented, making it possible to change the spirit and form of the city at many locations.

I end this book with a prayer, by imagining a journey I may not live to undertake, a journey to a potential future Athens, no longer so polluted that acids in its air melt stone, with its heritage returned from foreign lands, and with the parts of the Parthenon reassembled in the geographic setting that gave them birth, standing above the city on top of the Acropolis. Only then, when the remains of one of history's greatest integrated works of architecture and sculpture are once more gathered together, will we truly comprehend the human achievement of the city, and the past will assume a singular coloration perhaps beyond our capacity to anticipate. To achieve this greater understanding of the human heritage will require an international effort of goodwill, multinational recognition of our shared universal interests, and a moment of human invention similar to the myriad creative acts that have made the world's great cities so distinct, extraordinary, and important to preserve.

BIBLIOGRAPHIC SOURCES

THE CENTURY OF DESTRUCTION

FOR A HISTORY OF MODERN CITY PLANNING SINCE THE INDUSTRIAL REVOLUTION, SEE:
Peter Hall, *Cities of Tomorrow: An Intellectual History of Urban Planning in the Twentieth Century.* Cambridge, Mass.: Blackwell, 1988.

FOR THE INTELLECTUAL EVOLUTION OF MODERN ARCHITECTURE, SEE:
Reyner Banham, *Theory and Design in the First Machine Age.* Cambridge, Mass.: MIT Press, 1980.

FOR THE DEMOGRAPHICS OF OUR EXPANDING URBAN WORLD, SEE:
Eugene Linden, "The Exploding Cities of the Developing World." *Foreign Affairs* magazine, vol. 75, No. 1, 1996.

ROME

FOR A GENERAL ARCHITECTURAL SURVEY OF THE IMPERIAL AND RENAISSANCE CITY AND A DISCUSSION OF MICHELANGELO'S WORK ON THE CAMPIDOGLIO, SEE:
Spiro Kostof, *A History of Architecture: Settings and Rituals.* New York: Oxford University Press, 1985.

FOR AN ARCHITECTURAL HISTORY OF THE RENAISSANCE, SEE:
Peter Murray, *The Architecture of the Italian Renaissance.* New York: Schocken Books, 1986.

FOR THE URBAN DEVELOPMENT OF IMPERIAL ROME, SEE:
Lewis Mumford, *The City in History: Its Origins, Its Transformations, and Its Prospects.* New York: Harcourt, Brace and World, 1961.

FOR THE URBAN DEVELOPMENT OF RENAISSANCE ROME, SEE:
Mark Girouard, *Cities and People: A Social and Architectural History.* New Haven: Yale University Press, 1985.

FOR A LANDMARK HISTORICAL ACCOUNT OF THE EMERGENCE OF PRESERVATION THOUGHT IN ROME AND IN EUROPEAN CIVILIZATION, SEE:
Cevat Erder, *Our Architectural Heritage: From Consciousness to Conservation.* Paris: United Nations Educational, Scientific and Cultural Organization, 1986.

FOR THE SEMINAL DETAILED ACCOUNT OF THE DECONSTRUCTION OF IMPERIAL ROME, SEE:
Rodolfo Lanciani, *The Roman Forum.* New York: Frank, 1910.
Rodolfo Lanciani, *Ancient Rome in the Light of Recent Discoveries.* New York: Houghton Mifflin, 1989.

FOR A DETAILED DESCRIPTION OF THE FASCIST RECONSTRUCTION OF ROME, SEE:
Spiro Kostof, *The Third Rome, 1870–1950: Traffic and Glory.* Berkley, California: University Art Museum, 1973.

FOR THE DEVELOPMENT OF CONTEMPORARY CONSERVATION THINKING IN ITALY, SEE:
Jukka Jokilehto, *History of Architectural Conservation: Development of National Thought into an International Approach.* Rome: ICROM, unpublished manuscript, 1997.

FOR THE POLITICAL, ECONOMIC, AND SOCIAL MORES OF MODERN ITALY, SEE:
Mario B. Migone, *Italy Today: A Country in Transition.* New York: P. Lang, 1995.

INTERVIEWS

ON THE LEGAL STRUCTURE FOR CONSERVATION IN ITALY AND ROME:
Alberta Campitelli, Landmarks Office, City of Rome Building Department, Rome, March 8
and 11, 1996. Dottoressa Campitelli undertook the heroic task of outlining the complex
bureaucratic overlay of national, regional, and municipal conservation authorities that
protect the historic properties of Rome.

ON THE INTERRELATIONSHIP OF URBAN PLANNING WITH ITALIAN CONSERVATION
THEORY:
Paola Falini, professor, University La Sapienza, Rome, March 12, 1996.

ON THE CONTEMPORARY ADMINISTRATION OF PRESERVATION POLICY IN ROME:
Cristina Puglisi, assistant director for properties, American Academy in Rome, March 8,
1996.
Fabiana Zeli, architect in private practice, Rome, March 13, 1996.

ON HOW CONSERVATION PRACTICE IN ROME COMPARES WITH THAT IN OTHER EUROPEAN
CITIES:
Jukka Jokilehto, assistant to the director general, ICROM, Rome, March 12,1996.

WARSAW

FOR A GENERAL ARCHITECTURAL HISTORY OF THE HISTORIC CORE, SEE:
Maria Lewicka, *The Old Town in Warsaw.* Warsaw: Wydawnicto Arkady, 1992.

FOR PHOTOGRAPHIC IMAGES OF THE PRE–WORLD WAR II CITY, SEE:
Krystyna Lejko, *Warsaw Photographs from the Turn of the 19th and 20th Centuries.* Warsaw: VIA
Wydawnictwo, 1992.

ON LIFE IN THE JEWISH GHETTO UNDER THE GERMANS, SEE:
Ulrich Keller, *The Warsaw Ghetto in Photographs.* New York: Dover Publications, 1984.
Michel Mazor, *The Vanished City: Everyday Life in the Warsaw Ghetto.* New York: Marsilio, 1993.

ON THE EVOLUTION OF CONSERVATION LAW AND PRACTICE IN POLAND, SEE:
Gleye and Waldemar Szcerba, *Historic Preservation in Other Countries.* Vol. 2, *Poland.* Washington,
D.C.: U.S. Committee of the International Council on Monuments and Sites, 1989.

ON THE RECONSTRUCTION OF WAR-TORN CITIES AFTER WORLD WAR II, SEE:
Jeffry M. Diefendorf, ed., *Rebuilding Europe's Bombed Cities.* London: Macmillan, 1990.

ON TOWN PLANNING EFFORTS IN WARSAW BEFORE, DURING, AND AFTER THE WAR, SEE:
Barbara Klain, "City Planning in Warsaw," in Koos Bosma and Helma Hellinga, eds., *Mastering
the City: North European City Planning 1900–2000,* part IV, The Design of the Socialist City. The
Hague, NAI, 1997.

ON THE GERMAN DESTRUCTION AND POLISH RE-CREATION OF HISTORIC WARSAW, SEE:
Boleslaw Bierut, *The 6-Year Plan for the Reconstruction of Warsaw: Report by the President of the Central
Committee of the Polish United Workers Party.* Warsaw: Polskie Wydawn, 1949.
Stanislaw Jankowski, "Warsaw: Destruction, Secret Town Planning, 1939–44, and Postwar
Reconstruction," in Jeffry Diefendorf, ed., *Rebuilding Europe's Bombed Cities.* London,
Macmillan, 1990.

ON SOVIET ARCHITECTURE BEHIND THE IRON CURTAIN, SEE:
Anders Aman, *Architecture and Ideology in Eastern Europe during the Stalin Era: An Aspect of Cold War History.*
Cambridge, Mass.: MIT Press, 1992.

INTERVIEWS

ON THE REBUILDING OF HISTORIC WARSAW:

Anna Naruszewicz, architect, Polytechnika Warazawska. Warsaw, June 26, 1995. Ms. Naruszewicz had just completed a doctoral thesis documenting the oral histories of Varsovians who lived through the destruction during the war and the rebuilding that followed.

ON GERMAN EXECUTION SITES IN POLAND:

Jean Hoenninger, an American artist working in collaboration with the Polish government archives on the location of execution sites, Warsaw: June 27, 1995.

ON THE INVOLVEMENT OF GERMAN HISTORIANS IN THE DESTRUCTION OF WARSAW:

Dr. Peter Krieger, German architectural historian, New York: November 1997. Dr. Kreiger cited a recent study, published in German and Polish, that described how German architectural historians collaborated with the Nazis: Niels Gutschow and Barbara Klain, *Vernichtung und Utopie: Stadtplanung Warschau 1939–1945.* Hamburg: Junius Verlag, 1994. Dirk Hebel provided an oral translation of relevant sections of this study, New York, December 2000.

CAIRO

An abundance of material, in English, on the preservation, planning, and economic and social development of Cairo is available via a long tradition of scholarship in the city and through the publishing efforts of institutions such as the American University in Cairo.

FOR A GENERAL ARCHITECTURAL SURVEY OF ANCIENT EGYPT, ISLAM, AND ISLAMIC CAIRO, SEE:

Spiro Kostof, *A History of Architecture: Settings and Rituals.* New York: Oxford University Press, 1985.

FOR A DETAILED HISTORY OF ISLAMIC ARCHITECTURE IN THE MIDDLE EAST, SEE:

Martin S. Briggs, *Muhammadan Architecture in Egypt and Palestine.* New York: Da Capo Press, 1974.

FOR HISTORICAL VIEWS OF ISLAMIC CAIRO AND THE PYRAMIDS PRIOR TO THE INVENTION OF PHOTOGRAPHY, SEE:

David Roberts, *Egypt Yesterday and Today.* New York: Stewart, Tabori and Chang, 1996.

FOR A PHOTOGRAPHIC RECORD OF THE PHYSICAL DETERIORATION OF CAIRO, SEE:

Barry Iverson, *Comparative Views of Egypt: Cairo One Hundred Years Later.* Cairo: Boraïe Shaalan, 1994.

FOR ONE OF THE FINEST URBAN PLANNING HISTORIES OF ANY CITY, SEE:

Janet L. Abu-Lughod, *Cairo: 1001 Years of the City Victorious.* Princeton, N.J.: Princeton University Press, 1971.

FOR ONE OF THE MOST THOROUGH STUDIES OF CONSERVATION PLANNING IN ANY CITY, SEE:

Aga Khan Award for Architecture, *The Expanding Metropolis: Coping with the Urban Growth of Cairo.* Singapore: Concept Media for the Aga Khan Award for Architecture, 1984.

FOR DETAILED TECHNICAL EXPLANATIONS OF CONTEMPORARY CONSERVATION EFFORTS, SEE:

Jere L. Bacharach, *The Restoration and Conservation of Islamic Monuments in Egypt.* Cairo: American University in Cairo Press, 1995.

ON THE PHENOMENON OF INFORMAL SETTLEMENTS IN CAIRO, SEE:

Belgin Tekce, Linda Oldham, and Frederic C. Shorter, *A Place to Live: Families and Child Health in a Cairo Neighborhood.* Cairo: American University in Cairo Press, 1994.

ON THE PROBLEMS OF MODERN GOVERNANCE IN EGYPT, SEE:

Monte Palmer, Ali Leila, and El Sayed Yassin, *The Egyptian Bureaucracy.* Cairo: American University in Cairo Press, 1989.

ON LOCAL ADVOCACY EFFORTS TO SAVE THE HERITAGE OF CAIRO, SEE:

John Rodenbeck, *SPARE Newsletters* 1 to 13. Cairo: Society for the Preservation of the Architectural Resources of Egypt, 1979–1990.

ON THE CONTEMPORARY PHENOMENON OF MEGACITY GROWTH, THE GLOBAL ECONOMY, AND URBAN MARGINALIZATION, SEE:

Saskia Sassen, *Cities in a World Economy.* Thousand Oaks, Calif.: Pine Forge Press, 1994.

Ronald J. Fuchs, Ellen Brennan, Joseph Chamie, Fu-Chen Lo, and Juha I. Uitto, ed., *Mega-City Growth and the Future.* Tokyo: United Nations University Press, 1994.

Michael A. Cohen, Blair A. Ruble, Joseph S. Tulchin, Allison M. Garland, ed., *Preparing for the Urban Future: Global Pressures and Local Forces.* Washington, D.C.: Woodrow Wilson Center Press, 1996.

Hernando de Soto, *The Mystery of Capital: Why Capitalism Triumphs in the West and Fails Everywhere Else.* New York: Basic Books, 2000.

INTERVIEWS

ON CONSERVING EGYPTIAN ANTIQUITIES DURING THE CONSTRUCTION OF THE ASWAN DAM:

Hiroshi Daifuku, former chief of the Monuments and Sites Division of UNESCO, Washington, D.C., January 1995.

ON CITIZEN ADVOCACY FOR THE ARCHITECTURAL PRESERVATION OF CAIRO:

John Rodenbeck, director, Society for the Preservation of the Architectural Resources of Egypt, Cairo, April 3, 1995.

ON THE EXPERIENCES OF FOREIGN CONSERVATION MISSIONS IN CAIRO:

Robert K. Vincent, project director, American Research Center in Egypt, Cairo, April 5, 1995.

ON THE PRACTICE OF CONSERVATION ARCHITECTURE IN CAIRO:

Dr. Saleh Lamei-Mostafa, architect and consultant to UNESCO, Cairo, April 6, 1995.

ON UNESCO'S EFFORTS TO HELP EGYPT CONSERVE ISLAMIC CAIRO:

Dr. Said Zulficar, program specialist, UNESCO, Paris, May 19, 1995.

IDEOLOGICAL CONFLICT WITH THE PAST

MOSCOW

FOR AN ENCYCLOPEDIC HISTORY OF RUSSIAN ARCHITECTURE, SEE:

William Craft Brumfield, *A History of Russian Architecture.* New York: Cambridge University Press, 1993.

FOR AN URBAN ARCHITECTURAL HISTORY TRACING THE DEVELOPMENT OF MOSCOW, SEE:

Kathleen Berton, *An Architectural History.* London: I. B. Tauris, 1990.

FOR A CONCISE BUT USEFUL GUIDE TO THE URBAN PLANNING OF MOSCOW, SEE:

Aleksander V. Anismov, *Architectural Guide to Moscow.* Rotterdam: Uitgeverij 010, 1993.

FOR TWO CONTRASTING DESCRIPTIONS OF THE 1935 MASTER PLAN FOR MOSCOW, SEE:
Koos Bosma and Helma Hellinga, ed., *Mastering the City II: North-European City Planning 1900–2000*. Rotterdam: NAI, 1997.

FOR THE EFFECTS OF SOCIALIST REALISM ON THE ARCHITECTURE OF COMMUNIST CITIES, SEE:
Anders Åman, *Architecture and Ideology in Eastern Europe during the Stalin Era*. Cambridge, Mass.: MIT Press, 1992.

FOR AN INSIGHTFUL REVIEW OF SOVIET ARCHITECTURE IN THE YEARS OF COMMUNISM, SEE:
Alexei Tarkhanov and Sergei Kavtaradze, *Architecture of the Stalin Era*. New York: Rizzoli, 1992.

FOR THE EFFECTS AND AFTERMATH OF COMMUNIST PLANNING ON MOSCOW, SEE:
Gregory Andrusz, Michael Harloe, and Ivan Szelenyi, ed., *Cities After Socialism: Urban and Regional Change and Conflict in Post-Socialist Societies*. Oxford: Blackwell, 1996.

FOR A PASSIONATE ESSAY ON THE SANCTIONING OF MOSCOW'S DESTRUCTION BY MODERNIST ARCHITECTS, SEE:
Natalya Dushkina, *Some Thoughts on the Historical Fate of Twentieth Century Moscow*. Transition, Volume 33, 1990.

FOR AN ASSESSMENT OF COMMUNIST PURGES UNDER STALIN, SEE:
Robert Conquest, *The Great Terror*. New York: Oxford University Press, 1990.
Stephane Courtois et al., *The Black Book of Communism: Crimes, Terror, Repression*. Cambridge Mass.: Harvard University Press, 1999.

INTERVIEWS

ON THE CONSTRUCTION AND EXTENSIVE DETERIORATION OF COMMUNIST HOUSING IN MOSCOW AS WELL AS CONTEMPORARY EFFORTS TO PRESERVE HISTORIC STRUCTURES:
Vyacheslav Glazychev, president, Academy of the Urban Environment, Moscow, June 15 and 16, 1995 (two highly informative three-hour interviews).

ON THE CURRENT CONSERVATION BUREAUCRACY OF MOSCOW
Vladimir R. Krogius, deputy director, Central Research and Design Institute for the Reconstruction of Historical Towns, Moscow, June 17, 1995.

ON THE PRACTICE OF ARCHITECTURE IN MOSCOW TODAY:
Theodore Liebman, AIA, The Liebman Melting Partnership (an architect currently practicing in the United States and Russia), New York, 1998.

BEIJING

FOR A THOROUGH DESCRIPTION OF THE PLANNING AND HISTORY OF BEIJING, SEE:
Victor F. S. Sit, *Beijing: The Nature and Planning of a Chinese Capital City*. West Sussex, England: John Wiley and Sons, 1995.

FOR A COMPARATIVE ANALYSIS OF THE PLANNING OF MAJOR CITIES UNDER THE CHINESE COMMUNIST PARTY, SEE:
Victor F. S. Sit, *Chinese Cities: The Growth of the Metropolis Since 1949*. Hong Kong: Oxford University Press, 1985.

FOR A DESCRIPTION OF THE COMMUNIST EFFORT TO CONSERVE HISTORIC BEIJING, SEE:
Ke Huanzhang, *Preservation and Development of Beijing*. Town Planning Review, Vol. 4, Num.4.

FOR A BRIEF SURVEY OF THE HISTORY OF TRADITIONAL CHINESE ARCHITECTURE, SEE:
Henri Stierlin, *Architecture of the World: China*. Lausanne: Benedikt Taschen, 1958.

FOR A DETAILED AND PICTURESQUE DESCRIPTION OF BEIJING BEFORE WORLD WAR II, SEE:
L. C. Arlington and William Lewisohn, *In Search of Old Peking.* Hong Kong: Oxford University Press, 1991.

FOR A CURRENT DESCRIPTION OF THE HUTONGS OF BEIJING, SEE:
Weng Li, *Hutongs of Beijing.* Beijing: Beijing Arts and Photography, 1993.

FOR A RECENT DESCRIPTION OF THE COURTYARD HOUSES OF BEIJING, SEE:
Ma Bingjian, *Quadrangles of Beijing.* Beijing: Beijing Arts and Photography, 1993.

FOR A CONCISE STUDY OF THE TRADITIONAL COURTYARD IN CHINA, SEE:
Werner Blaser, *Courtyard House in China: Tradition and Present.* Basel, Swizterland: Birkhäuser—Verlag für Architektur, 1995.

FOR EARLY PHOTOGRAPHS OF THE FINAL DAYS OF IMPERIAL CHINA, SEE:
Clark Worswick and Jonathan D. Spence, *Imperial China: Photographs 1850–1912.* New York: Penwick, Inc., 1978.

FOR A TECHNICAL CRITIQUE OF CURRENT CHINESE CONSERVATION PRACTICE, SEE:
UNESCO, *Report and Recommendations of the UNESCO Monitoring Mission on Cultural Sites in the People's Republic of China.* Paris: UNESCO 1994.

FOR AN ENCYCLOPEDIC PHOTOGRAPHIC RECORD OF BEJING BEFORE 1949, SEE:
Official government publication: *Old Beijing in Panorama.*

FOR AN ENGLISH-LANGUAGE REVIEW OF THE CURRENT PLANNING LAWS OF BEIJING, SEE:
Official government publication: *A Brief Introduction to the City Planning of Beijing.*

FOR AN ENGLISH-LANGUAGE REVIEW OF ARCHITECTURAL CONSERVATION POLICY IN BEIJING, SEE:
Official government publication: *Protection of the Historical Relics in Beijing.*

FOR THE HUMAN TOLL OF REPRESSIVE POLICIES IN COMMUNIST CHINA, SEE:
Stephan Courtois, et al. *The Black Book of Communism: Crimes, Terror, Repression.* Cambridge, Mass.: Harvard University Press, 1999.

INTERVIEWS

On September 18, 1995, a day-long roundtable interview, with several government officials in charge of different aspects of Beijing's cultural heritage, spelled out in detail current conservation policy, proposed initiatives for the future, and appraised the mistakes of the past. The participants were Guo Zhan, vice research fellow, State Bureau of Cultural Property, secretary general of China ICOMOS, director of cultural relics, first section; Shan Ji Xiang, senior architect, director of Beijing Administrative Bureau for Cultural Relics; Kong Fan Zhi, deputy director of Beijing Administrative Bureau for Museum and Archaeological Data; and Shen Shujie, Foreign Affairs Division of the State Bureau of Cultural Property.

On September 19, 1995, Shan Ji Xiang, director of the Beijing Administrative Bureau for Cultural Relics, and several English-speaking staff members took the author on a day-long tour of cultural sites in Beijing with a special focus on the city's hutong courtyard houses.

SINGAPORE

FOR A SENSITIVE EXAMINATION OF THE CULTURE OF CONTEMPORARY AUTHORITARIAN RULE IN SOUTHEAST ASIA AND SINGAPORE, SEE:
Stan Sesser, *The Lands of Charm and Cruelty: Travels in Southeast Asia.* London: Picador, 1994.

FOR FURTHER EXAMINATION OF THE CITY'S CULTURE OF GOVERNANCE, SEE:
Kevin Hewison, Richard Robison, and Gary Rodan, eds., *Southeast Asia in the 1990s: Authoritarianism, Democracy and Capitalism.* Sydney: Allen and Unwin, 1993.

FOR AN IN-DEPTH HISTORY OF SINGAPORE, SEE:
Ernest C. T. Chew and Edwin Lee, eds., *A History of Singapore.* Singapore: Oxford University Press, 1991.

FOR AN ARCHITECTURAL HISTORY OF THE CITY, SEE:
Jane Beamish and Jane Ferguson, *A History of Singapore Architecture: The Making of a City.* Singapore: Graham Brash, 1989.

FOR A DIRECTORY TO THE CITY'S ARCHITECTURE, SEE:
Norman Edwards and Peter Keys, *Singapore: A Guide to Buildings, Streets, Places.* Singapore: Times Books International, 1988.

FOR A DETAILED STUDY OF THE CITY'S PLANNING, SEE:
Martin Perry, Lily Kong, and Brenda Yeoh, *Singapore: A Developmental City State.* New York: John Wiley and Sons, 1997.

FOR THE DEVELOPMENT OF A MULTIETHNIC CULTURE IN THE CITY, SEE:
Brenda S. A. Yeoh, *Contesting Space: Power Relations and the Urban Built Environment in Colonial Singapore.* Kuala Lampur: Oxford University Press, 1996.

ON THE ECONOMIC MOTIVE FOR CONSERVING THE CITY, SEE:
Russel A. Smith, "The Role of Tourism in Urban Conservation: The Case of Singapore." *Cities* (August 1988).

FOR A PHOTOGRAPHIC COMPARISON OF THE OLD CITY AND THE NEW CITY, SEE:
Siow Jin Hua, *Ray Tyers' Singapore: Then and Now.* Singapore: Landmark Books, 1993.

FOR THE STATISTICS OF URBAN CHANGE, SEE:
Sng Poey Siong, *Singapore Facts and Pictures 1995.* Singapore: Ministry of Information and the Arts, 1995.
Rodolphe De Koninck, *Singapore: An Atlas of the Revolution of Territory.* Montpellier: Groupement d'Intérêt Public (RECLUS), Maison de la Géographie, 1992.

FOR A DETAILED DESCRIPTION OF THE LAWS AND POLICIES INVOLVING THE CONSERVA-TION OF THE CITY, SEE:
Urban Redevelopment Authority, Preservation of Monuments Board, *Conservation Guidelines for Historic Districts, Secondary Settlements, and Specific Building Types.* Singapore: URA, 1993.

INTERVIEWS

ON THE COORDINATION OF CITY PLANNING AND HISTORIC CONSERVATION I SPOKE WITH THE FOLLOWING OFFICIALS, WHO ALSO ARRANGED A SITE INSPECTION OF CURRENT CONSERVATION PROJECTS:
Lim-Qyuah Soon Hong, senior administrative officer: Urban Redevelopment Authority. Singapore, September 28, 1995.
Adeline Tan Choon Yee, senior administrative assistant: Urban Redevelopment Authority. Singapore, September 28, 1995.
Cheong-Chua Koon Hean, director project services: Urban Redevelopment Authority. Singapore, September 28, 1995.

ON THE EFFORTS OF CITIZEN ADVOCATES OF PRESERVATION IN THE CITY, SEVERAL MEETINGS WERE ARRANGED AND ATTENDED BY
William Lim, Singapore Heritage Society, Singapore, September 26 to October 1, 1995.

PRESERVATION AND SOCIAL CONSCIENCE

FOR AN EXCELLENT SURVEY OF SOCIAL HOUSING REFORM IN THE EARLY INDUSTRIAL CITY, SEE:

Peter Hall, *Cities of Tomorrow*. Cambridge: Blackwell, 1993.

VIENNA

FOR AN ARCHITECTURAL AND URBAN PLANNING HISTORY OF VIENNA'S DEVELOPMENT, SEE:

Elisabeth Lichtenberger, *Vienna: Bridge Between Cultures*. London: Belhaven Press, 1993.

FOR A REVEALING URBAN STUDY OF THE CULTURAL FLORESCENCE OF VIENNA, SEE:

Sir Peter Hall, *Cities in Civilization*. New York: Random House, 1998.

FOR A DETAILED SOCIAL-ARCHITECTURAL DESCRIPTION OF FIN DE SIÈCLE VIENNA, SEE:

Donald J. Olsen, *The City As a Work of Art: London, Paris, Vienna*. New Haven: Yale University Press, 1986.

FOR A MASTERFUL CULTURAL HISTORY OF THE RINGSTRASSE ERA IN VIENNA, SEE:

Carl E. Schorske, *Fin-De-Siècle Vienna: Politics and Culture*. New York: Knopf, 1980.

FOR BRIEF ACCOUNT OF THE PLANNING OF THE RINGSTRASSE, SEE:

Thomas Hall, *Planning Europe's Capital Cities: Aspects of Nineteenth Century Urban Development*. Oxford: Alexandrine Press, 1997.

FOR AN ILLUMINATING STUDY OF INTERWAR SOCIAL HOUSING IN VIENNA, SEE:

Eve Blau, *The Architecture of Red Vienna, 1919–1934*. Cambridge, Mass.: MIT Press, 1999.

FOR A DETAILED DESCRIPTION OF AUSTRIAN CONSERVATION LAWS, SEE:

Margret T. Will, *Historic Preservation in Other Countries: Volume II*. Washington, D.C.: US/ICOMOS, 1984.

FOR A DESCRIPTION OF CONTEMPORARY CONSERVATION POLICY IN VIENNA, SEE:

Joseph Matousek and Peter Scheuchel, *Vienna: Preservation and Renewal of the Urban Environment*. Vienna: Municipal Department 18, Vienna Urban Development and Planning, 1995.

FOR A DESCRIPTION OF THE DISPOSITION OF THE HISTORIC DISTRICTS OF VIENNA, SEE:

Scheuchel and Reinberger, *Register of Protection Zones in Force in Vienna*. Vienna: Municipal Department 18, Vienna Urban Development and Planning, 1992.

FOR A GUIDE TO THE ARCHITECTURE OF VIENNA, SEE:

James Roderick O' Donovan, English translation, *Architecture in Vienna*. Vienna: Municipal Department 19, 1992.

FOR DESCRIPTIONS OF VIENNA'S POSTWAR HOUSING PROGRAMS, SEE:

Forster, Gruber-Renezeder, Koppl, and Wurm, *Vienna Paper on Urban Renewal: United Nations Economic Commission for Europe*. Vienna: Municipal Land Procurement and Urban Renewal Fund, 1994.

ON THE JEWISH CONTRIBUTION TO VIENNA'S CULTURAL FLORESCENCE, SEE:

Fredric V. Grunfeld, *Prophets Without Honor*. New York: Holt, Rinehart and Winston, 1979.

ON ANTI-SEMITISM IN AUSTRIA AND JEWISH INVOLVEMENT IN SOCIALISM, SEE:

Josef Fraenkel, *The Jews of Austria*. London: Vallentine, Mitchell, 1967.

INTERVIEWS

The Magistrat der Stadt Wien, Magistratsabteilung 19, was remarkably generous, providing several group discussions on conservation and urban policy, arranging for meetings with other urban planning officials, giving a guided tour of the city, and providing numerous documents in English and German.

OF PARTICULAR NOTE WERE DISCUSSIONS ON THE CREATION OF HISTORIC PROTECTION ZONES:
Peter Scheuchel, Stadtbaurat, MA 19, Vienna, July 7, 1995.
Josef Matousek, Oberstadtbaurat, MA 19, Vienna, July 7, 1995.

AND ON THE REGULATION OF PROTECTION ZONES:
Bettina Nezval, MA 19, Vienna, July 8, 1995.

AMSTERDAM

FOR A COMPREHENSIVE HISTORY OF AMSTERDAM'S RISE TO POWER IN THE SEVENTEENTH CENTURY, SEE:
Renee Kistemaker and Roelof Van Gelfer, *Amsterdam: The Golden Age, 1275–1795*. New York: Abbeville Press, 1983.

FOR A EVOCATIVE LOOK AT AMSTERDAM DURING ITS GOLDEN AGE, SEE:
Mark Girouard, *Cities and People: A Social and Architectural History*. New Haven: Yale University Press, 1985.

FOR A CONCISE TECHNICAL DESCRIPTION OF THE CITY'S CONSTRUCTION METHOD-OLOGY, SEE:
Herman Janse, *Building Amsterdam*. Amsterdam: De Brink, 1990.

FOR A PORTRAIT OF RELIEF FOR THE POOR IN AMSTERDAM DURING THE GOLDEN AGE, SEE:
Peter van Kessel and Elisja Schulte, *Rome, Amsterdam: Two Growing Cities in Seventeenth-Century Europe*. Amsterdam: Amsterdam University Press, 1997.

FOR AN EXCELLENT SOCIOLOGICAL AND ARCHITECTURAL HISTORY OF AMSTERDAM SCHOOL HOUSING, SEE:
Nancy Stieber, *Housing Design and Society in Amsterdam: Reconfiguring Urban Order and Identity, 1900–1920*. Chicago: University of Chicago Press, 1998.

FOR AN ARCHITECTURAL SURVEY OF AMSTERDAM SCHOOL HOUSING, SEE:
Maristella Casciato, *The Amsterdam School*. Rotterdam: Uitgeverij 010, 1996.

FOR A REVIEW AND STATISTICS OF SUBSIDIZED PUBLIC HOUSING IN AMSTERDAM. SEE:
Francoise Paulen, *The Amsterdam Social Housing Atlas*. Amsterdam: Architectura & Natura, 1997.

FOR THE EVOLUTION OF CONSERVATION LAW IN AMSTERDAM, SEE:
Antony Dale, *Historic Preservation in Foreign Countries*, vol. 2. Washington, D.C.: US/ICOMOS, 1982.

FOR AN OVERVIEW OF MODERN PRESERVATION EFFORTS IN AMSTERDAM, SEE:
Richter Roegholt, *Living Amsterdam: A City Protects Its Historic Past*. Amsterdam: Stichting Amsterdam, 1987.

FOR A DESCRIPTION OF THE RESTORATION OF AN OFFICIAL REHABILITATION AREA, SEE:
Donald Appleyard, *The Conservation of European Cities*. Cambridge, Mass.: MIT Press, 1979.

FOR AN EXCELLENT CONDENSED URBAN HISTORY AND ARCHITECTURAL SURVEY, SEE:
Guus Kemme, *Amsterdam Architecture: A Guide*. Amsterdam: Uitgeverij Thoth, 1992.

FOR A DESCRIPTION OF CONTEMPORARY ARCHITECTURE AND CITY PLANNING, SEE:
Paul Groenendijk and Piet Vollaard, *Guide to Modern Architecture in Amsterdam*. Rotterdam: Uitgeverij 010, 1996.

INTERVIEWS

The Bureau Monumentenzorg of Amsterdam arranged a group interview with its staff on conservation policy and practice, as well as a guided tour of conservation sites. Its director, Rob Apell, provided up-to-date statistics in a follow-up document.

ON THE COLLABORATION BETWEEN GOVERNMENT AND THE PRESERVATION SOCIETIES OF AMSTERDAM:
Rob Apell, director, Bureau Monumentenzorg, Amsterdam, May 10, 1995.

ON THE URBAN PLANNING STRATEGY OF STADSHERSTEL:
W. M. N. Eggenkamp te Heemstede, director, Amsterdamse Maatschappij Tot Stadsherstel N.V. May 9, 1995.

THE CITY OF THE GODS BESIEGED

ATHENS

FOR A GENERAL ARCHITECTURAL AND URBAN HISTORY OF CLASSICAL GREECE, SEE:
Spiro Kostoff, *A History of Architecture.* New York: Oxford University Press, 1995.

FOR A DESCRIPTION OF THE CULTURAL LIFE OF CLASSICAL ATHENS, SEE:
Lewis Mumford, *The City in History.* New York: Harcourt, Brace, 1989.

FOR AN EXCELLENT HISTORY OF THE ACROPOLIS AND ITS CONSERVATION, SEE:
Richard Economakis, *Acropolis Restoration: The CCAM Interventions.* London: Academy Editions, 1994.

FOR A TECHNICAL DESCRIPTION OF THE DESIGN AND CONSTRUCTION OF GREEK TEMPLES, SEE:
Roland Martin, *Living Architecture: Greek.* New York: Grosset and Dunlap, 1967.

FOR REFERENCES TO ANCIENT GREEK MANAGEMENT OF THE PHYSICAL CITY, SEE:
Cevat Erder, *Our Architectural Heritage: From Consciousness to Conservation.* Paris: UNESCO, 1986.

FOR A DESCRIPTION OF THE PLANNING OF ATHENS IN THE NINETEENTH CENTURY, SEE:
Thomas Hall, *Planning Europe's Capital Cities.* London: E & FN Spon, 1997.

FOR THE PLANNING ISSUES RAISED IN PROPOSALS FOR THE NINETEENTH-CENTURY CAPITAL, SEE:
Alexander Papageorgiou-Venetas, "Green Spaces, Archaeological Excavation Areas and the Historic Site in the Town Planning Schemes for the City of Athens." *Planning Perspectives* magazine, 1991.

FOR A REVIEW OF CONTEMPORARY CONSERVATION PROBLEMS IN THE PLAKA DISTRICT, SEE:
Donald Appleyard, *The Conservation of European Cities.* Cambridge, Mass.: MIT Press, 1981.

INTERVIEWS

ON GOVERNMENTAL EFFORTS TO SAVE THE BUILT HERITAGE OF ATHENS:
Louisa Matha and Nicolas Agriantonis of ICOMOS Greece arranged two interviews with administrators in the Greek conservation bureaucracy. Each interview was a group affair, with four Greek professionals helping one another to translate accurately into English.
The interview on March 17, 1995, delineated the many conservation programs that affect the city, the absence of coordination between these different branches of government at national and municipal levels, the lack of continuity when different parliamentary

administrations assume power, and the corruption that compromises conservation efforts at every level.

The interview on March 18, 1995, clarified the spheres of responsibility of the many municipal agencies responsible for the planning of Athens, as well as describing the problems in administering the illegal settlements that surround the modern city.

ON CITIZEN CONSERVATION ADVOCACY IN ATHENS:

Pantelis Nicolacopoulos, architect, Athens, March 16, 1995, described citizen efforts to induce the government to protect the modern architectural monuments of the city.

THE COMPREHENSIBLE URBAN VISAGE

LONDON

FOR AN EXCELLENT ARCHITECTURAL AND URBAN PLANNING HISTORY OF THE CITY, SEE:
Michael Hebbert, *London: More by Fortune Than Design.* Chichester, U.K.: John Wiley, 1998.

FOR AN ILLUMINATING STUDY OF THE DEVELOPMENT OF THE GREAT ESTATES, SEE:
Donald J. Olsen, *Town Planning in London: The Eighteenth and Nineteenth Centuries.* New Haven: Yale University Press, 1984.

FOR AN ARCHITECTURAL GUIDE WITH AN EXCELLENT SYNOPSIS OF LONDON'S URBAN HISTORY, SEE:
Edward Jones and Christopher Woodward, *A Guide to the Architecture of London.* London: Orion, 1992.

FOR AN INSIGHTFUL ANALYSIS OF LONDON AT VARIOUS STAGES OF ITS GROWTH, SEE:
Peter Hall, *Cities in Civilization.* New York: Random House, 1998.

FOR THE INFLUENCE OF LE CORBUSIER ON THE CONSTRUCTION OF POST-WAR RESIDENTIAL TOWERS IN LONDON, SEE:
Peter Hall, *Cities of Tomorrow: An Intellectual History of Urban Planning and Design in the Twentieth Century.* Oxford: Blackwell, 1988.

FOR A CRITICAL REVIEW OF POSTWAR PLANNING IN LONDON, SEE:
Peter Hall, *London 2001.* London: Unwin Hyman, 1989.

FOR THE EVOLUTION OF CONSERVATION LAW IN GREAT BRITAIN, SEE:
Anthony Dale, *Historic Conservation in Foreign Countries: France, Great Britain, Ireland, the Netherlands, Denmark.* Washington, D.C.: US/ICOMOS, 1982.

FOR A DETAILED OVERVIEW OF CURRENT CONSERVATION PRACTICE IN THE LONDON AGGLOMERATION, SEE:
Kate Macdonald, *Conservation in London: A Study of Strategic Planning Policy in London.* London: English Heritage and London Planning Advisory Committee, 1995.

FOR AN EXCELLENT ENCAPSULATED HISTORY AND OVERVIEW OF CONSERVATION IN THE INCORPORATED CITY, SEE:
Peter Wynne Rees, *Conservation Areas in the City of London.* London: Corporation of London, 1994.

INTERVIEWS

ON THE GENERAL PRACTICE OF CONSERVATION IN LONDON AND GREAT BRITAIN AND TOURS OF THE OUTER AGGLOMERATION:
Sherban Cantacuzino, president ICOMOS UK, London. April 17–25, 1995.

ON THE POLITICAL EMPOWERMENT OF AMENITY SOCIETIES IN LONDON:
Lionel Block, former chair of the Richmond Society, London. April 20, 1995.

ON THE COORDINATION OF NATIONAL AND LOCAL CONSERVATION EFFORTS:
Paul Drury, head of the London Division of English Heritage, London. April 21, 1995.
Andrew Saint, historian, London and Southeast Region of English Heritage, London. April 21, 1995.

ON CONSERVATION PRACTICE IN THE CITY OF WESTMINSTER:
Rosemarie A. MacQueen, assistant divisional director of development, city of Westminster, London. April 24, 1995.

ON CONSERVATION PRACTICE IN THE BOROUGH OF KENSINGTON AND CHELSEA:
Michael J. French, executive director, planning and conservation group, Royal Borough of Kensington and Chelsea, London. April 26, 1995.

ON CONSERVATION PRACTICE IN THE INCORPORATED CITY:
Peter Wynne Rees, city planning officer, Corporation of London, London. April 25, 1995.

ON CONSERVATION PRACTICE IN THE BOROUGH OF ISLINGTON:
Alec Forshaw, conservation officer, borough of Islington, London. April 26, 1995.

PARIS

ON THE EVOLUTION OF ARCHITECTURE AS AN ART FORM AND PROFESSION, AND THE EMERGENCE OF FRENCH CLASSICISM, THE ROYAL BUILDING ADMINISTRATION, AND THE ÉCOLE DES BEAUX-ARTS, SEE:
Spiro Kostof, *The Architect: Chapters in the History of the Profession*. New York: Oxford University Press, 1977.

FOR A DETAILED AND ILLUMINATING STUDY OF THE BUILT ENVIRONMENT OF PARIS, SEE:
Anthony Sutcliffe, *Paris: An Architectural History*. New Haven: Yale University Press, 1993.

FOR AN IN-DEPTH AND INSIGHTFUL ACCOUNT OF THE CITY SINCE HAUSSMANN, SEE:
Norma Everson, *Paris: A Century of Change, 1878–1978*. New Haven: Yale University Press, 1979.

FOR A PROFILE OF MODERN PLANNING PROBLEMS OF THE CITY, SEE:
Daniel Noin and Paul White, *Paris*. Chichester, U.K.: John Wiley & Sons, 1997.

FOR A DETAILED EXAMINATION OF CONSERVATION LAWS IN FRANCE, SEE:
Robert E. Stripe, *Historic Preservation in Foreign Countries: Volume I*. Washington, D.C.: US/ICOMOS, 1982.

FOR THE EMERGENCE OF THE CONSERVATION ETHIC IN FRANCE, SEE:
Cervat Erder, *Our Architectural Heritage: From Consciousness to Conservation*. Paris: UNESCO, 1986.

FOR A COMPARATIVE URBAN PORTRAIT OF PARIS DURING THE BELLE EPOQUE, SEE:
Mark Girouard, *Cities and People: A Social and Architectural History*. New Haven: Yale University Press, 1985.

FOR A REVEALING ANALYSIS OF THE WORK OF HAUSSMANN AND THE FLORESCENCE OF PAINTING IN THE CITY, SEE:
Sir Peter Hall, *Cities in Civilization*. New York: Random House, 1998.

FOR A REVEALING VISUAL PORTRAIT OF THE CITY, SEE:
Robert Cameron and Pierre Salinger, *Above Paris* (revised). San Francisco: Cameron, 1992.

FOR EARLY PHOTOGRAPHIC IMAGES OF THE CITY, SEE:
François Loyer, *Paris XIXE Siecle: L'immeuble et la Rue*. Milanostampa: Hazan, 1994.

INTERVIEWS

ON THE APPLICATION OF CONSERVATION STATUTES IN CONTEMPORARY PARIS:
Pierre Chatauret, Architecte des Bâtiments de France, Conseiller Technique auprès du Sour-
Director, Paris, March 26, 1996. Louis Decazes, ICOMOS Francais, interpreter.

ON THE COORDINATION OF URBAN PLANNING AND HISTORIC CONSERVATION IN PARIS:
Elsa Martayan, Communication/Documentation, Atelier Parisen d' Urbanisme (APUR). May
22, 1995.

ON THE CONSERVATION OF THE MARAIS:
François Comméngé, Architecte de Secteur Sauvegardé de Marais, May 23, 1995.

TOURISM VERSUS THE HABITABLE CITY

VENICE

FOR AN EXCELLENT ARCHITECTURAL AND URBAN HISTORY OF VENICE, SEE:
Richard Goy, *Venice: The City and Its Architecture.* London: Phaidon Press, 1997.

FOR A GENERAL SOCIAL, CULTURAL, AND POLITICAL HISTORY OF VENICE, SEE:
Alvise Zorzi, *Venice: The Golden Age, 697–1797.* New York: Abbeville Press, 1980.

FOR AN EXCELLENT ARCHITECTURAL GUIDE TO VENICE, SEE:
Antonio Salvadori, *Venice: A Guide to the Principal Buildings.* Venice: Canal & Stamperia Editrice,
1995.

FOR A GUIDE TO ART IN SITU IN VENICE, SEE:
Terisio Pignatti, Venice: *A Guide to Paintings in Original Settings.* Venice: Canal & Stamperia Editrice,
1995.

FOR A COMPREHENSIVE DESCRIPTION OF THE UNESCO CAMPAIGN IN VENICE, SEE:
UNESCO, *UNESCO for Venice: International Campaign for the Safeguarding of Venice, 1966–1992.* Rome:
Dipartimento per l'informazione e l'editoria, Presidenza del Consiglio dei Ministri, 1992.

FOR AN ANALYSIS OF THE EFFECTS OF GENTRIFICATION ON THE CONSERVATION OF
VENICE, SEE:
Donald Appleyard, *The Conservation of European Cities.* Cambridge, Mass.: MIT Press, 1979.

FOR AN ANALYSIS OF THE HOUSING PROBLEMS OF VENICE, SEE:
Hiroshi Daifuku, *The Conservation of Cities.* Paris: UNESCO Press, 1975.

FOR A DESCRIPTION OF THE FIRST EFFORTS TO MODERNIZE VENICE, SEE:
Margaret Plant, "Bereft of All but Her Loveliness: Change and Conservation in Nineteenth-
Century Venice." *Transition* 33.

FOR EARLY PHOTOGRAPHIC IMAGES OF VENICE, SEE:
Dorothea Ritter, *Ottocento: Immagini di Venezia, 1841–1920.* Venice: Arsenale Editrice, 1997.

FOR A DESCRIPTION OF THE PROGRAM TO REESTABLISH THE LAGOONS, SEE:
Consorzio Venezia Nuova, *Interventi per la Salvaguardia di Venezia e il Riequilibrio della Laguana.* Venice:
Consorzio Venezia Nuova, 1994.

FOR A DESCRIPTION OF THE LOSS OF RESIDENT VENETIANS, SEE:
Reports of the UNESCO Liaison Office for the Safeguarding of Venice.

INTERVIEWS

ON THE UNESCO EFFORT TO SAVE VENICE:

John Millerchip, secretary, Private Committees for the Safeguarding of Venice. Venice, March 18, 1996.

ON THE EFFORT BY PRIVATE COMMITTEES TO SAVE THE CITY:

Donatella Asta, program representative, World Monuments Fund in Italy. Venice, March 18, 1996.

ON THE PROGRAM TO STABILIZE THE VENETIAN LAGOON:

Dottoressa ssa Francesca de Pol, Consorzio Venezia Nuova. Venice, March 20, 1996.

Franco Miracco, Consorzio Venezia Nuova. Venice, March 20, 1996.

Dottor Mossetto, Assessore alla Cultura per il Commune di Venezia. Venice, March 20, 1996.

ON CURRENT TECHNICAL METHODS OF RESTORING HISTORIC ARCHITECTURE:

Franco Mancuso, architect in private practice. Venice, March 21, 1996.

POLITICS AND PRESERVATION IN THE MODERN METROPOLIS

NEW YORK

My experience as a New York City landmarks commissioner from 1979 to 1988 under Mayor Edward I. Koch was a primary source of information for this chapter.

FOR AN ENCYCLOPEDIC GUIDE TO THE ARCHITECTURE OF NEW YORK'S FIVE BOROUGHS, SEE:

Elliot Willensky and Norval White, *AIA Guide to New York City: Fourth Edition.* New York: Crown Publishers, 2000.

FOR A DETAILED ACCOUNT OF THE EMERGENCE OF THE ARCHITECTURAL PRESERVATION MOVEMENT IN NEW YORK, SEE:

Robert A. M. Stern, Thomas Mellins, David Fishman, *New York 1960: Architecture and Urbanism Between the Second World War and the Bicentennial.* New York: Monacelli Press, 1995.

FOR A MASTERFUL ARCHITECTURAL HISTORY OF CONTEMPORARY NEW YORK, SEE:

Robert A. M. Stern, Gregory Gilmartin, Thomas Mellins, *New York 1930: Architecture and Urbanism Between the Two World Wars.* New York: Rizzoli International, 1987.

Robert A. M. Stern, Gregory Gilmartin, and John Massengale, *New York 1900: Metropolitan Architecture and Urbanism: 1890–1915.* New York: Rizzoli International, 1983.

FOR AN EVOCATIVE CHRONICLE OF BEAUTIFUL MONUMENTS DESTROYED IN NEW YORK, SEE:

Nathan Silver, *Lost New York.* New York: American Legacy Press, 1967.

FOR AN INSIGHTFUL SOCIOLOGICAL AND TECHNICAL ESSAY ON THE EMERGENCE OF MODERN NEW YORK, SEE:

Sir Peter Hall, *Cities in Civilization.* New York: Pantheon Books, 1998.

FOR A REVEALING EXPLICATION OF THE MARKET FORCES THAT PROPELLED NEW YORK SKYWARD, SEE:

Carol Willis, *Form Follows Finance: Skyscrapers and Skylines in New York and Chicago.* Princeton, N.J.: Princeton Architectural Press, 1995.

FOR AN ILLUMINATING STUDY OF THE DEVELOPMENT OF THE TALL BUILDING IN NEW YORK, SEE:

Sarah Bradford Landau and Carl W. Condit, *Rise of the New York Skyscraper: 1865–1913.* New Haven, Conn.: Yale University Press, 1996.

FOR METICULOUS REPORTAGE OF RECENT PRESERVATION ISSUES IN NEW YORK, SEE:
Christabel Gough, Ronald Kopnicki, and Matt McGhee, *Village Views: A Quarterly Review of Architecture and Historic Preservation in New York.* New York: Society for the Architecture of the City, 1984–2000.

FOR A LISTING OF NEW YORK'S OFFICIAL LANDMARKS AND HISTORIC DISTRICTS, SEE:
Andrew S. Dolkart, *Guide to New York City Landmarks.* New York: John Wiley and Sons, 1998.

FOR A THOROUGH ILLUSTRATED GUIDE TO NEW YORK'S OFFICIALLY PROTECTED PROPERTIES, SEE:
Barbaralee Diamondstein, *The Landmarks of New York,* vol. 3. New York: Harry N. Abrams, 1988.

FOR DETAILED INFORMATION ON THE PRACTICES OF THE LANDMARKS PRESERVATION COMMISSION IN THE 1970S, SEE:
Adele Chatfield-Taylor, ed., *The Commissioners' Handbook.* New York: Landmarks Preservation Commission, 1979.

INTERVIEWS

ON THE NATIONAL LEGAL SIGNIFICANCE OF NEW YORK'S CONSERVATION LAW I SPOKE WITH:
Steven Dennis, former executive director, National Center for Preservation Law. Washington, D.C., Fall 1994.

ON THE EVOLUTION OF SPECIAL PERMITS AND DEVELOPMENT RIGHT TRANSFERS ON BEHALF OF ARCHITECTURAL CONSERVATION IN NEW YORK:
Dorothy Miner, former counsel of the New York City Landmarks Preservation Commission Commission. New York, Fall 1999.

ON RECENT PRESERVATION ISSUES AND THE CHANGING PRACTICES OF THE COMMISSION:
Christabel Gough, secretary, Society for the Architecture of the City. New York, numerous intermittent discussions from 1996 through 2000.

REVERSING THE CULTURE OF DESTRUCTION

KYOTO

FOR A BRIEF BUT EXCELLENT ARCHITECTURAL AND URBAN HISTORY OF THE CITY, SEE:
Hiroshi Mimura, *Development and Conservation of the Traditional Inner City of Kyoto and Its Wooden Houses.* Kyoto: Kyoto University Department of Architecture, 1989.

FOR THE CONFLICT BETWEEN MODERNIZATION AND HISTORIC CONSERVATION IN KYOTO, SEE:
Masahumi Yamasaki, *Kyoto: Its Cityscape Traditions and Heritage: Process Architecture,* no. 116. 1994.

FOR AN EARLY POSTWAR STUDY OF CONSERVATION PROBLEMS IN KYOTO AND NARA, SEE:
Hiroshi Daifuku, ed., *The Conservation of Cities.* Paris: UNESCO Press, 1975.

FOR AN INSIGHTFUL ANALYSIS OF THE CULTURAL ROOTS OF THE NEW URBANISM OF JAPAN, SEE:
Barrie Shelton, *Learning from the Japanese City: West Meets East in Urban Design.* London: Spon, 1999.

FOR DETAILS OF THE EVOLUTION OF CONSERVATION PRACTICE IN JAPAN, SEE:
Nobuo Ito and Knut Einar Larsen, *Dialogue on the Protection of Architectural Monuments in Japan.* Paris: ICOMOS magazine, September 1990.

FOR A GUIDE TO THE HISTORIC NEIGHBORHOODS OF KYOTO, SEE:
Diane Durston, *Kyoto: Seven Paths to the Heart of the City.* Kyoto: Mitsumura Suiko Shoin, 1987.

FOR DETAILS ON THE OVERLAY OF CURRENT CONSERVATION INITIATIVES, SEE:
City Planning Office, Kyoto City Hall. *Recent publications on the implementation of local and nationwide conservation laws.* Kyoto.

FOR A CONCISE INTRODUCTION TO THE HISTORY OF JAPANESE ARCHITECTURE, SEE:
William Alex, *Japanese Architecture: The Great Ages of World Architecture series.* New York, George Braziller, 1975.

INTERVIEWS

ON THE EVOLUTION OF CONSERVATION LAWS IN KYOTO AND THE CREATION OF PROTYPICAL FACADE DESIGNS FOR KYOTO'S HISTORIC DISTRICTS:
Professor Hiroshi Mimura, Department of Architecture and School of Global Engineering, Kyoto University, August 3–5, 1995.

ON THE APPLICATION OF CURRENT CONSERVATION LAWS IN KYOTO:
Hideo Yoshida and Eiko Kameyama, Kyoto City Hall, Departments of Planning and International Relations, August 4, 1995.

ON THE GENERAL PHENOMENON OF HISTORIC CONSERVATION IN MODERN JAPAN:
Hideo Noguchi, chief for Asia–Pacific, Division of Physical Heritage, UNESCO, May 20, 1995, and March 26, 1996.

THE CITY REDEEMED

FOR A SURVEY OF ANTI-SEMITISM AND JEWISH LIFE IN HISTORIC CITIES, SEE:
Alan M. Tigay, *The Jewish Traveler.* Northvale, N.J.: *Hadassah* magazine, 1994.

THE TOPOGRAPHY OF TERROR IN BERLIN

FOR A STUDY OF SOCIETAL CAUSES OF THE HOLOCAUST, SEE:
Daniel Jonah Goldhagen, *Hitler's Willing Executioners: Ordinary Germans and the Holocaust.* New York: Vintage Books, 1997.

FOR THE CONDITIONS IN BERLIN IMMEDIATELY AFTER WORLD WAR II, SEE:
Reinhart Rürup, *Berlin 1945.* Berlin: Willmuth Arenhövel, 1995.

FOR AN ANALYSIS OF THE CONFLICTS OF COLLECTIVE REMEMBRANCE IN THE CITY, SEE:
Brian Ladd, *The Ghosts of Berlin: Confronting German History in the Urban Landscape.* Chicago: University of Chicago Press, 1997.
Michael Z. Wise, *Capital Dilemma: Germany's Search for a New Architecture of Democracy.* New York: Princeton Architectural Press, 1998.

FOR A DESCRIPTION OF THE EXHIBITION AT *THE TOPOGRAPHY OF TERROR*, SEE:
Reinhart Rürup, *Topography of Terror: Gestapo, SS and Reich Security Main Office on the Prinz Albrecht Terrain.* Berlin: Willmuth Arenhövel, 1989.

FOR A CONCISE URBAN HISTORY AND GUIDEBOOK TO THE CITY'S ARCHITECTURE, SEE:
Derek Fraser, *The Buildings of Europe: Berlin.* Manchester: Manchester University Press, 1996.

THE AFRICAN BURIAL GROUND

FOR AN OVERVIEW OF BLACK HISTORY IN THE UNITED STATES, SEE:
Robin D. G. Kelley and Earl Lewis, *To Make Our World Anew: A History of African Americans.* New York: Oxford University Press, 2000.

FOR A SURVEY OF AFRICAN-AMERICAN SITES ON THE NATIONAL REGISTER OF HISTORIC
PLACES, SEE:
Beth L. Savage, *African American Historic Places*. Washington D.C.: Preservation Press, 1994.

FOR A STUDY OF SLAVE BUILDINGS DOCUMENTED BY THE HISTORIC AMERICAN
BUILDINGS SURVEY, SEE:
John Michael Vlach, *Back of the Big House: The Architecture of Plantation Slavery*. Chapel Hill: University
of North Carolina Press, 1993.

THE AZTEC PYRAMID SITE

FOR AN IN-DEPTH ANALYSIS OF THE MODERN METROPOLIS, SEE:
Peter M. Ward, *Mexico City*. New York: John Wiley & Sons, 1998.

FOR A DISCUSSION OF PROBLEMS IN CONTEMPORARY CITIES IN SOUTH AMERICA, SEE:
Richard M. Morse and Jorge E. Hardoy, *Rethinking the Latin American City*. Baltimore, Md.: Johns
Hopkins University Press, 1992.

FOR AN ARCHITECTURAL AND URBAN HISTORY OF HISTORIC MEXICO, SEE:
James Early, *The Colonial Architecture of Mexico*. Albuquerque: University of New Mexico Press,
1994.

FOR THE DEVELOPMENT OF MESTIZO ARCHITECTURAL CULTURE, SEE:
Elizabeth Wilder Weismann, *Art and Time in Mexico: Architecture and Sculpture in Colonial Mexico*. New
York: HarperCollins, 1995.

FOR A DESCRIPTION OF THE ARCHAEOLOGY OF THE AZTEC PYRAMID SITE, SEE:
Eduardo Matos Moctezuma, *The Great Temple of the Aztecs: Treasures of Tenochtitlán*. London: Thames
and Hudson,1988.

INTERVIEWS

Berlin

ON THE PRESERVATION OF HISTORIC SITES IN THE REUNITED CITYSCAPE OF BERLIN:
Dr. Berhard Kohlenback, Landeskonservator: Senatsverwaltung f. Stadtentwicklung u.
Umweltschutz. April 24, 1995.

ON THE ADAPTATION OF FORMER WALL AREAS AS PUBLIC PARKS AND GARDENS:
Dr. Klaus von Krosig, Senatsverwaltung für Stadtentwicklung and Umweltschutz:
Fachabteilung Bau-u. Gartendenkmalpflege. Berlin: April 25, 1995.

ON THE CRITICAL RECONSTRUCTION OF THE CAPITAL:
Dr. Hans Stimmann: Senatsverwaltung für Stadtentwicklung, Umweltschutz und Technologie.
Mexico City: March 28–29, 1998.

Monuments of Conscience in the Soviet Union

ON THE MEMORIALIZATION OF HISTORIC SITES ASSOCIATED WITH CRIMES AGAINST
HUMANITY, A TOUR BY VIDEOTAPE OF SITES IN KIEV, RIGA, AND MOSCOW:
Leo Kaplan, Professor of Social and Behavioral Sciences, Cooper Union Faculty of Liberal
Arts and Social Sciences. New York: June 15, 2000.

The Negroes' Burial Ground

ON DISCUSSION AT THE PUBLIC MEETINGS OF THE U.S. CONGRESS, NEW YORK CITY
COUNCIL, AND NEW YORK CITY LANDMARKS PRESERVATION COMMISSION:
Christabel Gough, Society for the Architecture of the City. New York: August 2000.

ON THE PRESERVATION OF SITES ASSOCIATED WITH SLAVERY IN THE SOUTHERN UNITED
STATES:
George McDaniel, director of Drayton Hall Plantation. Charleston: By phone.

Mexico City

While attending an international colloquium: *Megalopolis: The Modernization of Mexico City in the
Twentieth Century,* March 31 to April 2, 1998, sponsored by the Goethe Institute in Mexico
and CURARE, an organization of Mexico City artists, I heard more than twenty papers on
the history, preservation, planning, and social conditions of the city. Of special
importance to my research were:
Peter Krieger, Hamburg: *Megalopolis Mexico City.*
Margarito Nolasco, Mexico City: *Social Spaces and Urban Modernization.*
Ekkehart Ribbeck, Stuttgart: *Consolidation of Informal Settlements in Mexico City.*
Rita Eder, Mexico City: *Window Dressing as a Symbol of Urban Modernization.*
Felipe Real Fernández, Mexico City: *The Architecture of the Megalopolis.*
Carlos Tejeda, Mexico City: *Urban Planning and Political Responsibilities.*
Mario Schjetnan, Mexico City: *The Ecological Park at Xochimilco.*

THE CITY AS A LIVING MUSEUM

Charleston

FOR A DETAILED URBAN HISTORY WITH PARTICULAR FOCUS ON THE STORY OF BLACK AND
WHITE CHARLESTONIANS, SEE:
Robert N. Rosen, *A Short History of Charleston.* Charleston: Peninsula Press, 1992.

FOR AN EARLY STUDY OF THE ARCHITECTURAL LANDMARKS OF THE CITY, SEE:
Samuel Gaillard Stoney, *This Is Charleston: A Survey of the Architectural Heritage of a Unique American City.*
Charleston: Carolina Art Association, 1995.

FOR A STUDY OF CHARLESTON'S NEIGHBORHOODS, VERNACULAR AND HIGH ARCHITEC-
TURE, AND THE HISTORY OF AFRICAN-AMERICAN SETTLEMENT IN THE CITY, SEE:
Margaret and Truman Moore, *Complete Charleston: A Guide to the Architecture, History, and Gardens of
Charleston and the Low Country.* Charleston: TM Photography, 2000.

ON THE GENESIS OF PRESERVATION LAW AND PRACTICE IN CHARLESTON, SEE:
Mary Moore Jacoby, ed., *Preservation Progress: Charleston and the Board of Review: Special Edition.*
Charleston: Preservation Society of Charleston, Spring 1993.

Jerusalem

FOR AN EXCELLENT ARCHITECTURAL HISTORY OF JERUSALEM, SEE:
David Kroyanker, *Jerusalem Architecture.* New York: Vendome Press, 1994.

FOR A DETAILED HISTORY OF THE WALLS OF THE ANCIENT CITY, SEE:
Rommie Ellenman and Amnon Ramon, *The Walls of Jerusalem: A Guide to the Ramparts Walking Tour.* Jerusalem: Yad Izhak Ben-Zvi, 1995.

FOR A BRIEF OVERVIEW OF THE HISTORIC CITY'S PHYSICAL EVOLUTION, SEE:
Dan Bahat, *Carta's Historical Atlas of Jerusalem.* Jerusalem: Carta, 1992.

ON THE EARLY ISRAELI PLANNING OF THE CITY, SEE:
Arthur Kutcher, *The New Jerusalem: Planning and Politics.* London: Thames and Hudson, 1973.

ON THE DESTRUCTION OF THE JEWISH QUARTER DURING ARAB RULE, SEE:
Israel Information Center, *The Jewish Quarter: Ruins and Restoration.* Jerusalem: Israel Information
Centre, 1973.

ON THE RESTORATION OF THE JEWISH QUARTER, SEE:

David Kroyanker, *Jerusalem: Planning and Development: New Trends: 1982 to 1985*. Jerusalem: Jerusalem
   Foundation, 1985.

FOR A CRITICAL REVIEW OF PRESERVATION EFFORTS IN THE OLD CITY, SEE:

R. M. Lemaire, *Synoptic Report on the Application of UNESCO Resolutions and Decisions Regarding the Cultural
   Heritage of Jerusalem (Hundred and Twenty-seventh Session)*. Paris: United Nations Educational,
   Scientific and Cultural Organization, 1987.

ON ISRAELI EXPROPRIATION OF DISPUTED LAND AND THE UNEQUAL DISTRIBUTION OF
   NEW PUBLIC HOUSING, SEE:

Aaron Back and Eitan Felner, *The Battle for Jerusalem*. Tikkun, Vol. 10, No. 4.

INTERVIEWS

Charleston

ON THE PROCEDURES OF THE BOARD OF REVIEW:

Charles Chase, preservation officer, Department of City Planning. Charleston: January 10,
   1997.

ON THE DEVELOPMENT OF SCATTERED-SITE HOUSING AND THE RESTORATION OF
   HISTORIC BUILDINGS AS PUBLIC HOUSING:

Donald Cameron, director, Housing Authority of Charleston. Charleston: January 13, 1997.

ON THE ADAPTATION OF HISTORIC BUILDINGS AS PUBLIC HOUSING:

Patricia Crawford, director of housing and community development, Department of Planning
   and Urban Development. Charleston: January 13, 2000.

ON THE COORDINATION OF PLANNING AND HISTORIC PRESERVATION:

Yvonne Fortenberry, director of planning and zoning, Department of Planning and Urban
   Development. Charleston: January 13, 1997.

Lee Batchelder, director of zoning, Department of Planning and Urban Development.
   Charleston: January 13, 1997.

Jerusalem

ON THE RESTORATION OF THE OLD CITY, THE JEWISH QUARTER, AND OTHER HISTORIC
   AREAS IN JERUSALEM:

Yitzhak Jacobi, former director, East Jerusalem Development Corporation. Jerusalem: March
   24 1995.

ON THE DIFFICULTY OF ISRAELI ADMINISTRATORS IN APPLYING PRESERVATION
   REGULATIONS IN MUSLIM NEIGHBORHOODS:

Henry Cleere, World Heritage Coordinator, ICOMOS. Paris: March 29, 1996.

ACKNOWLEDGMENTS

The creation of this book presented daunting hurdles. A physical and intellectual journey around the world was required to gather the documentation, all in English, in oral, written, and visual forms. This was accomplished only through the generosity of numerous people.

INITIAL RESEARCH
The following people in the United States helped identify historic cities with important conservation stories: Dorothy Miner and Stephen Dennis, and Bonnie Burnham and John Stubbs at the World Monuments Fund. The aid of Ellen Delage at U.S. ICOMOS was crucial in contacting ICOMOS committees in numerous cities and in arranging a remarkable interview with Hiroshi Daifuku, former chief of the Monuments and Sites Division of UNESCO.

INVESTIGATING THE CITIES
Many people in foreign cities were exceedingly generous: setting up interviews, translating, providing documentation, taking me to obscure and hard-to-reach places, and arranging for me to lecture—which was an opportunity for cross-cultural exchange. Most important, my foreign hosts let see through their eyes the cities where they live. I am indebted to all the people listed in the bibliography under "Interviews." Of especially invaluable help were the following: in Athens, Pantelis Nicolacopoulos and Louisa Matha (ICOMOS Greece); in Istanbul, Nevzat Ilhan (ICOMOS Turkey); in Jerusalem, Yitzhak Jacobi; in Cairo, Saleh Lamei-Mostafa, and Mark Easton and Robert Vincent (American Research Center in Egypt); in London, Sherban Cantacuzino (ICOMOS U.K.) and Peter Wynne Rees (Corporation of London); in Edinburgh, Richard Emerson (Historic Scotland); in Amsterdam, Rob Apell (Amsterdam Bureau of Monuments); in Moscow, Barbara Finamore and Vyacheslav Glazychev (Academy of the Urban Environment); in Vienna, Peter Scheuchel, Josef Matousek, and Bettina Nezal (Stadtplanung Wien); in Prague, Jiri Hurza; in Berlin, Bernhard Kohlenback (Landeskonservator) and Klaus von Krosigk (Senatsverwaltung für Stadtentwicklung und Umweltschutz); in Kyoto, Hiroshi

Mimura (Kyoto University); in Beijing, Guo Zhan (State Bureau of Cultural Properties) and Shan Ji Xiang (Beijing Administrative Bureau for Cultural Relics); in Singapore, William Lim (Singapore Heritage Society) and the professionals at the Urban Redevelopment Authority; in Rome, Paola Falini and Alberta Campitelli (City of Rome Building Department); in Venice, Donatella Asta (World Monuments Fund); and in Charleston, Donald Cameron (Housing Authority of Charleston) and Margaret Moore and Truman Moore (Committee to Save the City).

The following people and organizations arranged important contacts and documentation: Carole Alexandre, Henry Cleere, and Louis Decazes of the International Council on Monuments and Sites; Bernd von Droste, Breda Pavlic, and Minja Yang of the World Heritage Center; Michael Pezet and Gabi Dolff-Bonekamper of ICOMOS Germany; Hideo Noguchi of the UNESCO Division of Physical Heritage; Cristina Puglisi and Adele Chatfield-Taylor of the American Academy in Rome; Peter Krieger and Edda Webels-Wolf at the Goethe Institute of Mexico; Dutch ICOMOS, Czech ICOMOS; and Luisa Vassallo of the University of Bologna.

FROM CONCEPT TO MANUSCRIPT TO BOOK

My editor at Clarkson Potter, Roy Finamore, championed the project and was my true and farsighted guide through the rigorous metamorphosis from first draft to finished book. I am deeply indebted to Maria Ascher, who was the principal reader of the first draft, offering astute editorial counsel as the manuscript developed. My wife, Janet Vicario, taught me how to use a camera, collaborated on the photographs, and expanded the compass of my research in foreign cities. My agent, Faith Hamlin, transformed a dream into a reality. Each of them was an indispensable partner.

My thanks to the professionals at Clarkson Potter who contributed their talents to the making of the book: Marysarah Quinn, creative director; Carol Divine Carson, jacket designer; Caitlin Daniels Israel, interior designer; Mark McCauslin, associate managing editor; Donna Ryan, copy editor; Joy Sikorski, production supervisor; and Martin Patmos, editorial assistant.

Finally, a lifetime of study was obligatory before attempting such a broad and complex subject. The following people have significantly expanded my critical understanding of art, architecture, preservation, urban governance, and the planning of cities: John Hejduk, Robert Slutzky, Ricardo Scofidio, Anthony Eardley and Leo Kaplan from my days at Cooper Union; Kent Barwick, Gene Norman, Elliot Willensky and Dewey Ebbin during my tenure as a landmarks commissioner; Rika Burnham at the Metropolitan Museum of Art; and my mother, Rosemary Tung, who is also an unfailing source for rare pictures of vanished beautiful cityscapes.

INDEX

ABOUT THE AUTHOR

Anthony M. Tung has been a New York City Landmarks Preservation Commissioner and an instructor at the Metropolitan Museum of Art. He has written for *New York Newsday* and lectured on urban preservation throughout the world. He lives in Greenwich Village in New York City.